SECOND EDITION

DIGITAL VIDEO AND HD

ALGORITHMS AND INTERFACES

SECOND EDITION

DIGITAL VIDEO AND HD

ALGORITHMS AND INTERFACES

CHARLES POYNTON

AMSTERDAM • BOSTON • HEIDELBERG • LONDON
NEW YORK • OXFORD • PARIS • SAN DIEGO
SAN FRANCISCO • SINGAPORE • SYDNEY • TOKYO

Morgan Kaufmann is an imprint of Elsevier

Acquiring editor: Laura Lewin
Development Editor: Graham Smith
Project Manager: Sarah W. Binns
Design, illustration, and composition: Charles Poynton
Copy editor/proofreader: Charles Roumeliotis
Cover Design: Joanne Blank

Morgan Kaufmann Publishers is an imprint of Elsevier
225 Wyman Street, Waltham MA 02451 USA

Library of Congress Cataloging-in-Publication Data
Application submitted.

British Library Cataloguing-in-Publication Data:
A catalogue record for this book is available from the British Library.

ISBN: 978-0-12-391926-7

For information on all Morgan Kaufmann publications, visit our Web site at www.mkp.com or www.elsevierdirect.com

Printed in the United States of America on acid-free paper.

2012 2013 2014 2015 2016 2017 2018   9 8 7 6 5 4 3 2 1

Working together to grow
libraries in developing countries

www.elsevier.com | www.bookaid.org | www.sabre.org

ELSEVIER   BOOK AID International   Sabre Foundation

Dedicated to
my dear friend
James C. (Jamie) Avis
1949–2011

Contents

List of Figures xxi

List of Tables xxxi

Preface xxxvii
Legacy technology xxxix
Layout and typography xxxix
Formulas xxxix
Spelling xl

Acknowledgments xli

Part 1 – Introduction 1

1 Raster images 3

Aspect ratio 4
Geometry 6
Image capture 7
Digitization 7
Perceptual uniformity 8
Colour 10
Luma and colour difference components 11
Digital image representation 11
SD and HD 13
Square sampling 14
Comparison of aspect ratios 14
Aspect ratio 15
Frame rates 18

2 Image acquisition and presentation 19

Image state 20
EOCF standards 22
Entertainment programming 22

Acquisition 24
Consumer origination 24
Consumer electronics (CE) display 24

3 Linear-light and
  perceptual uniformity
  27
Contrast 28
Contrast ratio 29
Perceptual uniformity 30
The "code 100" problem and nonlinear image coding
    31
Linear and nonlinear 36

4 Quantization 37
Linearity 37
Decibels 38
Noise, signal, sensitivity 40
Quantization error 40
Full-swing 41
Studio-swing (footroom and headroom) 42
Interface offset 44
Processing coding 45
Two's complement wrap-around 46

5 Contrast, brightness,
  CONTRAST, and
  BRIGHTNESS 47
Perceptual attributes 47
History of display signal processing 48
Digital driving levels 51
Relationship between signal and lightness 51
Algorithm 52
Black level setting 56
Effect of CONTRAST and BRIGHTNESS on contrast and
    brightness 56
An alternate interpretation 59
BRIGHTNESS and CONTRAST controls in LCDs 62
BRIGHTNESS and CONTRAST controls in PDPs 62
BRIGHTNESS and CONTRAST controls in desktop
    graphics 62

6 Raster images
  in computing 65
Symbolic image description 66
Raster images 67
Conversion among types 72
Image files 72
"Resolution" in computer graphics 73

7 Image structure 75
Image reconstruction 76
Sampling aperture 78
Spot profile 80

DIGITAL VIDEO AND HD ALGORITHMS AND INTERFACES

Box distribution   80
Gaussian distribution   81

8   Raster scanning 83   Flicker, refresh rate, and frame rate   83
                          Introduction to scanning   85
                          Scanning parameters   86
                          Interlaced format   88
                          Twitter   89
                          Interlace in analog systems   90
                          Interlace and progressive   90
                          Scanning notation   92
                          Motion portrayal   93
                          Segmented-frame (24PsF)   94
                          Video system taxonomy   94
                          Conversion among systems   95

9   Resolution 97   Magnitude frequency response and bandwidth   97
                          Visual acuity   99
                          Viewing distance and angle   100
                          Kell effect   102
                          Resolution   103
                          Resolution in video   104
                          Viewing distance   104
                          Interlace revisited   105

10 Constant luminance 107 The principle of constant luminance   108
                          Compensating for the CRT   109
                          Departure from constant luminance   110
                          Luma   111
                          "Leakage" of luminance into chroma   112

11 Picture rendering 115   Surround effect   116
                          Tone scale alteration   117
                          Incorporation of rendering   117
                          Rendering in desktop computing   119

12 Introduction to luma and   Luma   121
    chroma 121   Sloppy use of the term *luminance*   122
                          Colour difference coding (chroma)   123
                          Chroma subsampling   124
                          Chroma subsampling notation   125
                          Chroma subsampling filters   127
                          Chroma in composite NTSC and PAL   128

13 Introduction to component SD 129

Scanning standards 129
Widescreen (16:9) SD 133
Square and nonsquare sampling 133
Resampling 134

14 Introduction to composite NTSC and PAL 135

NTSC and PAL encoding 136
NTSC and PAL decoding 137
S-video interface 137
Frequency interleaving 137
Composite analog SD 139

15 Introduction to HD 141

HD scanning 141
Colour coding for BT.709 HD 144

16 Introduction to video compression 147

Data compression 147
Image compression 148
Lossy compression 148
JPEG 149
Motion-JPEG 150
JPEG 2000 150
Mezzanine compression 151
MPEG 152
Picture coding types (I, P, B) 153
Reordering 156
MPEG-1 157
MPEG-2 157
Other MPEGs 158
MPEG IMX 158
MPEG-4 159
H.264 160
AVC-Intra 160
WM9, WM10, VC-1 codecs 160
Compression for CE acquisition 161
HDV 161
AVCHD 162
Compression for IP transport to consumers 162
VP8 ("WebM") codec 162
Dirac (basic) 162

17 Streams and files 163

Historical overview 164
Physical layer 166
Stream interfaces 166
IEEE 1394 (FireWire, i.LINK) 167
HTTP live streaming (HLS) 168

18 Metadata 171   Conclusions 179

19 Stereoscopic ("3-D")   Acquisition 181
    video 181   S3D display 181
                                     Anaglyph 182
                                     Temporal multiplexing 183
                                     Polarization 183
                                     Wavelength multiplexing (Infitec/Dolby) 184
                                     Autostereoscopic displays 185
                                     Parallax barrier display 185
                                     Lenticular display 185
                                     Recording and compression 186
                                     Consumer interface and display 186
                                     Ghosting 187
                                     Vergence and accommodation 188

                                     Part 2 – Theory 189

20 Filtering and sampling   Sampling theorem 192
    191   Sampling at exactly $0.5f_S$ 193
                                     Magnitude frequency response 196
                                     Magnitude frequency response of a boxcar 197
                                     The sinc weighting function 198
                                     Frequency response of point sampling 199
                                     Fourier transform pairs 200
                                     Analog filters 202
                                     Digital filters 202
                                     Impulse response 207
                                     Finite impulse response (FIR) filters 207
                                     Physical realizability of a filter 208
                                     Phase response (group delay) 209
                                     Infinite impulse response (IIR) filters 210
                                     Lowpass filter 211
                                     Digital filter design 214
                                     Reconstruction 216
                                     Reconstruction close to $0.5f_S$ 217
                                     "$(\sin x)/x$" correction 218
                                     Further reading 220

21 Resampling,   2:1 downsampling 224
    interpolation, and   Oversampling 224
    decimation 221   Interpolation 226
                                     Lagrange interpolation 227
                                     Lagrange interpolation as filtering 229

Polyphase interpolators   231
Polyphase taps and phases   232
Implementing polyphase interpolators   233
Decimation   234
Lowpass filtering in decimation   234

22   Image digitization and   Spatial frequency domain   238
reconstruction   237   Comb filtering   241
Spatial filtering   242
Image presampling filters   242
Image reconstruction filters   243
Spatial (2-D) oversampling   244

23   Perception and visual   Retina   247
acuity   247   Adaptation   247
Contrast sensitivity   249
Contrast sensitivity function (CSF)   251

24   Luminance and   Radiance, intensity   255
lightness   255   Luminance   256
Relative luminance   258
Luminance from red, green, and blue   258
Lightness (CIE L^*)   259

25   The CIE system   Fundamentals of vision   266
of colorimetry   265   Definitions   266
Spectral power distribution (SPD) and tristimulus   267
Spectral constraints   268
CIE *XYZ* tristimulus   272
CIE [x, y] chromaticity   275
Blackbody radiation   276
Colour temperature   277
White   278
Chromatic adaptation   280
Perceptually uniform colour spaces   280
CIE L*u*v*   281
CIE L*a*b* (CIELAB)   283
CIE L*u*v* and CIE L*a*b* summary   284
Colour specification and colour image coding   285
Further reading   285

26   Colour science for video   Additive reproduction (*RGB*)   288
287   Characterization of *RGB* primaries   290
BT.709 primaries   290

Leggacy SD primaries   293
sRGB system   294
SMPTE Free Scale (FS) primaries   294
AMPAS ACES primaries   294
SMPTE/DCI P3 primaries   295
CMFs and SPDs   296
Normalization and scaling   299
Luminance coefficients   306
Transformations between *RGB* and CIE *XYZ*   307
Noise due to matrixing   308
Transforms among *RGB* systems   309
Camera white reference   310
Display white reference   310
Gamut   311
Wide-gamut reproduction   312
Free Scale Gamut, Free Scale Log (FS-Gamut, FS-Log)   312
Further reading   313

27 Gamma 315

Gamma in CRT physics   316
The amazing coincidence!   318
Gamma in video   318
Opto-electronic conversion functions (OECFs)   320
BT.709 OECF   320
SMPTE ST 240M transfer function   322
sRGB transfer function   323
Transfer functions in SD   324
Bit depth requirements   325
Gamma in modern display devices   326
Estimating gamma   326
Gamma in video, CGI, and Macintosh   328
Gamma in computer graphics   332
Gamma in pseudocolour   332
Limitations of 8-bit linear coding   333
Linear and nonlinear coding in CGI   333

28 Luma and colour differences 335

Colour acuity   335
RGB and *R'G'B'* colour cubes   337
Conventional luma/colour difference coding   341
Luminance and luma notation   342
Nonlinear red, green, blue (*R'G'B'*)   345
BT.601 luma   346
BT.709 luma   346
Chroma subsampling, revisited   347

Luma/colour difference summary   347
SD and HD luma chaos   350
Luma/colour difference component sets   352

Part 3 – Practical matters   355

29   Component video colour coding for SD   357

$B'{-}Y'$, $R'{-}Y'$ components for SD   359
P_BP_R components for SD   359
C_BC_R components for SD   361
$Y'C_BC_R$ from studio RGB 364
$Y'C_BC_R$ from computer RGB 365
"Full-swing" $Y'C_BC_R$ 365
$Y'UV$, $Y'IQ$ confusion   367

30   Component video colour coding for HD   369

$B'{-}Y'$, $R'{-}Y'$ components for BT.709 HD   369
P_BP_R components for BT.709 HD   370
C_BC_R components for BT.709 HD   371
C_BC_R components for xvYCC   373
$Y'C_BC_R$ from studio RGB 374
$Y'C_BC_R$ from computer RGB 374
Conversions between HD and SD   375
Colour coding standards   376

31   Video signal processing   377

Edge treatment   377
Transition samples   378
Picture lines   379
Choice of S_{AL} and S_{PW} parameters   380
Video levels   381
Setup (pedestal)   381
BT.601 to computing   383
Enhancement   383
Median filtering   385
Coring   385
Chroma transition improvement (CTI)   387
Mixing and keying   387

32   Frame, field, line, and sample rates   389

Field rate   389
Line rate   390
Sound subcarrier   391
Addition of composite colour   391
NTSC colour subcarrier   391
576i PAL colour subcarrier   393
$4f_{SC}$ sampling   393
Common sampling rate   394

DIGITAL VIDEO AND HD ALGORITHMS AND INTERFACES

Numerology of HD scanning   395
Audio rates   398

33 Timecode 399   Introduction   399
                           Dropframe timecode   400
                           Editing   401
                           Linear timecode (LTC)   402
                           Vertical interval timecode (VITC)   402
                           Timecode structure   402
                           Further reading   404

34 2-3 pulldown 405   2-3-3-2 pulldown   407
                           Conversion of film to different frame rates   408
                           Native 24 Hz coding   411
                           Conversion to other rates   412

35 Deinterlacing 413   Spatial domain   413
                           Vertical-temporal domain   415
                           Motion adaptivity   416
                           Further reading   418

36 Colourbars 419   SD colourbars   419
                           SD colourbar notation   421
                           PLUGE element   421
                           Composite decoder adjustment using colourbars   422
                           –I, +Q, and PLUGE elements in SD colourbars   423
                           HD colourbars   423

                           Part 4 – Studio standards   425

37 Reference display and References   428
    viewing conditions 427

38 SDI and HD-SDI   Component digital SD interface (BT.601)   430
    interfaces 429   Serial digital interface (SDI)   432
                           Component digital HD-SDI   432
                           SDI and HD-SDI sync, TRS, and ancillary data   433
                           TRS in 4:2:2 SD-SDI   434
                           TRS in HD-SDI   436
                           Analog sync and digital/analog timing
                             relationships   437
                           Ancillary data   437
                           SDI coding   439
                           HD-SDI coding   440

Interfaces for compressed video   441
SDTI   441
Switching and mixing   442
Timing in digital facilities   442
ASI   443
Summary of digital interfaces   443

39   480*i* component video   445

Frame rate   445
Interlace   445
Line sync   447
Field/frame sync   447
R'G'B' EOCF and primaries   448
Luma (*Y'*)   450
Picture center, aspect ratio, and blanking   450
Halfline blanking   451
Component digital 4:2:2 interface   452
Component analog *R'G'B'* interface   452
Component analog $Y'P_BP_R$ interface, EBU N10   453
Component analog $Y'P_BP_R$ interface, industry standard   455

40   576*i* component video   457

Frame rate   457
Interlace   457
Line sync   459
Analog field/frame sync   459
R'G'B' EOCF and primaries   460
Luma (*Y'*)   462
Picture center, aspect ratio, and blanking   462
Component digital 4:2:2 interface   463
Component analog 576*i* interface   464

41   1280×720 HD   467

Scanning   467
Analog sync   468
Picture center, aspect ratio, and blanking   469
R'G'B' EOCF and primaries   469
Luma (*Y'*)   471
Component digital 4:2:2 interface   471

42   1920×1080 HD   473

Scanning   473
Analog sync   475
Picture center, aspect ratio, and blanking   478
R'G'B' EOCF and primaries   478
Luma (*Y'*)   480
Component digital 4:2:2 interface   480

43 HD videotape 481

D-5 HD (HD-D5, D-15) 482
D-6 482
HDCAM (D-11) 482
DVCPRO HD (D-12) 482
HDCAM SR (D-16) 483

44 Component analog HD interface 485

Pre- and postfiltering characteristics 487

Part 5 – Video compression 489

45 JPEG and motion-JPEG (M-JPEG) compression 491

JPEG blocks and MCUs 492
JPEG block diagram 494
Level shifting 495
Discrete cosine transform (DCT) 495
JPEG encoding example 496
JPEG decoding 500
Compression ratio control 501
JPEG/JFIF 502
Motion-JPEG (M-JPEG) 503
Further reading 504

46 DV compression 505

DV chroma subsampling 506
DV frame/field modes 507
Picture-in-shuttle in DV 508
DV overflow scheme 508
DV quantization 510
DV digital interface (DIF) 511
Consumer DV recording 512
Professional DV variants 512

47 MPEG-2 video compression 513

MPEG-2 profiles and levels 514
Picture structure 517
Frame rate and 2-3 pulldown in MPEG 518
Luma and chroma sampling structures 519
Macroblocks 520
Picture coding types – I, P, B 520
Prediction 521
Motion vectors (MVs) 524
Coding of a block 525
Frame and field DCT types 525
Zigzag and VLE 527
Refresh 528
Motion estimation 528

Rate control and buffer management   531
Bitstream syntax   533
Transport   535
Further reading   535

48 H.264 video
    compression 537

Algorithmic features, profiles, and levels   538
Baseline and extended profiles   540
High profiles   541
Hierarchy   541
Multiple reference pictures   541
Slices   542
Spatial intra prediction   542
Flexible motion compensation   542
Quarter-pel motion-compensated interpolation   543
Weighting and offsetting of MC prediction   543
16-bit integer transform   543
Quantizer   544
Variable-length coding   544
Context adaptivity   546
CABAC   546
Deblocking filter   546
Buffer control   547
Scalable video coding (SVC)   547
Multiview video coding (MVC)   548
AVC-Intra   548
Further reading   548

49 VP8 compression 549

Algorithmic features   550
Further reading   552

Part 6 – Distribution standards   553

50 MPEG-2 storage and
    transport 555

Elementary stream (ES)   556
Packetized elementary stream (PES)   556
MPEG-2 program stream   556
MPEG-2 transport stream   556
System clock   557
Further reading   558

51 Digital television
    broadcasting 559

Japan   560
United States   560
ATSC modulation   561
Europe   563
Further reading   563

Appendices 565

A *YUV* and *luminance* considered harmful 567

Cement *vs.* concrete 567
True CIE luminance 568
The misinterpretation of luminance 568
The enshrining of luma 570
Colour difference scale factors 571
Conclusion: A plea 572

B Introduction to radiometry and photometry 573

Radiometry 574
Photometry 575
Light level examples 578
Image science 578
Units 579
Further reading 580

Glossary 581

Index 669

Index of authors 709

Figures

Preface   P.1   Scanning a raster   xxxvii

Part 1 – Introduction 1

1 Raster images   1.1   Pixel arrays   3
                               1.2   Aspect ratio   4
                               1.3   The choice of 16:9 aspect ratio   5
                               1.4   Cartesian coordinates   6
                               1.5   Scene, lens, image plane   7
                               1.6   Digitization   7
                               1.7   Audio taper   8
                               1.8   Grey paint samples   9
                               1.9   Comparison of aspect ratios   15
                               1.10 SD to HD pixel mapping   16
                               1.11 Aspect ratio changes   16
                               1.12 When centre-cut   16
                               1.13 Pan-and-scan   17
                               1.14 Letterbox format   17
                               1.15 Pillarbox format   17
                               1.16 Squeeze to $^3/_4$ 17
                               1.17 A normal image   17
                               1.18 Stretch to $^4/_3$ 17

2 Image acquisition and   2.1   Image acquisition   19
   presentation   2.2   Colour as a dramatic device   21
                               2.3   Image approval   22
                               2.4   Stages of production   23
                               2.5   Consumer origination   25

3 Linear-light and   3.1   The ITU-R BT.815 pattern   30
   perceptual uniformity   3.2   A contrast sensitivity test pattern   31

		3.3	The "code 100" problem 31
		3.4	The "code 100" problem is mitigated 31
		3.5	A greyscale ramp 35
		3.6	A greyscale ramp, augmented 35
4	Quantization	4.1	A Quantizer transfer function 37
		4.2	Peak-to-peak, peak, and RMS values 40
		4.3	Full-swing 8-bit quantization 42
		4.4	Footroom and headroom 42
		4.5	A Mid-tread quantizer for C_B and C_R 46
5	Contrast, brightness, CONTRAST, and BRIGHTNESS	5.1	Relationship between pixel value and L^* 52
		5.2	Effect of gain control 53
		5.3	Effect of offset control 53
		5.4	Effect of gain control 55
		5.5	Effect of offset control 55
		5.6	Contrast ratio and lightness (L^*) 58
		5.7	BLACK LEVEL and WHITE LEVEL controls 60
		5.8	The BRIGHTNESS (or BLACK LEVEL) control in video 61
		5.9	The CONTRAST (or VIDEO LEVEL) control in video 61
		5.10	The BRIGHTNESS control in Photoshop 63
		5.11	The CONTRAST control in Photoshop 63
		5.12	Photoshop CONTRAST control's gain factor 64
6	Raster images in computing	6.1	Raster image data 66
		6.2	Truecolour (24-bit) graphics 69
		6.3	Pseudocolour (8-bit) graphics 71
7	Image structure	7.1	"Box" reconstruction 76
		7.2	Gaussian reconstruction 76
		7.3	Diagonal line reconstruction 77
		7.4	Contone image reconstruction 77
		7.5	One frame of an animated sequence 78
		7.6	A Moiré pattern 78
		7.7	Bitmapped graphic image, rotated 79
		7.8	Gaussian spot size 81
8	Raster scanning	8.1	A dual-bladed shutter 84
		8.2	Blanking intervals 85
		8.3	The Production aperture 87
		8.4	The Clean aperture 87
		8.5	Interlaced format 88

8.6 Twitter 89
8.7 Horizontal and vertical drive 90
8.8 Progressive and interlaced scanning 91
8.9 Modern image format notation 92

9 Resolution

9.1 Magnitude frequency response 98
9.2 Snellen chart 99
9.3 The astronomers' rule of thumb 100
9.4 The viewing distance 101
9.5 The picture angle 101
9.6 Picture height 101
9.7 A Resolution wedge 104

10 Constant luminance

10.1 Formation of relative luminance 108
10.2 Hypothetical chroma components (linear-light) 109
10.3 Encoding nonlinearly coded relative luminance 109
10.4 Decoding nonlinearly coded relative luminance 109
10.5 The CRT transfer function 110
10.6 Compensating the CRT transfer function 110
10.7 Rearranged decoder 110
10.8 Simplified decoder 111
10.9 Rearranged encoder 111
10.10 Chroma components 112
10.11 Subsampled chroma components 112
10.12 Y' and C_B/C_R waveforms at the green-magenta transition 113
10.13 Luminance waveform at the green-magenta transition 113
10.14 Failure to adhere to constant luminance 113

11 Picture rendering

11.1 Surround effect 116
11.2 Imposition of picture rendering at decoder, hypothetical 118
11.3 Imposition of picture rendering at encoder 118

12 Introduction to luma and chroma

12.1 Chroma subsampling 124
12.3 Chroma subsampling notation 125
12.2 Subsampling schemes 126
12.4 An Interstitial chroma filter for JPEG/JFIF 127
12.5 A cosited chroma filter for BT.601, 4:2:2 127
12.6 A cosited chroma filter for MPEG-2, 4:2:0 127

13 Introduction to   13.1 SD digital video rasters   130
    component SD   13.2 SD sample rates   131
                            13.3 Interlacing in 480*i*   132
                            13.4 Interlacing in 576*i*   132
                            13.5 Interlacing in MPEG-2   132

14 Introduction to   14.1 NTSC chroma modulation and frequency
    composite NTSC and   interleaving   138
    PAL   14.2 The S-video interface   139

15 Introduction to HD   15.1 HD rasters at 30 and 60 frames per second   142
                            15.2 HD rasters at 24 Hz and 25 Hz   144

16 Introduction to video   16.1 Interpicture coding   152
    compression
                            16.3 An MPEG P-picture   154
                            16.4 An MPEG B-picture   155
                            16.5 The three-level MPEG picture hierarchy   155
                            16.6 Example GoP   156
                            16.7 Example 9-picture GoP without B-pictures   156
                            16.8 GoP reordered for transmission   157

                            Part 2 – Theory 189

20 Filtering and sampling   20.1 Cosine waves less than and greater than
                                   $0.5f_S$ 192
                            20.2 Cosine waves at exactly $0.5f_S$ 193
                            20.3 Point sampling   194
                            20.4 The Box weighting function   194
                            20.5 Boxcar filtering   194
                            20.6 Aliasing due to boxcar filtering   195
                            20.7 Frequency response of a boxcar filter   197
                            20.8 The sinc weighting function   199
                            20.9 A Gaussian function   200
                            20.10 Waveforms of three temporal extents   200
                            20.11 Fourier transform pairs   201
                            20.12 A [1, 1] FIR filter   203
                            20.13 A [1, –1] FIR filter   203
                            20.14 A [1, 0, 1] FIR filter   203
                            20.15 A [1, 0, –1] FIR filter   203
                            20.16 A very simple 5-tap FIR filter   204
                            20.17 A 5-tap FIR filter including multipliers   205
                            20.18 5-tap FIR filter responses   205
                            20.19 A simple comb filter   206

		20.20	The simple comb filter's response 206
		20.21	Linear phase 209
		20.22	An IIR ("recursive") filter 210
		20.23	Lowpass filter characterization 212
		20.24	BT.601 filter templates 213
		20.25	Halfband filter 215
		20.26	A 25-tap lowpass FIR filter 216
		20.27	Sampling and reconstruction 217
		20.28	Reconstruction close to $0.5f_S$ 217
		20.29	D-to-A conversion with a boxcar waveform 218
		20.30	"$(\sin x)/x$" correction 219
21	Resampling, interpolation, and decimation	21.1	Two-times upsampling 223
		21.2	An original signal 223
		21.3	Two-to-one downsampling 223
		21.4	An analog filter for direct sampling 225
		21.5	An analog filter for 2×-oversampling 225
		21.6	Cubic interpolation 228
22	Image digitization and reconstruction	22.1	Spatiotemporal domains 237
		22.2	Horizontal domain 238
		22.3	Vertical domain 238
		22.4	Temporal domain 238
		22.5	Spatial domain 238
		22.6	Horizontal spatial frequency domain 239
		22.7	Vertical spatial frequency domain 240
		22.8	The spatial frequency spectrum of 480i luma 240
		22.9	Two samples, vertically arranged 241
		22.10	The response of a [1, 1] FIR filter 242
		22.11	Separable spatial filter examples 242
		22.12	Inseparable spatial filter examples 242
23	Perception and visual acuity	23.1	Luminance range of vision 248
		23.2	Adaptation 248
		23.3	A contrast sensitivity test pattern 249
		23.4	Contrast sensitivity 250
		23.5	The contrast sensitivity function (CSF) 252
24	Luminance and lightness	24.1	Luminous efficiency functions 257
		24.2	Luminance and lightness 260
25	The CIE system of colorimetry	25.1	Example coordinate system 265

25.2 Spectral and tristimulus colour reproduction 267

25.3 Spectral constraints 269

25.4 The HPE colour-matching functions 270

25.5 CIE 1931, 2° colour-matching functions 271

25.6 Calculation of tristimulus values by matrix multiplication 273

25.7 CIE 1931 2° [x, y] chromaticity diagram 274

25.8 CIE [x, y] chart features 275

25.9 SPDs of blackbody radiators 276

25.10 SPDs of blackbody radiators, normalized 277

25.11 CIE illuminants 279

25.12 Colour systems 286

26 Colour science for video

26.1 Additive reproduction 289

26.2 The primaries of BT.709 and SMPTE/DCI P3 291

26.3 CMFs for CIE *XYZ* primaries 300

26.4 SPDs for CIE *XYZ* primaries 301

26.5 CMFs for BT.709 primaries 302

26.6 SPDs for BT.709 display primaries 303

26.7 Relative spectral responses (RSRs) for a real camera 304

26.8 Effective response after matrixing 305

27 Gamma

27.1 Display electro-optical function (EOCF) 317

27.2 Image reproduction in video 319

27.3 BT.709 OECF 321

27.4 BT.709, sRGB, and CIE *L** encoding functions 324

27.5 Gamma in video, CGI, and Macintosh 329

27.6 Gamma PC and in classic Mac 331

27.7 Linear and nonlinear coding in imaging standards 334

28 Luma and colour differences

28.1 *RGB* and *R'G'B'* cubes 336

28.2 A $Y'P_BP_R$ cube 339

28.3 Y', $B'-Y'$, $R'-Y'$ orthographic views 340

28.4 Conventional luma/colour difference encoder 341

28.5 Conventional luma/colour difference decoder 342

28.6 Luminance and luma notation 343

28.7 Typesetting $Y'C_BC_R$ 344

	28.8	A luma/colour difference encoder 348
	28.9	A luma/colour difference decoder 349
	28.10	Luma/colour difference flavors 350

Part 3 – Practical matters 355

29	Component video colour coding for SD	29.1	$B'-Y'$, $R'-Y'$ components for SD 359
		29.2	P_BP_R components for SD 360
		29.3	C_BC_R components for SD 363
		29.4	A "full-swing" C_BC_R quantizer 366
		29.5	C_BC_R "full-range" components 366

30	Component video colour coding for HD	30.1	$B'-Y'$, $R'-Y'$ components for BT.709 HD 370
		30.2	P_BP_R components for BT.709 HD 371
		30.3	C_BC_R components for BT.709 HD 372

31	Video signal processing	31.1	Transition samples 379
		31.2	Comparison of 7.5% and zero setup 382
		31.3	The 8-bit BT.601 to full-range (computer) $R'G'B'$ conversion 384
		31.4	A coring circuit 386
		31.5	This matte image example 388

| 32 | Frame, field, line, and sample rates | 32.1 | Numerology of HD scanning   395 |

| 33 | Timecode | 33.1 | Periodic dropped timecode numbers   401 |
| | | 33.2 | Timecode as displayed   401 |

34	2-3 pulldown	34.1	"2-3 pulldown" 405
		34.2	"2-3-3-2 pulldown" 407
		34.3	Vertical/temporal relationships of 2-3 pulldown 409
		34.4	2-3 pulldown, spatial view 410

35	Deinterlacing	35.1	Test scene 413
		35.2	Interlaced capture 413
		35.3	The weave technique 414
		35.4	Line replication 414
		35.5	Interfield averaging 414
		35.6	$V{\cdot}T$ development 415
		35.7	$V{\cdot}T$ domain 415
		35.8	Static lattice in the $V{\cdot}T$ domain 415
		35.9	Interframe averaging in the $V{\cdot}T$ domain 415

	35.10	Line replication in the *V·T* domain 416
	35.11	Intrafield averaging in the *V·T* domain 416
	35.12	Interstitial spatial filter coefficients 417
	35.13	Cosited spatial filter coefficients 417
	35.14	A window function 418

36   Colourbars
36.1	The SMPTE EG 1 SD colourbar test signal 419
36.2	Colourbar *R'G'B'* primary components 420
36.3	The PLUGE element 421
36.4	HUE and CHROMA are adjusted 422
36.5	The SMPTE RP 219 SD colourbar test signal 424

Part 4 – Studio standards 425

38   SDI and HD-SDI interfaces
38.1	Scan-line waveform for 480*i*29.97, 4:2:2 component luma 431
38.2	The BT.656 component digital interface 431
38.3	Scan-line waveform for 1080*i*30 HD component luma 433
38.4	BNC connector 440

39   480*i* component video
39.1	480*i* raster, vertical 449
39.1	480*i* raster, vertical 449
39.2	480*i* component digital 4:2:2 luma waveform 452
39.3	480*i* component analog luma waveform 454

40   576*i* component video
40.1	576*i* raster, vertical 461
40.2	576*i* component digital 4:2:2 luma waveform 464
40.3	576*i* component analog luma waveform 465

41   1280×720 HD
| 41.1 | 720*p* raster, vertical   470 |

42   1920×1080 HD
| 42.1 | 1080*i*30 analog line details   477 |
| 42.2 | 1080*i* and 1080*p* vertical blanking interval   479 |

44   Component analog HD interface
44.1	720*p*60 component analog luma waveform 486
44.2	1080*i*30/1080*p*30 component analog luma waveform 486
44.3	Filter template for *Y'* and *R'G'B'* components 488

Part 5 – Video compression 489

45   JPEG and motion-JPEG   45.1   A JPEG 4:2:0 minimum coded unit 492
    (M-JPEG) compression   45.2   The DCT concentrates image power 493
    45.3   The JPEG block diagram 494
    45.4   An 8×8 array of luma samples 496
    45.5   The DCT tends to concentrate 496
    45.6   A typical JPEG quantizer matrix 497
    45.7   DCT coefficients after quantization 498
    45.8   Zigzag scanning 499
    45.9   Zigzag-scanned coefficient string 499
    45.10   VLE {run length, level} pairs 499
    45.11   Reconstruction error 500
    45.12   Compression ratio control in JPEG 501
    45.13   Because the quantizer is adjustable 502

46   DV compression   46.1   DV superblocks 506
    46.2   Chroma samples in 4:1:1 DV 507

47   MPEG-2 video   47.1   An MPEG-2 frame picture 518
    compression   47.2   An MPEG-2 field picture pair 518
    47.3   Chroma subsampling in field-structured
    pictures 519
    47.4   The frame DCT type 526
    47.5   The field DCT type 527
    47.6   Zigzag *scan*[0] 528
    47.7   Zigzag *scan*[1] 528
    47.8   MPEG encoder and decoder 529
    47.9   Buffer occupancy 532

Appendices 565

B   Introduction to   B.1   Geometry associated with the definition of
    radiometry and   radiance 575
    photometry   B.2   Radiometric and photometric quantities 577

Tables

Part 1 – Introduction   1

3   Linear-light and   3.1 Typical contrast ratios   30
    perceptual uniformity

4   Quantization   4.1 Decibel examples   39

5   Contrast, brightness,   5.1 Effect of adjusting CONTRAST and BRIGHTNESS   57
    CONTRAST, and
    BRIGHTNESS

8   Raster scanning   8.1 Refresh rate   84
                                8.2 Scanning in computing   92
                                8.3 Video systems are classified   94

11 Picture rendering   11.1 End-to-end power functions   119

13 Introduction to   13.1 Gratuitous differences   132
    component SD

15 Introduction to HD   15.1 ATSC A/53 Table 3   143
                                15.2 HD scanning parameters   145

16 Introduction to video   16.1 Approximate compression ratios   149
    compression   16.2 Approximate compression ratios of
                                     M-JPEG   150

17 Streams and files   17.1 Files and streams   163

18 Metadata   18.1 *Color primaries*   177
                                18.2 *Transfer characteristics*   177

18.3 *Matrix coefficients*   177
18.4 *Color primaries* interpretation   179
18.5 *Transfer characteristics* interpretation   179
18.6 *Matrix coefficients* interpretation   179

Part 2 – Theory   189

23 Perception and visual   23.1 Power functions in perception   251
    acuity

25 The CIE system   25.1 White references   279
    of colorimetry

26 Colour science for video   26.1 BT.709 primaries   292
                                26.2 Luminance and chromaticities of BT.709
                                      colourbars   292
                                26.3 NTSC primaries (obsolete)   293
                                26.4 EBU Tech. 3213 primaries   293
                                26.5 SMPTE RP 145 primaries   293
                                26.6 SMPTE "Free Scale" default primaries   294
                                26.7 AMPAS ACES primaries   295
                                26.8 SMPTE/DCI P3 primaries   295
                                26.9 Example primaries   297

28 Luma and colour   28.1 luma coefficients, EOCF, and primary
    differences   chromaticities   351
                                28.2A Colour difference systems for analog SD   353
                                28.2B Colour difference systems for digital SD and
                                       computing   354
                                28.2C Colour difference systems for HD   354

Part 3 – Practical matters   355

32 Frame, field, line, and   32.1 Derivation of 13.5 MHz common sampling
    sample rates   rate   394

33 Timecode   33.1A Timecode bit assignment table   403
                                33.1B Timecode flag bits   403
                                33.1C Timecode binary group flags   404

35 Deinterlacing   35.1 Weston deinterlacer   416

Part 4 – Studio standards 425

38 SDI and HD-SDI
interfaces

38.1 Analog video levels 429
38.2 Digital video levels 429
38.3 Timing reference sequence (TRS) 435
38.4 Protection bits for SAV and EAV 435
38.5 Line number and CRC in HD-SDI 437
38.6 Digital to analog timing relationships 438
38.7 SD and HD interface standards 444

39 480*i* component video

39.1 480*i* line assignment 446

40 576*i* component video

40.1 576*i* line assignment 458

41 1280×720 HD

41.1 720*p* scanning parameters 467
41.2 1280×720 line assignment 468

42 1920×1080 HD

42.1 1920×1080 scanning parameters 474
42.2 1080*i* and 1080*p* line assignment 475

43 HD videotape

43.1 Digital videotape formats for HD 481

Part 5 – Video compression 489

46 DV compression

46.1 DV chroma subsampling 505

47 MPEG-2 video
compression

47.1 MPEG-2 profiles 515
47.2 MPEG-2 main and 4:2:2 profiles 516
47.3 GoP restrictions in SMPTE ST 308M 517
47.4 MPEG-2 *aspect ratio information* 517
47.5 MPEG-2 *frame rate code* 518
47.6 2-3 pulldown sequence in MPEG-2 519
47.7 MPEG macroblock types 523
47.8 MPEG picture coding types 523
47.9 MPEG-2 prediction modes 523

48 H.264 video
compression

48.1 H.264 features 539
48.2 H.264 levels 540
48.3 Two hypothetical coding schemes 544
48.4 An example of exponential Golomb coding 545
48.5 Exp-Golomb coding can be generalized 545
48.6 AVC-Intra profile/level combinations 548

Part 6 – Distribution standards   553

50 MPEG-2 storage and
    transport

50.1 MPEG-2 PCR counts per frame   558

Appendices   565

B Introduction to
   radiometry and
   photometry

B.1 Quantities, symbols, and units of radiometry and
        photometry   573
B.2 Light level examples   578
B.3 Conversion of illuminance into lux   579
B.4 Conversion of luminance into cd·m^{-2} 579

Preface

Video technology continues to advance since the publication, in early 2003, of the first edition of this book. Further "convergence" – Jim Blinn might say collision – between video and computer graphics has occurred. Television is losing; computing and internet transport are winning. Even the acronym "TV" is questionable today: Owing to its usage over the last half century, *TV* implies broadcast, but much of today's video – from the Apple iTunes store, Hulu, NetFlix, YouTube – is not broadcast in the conventional sense. In this edition, I have replaced *SDTV* with *SD* and *HDTV* with *HD*.

Digital video is now ubiquitous; analog scanning, as depicted by Figure P.1 below, is archaic. In this edition, I promote the pixel array to first-class status. The first edition described scan lines; I have retrained myself to speak of image rows and image columns instead. I expunge microseconds in favour of sample counts; I expunge millivolts in favour of pixel values. Phrases in the previous edition such as "immense data capacity" have been replaced by "fairly large" or even "modest data capacity."

Figure P.1 **Scanning a raster,** as suggested by this sketch, is obsolete. In modern video and HD, the image exists in a pixel array. Any book that describes image acquisition or display using a drawing such as this doesn't accurately portray digital video.

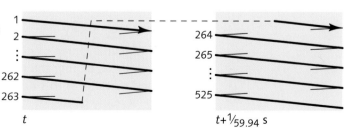

In my first book *Technical Introduction to Digital Video,* published in 1996, and in the first edition of the present book, I described encoding and then decoding. That order made sense to me from an engineering perspective. However, I now think it buries a deep philosophical flaw. Once program material is prepared, decoded, and viewed on a reference display in the studio, and mastered – that is, downstream of final approval – only the decoding and display matters. It is convenient for image data to be captured and encoded in a manner that displays a realistic image at review, but decoding and presentation of the image data at mastering is preeminent. If creative staff warp the colours at encoding in order to achieve an æsthetic effect – say they lift the black levels by 0.15, or rotate hue by 123° – the classic encoding equations no longer apply, but those image data modifications are not evidence of faulty encoding, they are consequence of the exercise of creative intent. The traditional explanation is presented in a manner that suggests that the encoding is fixed; however, what really matters is that *decoding* is fixed. The principle that I'm advocating is much like the principle of MPEG, where the *decoder* is defined precisely but the *encoder* is permitted to do anything that produces a legal bitstream. In this edition I emphasize decoding. A new chapter – Chapter 2, on page 19 – outlines this philosophy.

Many chapters here end with a *Further reading* section if extensive, authoritative information on the chapter's topic is available elsewhere.

Video technology is a broad area. There are entire books that cover subject matter for which this book provides only a chapter. My expertise centres on image coding aspects, particularly the relationship between vision science, colour science, image science, signal processing, and video technology. Chapters of this book on those topics – mainly, the topics of the *Theory* part of this book – have (as far as I know) no textbook counterpart.

Legacy technology

SMPTE is the source of many standards, both legacy and modern. During the interval between the first and second editions of this book, SMPTE abolished the *M* suffix of many historical standards, and prepended *ST* to standards (paralleling *EG* for Engineering Guideline and

RP for Recommended Practice). I cite recent SMPTE standards according to the new nomenclature.

As of 2012, we can safely say that analog television technology and composite (NTSC/PAL) television technology are obsolete. When writing the first edition of this book, I concentrated my efforts on the things that I didn't expect to change rapidly; nonetheless, perhaps 15 or 20 percent of the material in the first edition represents technology – mainly analog and composite and NTSC and PAL – that we would now classify as "legacy." It is difficult for an author to abandon work that he or she has written that represents hundreds or thousands of hours of work; nonetheless, I have removed this material and placed it in a self-contained book entitled *Composite NTSC and PAL: Legacy Video Systems* that is freely available on the web.

www.poynton.com/CNPLVS/

Layout and typography

I designed this book with wide margins. I write notes here, and I encourage you to do the same!

Many years ago, when my daughter Quinn was proofreading a draft chapter of the first edition of this book, she circled, in red, two lines at the top of a page that were followed by a new section. She drew an arrow indicating that the two lines should be moved to the bottom of the previous page. She didn't immediately realize that the lines had wrapped to the top of the page because there was no room for them earlier. She marked them nonetheless, and explained to me that they needed to be moved because that section should start at the top of the page. Quinn intuitively understood the awkward page break – and she was only twelve years old! I have spent a lot of time executing the illustration, layout, and typesetting for this book, based upon my belief that this story is told not only through the words but also through pictures and layout.

In designing and typesetting, I continue to be inspired by the work of Robert Bringhurst, Jan Tschichold, and Edward R. Tufte; their books are cited in the margin.

BRINGHURST, ROBERT (2008), *The Elements of Typographic Style*, version/edition 3.1, (Vancouver, B.C.: Hartley & Marks).

TSCHICHOLD, JAN (1991), *The Form of the Book* (London: Lund Humphries). [Originally published in German in 1975.]

TUFTE, EDWARD R. (1990), *Envisioning Information* (Cheshire, Conn.: Graphic Press).

Formulas

It is said that every formula in a book cuts the potential readership in half. I hope readers of this book can compute that after a mere ten formulas my readership would drop to 2^{-10}! I decided to retain formulas, but they are not generally necessary to achieve an understanding of the concepts. If you are intimidated by a formula, just skip it and come back later if you wish. I hope that you will treat the mathematics the way that Bringhurst recommends that you treat his mathematical description of the principles of page composition. In Chapter 8 of his classic book, *Elements of Typographic Style*, Bringhurst says,

> "The mathematics are not here to impose drudgery upon anyone. On the contrary, they are here entirely for pleasure. They are here for the pleasure of those who like to examine what they are doing, or what they might do or have already done, perhaps in the hope of doing it still better. Those who prefer to act directly at all times, and leave the analysis to others, may be content in this chapter to study the pictures and skim the text."

Spelling

At the urging of my wife Barbara and my two daughters, I have resumed spelling colour with a *u.* However, *colorimetric* and *colorimetry* are without. *Greyscale* is now spelled with an *e* (for English), not with an *a* (for American). The world is getting smaller, and Google's reach is worldwide; however, cultural diversity shouldn't suffer.

I tried carefully to avoid errors while preparing this book. Nonetheless, despite my efforts and the efforts of my reviewers, a few errors may have crept in. As with my previous book, I will compile errata for this book and make the corrections available at the URL indicated in the margin. Please report any error that you discover, and I will endeavour to repair it and attribute the correction to you!

www.poynton.com/DVAI2/

Charles Poynton
Toronto, Jan. 2012

Acknowledgments

My introduction to digital video was writing microcode many years ago for hardware conceived by John Lowry and engineered by Richard Kupnicki. John Ross, founder of Ross Video, continued my education in video. I thank all three.

I spent many hours at CJOH-TV in Ottawa, Canada, testing my theories at the invitation of CJOH's Vice-President of Engineering, Austin Reeve. I thank him for his confidence, good humor, and patience.

I owe a debt of gratitude to four people who have been not only colleagues but close personal friends for a few decades: C.R. Caillouet, Pierre Deguire, Charlie Pantuso, and Mark Schubin.

I thank the colleagues who encouraged me in this project, all of whom reviewed the manuscript at various stages: David Bancroft, George Joblove, Peter Symes and especially Dave LeHoty – who suggested the title, long ago!

Portions of the manuscript were reviewed, and error reports were provided by the following people, who I thank: Don Craig, Joseph Goldstone, and Adam Wilt. My apologies to them, also, because not all of their suggestions could be included this time around.

I thank the netizens that contributed error reports to the first edition, especially Ken Greenebaum, Dragan Matković, and Andrew Murray; thanks especially to Jay Zipnick for contributing several suggestions regarding colour calculations.

While writing this book, I was working in a Ph.D. program under the supervision of Brian Funt. I thank him for his contributions to that effort, many of which have found their way into this book.

Diane Cerra was my patient and thoughtful editor for my first book, and for the first edition of this one. Her ideas and hard work shaped this second edition. Sara Binns, Laura Lewin, Sara Scott, and Graham Smith comprised my thoroughly professional editorial staff at Morgan Kaufmann; I thank them. I also thank my superb copy editor, Charles Roumeliotis.

Thanks to my family, for their love and encouragement: Peg, Al, Kim, Brenna, Alana, Dad, and Jean. Thanks also to Jeri, Corot, Ben, and Paige.

Thanks to Barbara, the love of my life, and our daughters Quinn and Georgia.

Part 1

Introduction

1 Raster images 3
2 Image acquisition and presentation 19
3 Linear-light and perceptual uniformity 27
4 Quantization 37
5 Contrast, brightness, CONTRAST, and BRIGHTNESS 47
6 Raster images in computing 65
7 Image structure 75
8 Raster scanning 83
9 Resolution 97
10 Constant luminance 107
11 Picture rendering 115
12 Introduction to luma and chroma 121
13 Introduction to component SD 129
14 Introduction to composite NTSC and PAL 135
15 Introduction to HD 141
16 Introduction to video compression 147
17 Streams and files 163
18 Metadata 171
19 Stereoscopic ("3-D") video 181

Raster images

A *vector* image comprises data describing a set of geometric primitives, each of which is associated with grey or colour values.
A process of interpretation – *rasterizing, or raster image processing, or ripping* – is necessary to convert a vector image to a raster. *Vector* suggests a straight line but paradoxically, "vector" images commonly contain primitives describing curves.

A digital image is represented by a rectangular array (matrix) of *picture elements* (*pels,* or *pixels*). Pixel arrays of several image standards are sketched in Figure 1.1. In a greyscale system each pixel comprises a single component whose value is related to what is loosely called brightness. In a colour system each pixel comprises several components – usually three – whose values are closely related to human colour perception.

Historically, a video image was acquired at the camera, conveyed through the channel, and displayed using analog scanning; there was no explicit pixel array. Modern cameras and modern displays directly represent the discrete elements of an image array having fixed structure. Signal processing at the camera, in the pipeline, or at the display may perform spatial and/or temporal resampling to adapt to different formats.

Figure 1.1 **Pixel arrays** of several imaging standards are shown, with their counts of image columns and rows. The 640×480 square sampled structure common in computing is included; however, studio and consumer 480*i* standards are sampled 704×480 or 720×480 with nonsquare sampling.

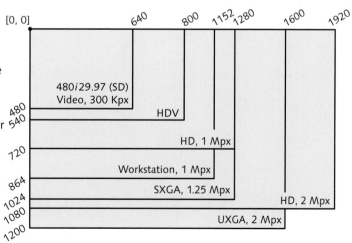

In art, the frame surrounds the picture; in video, the frame *is* the picture.

The pixel array is for one image is a *frame*. In video, digital memory used to store one image is called a *framestore;* in computing, it's a *framebuffer*. The total pixel count in an image is the number of image columns N_C (or in video, *samples per active line*, S_{AL}) times the number of image rows N_R (or *active lines*, L_A). The total pixel count is usually expressed in megapixels (Mpx).

In video and in computing, a pixel comprises the set of *all* components necessary to represent colour (typically red, green, and blue). In the mosaic sensors typical of digital still cameras (DSCs) a pixel is *any* colour component individually; the process of *demosaicking* interpolates the missing components to create a fully populated image array. In digital cinema cameras the DSC interpretation of *pixel* is used; however, in a digital cinema projector, a pixel is a triad.

A computer enthusiast refers to the image column and row counts (*width × height*) as *resolution*. An image engineer reserves the term *resolution* for the image detail that is acquired, conveyed, and/or delivered. Pixel count imposes an upper limit to the image detail; however, many other factors are involved.

The value of each pixel component represents brightness and colour in a small region surrounding the corresponding point in the sampling lattice.

Pixel component values are quantized, typically to an integer value that occupies between 1 and 16 bits – and often 8 or 10 bits – of digital storage. The number of bits per component, or per pixel, is called the *bit depth*. (We use *bit depth* instead of *width* to avoid confusion: The term *width* refers to the entire picture.)

Aspect ratio

Aspect ratio is simply the ratio of an image's width to its height. Standard aspect ratios for film and video are sketched, to scale, in Figure 1.2. What I call simply *aspect ratio* is sometimes called *display aspect ratio*

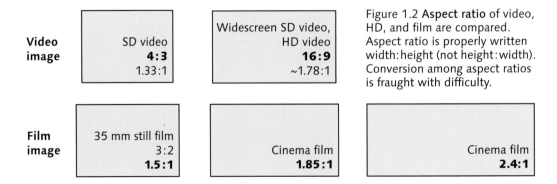

| Video image | SD video **4:3** 1.33:1 | Widescreen SD video, HD video **16:9** ~1.78:1 | Figure 1.2 **Aspect ratio** of video, HD, and film are compared. Aspect ratio is properly written width:height (not height:width). Conversion among aspect ratios is fraught with difficulty. |

| Film image | 35 mm still film 3:2 **1.5:1** | Cinema film **1.85:1** | Cinema film **2.4:1** |

DIGITAL VIDEO AND HD ALGORITHMS AND INTERFACES

$$\frac{width}{height} = \frac{AR}{SAR} \qquad \text{Eq 1.1}$$

$$N_C = \sqrt{n \cdot AR}; \quad N_R = \sqrt{\frac{n}{AR}} \qquad \text{Eq 1.2}$$

In Europe and Asia, 1.66:1 was the historical standard for cinema, though 1.85 is increasingly used owing to the worldwide market for entertainment imagery.

FHA: Full-height anamorphic

SCHUBIN, MARK (1996), "Searching for the perfect aspect ratio," in *SMPTE Journal* **105** (8): 460–478 (Aug.).

(DAR) or *picture aspect ratio* (PAR). *Standard-definition* (SD) television has an aspect ratio of 4:3.

Equation 1.1 relates picture and sample aspect ratios. To assign *n* square-sampled pixels to a picture having aspect ratio *AR*, choose image column and image row counts (*c* and *r*, respectively) according to Equation 1.2.

Cinema film commonly uses 1.85:1 (which for historical reasons is called either *flat* or *spherical*), or 2.4:1 ("CinemaScope," or colloquially, '*scope*). Many films are 1.85:1, but "blockbusters" are usually 2.4:1. Film at 2.4:1 aspect ratio was historically acquired using an aspherical lens that squeezes the horizontal dimension of the image by a factor of two. The projector is equipped with a similar lens, to restore the horizontal dimension of the projected image. The lens and the technique are called *anamorphic*. In principle, an anamorphic lens can have any ratio; in practice, a ratio of exactly two is ubiquitous in cinema.

Widescreen refers to an aspect ratio wider than 4:3. *High-definition* (HD) television is standardized with an aspect ratio of 16:9. In video, the term *anamorphic* usually refers to a 16:9 widescreen variant of a base video standard, where the horizontal dimension of the 16:9 image occupies the same width as the 4:3 aspect ratio standard. Consumer electronic equipment rarely recovers the correct aspect ratio of such conversions (as we will explore later in the chapter.)

HD is standardized with an aspect ratio of 16:9 (about 1.78:1), fairly close to the 1.85:1 ordinary movie aspect ratio. Figure 1.3 below illustrates the origin of the 16:9 aspect ratio. Through a numerological coincidence apparently first revealed by Kerns Powers, the

Figure 1.3 **The choice of 16:9 aspect ratio** for HD came about because 16:9 is very close to the geometric mean of the 4:3 picture aspect ratio of conventional television and the 2:4:1 picture aspect ratio of CinemaScope movies.

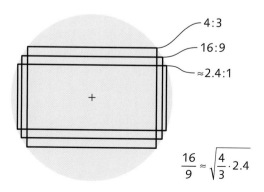

$$\frac{16}{9} \approx \sqrt{\frac{4}{3} \cdot 2.4}$$

geometric mean of 4:3 (the standard aspect ratio of conventional television) and 2.4 (the aspect ratio of a CinemaScope movie) is very close – within a fraction of a percent – to 16:9. (The calculation is shown in the lower right corner of the figure.) A choice of 16:9 for HD meant that SD, HD, and CinemaScope shared the same "image circle": 16:9 was a compromise between the vertical cropping required for SD and the horizontal cropping required for CinemaScope.

Geometry

In mathematics, coordinate values of the (two-dimensional) plane range both positive and negative. The plane is thereby divided into four quadrants (see Figure 1.4). Quadrants are denoted by Roman numerals in the counterclockwise direction. In the continuous image plane, locations are described using Cartesian coordinates [x, y] – the first coordinate is associated with the horizontal direction, the second with the vertical. When both x and y are positive, the location is in the *first quadrant* (quadrant I). In image science, the image lies in this quadrant. (Adobe's Postscript system uses first-quadrant coordinates.)

In matrix indexing, axis ordering is reversed from Cartesian coordinates: A matrix is indexed by *row* then *column*. The top row of a matrix has the smallest index, so matrix indices lie in quadrant IV. In mathematics, matrix elements are ordinarily identified using 1-origin indexing. Some image processing software packages use 1-origin indexing – in particular, MATLAB and Mathematica, both of which have deep roots in mathematics. The scan line order of conventional video and image processing usually adheres to the matrix convention, but with zero-origin indexing: Rows and columns are usually numbered [r, c] from [0, 0] at the top left. In other words, the image is in quadrant IV (but eliding the negative sign on the y-coordinate), but ordinarily using zero-origin indexing.

Digital image sampling structures are denoted *width* × *height*. For example, a 1920×1080 system has columns numbered 0 through 1919 and rows (historically, "picture lines") numbered 0 through 1079.

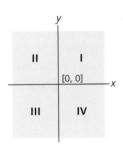

Figure 1.4 **Cartesian coordinates** [x, y] define four quadrants. *Quadrant I* contains points having positive x and y values. Coordinates in quadrant I are used in some imaging systems. *Quadrant IV* contains points having positive x and negative y. Raster image coordinates are ordinarily represented with image row numbers increasing down the height of the image – that is, in quadrant IV, but omitting the negative sign on the y values.

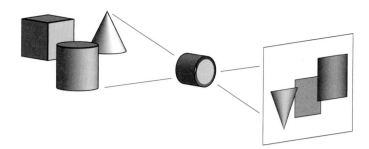

Figure 1.5 **Scene, lens, image plane**

Image capture

In human vision, the three-dimensional world is imaged by the lens of the eye onto the retina, which is populated with photoreceptor cells that respond to light having wavelengths ranging from about 400 nm to 700 nm. In video and in film, we build a camera having a lens and a photosensitive device, to mimic how the world is perceived by vision. Although the shape of the retina is roughly a section of a sphere, it is topologically two dimensional. In a camera, for practical reasons, we employ a flat *image plane,* sketched in Figure 1.5 above, instead of a section of a sphere. Image science involves analyzing the continuous distribution of optical power that is incident on the image plane.

Digitization

Signals captured from the physical world are translated into digital form by *digitization,* which involves two processes: *sampling* (in time or space) and *quantization* (in amplitude), sketched in Figure 1.6 below. The operations may take place in either order, though sampling usually precedes quantization.

Figure 1.6 **Digitization** comprises *sampling* and *quantization*, in either order. Sampling density, expressed in units such as pixels per inch (ppi), relates to resolution. Quantization relates to the number of bits per pixel (bpp) or bits per component/channel (bpc). Total data rate or data capacity depends upon the product of these two factors.

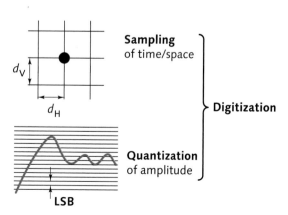

Quantization

Quantization assigns an integer to signal amplitude at an instant of time or a point in space, as I will explain in *Quantization,* on page 37. Virtually all image exchange standards – TIFF, JPEG, SD, HD, MPEG, H.264 – involve pixel values that are *not* proportional to light power in the scene or at the display: With respect to light power, pixel values in these systems are nonlinearly quantized.

1-D sampling

A continuous one-dimensional function of time, such as audio sound pressure level, is sampled through forming a series of discrete values, each of which is a function of the distribution of a physical quantity (such as intensity) across a small interval of time. *Uniform sampling,* where the time intervals are of equal duration, is nearly always used. (Details will be presented in *Filtering and sampling,* on page 191.)

2-D sampling

A continuous two-dimensional function of space is sampled by assigning, to each element of the image matrix, a value that is a function of the distribution of intensity over a small region of space. In digital video and in conventional image processing, the samples lie on a regular, rectangular grid.

Analog video was not sampled horizontally; however, it was sampled vertically by scanning and sampled temporally at the frame rate. Historically, samples were not necessarily digital: CCD and CMOS image sensors are inherently sampled, but they are not inherently quantized. (On-chip analog-to-digital conversion is now common in CMOS sensors.) In practice, though, sampling and quantization generally go together.

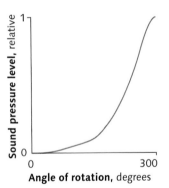

Figure 1.7 **Audio taper** imposes perceptual uniformity on the adjustment of volume. I use the term perceptual uniformity instead of perceptual linearity: Because we can't attach an oscilloscope probe to the brain, we can't ascribe to perception a mathematical property as strong as linearity. This graph is redrawn from BOURNS, INC. (2005), *General Application Note – Panel Controls – Taper.*

Perceptual uniformity

A perceptual quantity is encoded in a *perceptually uniform* manner if a small perturbation to the coded value is approximately equally perceptible across the range of that value. Consider the volume control on your radio. If it were physically linear, the roughly logarithmic nature of loudness perception would place most of the perceptual "action" of the control at the bottom of its range. Instead, the control is designed to be perceptually uniform. Figure 1.7 shows the transfer function of a potentiometer with standard *audio taper:* Angle of rotation is mapped to sound pressure level such that rotating the knob 10 degrees produces

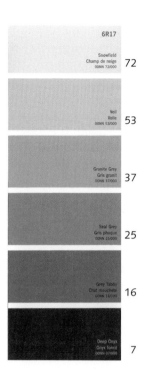

6R17

Snowfield
Champ de neige
00NN 72/000   72

Veil
Voile
00NN 53/000   53

Granite Grey
Gris granit
00NN 37/000   37

Seal Grey
Gris phoque
00NN 25/000   25

Grey Tabby
Chat moucheté
00NN 16/000   16

Deep Onyx
Onyx foncé
00NN 07/000   7

Figure 1.8 **Grey paint samples** exhibit perceptual uniformity: The goal of the manufacturer is to cover a reasonably wide range of reflectance values such that the samples are uniformly spaced as judged by human vision. The manufacturer's code for each chip typically includes an approximate *L** value. In image coding, we use a similar scheme, but with code (pixel) value *V* instead of *L**, and a hundred or a thousand codes instead of six.

CIE: *Commission Internationale de L'Éclairage.* See Chapter 25, on page 265.

$$0.495 \approx L^*(0.18)$$
$$0.487 \approx 0.18^{0.42}$$

EOCF: *Electro-optical conversion function.* See Chapter 27, *Gamma,* on page 315.

a similar perceptual increment in volume across the range of the control. This is one of many examples of perceptual considerations built into the engineering of electronic systems. (For another example, see Figure 1.8.)

Compared to linear-light encoding, a dramatic improvement in signal-to-noise performance can be obtained by using nonlinear image coding that mimics human lightness perception. Ideally, coding for distribution should be arranged such that the step between pixel component values is proportional to a *just noticeable difference* (JND) in physical light power. The CIE standardized the *L** function in 1976 as its best estimate of the lightness sensitivity of human vision. Although the *L** equation incorporates a cube root, *L** is effectively a power function having an exponent of about 0.42; 18% "mid grey" in relative luminance corresponds to about 50 on the *L** scale from 0 to 100. The inverse of the *L** function is approximately a 2.4-power function. Most commercial imaging systems incorporate a mapping from digital code value to linear-light luminance that approximates the inverse of *L**.

Different EOCFs have been standardized in different industries:

• In digital cinema, DCI/SMPTE standardizes the reference (approval) projector; that standard is closely approximated in commercial cinemas. The standard digital cinema reference projector has an EOCF that is a pure 2.6-power function.

• In SD and HD, EOCF was historically poorly standardized or not standardized at all. Consistency has been achieved only through use of *de facto* industry-standard CRT studio reference displays having EOCFs well approximated by a 2.4-power function. In 2011, BT.1886 was adopted formalizing the 2.4-power, but reference white luminance and viewing conditions are not [yet] standardized.

• In high-end graphics arts, the Adobe RGB 1998 industry standard is used. That standard establishes a reference display and its viewing conditions. Its EOCF is a pure 2.2-power function.

• In commodity desktop computing and low-end graphics arts, the sRGB standard is used. The sRGB standard establishes a reference display and its viewing conditions. Its EOCF is a pure 2.2-power function.

Colour

To be useful for colour imaging, pixel components represent quantities closely related to human colour vision. There are three types of photoreceptor *cone* cells in the retina, so human vision is trichromatic: Three components are necessary and sufficient to represent colour for a normal human observer. Rod cells constitute a fourth photoreceptor type, responsible for what can loosely be called night vision. When you see colour, cone cells are responding. Rod (scotopic) vision is disregarded in the design of virtually all colour imaging systems.

Colour images are generally best captured with sensors having spectral responsivities that peak at about 630, 540, and 450 nm – loosely, red, green, and blue – and having spectral bandwidths of about 50, 40, and 30 nm respectively. Details will be presented in Chapters 25 and 26.

In *multispectral* and *hyperspectral* imaging, each pixel has 4 or more components each representing power from different wavelength bands. Hyperspectral refers to a device having more than a handful of spectral components. There is currently no widely accepted definition of how many components constitute multispectral or hyperspectral. I define a multispectral system as having between 4 and 10 spectral components, and a hyperspectral system as having 11 or more. Hyper-

Vision when only the rod cells are active is termed *scotopic*. When light levels are sufficiently high that the rod cells are inactive, vision is *photopic*. In the *mesopic* realm, both rods and cones are active.

The term *multispectral* refers to cameras and scanners, or to their data representations. Display systems using more than three primaries are called *multiprimary*.

spectral systems may be described as having colour, but they are usually designed for purposes of science, not vision: A set of pixel component values in a hyperspectral system usually has no close relationship to colour perception. Apart from highly specialized applications such as satellite imaging and the preservation or reproduction of fine art, multispectral and hyperspectral techniques are not used in commercial imaging.

Luma and colour difference components

Some digital video equipment uses $R'G'B'$ components directly. However, human vision has considerably less ability to sense detail in colour information than in lightness. Provided achromatic detail is maintained, colour detail can be reduced by *subsampling*, which is a form of spatial filtering (or averaging).

A colour scientist might implement subsampling by forming relative luminance as a weighted sum of linear *RGB* tristimulus values, then imposing a nonlinear transfer function approximating CIE lightness ($L*$). In video, we depart from the theory of colour science, and implement an engineering approximation that I will describe in *Constant luminance,* on page 107. Briefly, component video systems convey image data as a luma component, Y', approximating lightness and coding the achromatic component, and two colour difference components – in the historical analog domain, P_B and P_R, and in digital systems, C_B and C_R – that represent colour disregarding lightness. The colour difference components are subsampled (horizontally, or both horizontally and vertically) to reduce their data rate. $Y'C_BC_R$ and $Y'P_BP_R$ components are explained in *Introduction to luma and chroma,* on page 121.

Digital image representation

Many different file, memory, and stream formats are used to convey still digital images and motion sequences. Most formats have three components per pixel (representing additive red, green, and blue colour components). In consumer electronics and commodity computing, most formats have 8 bits per component. In professional applications such as studio video and digital cinema, 10, 12, or more bits per component are typically used.

Imaging systems are commonly optimized for other aspects of human perception; for example, the JPEG and MPEG compression systems exploit the spatial frequency characteristics of vision. Such optimizations can also be referred to as perceptual coding.

Virtually all commercial imaging systems use perceptual coding, whereby pixel values are disposed along a scale that approximates the capability of human vision to distinguish greyscale shades. In colour science, capital letter symbols *R, G,* and *B* are used to denote *tristimulus values* that are proportional to light power in three wavelength bands. Tristimulus values are not perceptually uniform. It is explicit or implicit in nearly all commercial digital imaging systems that pixel component values are coded as the desired display *RGB* tristimuli raised to a power between about $1/2.2$ (that is, about 0.45) and $1/2.6$ (that is, about 0.38). Pixel values so constructed are denoted with primes: *R'G'B'* (though the primes are often omitted, causing confusion).

In order for image data to be exchanged and interpreted reasonably faithfully, digital image standards define pixel values for reference black and reference white. Digital image standards typically specify a target luminance for reference white. Most digital image standards offer no specific reflectance or relative luminance for reference black; it is implicit that the display system will make reference black as dark as possible.

It is a mistake to place a linear segment at the bottom of the sRGB EOCF. (A linear segment *is* called for in the OECF defined in sRGB, but that's a different matter.)

In computing, 8-bit digital image data ranges from reference black at code 0 to reference white at code 255. The sRGB standard calls for an exponent ("gamma") of 2.2 at the display. Reference white is supposed to display luminance of 80 cd·m^{-2}, though in practice values up to about 320 cd·m^{-2} are common.

In consumer digital video, image data is coded in 8-bit components ranging from reference black at code 16 to reference white at code 235. (In the studio, 10-bit coding is common.) Studio standards call for an exponent ("gamma") of about 2.4 at the display. Common practice places reference white at luminance of about 100 cd·m^{-2}, with a dark viewing environment (about 1 lx) and a dark surround (1%). Faithful display is obtained at the consumers' premises when these conventions are followed. It is common for consumer displays to be brighter than 100 cd·m^{-2}; consumers' viewing environments are often fairly bright (often around 100 lx) and the surround is often dim (5%). In cases where the consumer display and viewing conditions differ from those at the studio, preserving picture appearance requires display adjustment.

The DVI computer display interface is defined to carry $R'G'B'$ values having reference range 0 through 255. The HDMI and DisplayPort interfaces also accommodate that coding, but in addition they accommodate $R'G'B'$ values having reference range 16 through 235, they accommodate bit depths deeper than 8 bits, and they accommodate $Y'C_BC_R$ coding. The SDI and HD-SDI interfaces common in studio video accommodate 10-bit $R'G'B'$ or $Y'C_BC_R$ values having reference range 64 through 940 (that is, $16 \cdot 4$ and $219 \cdot 4$).

Image data for offset printing is typically represented as 8-bit code values for the relative amounts of cyan, magenta, yellow, and black (*CMYK*) inks required at a pixel location, where [0, 0, 0, 0] defines no ink (that is, producing the colour of the printing substrate, typically white) and [0, 0, 0, 255] defines black. Perceptual uniformity is imposed by what a printer calls *dot gain*. User interfaces typically present the 0 to 255 range as 0 to 100 – that is, the interface expresses percentage.

In some circles, dot gain is now called *tone value increase* (TVI). The *increase* makes things darker: Printers are more concerned with ink than with light.

SD and HD

Until about 1995, the term *television* referred to either 480*i* (historically denoted 525/59.94, or "NTSC") or 576*i* (625/50, or "PAL"). The emergence of widescreen television, high-definition television (HDTV), and other new systems introduced ambiguity into the unqualified term *television*. What we used to call "television" is now *standard-definition television* (SDTV). Video technology was and is widely used to distribute entertainment programming – historically, "television," TV – but applications are now so diverse that I omit the letters *TV* and refer simply to *SD* and *HD*.

My definition excludes 480*p*, 540*p*, and 576*p* as HD, but admits 720*p*. (My threshold of image rows is the geometric mean of 540 and 720.)

Surprisingly, there are no broadly agreed definitions of SD and HD. I classify as SD any video system having a frame rate of 23.976 Hz or more whose digital image has fewer than 1152 image columns or fewer than 648 image rows – that is, fewer than about ¾ million total pixels. I classify as HD any video system with a native aspect ratio of 16:9 and frame rate of 23.976 Hz or more, whose digital image has 1152 or more image columns and 648 or more image rows – that is, a digital image comprising 729 Kpixels (about ¾-million pixels) or more.

A 16:9 image having area of 1 m^2 has dimensions $^4/_3$ m by $^3/_4$ m (about 1.33 m by 0.75 m) and a diagonal of about 1.53 m (60 in). Today, this size represents the largest practical consumer direct-view display.

A 16:9 image having width of 1 m has height of 0.5625 m, and area of 0.5625 m^2. Its diagonal is about 1.15 m, or 45 inches; this is approximately the median size of HD receivers purchased today. At 1920×1080, pixel pitch is $^1/_{1920}$ m, or about 520 μm; each RGB "subpixel" has dimensions roughly 174 μm by 520 μm.

Square sampling

The term *square* refers to the sample arrangement: *Square* does not mean that image information is uniformly distributed throughout a square area associated with each pixel! Some 1080*i* HD compression systems re-sample to $^4/_3$ or $^3/_2$ pixel aspect ratio.

In modern digital imaging, including computing, digital photography, graphics arts, and HD, samples (pixels) are ordinarily equally spaced vertically and horizontally – they have equal horizontal and vertical sample density. These systems have *square sampling* ("square pixels"); they have *sample aspect ratio* (*SAR*) of unity. With square sampling, the count of image columns is simply the aspect ratio times the count of image rows.

Legacy imaging and video systems including digital SD systems had unequal horizontal and vertical sample pitch (nonsquare sampling). That situation was some-times misleadingly referred to as "rectangular sampling," but a square is also a rectangle! A heated debate in the early 1990s led to the adoption of square sampling for HD. In 1995 the New York Times wrote,

If you use the term *pitch*, it isn't clear whether you refer to the dimension of an element or to the number of elements per unit distance. I prefer the term *density*.

> HDTV signals can be sent in a variety of formats that rely not only on progressive or interlaced signals, but on features like square versus round pixels …

NEW YORK TIMES (1995, Sep. 11), "Patents; The debate over high-definition TV formats is resolved with a system that provides both"

A technical person finds humour in that statement; surprisingly, though – and unintentionally – it contains a technical grain of truth: In sampled continuous-tone imagery, the image information associated with each sample is spread out over a neighbourhood which, ideally, has circular symmetry.

Comparison of aspect ratios

Concerning the origin of the 16:9 aspect ratio, see page 5.

In the mid-1990s, when HD was undergoing standard-ization, SD and HD were compared using various measures, depicted in Figure 1.9 at the top of the facing page, based upon the difference in aspect ratio between 4:3 and 16:9. Comparisons were made of equal height,

Figure 1.9 **Comparison of aspect ratios** between conventional television (now SD) and HD was attempted using various measures: equal height, equal width, equal diagonal, and equal area. All of these comparisons overlooked the fundamental improvement of HD: its increased pixel count. The correct comparison is based upon equal picture detail. It is the angular subtense of a pixel that should be preserved.

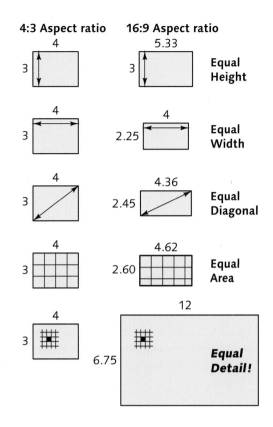

equal width, equal diagonal, and equal area. All of those measures overlooked the fundamental improvement of HD: Its "high definition" (or "resolution") does not squeeze six times the number of pixels into the same visual angle! Instead, the angular subtense of a single pixel should be maintained, and the entire image can now occupy a much larger area of the viewer's visual field. HD allows a greatly increased picture angle. The correct comparison between conventional television and HD is not based upon picture aspect ratio; it is based upon picture detail.

Aspect ratio

With the advent of HD consumer television receivers, it became necessary to display 4:3 (SD) material on 16:9 (HD) displays and 16:9 material on 4:3 displays. During the standardization of HD, I proposed – not entirely facetiously – that SD content at 4:3 should be "pixel-mapped" into the HD frame as sketched in Figure 1.10, preserving aspect ratio and equal detail. I anticipated

Figure 1.10 **SD to HD pixel mapping** is one way to convert 4:3 material to 16:9. The angular subtense of SD pixels is preserved. If CE vendors had adopted this approach at the introduction of HD, today's aspect ratio chaos would have been avoided.

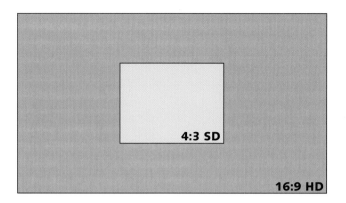

that provisions would be made for the consumer to enlarge the SD image – but the consumer would have been aware of two qualitatively different image sources. (My idea wasn't adopted!)

Widescreen 16:9 material can be adapted to 4:3 by cropping the image width; however, picture content is lost, and creative intent is liable to be compromised. Figures Figure 1.11 and 1.12 below show the result of centre-cropping 16:9 material. The plot might suffer!

Pan-and-scan, sketched in Figure 1.13 at the top of the facing page, refers to choosing on a scene-by-scene basis the 4:3 region to be maintained, to mitigate the creative loss that might otherwise result from cropping.

Figure 1.11 **Aspect ratio changes** can compromise creative intent. Consider this frame at 1.78:1 aspect ratio. The two figures survey the water prior to embarking on an adventure.

Figure 1.12 **When centre-cut** to 4:3 aspect ratio, one character is deleted; the story has changed. Much drama and much comedy depends upon action at the edges of the frame.

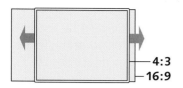

Figure 1.13 **Pan-and-scan** crops the width of widescreen material – here, 16:9 – for a 4:3 aspect ratio display.

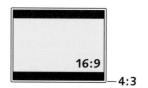

Figure 1.14 **Letterbox format** fits widescreen material – here, 16:9 – to the width of a 4:3 display.

Figure 1.15 **Pillarbox format** (sometimes called *sidebar*) fits narrow-aspect-ratio material to the height of a 16:9 display.

Many directors and producers refuse to allow their films to be altered by cropping; consequently, many movies on DVD are released in *letterbox* format, sketched in Figure 1.14 below. In letterbox format, the entirety of the widescreen image is maintained, and the top and bottom of the 4:3 frame are unused. (Typically, either grey or black is displayed.)

Conventional 4:3 material can be adapted to 16:9 in *pillarbox* format, shown in Figure 1.15. The full height of the display is used; the left and right of the widescreen frame are blanked. However, consumer electronics (CE) manufacturers were concerned about consumers complaining about unused screen area after upconversion of SD. So, CE vendors devised schemes to stretch the image horizontally to eliminate the side panels.

The centre panel below, Figure 1.17, shows an image with correct geometry. To its left (Figure 1.16), the image is squeezed horizontally to 75%; to its right (Figure 1.18), it is stretched horizontally to 133.3%. The distortion is so blatant that you may suspect that I have

Some consumer HD receivers have nonlinear stretching where the horizontal expansion ratio is a function of position. The intended image geometry is distorted; horizontal panning looks wonky.

Figure 1.16 **Squeeze to ³/₄** is necessary if 16:9 material is crudely resized to fit a 4:3 frame.

Figure 1.17 **A normal image** of Barbara Morris is shown here for comparison.

Figure 1.18 **Stretch to ⁴/₃** is necessary if 4:3 material is crudely resized to fit 16:9.

exaggerated the effect – but the images here are distorted by exactly the amounts that would be used for SD-to-HD and HD-to-SD conversion to fit the frame width. Such shrinking and stretching is disastrous to picture integrity – but it has been commonplace since the introduction of HD to consumer television in North America. Failure of content distributors and consumer electronics manufacturers to properly respect picture aspect ratio has been, in my opinion, the most serious engineering error made in the introduction of HD systems to North America.

Frame rates

Details concerning frame rates and interlace are found in *Flicker, refresh rate, and frame rate,* on page 83.

SD broadcast television historically used interlaced scanning. In 480*i* ("NTSC") systems, a frame rate of $30/_{1.001}$ Hz ("29.97 Hz") is standard; in 576*i* ("PAL") systems, a frame rate of 25 Hz is standard. The frame rates of composite NTSC and PAL video are rigid. Component video systems potentially have flexibility in the choice of frame rate. However, production and distribution infrastructure is generally locked-in to one of two frame rates, 25 Hz or 29.97 Hz. For international distribution of programming, frame-rate conversion is necessary either in the distribution infrastructure or in consumer equipment.

Frame rates have historically been chosen on a regional basis to match the prevailing AC power line frequency. Efforts were made in the 1990s to establish a single worldwide frame rate for HD; these efforts were unsuccessful. Origination and broadcasting of HD typically takes place at the prevailing power-line frequency, 50 Hz or (nominally) 60 Hz. Certain lighting units used for acquisition flash at twice the AC power line frequency (though well above the perceptual flicker sensitivity). If a camera operates at a frame rate different from the AC line frequency, such flashing is liable to "beat" with the frame rate of the camera to produce an objectionable low-frequency strobing.

With distribution of video across commodity IP networks to consumer PCs, decoding recovers the native frame rate of the program, but generally no attempt is made to synchronize the display system. Poor motion portrayal often results.

Image acquisition

and presentation   2

The basic proposition of digital imaging is summarized in Figure 2.1. Image data is captured, processed, and/or recorded, then presented to a viewer. As outlined in the caption, and detailed later, appearance depends upon display and viewing conditions. Viewing ordinarily takes place in conditions different from those in effect at the time of capture of a scene. If those conditions differ, a nontrivial mapping of the captured image data – *picture rendering* – must be imposed in order to achieve faithful portrayal, to the ultimate viewer, of the appearance of the scene (as opposed to its physical stimulus).

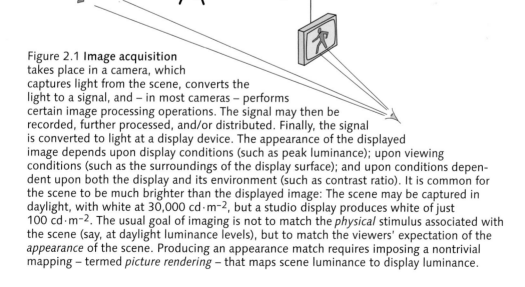

Figure 2.1 **Image acquisition** takes place in a camera, which captures light from the scene, converts the light to a signal, and – in most cameras – performs certain image processing operations. The signal may then be recorded, further processed, and/or distributed. Finally, the signal is converted to light at a display device. The appearance of the displayed image depends upon display conditions (such as peak luminance); upon viewing conditions (such as the surroundings of the display surface); and upon conditions dependent upon both the display and its environment (such as contrast ratio). It is common for the scene to be much brighter than the displayed image: The scene may be captured in daylight, with white at 30,000 cd·m^{-2}, but a studio display produces white of just 100 cd·m^{-2}. The usual goal of imaging is not to match the *physical* stimulus associated with the scene (say, at daylight luminance levels), but to match the viewers' expectation of the *appearance* of the scene. Producing an appearance match requires imposing a nontrivial mapping – termed *picture rendering* – that maps scene luminance to display luminance.

Examine the flowers in a garden at noon on a bright, sunny day. Look at the same garden half an hour after sunset. Physically, the spectra of the flowers have not changed, except by scaling to lower luminance levels. However, the flowers are markedly less colourful after sunset: Colourfulness decreases as luminance decreases. This is the *Hunt effect,* named after the famous colour scientist R.W.G. Hunt. Images are usually viewed at a small fraction, perhaps $\frac{1}{100}$ or $\frac{1}{1000}$, of the luminance at which they were captured. If the image is presented with luminance proportional to the scene luminance, the presented image would appear less colourful, and lower in contrast, than the original scene.

To present contrast and colourfulness comparable to the original scene, we *must* alter the characteristics of the image. An engineer or physicist might strive to achieve mathematical linearity in an imaging system; however, the required alterations cause the displayed relative luminance to depart from proportionality with scene luminance. The dilemma is this: We can achieve mathematical linearity, or we can achieve correct appearance, but we cannot simultaneously achieve both! Successful commercial imaging systems sacrifice mathematics to achieve the correct perceptual result.

Giorgianni, Edward J., and Thomas E. Madden (2008), *Digital Color Management: Encoding Solutions,* Second Edition (Chichester, U.K.: Wiley).

Image state

In many professional imaging applications, imagery is reviewed and/or approved prior to distribution. Even if the image data originated with a colorimetric link from the scene, any technical or creative decision that results in alteration of the image data will break that link. Consider the movie *Pleasantville.* Colour is used as a storytelling device. The story hinges upon characters depicted in greyscale and characters depicted in colour. (See Figure 2.2.) The $R'G'B'$ values of the final movie do not accurately represent what was in front of the camera! This example is from the entertainment industry, however, examples abound whereever colour is adjusted for æsthetic purposes.

Picture rendering is ordinarily a nonlinear operation, not easily described in a simple equation or even a set of equations. Once picture rendering is imposed, its parameters aren't usually preserved. In many applications of imaging, image data is manipulated to achieve

Figure 2.2 **Colour as a dramatic device**. This image mimics the visual style of the 1998 New Line Cinema movie, *Pleasantville*. When the scene was captured, the characters in the background weren't grey; they were rotoscoped in post-production. Image data has been altered to achieve an artistic goal.

ISO 22028-1 (2004), *Photography and graphic technology– Extended colour encodings for digital image storage, manipulation and interchange.*

High-end D-SLR cameras have provisions to capture "raw" data that has *not* been subject to picture rendering operations. These cameras are capable of capturing "science."

an artistic effect – for example, colours in a wedding photograph may be selectively altered by the photographer. In such cases, data concerning picture rendering is potentially as complex as the whole original image!

The design of an imaging system determines where picture rendering is imposed:
• In consumer digital photography and in video production, picture rendering is typically imposed in the camera.
• In movie making, picture rendering is typically imposed in the processing chain.

If an imaging system has a direct, deterministic link from luminance in the scene to image code values, in colour management terminology the image data is said to have an *image state* that is *scene referred*. If there is a direct, deterministic linkage from image code values to the luminance intended to be produced by a display, then image data is said to be *display referred*.

Video standards such as BT.709 and SMPTE ST 274 (both to be detailed later) are at best unclear and at worst wrong concerning image state. Consequently, video engineers often mistakenly believe that video data is linked colorimetrically to the scene. Users of digital still cameras may believe that their cameras capture "science"; however, when capturing TIFF or JPEG images, camera algorithms perform rendering, so the colorimetric link to the scene is broken. What is important in these applications is not the OECF that once mapped light from the scene to image data values, but rather the EOCF that is expected to map image data values to light presented to the viewer.

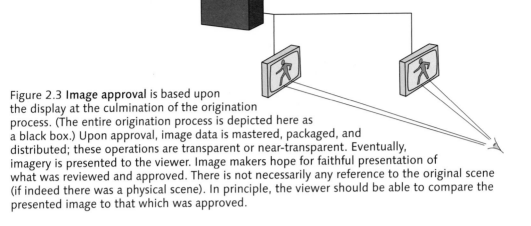

Figure 2.3 **Image approval** is based upon the display at the culmination of the origination process. (The entire origination process is depicted here as a black box.) Upon approval, image data is mastered, packaged, and distributed; these operations are transparent or near-transparent. Eventually, imagery is presented to the viewer. Image makers hope for faithful presentation of what was reviewed and approved. There is not necessarily any reference to the original scene (if indeed there was a physical scene). In principle, the viewer should be able to compare the presented image to that which was approved.

EOCF standards

In imaging systems where imagery is subject to review or approval at origination, faithful presentation requires consistent mapping from image data to light – and in entertainment applications, from audio signal to sound – between the origination environment and the ultimate viewing environment.

Figure 2.3 depicts the basic chain of origination, approval, distribution, and presentation. Origination is depicted as a "black box." The mapping from image data to displayed light involves an *electro-optical conversion function* (EOCF). It is clear from the sketch that faithful presentation requires matching EOCFs at the approval display and the presentation display. EOCF is thereby incorporated – explicitly or implicitly – in any image interchange standard. Faithful presentation also requires agreement – again, implicit or explicit – upon reference viewing conditions.

To make the most effective use of limited capacity in the "channel," the EOCFs common in commercial imaging incorporate perceptual uniformity, a topic to which we now turn.

Entertainment programming

Entertainment represents an economically important application of imaging, so it deserves special mention here. Digital video, HD, and digital cinema all involve acquisition, recording, processing, distribution, and

Production → Post-production ———→ Distribution ———→ Consumer
                  (Digital intermediate)   presentation
                                                                             (Exhibition)

Figure 2.4 **Stages of production** are depicted. In video, the final stage is *presentation;* in cinema, it's called *exhibition.*

presentation of programs. I'll use the generic word "program" as shorthand for a movie, a television show, or a short piece such as a commercial. Figure 2.4 above presents a sketch of the entire chain.

Production refers to acquisition, recording, and processing. In a live action movie, the term *production* may be limited to just the acquisition of imagery (on set or on location); processes that follow are then postproduction ("post"). In the case of a movie whose visual elements are all represented digitally, post production is referred to as the *digital intermediate* process, or DI.

Production culminates with display and approval of a program on a studio reference display – or, in the case of digital cinema, approval on a cinema reference projector in a review theatre. (If distribution involves compression, then approval properly includes review of compression at the studio and decompression by a reference decompressor.) Following approval, the program is mastered, packaged, and distributed.

Professional content creators rarely seek to present, at the viewer's premises, an accurate representation of the scene in front of the camera. Apart from makers of documentaries, movie makers often make creative choices that alter that reality. They hope that when the program completes its journey through the distribution chain, the ultimate consumer will be presented with a faithful approximation *not* of the original scene, but rather of what the director saw on his or her studio display when he or she approved the final product of postproduction. In colour management terms, movie and video image data is display-referred.

If a movie is "in production," then principal photography is not yet complete.

The word *reproduction,* taken literally, suggests production again! I propose *presentation.*

Acquisition

A person using a camera to acquire image data from a scene expects that when the acquired material is displayed it will approximately match the appearance of the scene. Luminance of white in an outdoor scene might reach 30,000 $cd \cdot m^{-2}$, but it is rare to find an electronic display whose luminance exceeds 450 $cd \cdot m^{-2}$, and professional HD content mastering and approval is performed with a reference white around 100 $cd \cdot m^{-2}$. Linear transfer of the scene luminance to the display – in effect, scaling absolute luminance by a factor of 0.015 or 0.01 – won't present the same appearance as the outdoor scene. The person using the camera expects an approximate apppearance match upon eventual display; consequently, picture rendering must be imposed. In HD, and in consumer still photography, rendering is imposed at the camera; in digital cinema and in professional ("raw") still photography, rendering is imposed in postproduction.

Some people use the phrase "scene-to-screen" to describe the goal of delivering an accurate representation of scene luminance and colour to the display. Unless proper account is taken of appearance phenomena – that is, unless picture rendering is imposed – this effort is doomed to failure.

Consumer origination

Figure 2.5 summarizes consumer-originated video. Consumers may exercise creative control through signal processing after acquisition; however, picture rendering is imposed by algorithms in the camera. The camera is engineered to encode signals for presentation in the consumers' living room. Studio origination is built on an assumption of viewing at 100 $cd \cdot m^{-2}$ in a dark surround (today, around 1%). Consumer camcorders incorporate picture rendering based upon comparable parameters.

Consumer electronics (CE) display

In the consumer electronics domain, there is a diversity of display devices (having different contrast ratios, different peak luminance values, and different colour gamuts), and there is a diversity of viewing environ-

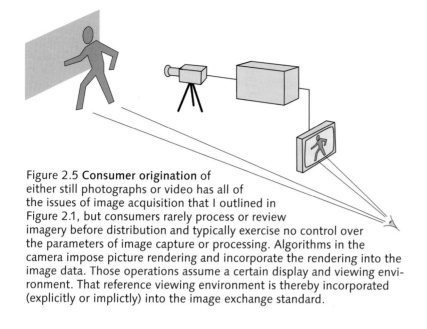

Figure 2.5 **Consumer origination** of either still photographs or video has all of the issues of image acquisition that I outlined in Figure 2.1, but consumers rarely process or review imagery before distribution and typically exercise no control over the parameters of image capture or processing. Algorithms in the camera impose picture rendering and incorporate the rendering into the image data. Those operations assume a certain display and viewing environment. That reference viewing environment is thereby incorporated (explicitly or implictly) into the image exchange standard.

ments (some bright, some dark; some having bright surround, some dim, and some dark).

Different consumer display devices have different default EOCFs. The EOCF for a particular product is preset at the factory in a manner suitable for the viewing conditions expected for that product. Traditional domestic television receivers had EOCFs approximating the 2.4-power function used in the studio; however, modern consumer receivers are considerably brighter than 100 cd·m^{-2} (up to 350 cd·m^{-2} today) and the higher brightness necessitates a somewhat lower value of gamma, today typically between 2.1 and 2.3. A home theatre projector used in a rather dark environment will have characteristics comparable to those of a studio reference display (see *Reference display and viewing conditions,* on page 427), and will typically have "gamma" of about 2.4. A PC has a default sRGB EOCF, with gamma of 2.2.

Consumer television receiver vendors commonly impose signal processing claimed to "improve" the image – often described by adjectives such as "naturalness" or "vividness." However, the director may have thoughtful reasons for wanting the picture to look unnatural, pale, or noisy! Creative control is properly

Digital Reality Creation (DRC) is a trademark of Sony Electronics Inc.

DNIe is a trademark of Samsung Electronics Co., Ltd.

exercised at production, not at presentation. Creative staff generally despise consumer processing that goes by such names as Digital Reality Creation (DRC) or Digital Natural Image engine (DNIe).

Linear-light and
perceptual uniformity 3

Each pixel value in a greyscale image represents what is loosely called *brightness*. However, brightness is defined formally as *the attribute of a visual sensation according to which an area appears to emit more or less light*. This definition is obviously subjective: *Brightness* can't be measured, so is an inappropriate metric for image data. Also, according to colour appearance theory, brightness has no top end: Brightness is not relative to anything.

Intensity is radiant power in a particular direction, that is, power per unit solid angle [$W \cdot sr^{-2}$]; *radiance* is intensity per unit projected area. These terms disregard wavelength composition, but in colour imaging, wavelength is important! Neither of these quantities is a suitable metric for colour image data.

Luminance is radiance weighted by the spectral sensitivity associated with the lightness sensation of vision. Luminance is proportional to intensity; in the SI system, it carries units of candelas per meter squared [$cd \cdot m^{-2}$], commonly called *nits* [nt]. Imaging systems rarely use pixel values proportional to luminance; values nonlinearly related to luminance are usually used.

Illuminance describes light falling on an object; technically, it is luminance integrated over a half-sphere.

Lightness is defined by the CIE as *the brightness of an area judged relative to the brightness of a similarly illuminated area that appears to be white or highly transmitting*. A purist may claim this definition to be subjective; however, an objective quantity L^* is defined as the standard estimate of the perceptual response to relative luminance. It is computed by subjecting relative luminance to a nonlinear transfer function that mimics the

See Appendix B, *Introduction to radiometry and photometry,* on page 601. Sound intensity is conceptually very different from light intensity. ·

Old texts use "brightness," symbolized *B*, where today we would use (absolute) *luminance*, symbolized *L*. In image reproduction, we are usually concerned not with (absolute) luminance, but with *relative luminance*, symbolized *Y*, as I will describe on page 206. The term *luminance* is often carelessly and incorrectly used by video engineers to refer to *luma*, as I will describe.

response of vision at a certain state of adaptation. A few greyscale imaging systems have pixel values proportional to $L*$.

Value refers to measures of lightness roughly equivalent to CIE $L*$ (but typically scaled 0 to 10, not 100). In image science, *value* is rarely – if ever – used in any sense consistent with accurate colour. (Several different value scales are graphed in Figure 20.2 on page 208.)

Regrettably, many practitioners of digital image processing and computer graphics have a cavalier attitude toward the terms described here. In the *HSB, HSI, HSL,* and *HSV* systems, *B* allegedly stands for brightness, *I* for intensity, *L* for lightness, and *V* for value; however, none of these systems is associated with brightness, intensity, luminance, or value according to any definition that is recognized in colour science!

Colour images are sensed and reproduced based upon *tristimulus values* (*tristimuli*), whose amplitudes are proportional to intensity but whose spectral compositions are carefully chosen according to the principles of colour science. Relative luminance can be regarded as a distinguished tristimulus value useful on its own; apart from that, tristimulus values come in sets of three.

The image sensor of a digital camera produces values, proportional to radiance, that approximate red, green, and blue (*RGB*) tristimulus values. I call these values *linear-light*. However, in most imaging systems, *RGB* tristimulus values are coded using a nonlinear transfer function – *gamma correction* – that mimics the perceptual response of human vision. Most image coding systems use *R'G'B'* values that are *not* proportional to intensity; the primes in the notation denote imposition of a perceptually motivated nonlinearity.

Luma (*Y'*) is formed as a suitably weighted sum of *R'G'B'*; it is the basis of luma/colour difference coding in video, MPEG, JPEG, and similar image coding systems. In video, the nonlinearity implicit in gamma correction that forms *R'G'B'* components is subsequently incorporated into the luma and chroma ($Y'C_BC_R$) components.

Luma is comparable to lightness; it is often carelessly and incorrectly called *luminance* by video engineers. See Appendix A, *YUV and luminance considered harmful,* on page 567.

Contrast

The term *contrast,* as used in imaging, is heavily overloaded. "Contrast" can relate to physical properties of light in a scene, physical properties of light in an image, properties of an imaging system's mapping between the two, physical properties of a display system (independent of any image), or various attributes of perception.

Photographers speak of scenes having "high contrast" or "low contrast." A scene's contrast can be characterized by the coefficient of variation of its luminance – that is, by the standard deviation of its luminance divided by its mean luminance. Scene contrast is closely related to the width of the scene's luminance histogram with respect to its "centre of gravity." A dark scene and a light scene may have identical scene contrast. Scene contrast is unaffected by noise.

Photographers also speak of "high key" and "low key" scenes. Loosely speaking, these are predominantly light or dark (respectively). From a cumulative histogram of log luminance, key can be quantified as the fraction of the interval along the *x*-axis between the 10th and 90th percentile where the 50th percentile falls.

Contrast ratio

A basic property of a display is its *contrast ratio,* the ratio between specified light and dark luminances – typically the luminance associated with reference (or peak) white and the luminance associated with reference black. *Inter-image* (or *on-off,* or *sequential*) contrast ratio is measured between fully-white and fully-black images presented individually. Intra-image contrast ratio is measured from white and black regions of a single test image such as that specified by ANSI IT7.228-1997 (now withdrawn, for projectors) or ITU-R BT.815. Visual performance of a display system is best characterized by intra-image contrast ratio.

BT.815 specifies a test image, having 16:9 aspect ratio, useful for measuring contrast ratio ;see Figure 3.1. Contrast ratio is the luminance of the white square divided by the average luminance of the black squares.

In practical imaging systems, many factors conspire to increase the luminance of black, thereby lessening contrast ratio and impairing picture quality. On an electronic display or in a projected image, intra-image contrast ratio is typically less than 800:1 owing to flare in the display system and/or spill light (stray light) in the ambient environment. Typical contrast ratios are shown in Table 3.1. Contrast ratio is a major determi-

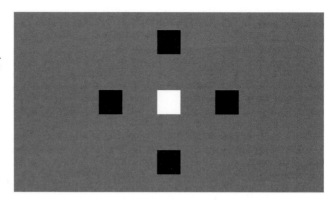

Figure 3.1 **The ITU-R BT.815 pattern** is used to characterize intra-image contrast ratio. The grey background is at 8-bit interface code 126. A small square of reference white lies at the centre of the image; it occupies $^{2}/_{15}$ of the image height. Four identical small squares of reference black are disposed around the centre, offset by $^{1}/_{3}$ of the image height, at 12 o'clock, 3 o'clock, 6 o'clock, and 9 o'clock.

Application	Max. (Ref.) luminance [cd·m⁻²]	Typ. PDR luminance [cd·m⁻²]	Typical inter-image contrast ratio	Typical BT.815 intra-image contrast ratio	Minimum L*
Cinema (projection)	48 (48)	24	1 000:1	100:1	9
HD, studio mastering	120 (100)	90	10 000:1	1000:1	0.9
HD, living room (typ.)	200	200	1 000:1	400:1	2.3
Office (sRGB, typ.)	320	320	100:1	100:1	16

Table 3.1 **Typical contrast ratios** are summarized. PDR refers to perfect diffuse reflector.

nant of subjective image quality, so much so that an image reproduced with a high simultaneous contrast ratio may be judged sharper than another image that has higher measured spatial frequency content.

Because contrast ratio involves measurement of just two quantities – reference white and reference black – it is independent of transfer function. Contrast ratio (and its first cousin, dynamic range) say nothing about bit depth: A bilevel image contains both reference white and reference black, and suffices to produce the optical stimulus necessary to measure contrast ratio.

Perceptual uniformity

I introduced perceptual uniformity on page 8. Coding of a perceptual quantity is *perceptually uniform* if a small perturbation to the coded value is approximately equally perceptible across the range of that value. Vision cannot distinguish two luminance levels if the ratio between them is less than about 1.01 – in other words, the visual threshold for luminance difference is about 1%. This *contrast sensitivity* threshold is established by experiments using the test pattern such as the

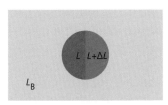

Figure 3.2 **A contrast sensitivity test pattern** reveals that a difference in luminance will be observed in certain conditions when ΔL exceeds about 1% of L. This threshold is called a *just-noticeable difference* (JND).

one sketched in Figure 3.2 in the margin; details will be presented in *Contrast sensitivity,* on page 249. Ideally, pixel values are placed at these *just noticeable difference* (JND) increments along the scale from reference black to reference white.

The "code 100" problem and nonlinear image coding

Consider 8-bit pixel values proportional to luminance, where code zero represents black, and the maximum code value of 255 represents white, as in Figure 3.3 below. Code 100 lies at the point on the scale where the ratio between adjacent luminance values is 1%: Owing to the approximate 1% contrast threshold of vision, the boundary between a region of code-100 samples and a region of code-101 samples is liable to be visible.

As pixel value decreases below 100, the difference in luminance between adjacent codes becomes increasingly perceptible: At code 20, the ratio between adjacent luminance values is 5%. In a large area of smoothly

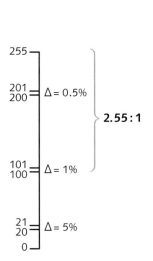

Figure 3.3 **The "code 100" problem** with linear-light coding is that for code levels below 100 the steps between code values have ratios larger than the visual threshold: With just 256 steps, some steps are liable to be visible as banding.

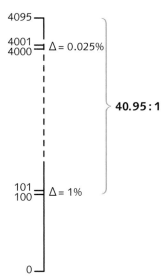

Figure 3.4 **The "code 100" problem is mitigated** by using more than 8 bits to represent luminance. Here, 12 bits are used, placing the top end of the scale at 4095. However, the majority of these 4096 codes cannot be distinguished visually.

varying shades of grey, these luminance differences are likely to be visible or even objectionable. Visible jumps in luminance produce *contouring* or *banding* artifacts.

Linear-light codes above 100 suffer no banding artifacts. However, as code value increases toward white, the codes have decreasing perceptual utility: At code 200, the luminance ratio between adjacent codes is just 0.5%, below the threshold of visibility. Codes 200 and 201 are visually indistinguishable; code 201 could be discarded without its absence being noticed.

High-quality image display requires a contrast ratio of at least 30 to 1 between the luminance of white and the luminance of black. In 8-bit linear-light coding, the ratio between the brightest luminance (code 255) and the darkest luminance that can be reproduced without banding (code 100) is only 2.55:1. Linear-light coding in 8 bits is therefore unsuitable for high-quality images.

One way to mitigate the "code 100" problem is to place the top end of the scale at a code value much higher than 100, as sketched in Figure 3.4. If luminance is represented in 12 bits, with white at code 4095, the luminance ratio between code 100 and white reaches 40.95:1. However, the vast majority of those 4096 code values cannot be distinguished visually; for example, codes 4000 through 4039 are visually indistinguishable. Rather than coding luminance linearly with a large number of bits, we can use many fewer code values, and assign them on a perceptual scale that is nonlinear with respect to light power. Such nonlinear-light – or *perceptually uniform* – coding is pervasive in digital imaging; it works so beautifully that many practitioners don't even know it's happening.

In video (including motion-JPEG, MPEG, and H.264/AVC), and in digital photography (including JPEG/JFIF/Exif), $R'G'B'$ components are coded in a perceptually uniform manner. A video display has a nonlinear transfer function from code value to luminance. That function is comparable to the function graphed in Figure 1.7 on page 8, and approximates the inverse of the lightness sensitivity of human vision. Perceptual uniformity is effected by applying a nonlinear transfer function – *gamma correction* – to each tristimulus estimate sensed from the scene. Gamma correction parameters are chosen – by default, manually, or automatically – such that the intended image appearance is obtained on the reference display in the reference viewing environment. Gamma correction thereby incorporates both considerations of perceptual uniformity and considerations of picture rendering.

A truecolour image in computing is usually represented in R'G'B' components of 8 bits each, as I will explain further on page 36. Each component ranges from 0 (black) through 255 (white). Greyscale and true-colour data in computing is usually coded so as to exhibit approximate perceptual uniformity: The steps are not proportional to intensity, but are instead uniformly spaced perceptually. The number of steps required depends upon properties of the display system, of the viewing environment, and of perception.

An example of 8-bit quantization as commonly used in computing is shown in the right-hand sketch of Figure 4.1, on page 37.

Reference display and viewing parameters for studio video have historically been either poorly standardized or not standardized at all. In *Reference display and viewing conditions,* on page 427, I summarize a set of realistic parameters.

Video standards such as BT.709 and SMPTE ST 274 have historically established standard *opto-electronic conversion functions* (OECFs), as if video had scene-referred image state and as if cameras had no adjustments! In fact, video is effectively *output* (display) referred, and what matters most is not the OECF but the *electro-optical conversion function,* EOCF! Nonlinear coding is the central topic of Chapter 27, *Gamma,* on page 315; that chapter discusses OECF and EOCF.

If the threshold of vision behaved strictly according to the 1% relationship across the whole tone scale, then luminance could be coded logarithmically. For a contrast ratio of 100:1, about 462 code values would be required, corresponding to about 9 bits.

$$\frac{\log 100}{\log 1.01} \approx 462; \quad 1.01^{462} \approx 100$$

For reasons to be explained in *Luminance and lightness,* on page 255, instead of modelling the lightness sensitivity of vision as a logarithmic function, in most digital imaging systems we model it as a power function. The luminance of the red, green, or blue primary light produced by a display is made proportional to code value raised to approximately the 2.4-power. The equation in the margin computes the ratio of linear-light value between the highest 8-bit code value (255) and the next-lowest value (254): The 1.01-requirement

Conversely, display R'G'B' values are proportional to displayed luminance raised to approximately the 0.42-power.-See *Gamma,* on page 315.

$$\frac{\left(\dfrac{255}{255}\right)^{2.4}}{\left(\dfrac{254}{255}\right)^{2.4}} \approx 1.01$$

A related claim is that 8-bit imaging
has an optical density range of about
2.4, where 2.4 is the base-10 log of
$^1/_{255}$. This claim similarly rests upon
linear-light coding.

$$\left(\frac{1}{255}\right)^{2.4} \approx 0.0000016$$

of human vision is met. As code values decrease, the
ratio gets larger; however, as luminance decreases the
luminance ratio required to maintain the "JND" of
vision gets larger. The 2.4-power function turns out to
be a very good match to the perceptual requirement.

Eight-bit imaging systems are often claimed to have
"dynamic range" of 255:1 or 256:1. Such claims arise
from the assumption that image data codes are linearly
related to light. However, most 8-bit image data is
coded perceptually, like sRGB, assuming a 2.2- or 2.4-
power function at the display: For an ideal display, the
dynamic range associated with code 1 would be close
to a million to one. In practice, physical parameters of
the display and its environment limit the dynamic range.

The cathode ray tube (CRT) was, for many decades,
the dominant display device for television receivers and
for desktop computers. Amazingly, a CRT exhibits an
EOCF that is very nearly the inverse of vision's lightness
sensitivity! The nonlinear lightness response of vision
and the power function intrinsic to a CRT combine to
cause the display code value (historically, voltage) to
exhibit perceptual uniformity, as demonstrated in
Figures 3.5 and 3.6 (opposite). The CRT's characteristics were the basis for perceptual uniformity for the first
half century of electronic imaging. Most modern display
devices – such as LCDs, PDPs, and DLPs – do not have
a native, physical power function like that of a CRT;
however, signal processing circuits impose whatever
transfer function is necessary to make the device
behave as if it had a 2.2- or 2.4-power function from
signal value to displayed tristimulus value.

In video, this perceptually uniform relationship is
exploited by *gamma correction* circuitry incorporated
into every video camera. The *R'G'B'* values that result
from gamma correction – the values that are processed,
recorded, and distributed in video – are roughly proportional to the 0.42-power of the intended display luminance: *R'G'B'* values are nearly perceptually uniform.
Perceptual uniformity allows as few as 8 bits to be used
for each *R'G'B'* component. Without perceptual uniformity, each component would need 11 bits or more.
Image coding standards for digital still cameras – for
example, JPEG/Exif – adopt a similar approach.

See *Bit depth requirements,*
on page 326.

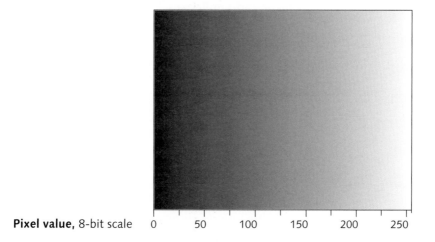

Pixel value, 8-bit scale   0   50   100   150   200   250

Figure 3.5 **A greyscale ramp** on a CRT display is generated by writing successive integer values 0 through 255 into the columns of a framebuffer. When processed by a digital-to-analog converter (DAC), and presented to a CRT display, a perceptually uniform sweep of lightness results. A naive experimenter might conclude – mistakenly! – that code values are proportional to intensity.

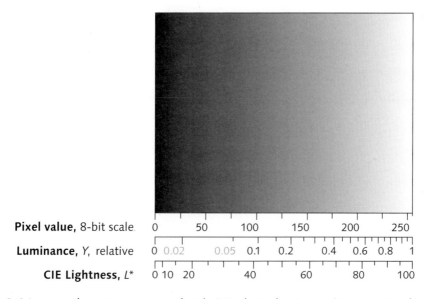

Pixel value, 8-bit scale   0   50   100   150   200   250

Luminance, Y, relative   0   0.02   0.05   0.1   0.2   0.4   0.6   0.8   1

CIE Lightness, L^* 0 10   20   40   60   80   100

Figure 3.6 **A greyscale ramp, augmented** with CIE relative luminance (Y, proportional to intensity, on the middle scale), and CIE lightness (L^*, on the bottom scale). The point midway across the screen has lightness value midway between black and white. There is a near-linear relationship between code value and lightness. However, luminance at the midway point is only about 18% of white! Luminance produced by a CRT is approximately proportional to the 2.4-power of code value. Lightness is approximately the 0.42-power of luminance. Amazingly, these relationships are near inverses. Their near-perfect cancellation has led many workers in video, computer graphics, and digital image processing to misinterpret the term *intensity*, and to underestimate – or remain ignorant of – the importance of nonlinear transfer functions.

Linear and nonlinear

Modern image sensor devices such as CCD and CMOS sensors effectively convert photons to electrons: They produce signals whose amplitude is proportional to physical intensity; they are said to be linear.

Video signals were historically processed through analog circuits that had linear response to voltage. Today's digital video systems are often linear with respect to the arithmetic performed on the pixel values. Video systems are said to be linear.

Linear is an adjective, not a noun!

However, linearity in one domain cannot be carried across to another domain if a nonlinear function separates the two. In video, scene luminance is in a linear optical domain, and the video signal is subject to linear operations in the electrical signal domain. However, OECF and EOCF functions are imposed between the domains. Luminance and pixel value are therefore *not* linearly related. When you ask an optical engineer if her system is linear, she will say, "Of course!" – referring to intensity, radiance, or luminance. When you ask a video engineer if his system is linear, he will say, "Of course!" – referring to arithmetic on pixel values. However, a nonlinear transform lies between the two systems: A linear operation performed in one domain is not linear in the other.

If your computation involves perception, nonlinear representation may be required. If you perform a discrete cosine transform (DCT) on image data as part of image compression, as in JPEG, you should use coding that exhibits perceptual uniformity, in order to minimize the perceptibility of the errors that will be introduced by the coding process.

Quantization   4

Resolution properly refers to spatial phenomena; see page 65. In my view, it is a mistake to refer to a sample as having "8-bit resolution": Say *quantization* or *precision* instead. To make a 100-foot-long fence with fence posts every 10 feet, you need 11 posts, not 10! Take care to distinguish *levels* (in the left-hand portion of Figure 4.1, 11) from *steps* or *risers* (here, 10).

A signal whose amplitude takes a range of continuous values is *quantized* by assigning to each of several (or several hundred or several thousand) intervals of amplitude a discrete, numbered level. In *uniform quantization*, the *steps* between levels have equal amplitude. Quantization discards signal information lying between quantizer levels. Quantizer performance is characterized by the extent of this loss. Figure 4.1 shows, on the left, the transfer function of a uniform quantizer.

Linearity

Electronic systems are often expected to satisfy the *principle of superposition;* in other words, they are expected to exhibit *linearity*. A system g is linear *if and only if* (iff) it satisfies both of these conditions:

Eq 4.1

$$g(a \cdot x) \equiv a \cdot g(x) \qquad \text{[for scalar } a\text{]}$$

$$g(x + y) \equiv g(x) + g(y)$$

    The function g can encompass an entire system: A system is linear iff the sum of the individual responses of the system to any two signals is identical to its response to the sum of the two. Linearity can pertain to

Figure 4.1 **A Quantizer transfer function** is shown on the left. The usual 0 to 255 range of quantized *R'G'B'* components in computing is sketched on the right.

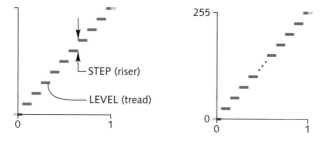

STEP (riser)

LEVEL (tread)

steady-state response, or to the system's temporal response to a changing signal.

Linearity is a very important property in mathematics, signal processing, and video. Many electronic systems operate in the linear intensity domain, and use signals that directly represent physical quantities. One example is compact audio disc (CD) coding: *Sound pressure level* (SPL), proportional to physical intensity, is quantized linearly into 16-bit samples.

Human perception, though, is nonlinear, and in applications where perceptual quantities are being encoded or transmitted, the perceptual nonlinearity can be exploited to achieve coding more efficient than coding the raw physical quantity. For example, audio for digital telephony is nonlinearly coded using just 8 bits per sample. (Two coding laws are in use, A-law and μ-law; both of these involve decoder transfer functions that are comparable to bipolar versions of Figure 4.1.) Image signals that are captured, recorded, processed, or transmitted can similarly be coded in a nonlinear, perceptually uniform manner in order to optimize perceptual performance.

BELLAMY, JOHN C. (2000), *Digital Telephony*, Third Edition (New York: Wiley): 98–111 and 472–476.

Decibels

In the following sections, I will describe signal amplitude, noise amplitude, and the ratio between these – the *signal to noise ratio* (SNR). In engineering, ratios such as SNR are usually expressed in logarithmic units. A power ratio of 10:1 is defined as a *bel* (B), in honour of Alexander Graham Bell. A more practical measure is one-tenth of a bel – a *decibel* (dB), which represents a power ratio of $10^{0.1}$, or about 1.259. The ratio (expressed in decibels) of a power P_1 to a power P_2 is given by Equation 4.2. Signal power is often given with respect to a reference power P_{REF}, which must either be specified (often as a letter following dB) or implied by the context; the computation is expressed in Equation 4.3. An increase of 3 dB in power represents very nearly a doubling of power ($10^{0.3} = 1.995$). An increase of +10 dB multiplies power exactly tenfold; a change of –10 dB reduces power to a tenth.

Eq 4.2 Power ratio, in decibels:

$$m = 10 \log_{10} \frac{P_1}{P_2} \quad \text{(dB)}$$

Eq 4.3 Power ratio, with respect to a reference power:

$$m = 10 \log_{10} \frac{P}{P_{REF}} \quad \text{(dB)}$$

Consider a cable conveying a 100 MHz radio frequency signal. After 100 m of cable, power has diminished to some fraction, perhaps $\frac{1}{8}$, of its original

Eq 4.4 Power ratio, in decibels, as a function of voltage:

$$m = 20 \log_{10} \frac{V_1}{V_2} \quad \text{(dB)}$$

Voltage ratio	Decibels
10	20 dB
2	6 dB
1.112	1 dB
1.0116	0.1 dB
1	0 dB
0.5	–6 dB
0.1	–20 dB
0.01	–40 dB
0.001	–60 dB

Table 4.1 Decibel examples

In photography, a stop is taken to be a ratio of 2. For scientific and engineering purposes it is more convenient to define a stop as exactly three tenths of a density unit, that is, $10^{0.3}$, or about 1.995.

value. After another 100 m, power will be reduced by the same fraction again. Rather than expressing this cable attenuation as a unitless fraction 0.125 per 100 m, we express it as 9 dB per 100 m; power at the end of 1 km of cable is –90 dB referenced to the source power.

The decibel is defined as a power ratio. If a voltage source is applied to a constant impedance, and the voltage is doubled, current doubles as well, so power increases by a factor of four. More generally, if voltage (or current) into a constant impedance changes by a ratio r, power changes by the ratio r^2. (The log of r^2 is $2 \log r$.) To compute decibels from a voltage ratio, use Equation 4.4. In digital signal processing (DSP), digital code levels are treated equivalently to voltage; the decibel in DSP is based upon voltage ratios. In historical analog systems it was common to use a reference of 1 mV (dBmV); in digital systems, the reference is usually the "full scale" range from reference black to reference white (dB_{FS}), equivalent to 219 codes at 8-bit interface levels. Beware: Historical 8-bit computer graphics processed 8-bit signals with no footroom and no headroom, and that practice found its way into PSNR calculations in the MPEG community, where it is common to have full scale interpreted as 0–255 instead of 0–219.

Table 4.1 gives numerical examples of decibels used for voltage ratios.

A 2:1 ratio of frequencies is an *octave*, referring to the eight whole tones in music, *do, re, me, fa, sol, la, ti, do,* that cover a 2:1 range of frequency. When voltage halves with each doubling in frequency, an electronics engineer refers to this as a loss of *6 dB per octave*. If voltage halves with each doubling, then it is reduced to one-tenth at ten times the frequency; a 10:1 ratio of quantities is a *decade*, so 6 dB/octave is equivalent to 20 dB/decade. (The base-2 log of 10 is very nearly $20\!/\!6$.)

A *stop* in photography is a 2:1 ratio of light power. As mentioned above, a decibel is a power ratio of $10^{0.1}$, or about 1.259. Sensor and camera engineers prefer to use units that are equivalent between the optical and electrical domains: They treat digital code level as signal (like voltage), and they describe an optical power of 2 as 6 dB. It is a numerological coincidence that $10^{0.3}$ is very nearly equal to 2; so 6 dB corresponds to one stop, and 2 dB corresponds to $1/3$ stop.

Noise, signal, sensitivity

Analog electronic systems are inevitably subject to noise introduced from thermal and other sources. Thermal noise is unrelated to the signal being processed. A system may also be subject to external sources of interference. As signal amplitude decreases, noise and interference make a larger relative contribution.

Processing, recording, and transmission may introduce noise that is uncorrelated to the signal. In addition, *distortion* that is correlated to the signal may be introduced. As it pertains to objective measurement of the performance of a system, distortion is treated like noise; however, a given amount of distortion may be more or less perceptible than the same amount of noise. Distortion that can be attributed to a particular process is known as an *artifact*, particularly if it has a distinctive perceptual effect.

In video, *signal-to-noise ratio* (SNR) is the ratio of the peak-to-peak amplitude of a specified signal, often the reference amplitude or the largest amplitude that can be carried by a system, to the root mean square (RMS) magnitude of undesired components including noise and distortion. (It is sometimes called PSNR, to emphasize *peak* signal; see Figure 4.2.) SNR is expressed in units of decibels. In many fields, such as audio, SNR is specified or measured in a physical (intensity) domain. In video, SNR usually applies to gamma-corrected components R', G', B', or Y' that are in the perceptual domain; so, SNR correlates with perceptual performance.

Sensitivity refers to the minimum source power that achieves acceptable (or specified) SNR performance.

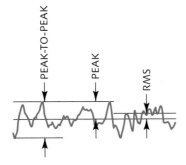

Figure 4.2 **Peak-to-peak, peak, and RMS values** are measured as the total excursion, half the total excursion, and the square root of the average of squared values, respectively. Here, a noise component is shown.

Quantization error

A quantized signal takes only discrete, predetermined levels: Compared to the original continuous signal, *quantization error* has been introduced. This error is correlated with the signal, and is properly called *distortion*. However, classical signal theory deals with the addition of noise to signals. Providing each quantizer step is small compared to signal amplitude, we can consider the loss of signal in a quantizer as addition of an equivalent amount of noise instead: Quantization

Eq 4.5 Theoretical SNR limit
for a *k*-step quantizer:

$$20 \log_{10} \left(k \sqrt{12} \right)$$

The factor of root-12, about
11 dB, accounts for the ratio
between peak-to-peak and
RMS; for details, see Schreiber
(cited below).

Some people use the word *dither*
to refer to the technique of adding
noise prior to quantization; other
people restrict the term *dither to*
schemes that involve spatial distribution of the noise. The technique
was first described by ROBERTS,
LAWRENCE G. (1962), "Picture
coding using pseudorandom
noise," *IRE Trans.* **IT-8** (2): 145–
154. Roberts' work is summarized in SCHREIBER, WILLIAM F.
(1993), *Fundamentals of Electronic
Imaging Systems,* Third Edition
(Berlin: Springer-Verlag).

diminishes signal-to-noise ratio. The theoretical SNR
limit of a *k*-step quantizer is given by Equation 4.5.
Eight-bit quantization, common in consumer video, has
a theoretical SNR limit (peak-to-peak signal to RMS
noise) of about 56 dB.

If an analog signal has very little noise, then its quantized value can be nearly exact when near a step, but
can exhibit an error of nearly $\pm\frac{1}{2}$ of a step when the
analog signal is midway between quantized levels. In
video, this situation can cause the reproduced image to
exhibit *noise modulation*. It is beneficial to introduce,
prior to quantization, roughly $\pm\frac{1}{2}$ of a quantizer step's
worth of high-frequency random or pseudorandom
noise to avoid this effect. This introduces a little noise
into the picture, but this noise is less visible than low-
frequency "patterning" of the quantization that would
be liable to result without it. SNR is slightly degraded,
but subjective picture quality is improved. Historically,
video digitizers implicitly assumed that the input signal
itself arrived with sufficient analog noise to perform this
function; nowadays, analog noise levels are lower, and
the noise should be added explicitly at the digitizer.

The degree to which noise in a video signal is
visible – or objectionable – depends upon the properties of vision. To minimize noise visibility, we digitize
a signal that is a carefully chosen nonlinear function of
luminance (or tristimulus values). The function is chosen
so that a given amount of noise is approximately
equally perceptible across the whole tone scale from
black to white. This concept was outlined in *Nonlinear
image coding,* on page 12; in the sections to follow,
linearity and perceptual uniformity are elaborated.

Full-swing

Excursion (or colloquially, *swing*) refers to the range of
a signal – the difference between its maximum and
minimum levels. In video, reference excursion is the
range between standardized *reference white* and *reference black* signal levels.

Computer graphics image data ordinarily has *full-
swing* (or *full-range*), where reference black is assigned
to the lowest code level and reference white is assigned
to the highest code level. In desktop graphics, *R'G'B'*

Figure 4.3 **Full-swing 8-bit quantization** is depicted in this sketch. A nominally continuous input signal, here represented by values ranging 0 to 1 on the x-axis, is quantized to 8 bits – that is, 256 steps – for storage or transmission. The coding provides no footroom or headroom.

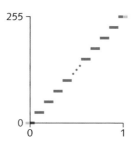

components typically have 8 bits each and range 0 through 255. Figure 4.3 depicts 8-bit full-swing coding.

Studio-swing (footroom and headroom)

In high-quality video, it is necessary to preserve transient signal excursions below black and above white that are liable to result from processing by digital and analog filters. Studio video standards therefore provide footroom below reference black, and headroom above reference white. Since headroom allows code values that exceed reference white, *reference* white and *peak* white refer to different signal levels.

When the BT.601 standard was established in 1984, an engineering error was made. Luma should have been assigned interface codes from 16 to 240 to match the chroma excursion. Instead, the range 16 to 235 was chosen, for no good reason.

I have described signals in the abstract range 0 to 1. When $R'G'B'$ or Y' components are interfaced in 8 bits, the 0 to 1 values are scaled by 219 and offset by +16. Eight-bit studio standards thus have 219 steps between reference black and reference white. Interface codes below 16 and above 235 are used for footroom and headroom. Unfortunately, footroom and headroom are not symmetrical. Figure 4.4 below shows the standard coding range for 8-bit R', G', or B', or luma. Codes

Figure 4.4 **Footroom and headroom** is provided in digital video standards. For processing, reference black is considered to lie at code 0; in an 8-bit system, R', G', B', and luma (Y') range 0 through reference white at code 219. At an 8-bit interface according to BT.601, an offset of +16 is added (indicated in italics). Interface codes 0 and 255 are reserved for synchronization; those codes are prohibited in video data.

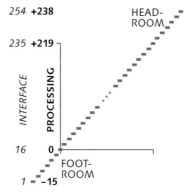

having the 8 most-significant bits (MSBs) all-zero or all-one 0 and 255 are used for synchronization; these codes are prohibited within video data.

Historically, there were essentially two reasons for footroom and headroom:

• It was necessary to accommodate video whose analog levels were misadjusted.

• It was very useful to preserve filter transients (undershoot and overshoot) through as much of the system as possible (even though undershoots would eventually be clipped at the display).

As use of analog decreased, the first reason vanished. The second remained important, and three additional reasons emerged:

PLUGE: Picture line-up generator. See page 421.

• The footroom region enables conveyance of the PLUGE pattern used to set black level.

• When black is set correctly, reference black level produces luminance that is visually indistinguishable from reference black, but still nonzero. A pure 2.4-power function EOCF produces relative luminance of around 0.0003 at this point. The idealized, theoretical zero luminance occurs at a level below reference black. That level is coded in the footroom region.

• Image sensors produce noise, including noise at black. If footroom is provided, the noise averages to black. If lack of footroom clips the negative-going excursion of the noise, then the noise average rises. Provision of footroom prevents *noise modulation.*

So, the first reason for footroom is archaic, but the other four remain important.

Program creators routinely hire *quality control* (QC) contractors to vet finished programs. QC contractors have and come to believe, mistakenly, that excursions outside the 0-to-1 range are "illegal" and should be rejected. Many studios now thoughtlessly believe their QC houses instead of developing their own understanding of the issue.

Concerning headroom, reference black was originally established at a level somewhat below peak white to accommodate analog misadjustment. As digitization prevailed, that reason vanished. But reference white stands firm for digital video, and with a pure 2.4-power EOCF, peak white lies at relative luminance of $(955/876)^{2.4}$, or about 1.23. A studio reference display should follow the 2.4-curve all the way to peak white. The consumer electronic industry is always keen to maximize average brightness, and that goal is routinely aided by their flattening the EOCF at the high end. The working assumption in program creation is that CE equipment will reasonably reliably display levels up to reference white, then cheat.

In interfaces having κ bits ($8 \leq \kappa$), reference black and white levels are multiplied by $2^{\kappa-8}$. For example, when *R'G'B'* or *Y'* components occupy 10 bits, the 0 to 1 range is scaled by 219·4 (i.e., to 0 to 876); the interface offset is +64 instead of +16.

The terms *superblack* and *superwhite* are used in the consumer arena to refer to excursions into the footroom and headroom regions respectively. In some consumer gear (e.g., PS3), *Superwhite* is an option that enables an interface to carry footroom and headroom codes; when *not* set, interface codes are clipped, and the quality of studio-standard material is liable to suffer.

I use the term *studio-swing* for the levels used in studio equipment; I use the term *full-swing* for coding that places the reference levels at the interface extremes, leaving no room for footroom or headroom. Historically, desktop graphics coding had full-swing (between 0 and 255). A realtime HD-SDI interface prohibits codes 0 and 255, or in a 10-bit system, codes 0–3 and codes 1020–1023. If full-swing coding is to be used across an HD-SDI interface, then codes 0–3 and codes 1020–1023 must be avoided.

In digital cinema acquisition and postproduction, it is common to preserve the bottom 64 codes for footroom, but use all of the headroom region up to code 1019. Some digital cinema systems call this "extended" range; however, to my mind using the word "extended" runs the risk of suggesting that using that range is a good idea. (Who wouldn't want "extended?") In my view, the option should be labelled "extreme."

Interface offset

In hardware, an 8-bit interface is considered to convey values 0 through 255. In serial digital video interfaces (SDI, or its HD variant, HD-SDI), the all-zeros and all-ones 8-bit codes are prohibited from data. At an 8-bit digital video interface, an offset of +16 is added to the code values shown in boldface in Figure 4.4: Reference black is placed at interface code 16, and white at 235. I consider the offset to be added or removed at the interface, because a signed representation is necessary for many processing operations (such as changing gain). However, hardware designers often consider 8-bit digital video to have black at code 16 and white at 235.

Taking black as code 16 makes interface design easy, but makes signal arithmetic design more difficult.

Processing coding

In signal processing, it is often convenient (and sometimes necessary) to use a coding that represents reference black at zero independent of coding range. To accommodate footroom, the number representation must allow negative numbers. In describing signal processing at an abstract level – or implementing signal processing in floating point arithmetic – it is simplest to use the range 0 to 1. The reference points 0 and 1 are taken to be reference black and reference white. (The range is also referred to as *units,* where there are 100 units from reference black to reference white.) To accommodate signals in the headroom region, the number representation must allow numbers greater than unity, and in the footroom region, less than zero.

In processing hardware, a sample is ordinarily represented as a fixed-point integer with a limited number of bits. It is usually most convenient to use two's complement arithmetic. The bit depth required in processing is usually greater than that required at an interface. Black will ordinarily be coded at 0. Reference white will be coded to an appropriate value such as 219 in an 8-bit system or 876 in a 10-bit system.

In signal processing, even without the interface offset, it may be necessary to handle negative numbers. Two's complement binary representation is common.

$R'G'B'$ or $Y'C_BC_R$ components of 8 bits each suffice for distribution of consumer video. However, if a video signal must be processed many times, say for inclusion in a multiple-layer composited image, then roundoff errors are liable to accumulate. To avoid roundoff error, studio video data typically carries 10 bits each of $Y'C_BC_R$. Ten-bit studio interfaces have the reference levels of Figures 4.4 and 4.5 multiplied by 4: The extra two bits are appended as least-significant bits to provide increased precision. Within processing equipment, intermediate results may need to be maintained to 12, 14, or even 16 bits.

Figure 4.4 showed a quantizer for a unipolar signal such as luma. C_B and C_R signals are bipolar, ranging positive and negative. For C_B and C_R it is standard to

One one-hundredth of the range from blanking to reference white was historically referred to as an *IRE* unit, for the Institute of Radio Engineers, the predecessor of today's IEEE. Now it is best to say *units.* The mapping from units to 8-bit digital video interface code is this:

$$V_{709} = 16 + 219 \cdot \frac{units}{100}$$

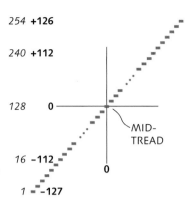

Figure 4.5 A **Mid-tread quantizer for** C_B **and** C_R bipolar signals allows zero chroma to be represented exactly. (*Mid-riser* quantizers are rarely used in video.) For processing, C_B and C_R abstract values have a range of ±112. At an 8-bit studio video interface according to BT.601, an offset of +128 is added, indicated by the values in italics. Interface codes 0 and 255 are reserved for synchronization, as they are for luma.

use a *mid-tread* quantizer, such as the one graphed in Figure 4.5, so that zero chroma has an exact representation. For processing, a signed representation is necessary; at a studio video interface, it is standard to scale 8-bit colour difference components to an excursion of 224, and add an offset of +128. (Note that chroma occupies five more 8-bit codes than luma.)

Two's complement wrap-around

Modern computers use binary number representation. Signed integer arithmetic is implemented using two's complement representation. When the result of an arithmetic operation such as addition or subtraction overflows the fixed bit depth available, two's complement arithmetic wraps around. For example, in 16-bit two's complement arithmetic, taking the largest positive number, 32,767 (in hexadecimal, $7fff_h$) and adding one produces the smallest negative number, –32,768 (in hexadecimal, 8000_h). It is an insidious problem with computer software implementation of video algorithms that wrap-around is allowed in integer arithmetic. In video signal processing, such wrap-around must be prevented, and *saturating arithmetic* must be used.

I use the subscript h to denote a hexadecimal (base 16) integer.

Contrast, brightness,

CONTRAST, and BRIGHTNESS   5

User-accessible controls labelled CONTRAST and BRIGHT-NESS are found on nearly all electronic displays. These labels are indirectly and confusingly connected to the perceptual attributes *brightness* and *contrast*. In a CRT, adjusting BRIGHTNESS upwards from its optimum setting affects visual contrast much more than a comparable adjustment of the CONTRAST control. Adjusting CONTRAST affects visual brightness much more than a comparable adjustment of the BRIGHTNESS control. BRIGHTNESS and CONTRAST are therefore misleading labels. Today, CONTRAST and BRIGHTNESS controls are implemented in literally *billions* of pieces of equipment. Hundreds of millions of people have a poor understanding of these controls, and have had it for half a century: Imaging system designers are faced with a big problem.

This chapter describes the perceptual attributes *brightness* and *contrast.* I describe conventional CONTRAST and BRIGHTNESS controls, I explain how those controls came to do what they do, and I conclude by making some recommendations to reduce the confusion.

Perceptual attributes

HEYNDERICKX, INGRID and LANGENDIJK, ERNO (2005), "Image-quality comparison of PDPs, LCDs, CRTs and LCoS projection displays," in *SID Symposium Digest* **36** (1): 1502–1505.

According to two well respected vision and display system researchers,

> The four most important image quality attributes, at least for non-expert viewers when assessing image quality of high-end TVs, are brightness, contrast, color rendering and sharpness.

Here we address the first two image attributes, *brightness* and *contrast*, which presumably the authors consider the most important. Heynderickx and her colleague are referring to brightness and contrast as perceptual attributes. There are like-named controls on display equipment; however, I argue that the controls don't affect the perceptual attributes of a displayed image in the obvious manner. In the present chapter, including its title, we have to distinguish the names of the controls from the perceptual attributes. I typeset the names of the controls in small capitals – CONTRAST and BRIGHTNESS – and typeset normally the visual attributes brightness and contrast.

Contrast refers to a measured or visual distinction between colours or grey shades. Contrast is usually quantified by the ratio of a higher-valued luminance (or reflectance) to a lower-valued luminance (or reflectance). The ratio can be computed between widely different luminances; for example, when evaluating a display system we generally seek *contrast ratio* (the ratio of maximum to minimum luminance) of 100 or better, and perhaps up to 10,000. The ratio can be computed between similar luminances. Vision cannot distinguish two luminance levels when their contrast ratio falls below about 1.01 ("Weber's Law"), and the ratio between two luminances near the threshold of human detection is sometimes called *Weber contrast.*

History of display signal processing

Television originated with analog vacuum tube circuits; CRTs are themselves vacuum tubes. Vacuum tubes and the associated analog components (primarily resistors and capacitors) were subject to drift owing to operating temperature variation and owing to age-induced component degradation. The main effects of drift were to alter the gain and offset of the video signal; so, gain and offset controls were provided. Drift was such a serious problem that the controls were located on the front panel; consumers were expected to use them.

User-adjustable CONTRAST and BRIGHTNESS controls were implemented in vacuum tube television receivers of the early 1940s. Gain of the video amplifier circuitry was adjusted by a control that came to be called CONTRAST. Control of offset (bias) was implemented at

DRIVE historically referred to separate gain adjustments internally in the *R*, *G*, and *B* signal paths; SCREEN or BIAS referred to independent internal *R*, *G*, and *B* offset adjustments. In home theatre calibration circles these are respectively RGB-HIGH and RGB-LOW.

KALLMANN, HEINZ. E. (1940), "The gradation of television pictures," in *Proc. IRE* **28** (4): 170–174 (Apr.).

the CRT itself, by a control called BRIGHTNESS. Gain control took effect earlier in the signal path than offset. Kallmann described a typical implementation:

> … the so-called contrast control … is a voltage divider controlling signal amplitude … the background-light control … adjusts bias on the cathode-ray tube.

The scheme described by Kallmann prevailed for the whole CRT era. CONTRAST and BRIGHTNESS circuitry operated in the *R'G'B'* domain – that is, operated on gamma-encoded signals. Historically, the CRT itself imposed the power function associated with display "gamma." In CRTs, gamma wasn't adjustable.

I have been unable to find any historical documents that discuss how the names CONTRAST and BRIGHTNESS came about. Some early television receivers used the label BRILLIANCE for the gain control and some used BACKGROUND for the offset control. Some early television models had concentric CONTRAST and VOLUME controls, suggesting a single place for the user to alter the magnitude of the sound and the magnitude of the picture. One model had BRIGHTNESS on the front panel between VERTICAL HOLD and FOCUS!

Video scientists, engineers, and technicians have been skeptical about the names CONTRAST and BRIGHTNESS for many, many decades. Sixty years ago, Oliver wrote:

OLIVER, B.M. (1950), "Tone rendition in television," in *Proc. IRE* **38** (11): 1288–1300 (Nov.).

> … the gain ("contrast") control certainly produces more nearly a pure brightness change than does the bias ("brightness") control, so the knobs are, in a sense, mislabeled.

The parentheses and quotes are in the original. Concerning BRIGHTNESS, Oliver stated:

> … A good name for this knob might be "blacks," or "background," or "shadows."

That these controls are misnamed was observed a few years later by the preeminent electronics engineer Donald Fink:

Fink, Donald G. (1952), Television Engineering, Second Edition (New York: McGraw-Hill)

> "Unfortunately, in television systems of the present day, … the separate manipulation of the receiver

brightness and contrast controls (both of which are misnamed, photometrically speaking) by the nontechnical viewer may readily undo the best efforts of the system designers and the operating technicians."

In some modern television receivers, the gain control is labelled PICTURE instead of CONTRAST.

Despite researchers of the stature of Oliver and Fink complaining many decades ago, the names stuck – unfortunately, in my opinion.

Over 70 years, video signal processing technology shifted, first in about 1965 to transistors used in analog mode, then in about 1975 to analog integrated circuits, and then in about 1985 to digital integrated circuits, whose complexity has increased dramatically over the last 25 years. Around 2000, display technology started to shift from CRTs to LCD and PDP technology. With all of these shifts, the need for adjustment diminished. Nonetheless, CONTRAST and BRIGHTNESS have been carried forward (thoughtlessly, some would say) into successive generations of technology. Today, these controls are in use in around a billion CRT-based television receivers and another billion CRT displays in use with computers. The controls have been carried over (again, without much thought) into fixed-pixel displays; around a billion LCD displays are in use today, and virtually all have BRIGHTNESS and CONTRAST controls implemented in the digital signal processing path.

In video processing equipment, gain and offset controls have historically been available; they operate comparably to the display controls, but the associated controls are usually labelled GAIN and BLACK LEVEL.

LCD and plasma displays typically have CONTRAST and BRIGHTNESS controls. Despite the professional users' expectation that the controls would be implemented similarly to the like-named controls on a CRT display, and despite consumers' expectations that such controls should function in a comparable manner to CRTs, the LCD controls often have quite different effect.

CONTRAST and BRIGHTNESS controls are widespread in image applications in computers. The effect of CONTRAST and BRIGHTNESS controls in these domains is not necessarily comparable to the effect of like-named controls on display equipment. In particular, CONTRAST in Photoshop behaves very differently than CONTRAST in typical displays: Photoshop CONTRAST controls gain, but it "pivots" the gain around a certain formulation of the average pixel level instead of pivoting at zero as is usual in video equipment and in displays. For other computer imaging applications, there are no standards; it's often difficult or impossible to tell exactly how a particular application implements these controls.

Digital driving levels

The term *pixel value* is ambiguous because pixel values accessible to application software can be altered by the graphics subsystem on the way to the display – for example, they can be altered by the lookup table in a graphics adapter. DDL numbers are not necessarily those passed to the display panel column drivers and "glass": Modern display equipment ordinarily incorporates signal processing – often including lookup tables (LUTs) – to compensate for the native display panel response.

The term *digital driving level* (DDL) refers to a pixel component data value (typically produced by a PC graphics subsystem, or by a consumer electronics signal source such as a Blu-ray player) that crosses an interface (typically DVI, HDMI, or DisplayPort) and drives a display device. A DDL is interpreted as an integer value from 0 to $2^K - 1$ (where K is the bit depth at the interface, typically 8, but potentially 10 or 12).

Computer interfaces such as DVI carry 8-bit DDLs where DDL 0 is reference black and DDL 255 is reference white.

Video interface standards such as HD-SDI in the studio and HDMI in consumer equipment allow footroom below reference black and headroom above reference white. HD-SDI is standardized with 10-bit values; interface code 64 corresponds to reference black and interface code 940 corresponds to reference white. In consumer use, eight-bit HDMI is commonly used; interface code 16 corresponds to reference black and interface code 235 corresponds to reference white.

To simplify the rest of the discussion I'll refer to pixel values in terms of *normalized DDLs* (NDDLs) where reference black at the interface corresponds to NDDL 0 and reference white at the interface corresponds to NDDL 1. Pixel values in video are permitted to have modest excursions outside the reference 0 to 1 range, $-^{15}/_{219}$ to $^{235}/_{219}$ (about –0.07 to +1.09). The NDDL range 0 to 1 corresponds to what an HD engineer might call *IRE levels* 0 through 100.

Relationship between signal and lightness

The sRGB standard requires an electro-optical conversion function (EOCF) comprising a 2.2-power function.

Documentation associated with sRGB makes clear that the fundamental EOCF – the mapping from pixel value to display luminance – is supposed to be a pure 2.2-power function, followed by the addition of

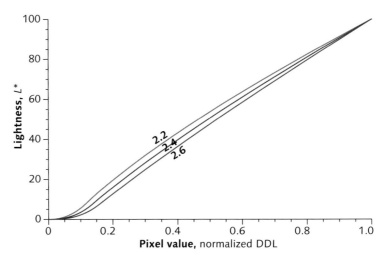

Figure 5.1 Relationship between pixel value and L^*. The *x*-axis plots normalized pixel (or video signal) value. The corresponding L^* values are plotted for display power functions ("gamma") of 2.2 (typical of computer imaging, e.g., sRGB), 2.4 (typical of studio video), and 2.6 (standard for digital cinema). This graph, and those to follow, apply to three channels when $R = G = B$, or to individual channels scaled appropriately (where the other two channels are zero). Adapted from Poynton's "Perceptual uniformity in digital imaging."

POYNTON, CHARLES (2009), "Perceptual uniformity in digital imaging," in *Proc. Gjøvik Color Imaging Symposium* (GCIS 2009): 102–109.

a veiling glare term. The sRGB standard also documents an OECF that is intended to describe a mapping from display luminance to pixel value, suitable to simulate a camera where the inverse power function's infinite slope at black would be a problem. The OECF has a linear segment near black, and has an power function segment with an exponent of $1/2.4$. The OECF should *not* be inverted for use as an EOCF; the linear slope near black is not appropriate for an EOCF.

The sRGB 2.2-power function, the *de facto* 2.4-power function of today's studio reference displays, and the 2.6-power function of digital cinema all almost perfectly invert L^*, as depicted in Figure 5.1. The 2.4-curve, which typifies video and HD practice, has a highly linear relationship with L^* for NDDL 0.2 and above (that is, for 8-bit interface codes above 59). An NDDL of 0.2 yields an L^* value of 16. The line from [0.2, 16] through reference white has slope of 105; extending that line back towards the *x*-axis yields an *x*-intercept of 0.0475, and back further, a *y*-intercept of almost exactly –5.

Algorithm

The effect of conventional CONTRAST and BRIGHTNESS controls in video is approximated by the following

Figure 5.2 **Effect of gain control** ("CONTRAST") for nominal offset ("BRIGHT-NESS") setting ($b = 0$). Gain values 0.8, 1.0, and 1.25 are shown; these are values of m in Equation 5.1. The y-axis is tristimulus value, a linear-light quantity that is not directly perceptually meaningful.

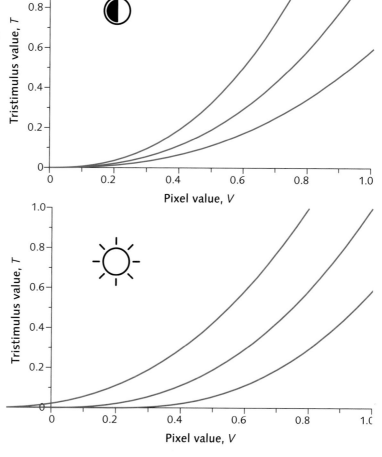

Figure 5.3 **Effect of offset control** ("BRIGHTNESS") for nominal gain ("CONTRAST") setting ($m = 1$). Offset values –0.2, 1.0, and +0.2 are shown; these are values of b in Equation 5.1.

equation, where x represents NDDL (one of R', G', or B') scaled to the range 0 to 1.

$$y = m\,x + b \qquad\qquad \text{Eq 5.1}$$

CONTRAST alters the m parameter – Oliver and Fink (cited on page 49) would have called it *gain* – over a range approximately 0.5 to 2. BRIGHTNESS alters the b parameter – Oliver and Fink would have called it *offset* or *bias* – over a range approximately ±0.2.

Figures 5.2 and 5.3 show the effect on the display tristimuli of changing gain and offset respectively.

The result y of equation 5.1 is clipped (historically by the action of the CRT itself, or now by signal processing) so as not to fall below zero. At a sufficiently high signal value, probably not too much over 1.09, saturation is likely to set in. The user adjusting gain or offset should be careful that his or her settings don't induce clipping or saturation.

The x and y signals in equation 5.1 are in the gamma-corrected ($R'G'B'$) domain. The result is then raised to a modest power γ (*gamma*, ranging from about 2.0 to 2.6) to produce a displayed tristimulus value (R, G, or B, on the y-axes of Figures 5.2 and 5.3).

Historical analog gain control circuitry implemented CONTRAST as a "one-quadrant" multiplier on $R'G'B'$ video signals clamped at blanking level (0). In PAL video, black and blanking levels were identically 0; consequently, adjusting CONTRAST in a PAL receiver left black of a properly coded signal where it was supposed to be (having minimal interaction with BRIGHTNESS). In NTSC encoding, +7.5-unit "setup" was inserted, causing black level of a properly encoded signal to lie at 0.075 on the 0 to 1 scale. However, clamping was still at blanking level (0). With gain "hinged" at zero, adjusting gain from 0.5 to 2 would alter black level from 0.0375 to 0.15, thereby causing CONTRAST and BRIGHTNESS to interact.

There is no standard or convention for the range of m and b, for the relationship of m and b values to the controls, or for numerical control values presented to the user. Today's video studio reference displays ("BVMs") are adjustable allowing m to range between about 0.5 and 2, and b to range about ±0.2; however in studio practice it is common for both controls to lack numerical control values. In today's consumer equipment, CONTRAST is typically presented to the user as a value (here denoted C) from 0 through 100 – shown for example on an on-screen display (OSD) – and BRIGHTNESS as a value (here, B) from 0 through 100. Suitable mappings from those control values to parameters m ranging 0.5 and 2 and b ranging ±0.2 are these:

$$m = 2^{\frac{C-50}{50}} \; ; \quad b = \frac{B-50}{250} \qquad\qquad \text{Eq 5.2}$$

BRIGHTNESS values might alternatively be presented in the range –50 through +50, in which case the second mapping would be $b = {}^{B}\!/_{250}$.

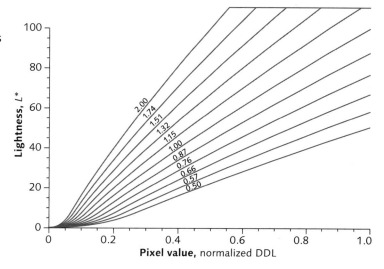

Figure 5.4 **Effect of gain control** ("CONTRAST") on lightness, for nominal bias setting ($b = 0$), with gain control viewed as setting the display function. Gain values correspond to values of m in Equation 5.1.

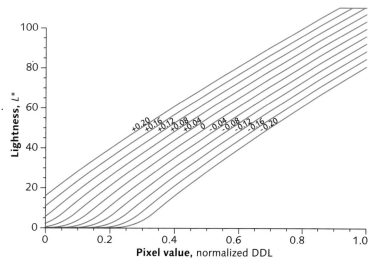

Figure 5.5 **Effect of offset control** ("BRIGHTNESS") for nominal gain setting ($m = 1$), with bias control viewed as setting the display function. Bias values correspond to values of b in Equation 5.1.

Figure 5.4 graphs the lightness produced for various settings of the gain parameter m, with the display characteristic considered a function of that parameter. The range of values in the graph corresponds to a CONTRAST range of 0 to 100 under the mapping of Equation 5.2.

Figure 5.5 graphs the lightness produced for various settings of the offset parameter b, with the display characteristic considered a function of that parameter. The range of values in the graph corresponds to a BRIGHTNESS range of 0 to 100 under the mapping of Equation 5.2.

Black level setting

PLUGE: Picture line-up generator, see page 421. ITU-R BT-814.2 standardizes a suitable test pattern. My procedure involves only the negative PLUGE bar, and is independent of its excursion. Traditional standards such as SMPTE RP 167 call for setting "so that the darker [negative] patch of the PLUGE just merges with the reference black level, but the brighter [positive] patch is clearly distinguishable." In my view the "but" phrase is not properly part of the optimization; instead, it provides a cross-check after the fact.

To set BRIGHTNESS (or BLACK LEVEL) in the studio, display a pattern containing PLUGE (levels –0.02, 0, +0.02) on a test image having average relative luminance of about 0.01 (1%). Set BLACK LEVEL high, then reduce it until the –0.02 and 0 PLUGE levels become just barely indistinguishable. You're finished.

If you have no PLUGE pattern, display a picture that is predominantly or entirely black. Set BLACK LEVEL to its minimum, then increase its level until the display barely shows a hint of dark grey, then back off a smidge.

Historically, BLACK LEVEL setting was somewhat dependent upon ambient light. However, modern displays have such low faceplate reflectance that ambient light contributes very little unwanted luminance, and the BLACK LEVEL setting is no longer very sensitive to ambient light. Modern display equipment is very stable; frequent adjustment is unnecessary.

Here I use standard digital studio video levels, not computing levels.

In the end, eight-bit codes 0 through 16 are expected to be indistinguishable. Code 16 (NDDL 0) is supposed to produce luminance that is visually indistinguishable from that of the negative-going bar of PLUGE (8-bit interface code 12, NDDL –0.02): The positive-going bar of PLUGE (8-bit interface code 20, NDDL +0.02) is expected to be visible.

See *Relative luminance,* on page 258, and *Display white reference,* on page 310. Astonishingly, no current studio standard specifies the luminance of reference white. I suggest 100 nt.

Once BLACK LEVEL is set correctly, CONTRAST can be set to whatever level is appropriate for comfortable viewing, provided that clipping is avoided. In the studio, the CONTRAST control can be used to achieve the desired luminance of reference white, typically around 100 cd·m^{-2}. (Historically, Europe used a somewhat lower reference white luminance, perhaps 80 cd·m^{-2}.)

Effect of CONTRAST and BRIGHTNESS on contrast and brightness

To explore the visual effect of CONTRAST and BRIGHTNESS controls, consider an ideal, properly adjusted 8-bit HD studio display.

Decreasing BRIGHTNESS leads to a darker image. Ignoring "shadow detail," a naïve viewer may find the resulting picture superior!

Decreasing BRIGHTNESS from its optimum setting causes clipping of video content lying just above reference black. Clipping doesn't impair contrast ratio *per se,* but stripping out image content "in the shadows" produces obvious artifacts, so we won't explore decreasing BRIGHTNESS.

Let's compute the effect of CONTRAST on contrast ratio. Assume a typical studio contrast ratio of 3333 (100 nt white, 0.03 nt black). Decreasing CONTRAST by 20% reduces the white video signal to 0.8, yielding a relative luminance of 0.585. Increasing CONTRAST by 20% increases the white signal to 1.25, yielding a relative luminance of 1.71. Starting with a contrast ratio of 3333, adjusting CONTRAST ±20% decreases contrast ratio to about 1950 or increases it to about 5700.

Let's compute the effect of CONTRAST on "brightness," as estimated by L^*. Adjusting CONTRAST ±20% yields L^* ranging from 81 to 118.

To compute the effect of increasing BRIGHTNESS on contrast ratio, increasing BRIGHTNESS by 20% takes the y-intercept of the 2.4-gamma curve of Figure 5.1 from −5 to +3. Reference black code now produces relative luminance of about 0.00332; reference white produces relative luminance of about 1.08. Increasing BRIGHTNESS thus causes contrast ratio to drop from 3333 to $1/_{0.00332}$, that is, to 325.

Finally, increasing BRIGHTNESS by +20% causes the reference white signal to increase L^* to 103.

Increasing CONTRAST by 20% takes contrast ratio from 3333 to 5700, roughly a factor of 2. Increasing BRIGHTNESS by 20% drops contrast ratio from 3333 to 325, roughly a factor of 10. A 20% change in BRIGHTNESS has much more effect on contrast ratio than a 20% change in CONTRAST.

Increasing BRIGHTNESS by 20% takes L^* from 100 to 103, but increasing CONTRAST by 20% takes L^* from 100 to 118. The results are summarized in table 5.1:

	Contrast ratio	Ref. black L*	Ref. white L*
Nominal	3333	0 3	100
Decrease CONTRAST 20%	1950	0.5	81
Increase CONTRAST 20%	5700	0.2	118
Increase BRIGHTNESS 20%	325	2.8	103

Table 5.1 **Effect of adjusting CONTRAST and BRIGHTNESS**

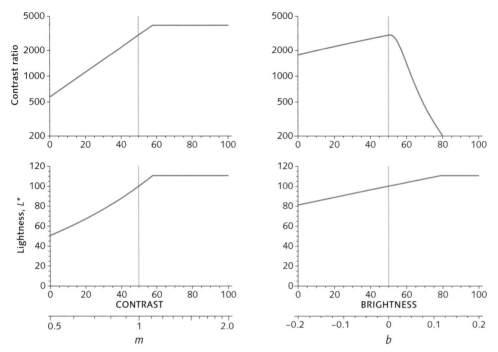

Figure 5.6 **Contrast ratio and lightness (L*)** are graphed in the upper and lower pairs, as a function of the *m* parameter ranging from 0.5 to 2 (with the typical CONTRAST setting 0 to 100) graphed at the left, and the *b* parameter with a range of ±0.2 (with the typical BRIGHTNESS setting 0 to 100) graphed at the right. The display EOCF underlying these graphs clips at about 109% of the video signal, that is, at a relative luminance of about $1.09^{2.4}$ or 1.23. The light grey vertical lines indicate the default *m* = 1, *b* = 0 (that is, CONTRAST 50 and BRIGHTNESS 50).

This numerical example is elaborated by the four graphs of Figure 5.6, which show the effect on contrast ratio (at the top) and lightness (L*, at the bottom) of adjusting CONTRAST (at the left) and BRIGHTNESS (at the right), with the CONTRAST and BRIGHTNESS scales corresponding to the mappings to *m* and *b* of Equation 5.2. The optimization of contrast ratio by choosing the appropriate BRIGHTNESS setting is clearly evident in the peak of the top-right graph. The other three graphs show saturation (clipping), which for this example is taken to set in at the studio video level of 109% of reference white, corresponding to relative luminance of about 1.23.

From the right-hand halves of the two top graphs it is evident that an adjustment to BRIGHTNESS above its optimum setting causes contrast ratio to decrease at roughly three times the rate that contrast ratio increases when CONTRAST is adjusted (in its nonclipped region):

$$\left(\frac{1019-64}{940-64}\right)^{2.4} \approx 1.23$$

Contrast ratio is more responsive to BRIGHTNESS than to CONTRAST. From the bottom graphs, adjusting either CONTRAST or BRIGHTNESS upwards increases the lightness of white (until clipping sets in), but the CONTRAST control is more responsive.

An alternate interpretation

In Figures 5.4 and 5.5, I interpreted the CONTRAST and BRIGHTNESS controls as changing the display's characteristics for a fixed scale of input pixel values (normalized DDLs). Let's turn that around, and consider the display characteristic to be a fixed function of display reference values ranging 0 through 1. equation 5.1 implements a linear operation on the x-axis of figure 5.1. Adjustment of CONTRAST and BRIGHTNESS can be interpreted as scaling and offsetting along that axis.

We can establish a parameter B (accessible to the user as BLACK LEVEL) to control the display reference value intended to be produced by NDDL 0, and parameter W (accessible to the user as WHITE LEVEL) to control the display reference value intended to be produced by NDDL 1.

Figure 5.7 overleaf shows the new interpretation. The x-axis in Figures 5.4 and 5.5 has been relabelled *Display reference value;* underneath that is the *Pixel value (normalized DDL)* scale. The NDDL scale is now squeezed and offset. The example of Figure 5.5 has BLACK LEVEL of 0.1 and WHITE LEVEL of 0.9. BLACK LEVEL has been elevated so that NDDL 0 produces an L^* value of about 3; WHITE LEVEL is set so that NDDL 1 produces an L^* value of about 90.

The reparameterized version of Equation 5.1 is this:

$$y = (W - B) \cdot x + B \hspace{3cm} \text{Eq 5.3}$$

To implement an offset range comparable to a conventional BRIGHTNESS control, and to allow treatment of input signals that have black-level errors, settings for B should have a range of about ±0.2. To be comparable to the gain range of a conventional CONTRAST control, settings for W should extend from 0.5 to 2.0. Most displays will be expected to exhibit clipping at W values greater than about 1.1, and it may be desirable to limit the user setting to such a value.

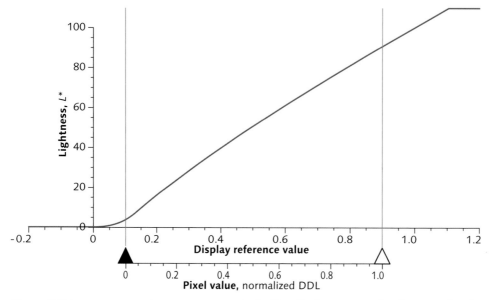

Figure 5.7 **BLACK LEVEL and WHITE LEVEL controls.** The display is viewed as having a fixed conversion from display reference values (0 to slightly more than 1) to lightness. BLACK LEVEL and WHITE LEVEL controls (indicated by the black and white triangles) set the display values corresponding to normalized interface pixel values 0 and 1. In this example, BLACK LEVEL is set to 0.1 and WHITE LEVEL to 0.9; *m* is computed as 0.8 and *b* as 0.1.

Concerning user adjustment of "poor sources," consider Poynton's Fourth Law: *Once a program is approved and packaged, errors in mastering are indistinguishable from expressions of creative intent.*

For consumer equipment, the black levels of modern source material are quite stable, and user adjustment to compensate for poor sources is no longer required. The diffuse ambient reflectance of modern displays is so low – around 0.01 – that ambient illuminance has a minor effect on contrast ratio. User adjustment to compensate for ambient light is now rarely necessary. Manufacturers should therefore consider relegating BLACK LEVEL to an internal or service adjustment.

In a display, BLACK LEVEL is normally used to compensate for the display, not the input signal, and so it should be effected downstream of the gain (CONTRAST) control.

In processing equipment, it is sometimes necessary to correct errors in black level in an input signal while maintaining unity gain: A BLACK LEVEL control should be implemented prior to the application of gain (and should not be called BRIGHTNESS). Figures 5.8 and 5.9 plot the transfer functions of CONTRAST and BRIGHTNESS controls in the video signal path, disregarding the typical 2.4-power function of the display.

DIGITAL VIDEO AND HD ALGORITHMS AND INTERFACES

Figure 5.8 **The BRIGHTNESS (or BLACK LEVEL) control in video** applies an offset, roughly ±20% of full scale, to *R'G'B'* components. Though this function is evidently a straight line, the input and output video signals are normally in the gamma-corrected (perceptual) domain; the values are *not* proportional to intensity. At the minimum and maximum settings, I show clipping to the BT.601 footroom of $-15/219$ and headroom of $238/219$. (Light power cannot go negative, but electrical and digital signals can.)

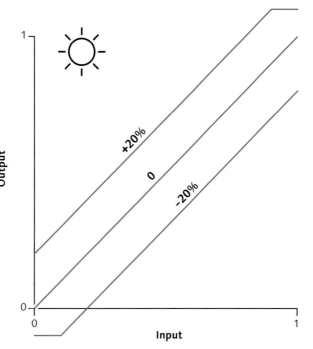

Figure 5.9 **The CONTRAST (or VIDEO LEVEL) control in video** applies a gain factor between roughly 0.5 and 2.0 to *R'G'B'* components. The output signal clips if the result would fall outside the range allowed for the coding in use. Here I show clipping to the BT.601 headroom limit.

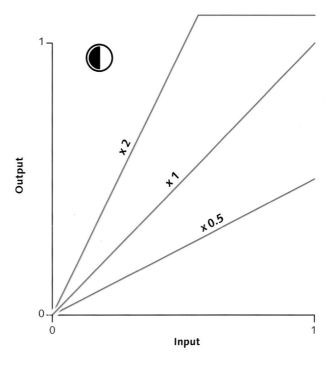

BRIGHTNESS and CONTRAST controls in LCDs

LCD: liquid crystal display

In LCD displays, BRIGHTNESS typically alters the luminance of the backlight; its function is comparable to the CONTRAST control of a CRT display. LCD displays produce luminance that is a nonlinear function of drive voltage. In early LCDs, CONTRAST adjusted an electrical bias voltage at the panel. In modern LCDs, CONTRAST adjusts gain in the signal path. There is no good reason for LCDs to have separate R, G, and B bias controls (RGB-LOW).

BRIGHTNESS and CONTRAST controls in PDPs

PDP: plasma display panel

In PDP displays, maximum luminance is fixed by the electronic design of the panel; BRIGHTNESS and CONTRAST are implemented by digital signal processing. PDP displays produce luminance that is a linear function of drive level. DDL 0 produces the smallest possible luminance from the display, so reference black video code should produce DDL 0 – there is no good reason to have it otherwise. There is no good reason for PDPs to have separate R, G, and B bias controls (RGB-LOW).

BRIGHTNESS and CONTRAST controls in desktop graphics

This section describes Photoshop BRIGHTNESS and CONTRAST controls for versions up to and including CS2, and for later versions when the "Use Legacy" option is enabled. The default brightness and contrast controls for versions CS3 and above behave differently.

Adobe's Photoshop software established the *de facto* effect of BRIGHTNESS and CONTRAST controls in desktop graphics. Photoshop's BRIGHTNESS control is similar to the BRIGHTNESS control of video; however, Photoshop's CONTRAST differs dramatically from that of video.

The transfer functions of Photoshop's controls are sketched in Figures 5.10 and 5.11 (opposite). R', G', and B' component values in Photoshop are presented to the user as values between 0 and 255. BRIGHTNESS and CONTRAST controls have sliders with a range of ±100.

BRIGHTNESS effects an offset between –100 and +100 on the R', G', and B' components. Any result outside the range 0 to 255 clips to the nearest extreme value, 0 or 255. Photoshop's BRIGHTNESS control is comparable to that of video, but its range (roughly ±40% of full scale) is greater than the typical video range (of about ±20%).

Photoshop's (legacy) CONTRAST control follows the application of BRIGHTNESS; it applies a gain factor. Instead of leaving reference black (code zero) fixed, as

Figure 5.10 **The BRIGHTNESS control in Photoshop** applies an offset of –100 to +100 to *R'G'B'* components ranging from 0 to 255. If a result falls outside the range 0 to 255, it saturates; headroom and footroom are absent. The function is evidently linear, but depending upon the image coding standard in use, the input and output values are generally nonlinearly related to luminance (or tristimulus values).

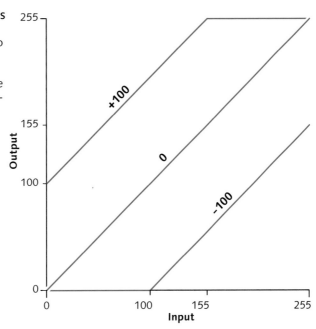

Figure 5.11 **The CONTRAST control in Photoshop** applies a gain factor between zero (for CONTRAST setting of –100) and infinity (for CONTRAST setting of +100) to image data, but "pivoted" around a weighted average pixel level (APL) of the image data, instead of "pivoting" around zero (as is the case for GAIN and CONTRAST controls in video). Each component result saturates if it falls outside the range 0 to 255.

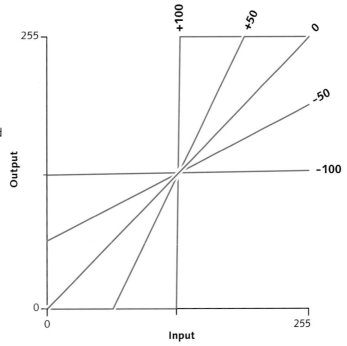

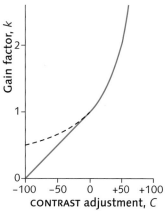

Figure 5.12 **Photoshop**
**CONTRAST control's gain
factor** depends upon the
CONTRAST setting according
to this function.

$$0.66 = \frac{1.45}{2.2}$$

a video CONTRAST control does, Photoshop "pivots" the gain adjustment around a weighted average of the image data formed as 0.299 R'+0.587 G'+0.114 B'. (For image data having the "gamma correction" of video, the weighted average corresponds to BT.601 luma, or *average pixel level,* APL.) The transfer function for various settings of CONTRAST adjustment, for a weighted image average of 127.5, is graphed in Figure 5.11.

The gain available from Photoshop's CONTRAST control ranges from zero to infinity, far wider than the typical range of 0.5 to 2 of studio GAIN. The function that relates Photoshop's CONTRAST to gain is graphed in Figure 5.12. From the –100 setting to the 0 setting, gain ranges linearly from zero through unity. From the 0 setting to the +100 setting, gain ranges nonlinearly from unity to infinity, following the reciprocal curve described by Equation 5.4:

$$k = \begin{cases} 1+\dfrac{C}{100}, & -100 \leq C < 0 \\[3ex] \dfrac{1}{1-\dfrac{C}{100}}, & 0 \leq C < 100 \end{cases}$$

Eq 5.4

In desktop graphics applications such as Photoshop, image data is usually coded in a perceptually uniform manner, comparable to video R'G'B'. On a PC, R'G'B' components are by default proportional to the $1/_{2.2}$-power of reproduced luminance (or tristimulus) values. On Macintosh computers prior to Mac OS X 10.6, QuickDraw R'G'B' components were by default proportional to the 0.66-power of displayed luminance (or tristimulus). Modern Macintosh computers conform to the sRGB standard. However, on both PC and Macintosh computers, the user, system software, or application software can set the transfer function to nonstandard functions – perhaps so far as effecting linear-light coding – as will be described in *Gamma,* on page 315.

Raster images

in computing 6

This chapter places video into the context of computing. Images in computing are represented in three forms, depicted schematically in the three rows of Figure 6.1: *symbolic image description, raster image,* and *compressed image.*

• A **symbolic image description** does not directly contain an image, but contains a high-level 2-D or 3-D geometric description of an image, such as its objects and their properties. A two-dimensional image in this form is sometimes called a *vector graphic*, though its primitive objects are usually much more complex than the straight-line segments suggested by the word *vector*.

• A **raster image** enumerates the greyscale or colour content of each pixel directly, in scan-line order. There are four fundamental types of raster image: *bilevel, pseudocolour, greyscale,* and *truecolour*. In Figure 6.1, the four types are arranged in columns, from low quality at the left to high quality at the right.

• A **compressed image** originates with raster image data, but the data has been processed to reduce storage and/or transmission requirements. The bottom row of Figure 6.1 indicates several compression methods. At the left are lossless (data) compression methods, generally applicable to bilevel and pseudocolour image data; at the right are lossy (image) compression methods, generally applicable to greyscale and truecolour.

The greyscale, pseudocolour, and truecolour systems used in computing involve lookup tables (LUTs) that map pixel values into display $R'G'B'$ values. Most computing systems use perceptually uniform image coding; however, some systems use linear-light coding,

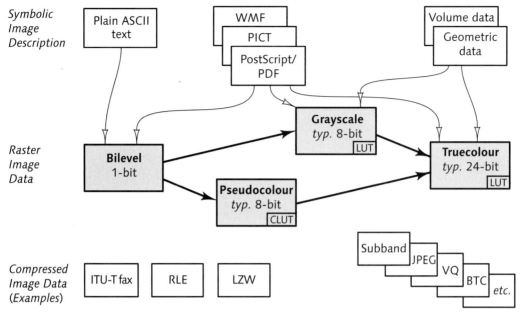

Plain ASCII text

WMF
PICT
PostScript/ PDF

Volume data
Geometric data

*Raster
Image
Data*

Bilevel 1-bit

Grayscale *typ.* 8-bit LUT

Truecolour *typ.* 24-bit LUT

Pseudocolour *typ.* 8-bit CLUT

*Compressed
Image Data
(Examples)*

ITU-T fax   RLE   LZW

Subband
JPEG
VQ
BTC
etc.

Figure 6.1 **Raster image data** may be captured directly, or may be rendered from symbolic image data. Traversal from left to right corresponds to conversions that can be accomplished without loss. Some raster image formats are associated with a lookup table (LUT) or colour lookup table (CLUT).

and some systems use other techniques. For a system to operate in a perceptually uniform manner, similar to or compatible with video, its LUTs need to be loaded with suitable transfer functions. If the LUTs are loaded with transfer functions that cause code values to be proportional to intensity, then the advantages of perceptual uniformity will be diminished or lost.

Many different file formats are in use for each of these representations. Discussion of file formats is outside the scope of this book. To convey photographic-quality colour images, a file format must accommodate *at least* 24 bits per pixel. To make maximum perceptual use of a limited number of bits per component, nonlinear coding should be used, as I outlined in *Perceptual uniformity,* on page 30.

Symbolic image description

Many methods are used to describe the content of a picture at a level of abstraction higher than directly enumerating the value of each pixel. Symbolic image data is converted to a raster image by the process of *rasterizing*. Images are *rasterized* (or *imaged* or *rendered*)

MURRAY, JAMES D., and WILLIAM VANRYPER (1996), *Encyclopedia of Graphics File Formats,* Second Edition (Sebastopol, Calif.: O'Reilly & Associates).

by interpreting symbolic data and producing raster image data. In Figure 6.1, this operation passes information from the top row to the middle row.

Geometric data describes the position, size, orientation, and other attributes of objects; 3-D geometric data may be interpreted to produce an image from a particular viewpoint. Rasterizing from geometric data is called *rendering;* truecolour images are usually produced.

Adobe's PostScript system is widely used to represent 2-D illustrations, typographic elements, and publications. PostScript is essentially a programming language specialized for imaging operations. When a PostScript file is executed by a PostScript interpreter, the image is rendered. (In PostScript, the rasterizing operation is often called raster image processing, or *RIPping*.) An encapsulated PostScript file (EPS or EPSF) is a special case of a PostScript file that describes one image; Adobe's PDF format is essentially a nonprogrammable variant of PostScript.

Once rasterized, there is no general method of converting raster image data back into a symbolic description: A raster image – in the middle row of Figure 6.1 – generally cannot be returned to its description in the top row. If your application involves rendered images, you may find it useful to retain the symbolic data even after rendering, in case the need arises to rerender the image, at a different size, perhaps, or to perform a modification such as removing an object.

Images from a fax machine, a video camera, or a greyscale or colour scanner originate in raster image form: No symbolic description is available. Optical character recognition (OCR) and raster-to-vector techniques make brave but generally unsatisfying attempts to extract text or geometric data from raster images.

Raster images

There are four distinct types of raster image data:
- *Bilevel,* by definition 1 bit per pixel;
- *Greyscale,* typically 8 bits per pixel;
- *Pseudocolour,* typically 8 bits per pixel; and
- *Truecolour,* typically 24 bits per pixel.

Greyscale and truecolour systems are capable of representing continuous tone. Video systems use only truecolour (and perhaps greyscale as a special case).

In the following sections, I will explain bilevel, greyscale, truecolour, and pseudocolour in turn. The truecolour and pseudocolour descriptions are accompanied by block diagrams that represent the hardware at the back end of the framebuffer or graphics card. (Historically, this hardware would have included *digital-to-analog converters*, DACs; today, digital display interfaces such as DVI, HDMI, and DisplayPort are used.) Alternatively, you can consider each block diagram to represent an algorithm that converts image data to display R', G', and B' components.

Bilevel

Each pixel of a bilevel (or two-level) image comprises one bit, which represents either black or white – but nothing in between. In computing this is often called *monochrome*. (That term ought to denote shades of a single hue; however, in common usage – and particularly in video – *monochrome* denotes the black-and-white, or greyscale, component of an image.)

Since the invention of data communications, binary zero (0) has been known as *space,* and binary one (1) has been known as *mark*. A "mark" on an electronic display device emits light, so in video and in computer graphics a binary one (or the maximum code value) conventionally represents white. In printing, a "mark" deposits ink on the page, so in printing a binary one (or in greyscale, the maximum pixel value) conventionally represents black.

Greyscale

A greyscale image represents an effectively continuous range of tones, from black, through intermediate shades of grey, to white. A greyscale system with a sufficient number of bits per component, 8 bits or more, can represent a black-and-white photograph. A greyscale system may or may not have a lookup table (LUT); it may or may not be perceptually uniform.

In printing, a greyscale image is said to have *continuous tone*, or *contone* (distinguished from *line art* or *type*). When a contone image is printed, *halftoning* is ordinarily used.

Truecolour

A truecolour system has separate red, green, and blue components for each pixel. In most truecolour systems, each component is represented by a *byte* of 8 bits (known as 8 *bits per channel,* or bpc). Each pixel has three components (channels), so this mode is often called "24-bit colour" (or "millions of colours"). The *RGB* values of each pixel can represent 2^{24}, or about 16.7 million, distinct codes. In computing, a truecolour framebuffer usually has three *lookup tables* (LUTs), one for each component. The LUTs and DACs of a 24-bit truecolour system are sketched in Figure 6.2 below.

The mapping from image code value to display voltage is determined by the content of the LUTs. Owing to the perceptually uniform nature of the display, the best perceptual use is generally made of truecolour pixel values when each LUT contains an identity function ("ramp") that maps input to output, unchanged.

In computing, the LUTs can be set to implement an arbitrary mapping from code value to tristimulus value (and so, to intensity). The total number of pixel values that represent distinguishable colours depends upon the transfer function used. If the LUT implements a power function to impose gamma correction on linear-light data, then the code-100 problem will be at its worst. With 24-bit colour and a properly chosen transfer function, photographic quality images can be displayed and geometric objects can be rendered smoothly shaded with sufficiently high quality for many applications. But if the LUTs are set for linear-light representation with 8 bits per component, contouring

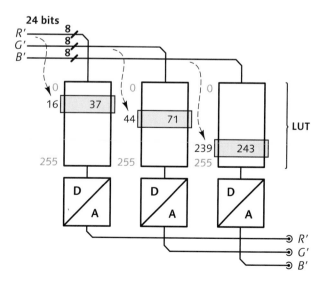

Figure 6.2 **Truecolour (24-bit) graphics** usually involves three programmable lookup tables (LUTs). The numerical values shown here are from the default Macintosh LUT (prior to Mac OS X 10.6). In video, *R'G'B'* values are transmitted to the display with no intervening lookup table. To make a truecolour computer system display video properly, the LUTs must be loaded with ramps that map input to output unchanged. Such a "unity" mapping (or "ramp") is the default in PCs.

will be evident in many images, as I mentioned on page 30. Having 24-bit truecolour is *not* a guarantee of good image quality. If a scanner claims to have 30 bits (or 36 bits) per pixel, obviously each component has 10 bits (or 12 bits). However, it makes a great deal of difference whether these values are coded physically (as linear-light luminance, loosely "intensity"), or coded perceptually (as a quantity comparable to lightness).

POYNTON, CHARLES (1998), "The rehabilitation of *gamma*," in Proc. SPIE **3299** (*Human Vision and Electronic Imaging III*, Bellingham, Wash.: SPIE).

In video, either the LUTs are absent, or each is set to the identity function. Studio video systems are effectively permanently wired in truecolour mode with perceptually uniform coding: Code values are presented directly to the DACs, without intervening lookup tables.

It is easiest to design a framebuffer memory system where each pixel has a number of bytes that is a power of two; so, a truecolour framebuffer often has four bytes per pixel – "32-bit colour." Three bytes comprise the red, green, and blue colour components; the fourth byte is used for purposes other than representing colour. The fourth byte may contain overlay information, or it may store an *alpha* (α) or *key* component representing opacity from black (0, fully transparent) to white (1, fully opaque). In computer graphics, the alpha component modulates components (usually *RGB*) that are coded in the linear-light domain. In video, the *linear key* signal modulates nonlinear (gamma-corrected) *R'G'B'* signals or luma and colour difference components such as $Y'C_BC_R$.

Concerning alpha, see page 387.

Pseudocolour

In a *pseudocolour* (or *indexed colour*, or *colour-mapped*) system, several bits – usually 8 – comprise each pixel in an image or framebuffer. This provides a moderate number of unique codes – usually 256 – for each pixel. Pseudocolour involves "painting by numbers," where the number of colours is rather small. In an 8-bit pseudocolour system, any particular image, or the content of the framebuffer at any instant in time, is limited to a selection of just 2^8 (or 256) colours from the universe of available colours.

I reserve the term *CLUT* for pseudocolour. In greyscale and truecolour systems, the LUTs store transfer functions, not colours. In Macintosh, pseudocolour CLUT values are roughly, but not optimally, perceptually coded.

Each code value is used as an index into a *colour lookup table* (CLUT, *colourmap*, or *palette*) that retrieves *R'G'B'* components; the DAC translates these linearly into voltage levels that are applied to the display. (Macintosh is an exception: Image data read from the

DIGITAL VIDEO AND HD ALGORITHMS AND INTERFACES

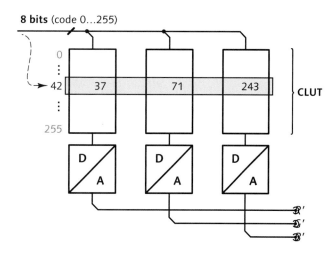

8 bits (code 0...255)

CLUT

0
⋮
42 | 37 | 71 | 243
⋮
255

D/A   D/A   D/A

R'
G'
B'

Figure 6.3 **Pseudocolour (8-bit) graphics** systems use a limited number of integers, usually 0 through 255, to represent colours. Each pixel value is processed through a *colour lookup table* (CLUT) to obtain red, green, and blue output values to be delivered to the display.

The browser-safe palette forms a radix-6 number system with *RGB* digits valued 0 through 5.

$216 = 6^3$

CLUT is in effect passed through a second LUT.) Pseudocolour CLUT values are effectively perceptually coded.

The CLUT and DACs of an 8-bit pseudocolour system are sketched in Figure 6.3 above. A typical lookup table retrieves 8-bit values for each of red, green, and blue, so each of the 256 different colours can be chosen from a universe of 2^{24}, or 16777216, colours. (A CLUT may return 4, 6, or more than 8 bits for each component.)

Pseudocolour image data is always accompanied by the associated colourmap (or *palette*). The colourmap may be fixed, independent of the image, or it may be specific to the particular image (*adaptive* or *optimized*).

A popular choice for a fixed CLUT is the *browser safe* palette comprising the 216 colours formed by combinations of 8-bit *R'*, *G'*, and *B'* values chosen from the set {0, 51, 102, 153, 204, 255}. This set of 216 colours fits nicely within an 8-bit pseudocolour CLUT; the colours are perceptually distributed throughout the *R'G'B'* cube.

Pseudocolour is appropriate for images such as maps, schematic diagrams, or cartoons, where each colour or combination is either completely present or completely absent at any point in the image. In a typical CLUT, adjacent pseudocolour codes are generally completely unrelated; for example, the colour assigned to code 42 has no necessary relationship to the colour assigned to code 43.

Conversion among types

In Figure 6.1, traversal from left to right corresponds to conversions that can be accomplished without loss.

Disregarding pseudocolour for the moment, data in any of the other three schemes of Figure 6.1 can be "widened" to any scheme to the right simply by assigning the codes appropriately. For example, a grey-scale image can be widened to truecolour by assigning codes from black to white. Widening adds bits but not information.

A pseudocolour image can be converted to truecolour through software application of the CLUT. Conversion to truecolour can be accomplished without loss, provided that the truecolour LUTs are sensible.

Concerning conversions in the reverse direction, an image can be "narrowed" without loss only if it contains only the colours or shades available in the mode to its left in Figure 6.1; otherwise, the conversion will involve loss of shades and/or loss of colours.

ASHDOWN, IAN, *Color Quantization Bibliography,* available at <http://liinwww.ira.uka.de/bibliogr aphy/Graphics/cquant.html>

A truecolour image can be approximated in pseudocolour through software application of a fixed colourmap. Alternatively, a *colourmap quantization* algorithm can be used to examine a particular image (or sequence of images), and compute a colourmap that is optimized or adapted for that image or sequence.

Image files

Images in bilevel, greyscale, pseudocolour, or truecolour formats can be stored in files. A general-purpose image file format stores, in its header information, the count of columns and rows of pixels in the image.

Many file formats – such as TIFF and EPS – store information about the intended size of the image. The intended image width and height can be directly stored, in absolute units such as inches or millimeters. Alternatively, the file can store sample density in units of *pixels per inch* (ppi), or less clearly, *dots per inch* (dpi). Sample density is often confusingly called "resolution."

Image width is the product of so-called resolution and the count of image columns; height is computed similarly from the count of image rows.

In some software packages, such as Adobe Illustrator, the intended image size coded in a file is respected. In other software, such as Adobe Photoshop, viewing at 100% implies a 1:1 relationship between file pixels and display device pixels, disregarding the number of pixels per inch in the file and at the display. Image files

DIGITAL VIDEO AND HD ALGORITHMS AND INTERFACES

without size information are often treated as having 72 pixels per inch; application software unaware of image size information often uses a default of 72 ppi.

"Resolution" in computer graphics

In computer graphics, a pixel is often regarded as an intensity distribution uniformly covering a small square area of the screen. In fixed-pixel displays such as liquid crystal displays (LCDs), plasma display panels (PDPs), and digital light processing (DLP) displays, discrete pixels such as these are constructed on the display device. When such a display is driven digitally at native pixel count, there is a one-to-one relationship between framebuffer pixels and device pixels. However, a graphic subsystem may resample by primitive means when faced with a mismatch between framebuffer pixel count and display device pixel count. If framebuffer count is higher, pixels are dropped; if lower, pixels are replicated. In both instances, image quality suffers.

CRT displays typically have a Gaussian distribution of light from each pixel, as I will discuss in the next chapter. The typical spot size is such that there is some overlap in the distributions of light from adjacent pixels. You might think that overlap between the distributions of light produced by neighboring display elements is undesirable. However, image display requires a certain degree of overlap in order to minimize the visibility of pixel structure or scan-line structure. I will discuss this issue in *Image structure,* on page 75.

Two disparate measures are referred to as *resolution* in computing:
• The count of image columns and image rows – that is, columns and rows of pixels – in a framebuffer
• The number of pixels per inch (ppi) intended for image data (often misleadingly denoted dots per inch, dpi)

An image scientist considers *resolution* to be delivered to the viewer; resolution is properly estimated from information displayed at the display surface (or screen) itself. The two measures above all limit resolution, but neither of them quantifies resolution directly. In *Resolution,* on page 97, I will describe how the term is used in image science and video.

Image structure   7

A naïve approach to digital imaging treats an image as a matrix of independent pixels, disregarding the spatial distribution of light power across each pixel. You might think that optimum image quality is obtained when there is no overlap between the distributions of neighboring pixels; many computer engineers hold this view. However, continuous-tone images are best reproduced with a certain degree of overlap between pixels; sharpness is reduced slightly, but pixel structure is made less visible and image quality is improved.

Don't confuse point spread function (PSF) with *progressive segmented-frame* (PsF), to be described on page 94.

The distribution of intensity across a displayed pixel is referred to as its *point spread function* (PSF). A one-dimensional slice through the center of a PSF is colloquially called a *spot profile.* A display's PSF influences the nature of the images it reproduces. The effects of a PSF can be analyzed using filter theory, discussed for one dimension in the chapter *Filtering and sampling,* on page 191, and for two dimensions in *Image digitization and reconstruction,* on page 237.

Historically, the PSFs of greyscale ("black-and-white") CRTs were roughly Gaussian in shape: Intensity distribution peaked at the center of the pixel, fell off over a small distance, and overlapped neighboring pixels to some extent. The scanning spot of colour CRTs had this shape, too; but the PSF was influenced by the shadow mask or aperture grille. The introduction of direct-view colour CRTs shifted the requirement for spatial filtering to the viewer: The assumption was introduced that the viewers were sufficiently distant from the screens that the viewers' visual systems would perform the spatial integration necessary to obscure the triad structure.

Modern direct view fixed-pixel displays (FPDs) such as LCD and PDP displays have more or less uniform light emission over most of the area corresponding to each colour component (subpixel); their modulated light has a spatial structure comparable to that of a direct-view colour CRT, and similarly depends upon the viewers being located at a sufficient distance that their visual characteristics perform the spatial intergation necessary to obscure the triad structure.

A pixel whose intensity distribution uniformly covers a small square area of the screen has a point spread function referred to as a "box."

Image reconstruction

Figure 7.1 reproduces a portion of an idealized bitmapped (bilevel) graphic image, part of a computer's desktop display. Each sample is either black or white. The element with horizontal "stripes" is part of a window's titlebar; the checkerboard background is intended to integrate to grey. Figure 7.1 shows reconstruction of the image with a "box" distribution. Each pixel is uniformly shaded across its extent; there is no overlap between pixels. This figure exemplifies a *raster-locked* image as displayed on an LCD. By *raster-locked*, I refer to image data having the underlying image elements aligned with the pixel array.

A CRT's electron gun produces an electron beam that illuminates a spot on the phosphor screen. The beam is deflected to form a raster pattern of scan lines that traces the entire screen, as I will describe in the following chapter. The beam is not perfectly focused when it is emitted from the CRT's electron gun, and is dispersed further in transit to the phosphor screen. The intensity produced for each pixel at the face of the screen has a "bell-shaped" distribution resembling a two-dimensional Gaussian function. With a typical amount of spot overlap, the checkerboard area of this example will display as a nearly uniform grey as depicted in Figure 7.2. You might think that the blur caused by overlap between pixels would diminish image quality. However, for continuous-tone ("contone") images, some degree of overlap is not only desirable but necessary, as you will see from the following examples.

Figure 7.1 **"Box" reconstruction** of a bitmapped graphic image is shown.

Figure 7.2 **Gaussian reconstruction** is shown for the same bitmapped image as Figure 7.1. I will detail the one-dimensional *AGaussian function* on page 200.

Figure 7.3 **Diagonal line reconstruction.** At the left is a near-vertical line slightly more than 1 pixel wide, rendered as an array 20 pixels high that has been reconstructed using a box distribution. At the right, the line is reconstructed using a Gaussian distribution. Between the images I have placed a set of markers to indicate the vertical centers of the image rows.

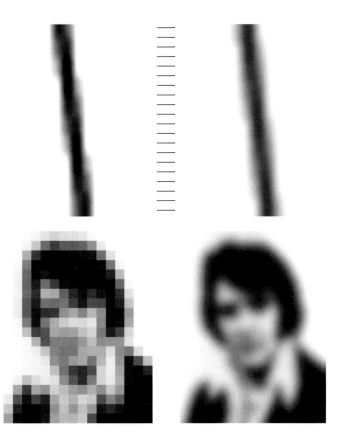

Figure 7.4 **Contone image reconstruction.** At the left is a continuous-tone image of 16×20 pixels that has been reconstructed using a box distribution. The pictured individual cannot be recognized. At the right is exactly the same image data, but reconstructed by a Gaussian function. The reconstructed image is very blurry but recognizable. Which reconstruction function do you think is best for continuous-tone imaging?

Visual acuity is detailed in *Contrast sensitivity function (CSF)*, on page 251.

Figure 7.3 shows a 16×20-pixel image of a dark line slightly more than one pixel wide, 7.2° off the vertical. At the left, the image data is reconstructed using a box distribution; a jagged and "ropey" nature is evident. At the right, the image data is reconstructed using a Gaussian. It is blurry, but less jagged.

Figure 7.4 shows two ways to reconstruct the same 16×20 pixels (320 bytes) of continuous-tone greyscale image data. The left-hand image is reconstructed using a box function, and the right-hand image with a Gaussian. The example was constructed so that each image is 4 cm (1.6 inches) wide. At typical reading distance of 40 cm (16 inches), a pixel subtends 0.4°, where visual acuity is near its maximum. At this distance, when reconstructed with a box function, the pixel structure of each image is highly visible; visibility of the pixel structure overwhelms the perception of the image itself. The right image is reconstructed using a Gaussian distribution. It is blurry, but easily recognizable as an American

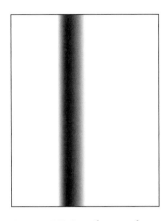

Figure 7.5 **One frame of an animated sequence,** reconstructed with a "box" filter.

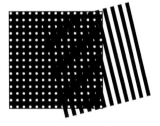

Figure 7.6 **A Moiré pattern** is a form of aliasing in two dimensions that results when a sampling pattern (here the perforated square) has a sampling density that is too low for the image content (here the dozen bars, 14° off-vertical). This figure is adapted from Fig. 3.12 of Wandell's *Foundations of Vision* (cited on page 195).

cultural icon. This example shows that sharpness is not always good, and blurriness is not always bad!

Figure 7.5 in the margin shows a 16×20-pixel image comprising 20 copies of the top row of Figure 7.3 (left). Consider a sequence of 20 animated frames, where each frame is formed from successive image rows of Figure 7.3. The animation would depict a narrow vertical line drifting rightward across the screen at a rate of 1 pixel every 8 frames. If image rows of Figure 7.3 (left) were used, the width of the moving line would appear to jitter frame-to-frame, and the minimum lightness would vary. With Gaussian reconstruction, as in Figure 7.3 (right), motion portrayal is much smoother.

Sampling aperture

In a practical image sensor, each element acquires information from a finite region of the image plane; the value of each pixel is a function of the distribution of intensity over that region. The distribution of sensitivity across a pixel of an image capture device is referred to as its *sampling aperture,* sort of a PSF in reverse – you could call it a point "collection" function. The sampling aperture influences the nature of the image signal originated by a sensor. Sampling apertures used in continuous-tone imaging systems usually peak at the center of each pixel, fall off over a small distance, and overlap neighboring pixels to some extent.

In 1915, Harry Nyquist published a landmark paper stating that a sampled analog signal cannot be reconstructed accurately unless all of its frequency components are contained strictly within half the sampling frequency. This condition subsequently became known as the *Nyquist criterion;* half the sampling rate became known as the *Nyquist rate.* Nyquist developed his theorem for one-dimensional signals, but it has been extended to two dimensions. In a digital system, it takes at least two elements – two pixels or two scanning lines – to represent a cycle. A *cycle* is equivalent to a *line pair* of film, or two "TV lines" (TVL).

In Figure 7.6, the black square punctured by a regular array of holes represents a grid of small sampling apertures. Behind the sampling grid is a set of a dozen black bars, tilted 14° off the vertical, representing image information. In the region where the image is sampled, you can see three wide dark bars tilted at 45°. Those bars represent spatial *aliases* that arise because the number of bars per inch (or mm) in the image is greater than half the number of apertures per inch (or mm) in the sampling lattice. Aliasing can be prevented – or at least minimized – by imposing a spatial filter in front of the sampling process, as I will describe for one-dimensional signals in *Filtering and sampling,* on page 191, and for two dimensions in *Image presampling filters,* on page 242.

Nyquist explained that an arbitrary signal can be reconstructed accurately only if more than two samples are taken of the highest-frequency component of the signal. Applied to an image, there must be at least twice as many samples per unit distance as there are image elements. The checkerboard pattern in Figure 7.1 (on page 76) doesn't meet this criterion in either the vertical or horizontal dimensions. Furthermore, the titlebar element doesn't meet the criterion vertically. Such elements can be represented in a bilevel image only when they are in precise registration – "locked" – to the imaging system's sampling grid. However, images captured from reality almost never have their elements precisely aligned with the grid!

Point sampling refers to capture with an infinitesimal sampling aperture. This is undesirable in continuous-tone imaging. Figure 7.7 shows what would happen if a physical scene like that in Figure 7.1 were rotated 14°, captured with a point-sampled camera, and displayed with a box distribution. The alternating on-off elements are rendered with aliasing in both the checkerboard portion and the titlebar. (Aliasing would be evident even if this image were to be reconstructed with a Gaussian.) This example emphasizes that in digital imaging, we must represent arbitrary scenes, not just scenes whose elements have an intimate relationship with the sampling grid.

A suitable presampling filter would prevent (or at least minimize) the Moiré artifact of Figure 7.6, and prevent or minimize the aliasing of Figure 7.7. When image content such as the example titlebar and the desktop pattern of Figure 7.2 is presented to a presampling filter, blurring will occur. Considering only bitmapped images such as Figure 7.1, you might think

Figure 7.7 Bitmapped graphic image, rotated.

the blurring to be detrimental, but to avoid spatial aliasing in capturing high-quality continuous-tone imagery, some overlap is necessary in the distribution of sensitivity across neighboring sensor elements.

Having introduced the aliasing artifact that results from poor capture PSFs, we can now return to the display and discuss reconstruction PSFs (spot profiles).

Spot profile

The designer of a display system for continuous-tone images seeks to make a display that allows viewing at a wide picture angle, with minimal intrusion of artifacts such as aliasing or visible scan-line or pixel structure. Picture size, viewing distance, spot profile, and scan-line or pixel visibility all interact. The display system designer cannot exert direct control over viewing distance; spot profile is the parameter available for optimization.

On page 77, I demonstrated the difference between a box profile and a Gaussian profile. Figures 7.3 and 7.4 showed that some overlap between neighboring distributions is desirable, even though blur is evident when the reproduced image is viewed closely.

When the images of Figure 7.3 or 7.4 are viewed from a distance of 10 m (33 feet), a pixel subtends a minute of arc ($\frac{1}{60}°$). At this distance, owing to the limited acuity of human vision, both pairs of images are apparently identical. Imagine placing beside these images an emissive display having an infinitesimal spot, producing the same total flux for a perfectly white pixel. At 10 m, the pixel structure of the emissive display would be somewhat visible. At a great viewing distance – say at a pixel or scan-line subtense of less than $\frac{1}{180}°$, corresponding to SD viewed at three times normal distance, or about 20·PH – the limited acuity of the human visual system causes all three displays to appear identical. As the viewer moves closer, different effects become apparent, depending upon spot profile. I'll discuss two cases: box distribution and Gaussian distribution.

Box distribution

A typical digital projector – such as an LCD or a PDP – has a spot profile resembling a box distribution covering nearly the entire width and nearly the entire height corresponding to the pixel pitch. There is no significant gap between image rows or image columns. Each pixel has three colour components, but the optics of the projection device are arranged to cause the distribution of light from these components to be overlaid. From a great distance, pixel structure will not be visible. However, as viewing distance decreases, aliasing ("the jaggies") will intrude. Limited performance of projection lenses mitigates aliasing somewhat; however, aliasing can be quite noticeable, as in the examples of Figures 7.3 and 7.4 on page 77.

In a typical direct-view digital display, such as an LCD or a PDP, each pixel comprises three colour components that occupy distinct regions of the area corresponding to each pixel. Ordinarily, these components are side-by-side. There is no significant gap between image rows. However, if one component (say green) is turned on and the others are off, there is a gap between columns. These systems rely upon the limited acuity of the viewer to integrate the components into a single coloured area. At a close viewing distance, the gap can be visible, and this can induce aliasing.

The viewing distance of a display using a box distribution, such as a direct-view LCD or PDP, is limited by the intrusion of aliasing.

Gaussian distribution

As I have mentioned, a CRT display has a spot profile resembling a Gaussian. The CRT designer's choice of spot size involves a compromise illustrated by Figure 7.8.

• For a Gaussian distribution with a very small spot, say a spot width less than $\frac{1}{2}$ the scan-line pitch, line structure will become evident even at a fairly large viewing distance.

• For a Gaussian distribution with medium-sized spot, say a spot width approximately equal to the scan-line pitch, the onset of scan-line visibility will occur at a closer distance than with a small spot.

• As spot size is increased beyond about twice the scan-line pitch, eventually the spot becomes so large that no further improvement in line-structure visibility is achieved by making it larger. However, there is a ser-

Figure 7.8 **Gaussian spot size.** Solid lines graph Gaussian distributions of intensity across two adjacent image rows, for three values of spot size. The areas under each curve are identical. The shaded areas indicate their sums. In progressive scanning, adjacent image rows correspond to consecutive scan lines. In interlaced scanning, the situation is more complex.

ious disadvantage to making the spot larger than necessary: Sharpness is reduced.

You saw at the beginning of this chapter that in order to avoid visible pixel structure in image display some overlap is necessary in the distributions of light produced by neighboring display elements. Such overlap reduces sharpness, but by how much? How much overlap is necessary? I will discuss these issues in the Chapter *Resolution,* on page 97. First, though, I will introduce the fundamentals of raster scanning.

Raster scanning

I introduced the pixel array on page 3. This chapter outlines the basics of this process of *raster scanning*, whereby the samples of the pixel array are sequenced uniformly in time to form scan lines, which are in turn sequenced in time throughout each frame interval. In Chapter 13, *Introduction to component SD,* on page 129, I will present details on scanning in conventional "525-line" and "625-line" video. In *Introduction to composite NTSC and PAL,* on page 135, I will introduce the colour coding used in these systems. In Chapter 15, *Introduction to HD,* on page 141, I will introduce scanning in high-definition television.

Flicker, refresh rate, and frame rate

A sequence of still pictures, captured and displayed at a sufficiently high rate, can create the illusion of motion.

The historical CRT display used for television emits light for a small fraction of the frame time: The display has a *short duty cycle;* it is black most of the time. If the flash rate – or *refresh* rate – is too low, flicker is perceived. The flicker sensitivity of vision is dependent upon display and viewing conditions: The brighter the environment, and the larger the angle subtended by the picture, the higher the flash rate must be to avoid flicker. Because picture angle influences flicker, flicker depends upon viewing distance.

Most modern displays – including LCDs and plasma displays – do not flash, and cannot flicker. Nonetheless, they may be subject to various motion impairments.

In a "flashing" display, the brightness of the displayed image itself influences the flicker threshold to some

Flicker is sometimes redundantly called *large-area flicker*. Take care to distinguish *flicker*, described here, from *twitter*, to be described on page 89. See FUKUDA, TADAHIKO (1987), "Some Characteristics of Peripheral Vision," *NHK Tech. Monograph No.* 36 (Tokyo: NHK Science and Technical Research Laboratories).

Application	Display luminance	Surround	Refresh (flash) rate [Hz]	Frame rate [Hz]
Cinema	48 nt	Dark ~0%	48	24
Television {	80 nt	Dim ~5%	50	25
	120 nt	Dim ~5%	≈60	≈30
Office	320 nt	"Average" ~20%	various, e.g., 66, 72, 76	same as refresh rate

Table 8.1 *Refresh rate* refers to the shortest interval over which the entire picture is updated. *Flash rate* refers to the rate at which the picture height is covered at the display. Different refresh rates and flash rates are used in different applications.

The fovea has a diameter of about 1.5 mm, and subtends a visual angle of about 5°.

Figure 8.1 **A dual-bladed shutter** in a film projector flashes each frame twice. Rarely, three bladed shutters are used; they flash each frame thrice.

Television refresh rates were originally chosen to match the local AC power line frequency. See *Frame, field, line, and sample rates*, on page 389.

FARRELL, JOYCE E., et al. (1987), "Predicting flicker thresholds for video display terminals," in *Proc. Society for Information Display* **28** (4): 449–453.

extent, so the brighter the image the higher the refresh rate must be. In a very dark environment, such as the cinema, flicker sensitivity is completely determined by the luminance of the image itself. Peripheral vision has higher temporal sensitivity than central (foveal) vision, so the flicker threshold increases to some extent with wider viewing angles. Table 8.1 summarizes refresh rates used in film, video, and computing.

In the darkness of a cinema, a flash rate of 48 Hz is sufficient to overcome flicker. In the early days of motion pictures, 24 frames per second were found to be sufficient for good motion portrayal. So, a conventional film projector uses a dual-bladed shutter, depicted in Figure 8.1, to flash each frame twice. Higher realism can be obtained with material at 48 frames per second or higher displayed with single-bladed shutters, but such schemes are nonstandard.

In the dim viewing environment typical of television, such as a living room, a flash rate of 60 Hz suffices. The interlace technique, to be described on page 88, provides for video a function comparable to the dual-bladed shutter of a film projector: Each frame is flashed as two fields. Refresh is established by the field rate (twice the frame rate). For a given data rate, interlace doubles the apparent flash rate, and provides improved motion portrayal by doubling the temporal sampling rate. Scanning without interlace is called *progressive*.

CRT computer displays used in office environments historically required refresh rates above 70 Hz to overcome flicker (see Farrell, 1987). CRTs have now been supplanted by LCD displays, which don't flicker. High refresh rates are no longer needed to avoid flicker.

Introduction to scanning

A moment ago, I outlined how refresh rate for television was chosen so as to minimize flicker. In *Viewing distance and angle,* on page 100, I will outline how spatial sampling determines the number of pixels in the image array. Video scanning represents pixels in sequential order, so as to acquire, convey, process, or display every pixel during the fixed time interval associated with each frame. In analog video, information in the image plane was scanned left to right at a uniform rate during a fixed, short interval of time – the *active line time*. Scanning established a fixed relationship between a position in the image and a time instant in the signal. Successive lines were scanned at a uniform rate from the top to the bottom of the image, so there was also a fixed relationship between vertical position and time. The stationary pattern of parallel scanning lines disposed across the image area is the *raster*.

Samples of a digital image matrix are usually conveyed in the same order that the image was historically conveyed in analog video: first the top image row (left to right), then successive rows. *Scan line* is an old-fashioned term; the term *image row* is now preferred. Successive pixels lie in *image columns*.

In cameras and displays, a certain time interval is consumed in advancing the scanning operation – historically, *horizontal retracing* – from one line to the next; several line times are consumed by vertical retrace, from the bottom of one scan to the top of the next. A CRT's electron gun had to be switched off (blanked) during these intervals, so these intervals were (and are) called *blanking intervals*. The *horizontal blanking interval* occurs between scan lines; the *vertical blanking interval* (VBI) occurs between frames (or fields). Figure 8.2 shows the blanking intervals of "525-line" video.

The word *raster* is derived from the Greek word *rustum* (rake), owing to the resemblance of a raster to the pattern left on newly raked earth.

Line is a heavily overloaded term. *Lines* may refer to the total number of raster lines: Figure 8.2 shows "525-line" video, which has 525 total lines. *Line* may refer to a line containing picture, or to the total number of lines containing picture – in this example, 480. *Line* may denote the AC power line, whose frequency is very closely related to vertical scanning. Finally, *lines* is a measure of resolution, to be described in *Resolution,* on page 97.

Figure 8.2 **Blanking intervals** for "525-line" video are indicated here by a dark region surrounding a light-shaded rectangle that represents the picture. The *vertical blanking interval* (VBI) consumes about 8% of each field time; horizontal blanking consumes about 15% of each line time.

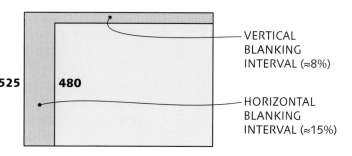

525   **480**

VERTICAL BLANKING INTERVAL (≈8%)

HORIZONTAL BLANKING INTERVAL (≈15%)

The horizontal and vertical blanking intervals required for a CRT were large fractions of the line time and frame time: In SD, vertical blanking consumes roughly 8% of each frame period. In HD, that fraction is reduced to about 4%.

In a video interface, whether analog or digital, synchronization information (*sync*) is conveyed during the blanking intervals. In principle, a digital video interface transmit just the active pixels accompanied by the minimum necessary sync information. Instead, digital video interfaces use interface rates that match the blanking intervals of historical analog equipment. What would otherwise be excess data capacity is put to good use conveying audio signals, captions, test signals, error detection or correction information, or other data or metadata.

The count of 480 picture lines in Figure 8.2 is a recent standard; some people will quote numbers between 481 and 487. See *Picture lines*, on page 379.

Scanning parameters

In *progressive* (or *sequential*) *scanning*, the image rows are scanned in order, from top to bottom, at a picture rate sufficient to portray motion. Figure 8.3 at the top of the facing page indicates four basic scanning parameters:

• *Total lines* (L_T) comprises all of the scan lines, including the vertical blanking interval and the picture lines.
• The image has N_R *image rows,* containing the picture. (Historically, this was the *active line* count, L_A.)
• *Samples per total line* (S_{TL}) comprises the sample intervals in the total line, including horizontal blanking.
• The image has N_C *image columns,* containing the picture. (Historically, some number of *samples per active line* (S_{AL}) were permitted to take values different from the blanking level.

The *production aperture*, sketched in Figure 8.3, comprises the array N_C columns by N_R rows. The samples in the production aperture comprise the pixel array; they are *active*. All other sample intervals comprise blanking; they are *inactive* or "*blanked.*"

VITS: Vertical interval test signal
VITC: Vertical interval timecode

The vertical blanking interval in analog signals typically carried vertical interval information such as VITS, VITC, and closed captions. Consumer display equipment must blank these lines. Both vertical and horizontal blanking intervals in a digital video interface may be used to convey ancillary (ANC) data such as audio.

Figure 8.3 **The Production aperture** comprises the image array, N_C columns by N_R rows. Blanking intervals lie outside the production aperture; here, blanking intervals are darkly shaded. The product of N_C and N_R yields the active pixel count per frame. Sampling rate (f_S) is the product of S_{TL}, L_T, and frame rate.

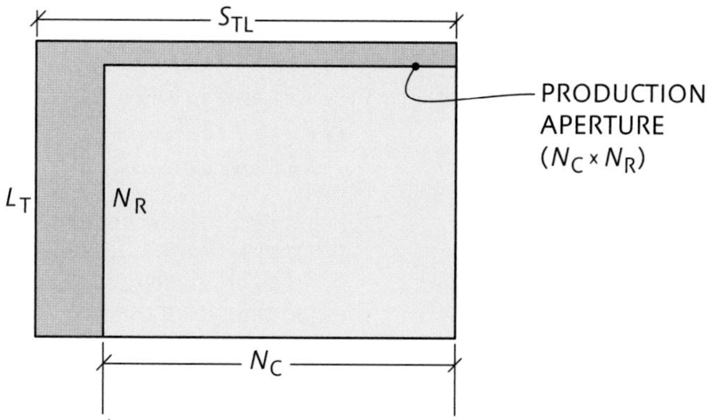

Figure 8.4 **The Clean aperture** should remain subjectively free from artifacts arising from filtering. The clean aperture excludes blanking transition samples, indicated here by black bands outside the left and right edges of the picture width, defined by the count of samples per picture width (S_{PW}).

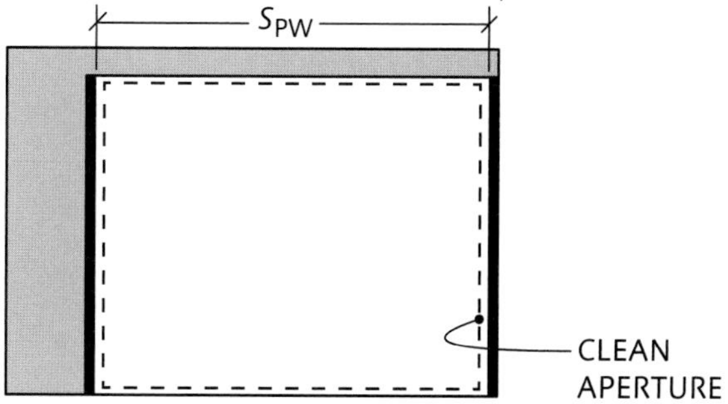

All standard SD and HD image formats have N_C and N_R both even. The horizontal center of the picture lies midway between the central two luma samples, and the vertical center of the picture lies vertically midway between the central two image rows.

See *Transition samples,* on page 378.

Only pixels in the image array are represented in acquisition, processing, storage, and display. However, some processing operations (such as spatial filtering) use information in a small neighbourhood surrounding the subject pixel. In the absence of any better information, we take the pixel of the image array to lie on black. At the left-hand edge of the picture, if the video signal of the leftmost pixel has a value greatly different from black, an artifact called *ringing* is liable to result when that transition is processed through an analog or digital filter. A similar circumstance arises at the right-hand picture edge. In studio video, the signal builds to full amplitude, or decays to blanking level, over several *transition* samples ideally having a raised cosine envelope.

Active samples encompass not only the picture, but also the transition samples; see Figure 8.4 above. Studio equipment should maintain the widest picture possible within the production aperture, subject to appropriate blanking transitions.

I have treated the image array as an array of pixels, without regard for the spatial distribution of light

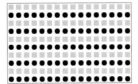 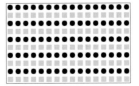

Figure 8.5 **Interlaced format** represents a complete picture – the *frame* – from two *fields,* each containing half of the total number of image rows. The second field is delayed by half the frame time from the first. This example shows 10 image rows. In analog scanning, interlace is effected by having an odd number of *total* scan lines (e.,g., 525, 625, or 1125).

power across each pixel – the pixel's *spot profile,* or more technically, *point spread function* (PSF). If the spot profile is such that there is a significant gap between the intensity distributions of adjacent image rows (scan lines), then image structure will be visible to viewers closer than a certain distance. The gap between scan lines is a function of image row (scan-line) pitch and spot profile. *Spot size* was historically characterized by spot diameter at 50% power. For a given image row pitch, a smaller spot size will force viewers to be more distant from the display if scan lines are to be rendered invisible.

Interlaced format

Interlacing is a scheme which – for given viewing distance, flicker sensitivity, and data rate – offered some increase in static spatial resolution over progressive scanning in historical CRT displays, which exhibited flicker. The full height of the image is scanned leaving gaps in the vertical direction. Then, $\frac{1}{50}$ or $\frac{1}{60}$ s later, the full image height is scanned again, but offset vertically so as to fill in the gaps. A frame thereby comprises two *fields,* denoted *first* and *second.* The scanning mechanism is depicted in Figure 8.5. Historically, the same scanning standard was used across an entire television system, so interlace was used not only for display but for the whole chain, including acquisition, recording, processing, distribution, and transmission.

Noninterlaced (*progressive*) scanning is universal in desktop computers and in computing; also, progressive scanning has been introduced for digital television and

To refer to fields as *odd* and *even* invites confusion. Use *first field* and *second field* instead. Some people refer to scanning first the odd lines then the even; however, scan lines in interlaced video were historically numbered in *temporal* order, not spatial order: Scan lines are *not* numbered as if they were rows in the frame's image matrix. Confusion on this point among computer engineers – and confusion regarding *top* and *bottom fields* – has led to lots of improperly encoded video where the top and bottom offsets are wrong.

DIGITAL VIDEO AND HD ALGORITHMS AND INTERFACES

HD. However, the interlace technique remains universal in SD, and is widely used in broadcast HD. Interlace-to-progressive (I-P) conversion, also called *deinterlacing,* is an unfortunate but necessary by-product of interlaced scanning.

CRTs are now obsolete. The dominant display technologies now used for video – LCD and plasma panels – have relatively long duty cycles, and they don't flicker. The *raison d'être* for interlace has vanished. Nonetheless, interlace remains in wide use.

Twitter

The flicker susceptibility of vision stems from a wide-area effect: In a display such as a CRT that flashes, as long as the complete height of the picture is flashed sufficiently rapidly to overcome flicker, small-scale picture detail, such as that in the alternate lines, can be transmitted at a lower rate. With progressive scanning, scan-line visibility limits the reduction of spot size. With interlaced scanning, this constraint is relaxed by a factor of two. However, interlace introduced a new constraint, that of *twitter.*

If an image has vertical detail at a scale comparable to the image row pitch – for example, if the fine pattern of horizontal line pairs in Figure 8.6 is scanned – then interlaced display causes the content of the first and the second fields to differ markedly. At usual field rates – 50 or 60 Hz – this causes twitter, a small-scale phenomenon that is perceived as a scintillation, or an extremely rapid up-and-down motion. If such image information occupies a large area, then flicker is perceived instead of twitter. Twitter is sometimes called *interline flicker*; however, flicker is by definition a wide-area effect, so *interline flicker* is a poor term.

Twitter is produced not only from degenerate images such as the fine black-and-white lines of Figure 8.6, but also from high-contrast vertical detail in ordinary images. High-quality video cameras include optical spatial lowpass filters to attenuate vertical detail that would otherwise be liable to produce twitter. When computer-generated imagery (CGI) is interlaced, vertical detail must be filtered in order to avoid flicker. Signal processing to accomplish this is called a *twitter filter.*

Figure 8.6 **Twitter** would result if this scene were scanned at the indicated line pitch by a camera without vertical filtering, then displayed using interlace on a short duty cycle display such as a CRT.

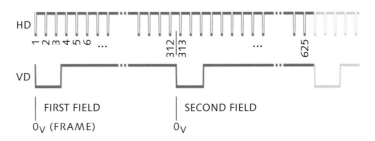

Figure 8.7 **Horizontal and vertical drive** pulses historically effected interlace in analog scanning. 0_V denotes the start of each field. The halfline offset of the second 0_V causes interlace. Here, 576*i* scanning is shown.

Interlace in analog systems

In analog video, interlace was historically achieved by scanning vertically at a constant rate, typically 50 or 60 Hz, and scanning horizontally at an odd multiple of half that rate. In SD in North America and Japan, the field rate is 59.94 Hz; the line rate (f_H) is $\frac{525}{2}$ ($262\frac{1}{2}$) times that rate. In Asia, Australia, and Europe, the field rate is 50 Hz; the line rate is $\frac{625}{2}$ ($312\frac{1}{2}$) times that rate.

Figure 8.7 shows the *horizontal drive* (HD) and *vertical drive* (VD) pulse signals that were once distributed in the studio to cause interlaced scanning in analog equipment. These signals have been superseded by a combined *sync* (or *composite sync*) signal; vertical scanning is triggered by *broad pulses* having total duration of $2\frac{1}{2}$ or 3 lines. Sync is usually imposed onto the video signal, to avoid separate distribution circuits. Analog sync is coded at a level "blacker than black."

Details are presented in Chapter 2, *Analog SD sync, genlock, and interface*, in *Composite NTSC and PAL: Legacy Video Systems*, and in the first edition of the present book.

Interlace and progressive

For a given viewing distance, sharpness is improved as spot size becomes smaller. However, if spot size is reduced beyond a certain point, depending upon the spot profile of the display, either scan lines or pixels will become visible, or aliasing will intrude. In principle, improvements in bandwidth or spot profile reduce potential viewing distance, enabling a wider picture angle. However, because consumers form expectations about viewing distance, we assume a constant viewing distance and say that *resolution* is improved instead.

A rough conceptual comparison of progressive and interlaced scanning is presented in Figure 8.8 at the top of the facing page. At first glance, an interlaced system offers twice the number of pixels – loosely, twice the

We'll take up resolution in interlaced systems on *Interlace revisited*, on page 105.

DIGITAL VIDEO AND HD ALGORITHMS AND INTERFACES

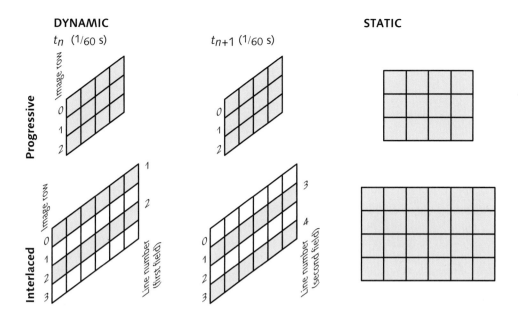

DYNAMIC

t_n (1/60 s) t_{n+1} (1/60 s)

STATIC

Progressive

Image row

0
1
2

Interlaced

Image row

0
1
2
3

Line number (first field)

1
2

0
1
2
3

Line number (second field)

3
4

Figure 8.8 **Progressive and interlaced scanning** are compared. The top left sketch depicts an image of 4×3 pixels transmitted during an interval of $^1/_{60}$ s. The top center sketch shows image data from the same 12 locations transmitted in the following $^1/_{60}$ s interval. The top right sketch. shows the spatial arrangement of the 4×3 image, totalling 12 pixels; the data rate is 12 pixels per $^1/_{60}$ s. At the bottom left, 12 pixels comprising image rows 0 and 2 of a 6×4 image array are transmitted in $^1/_{60}$ s. At the bottom center, the 12 pixels of image rows 1 and 3 are transmitted in the following $^1/_{60}$ s interval. At the bottom right, the spatial arrangement of the 6×4 image is shown: The 24 pixel image is transmitted in $^1/_{30}$ s. Interlaced scanning has the same data rate as progressive, but at first glance has twice the number of pixels, and potentially twice the resolution. In practice, the improvement is a factor of about 1.4 – about 1.2 horizontally and 1.2 verticallly.

spatial resolution – as a progressive system with the same data capacity and the same frame rate. Owing to twitter, spatial resolution in a practical interlaced system is not double that of a progressive system at the same data rate. Historically, cameras have been designed to avoid producing so much vertical detail that twitter would be objectionable. However, resolution is increased by a factor large enough that interlace has historically been considered worthwhile. The improvement comes at the expense of introducing some aliasing and some vertical motion artifacts. Also, interlace makes it difficult to process motion sequences, as will be explained on page 93.

Examine the interlaced (bottom) portion of Figure 8.8, and imagine an image element moving slowly down the picture at a rate of one row of the

Notation	Pixel array
VGA	640×480
SVGA	800×600
XGA	1024×768
WXGA	1366×768
SXGA	1280×1024
UXGA	1600×1200
WUXGA	1920×1200
QXGA	2048×1536

Table 8.2 **Scanning in computing** has no standardized notation, but these notations are widely used.

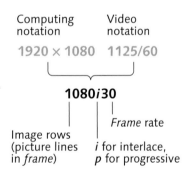

Figure 8.9 **Modern image format notation** gives the count of image rows (active/picture lines); *p* for progressive or *i* for interlace (or *psf* for progressive segmented-frame); then a rate. I write frame rate, but some people write field rate. Aspect ratio is not part of the notation.

pixel array every field time – in a 480*i*29.97 system, $\frac{1}{480}$ of the picture height in $\frac{1}{60}$ s, or one picture height in 8 seconds. Owing to interlace, half of that image's vertical information will be lost! At other rates, some portion of the vertical detail in the image will be lost. With interlaced scanning, vertical motion can cause serious motion artifacts. Techniques to avoid such artifacts will be discussed in *Deinterlacing,* on page 413.

Scanning notation

In computing, a display format may be denoted by a pair of numbers: the count of pixels across the width of the image – that is, the count of image columns – and the count of pixels down the height of the image – that is, the count of image rows. Square sampling is implicit. This notation does not indicate refresh rate. (Alternatively, a display format may be denoted symbolically – VGA, SVGA, XGA, etc., as in Table 8.2. This notation is utterly opaque to the majority of computer users.)

Traditionally, video scanning was denoted by the total number of lines per *frame* (picture lines plus sync and vertical blanking overhead), a slash, and the *field* rate in hertz. (Interlace was implicit unless a slash and *1:1* was appended to indicate progressive scanning; a slash and *2:1* make interlace explicit.) For SD, 525/59.94/2:1 scanning is used in North America and Japan; 625/50/2:1 prevails in Europe, Asia, and Australia. Before the advent of HD, these were the only scanning systems used for broadcasting.

Digital technology enabled new scanning and display standards. Conventional scanning notation could not adequately describe the new scanning systems. A new notation, depicted in Figure 8.9, emerged: Scanning is denoted by the count of image rows, followed by *p* for progressive or *i* for interlace, followed by the frame rate. I write the letter *i* in lowercase italics to avoid potential confusion with the digit 1. For consistency, I write the letter *p* in lowercase italics. Traditional video notation (such as 625/50) is inconsistent, juxtaposing lines per *frame* with *fields* per second. Some people – particularly historical proponents of interlaced scanning – seem intent upon carrying this confusion into the future, by denoting the old 525/59.94 as 480*i*59.94. I strongly prefer using frame rate.

DIGITAL VIDEO AND HD ALGORITHMS AND INTERFACES

Since all 480*i* systems have a frame rate of 29.97 Hz, I use 480*i* as shorthand for 480*i*29.97. Similarly, I use 576*i* as shorthand for 576*i*25.

Because some people write 480*p*60 when they mean 480*p*59.94, the notation *60.00* should be used to emphasize a rate of exactly 60 Hz.

In my notation, conventional 525/59.94/2:1 video is denoted 480*i*29.97; conventional 625/50/2:1 video is denoted 576*i*25. HD systems include 720*p*60 and 1080*i*30. Film-friendly versions of HD are denoted 720*p*24 and 1080*p*24. Aspect ratio is not explicit in the new notation: 720*p*, 1080*i*, and 1080*p* are implicitly 16:9 since there are no 4:3 standards for these systems, but 480*i* or 480*p* could potentially have either conventional 4:3 or widescreen 16:9 aspect ratio.

Motion portrayal

In *Flicker, refresh rate, and frame rate,* on page 83, I outlined the perceptual considerations in choosing refresh rate. In order to avoid objectionable flicker, it was historically necessary with CRT displays to flash an image at a rate higher than the rate necessary to portray its motion. Different applications have adopted different refresh rates, depending on the image quality requirements and viewing conditions. Refresh rate is generally engineered into a video system; once chosen, it cannot easily be changed.

Flicker is minimized by any display device that produces steady, unflashing light, or pulsed light lasting for the majority of the frame time. You might regard a nonflashing display to be more suitable than a device that flashes; many modern devices do not flash. However, with a display having a pixel duty cycle near 100% – that is, an *on-time* approaching the frame time – if the viewer's gaze tracks an element that moves across the image, that element will be seen as smeared. This problem becomes more severe as eye tracking velocities increase, such as with the wide viewing angle of HD. (For details of temporal characteristics of image acquisition and display, see my SMPTE paper.)

POYNTON, CHARLES (1996), "Motion portrayal, eye tracking, and emerging display technology," in *Proc. 30th SMPTE Advanced Motion Imaging Conference* (New York: SMPTE), 192–202.

Historically, this technique was called *3-2 pulldown*, but since the adoption of SMPTE RP 197 in 1998, it is now more accurately called *2-3 pulldown*.

Film at 24 frames per second is transferred to interlaced video at 60 fields per second by *2-3 pulldown*. The first film frame is transferred to two video fields, then the second film frame is transferred to three video fields; the cycle repeats. The 2-3 pulldown is normally used to produce video at 59.94 Hz, not 60 Hz; the film is run 0.1% slower than 24 frames per second. The scheme is detailed in *2-3 pulldown,* on page 405. The 2-3 technique can be applied to transfer to progressive video at 59.94 or 60 frames per second.

Film at 24 frames per second is transferred to *576i* video using *2-2 pulldown:* Each film frame is scanned into two video fields (or frames); the film is run 4% faster than the capture rate. The process is described more fully in Chapter 34, *2-3 pulldown,* on page 405.

Segmented-frame (24PsF)

The *progressive segmented-frame* (PsF) technique is known in consumer SD systems as *quasi-interlace.* PsF is not to be confused with *point spread function,* PSF.

Some camera sensors sample the entire scene at the same instant (*global shutter,* GS). With other sensors, sampling of the scene proceeds vertically at a uniform rate through the frame time (*rolling shutter,* RS).

A scheme called *progressive segmented-frame* is sometimes used in HD equipment that handles images at 24 frames per second. The scheme, denoted *24PsF,* uses progressive scanning: The entire image is sampled at once, and vertical filtering to reduce twitter is both unnecessary and undesirable. However, lines are rearranged to interlaced order for studio distribution and recording. The scheme offers some compatibility with interlaced processing and recording equipment.

Video system taxonomy

Insufficient channel capacity was available at the outset of television broadcasting to transmit three separate colour components. The NTSC and PAL techniques were devised to combine (*encode*) the three colour components into a single *composite* signal. Composite video remains in use in consumers' premises. However, modern video equipment – including all consumer digital video equipment, and all HD equipment – uses component video, either $Y'P_BP_R$ analog components or $Y'C_BC_R$ digital components.

A video system can be classified as component HD, component SD, or composite SD. Independently, a system can be classified as analog or digital. Table 8.3 indicates the six classifications, with the associated

Table 8.3 **Video systems are classified** as analog or digital, and component or composite (or S-video). SD may be represented in component, hybrid (S-video), or composite forms. HD is always in component form.

		Analog	Digital
HD	Component	R'G'B', 709$Y'P_BP_R$	4:2:2 709$Y'C_BC_R$
SD	Component	R'G'B', 601$Y'P_BP_R$	4:2:2 601$Y'C_BC_R$
	Hybrid	S-video	
	Composite	NTSC, PAL	4f_{SC} (obsolete)

colour encoding schemes. Composite NTSC and PAL video encoding is used only in 480*i* and 576*i* systems; HD systems use only component video. S-video is a hybrid of component analog video and composite analog NTSC or PAL; in Table 8.3, S-video is classified in its own seventh (hybrid) category.

Conversion among systems

In video, *encoding* traditionally referred to converting a set of $R'G'B'$ components into an NTSC or PAL composite signal. Encoding may start with $R'G'B'$, $Y'C_BC_R$, or $Y'P_BP_R$ components, or may involve matrixing from $R'G'B'$ to form luma (Y') and intermediate $[U, V]$ components. Quadrature modulation then forms modulated chroma (C); luma and chroma are then summed. *Decoding* historically referred to converting an NTSC or PAL composite signal to $R'G'B'$. Decoding involves luma/chroma separation, quadrature demodulation to recover $[U, V]$, then scaling to recover $[C_B, C_R]$ or $[P_B, P_R]$, or matrixing of luma and chroma to recover $R'G'B'$. *Encoding* and *decoding* have now become general terms that may refer to JPEG, M-JPEG, MPEG, or other encoding or decoding processes.

Transcoding traditionally referred to conversion among different colour encoding methods having the same scanning standard. Transcoding of component video involves chroma interpolation, matrixing, and chroma subsampling. Transcoding of composite video involves decoding, then reencoding to the other standard. With the emergence of compressed storage and digital distribution, the term *transcoding* is now applied toward various methods of recoding compressed bitstreams, or decompressing then recompressing.

Scan conversion refers to conversion among scanning standards having different spatial structures, without the use of temporal processing. In consumer video and desktop video, scan conversion is commonly called *scaling*.

If the input and output frame rates differ, the operation is said to involve *frame rate conversion*. Motion portrayal is liable to be impaired.

By NTSC, I do not mean 525/59.94 or 480*i*; by PAL, I do not mean 625/50 or 576*i*! See *Introduction to composite NTSC and PAL,* on page 135. Although SECAM is a composite technique in that luma and chroma are combined, it has little in common with NTSC and PAL. SECAM is obsolete.

Transcoding refers to the technical aspects of conversion; signal modifications for creative purposes are not encompassed by the term.

In radio frequency (RF) technology, *upconversion* refers to conversion of a signal to a higher carrier frequency; *downconversion* refers to conversion of a signal to a lower carrier frequency.

WATKINSON, JOHN (1994), *The Engineer's Guide to Standards Conversion* (Petersfield, Hampshire, England: Snell & Wilcox, now Snell Group).

Historically, *upconversion* referred to conversion from SD to HD; *downconversion* referred to conversion from HD to SD. Historically, these terms referred to conversion of a signal at the same frame rate as the input; nowadays, frame rate conversion might be involved. High-quality upconversion and downconversion require spatial interpolation. That, in turn, is best performed in a progressive format: If the source is interlaced, intermediate deinterlacing is required, even if the target format is interlaced.

Standards conversion is the historical term denoting conversion among scanning standards having different frame rates. Historically, the term implied similar pixel count (such as conversion between 480*i* and 576*i*), but nowadays a standards converter might incorporate upconversion or downconversion. Standards conversion requires a fieldstore or framestore; to achieve high quality, it requires several fieldstores and motion-compensated interpolation. The complexity of standards conversion between different frame rates has made it difficult for broadcasters and consumers to convert European material for use in North America or Japan, or vice versa.

Resolution 9

To avoid visible pixel structure in image display, some overlap is desirable in the distributions of light produced by neighboring display elements, as I explained in *Image structure,* on page 75. Also, to avoid spatial aliasing in image capture, some overlap is necessary in the distribution of sensitivity across neighboring sensor elements. Such overlap reduces sharpness, but is beneficial to continuous-tone imagery. In this chapter, I will explain *resolution,* which is closely related to sharpness.

Resolution is an overloaded and ambiguous term that properly refers to spatial phenomena. It is confusing to refer to a sample as having 8-bit *resolution;* use *precision* or *quantization* instead. In computing, it is usual to use the term "resolution" to specify the number of columns and rows in the image matrix – that is, to express pixel count. That use disregards effects of signal processing. To preempt *resolution* for *pixel count* makes it difficult to discuss the image detail that's actually represented or delivered to the viewer. I'll present the details of resolution, but first I must introduce the concepts of *magnitude frequency response* and *bandwidth*.

Magnitude frequency response and bandwidth

To characterize the acquisition, processing, or display of smalll elements, rather than analyzing an element of certain (small) dimensions, we analyze a group of closely spaced identical elements, characterizing the spacing between the elements. This allows mathematical analysis using *transforms*, particularly the Fourier transform and the *z*-transform.

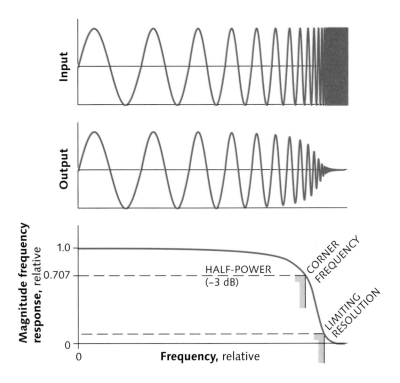

Figure 9.1 **Magnitude frequency response** of an electronic or optical system typically falls as frequency increases. Bandwidth is measured at the half-power point (–3 dB), where response has fallen to 0.707 of its value at a reference frequency (often zero frequency, or *DC*). Useful visible detail is obtained from signal power beyond the half-power bandwidth, that is, at depths of modulation less than 70.7%. I show *limiting resolution,* which might occur at about 10% response.

The top graph in Figure 9.1 shows a one-dimensional sine wave test signal "sweeping" from zero frequency up to a high frequency. (This could be a one-dimensional function of time such as an audio waveform, or the waveform of luma from one scan line of an image.) A typical optical or electronic imaging system involves temporal or spatial dispersion, which causes the response of the system to diminish at high frequency, as shown in the middle graph. The envelope of that waveform – the system's *magnitude frequency response* – is shown at the bottom. An electrical engineer may call this simply *frequency response.* The qualifier *magnitude* distinguishes it from other functions of frequency such as phase frequency response.

Bandwidth characterizes the range of frequencies that a system can capture, record, process, or transmit. *Half-power bandwidth* (also known as *3 dB bandwidth*) is specified or measured where signal magnitude has fallen 3 dB – that is, to the fraction 0.707 – from its value at a reference frequency (often zero frequency, or *DC*). Useful visual information is typically available at frequencies higher than the bandwidth. In image science, *limiting resolution* is determined visually.

The maximum rate at which an analog or digital electronic signal can change state – in an imaging system, between black and white – is limited by frequency response, and is therefore characterized by bandwidth.

Figure 9.1 shows abstract input and output signals. When bandwidth of an optical system is discussed, it is implicit that the quantities are proportional to intensity. When bandwidth of video signals is discussed, it is implicit that the input and output electrical signals are gamma-corrected.

Many digital technologists use the term *bandwidth* to refer to *data rate;* however, the terms properly refer to different concepts. *Bandwidth* refers to the frequency of signal content in an analog or digital signal. *Data rate* refers to digital transmission capacity, independent of any potential signal content. A typical studio HD luma signal has 30 MHz signal bandwidth and 74.25 MB/s data rate – the terms are obviously not interchangeable.

Visual acuity

When an optometrist measures your visual acuity, he or she uses a chart similar to the one shown in Figure 9.2 in the margin. The results of this test depend upon viewing distance. The test is standardized for a viewing distance of 20 feet. At that distance, the strokes of the letters in the 20/20 row subtend one sixtieth of a degree ($\frac{1}{60}°$, one minute of arc). This is roughly the limit of angular discrimination of normal vision.

Visual angles can be estimated using the astronomers' rule of thumb depicted in Figure 9.3: When held at arm's length, the joint of the thumb subtends about two degrees. The full palm subtends about ten degrees, and the nail of the little finger subtends about one degree. (The angular subtense of the full moon is about half a degree.)

Figure 9.2
Snellen chart

RESOLUTION

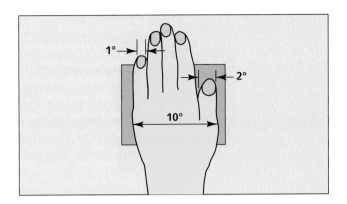

Figure 9.3 **The astronomers' rule of thumb** allows rough measurement of subtended angles. The hand is held at arm's length; the palm then subtends about 10°. Here I show the palm covering a rectangle having 4:3 aspect ratio. If that rectangle was an SD picture, the viewer would be located at roughly the optimal viewing distance.

Viewing distance and angle

If you display a white flatfield on a display with typical pixel pitch, pixel structure is likely to be visible if the viewer is located closer than the distance where adjacent image rows (or scan lines) at the display surface subtend an angle of one minute of arc ($\frac{1}{60}°$) or more.

To achieve viewing where pixel pitch subtends $\frac{1}{60}°$, viewing distance should be about 3400 times the distance d between image rows – that is, 3400 divided by the pixel density. For example, for pixels per inch (ppi):

$$distance \approx 3400 \cdot d \approx \frac{3400}{ppi}; \quad 3400 \approx \frac{1}{\sin\left(\frac{1}{60}\right)^{°}} \qquad \text{Eq 9.1}$$

So, at a distance of 3400 times the distance between image rows, there are about 60 pixels per degree. Viewing distance expressed numerically as a multiple of picture height is then 3400 divided by the number of image rows (N_R):

$$distance \approx \frac{3400}{L_A} \text{PH} \qquad \text{Eq 9.2}$$

SD has about 480 image rows (picture lines). An image row subtends $\frac{1}{60}°$ at a distance of about seven times picture height (PH), as sketched in Figure 9.4 at the top of the facing page, giving roughly 600 pixels across the picture width. Picture angle is about 11°, as shown in Figure 9.5. With your hand held at arm's length, your palm ought to just cover the width of the picture. This

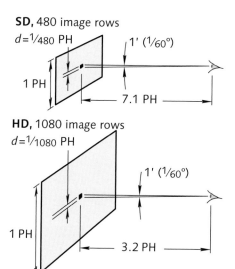

SD, 480 image rows

$d = 1/480$ PH

1' ($1/60°$)

1 PH

7.1 PH

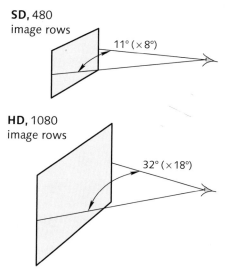

SD, 480
image rows

11° (×8°)

HD, 1080 image rows

$d = 1/1080$ PH

1' ($1/60°$)

1 PH

3.2 PH

HD, 1080
image rows

32° (×18°)

Figure 9.4 **The viewing distance** where pixels become invisible occurs approximately where the pixel pitch subtends an angle of about one minute of arc ($1/60°$) at the display surface. This is roughly the limit of angular discrimination for normal vision.

Figure 9.5 **The picture angle** of SD, sketched at the top, has a horizontal angle of about 11° and a vertical angle of about 8°, where pixel structure becomes invisible. In 1920×1080 HD, horizontal angle can increase to about 33°, and vertical angle to about 18°, preserving the pixel subtense.

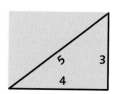

Figure 9.6 **Picture height** at an aspect ratio of 4:3 is ³⁄₅ of the diagonal; optimum viewing distance for conventional video is 4.25 times the diagonal. Picture height at 16:9 is about half the diagonal; optimum viewing distance for 2 Mpx HD is 1.5 times the diagonal.

distance is about 4.25 times the display diagonal, as sketched in Figure 9.6 in the margin. For HD with 1080 image rows, the viewing distance that yields the $1/60°$ pixel subtense is about 3.2 PH (see the bottom of Figure 9.4), about 1.5 times the display diagonal.

For SD, the total horizontal picture angle at that viewing distance is about 11°. Viewers tend to choose a viewing distance that renders pixel structure invisible; angular subtense of a pixel is thereby preserved. Thus, the main effect of higher pixel count is to enable viewing at a wide picture angle. For 1920×1080 HD, horizontal viewing angle is tripled to 33° compared to the 11° of SD as sketched in Figure 9.5. The "high definition" of HD does not squeeze six times the number of pixels into the same visual angle! Instead, the entire image can potentially occupy a much larger area of the viewer's visual field. This topic is addressed further in *Viewing distance,* on page 104.

Kell effect

Early television systems failed to deliver the maximum resolution that was to be expected from Nyquist's work (which was introduced on page 78). In 1934, Kell published a paper quantifying the fraction of the maximum theoretical resolution achieved by RCA's experimental television system. He called this fraction k; later – apparently without Kell's consent! – it became known as the *Kell factor* (less desirably denoted K). Kell's first paper gives a factor of 0.64, but he failed to completely describe his experimental method. A subsequent paper (in 1940) detailed the method, and gives a factor of 0.8, under somewhat different conditions.

Kell's k factor was determined by subjective, not objective, criteria. If the system under test had a spot profile resembling a Gaussian, closely spaced lines on a test chart would cease to be resolved as their spacing diminished beyond a certain value. If a camera under test had an unusually small spot size, or a display had a sharp distribution (such as a box), then k was determined by the intrusion of objectionable artifacts as the spacing reduced – also a subjective criterion.

Kell and other authors published various theoretical derivations that justify various numerical factors; Hsu has published a comprehensive review. In my opinion, such numerical measures are so poorly defined and so unreliable that they are now useless. Hsu says:

> Kell factor is defined so ambiguously that individual researchers have justifiably used different theoretical and experimental techniques to derive widely varying values of k.

Today I consider it poor science to quantify a numerical Kell *factor.* However, Ray Kell made an important contribution to television science, and I think it entirely fitting that we honour him with the Kell *effect:*

> *In a video system – including image capture, signal processing, transmission, and display – KELL EFFECT refers to the loss of resolution, relative to the Nyquist limit, caused by the spatial dispersion of light power. Some dispersion is necessary to avoid aliasing upon capture; some dispersion is necessary to avoid objectionable scan line or pixel structure at a display.*

Lowercase k for *Kell factor* is unrelated to K *rating,* sometimes called K *factor,* which I will describe on page 542; neither is related to 1000 or 1024.

KELL, RAY D., ALDA V. BEDFORD, and G. L. FREDENDALL (1940), "A determination of the optimum number of lines in a television system," in *RCA Review* **5**: 8–30 (July).

HSU, STEPHEN C. (1986), "The Kell factor: past and present," in *SMPTE Journal* **95** (2): 206–214 (Feb.).

Twitter is introduced on page 89.

MITSUHASHI, TETSUO (1982), "Scanning specifications and picture quality," in FUJIO, TAKASHI, et al., *High Definition Television*, NHK Science and Technical Research Laboratories Tech. Monograph **32** (June).

Kell's 1934 paper concerned only progressive scanning. With the emergence of interlaced systems, it became clear that twitter resulted from excessive vertical detail. To reduce twitter to tolerable levels, it was necessary to reduce vertical resolution to substantially below that of a well-designed progressive system having the same spot size – for a progressive system with a given k, an interlaced system having the same spot size had to have lower k. Many people have lumped this consideration into "Kell factor," but researchers such as Mitsuhashi identify this reduction separately as an *interlace factor* or *interlace coefficient*.

Resolution

SD (at roughly 720×480), HD at 1280×720, and HD at 1920×1080 all have different pixel counts. Image quality delivered by a particular number of pixels depends upon the nature of the image data (e.g., whether the data is raster-locked or Nyquist-filtered), and upon the nature of the display device (e.g., whether it has box or Gaussian reconstruction).

In computing, unfortunately, the term *resolution* has come to refer simply to the count of vertical and horizontal pixels in the pixel array, without regard for any overlap at capture, or overlap at display that may have reduced the amount of detail in the image. A system may be described as having "resolution" of 1152×864 – this system has a total of about one million pixels (one megapixel, or 1 Mpx). Interpreted this way, "resolution" doesn't depend upon whether individual pixels can be discerned ("resolved") on the face of the display.

Resolution in a digital image system is bounded by the count of pixels across the image width and height. However, as picture detail increases in frequency, signal processing and optical effects cause response to diminish even within the bounds imposed by sampling. In video, we are concerned with resolution that is delivered to the viewer; we are also interested in limitations of frequency response ("bandwidth") that may have been imposed in capture, recording, processing, and display. In video, resolution concerns the maximum number of line pairs (or cycles) that can be resolved on the display screen. This is a subjective criterion! Resolution is related to perceived sharpness.

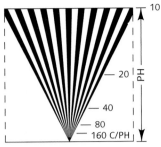

— 10

— 20 PH

— 40

— 80

— 160 C/PH

Figure 9.7 **A Resolution wedge** pattern sweeps various horizontal frequencies through an imaging system. This pattern is calibrated in terms of cycles per picture *height* (here signified PH); however, with the pattern in the orientation shown, *horizontal* resolution is measured.

Resolution is usually expressed in terms of spatial frequency, whose units are cycles per picture width (C/PW) horizontally, and cycles per picture height (C/PH) vertically, or units closely related to these. Figure 9.7 depicts a resolution test chart. In the orientation presented, it sweeps across horizontal frequencies, and can be used to estimate horizontal resolution. Turned 90°, it can be used to sweep through vertical frequencies, and thereby estimate vertical resolution.

Resolution in video

Spatial phenomena at an image sensor or at a display device may limit both vertical and horizontal resolution. Analog processing, recording, and transmission historically limits bandwidth, and thereby affects only horizontal resolution. *Resolution* in video historically refers to horizontal resolution:

> *Resolution in TVL/PH – colloquially, "TV lines" – is twice the number of vertical black and white line pairs (cycles) that can be visually discerned across a horizontal distance equal to the picture height.*

Vertical resampling has become common in consumer equipment; resampling potentially affects vertical resolution. In transform-based compression (such as JPEG, DV, and MPEG), dispersion comparable to overlap between pixels occurs; this affects horizontal and vertical resolution.

Viewing distance

Pixel count in SD and HD is fixed by the corresponding image format. On page 100, I explained that viewing distance is optimum where the scan-line pitch subtends an angle of about $\frac{1}{60}°$. If a sampled image is viewed closer than that distance, scan lines or pixels are liable to be visible. With typical displays, SD is suitable for viewing at about 7·PH; 1080*i* HD is suitable for viewing at a much closer distance of about 3·PH.

A computer user tends to position himself or herself where scan-line pitch subtends an angle greater than $\frac{1}{60}°$ – perhaps at half that distance. However, at such a close distance, individual pixels are likely to be discernible, perhaps even objectionable, and the quality of continuous-tone images will almost certainly suffer.

MTF: Modulation transfer function

Closest viewing distance is constrained by pixel count; however, visibility of pixel or scan-line structure in an image depends upon many other factors such as camera MTF, spot profile (PSF), and frequency response. In principle, if any of these factors reduces the amount of detail in the image, the optimum viewing distance is pushed more distant. However, consumers have formed an expectation that SD is best viewed at about 7·PH; as people become familiar with HD they will form an expectation that it is best viewed at about 3·PH.

Lechner worked at RCA Labs in Princeton, New Jersey. Jackson worked at Philips Research Laboratories, Redhill, Surrey, U.K.; he is unrelated to my like-named colleague who worked at Grass Valley Group, now at AJA Video.

A countervailing argument is based upon the dimensions of consumers' living rooms. In unpublished research, Bernie Lechner found that North American viewers tend to view SD receivers at about 9 ft. In similar experiments in England, Richard Jackson found a preference for 3 m. This viewing distance is sometimes called the *Lechner distance* – or in Europe, the *Jackson distance!* These numbers are consistent with Equation 9.2, on page 100 applied to an SD display with a 27-inch (70 cm) diagonal.

Rather than saying that improvements in bandwidth or spot profile enable decreased viewing distance, and therefore wider picture angle, we assume that viewing distance is fixed, and say that resolution is improved.

Interlace revisited

We can now revisit the parameters of interlaced scanning. With the luminance and surround conditions typical of consumer television receivers, a vertical scan rate of 50 or 60 Hz is sufficient to overcome flicker. As I mentioned on page 88, at practical vertical scan rates, it is possible to flash alternate image rows in alternate vertical scans without causing flicker. This is *interlace.* The scheme is possible owing to the fact that temporal sensitivity of the visual system decreases at high spatial frequencies.

Twitter is introduced, however, by vertical detail whose scale approaches the scan-line pitch. Twitter can be reduced to tolerable levels by reducing the vertical detail somewhat, to perhaps 0.7 times. On its own, this reduction in vertical detail would push the viewing distance back to 1.4 times that of progressive scanning.

However, to maintain the same sharpness as a progressive system at a given data capacity, all else being equal, in interlaced scanning only half the picture data needs to be transmitted in each vertical scan period (field). For a given frame rate, this reduction in data per scan enables pixel count per frame to be doubled.

The pixels gained could be exploited in one of three ways: by doubling the row count, by doubling the column count, or by distributing the additional pixels proportionally to image columns and rows. Taking the third approach, the doubled pixel count could be distributed equally horizontally and vertically, increasing column count by a factor of 1.4 and row count by a factor of 1.4. Viewing distance could thereby be reduced to 0.7 that of progressive scan, winning back the lost viewing distance associated with twitter, and yielding equivalent performance to progressive scan.

Ideally, though, the additional pixels owing to interlaced scan should not be distributed equally to both dimensions. Instead, the count of image rows should be increased by about 1.4×1.2 (i.e., 1.7), and the count of image columns by about 1.2. The factor of 1.4 increase in the row count alleviates twitter. The remaining 1.2 increase in both row and column count yields a modest but significant improvement in viewing distance – and therefore picture angle – over a progressive system.

Twitter and scan-line visibility are inversely proportional to the count of image rows, a one-dimensional quantity. However, sharpness is proportional to pixel count, a two-dimensional (areal) quantity. To overcome twitter at the same picture angle, 1.4 times as many image rows are required; however, 1.2 times as many rows and 1.2 times as many columns are still available to improve picture angle.

Interlaced scanning was chosen over progressive in the early days of television, half a century ago. All other things being equal – such as data rate, frame rate, spot size, and viewing distance – various advantages have been claimed for interlace scanning.

• Neglecting the introduction of twitter, and considering just the static pixel array, interlace offers twice the static resolution for a given bandwidth and frame rate.

• If you consider an interlaced image of the same size as a progressive image and viewed at the same distance – that is, preserving the picture angle – then there is a decrease in scan-line visibility.

Constant luminance

Video systems convey colour image data using one component that approximates lightness, and two other components that represent colour, absent lightness. In *Colour science for video,* on page 287, I will detail how luminance can be formed as a weighted sum of linear *RGB* values each of which is proportional to optical power. A colour scientist uses the term *constant luminance* to refer to this sum being constant. Transmitting a single component from which relative luminance can be reconstructed is the *principle of constant luminance.* Preferably a nonlinear transfer function acts on that component to impose perceptually uniform coding.

Standard video systems do not strictly adhere to that principle; instead, they implement an engineering approximation. The colour scientist's weighted sum of linear *RGB* is *not* computed. Instead, a nonlinear transfer function is applied to each linear-light *RGB* component individually, then a weighted sum of the nonlinear *gamma-corrected R'G'B'* components forms what I call *luma.* (Many video engineers carelessly call this quantity *luminance.*) In standard video systems, luma is encoded using the theoretical *RGB* weighting coefficients of colour science, but in a block diagram different from the one a colour scientist would expect: In video, gamma correction is applied *before* the matrix, instead of the colour scientist's preference, after.

Historically, transmission of a single component representative of greyscale enabled compatibility with "black-and-white" television. Human vision has poor acuity for colour compared to luminance. Placing "black-and-white" information into one component

The term *luminance* is widely misused in video. *See Relative luminance,* on page 258, and Appendix A, *YUV and luminance considered harmful,* on page 567.

107

enables *chroma subsampling* to take advantage of vision's low acuity for chroma in order to reduce data rate (historically, bandwidth) in the two other components. In colour imaging, it is sensible to code a "black-and-white" component even if "black-and-white" compatibility isn't required (for example, in JPEG).

I've been placing "black-and-white" in quotes. At the invention of television, the transmitted signal represented greyscale, not just black and white: Then, and now, *greyscale* would be a better term.

Historical video literature refers to the "signal representing luminance" or the "luminance signal" or the "luminance component." All of these terms were once justified; however, they are now dangerous: To use the term "luminance" suggests that relative luminance (Y) can be decoded from that component. However, without strict adherence to the principle of constant luminance, luminance *cannot* be decoded from the greyscale component alone: Two other components (typically C_B and C_R) are necessary.

In this chapter, I will explain why and how all current video systems depart from the principle of constant luminance. If you are willing to accept this departure from theory as a fact, then you may safely skip this chapter, and proceed to *Introduction to luma and chroma,* on page 121, where I will introduce how the luma and colour difference signals are formed and subsampled.

The term "monochrome" is sometimes used instead of "greyscale." However, in classic computer graphics terminology *monochrome* refers to bilevel (1-bit) images or display systems, so I avoid that term.

The principle of constant luminance

APPLEBAUM, SIDNEY (1952), "Gamma correction in constant luminance color television systems," in *Proc. IRE,* **40** (11): 1185–1195 (Oct.).

Ideally, the so-called monochrome component in colour video would mimic a greyscale system: Relative luminance would be computed as a properly weighted sum of (linear-light) R, G, and B tristimulus values, according to the principles of colour science that are explained in *Transformations between RGB and CIE XYZ,* on page 307. At the decoder, the inverse matrix would reconstruct linear R, G, and B tristimulus values:

Figure 10.1 **Formation of relative luminance**

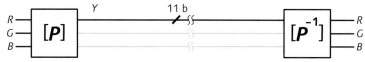

Two colour difference (chroma) components would be computed, to enable chroma subsampling; these would be conveyed to the decoder through separate channels:

Figure 10.2 **Hypothetical chroma components (linear-light)**

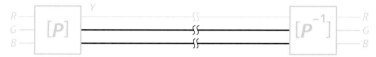

Set aside the chroma components for now: No matter how they are handled, in a true constant luminance system all of the relative luminance is recoverable from the greyscale component alone.

If relative luminance were conveyed directly, 11 bits or more would be necessary. Eight bits barely suffice if we use nonlinear image coding, introduced on page 31, to impose perceptual uniformity: We could subject relative luminance to a nonlinear transfer function that mimics vision's lightness sensitivity. Lightness can be approximated as CIE *L** (to be detailed on page 259); *L** is roughly the 0.42-power of relative luminance.

Figure 10.3 **Encoding nonlinearly coded relative luminance**

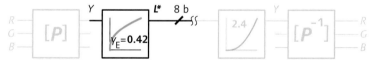

The decoder would apply the inverse transfer function:

Figure 10.4 **Decoding nonlinearly coded relative luminance**

If a video system were to operate in this manner, it would conform to the principle of constant luminance: All of the relative luminance would be present in, and recoverable from, the greyscale component.

Compensating for the CRT

Unfortunately for the theoretical block diagram – but fortunately for video, as you will see in a moment – the

electron gun of a historical CRT display introduces
a power function having an exponent of about 2.4:

Figure 10.5 **The CRT**
transfer function

In a constant luminance system, the decoder would
have to invert the display's power function. This would
require insertion of a compensating transfer function –
roughly a $\frac{1}{2.4}$-power function – in front of the CRT:

Figure 10.6 **Compensating**
the CRT transfer function

The decoder would now include two power functions:
An inverse *L** function with an exponent close to 2.4 to
invert the perceptually uniform coding, and a power
function with an exponent of $\frac{1}{2.4}$ – that is, about
0.42 – to compensate for the CRT's nonlinearity.
Figure 10.6 represents the block digram of an idealized,
true constant luminance video system.

Departure from constant luminance

Having two nonlinear transfer functions at every
decoder was historically expensive and impractical.
    Notice that the exponents of the power functions are
2.4 and $\frac{1}{2.4}$ – the functions are inverses! To avoid the
complexity of incorporating two power functions into
a decoder's electronics, we begin by rearranging the
block diagram, to interchange the "order of operations"
of the matrix and the CRT compensation:

Figure 10.7 **Rearranged decoder**

Upon rearrangement, the two power functions are
adjacent. Since the functions are effectively inverses,

the combination of the two has no net effect. Both functions can be dropped from the decoder:

Figure 10.8 **Simplified decoder**

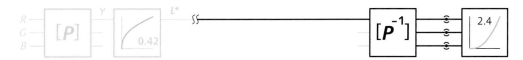

Decoder signal processing simply inverts the encoder matrix. The 2.4-power function is intrinsic to a CRT display; alternative display technologies exhibit comparable mapping from signal value to tristimulus.

Rearranging the decoder requires that the encoder also be rearranged, so as to mirror the decoder and achieve correct end-to-end reproduction of the original *RGB* tristimulus values:

Figure 10.9 **Rearranged encoder**

Figure 10.9 represents the basic signal flow for all video systems; it will be elaborated in later chapters.

Luma

Television engineers who are uneducated in colour science often mistakenly call luma (*Y'*) by the name *luminance* and denote it by the unprimed symbol *Y*. This leads to great confusion, as I explain in Appendix A, on page 567.

The rearranged flow diagram of Figure 10.9 is *not* mathematically equivalent to the arrangement of Figures 10.1 through 10.4! In Figure 10.9, the encoder's matrix does not operate on (linear-light) tristimulus signals, and relative luminance is not computed. Instead, a nonlinear quantity – denoted *luma* and symbolized *Y'* – is computed and transmitted. Luma involves an engineering approximation: The system no longer adheres strictly to the principle of constant luminance (though it is often mistakenly claimed to do so).

In the rearranged encoder, we no longer use CIE *L** to optimize for perceptual uniformity; instead, we use the inverse of the CRT's inherent transfer function. A 0.42-power function accomplishes approximately perceptually uniform coding, and reproduces tristimulus values proportional to those in the original scene.

The following chapter, *Picture rendering*, explains that the 0.42 value must be altered in a normal scene to about 0.5 to accommodate a perceptual effect. The alteration depends upon artistic intent, and upon display and viewing conditions. Ideally, display systems should have adjustments for picture rendering depending upon display and viewing conditions, but they rarely do!

"Leakage" of luminance into chroma

Until now, we have neglected the colour difference components. In the rearranged block diagram of Figure 10.9, colour difference components are "matrixed" from *nonlinear* (gamma-corrected) *R'G'B'*:

Figure 10.10 **Chroma components**

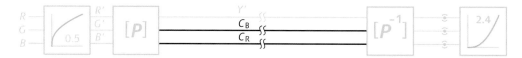

In a true constant luminance system, no matter how the colour difference signals are handled, all of the relative luminance is carried by the greyscale component. In the rearranged system, most of the relative luminance is conveyed through the *Y'* channel. However, to the extent that *Y'* isn't equal to *Y,* some relative luminance can be thought of as "leaking" into the colour difference components. If the colour difference components were not subsampled – for example, in a $Y'C_BC_R$, 4:4:4 system – this leakage would be inconsequential. However, the colour difference components are formed precisely to *enable* subsampling! So, we now turn our attention to subsampling.

Figure 10.11 below shows Figure 10.10's practical block diagram augmented with subsampling filters in the chroma paths. With conventional coding, some of

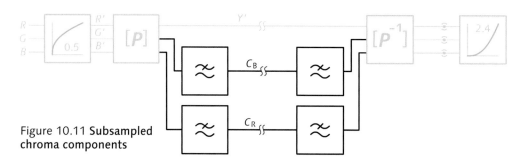

Figure 10.11 **Subsampled chroma components**

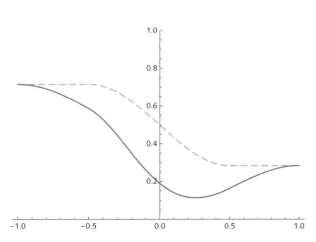

Figure 10.12 *Y'* and C_B/C_R waveforms at the green-magenta transition of SD colourbars are shown, following idealized 4:2:2 chroma subsampling. The luma waveform is plotted in grey; C_B and C_R share the same waveform, plotted in magenta. The transition rate (rise time) of the C_B and C_R components is half that of luma.

Figure 10.13 **Luminance waveform at the green-magenta transition** of colourbars is shown in the solid line. The dashed line reflects luminance in a hypothetical true constant-luminance system.

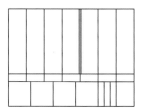

Figure 10.14 **Failure to adhere to constant luminance** is evident in the dark band in the green-magenta transition of colourbars. The dark band is found upon displaying any colourbar signal that has been subject to chroma subsampling.

the relative luminance traverses the chroma pathways. Figure 10.12 above shows the idealized $Y'C_BC_R$ waveforms at the green-magenta transition of colourbars, with 4:2:2 chroma subsampling. Figure 10.13 shows, in the solid line, the luminance that results after conventional decoding. Subsampling not only removes detail from the colour components, it removes detail from the "leaked" relative luminance. We have to ask, "What's lost?" The departure from theory is apparent in the dark band appearing between the green and magenta colour bars of the standard video test pattern, depicted in Figure 10.14 in the margin.

With conventional video coding, in areas where luminance detail is present in saturated colours, relative luminance is incorrectly reproduced: relative luminance is reproduced too dark, and saturation is reduced. This inaccurate conveyance of high-frequency

LIVINGSTON, DONALD C. (1954),
"Reproduction of luminance detail
by NTSC color television systems,"
in *Proc. IRE* **42** (1): 228–234.

luminance is the price that must be paid for lack of strict adherence to the principle of constant luminance. Such "Livingston" errors are perceptible by experts, but they are very rarely noticeable – let alone objectionable – in normal imagery.

To summarize signal encoding in video systems: First, a nonlinear transfer function, *gamma correction*, comparable to a square root, is applied to each of the linear R, G, and B tristimulus values to form R', G', and B'. Then, a suitably weighted sum of the nonlinear components is computed to form the luma signal (Y'). Luma approximates the lightness response of vision. Colour difference components *blue minus luma* ($B'-Y'$) and *red minus luma* ($R'-Y'$) are formed. (Luma, $B'-Y'$, and $R'-Y'$ can be computed from R', G', and B' simultaneously, through a 3×3 matrix.) The colour difference components are then subsampled (filtered), using one of several schemes – including 4:2:2, 4:1:1, and 4:2:0 – to be described starting on page 124.

This chapter has outlined how, in the development of NTSC, an engineering approximation to constant luminance was adopted rather than "true" constant luminance. This engineering decision has served spectacularly well, and has been carried into component video systems (SD and HD), and into modern compression systems such as JPEG, MPEG, and H.264.

Since about 2000, the majority of television receivers have incorporated digital signal processing that obviates the engineering argument made in 1950: The two nonlinear functions of Figure 10.6 could today be easily be implemented by lookup tables. Some purists believe that in the modern age we should abolish the approximation, and adopt the correct theoretical approach. However, the video infrastructure of SD and HD is built on Figure 10.9 (or with chroma subsampling, Figure 10.11). It seems unreasonable to change the block diagram of video, and impose a huge conversion burden, unless substantial benefit can be shown. I appreciate the theoretical argument; however, I am unaware of any significant benefit that would result from such a change, so I argue that we should not change the block diagram of video.

Picture rendering 11

Examine the flowers in a garden at noon on a bright, sunny day. Look at the same garden half an hour after sunset. Physically, the spectra of the flowers have not changed, except by scaling to lower luminance levels. However, the flowers are markedly less colourful after sunset: Colourfulness decreases as luminance decreases. This is the *Hunt effect,* first described (in 1952) by the famous colour scientist R.W.G. Hunt. Reproduced images are usually viewed at a small fraction, perhaps $\frac{1}{100}$ or $\frac{1}{1000}$, of the luminance at which they were captured. If reproduced luminance were made proportional to scene luminance, the reproduced image would appear less colourful, and lower in contrast, than the original scene.

GIORGIANNI, EDWARD J., and THOMAS E. MADDEN (2008), *Digital Color Management: Encoding Solutions,* Second Edition (Chichester, U.K.: Wiley).

To reproduce contrast and colourfulness comparable to the original scene, we *must* alter the characteristics of the image. An engineer or physicist might strive to achieve mathematical linearity in an imaging system; however, the required alterations cause reproduced luminance to depart from linearity. The dilemma is this: We can achieve mathematical linearity, or we can achieve correct appearance, but we cannot simultaneously do both! Successful commercial imaging systems sacrifice mathematics to achieve the correct perceptual result.

I use the term *white* to refer to diffuse white, which I will explain on page 117. A diffuse white reflector has a luminance of up to 30,000 $\text{cd} \cdot \text{m}^{-2}$ in daylight, and perhaps 100 $\text{cd} \cdot \text{m}^{-2}$ at twilight.

If "white" in the viewing environment has luminance significantly less than "white" in the environment in which it was captured, the tone scale of an image must be altered. An additional reason for correction is the surround effect, which I will now explain.

Figure 11.1 **Surround effect.** The three squares surrounded by light grey are identical to the three squares surrounded by black; however, each of the black-surround squares is apparently lighter than its counterpart. Also, the contrast of the black-surround series appears lower than that of the white-surround series.

DeMarsh, LeRoy E., and Edward J. Giorgianni (1989), "Color science for imaging systems," in *Physics Today* **42** (9): 44–52 (Sep.).

I use the term *glare* (or *viewing glare*, or *veiling glare*) to refer to uncontrolled, unwanted light that reflects from the display surface, either diffusely or specularly. Image-related scattered light is called *flare*. Some people use these terms interchangeably, thus failing to distinguish unmodulated and modulated light.

Unfortunately, *simultaneous contrast* has another meaning, where it is a contraction of *simultaneous contrast ratio*, preferrably called *intra-image contrast ratio*. See *Contrast ratio*, on page 29.

Surround effect

Human vision adapts to an extremely wide range of viewing conditions, as I will detail in *Adaptation*, on page 247. One of the mechanisms involved in adaptation increases our sensitivity to small brightness variations when the area of interest is surrounded by bright elements. Intuitively, light from a bright surround can be thought of as spilling or scattering into all areas of our vision, including the area of interest, reducing its apparent contrast. Loosely speaking, the visual system compensates for this effect by "stretching" its contrast range to increase the visibility of dark elements in the presence of a bright *surround*. Conversely, when the region of interest is surrounded by relative darkness, the contrast range of the vision system decreases: Our ability to discern dark elements in the scene decreases. The effect is demonstrated in Figure 11.1 above, from DeMarsh and Giorgianni. The surround effect stems from the perceptual phenomenon called the *simultaneous contrast effect*, also known as *lateral inhibition*.

The surround effect has implications for the display of images in dark areas, such as projection of movies in a cinema, projection of 35 mm slides, or viewing of television in your living room. If an image were reproduced with the correct relative luminance, then when viewed in a dark or dim surround, it would appear lacking in contrast.

Image reproduction is not simply concerned with physics, mathematics, chemistry, and electronics: Perceptual considerations play an essential role.

Tone scale alteration

Tone scale alteration is necessary mainly for the two reasons that I have described: The luminance of a reproduction is typically dramatically lower than the luminance of the original scene, and the surround of a reproduced image is rarely comparable to the surround of the original scene. Two additional reasons contribute to the requirement for tone scale alteration: limitation of contrast ratio, and specular highlights.

Intra-image contrast ratio is the ratio of luminances of the lightest and darkest elements of an image. For details, see *Contrast ratio,* on page 29.

A typical original scene has a ratio of luminance levels of more than 1000:1. However, contrast ratio in the captured image is limited by optical flare in the camera. Contrast ratio at a display is typically limited by physical factors and by display flare to perhaps 1000:1.

Diffuse white refers to the luminance of a diffusely reflecting white surface in a scene. Paper reflects diffusely, and white paper reflects about 90% of incident light, so a white card approximates diffuse white. However, most scenes contain shiny objects that reflect directionally. When viewed in certain directions, these objects reflect specular highlights having luminances perhaps ten times that of diffuse white. At the reproduction device, we can seldom afford to reproduce diffuse white at merely 10% of the maximum luminance of the display, solely to exactly reproduce the luminance levels of the highlights! Nor is there any need to reproduce highlights exactly: A convincing image can be formed with highlight luminance greatly reduced from its true value. To make effective use of luminance ranges that are typically available in image display systems, highlights must be compressed.

Incorporation of rendering

The correction that I have mentioned can be achieved by subjecting luminance – or, in the case of a colour system, tristimulus values – to an end-to-end power function having an exponent between about 1.1 and 1.5. The exponent depends primarily upon the ratio of scene luminance to reproduction luminance; it depends to some degree upon the display physics and the viewing environment. Nearly all image reproduction systems require some tone scale alteration.

In *Constant luminance,* on page 107, I outlined nonlinear coding in video. Continuing the sequence of sketches from Figure 10.9, on page 111, Figure 11.2 shows that correction for typical television viewing could be effected by including, in the decoder, a power function having an exponent of about 1.2:

Figure 11.2 **Imposition of picture rendering at decoder, hypothetical**

Observe that a power function is already a necessary part of the encoder. Instead of altering the decoder, we modify the encoder's power function to approximate a 0.5-power, instead of the physically correct 0.42-power:

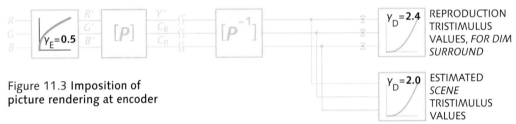

Figure 11.3 **Imposition of picture rendering at encoder**

Concatenating the 0.5-power at encoding and the 2.4-power at decoding produces the end-to-end 1.2-power required for television display in a dim surround. To recover scene tristimulus values, the encoding transfer function should simply be inverted; the decoding function then approximates a 2.0-power function, as sketched at the bottom right of Figure 11.3.

The effective power function exponent at a CRT varies depending upon the setting of the BRIGHTNESS control. In a dark viewing environment – such as a home theater – the display's BRIGHTNESS setting could be so low as to push the decoder's effective exponent up to about 2.6; the end-to-end power will be about 1.3. In a bright surround – such as a computer in a desktop environment – BRIGHTNESS will be increased; this will reduce the effective exponent to about 2.2, and thereby reduce the end-to-end exponent to about 1.1.

The encoding exponent, decoding exponent, and end-to-end power function for cinema, television, and office CRT viewing are shown in Table 11.1.

In film systems, the necessary correction was histori-cally designed into the transfer function of the camera

FAIRCHILD, MARK D. (2005), *Color Appearance Models,* Second Edition (Chichester, U.K.: Wiley).

JAMES, THOMAS H., ed. (1977), *The Theory of the Photographic Process,* Fourth Edition (Rochester, N.Y.: Eastman Kodak). See Ch. 19 (p. 537), *Preferred tone reproduction.*

Imaging system	Encoding exponent	"Advertised" exponent	Decoding exponent	Typ. surround	Contrast ratio	End-to-end exponent
Cinema (film projection)	0.6	0.6	2.5	Dark (0%)	100:1	1.5
HD, studio mastering (BT.709/BT.1886)	0.5	0.45	2.4	Very dim (1%)	1000:1	1.2
HD, living room (typ.)	0.5	0.45	2.4	Dim (5%)	400:1	1.2
Office (sRGB, typ.)	0.45	0.42	2.2	Avg (20%)	100:1	1.1

Table 11.1 **End-to-end power functions** for several imaging systems. The encoding exponent achieves approximately perceptual coding. (The "advertised" exponent neglects the scaling and offset associated with the straight-line segment of encoding.) The decoding exponent acts at the display to approximately invert the perceptual encoding. The product of the two exponents sets the end-to-end power function that imposes the rendering. Here, contrast ratio is intra-image.

negative and print films. Projected imagery is typically intended for viewing in a dark surround; arrangements are made to have an end-to-end power function exponent considerably greater than unity – typically about 1.5 – so that the contrast range of the scene is expanded upon display. In cinema film, the correction is achieved through a combination of the transfer function ("gamma" of about 0.6) built into camera negative film and the transfer function ("gamma" of about 2.5) built into print film.

Some people suggest that NTSC should be gamma-corrected with power of $\frac{1}{2.2}$, and PAL with $\frac{1}{2.8}$. I disagree with both interpretations; see page 325.

I have described video systems as if they use a pure 0.5-power law encoding function. Practical considerations necessitate modification of the pure power function by the insertion of a linear segment near black, as I will explain in *Gamma*, on page 315. The exponent in the BT.709 standard is written ("advertised") as 0.45; however, the insertion of the linear segment, and the offsetting and scaling of the pure power function segment of the curve, cause an exponent of about 0.51 to best describe the overall curve. (To describe gamma as 0.45 in this situation is misleading.)

Rendering in desktop computing

In the desktop computer environment, the ambient condition is considerably brighter, and the surround is brighter than is typical of television viewing. An end-to-end exponent lower than the 1.2 of video is called for; a value around 1.1 is generally suitable. However, desktop computers are used in a variety of different viewing conditions. It is not practical to originate every image in several forms, optimized for several potential

In the sRGB standard, the exponent is written ("advertised") as $1/2.4$ (about 0.42). However, the insertion of the linear segment, and the offsetting and scaling of the pure power function segment of the curve, cause an exponent of about 0.45 to best describe the overall curve. See *sRGB transfer function,* on page 324.

viewing conditions! A specific encoding function needs to be chosen. Achieving optimum reproduction in diverse viewing conditions requires selecting a suitable correction at display time. Technically, this is easy to achieve: Modern computer display subsystems have hardware lookup tables (LUTs) that can be loaded dynamically with appropriate curves. However, it is a challenge to train users to make a suitable choice. There is promise in sensors to detect ambient light, and algorithms to effect appropriate correction (largely by altering display gamma). Such schemes have been implemented commercially, but there are no standards.

When the sRGB standard for desktop computing was being developed, the inevitability of local, viewing-dependent correction was not appreciated. That standard promulgates decoding with a pure 2.2-power function, but the standard also described what is apparently an encoding standard with a linear segment near black and an effective exponent of about 0.45. A close reading of the sRGB standard confirms that sRGB is display referred; the video-like definition with the linear segment is a mapping from tristimulus values *at the display surface* into sRGB code values. The sRGB "encode" function is not comparable to BT.709's reference OECF. Display of sRGB material should be accomplished with the pure 2.2-power function, without any linear segment.

Video cameras, film cameras, motion picture cameras, and digital still cameras all capture images from the real world. When an image of an original scene or object is captured, it is important to introduce rendering. However, scanners used in desktop computing rarely scan original objects; they usually scan reproductions such as photographic prints or offset-printed images. When a reproduction is scanned, rendering has already been imposed by the first imaging process. It may be sensible to adjust the original rendering, but it is not sensible to introduce rendering that would be suitable for scanning a real scene or object.

Introduction to
luma and chroma 12

The statement is commonly made that "the human visual system is more sensitive to luma than chroma." That statement is incorrect. It is vision's sensitivity *to information at high spatial frequency* that is diminished for chroma. Chroma subsampling is enabled by poor *acuity* for chroma, not by poor *sensitivity*.

Video systems convey image data in the form of one component that represents lightness, and two components that represent colour, disregarding lightness. This scheme exploits the reduced colour acuity of vision compared to luminance acuity: As long as lightness is conveyed with full detail, detail in the colour components can be reduced by subsampling – that is, by filtering (averaging). This chapter introduces the concepts of luma and chroma encoding; details will be presented in *Luma and colour differences*, on page 335.

Luma

A certain amount of noise is inevitable in digital imaging systems. As explained in *Perceptual uniformity*, on page 8, encoding is arranged so that noise has a perceptually similar effect across the entire tone scale from black to white. The lightness component is conveyed in a perceptually uniform manner that minimizes the amount of noise (or quantization error) introduced in processing, recording, and transmission.

Ideally, noise would be minimized by forming a signal proportional to CIE luminance, as a suitably weighted sum of linear R, G, and B tristimulus signals. Then, this signal would be subjected to a transfer function that imposes perceptual uniformity, such as the CIE L^* function of colour science that will be detailed on page 259. As explained in *Constant luminance*, on page 107, there are practical reasons in video to perform these operations in the opposite order. First, a nonlinear transfer function – *gamma correction* – is applied to each of the linear R, G, and B tristimulus signals: We impose a transfer function similar to a square root, and roughly comparable to the CIE lightness (L*) function. Then a weighted sum of the resulting nonlinear R', G', and B' components is computed to form a *luma* signal (Y') representative of lightness. SD uses coefficients that are standardized in BT.601 (see page 131):

The prime symbols here, and in following equations, denote nonlinear components.

$$^{601}Y' = 0.299\,R' + 0.587\,G' + 0.114\,B' \qquad \text{Eq 12.1}$$

Unfortunately, luma for HD is coded differently from luma in SD! BT.709 specifies these coefficients:

$$^{709}Y' = 0.2126\,R' + 0.7152\,G' + 0.0722\,B' \qquad \text{Eq 12.2}$$

Sloppy use of the term *luminance*

CIE: Commission Internationale de l'Éclairage

The term *luminance* and the symbol Y were established 75 years ago by the CIE, the standards body for colour science. Unfortunately, in video, the term *luminance* has come to mean *the video signal representative of luminance* even though the components of the video signal have been subjected to a nonlinear transfer function. At the dawn of video, the nonlinear signal was denoted Y', where the prime symbol indicated the nonlinear treatment. But over the last 50 years the prime has not appeared consistently, and today, both the term *luminance* and the symbol Y conflict with their CIE definitions, making them ambiguous! This has led to great confusion, such as the incorrect statement commonly found in computer graphics textbooks and digital image-processing textbooks that in the *YIQ* or *YUV* colour spaces, the Y component is identical to CIE luminance!

See Appendix A, *YUV and luminance considered harmful,* on page 567.

I use the term *luminance* according to its CIE definition; I use the term *luma* to refer to the video signal; and I am careful to designate nonlinear quantities with a prime. However, many video engineers, computer graphics practitioners, and image-processing specialists use these terms carelessly. You must be careful to determine whether a linear or nonlinear interpretation is being applied to the word and the symbol.

Colour difference coding (chroma)

In component video, the three components necessary to convey colour information are transmitted separately. Rather than conveying $R'G'B'$ directly, the relatively poor colour acuity of vision is exploited to reduce data capacity accorded to the colour information, while maintaining full luma detail. First, luma is formed according to Equation 12.1 (or for HD, Equation 12.2). Then, two *colour difference* signals based upon gamma-corrected B' *minus luma* and R' *minus luma*, $B'-Y'$ and $R'-Y'$, are formed by "matrixing." Finally, subsampling (filtering) reduces detail in the colour difference (or *chroma*) components, as I will outline on page 127. Subsampling incurs no loss in sharpness at any reasonable viewing distance.

In component analog video, $B'-Y'$ and $R'-Y'$ were scaled to form colour difference signals denoted P_B and P_R, which were then analog lowpass filtered (horizontally) to about half the luma bandwidth. Y', P_B, and P_R each have unity excursion (i.e., 0 to 1, ±0.5, and ±0.5). In computing, these components are commonly denoted U and V.

In component digital video (including M-JPEG, MPEG, and H.264), $B'-Y'$ and $R'-Y'$ are scaled to form C_B and C_R components, which can then be subsampled by digital filtering denoted 4:2:2 or 4:2:0; I will describe the subsampling in a moment.

In composite NTSC or PAL video, $B'-Y'$ and $R'-Y'$ were scaled to form U and V components. U and V were then lowpass filtered and combined into a modulated chroma component, C. Luma was then summed with modulated chroma to produce the composite NTSC or PAL signal. Scaling of U and V was arranged so that the excursion of the composite signal ($Y'+C$) was constrained to the range $-\frac{1}{3}$ to $+\frac{4}{3}$ of the unity excursion of luma. The historical U and V components are now obsolete, and today UV denotes $Y'P_BP_R$ (see above).

Composite NTSC video was standardized in 1953 based upon I and Q components that were essentially U and V components rotated 33° and axis-exchanged. Excess detail was supposed to be removed from the Q component so as to improve colour quality. The scheme never achieved significant deployment; I and Q components have been completely obsolete for many decades.

Luma and colour differences can be computed from R', G', and B' through a 3×3 matrix multiplication.

$Y'P_BP_R$

$Y'C_BC_R$

$Y'UV$

$Y'IQ$

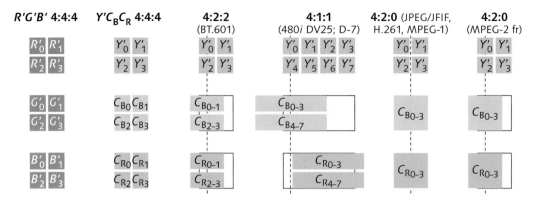

Figure 12.1 **Chroma subsampling.** A 2×2 array of *R'G'B'* pixels is matrixed into a luma component *Y'* and two colour difference components C_B and C_R. Colour detail is reduced by subsampling C_B and C_R; providing full luma detail is maintained, no degradation is perceptible. In this sketch, samples are shaded to indicate their spatial position and extent. In 4:2:2, in 4:1:1, and in 4:2:0 used in MPEG-2, C_B and C_R are cosited (positioned horizontally coincident with a luma sample). In 4:2:0 used in JPEG/JFIF, H.261, and MPEG-1, C_B and C_R are sited interstitially (midway between luma samples). In the 4:2:0 variant used in consumer 576*i* DV (not sketched here), C_B and C_R are vertically sited in line-alternate fashion in each field (starting with a C_R sample sited over the top left luma sample.)

Chroma subsampling

4:4:4

In Figure 12.1, the left-hand column sketches a 2×2 array of *R'G'B'* pixels. (Think of these 2×2 arrays as being overlaid on the display surface.) Prior to subsampling, this sampling is denoted *R'G'B'* 4:4:4. With 8 bits per sample, this 2×2 array of *R'G'B'* would consume 12 bytes. Each *R'G'B'* triplet (pixel) can be losslessly transformed ("matrixed") into $Y'C_BC_R$, as shown in the second column; this is denoted $Y'C_BC_R$ 4:4:4.

In component digital video, data capacity is reduced by subsampling C_B and C_R using one of three schemes.

4:2:2

$Y'C_BC_R$ studio digital video according to BT.601 uses 4:2:2 sampling: C_B and C_R components are each subsampled by a factor of 2 horizontally. C_B and C_R are sampled together, coincident (*cosited*) with even-numbered luma samples. The 12 bytes of *R'G'B'* are reduced to 8, effecting 1.5:1 lossy compression.

4:1:1

Certain digital video systems, such as 480*i*29.97 DV25, use 4:1:1 sampling, whereby C_B and C_R components are each subsampled by a factor of 4 horizontally, and cosited with every fourth luma sample. The 12 bytes of *R'G'B'* are reduced to 6, effecting 2:1 lossy compression.

4:2:0

ITU-T Rec. H.261 is a 1990s-vintage videoconferencing standard.

This scheme is used in JPEG/JFIF, MPEG-2, and H.264. C_B and C_R are each subsampled by a factor of 2 horizontally and a factor of 2 vertically. The 12 bytes of $R'G'B'$ are reduced to 6. C_B and C_R are effectively centered vertically halfway between image rows. There are three variants of 4:2:0, having different vertical and horizontal siting. In MPEG-2, C_B and C_R are cosited horizontally. In JPEG/JFIF, H.261, and MPEG-1, C_B and C_R are sited interstitially, halfway between alternate luma samples. In 4:2:0 DV, C_B and C_R alternate line by line. Figure 12.2 overleaf summarizes the various schemes.

Subsampling effects 1.5:1 or 2:1 lossy compression. However, in studio terminology, subsampled video is referred to as *uncompressed:* The word *compression* is reserved for techniques such as JPEG, M-JPEG, MPEG, or H.264 that use transform coding (DCT or wavelets).

Chroma subsampling notation

At the outset of digital video, subsampling notation was logical; unfortunately, technology outgrew the notation. In Figure 12.3 below, I strive to clarify today's nomenclature. Despite appearances, the notation doesn't specify a ratio! The first digit originally specified luma sample rate relative to $3\frac{3}{8}$ MHz; the leading digit is now relative to the sample rate in use. The initial digit is typically 4, since all common chroma ratios are small powers of two – 4, 2, or 1. (3:1:1 subsampling was commercialized in an HD production system – Sony's HDCAM – and 3 appeared as the leading digit. HDCAM has been superseded by HDCAM SR, which uses 4:2:2 or 4:4:4 subsampling.) Some people use 4:0:0 to denote greyscale ("monochrome").

The use of *4* as the numerical basis for subsampling notation is a historical reference to sampling at roughly four times the NTSC colour subcarrier frequency. The $4f_{SC}$ rate was already in use for composite digital video.

Figure 12.3 **Chroma subsampling notation** indicates, in the first digit, the luma horizontal sampling reference. The second digit specifies the horizontal subsampling of C_B and C_R with respect to luma. The third digit originally specified the horizontal subsampling of C_R. The notation developed without anticipating vertical subsampling; a third digit of zero now denotes 2:1 vertical subsampling of both C_B and C_R.

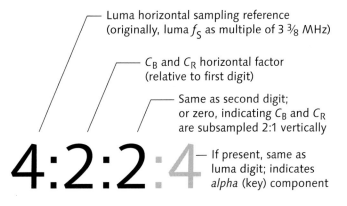

Luma horizontal sampling reference (originally, luma f_S as multiple of $3\frac{3}{8}$ MHz)

C_B and C_R horizontal factor (relative to first digit)

Same as second digit; or zero, indicating C_B and C_R are subsampled 2:1 vertically

If present, same as luma digit; indicates *alpha* (key) component

4:2:2:4

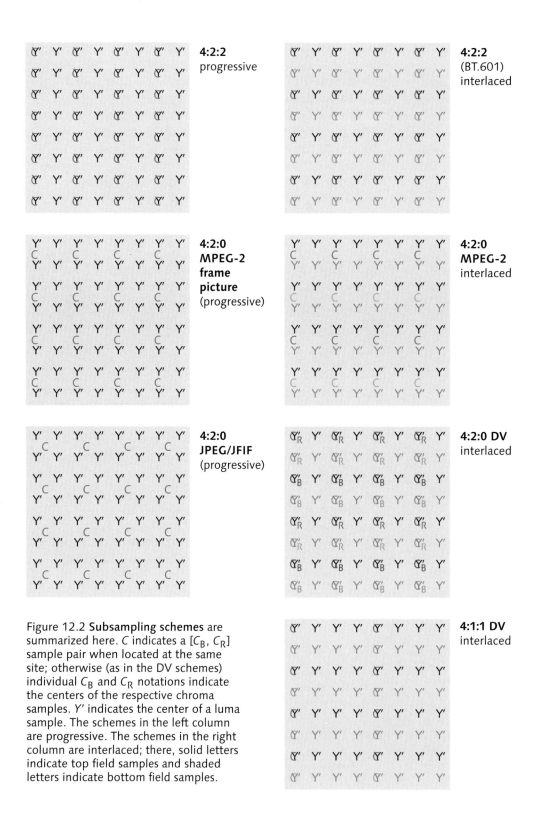

Figure 12.2 **Subsampling schemes** are summarized here. C indicates a $[C_B, C_R]$ sample pair when located at the same site; otherwise (as in the DV schemes) individual C_B and C_R notations indicate the centers of the respective chroma samples. Y' indicates the center of a luma sample. The schemes in the left column are progressive. The schemes in the right column are interlaced; there, solid letters indicate top field samples and shaded letters indicate bottom field samples.

Figure 12.4 **An Interstitial chroma filter for JPEG/JFIF** averages samples over a 2×2 block. Shading represents the spatial extent of luma samples. The black dot indicates the effective subsampled chroma position, equidistant from the four luma samples. The outline represents the spatial extent of the result.

Figure 12.5 **A cosited chroma filter for BT.601, 4:2:2** causes each filtered chroma sample to be positioned coincident – *cosited* – with an even-numbered luma sample.

Figure 12.6 **A cosited chroma filter for MPEG-2, 4:2:0** produces a filtered result sample that is cosited horizontally, but sited interstitially in the vertical dimension.

Chroma subsampling filters

In chroma subsampling, the encoder discards selected colour difference samples after filtering. A decoder approximates the missing samples by interpolation.

To perform 4:2:0 subsampling with minimum computation, some systems simply average C_B over a 2×2 block and average C_R over the same 2×2 block, as sketched in Figure 12.4 in the margin. To interpolate the missing chroma samples prior to conversion back to *R'G'B'*, low-end systems simply replicate the subsampled C_B and C_R values throughout the 2×2 quad. This technique is ubiquitous in JPEG/JFIF stillframes in computing, and is used in M-JPEG, H.261, and MPEG-1. This simple averaging process causes subsampled chroma to take an effective horizontal position halfway between two luma samples, what I call *interstitial* siting, not the cosited position standardized for studio video.

A simple way to perform 4:2:2 subsampling with horizontal cositing as required by BT.601 is to use weights of [$\frac{1}{4}$, $\frac{1}{2}$, $\frac{1}{4}$], as sketched in Figure 12.5. 4:2:2 subsampling has the advantage of no interaction with interlaced scanning.

A cosited horizontal filter can be combined with [$\frac{1}{2}$, $\frac{1}{2}$] vertical averaging, as sketched in Figure 12.6, to implement 4:2:0 as used in MPEG-2.

Simple averaging filters like those of Figures 12.4, 12.5, and 12.6 have acceptable performance for stillframes, where any alias components that are generated remain stationary, or for desktop-quality video. However, in a moving image, an alias component introduced by poor filtering is liable to move at a rate different from the associated scene elements, and thereby produce a highly objectionable artifact. High-end digital video equipment uses sophisticated subsampling filters, where the subsampled C_B and C_R of a 2×1 pair in 4:2:2 (or of a 2×2 quad in 4:2:0) take contributions from several surrounding samples. The relationship of filter weights, frequency response, and filter performance will be detailed in *Filtering and sampling,* on page 191. These coefficients implement a high quality FIR filter suitable for 4:2:2 subsampling: [−1, 3, −6, 12, −24, 80, 128, 80, −24, 12, −6, 3, −1]/256.

The video literature often calls these quantities *chrominance*. That term has a specific meaning in colour science, so in video I prefer the term *modulated chroma*.

See *Introduction to composite NTSC and PAL,* on page 135. Concerning SECAM, see *SECAM,* on page 126 of *Composite NTSC and PAL: Legacy Video Systems.*

Chroma in composite NTSC and PAL

I introduced the colour difference components P_BP_R and C_BC_R, often called *chroma components*. They accompany luma in a component video system. I also introduced *UV* and *IQ* components; these are intermediate quantities in the formation of *modulated chroma*.

Historically, insufficient channel capacity was available to transmit three colour components separately. The NTSC technique was devised to combine the three colour components into a single *composite* signal; the PAL technique is both a refinement of NTSC and an adaptation of NTSC to *576i* scanning. (In SECAM, the three colour components are also combined into one signal. SECAM is a form of composite video, but the technique has little in common with NTSC and PAL, and it is of little commercial importance today.)

NTSC and PAL encoders traditionally started with *R'G'B'* components. At the culmination of composite video, digital encoders started with $Y'C_BC_R$ components. NTSC or PAL encoding involves these steps:

• Component signals are matrixed and conditioned to form colour difference signals *U* and *V* (or *I* and *Q*).

• *U* and *V* (or *I* and *Q*) are lowpass-filtered, then *quadrature modulation* imposes the two colour difference signals onto an unmodulated colour subcarrier, to produce a *modulated chroma* signal, *C*.

• Luma and chroma are summed. In studio video, summation exploits the *frequency-interleaving* principle.

Composite NTSC and PAL signals were historically analog. During the 1990s, digital composite ($4f_{SC}$) systems were used; the $4f_{SC}$ scheme is now obsolete. As I mentioned in *Video system taxonomy,* on page 94, composite video has been supplanted by component video in consumers' premises and in industrial applications. For further information, see *Introduction to composite NTSC and PAL,* on page 135.

Introduction to

component SD   13

In *Raster scanning,* on page 83, I introduced the
concepts of raster scanning; in *Introduction to luma and
chroma,* on page 121, I introduced the concepts of
colour coding in video. This chapter combines the
concepts of raster scanning and colour coding to form
the basic technical parameters of the 480*i* and 576*i* SD
systems. This chapter concerns modern systems that
use component colour – digital $Y'C_BC_R$ (BT.601), or
analog $Y'P_BP_R$. In *Introduction to composite NTSC and
PAL,* on page 135, I will describe NTSC and PAL
composite video encoding.

Scanning standards

Two scanning standards are in use for conventional
analog television broadcasting in different parts of the
world. The 480*i*29.97 system is used primarily in North
America and Japan, and today accounts for roughly $\frac{1}{4}$
of all television receivers. The 576*i*25 system is used
primarily in Europe, Asia, Australia, and Central
America, and accounts for roughly $\frac{3}{4}$ of all television
receivers. 480*i*29.97 (or 525/59.94/2:1) is colloquially
referred to as *NTSC,* and 576*i*25 (or 625/50/2:1) as
PAL; however, the terms NTSC and PAL properly apply
to colour encoding and not to scanning standards. It is
obvious from the scanning nomenclature that the line
counts and field rates differ between the two systems:
In 480*i*29.97 video, the field rate is exactly $\frac{60}{1.001}$ Hz;
in 576*i*25, the field rate is exactly 50 Hz.

  Several different standards for 480*i*29.97 and 576*i*25
digital video are sketched in Figure 13.1 overleaf.

The notation *CCIR* is often
wrongly used to denote 576*i*25
scanning. The former CCIR (now
ITU-R) standardized many scanning systems, not just 576*i*25.

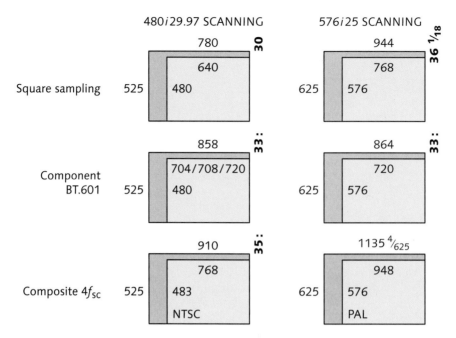

Figure 13.1 **SD digital video rasters** for 4:3 aspect ratio. 480*i*29.97 scanning is at the left, 576*i*25 at the right. The top row shows square sampling ("square pixels"). The middle row shows sampling at the BT.601 standard sampling frequency of 13.5 MHz. The bottom row shows sampling at four times the colour subcarrier frequency (4*f*~SC~). Above each diagram is its count of samples per total line (*S*~TL~); ratios among *S*~TL~ values are written vertically in bold numerals.

See *PAL-M, PAL-N* on page 125, and *SECAM* on page 126 of *Composite NTSC and PAL: Legacy Video Systems*. Consumer frustration with a diversity of functionally equivalent standards led to proliferation of multistandard TVs and VCRs in countries using these standards.

Analog broadcast of 480*i* usually uses NTSC colour coding with a colour subcarrier of about 3.58 MHz; analog broadcast of 576*i* usually uses PAL colour coding with a colour subcarrier of about 4.43 MHz. It is important to use a notation that distinguishes scanning from colour, because other combinations of scanning and colour coding are in use in large and important regions of the world. Brazil uses PAL-M, which has 480*i* scanning and PAL colour coding. Argentina uses PAL-N, which has 576*i* scanning and a 3.58 MHz colour subcarrier nearly identical to NTSC's subcarrier. In France, Russia, and other countries, SECAM is used. Production equipment is no longer manufactured for any of these obscure standards: Production in these countries is done using 480*i* or 576*i* studio equipment, either in the component domain or in 480*i* NTSC or 576*i* PAL. These studio signals are then *transcoded* prior to broadcast: The colour encoding is altered – for example, from PAL to SECAM – without altering scanning.

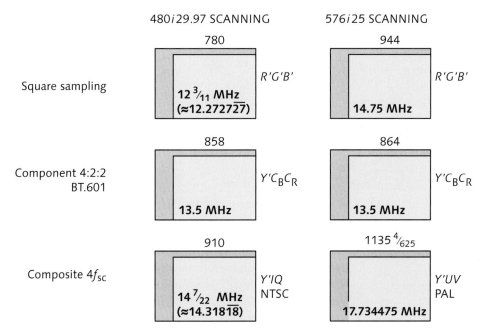

Square sampling

780

$12\,{}^{3}\!/_{11}$ **MHz**
(≈12.272727)

R'G'B'

944

14.75 MHz

R'G'B'

Component 4:2:2
BT.601

858

13.5 MHz

$Y'C_BC_R$

864

13.5 MHz

$Y'C_BC_R$

Composite 4f_{SC}

910

$14\,{}^{7}\!/_{22}$ **MHz**
(≈14.31818)

Y'IQ
NTSC

$1135\,{}^{4}\!/_{625}$

17.734475 MHz

Y'UV
PAL

Figure 13.2 **SD sample rates** are shown for six different 4:3 standards, along with the usual colour coding for each standard. There is no realtime studio interface standard for square-sampled SD.

ITU-R Rec. BT.601-5, *Studio encoding parameters of digital television for standard 4:3 and widescreen 16:9 aspect ratios.*

Figure 13.1 indicates S_{TL} and S_{AL} for each standard. The S_{AL} values are the result of some complicated issues to be discussed in *Choice of S_{AL} and S_{PW} parameters* on page 380. For details concerning my reference to 483 active lines (L_A) in 480*i* systems, see *Picture lines,* on page 379.

Figure 13.2 above shows the standard 480*i*29.97 and 576*i*25 digital video sampling rates, and the colour coding usually associated with each of these standards. The 4:2:2, $Y'C_BC_R$ system for SD is standardized in *Recommendation BT.601* of the ITU Radiocommunication Sector (formerly CCIR). I call it *BT.601*.

With one exception, all of the sampling systems in Figure 13.2 have a whole number of samples per total line; these systems are *line-locked*. The exception is composite 4f_{SC} PAL sampling, which has a noninteger number ($1135\,{}^{4}\!/_{625}$) of samples per total line; this creates a huge nuisance for the system designer.

480*i* and 576*i* have gratuitous differences in many technical parameters, summarized in Table 13.1 overleaf.

System	480i29.97	576i25
Picture:sync ratio	10:4[†]	7:3
Setup, percent	7.5[‡]	0
Count of equalization, broad pulses	6	5
Line number 1, and 0_V, defined at:	First equalization pulse of field	First broad pulse of frame
Bottom picture line in:	First field	Second field

Table 13.1 **Gratuitous differences.** between 480i and 576i

† The EBU N10 component analog interface for $Y'P_BP_R$, occasionally used for 480i, has 7:3 picture-to-sync ratio.

‡ 480i video in Japan, and the EBU N10 component analog interface, have zero setup. See page 381.

Different treatment of interlace between 480i and 576i imposes different structure onto the picture data. The differences cause headaches in systems such as MPEG that are designed to accommodate both 480i and 576i images. In Figures 13.3 and 13.4 below, I show how field order, interlace nomenclature, and image structure are related. Figure 13.5 at the bottom of this page shows how MPEG-2 identifies each field as either *top* or *bottom*. In 480i video, the bottom field is the first field of the frame; in 576i, the top field is first. Figures 13.3, 13.4, and 13.5 depict just the image array (i.e., the active samples), without vertical blanking lines; MPEG makes no provision for halflines.

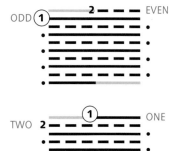

Figure 13.3 **Interlacing in 480i.** The first field (historically called *odd*, here denoted **1**) starts with a full picture line, and ends with a left-hand halfline containing the bottom of the picture. The second field (here dashed, historically called *even*), transmitted about $\frac{1}{60}$ s later, starts with a right-hand halfline containing the top of the picture; it ends with a full picture line.

Figure 13.4 **Interlacing in 576i.** The first field includes a right-hand halfline containing the top line of the picture, and ends with a full picture line. The second field, transmitted $\frac{1}{50}$ s later, starts with a full line, and ends with a left-hand halfline that contains the bottom of the picture. (In 576i terminology, the terms *odd* and *even* are rarely used, and are best avoided.)

Figure 13.5 **Interlacing in MPEG-2** identifies a picture according to whether it contains the *top* or *bottom* picture line of the frame. Top and bottom fields are displayed in the order that they are coded in an MPEG-2 data stream. For frame-coded pictures, display order is determined by a one-bit flag *top field first*, typically asserted for 576i and negated for 480i.

Widescreen (16:9) SD

Programming in SD is intended for display at 4:3 aspect ratio. Prior to (and during) the development of HD, several schemes were devised to adapt SD to widescreen (16:9) material – *widescreen SD*. That term is misleading, though: Because there is no increase in pixel count, a so-called widescreen SD picture cannot be viewed with a picture angle substantially wider than regular (4:3) SD. (See page 75.) So widescreen SD does not deliver HD's major promise – that of dramatically wider viewing angle – and a more accurate term would be *wide aspect ratio SD*. The various schemes devised in the transition period are now obsolete. A discussion is found in *Widescreen (16:9) SD* on page 5 of *Composite NTSC and PAL: Legacy Video Systems*.

Square and nonsquare sampling

Computer graphics equipment now universally employs *square sampling* – that is, a sampling lattice where pixels are equally spaced horizontally and vertically. Square sampling of 480*i* and 576*i* is diagrammed in the top rows of Figures 13.1 and 13.2 on page 131.

See Table 15.1, on page 143, and the associated discussion.

Although ATSC's notorious Table 3 includes a 640×480 square-sampled image, no studio standard or realtime interface standard addresses square sampling of SD. For desktop video applications, I recommend sampling 480*i* video with exactly 780 samples per total line, for a nominal sample rate of $12\frac{3}{11}$ MHz – that is, 12.272727 MHz. To accommodate full picture width in the studio, 648 samples are required; often, 640 samples are used with 480 picture lines. For square sampling of 576*i* video, I recommend using exactly 944 samples per total line, for a sample rate of exactly 14.75 MHz.

$$648 \approx 780 \cdot \left(1 - \frac{10.7 \ \mu s}{63.55\overline{5} \ \mu s} \right)$$

$$767 = 944 \cdot \frac{52 \ \mu s}{64 \ \mu s}$$

MPEG-1, MPEG-2, DVD, and DV all conform to BT.601, which specifies nonsquare sampling. BT.601 sampling of 480*i* and 576*i* is diagrammed in the middle rows of Figures 13.1 and 13.2.

Composite digital video systems historically sampled at four times the colour subcarrier frequency ($4f_{SC}$), resulting in nonsquare sampling whose parameters are shown in the bottom rows of Figures 13.1 and 13.2. As I stated on page 128, composite $4f_{SC}$ systems are obsolete.

In 480i, the sampling rates for square sampling, BT.601, and $4f_{SC}$ are related by the ratio $30:33:35$. The pixel aspect ratio of BT.601 480i is exactly $^{10}\!/_{11}$; the pixel aspect ratio of $4f_{SC}$ 480i is exactly $^{6}\!/_{7}$.

In 576i, the sampling rates for square sampling and 4:2:2 are related by the ratio $59:54$, so the pixel aspect ratio of 576i BT.601 is precisely $^{59}\!/_{54}$. BT.601 and $4f_{SC}$ sample rates are related by the ratio in the margin, which is fairly impenetrable to digital hardware.

$$\frac{f_{S,601}}{4f_{SC,PAL\text{-}I}} = \frac{540000}{709379}$$

Most of this nonsquare sampling business has been put behind us: Most HD studio standards call for square sampling, and it is difficult to imagine any future studio standard being established with nonsquare sampling.

Resampling

Analog video can be digitized with square sampling simply by using an appropriate sample frequency. However, SD already digitized at a standard digital video sampling rate such as 13.5 MHz must be *resampled* – or *interpolated*, or in PC parlance, *scaled* – when entering the square-sampled desktop video domain. If video samples at 13.5 MHz are passed to a computer graphics system and then treated as if the samples are equally spaced vertically and horizontally, then picture geometry will be distorted. BT.601 480i video will appear horizontally stretched; BT.601 576i video will appear squished. In desktop video, often resampling in both axes is needed.

The ratio $^{10}\!/_{11}$ relates 480i BT.601 to square sampling: Crude resampling could be accomplished by simply dropping every eleventh sample across each scan line! Crude resampling from 576i BT.601 to square sampling could be accomplished by replicating 5 samples in every 54 (perhaps in the pattern 11-R-11-R-11-R-11-R-10-R, where R denotes a repeated sample). However, such sample dropping and stuffing techniques introduce aliasing. I recommend that you use a more sophisticated interpolator, of the type explained in *Filtering and sampling*, on page 191. Resampling could potentially be performed along either the vertical axis or the horizontal (transverse) axis; horizontal resampling is the easier of the two, as it processes pixels in raster order and therefore does not require any linestores.

Introduction to composite NTSC and PAL 14

NTSC stands for *National Television System Committee*. PAL stands for *Phase Alternate Line*. (Some sources say that PAL stands for *Phase Alternation* at *Line* rate, or perhaps even *Phase Alternating Line*).

SECAM is a composite technique of sorts, though it has little in common with NTSC and PAL, and it is now obsolete. See "SECAM," in Chapter 12 of *Composite NTSC and PAL: Legacy Video Systems*.

In *component* video, the three colour components are kept separate. Video can use *R'G'B'* components directly, but three signals are expensive to record, process, or transmit. Luma (*Y'*) and colour difference components based upon *B'–Y'* and *R'–Y'* can be used to enable subsampling: Luma is maintained at full data rate, and the two colour difference components are subsampled. Even after chroma subsampling, video has a fairly high information rate (data rate, or "bandwidth"). To further reduce the information rate, the composite NTSC and PAL colour coding schemes use *quadrature modulation* to combine the two colour difference components into a single *modulated chroma* signal, then use *frequency interleaving* to combine luma and modulated chroma into a *composite* signal having roughly $\frac{1}{3}$ the data rate – or in an analog system, $\frac{1}{3}$ the bandwidth – of *R'G'B'*.

Composite encoding was invented to address three main needs. First, there was a need to limit transmission bandwidth. Second, it was necessary to enable black-and-white receivers already deployed by 1953 to receive colour broadcasts with minimal degradation. Third, it was necessary for newly introduced colour receivers to receive the then-standard black-and-white broadcasts. Composite encoding was necessary in the early days of television, and it has proven highly effective for broadcast. NTSC and PAL are entrenched in billions of consumer electronic devices. However, component digital video has overtaken composite techniques, and composite NTSC and PAL are now "legacy" techniques.

Composite NTSC or PAL encoding has three major disadvantages compared to component video. First, encoding introduces some degree of mutual interference between luma and chroma. Once a signal has been encoded into composite form, the NTSC or PAL *footprint* is imposed: *Cross-luma* and *cross-colour* errors are irreversibly impressed on the signal. Second, it is impossible to directly perform many processing operations in the composite domain; even to reposition or resize a picture requires decoding, processing, and reencoding. Third, digital compression techniques such as JPEG and MPEG cannot be directly applied to composite signals, and the artifacts of NTSC and PAL encoding are destructive to MPEG encoding.

The bandwidth to carry separate colour components is now easily affordable, and composite encoding is now obsolete in the studio. To avoid NTSC and PAL artifacts, to facilitate image manipulation, and to enable compression, composite video has been superseded by *component video*, where three colour components $R'G'B'$, or $Y'C_BC_R$ (in digital systems), or $Y'P_BP_R$ (in analog systems), are kept separate. I hope you can manage to avoid composite NTSC and PAL, and skip this chapter!

The terms *NTSC* and *PAL* properly denote colour encoding. Unfortunately, they are often used incorrectly to denote scanning standards. PAL encoding has been used with both 576*i* scanning (with two different subcarrier frequencies) and 480*i* scanning (with a third subcarrier frequency); PAL alone is ambiguous.

In principle, NTSC or PAL colour coding could be used with any scanning standard. However, in practice, NTSC and PAL are used only with 480*i* and 576*i* scanning, and the parameters of NTSC and PAL encoding are optimized for those scanning systems. This chapter introduces composite encoding. Details can be found in *Composite NTSC and PAL: Legacy Video Systems*.

NTSC and PAL encoding

NTSC or PAL encoding involves these steps:
- $R'G'B'$ component signals are matrixed and filtered, or $Y'C_BC_R$ or $Y'P_BP_R$ components are scaled and filtered,

By NTSC and PAL, I do not mean 480*i* and 576*i*, or 525/59.94 and 625/50!

When I use the term *PAL* in this chapter, I refer only to 576*i* PAL-B/G/H/I. Variants of PAL used for broadcasting in South America are discussed in *PAL-M, PAL-N*, on page 125 of *Composite NTSC and PAL: Legacy Video Systems*. PAL variants in consumer devices are discussed in *Consumer analog NTSC and PAL* in *Composite NTSC and PAL: Legacy Video Systems*.

DIGITAL VIDEO AND HD ALGORITHMS AND INTERFACES

to form luma (*Y'*) and colour difference signals (*U* and *V*, or in certain NTSC systems, *I* and *Q*).

• *U* and *V* (or *I* and *Q*) colour difference signals are modulated onto a pair of intimately related continuous-wave colour subcarriers, typically at a frequency of about 3.58 MHz in 480*i*29.97 or 4.43 MHz in 576*i*25, to produce a modulated chroma signal, *C*. (See the left side of Figure 14.1 overleaf.)

• Luma and modulated chroma are summed to form a composite NTSC or PAL signal. (See the right side of Figure 14.1.) Summation of luma and chroma is liable to introduce a certain degree of mutual interference, called *cross-luma* and *cross-colour;* these artifacts can be minimized through *frequency interleaving*, to be described.

NTSC and PAL decoding

NTSC or PAL decoding involves these steps:

• Luma and modulated chroma are separated. Crude separation can be accomplished using a *notch filter*. Alternatively, frequency interleaving can be exploited to provide greatly improved separation; in NTSC, such a separator is a *comb filter*. (In an S-video interface, luma and modulated chroma are already separate.)

• Chroma is demodulated to produce *UV*, *IQ*, P_BP_R, or C_BC_R baseband colour difference components.

• If *R'G'B'* components are required, the baseband colour difference components are interpolated, then luma and the colour difference components are dematrixed.

S-video interface

S-video involves NTSC or PAL chroma modulation; however, luma and modulated chroma traverse separate paths across the interface instead of being summed; the S-video interface bypasses the third step of *NTSC and PAL encoding* above. Cross-luma and cross-colour artifacts are avoided. Figure 14.2 sketches the encoder and decoder arrangement. The S-video interface is widely implemented in consumer video equipment.

Frequency interleaving

When luma and modulated chroma are summed, a certain amount of mutual interference is introduced.

HUE (or TINT, or PHASE) and CHROMA (or COLOUR, or SATURATION) controls properly apply only to NTSC/PAL decoding. They have no place in modern component video systems. See *Composite decoder adjustment using colourbars,* on page 422, and *NTSC and PAL Chroma modulation* in *Composite NTSC and PAL: Legacy Video Systems*.

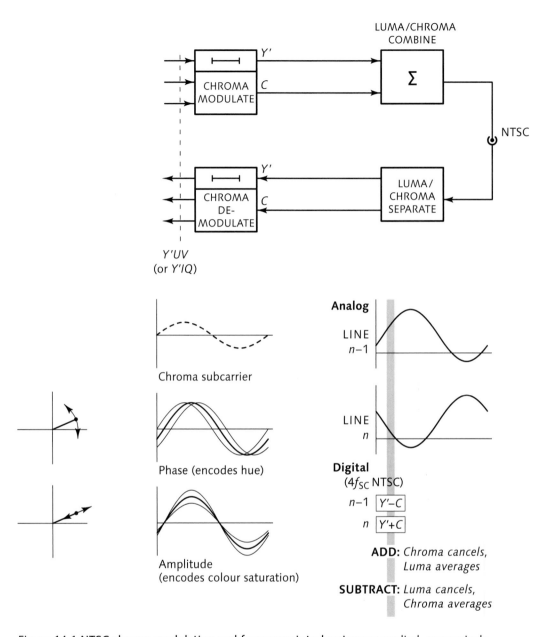

Figure 14.1 **NTSC chroma modulation and frequency interleaving** are applied, successively, to encode luma and a pair of colour difference components into NTSC composite video. First, the two colour difference signals are modulated onto a colour subcarrier. If the two colour differences are interpreted in polar coordinates, hue angle is encoded as subcarrier phase and colour saturation is encoded as subcarrier amplitude. (A sample of the unmodulated subcarrier, *burst*, is included in the composite signal.) Then, modulated chroma is summed with luma. Frequency interleaving leads to line-by-line phase inversion of the unmodulated colour subcarrier, thence to the modulated subcarrier. Summation of adjacent lines tends to cause modulated chroma to cancel, and tends to cause luma to average.

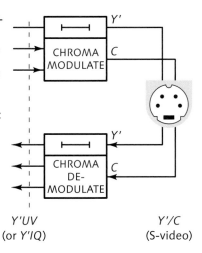

Figure 14.2 **The S-video interface** involves NTSC or PAL chroma modulation; however, luma and modulated chroma traverse separate paths across the interface instead of being summed. There are no fewer than three versions of S-video: S-video-525, S-video-525-J, and S-video-625; these are detailed in "480i NTSC composite video," in Chapter 7 of *Composite NTSC and PAL: Legacy Video Systems*.

Y'UV
(or Y'IQ)

Y'/C
(S-video)

In PAL, all but the most sophisticated comb filters separate *U* and *V*, not luma and chroma. See "NTSC and PAL Chroma modulation," Chapter 5 of *Composite NTSC and PAL: Legacy Video Systems*.

Interference is minimized by arranging for *frequency interleaving*, which is achieved when the colour subcarrier frequency and the line rate are *coherent* – that is, when the unmodulated colour subcarrier is phase-locked to a carefully chosen rational multiple of the line rate – an integer multiple of half the line rate for NTSC, and an integer multiple of $\frac{1}{4}$ the line rate in PAL. Coherence is achieved in the studio by deriving both the sync and colour subcarrier from a single master clock.

In NTSC, frequency interleaving enables use of a comb filter to separate luma and chroma: Adjacent lines are summed (to form vertically averaged luma) and differenced (to form vertically averaged chroma), as suggested at the bottom right of Figure 14.1.

In industrial and consumer video, the subcarrier often free-runs with respect to line rate, and the advantages of frequency interleaving are lost. Most forms of analog videotape recording introduce timebase error; left uncorrected, this also defeats frequency interleaving.

Composite analog SD

Composite analog 480*i* NTSC and 576*i* PAL is widely deployed in consumer equipment (such as television receivers and VCRs) and was used for terrestrial VHF/UHF broadcasting and cable television for many decades. Details are found in "Analog SD broadcast standards," Chapter 12 of *Composite NTSC and PAL: Legacy Video Systems*.

Introduction to HD 15

FUJIO, TAKASHI, J. ISHIDA, T. KOMOTO, and TAIJI NISHIZAWA (1980), *High definition television system – signal standards and transmission*, *SMPTE Journal*, **89** (8): 579–584 (Aug.).

FUJIO, TAKASHI (1981), "High definition television systems: desirable standards, signal forms, and transmission systems," in *IEEE Tr. Comm.* **29** (12): 1882–1891 (Dec.).

FUJIO, TAKASHI, et al. (1982), *High Definition television*, NHK Science and Technical Research Laboratories Technical Monograph 32 (June).

Developmental HD systems had 1125/60.00/2:1 scanning, an aspect ratio of 5:3, and 1035 active lines. The alternate 59.94 Hz field rate was added later. Aspect ratio was changed to 16:9 to achieve international agreement upon standards. A count of 1080 image rows was eventually agreed upon to provide square sampling. The developmental 1035*i* (1125/60) system, standardized in SMPTE 240M, was discussed in the first edition of this book.

This chapter outlines the 1280×720 and 1920×1080 image formats for high-definition (HD) television, and introduces the scanning parameters of the associated video systems such as 720*p*60 and 1080*i*30.

Today's HD systems stem from research directed by Dr. Fujio at NHK (Nippon Hoso Kyokai, the Japan Broadcasting Corporation). HD has about twice the vertical and twice the horizontal resolution of conventional television, a picture aspect ratio of 16:9, at least two channels of CD-quality audio, and a frame rate of 23.976 Hz or higher. By my definition, HD has ¾-million pixels or more. NHK conceived HD to have interlaced scanning; however, progressive HD systems have since emerged.

Studio HD has a sampling rate of 74.25 MHz, 5.5 times that of the BT.601 standard for SD. HD has a pixel rate of about 60 megapixels per second. Apart from a few annoying exceptions, parameters of *R'G'B'* coding are similar those of SD standards – in fact, several parameters adopted for HD in BT.709 have essentially been retrofitted into SD. Details concerning scanning, sample rates, and interface levels of HD will be presented in *1280×720 HD* on page 467 and *1920×1080 HD* on page 473. Unfortunately, the parameters for $Y'C_BC_R$ colour coding for HD differ from the parameters for SD! Details will be provided in *Component video colour coding for HD*, on page 369.

HD scanning

A great debate took place in the 1980s and 1990s concerning whether HD should have interlaced or

141

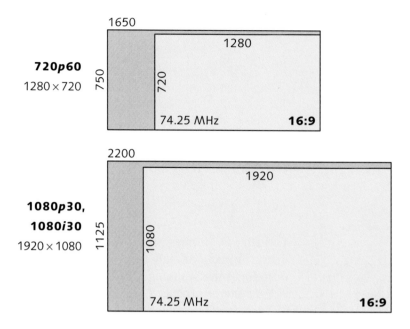

Figure 15.1 **HD rasters at 30 and 60 frames per second** are standardized in two formats, 1280×720 (1 Mpx, always progressive), and 1920×1080 (2 Mpx, interlaced or progressive). The latter is often denoted 1080*i*, but the standards accommodate progressive scan. These sketches are scaled to match Figures 13.1 and 13.2; pixels in these sketches have identical area.

progressive scanning. At given flicker and data rates, interlace offers some increase in static spatial resolution, as suggested by Figure 8.8 on page 91. Broadcasters have historically accepted the motion artifacts and spatial aliasing that accompany interlace, in order to gain some static spatial resolution. In the HD debate, the computer industry and the creative film community were resolutely set against interlace. Eventually, both camps compromised to some degree and HD standards were established to accommodate both interlaced and progressive image formats. To be commercially viable a receiver must decode both formats, though there is no "legal" requirement to do so.

In *Numerology of HD scanning,* on page 395, I explain the origin of the numbers in Figure 15.1.

Figure 15.1 above sketches the rasters of the 1 Mpx progressive system (1280×720, 720*p*60) and the 2 Mpx interlaced system (1920×1080, 1080*i*30) that were agreed upon. 1280×720 is very simply related to 1920×1080: 1280 is two thirds of 1920, and 720 is two thirds of 1080.

Image format	Progressive/interlace ‡Frame rate [Hz]		Image aspect ratio	Sampling
640×480	p	24, 30, 60	4:3	Square
	i	30		
704×480	p	24, 30, 60	4:3	Nonsquare
	i	30		
	p	24, 30, 60	16:9	Nonsquare
	i	30		
1280×720	p	24, 30, 60	16:9	Square
1920×1080	p	24, 30	16:9	Square
	i	30		

‡Frame rates modified by the ratio $\frac{1000}{1001}$ – that is, frame rates of 23.976 Hz, 29.97 Hz, and 59.94 Hz – are permitted.

Table 15.1 **ATSC A/53 Table 3** defines the so-called 18 formats – including 12 SD formats – for digital television in the U.S. I find the layout of ATSC's Table 3 to be hopelessly contorted, so I rearranged it. ATSC specifies 704 S_{AL} for several SD formats, instead of BT.601's 720 S_{AL}; see page 380. ATSC standard A/53 doesn't accommodate 25 Hz and 50 Hz frame rates, but A/63 does.

ATSC A/53, *Digital Television Standard.*

In addition to the 1 Mpx (progressive) and 2 Mpx (interlaced) systems, several SD scanning systems and several additional frame rates were included in the ultimate ATSC standards for U.S. digital television (DTV). Table 15.1 summarizes the "18 formats" that are found in Table 3 of the ATSC's A/53 standard.

The 1920×1080 system was conceived as interlaced-only (1080*i*30), but was adapted to 24 and 30 Hz progressive scan (1080*p*24, 1080*p*30) using the standard 74.25 MHz sample rate. The adaptation to 24 Hz was seminal to digital cinema. Figure 15.2 overleaf sketches raster structures for 24 Hz and 25 Hz systems; Table 15.2 summarizes the scanning parameters.

In Sony's legacy HDCAM system, the 1920×1080 image was downsampled to 1440×1080, and colour difference signals were subsampled 3:1:1, prior to compression. This was an internal representation only; there was no corresponding uncompressed external interface standard. The current Sony HDCAM SR format represents 1920×1080 image data directly at 4:2:2 (or in some variations 4:4:4), and alleviates the need for such downsampling.

SMPTE ST 274 provides for carriage of a 1920×1080 image at a frame rate of 25 Hz: 1125 total lines are

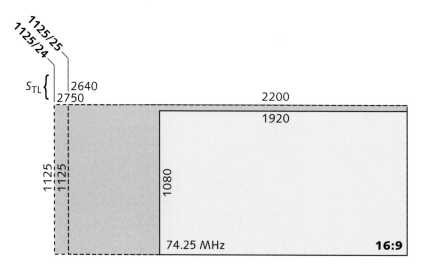

Figure 15.2 **HD rasters at 24 Hz and 25 Hz** carry an array of 1920×1080 active samples, using a 74.25 MHz sampling rate at the interface. For 24 Hz (1080p24), the 1920×1080 array is carried in an 1125/24 raster. For 25 Hz, the array is carried in an 1125/25 raster.

$$\frac{24}{1.001} \approx 23.976$$

retained, and S_{TL} is increased to 2640. This yields the 1080p25 format, using an 1125/25 raster. Scanning can be either progressive or interlaced; with progressive scanning, the signal is usually interfaced using the progressive segmented frame (PsF) scheme that I introduced on page 94.

For 24 Hz, 1125 total lines are retained, and S_{TL} is increased to 2750 to achieve the 24 Hz frame rate. This yields the 1080p24 format, in an 1125/24 raster. This system is used in digital cinema (D-cinema). A variant at 23.976 Hz is accommodated.

Table 15.2 summarizes the scanning parameters for 720p, 1080i, and 1080p systems. Studio interfaces for HD will be introduced in *SDI and HD-SDI interfaces,* on page 429.

Colour coding for BT.709 HD

The conventional view of BT.709 "encoding" involves the OECF in the standard. In *Image acquisition and presentation,* on page 19, the argument is made that what matters is the *display* process. Faithful presentation of completed program material requires that the display EOCF be standardized. A standard camera OECF (such as that in BT.709) is useful for engineering

System	Scanning	SMPTE standard	S_{TL}	L_T	N_C (S_{AL})	N_R (L_A)
720p60	750/60/1:1	SMPTE ST 296	1650	750	1280	720
1080i30	1125/60/2:1	SMPTE ST 274	2200	1125	1920	1080
1080p60¶	1125/60/1:1	SMPTE ST 274	2200	1125	1920	1080
1080p30	1125/30/1:1	SMPTE ST 274	2200	1125	1920	1080
1080i25	1125/25/2:1	SMPTE ST 274	2640	1125	1920	1080
1080p25	1125/25/1:1	SMPTE ST 274	2640	1125	1920	1080
1080p24	1125/24/1:1	SMPTE ST 274	2750	1125	1920	1080

Table 15.2 **HD scanning parameters.** are summarized. SMPTE ST 274 includes a progressive 2 Mpx, 1080p60 system with 1125/60/1:1 scanning, flagged with ¶ above; this system is not permitted for ATSC broadcasting. Each of the 24, 30, and 60 Hz systems above has an associated system at $\frac{1000}{1001}$ of that rate.

purposes, but has no impact upon faithful presentation. In practice, so-called BT.709 program material has $R'G'B'$ data values established so that the inrtended image appearance is obtained when those $R'G'B'$ values are displayed through a reference EOCF (for example, that of BT.1886) into a known set of viewing conditions (unfortunately, not yet standardized).

BT.709 defines $Y'C_BC_R$ colour coding. Unfortunately, the luma coefficients standardized in BT.709 – and the C_BC_R scale factors derived from them – differ from those of SD. $Y'C_BC_R$ coding now comes in two flavors: coding for small (SD) pictures, and coding for large (HD) pictures. I will present details concerning this troublesome issue in *SD and HD luma chaos*, on page 350.

Introduction to
video compression   16

Directly storing or transmitting digital video requires fairly high data capacity – about 20 megabytes per second for SD, or about 120 megabytes per second for HD. Here is a rule of thumb that relates storage capacity and data rate: Eight, 2000-ft reels of motion picture print film can carry a 133 $1/3$ minute movie; there are 8 bits in a byte and 60 seconds in a minute; and $60/8 \cdot 133\ 1/3$ is 1000. So one megabit per second equals one gigabyte per movie – whether compressed or not! Similarly, one gigabit per second equals one terabyte per movie.

Economical storage or transmission requires compression. This chapter introduces the JPEG, M-JPEG, MPEG, and H.264 compression techniques.

In previous chapters, we have discussed representation of image data in a rather small number of colour components (say, three); a rather small number of bits per component (say 8 or 10); perceptual coding by way of a nonlinear EOCF; and chroma subsampling yielding a data rate reduction of around 50%. In video terminology, all of these techniques are termed – paradoxically, perhaps – to be *uncompressed* video. *Compression* involves transform techniques such as the discrete cosine transform (DCT) and – in the case of JPEG 2000 – the discrete wavelet transform (DWT).

A rule of thumb that relates data rate to storage capacity:

$$Mb/_s = GB/_{movie}$$

$$Gb/_s = TB/_{movie}$$

Data compression

Data compression has the goal of reducing the number of bits required to store or convey text, numeric, binary, image, sound, or other data. High performance is obtained by exploiting statistical properties of the data.

The reduction comes at the expense of some computational effort to compress and decompress. Data compression is, by definition, lossless: Decompression recovers exactly, bit for bit (or byte for byte), the data that was presented to the compressor.

Binary data typical of general computer applications often has patterns of repeating byte strings. Most data compression techniques, including *run-length encoding* (RLE) and *Lempel-Ziv-Welch* (LZW), accomplish compression by taking advantage of repeated strings; performance is highly dependent upon the data being compressed.

Image compression

Image data typically has strong vertical, horizontal, and spatial correlations among samples of the same colour component. When the RLE and LZW algorithms are applied to bilevel or pseudocolour image data stored in scan-line order, horizontal correlation among pixels can be exploited to some degree; such techniques usually result in modest compression (perhaps 2:1).

A data compression algorithm can be designed to exploit the statistics of image data, as opposed to arbitrary binary data; improved compression is then possible. For example, the ITU-T fax standard for bilevel image data exploits vertical and horizontal correlation to achieve typical compression ratios higher than RLE or LZW typically achieve. In the absence of channel errors, data compression (even of images) is lossless, by definition: Decompression reproduces, bit-for-bit, the data presented to the compressor.

Lossy compression

Lossless data compression can be optimized to achieve modest compression of continuous-tone (greyscale or truecolour) image data. However, if exact reconstruction is not required, the characteristics of human perception can be exploited to achieve dramatically higher compression ratios: Image or sound data can be subject to *lossy* compression, provided that any impairments introduced are not overly perceptible. Lossy compression techniques are not appropriate for bilevel or pseudocolour images; however, they are very effective for greyscale or truecolour images, both stills and video.

SALOMON, DAVID (2008), *A Concise Introduction to Data Compression* (Springer).

SAYOOD, KHALID (2005), *Introduction to Data Compression,* Third edition (Elsevier/Morgan-Kaufmann).

The term "perceptually lossless" signifies an attempt to minimize the perceptibility of compression errors. There are no standards or industry practices to determine to what extent that goal is achieved. Thus, the term is indistinct.

	Uncompressed	Compression ratio		
Format	data rate [MB/s]	Motion-JPEG	MPEG-2	H.264
SD (480*i*30, 576*i*25)	20	15:1 (e.g., DV25)	45:1 (e.g,. DVD)	90:1
HD (720*p*60, 1080*i*30)	120	20:1	75:1 (e.g., ATSC)	100:1 (e.g., Blu-ray)

Table 16.1 **Approximate compression ratios** for SD and HD video distribution systems

Transform techniques are effective for compression of continuous-tone (greyscale or truecolour) image data. The *discrete cosine transform* (DCT) has been developed and optimized over the last few decades; it is the method of choice for continuous-tone image compression. *JPEG* refers to a lossy compression method for still images. *MPEG* refers to a lossy compression standard for video sequences; MPEG-2 is used in digital television distribution (e.g., ATSC and DVB), and in DVD. *H.264* refers to a lossy compression standard for video sequences. H.264 is highly effective for HD; it is used in satellite, cable, and telco (IPTV) systems, and in Blu-ray. These techniques will all be described in subsequent sections.

Internet protocol television (IPTV) concerns video and audio delivered over TCP/IP networks.

Table 16.1 compares typical compression ratios of M-JPEG and MPEG-2, for SD and HD.

In the context of compression of video or audio, the term *codec* refers to an en*CO*der and/or a *DEC*oder.

Encoders and decoders in compression systems are not to be confused with composite video (NTSC or PAL) encoders or decoders.

JPEG

In 1992, the JPEG committee adopted a standard based upon DCT transform coding, suitable for compressing greyscale or truecolour still images. This was before the world-wide web: The standard was expected to be used for colour fax! JPEG was quickly adopted and widely deployed for still images in desktop graphics and digital photography. The *M-JPEG* variant can be used for motion sequences; the DV scheme uses an M-JPEG-like algorithm. Details are presented in *JPEG and motion-JPEG (M-JPEG) compression*, on page 491.

JPEG stands for *Joint Photographic Experts Group*, constituted by ISO and IEC in collaboration with ITU-T (the former CCITT).

A JPEG compressor ordinarily transforms $R'G'B'$ to $Y'C_BC_R$, then applies 4:2:0 chroma subsampling to effect 2:1 compression prior to the transform coding steps. (In desktop graphics, this 2:1 factor is included in the compression ratio.) JPEG has provisions to compress $R'G'B'$ data directly, without subsampling.

Compression ratio	Quality/application	Example SD tape formats
2:1	"Visually lossless" studio video	Digital Betacam
3.3:1	Excellent-quality studio video	DVCPRO50, D-9 (Digital-S)
6.6:1	Good-quality studio video; consumer digital video	D-7 (DVCPRO), DVCAM, consumer DV

Table 16.2 **Approximate compression ratios of M-JPEG** for SD applications

Motion-JPEG

The JPEG algorithm – though not the ISO/IEC JPEG standard – has been adapted to compress motion video. Motion-JPEG simply compresses each field or frame of a video sequence as a self-contained compressed picture – each field or frame is *intra-coded*. Because pictures are compressed individually, an M-JPEG video sequence can be easily edited; however, no advantage is taken of temporal coherence.

JPEG and motion-JPEG (M-JPEG) compression is described on page 491. DV compression is described on page 505.

Video data is almost always presented to an M-JPEG compression system in $Y'C_BC_R$ subsampled form. (In video, the 2:1 factor due to chroma subsampling is generally not included in the compression ratio.)

The M-JPEG technique achieves compression ratios ranging from about 2:1 to about 20:1. The 20 MB/s data rate of SD can be compressed to about 20 Mb/s, suitable for recording on consumer digital videotape (e.g., DVC). M-JPEG compression ratios and tape formats are summarized in Table 16.2.

JPEG 2000

TAUBMAN, DAVID S. and MARCELLIN, MICHAEL W. (2002), *JPEG-2000: Image Compression Fundamentals, Standards and Practice* (Norwell, Mass.: Kluwer).

Between 1995 and 2000, the JPEG committee developed a compression standard for continuous-tone colour still images. The effort culminated in the JPEG 2000 standard, which is based upon discrete wavelet transform (DWT) techniques. DCI standards for digital cinema use JPEG 2000 compression. An adaptation of JPEG 2000 accommodates motion sequences, where each (progressive) frame is coded individually without reference to any other frame. Although the "core" JPEG 2000 coding system is intended to be royalty and license-free, intellectual property rights (IPR) concerns have inhibited JPEG 2000 commercialization.

DIGITAL VIDEO AND HD ALGORITHMS AND INTERFACES

Mezzanine compression

Uncompressed recording is taken to be the upper floor; formats for distribution are at ground level. The mezzanine lies between.

DV and its derivatives and relatives are common in the studio. In the last several years, several software-based codecs suitable for acquisition and postproduction have emerged: Dirac/VC-2, DNxHD/VC-3, and Apple ProRes. The term *mezzanine* is used for such codecs, signifying compression rates intermediate between uncompressed recording and consumer distribution.

Dirac PRO (VC-2)

An open-source development project led by the BBC developed video compression technology collectively named *Dirac* (in honour of the Nobel prize-winning physicist) for lossy mezzanine-level intra-frame wavelet compression. Dirac PRO handles a wide range of video formats, but is optimized to compress 10-bit, 4:2:2 1080*p* video to bit rates between about 50 Mb/s and 165 Mb/s. SMPTE has standardized Dirac PRO in the ST 2042 series of standards (also known as VC-2).

The Dirac PRO bitstream includes parameter values to identify the complexity of the coded bit-stream through the use of profiles and levels. These values enable a decoder to easily establish whether it has the capability to decode the bit-stream. Profiles and levels are defined.

DNxHD (VC-3)

Avid implemented a family of compression systems that are now widely deployed in postproduction. One of these, denoted DNxHD by Avid, has been standardized by SMPTE as ST 2042-1, colloquially called VC-3. Bit rate for HD ranges from about 60 Mb/s to 220 Mb/s. Compressed data is typically carried in MXF files.

Apple ProRes

Apple implemented a set of proprietary variable bit rate, intra-frame DCT-based codecs called *ProRes,* now used fairly widely in acquisition and in postproduction. ProRes resembles motion-JPEG; however, the scheme is proprietary and details aren't published. The scheme was designed for implementation in software; however, hardware-based codecs are commercially available.

RedCode; CineForm

Several intraframe wavelet-based codecs have been developed and deployed for digital cinema acquisition, and can be used for HD. Red's RedCode is a proprietary form of JPEG 2000; GoPro's CineForm also uses wavelet compression. Both of these schemes individually compress Bayer mosaic data prior to demosaicking.

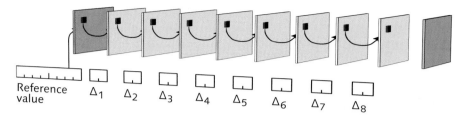

Figure 16.1 **Interpicture coding** exploits the similarity between successive pictures in video. First, a reference picture is transmitted (typically using intrapicture compression). Then, pixel differences to successive pictures are computed by the encoder and transmitted. The decoder reconstructs successive pictures by accumulating the differences. The scheme is effective provided that the difference information can be coded more compactly than the raw picture information.

MPEG

The M in MPEG stands for *moving*, not *motion!* If you read a document that errs in this detail, the accuracy of the document is suspect!

Apart from scene changes, there is a statistical likelihood that successive pictures in a video sequence are very similar. In fact, it is *necessary* that successive pictures are mostly similar: If this were not the case, human vision could make no sense of the sequence!

The efficiency of transform coding can be increased by a factor of 10 or more by exploiting the inherent temporal redundancy of video. The *MPEG* standard was developed by the *Moving Picture Experts Group* within ISO and IEC. In MPEG, intra-frame compression is used to provide an initial, self-contained picture – a *reference* picture, upon which predictions of succeeding pictures can be based. The encoder then transmits pixel differences, that is, prediction errors, or *residuals* – from the reference, as sketched in Figure 16.1. The method is termed *interframe coding*. (In interlaced video, differences between *fields* may be used, so the method is more accurately described as *interpicture* coding.)

Once a reference picture has been received by the decoder, it provides a basis for predicting succeeding pictures. This estimate is improved when the decoder receives the residuals. The scheme is effective provided that the residuals can be coded more compactly than the raw picture information.

Motion in a video sequence causes displacement of scene elements with respect to the image array. A fast-moving image element may easily move 20 pixels in one frame time. In the presence of motion, a pixel at a certain location may take quite different values in successive pictures. Motion is liable to cause prediction

DIGITAL VIDEO AND HD ALGORITHMS AND INTERFACES

Figure 16.2 **An MPEG group of pictures (GoP).** The GoP depicted here has nine pictures, numbered 0 through 8. Picture 9 is the first picture of the next GoP. I-picture 0 is decoded from the coded data depicted as a green block. Here, the *intra-count* (N) is 9.

One form of motion-compensated prediction forms an integer-valued MV, and copies a block of pixels from a reference picture for use as a prediction block. A more sophisticated form computes motion vectors to half-pixel precision, and interpolates between reference pixels (for example, by averaging). The latter is *motion-compensated interpolation.* Although the simple technique involves just copying, it's also called interpolation.

error information to grow in size to the point where the advantage of interframe coding would be negated.

However, image elements tend to retain their spatial structure even when moving. MPEG overcomes the problem of motion between pictures by using *motion-compensated prediction* (MCP). The encoder is equipped with *motion estimation* (ME) circuitry that computes *motion vectors*. The encoder then displaces the pixel values of the reference picture by the estimated motion – a process called *motion compensated interpolation* – then computes residuals from the motion-compensated reference. The encoder compresses the residuals using a JPEG-like technique, then transmits the motion vectors and the compressed residuals.

Based upon the received motion vectors, the decoder mimics the motion compensated interpolation of the encoder to obtain a predictor much more effective than the undisplaced reference picture. The received residuals are then applied (by simple addition) to reconstruct an approximation of the encoder's picture.

The MPEG suite of standards specifies the properties of a compliant bitstream and the algorithms that are implemented by a decoder. Any encoder that produces compliant ("legal") bitstreams is considered MPEG-compliant, even if it produces poor-quality images.

Picture coding types (I, P, B)

When encoding interlaced source material, an MPEG-2 encoder can choose to code each field as a picture or each frame as a picture, as I will describe on page 518. In this chapter, and in Chapter 47, the term *picture* can refer to either a field or a frame.

In MPEG, a video sequence is partitioned into successive *groups of pictures* (GoPs). The first picture in each GoP is coded using a JPEG-like algorithm, independently of other pictures. This is an *intra* or *I-picture*. Once reconstructed, an I-picture becomes a reference picture available for use in predicting neighboring (*nonintra*) pictures. The example GoP sketched in Figure 16.2 above comprises nine pictures.

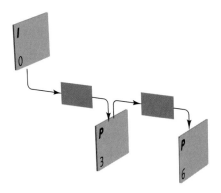

Figure 16.3 **An MPEG P-picture** contains elements forward-predicted from a preceding reference picture, which may be an I-picture or a P-picture. Here, a P-picture (3) is predicted from an I-picture (0). Once decoded, that P-picture becomes the predictor for a following P-picture (6).

A *P-picture* contains elements that are predicted from the most recent anchor frame. Once a P-picture is reconstructed, it is displayed; in addition, it becomes a new anchor. I-pictures and P-pictures form a two-layer hierarchy. An I-picture and two dependent P-pictures are depicted in Figure 16.3 above.

MPEG provides an optional third hierarchical level whereby *B-pictures* may be interposed between anchor pictures. Elements of a B-picture are typically *bipredicted* by averaging motion-compensated elements from the past reference picture and motion-compensated elements from the future reference picture. (At the encoder's discretion, elements of a B-picture may be unidirectionally forward-interpolated from the preceding reference, or unidirectionally backward-predicted from the following reference.) Each B-picture is reconstructed, displayed, then discarded: No decoded B-picture forms the basis for any prediction. Using B-pictures delivers a substantial gain in compression efficiency compared to encoding with just I- and P-pictures, but incurs a coding latency.

Figure 16.4 below depicts two B-pictures.

The term *bidirectional prediction* was historically used, suggesting reverse and forward directions in time. It is often the case that pairs of motion vectors associated with B-pictures point in opposite directions in the image plane. In H.264, the term *bipredictive* is used, and is more accurate in H.264's context.

Figure 16.4 **An MPEG B-picture** is generally predicted from the average of the preceding reference picture and the following ("future") reference picture. (At the encoder's option, a B-picture may be unidirectionally forward-predicted from the preceding reference, or unidirectionally backward-predicted from the following reference.)

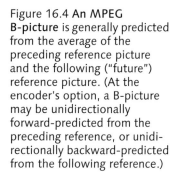
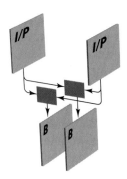

Figure 16.5 **The three-level MPEG picture hierarchy.** This sketch shows a regular GoP structure with an I-picture interval of $N=9$, and a reference picture interval of $M=3$. This example represents a simple encoder that emits a fixed schedule of I-, B-, and P-pictures; this structure can be described as IBBPBBPBB. The example shows an *open GoP:* B-pictures following the GoP's last P-picture are permitted to use backward prediction from the I-picture of the following GoP. Such prediction precludes editing of the bitstream between GoPs. A *closed GoP* permits no such prediction, so the bitstream can be edited between GoPs. Closed GoPs lose some efficiency.

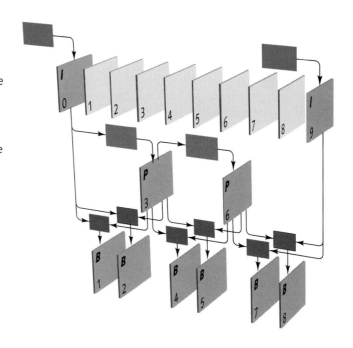

A 15-frame "long" GoP structured IBBPBBPBBPBBPBB is common for broadcasting. A sophisticated encoder may produce irregular GoP patterns.

The three-level MPEG picture hierarchy is summarized in Figure 16.5 above; this example has the structure IBBPBBPBB.

A simple encoder typically produces a bitstream having a fixed schedule of I-, P-, and B-pictures. A typical GoP structure is denoted IBBPBBPBBPBBPBB. At 30 pictures per second, there are two such GoPs per second. Periodic GoP structure can be described by a pair of integers N and M; N is the number of pictures from one I-picture (inclusive) to the next (exclusive), and M is the number of pictures from one anchor picture (inclusive) to the next (exclusive). If $M=1$, there are no B-pictures. Figure 16.5 shows a regular GoP structure with an I-picture interval of $N=9$ and an anchor-picture interval of $M=3$. The $M=3$ component indicates two B-pictures between anchor pictures. Rarely do more than 2 B-pictures intervene between reference pictures.

Coded B-pictures in a GoP depend upon P- and I-pictures; coded P-pictures depend upon earlier P-pictures and I-pictures. Owing to these interdependencies, an MPEG sequence cannot be edited, except at GoP boundaries, unless the sequence is decoded, edited, and subsequently reencoded. MPEG is very suitable for distribution, but owing to its inability to be edited without impairment at arbitrary points, MPEG is generally unsuitable for production. In the specialization of MPEG-2 called *I-frame only MPEG-2*, every GoP is a single I-frame. This is conceptually equivalent to Motion-JPEG, but has the great benefit of an international standard. (Another variant of MPEG-2, the *simple profile*, has no B-pictures.)

I have introduced MPEG as if all elements of every P-picture and all elements of every B-picture are coded similarly. But even a picture that is generally well predicted by the past reference picture may have a few regions that cannot effectively be predicted. In MPEG, the image is tiled into *macroblocks* of 16×16 luma samples, and the encoder is given the option to code *any* particular macroblock in *intra* mode – that is, independently of any prediction. A compact code signals that a macroblock should be *skipped*, in which case the motion-compensated prediction is used without modification. In a B-picture, the encoder can decide on a macroblock-by-macroblock basis to code using forward prediction, backward prediction, or biprediction. Formally, an I-picture contains only I-macroblocks; a P-picture has at least one P-macroblock, and a B-picture has at least one B-macroblock.

Reordering

In a sequence without B-pictures, I- and P-pictures are encoded then stored or transmitted in the obvious order. However, when B-pictures are used, the decoder typically needs to access the past anchor picture and the future anchor picture to reconstruct a B-picture.

Consider an encoder about to compress the sequence in Figure 16.6 (where anchor pictures I_0, P_3, and P_6 are written in boldface). The coded B_1 and B_2 pictures may be backward predicted from P_3, so the encoder must buffer the uncompressed B_1 and B_2 pictures until P_3 is coded: Only when coding of P_3 is complete can coding of B_1 start. Using B-pictures incurs a penalty in encoding delay. (If the sequence were coded without B-pictures, as depicted in Figure 16.7, transmission of the coded information for P_1 would not be subject to this two-picture delay.) Coding delay

Figure 16.6 Example GoP

$I_0B_1B_2P_3B_4B_5P_6B_7B_8$

Figure 16.7 Example 9-picture GoP without B-pictures

$I_0P_1P_2P_3P_4P_5P_6P_7P_8$

DIGITAL VIDEO AND HD ALGORITHMS AND INTERFACES

(latency) can make MPEG with B-pictures unsuitable for realtime two-way applications such as teleconferencing.

If the coded 9-picture GoP of Figure 16.6 were transmitted in the order shown, then the decoder would have to hold the coded B_1 and B_2 data in a buffer while receiving and decoding P_3; only when decoding of P_3 was complete could decoding of B_1 start. The encoder must buffer the B_1 and B_2 pictures no matter what; however, to minimize buffer memory at the decoder, MPEG-2 specifies that coded B-picture information is transmitted after the coded reference picture. Figure 16.8 indicates picture data as reordered for transmission. I have placed I_9 in parentheses because it belongs to the next GoP (the GoP header precedes it). Here, B_7 and B_8 follow the GoP header.

Figure 16.8 **GoP reordered for transmission**

$$I_0P_3B_1B_2P_6B_4B_5(I_9)B_7B_8$$

ISO/IEC 11172-1, *Coding of moving pictures and associated audio for digital storage media at up to about 1,5 Mbit/s – Part 1: Systems* [MPEG-1].

MPEG-1

The original MPEG effort resulted in a standard now called MPEG-1, which was deployed in multimedia applications. MPEG-1 was optimized for the coding of progressive 352×240 images at 30 frames per second (240*p*30). MPEG-1 has no provision for interlace. When 480*i*29.97 or 576*i*25 video is coded with MPEG-1 at typical data rates, the first field of each frame is coded as if it were progressive, and the second field is dropped. At its intended data rate of about 1.5 Mb/s, MPEG-1 delivers VHS-quality images.

For broadcast, MPEG-1 has been superseded by MPEG-2. An MPEG-2 decoder must decode MPEG-1 *constrained-parameter bitstream* (CPB) sequences – to be discussed in the caption to Table 47.1, on page 515 – so I will not discuss MPEG-1 further.

MPEG-2

The MPEG-2 effort was initiated to extend MPEG-1 to interlaced scanning, to larger pictures, and to data rates much higher than 1.5 Mb/s. MPEG-2 is standardized in a series of documents from ISO/IEC; MPEG-2 is widely deployed for the distribution of digital television (DTV) including SD and HD (for example, ATSC), and is the (only) video compression scheme for DVD.

Many MPEG terms – such as *frame, picture,* and *macroblock* – can refer to elements of the source video, to the corresponding elements in the coded bitstream, or to the corresponding elements in the reconstructed video. It is generally clear from context which is meant.

MPEG-2 accommodates both progressive and interlaced material. A video frame can be coded directly as a *frame-structured picture*. Alternatively, a video frame (typically originated from an interlaced source) may be coded as a pair of *field-structured pictures* – a top-field picture and a bottom-field picture. The two fields are time-offset by half the frame time, and are intended for interlaced display. Field pictures always come in pairs having opposite parity (top/bottom or bottom/top). Both pictures in a field pair have the same picture coding type (I, P, or B), except that an I-field may be followed by a P-field (in which case the pair effectively serves as an I-frame).

The MPEG IMX variant of MPEG-2, for studio use, is described below. The HDV variant of MPEG-2, for consumer use, is described on page 161. MPEG-2 video compression is detailed starting on page 513.

Other MPEGs

While the MPEG-2 work was underway, an MPEG-3 effort was launched to address HD. The MPEG-3 committee concluded early on that MPEG-2, at high data rate, would accommodate HD; consequently, the MPEG-3 effort was abandoned. I'll discuss MPEG-4 below. MPEG numbers above 4 are capricious.

ISO/IEC 15938-1, *Information technology – Multimedia content description interface – Part 1: Systems.*

MPEG-7, titled *Multimedia Content Description Interface,* standardizes a description of various types of multimedia information (metadata). In my view, MPEG-7 is not relevant to handling studio- or distribution-quality video signals.

ISO/IEC 21000, *Multimedia framework (MPEG-21).*

According to ISO, MPEG-21 "defines an open framework for multimedia delivery and consumption, with both the content creator and content consumer as focal points. The vision for MPEG-21 is to define a multimedia framework to enable transparent and augmented use of multimedia resources across a wide range of networks and devices used by different communities." In my view, MPEG-21 is not relevant to handling studio- or distribution-quality video.

MPEG IMX

MPEG IMX is a Sony trademark; IMX is not an MPEG designation.

Sony's original Digital Betacam for 480*i* and 576*i* SD used proprietary motion-JPEG-like compression. The first products were videotape recorders denoted

Betacam SX, having a data rate of about 18 Mb/s. Follow-on products adopted I-frame-only MPEG-2 422P@ML, denoted MPEG IMX, having data rates of 30 Mb/s, 40 Mb/s, or 50 Mb/s (IMX30, IMX40, IMX50). MPEG IMX videotape recorders were commercialized. Today it is common to place or wrap IMX compressed video in an MXF file.

XDCAM is Sony's designation for a line of products using a variety of compression systems and a variety of physical media. MPEG IMX compression is one of the compression systems available in the XDCAM line. Recording on optical disc media is possible.

MPEG-4

ISO/IEC 14496, *Information technology – Coding of audio-visual objects.*

The original goal of the MPEG-4 effort was video coding at very low bit rates. The video compression system that resulted is standardized as MPEG-4 Part 2 *Visual; it differes from MPEG-2 and from H.264.* ISO/IEC co-published the ITU-T H.264 standard as MPEG-4 Part 10, so the term *MPEG-4* alone is ambiguous.

MPEG-4 Part 2 defines the *advanced simple profile* (ASP), implemented by DivX and Xvid. ASP is not useful for professional quality video. Even in ASP's intended application domain, low bit-rate video, H.264 – to be described in a moment – has proven to have better performance. Consequently, ASP has fallen out of favour.

MPEG-4 Part 2 also defines a profile called *Simple Studio Profile* (SStP). This profile is used in Sony's HDCAM SR, at very high bit rates (the other end of the bit rate spectrum for which MPEG-4 was conceived). HDCAM SR is widely used in HD, both on tape and in files. Apart from HDCAM SR, the simple studio profile of MPEG-4 sees very limited use.

ISO/IEC 14496-12:2004, *Information technology – Coding of audio-visual objects – Part 12: ISO base media file format.*

Part 12 of the MPEG-4 suite of standards defines the *ISO Base Media File Format,* which defines a general container structure for time-based media files. The format is used in desktop video (most commonly with MPEG-4 Part 2/ASP video, in *mp4* files), but is rarely if ever used in professional video distribution.

H.264

ISO/IEC 14496-10:2009, *Coding of audio-visual objects – Part 10: Advanced Video Coding* [AVC].

ITU-T Rec. H.264, *Advanced video coding for generic audiovisual services.*

An effort to extend MPEG-2 coding was undertaken by the *Joint Video Team* (JVT). During development, this effort worked toward *advanced video coding* (AVC). The resulting standard is promulgated jointly by by ITU-T (who call it H.264) and by ISO/IEC (who call it MPEG-4 Part 10, despite its having little to do with the rest of MPEG-4). H.264 encoding is roughly 1.5 or 2 times as efficient as MPEG-2 – that is, H.264 typically allows encoding at somewhat more than half the bit rate of MPEG-2 for similar picture quality levels. The Blu-ray standard mandates inclusion of H.264 decoding in consumer players. Details are found in *H.264 video compression,* on page 537.

AVC-Intra

An I-frame-only specialization of H.264 has been intro-duced for professional video acquisition and produc-tion, called *AVC-Intra.* Ten-bit vIdeo in *720p, 1080i,* or *1080p*24 format is compressed to data rates of 50 Mb/s or 100 Mb/s.

In *AVC-Intra 50,* 1920×1080 images are subsampled to 1440×1080, 4:2:0 prior to compression; H.264 Hi10P Intra profile at level 4 is used. 1280×720 images are subsampled to 960×720; 4:2:0; H.264 level 3.2 is used.

AVC-Intra 100 codes 1280×720 and 1920×1080 natively, uses 4:2:2 chroma subsampling, and codes to H.264 Hi422P Intra profile at level 4.1.

WM9, WM10, VC-1 codecs

SMPTE 421M, *VC-1 Compressed Video Bitstream Format and Decoding Process.*

SMPTE RP 227, *VC-1 Bitstream Transport Encodings.*

SMPTE RP 228, *VC-1 Decoder and Bitstream Conformance.*

Microsoft developed a series of video codecs culmi-nating in Windows Media Video versions 9 and 10 (WMV9 and WMV10). These codecs are conceptually similar to – but differ in detail from – H.264. Microsoft submitted the WMV9 codec to SMPTE, where with slight changes it was standardized as VC-1 (corre-sponding to Windows Media Video 9 – WMV9 or WM9 – Studio profile).

Microsoft developed a proprietary implementation of an encoder and decoder for WM9 (and its successor, Windows Media Video 10). The VC-1 specification was used to produce a "clean-room" implementation of a decoder whose reference source code is publicly available.

The Blu-ray standard mandates VC-1 decoding capability in consumer players, and hundreds of Blu-ray discs were mastered using VC-1. If you're developing Blu-ray players, you'll need to implement VC-1 decoding. However, Microsoft stopped development of the system. VC-1 is now moribund, and VC-1 will not be discussed further here.

Compression for CE acquisition

Traditional consumer electronics equipment has been hardware-based. Two video compression schemes dominate CE today: the HDV scheme, based upon MPEG-2, and the AVCHD scheme, based upon H.264. However, delivery of video across IP networks for display on PCs now has huge economic importance. In a few moments, I'll discuss compression technologies optimized for IP transport and software-based decoding.

HDV

HDV – high definition video, presumably – refers to a compression system suitable for consumer electronic equipment. Long-GoP interframe MPEG-2 compression is used, with $Y'C_BC_R$ 8-bit 4:2:0 video at several different frame rates.

720*p* HDV (sometimes called *HDV1*) offers frame rates of 25, 30, 50, or 60 Hz, has an image structure of 1280×720 with 4:2:0 chroma subsampling, compresses according to MP@HL, and records an MPEG-2 transport stream (TS) with a short (6-frame) GoP at a data rate of about 19 Mb/s.

1080*i* HDV at 25 Hz or 29.97 Hz (sometimes called *HDV2*) downsamples to 1440×1080 with 4:2:0 chroma subsampling, compresses according to MP@H14, and records a packetized elementary stream (PES) with a long (15-frame) GoP at a data rate of about 25 Mb/s. The luma sample rate is 55.6875 MHz – three-quarters of the studio-standard 74.25 MHz rate.

HDV accommodates MPEG-1 Layer II stereo audio. Consumer camcorders are available using MiniDV cassette media, hard drive media, and flash media.

AVCHD

A specialization of H.264 for consumer use is called *AVCHD*. AVCHD compresses 720*p*, 1080*i*, and 1080*p*24 video using long-GoP H.264 coding, to bit rates between about 6 Mb/s and 18 Mb/s. Dolby Digital audio coding is used. AVCHD has been adapted to semi-professional use for recording on 12 cm DVD-R media, SDHC flash memory cards, or hard disk drives.

Compression for IP transport to consumers

The proliferation of personal computers, notebook computers, handheld devices, and tablets, most having WiFi connection and all able to execute software-based video decompression, has led to software-based codec implementations having performance beyond MPEG-2.

Apple has invested in, and has widely deployed, H.264 codecs. H.264 was outlined earlier in this chapter, and is detailed in Chapter 48 on page 537.

Google prefers WebM, to be outlined below.

There is a handful of proprietary codecs in this application domain, including RealPlayer and Adobe Flash Video. (Recent Flash players include H.264 decoding.)

VP8 ("WebM") codec

www.webmproject.org

In 2010, Google acquired a company called On2 that had, over a decade or more, developed a series of proprietary software-based codecs for video distribution. Google released the VP8 codec as open-source, and introduced the *WebM* system for web (IP-based) distribution of video to consumers. WebM comprises video encoded by the VP8 codec and audio encoded by the *Vorbis* codec, both wrapped in the *Matroska* file wrapper. Google's motivation is to avoid paying royalties – and to avoid having its customers pay royalties – on MPEG-2 or H.264 intellectual property (patent) licences.

Dirac (basic)

Dirac seems to be the BBC's preferred designation for the long-GoP wavelet codec intended for use in video distribution. Here we use the qualifier *basic* to distinguish it from Dirac PRO (see page 151).

Basic Dirac is a long-GoP motion-compensated interframe wavelet codec developed by the BBC and its partners. It has been widely deployed by the BBC for SD distribution between 2–4 Mb/s and for HD distribution between 15–18 Mb/s.

DIGITAL VIDEO AND HD ALGORITHMS AND INTERFACES

Streams and files 17

A file is an ordered sequence of bytes explicitly having a start and an end, characterized by storage. A stream is characterized by realtime data transfer of unbounded duration on a unidirectional channel – that is, with no upstream channel for flow control, acknowledgement, or retransmission request. Table 17.1 provides a general summary of the characteristics of files and streams.

A file ...	A stream ...
... has predefined beginning and end	... has indeterminate beginning and end
... usually involves storage media	... usually involves an external data interconnect
... permits "random access" to data	... involves sequential data access, typically starting midstream
... has structure imposed at a high level; data is arranged arbitrarily	... has structure imposed at a low level; data is arranged to minimize buffering
... has no need for embedded delimiters	... contains embedded delimiters by which essence elements can be identified "on the fly"
... transfer usually occurs across a general-purpose network	... transfer usually occurs across a data interconnect
... transfer is usually free-running	... transfer is usually synchronized to a timing reference
... transfer typically has variable data (bit) rate (VBR)	... transfer typically has constant data (bit) rate (CBR)
... transfer data integrity is guaranteed, but data transfer rate isn't (best effort)	... transfer data rate is guaranteed, but data integrity isn't (errors may intrude)
... transfer typically involves upstream communication; transfers are generally acknowledged	... transfer typically has no upstream communication; transfers are generally not acknowledged

Table 17.1 **Files and streams** are compared.

A stream is "live," and suitable for realtime interface. A file is not intrinsically "live." A file may be operated on or exchanged slower than realtime, in realtime, or faster than realtime. A portion of a stream can be recorded as a file, and a file can be streamed across an interface; however, generally, streams are structured for realtime use across interfaces and files are structured for nonrealtime use on storage media. Generally, video interfaces (and videotape recorders) are characterized as streams; video storage is characterized as files.

Historical overview

Video signals were historically conceived as streams. VTRs recorded continuous streams (traditionally omitting the vertical blanking interval, and in DVTRs, omitting the horizontal blanking intervals as well).

A stream interface conveys elements (analogous to historical analog video sync) that permit synchronization on the fly: A receiver can connect to a stream at any time, and begin operation within a fraction of a second. Stream formats are designed to have a property of locality whereby essence elements to be presented simultaneously – typically, video and the associated audio – are located nearby in the stream, so as to bound the required buffer storage capacity, and to bound latency to access the essence required for presentation.

Historically, uncompressed digital video was streamed in the studio in realtime across SDI or HD-SDI interfaces. SDI and HD-SDI timing was designed such that analog video could be obtained simply by stripping off the stream synchronization and ancillary elements, performing digital-to-analog conversion, and inserting analog sync. Almost no buffer storage was required.

As digital recording and playback of compressed digital video became possible, the SDTI specialization of SDI was designed to "wrap" compressed video, then audio, for conveyance across SDI. Various compression schemes such as MPEG IMX and DV100 were accommodated. DV video can be conveyed in streaming mode across IEEE 1394 interfaces.

As computing and networking technology advanced, it became feasible to store compressed video, then uncompressed video, in files. It became common to exchange these files across TCP/IP Ethernet networks – first at 100 Mb/s, then 1 Gb/s, and soon, 10 Gb/s.

As commodity IT networking technology improved, the schemes that were used to package compressed video for transport across specialized interfaces such as SDTI were adapted to general-purpose networking. Compressed video in formats such as MPEG IMX and DV100 were stored in files as raw bytestreams. The MXF file format emerged as a mechanism to store video and audio essence in a more structured manner. Standards emerged to store compressed video in MXF files. An MXF file need not contain essence: It can refer to essence stored in separate files. Some formats for A/V storage in MXF files are "stream-friendly" in the sense that video and audio essence is stored in the MXF file in proximity to each other, suitable for playout with a minimum of restructuring. Other formats have higher-level structure more suitable to postproduction (for example, storing video and audio in separate files referred to by the main MXF file).

Today, file-based workflows are widely used in production and postproduction; however, stream-based techniques continue to dominate distribution of professionally produced content. Services such as YouTube, Hulu, and Netflix distribute video to consumers across what I call the big wooly internet – however, service and quality levels of these systems are lower than those associated with television broadcasting: The pictures aren't at HD quality level. They stutter, and the audio loses sync. *Internet-protocol television* (IPTV) refers to adaptations of commodity TCP/IP-based networking to achieve the service and quality levels of broadcasting.

In professional video distribution, the file-based production/postproduction world and the stream-based distribution world meet at the playout server. The playout server includes a disk store with an associated file system. On the production side, the server is accessed asynchronously using IT networking. On the distribution side, a stream access mechanism reads files according to a timeline driven by house sync and time-code, and throttles playback accordingly. Realtime decompression of compressed video may be required. Dedicated stream interfaces then launch the content into the distribution network.

The Apple iTunes model differs: Files are transferred for later playback.

Physical layer

Serial digital video SDI and HD-SDI interfaces are based upon 10-bit words that are serialized, "scrambled," then conveyed unidirectionally as a bitstream onto a single wire. The scrambling technique permits payload data transfer rate to equal the bit rate on the wire; however, signalling sync requires certain data values to be prohibited from appearing in video.

Commodity computer interfaces are based upon 8-bit bytes. Historically, data was serialized onto a single conductor (e.g., Ethernet); however, a number of computer-oriented interfaces (e.g., PCIe and Thunderbolt) serialize data onto multiple "lanes." In some physical interfaces, data is typically mapped – for example, using the 8b/10b scheme – so that all 8-bit byte values can be conveyed across the interface, while allowing the receiver to recover the clock and the data framing for arbitrary data. The bit rate in the channel of such encodings is somewhat higher than the payload rate – in the case of 8b/10b mapping, 1.25 times higher. Other interfaces (e.g., DVI and HDMI) use a dedicated clock wire to establish timing; arbitrary data can then be serialized and transferred without data value restrictions. Some interfaces reverse the direction of data transfer across each conductor (or pair); others have dedicated wires (or pairs) in each direction.

Stream interfaces

SDI, HD-SDI

SDI was designed for uncompressed 4:2:2 SD; it has a data rate of 270 Mb/s. (SDI was adapted to SDTI for compressed video; however, SDTI is now largely obsolete.) HD-SDI was designed for uncompressed 4:2:2 HD; it has a data rate of about 1.5 Gb/s. Recently, a 3 Mb/s adaptation of HD-SDI has been standardized and commercialized. Details are found in SDI and HD-SDI interfaces, on page 429.

DVI, HDMI, and DisplayPort

DVI, HDMI, and *DisplayPort* are digital interfaces designed for connection of computer graphics subsystems to displays, across cables at lengths up to 3 m. Apart from a very low-rate reverse channel – *display data channel,* DDC – that communicates display characteristics upstream to the graphics subsystem, DVI and HDMI are unidirectional.

DIGITAL VIDEO AND HD ALGORITHMS AND INTERFACES

Thunderbolt

The Thunderbolt logo depicts lightning, not thunder! The trademark is registered to Intel.

MPEG-2

IEEE 1394, *Standard for a High Performance Serial Bus*.

Thunderbolt refers to a bidirectional interface designed by Intel (apparently in collaboration with Apple). The scheme is intended to connect a computer and its peripheral devices; it achieves a data rate of about 10 Gb/s in each direction, and drives cables up to 3 m. Thunderbolt links can be daisy-chained. Display-Port predates Thunderbolt; nevertheless, DisplayPort (with a Mini DisplayPort connector) is a specialization of Thunderbolt in which – apart from a very low-speed reverse channel to implement DDC – the data flow is unidirectional. A Thunderbolt link is capable of carrying two uncompressed 1080*p*60 *R'G'B'* signal sets. Data flow across Thunderbolt is organized into packets; data exchange is based upon the protocols of PCI Express (PCIe), a commodity computer interface.

Part 2, *Systems,* of the MPEG-2 specification defines two multiplexing schemes. An MPEG-2 *program stream* is a multiplexing scheme appropriate for one program stored on or conveyed across relatively error-free media; an MPEG-2 *transport stream* is a multiplexing scheme appropriate for one or more programs stored on or conveyed across relatively error-prone media. Both of these schemes are outlined in MPEG-2 storage and transport, on page 555. They are generally appropriate for distribution, but not for acquisition or production. (An exception is Sony's MPEG IMX scheme for SD, whose I-B frame structure and fairly high data rate enable use in production.)

IEEE 1394 (FireWire, i.LINK)

In 1995, the IEEE standardized a general-purpose high-speed serial bus capable of connecting up to 63 devices in a tree-shaped network through point-to-point connections. The link conveys data across two shielded twisted pairs (STP), and operates at 100 Mb/s, 400 Mb/s, or 800 Mb/s. Each point-to-point segment is limited to 4.5 m; there is a limit of 72 m across the breadth of a network. Asynchronous and isochronous modes are provided; the latter accommodates realtime traffic. Apple computer refers to the interface by their trademark *FireWire*. Sony's trademark is *i.LINK*.

Though not practical for uncompressed video, IEEE 1394 has performance and features that make it highly practical for compressed video streams, particularly DV.

The standard 6-pin connector provides power for peripheral devices. Sony commonly uses a 4-pin connector not compliant with the IEEE standard. A node may have either 4-pin or 6-pin connectors. Power is absent from the 4-pin connector; many people find the 4-pin connector to be mechanically flimsy.

IEC 61883-1, *Consumer audio/video equipment – Digital interface – Part 1: General.* See also parts 2 through 5.

IEC has standardized the transmission of digital video over IEEE 1394. Video is digitized according to BT.601, then motion-JPEG coded (using the DV standard) at about 25 Mb/s; this is colloquially known as 1394/DV25 (or DV25-over-1394). DV coding has been adapted to 100 Mb/s for HD (DV100); a standard for DV100-over-1394 has been adopted by IEC.

HTTP live streaming (HLS)

http: hypertext transfer protocol

Apple has introduced a streaming adaptation of the *http* protocol that was devised for the World Wide Web. The scheme has aspects of stream transfer and aspects of file transfer.

The playlist is an Extended M3U Playlist file, either an .m3u file encoded in US-ASCII or an .m3u8 file encoded in UTF-8.

The server segments programs into a sequence of media files each having short playback duration, typically a small integer number of seconds, 10 or so. Typically, a segment is represented by several media files containing the same program material coded at different bit rates. Each media file is an MPEG-2 transport stream including a program association table (PAT) and a program mapping table (PMT); these alllow stream decoding to start at any segment without requiring access to any earlier segment.

The server also prepares a playlist (index) file that associates time offsets to a set of filenames (actually, URLs) of media files along with their associated bit rates and sequence numbers. The playlist file can be gzip-compressed.

gzip: Gnu zip, a lossless data compression technique

The client establishes the bit rate that it expects to be sustained, then accesses the playlist file to establish the filenames of the content at the desired time and the desired bit rate. The client issues an http request for the named file, and plays it.

There is no predetermined bound on program length: The server is free to add additional media files, and (atomically) update the playlist file accordingly. To continue playing, at some suitable time before that file has played out (making provision for estimated latencies), a request is issued for the next file in the playlist. The client can dynamically switch between different bit rates as required by network performance. Random access and "trick" mode access is permitted.

Audio-only files are accommodated. Provisions are made for encryption.

The scheme is called *live* streaming. For a truly live "broadcast," the playlist file can contain as few as three segments, with clients accessing segments according to their time of joining and their data rate requirements. The playlist file is updated every few seconds, appending and removing media files as necessary. There is a certain latency in access – typically several seconds, much longer than the typical latency of a live television broadcast using MPEG-2. There's no requirement for content to be "live": All of the segments of a show can be present in the playlist file; a playlist can be appended to as a program proceeds, with older segments being retained.

All data – both playlist files and media files – is transferred using normal web protocols on port 80: The upstream http GET request for a playlist file looks like a request for a web page, and the downstream transfer of a media file looks like transfer of an admittedly large web page. Router, proxy, and firewall issues are rare.

HTTP live streaming is implemented in Mac OS X and in iPhones.

A comparable scheme called *dynamic adaptive streaming over http* (DASH) is in the process of being standardized by ISO/IEC MPEG.

Metadata   18

This chapter differs in tone from other chapters in this book. I'm a skeptic concerning metadata.

You know you're in trouble when the Wikipedia page for *Metadata* starts "The term metadata is an ambiguous term …" [accessed 2011-10-18].

Metadata presents problems – therefore opportunities, therefore commercial activities, therefore products. However, in my view the video industry hasn't achieved a sufficiently broad understanding of the deep principles of metadata that any general approach can be set out.

Consider an audio file, storing 200 million audio sample pairs at 44.1 kHz representing a performance of Beethoven's Symphony No. 9, *Choral.* To recreate that sound approximating the way it was experienced by the original audience, you'll need to know the sample rate.

The sample rate could be provided in a paper document, perhaps a standard. To enable general purpose decoders and players, it makes sense to encode sample rate in the file, perhaps in the file header.

Is such an encoded sample rate *data* or *metadata?*

I argue that it's *data,* because the intended auditory experience cannot be attained without knowing it.

You may feel that this example – call it Example 0 – is contrived and irrelevant. Let me present five further examples. Example 1 is conceptually a small step from Example 0; we proceed (with increasing complexity and increasing relevance to professional video) to Example 5, which concerns a highly topical issue in video engineering. I claim that Example 5 exhibits the same philosophical dilemma as Example 0:

What's *data,* and what's *metadata?*

While this dilemma persists, a chapter entitled *Metadata* must ask questions instead of providing answers.

Metadata Example 1: CD-DA

CD-DA was defined by the Sony and Philips "Red Book," which IEC subsequently standardized as IEC 60908.

After a few years, the CD proponents adopted the *CD Text* standard, augmenting the Red Book to allow recording text-based metadata. But by then it was too late.

Today some people would call the table of contents *technical metadata*. I consider it to be data: Without the ToC, the user cannot put the system to its intended use – playing songs.

CD-DA abbreviates *compact disc-digital audio.* CD-DA was conceived by Philips and Sony to store hi-fi digital stereo audio at 16 bits per sample and 44.1 kHz sample rate (that is, a data rate of about 1.5 Mb/s) on optical media having capacity of about 660 MB.

The original "Red Book" specification for CD-DA did not include any provision for album title, artist name, song titles, liner notes, or any other text information. This information was printed on the CD jacket; apparently Sony and Philips thought that providing such information in digital form would be redundant! The CD format not only lacked the metadata but also lacked any provisions for a unique ID.

The recorded CD-DA media did – of necessity – include a table of contents giving track count, track start times, and track durations (to $^1/_{75}$ s accuracy). The audiophile and software engineer Ti Kan realized that this information could be "hashed" into a 32-bit number and treated as an ersatz unique ID. As CDs became popular, Kan (assisted by Steve Scherf) created the CDDB service, a database to store community-contributed metadata associated with their codes. CDDB was originally a community-driven service, but became a commercial entity – first CDDB, Inc. (in 1995), then Gracenote (in 2000, acquired by Sony in 2008).

So, CD albums have metadata – but not reliably sourced by, or under direct control of, content creators.

The lesson for the system designer is this: What constitutes "data" and what constitutes "metadata" is coloured by your view of the boundaries of your system. Sony and Philips apparently thought of the CD system as distributing prerecorded digital audio. Today, we think of the CD system as distributing music to consumers. There's a subtle difference that changes the notion of what's data and what's metadata.

When the MP3 audio compression system was created, the developers made provisions for ID3 tags to convey metadata sourced by the content creators.

ITU-R BR.1352-2, *Broadcast Wave Format (BWF).*

The BWF file format commonly used for broadcast audio includes a "parameter" called *nSamplesPerSec* giving the sample rate. The parameter is carried in a "BWF Metadata Chunk." Is the sample rate metadata?

Metadata Example 2: .yuv files

The ".yuv" file format was introduced by Abekas in the late 1980s to store uncompressed video. Given samples of 8-bit $Y'C_BC_R$, 4:2:2 interlaced video in raster order, the file format definition is essentially as follows:

> Store successive image rows, where each row is a sequence of 4-byte elements $[C_{B_0}, Y_0', C_{R_0}, Y_1']$ where subscript 0 signifies an even-numbered luma sample location and subscript 1 signifies odd.

There is no header in a .yuv file – in particular, there is no provision for storing the count of frames, image rows, or image columns. The format was introduced to store 720×480 video. Later, it was applied to 720×576. It could potentially be applied to 720×481, 720×483, 720×486, or 704×480. It has been used in the codec research community for 1280×720p and 1920×1080i.

Consider the reading of .yuv files constrained to be 720×480 or 720×576. Most of the time the format can be determined by dividing the file's bytecount by 1440, then dividing by 480 and 576 in turn to see which quotient is an integer. But that approach doesn't always work. For example, a 4,147,200-byte file could be six frames of 480i or five frames of 576i.

Reliable file interpretation is attained only by agreement between sender and receiver – or expressed more properly in terms of files, between writer and reader – that is, *outside* the scope of transfer of the file itself.

Imagine extending the .yuv file format by prepending a file header comprising three 32-bit words: a count of the number of frames, a count of the number of image rows, and a count of the number of image columns. Is the header data or metadata? If your "system" is defined in advance as being 480i, then the counts in the header are inessential, auxiliary information – call it metadata. But if your "system" is multiformat, then the counts are most certainly *data*, because reliable interpretation of the image portion of the file is impossible without the numbers in the header.

The conclusion is this: What comprises "metadata" depends upon what you consider to be your "system." The larger, more inclusive, and more general your system – the less you depend upon context – the more your metadata turns into data.

Metadata Example 3: RFF

See *2-3 pulldown*, on page 405.

Since about 1953, a dominant source of television content has been movies – first on photochemical film, then in digital form. For more than half a century, movies have been intended for display at a frame rate of 24 Hz. The expedient solution to match movie frame rate to the historical 59.94 Hz field rate of North American television is to slow the movie to 23.976 Hz, then impose *2-3 pulldown* whereby successive movie frames are displayed twice, then three times, twice, then three times, and so on. A certain degree of motion stutter results, but is not objectionable to consumers. Certain video frames – *M-frames,* see Figure 34.1 on page 405 – comprise fields from two different movie frames.

In about 1990 it became feasible for consumer television receivers to eliminate the display twitter artifact of interlaced display by deinterlacing (by digital means) and displaying frames at 59.94 Hz. Owing to the prevalence of "film" material, deinterlacing required detection and treatment of the M-frames.

The technique adopted compares elements of the image data of successive video fields to see if a 2-3 pattern can be discerned. If a sustained 2-3 sequence is detected, then the source is presumed to be 24 Hz; frames are assembled accordingly. As CE technology progressed, receivers became more and more dependent upon such algorithms, to the point today that a high-quality digital television processor chip may dedicate a hundred thousand gates to the task. The problem is that implementations aren't necessarily reliable, and different implementations aren't consistent.

The problem arose at a time when broadcasting of "line 21" closed caption data was becoming commonplace, transmitting roughly 16 bits per field. The 2-3 problem could have been nipped in the bud by including one bit per field signalling the film pulldown.

The MPEG-2 system accommodates 24 Hz material through the *repeat first field* (RFF) flag conveyed in the Picture Coding Extension. The flag causes the first decoded field of a field pair to be repeated. MPEG-2's RFF can be considered a metadata "hint": Satisfactory performance is obtained ignoring it, but improved performance is obtained by using it.

Metadata Example 4: JPEG/JFIF

JFIF mandates $Y'C_BC_R$ with BT.601 luma-chroma matrixing; however, 4:2:0 chroma subsampling in JFIF is sited interstitially both horizontally and vertically, unlike BT.601.

At its inception, the JPEG committee decided to avoid colour space wars: Its scope was established as compressing and decompressing image data, without concern for what colours the data represented. They accommodated one-channel greyscale image data, three-channel image data such as *RGB*, and four-channel image data such as *CMYK*. Chroma subsampling was recognized as providing a big compression gain – a 2:1 factor in the case of 4:2:0 – so allowance was made to enable luma-chroma encoding as a preprocessing step.

JPEG development culminated before the World Wide Web emerged – JPEG's original target application was colour facsimile! The founders expected that system integrators would make provisions outside JPEG for reliable colour transfer. However, JPEG was rapidly adopted as a method of *exchanging* colour images in files, not just compressing them.

HAMILTON, ERIC (1992), *JPEG File Interchange Format*, Version 1.02 (Milpitas, Calif.: C-Cube Microsystems). This informal document was endorsed by ECMA, who made slight modifications and in June 2009 published ECMA TR/98 having the same title.

It became clear to a JPEG proponent, C-Cube, that confusion regarding colour spaces in the *exchange* of JPEG files threatened to inhibit commercialization. C-Cube quickly drafted a document (paper metadata) defining a file format called *JFIF*, stating that image data was to be coded in the $Y'C_BC_R$ colour space of BT.601 (but without the footroom and headroom). JFIF is clear on the arithmetic. However, implementation according to JFIF calls for a C_B/C_R reference range of ±128, that is, 257 integers – but 8-bit coding permits only 256 values! Meeting the specification produces grey having noninteger C_B and C_R values; decoded grey is bound to be coloured. Implementations (particularly the widely used *libjpeg*) use the standard scale factors but clip the C_B/C_R range to +127, thereby clipping pure blue and pure red.

To use JFIF for BT.709 HD $Y'C_BC_R$, to conform to the standard you must recode to $^{601}Y'C_BC_R$, compress, transfer, decompress, and finally recode to $^{709}Y'C_BC_R$.

JFIF explicitly mandates the BT.601 luma-chroma matrix. BT.601 says nothing of primaries, and JFIF does *not* say what primaries are intended. JFIF was embraced by the computer industry at exactly the time that the sRGB standard was being formulated using BT.709 primaries. In practice, JFIF uses BT.709 primaries.

The JFIF specification states, "RGB components calculated by linear conversion from YCbCr shall not be gamma corrected (gamma = 1.0)." This passage does *not* mean that linear-light components are encoded; instead, *decoding* is intended to conform to BT.601

practice, which (after $Y'C_BC_R$-to-$R'G'B'$ dematrixing) imposes a 2.4-power function on $R'G'B'$ components to produce display tristimulus values.

So, we have the following mess:

• The spec says "BT.601 $Y'C_BC_R$" but contrary to BT.601, and for no good reason, "full-swing" is used.

• The spec says C_B and C_R values range ±128, a range unattainable in 8-bit integer arithmetic. Implementations cope by clipping pure blue and pure red.

• The spec says "gamma = 1.0," but the intention is clearly not linear-light coding. The spec is otherwise silent on "gamma," but a 2.4-power law EOCF is implicit.

• The spec says "BT.601," evidently taking that to define colour primaries, but BT.601 is silent on colour primaries. In practice, the primaries of BT.709 are used.

You may be thinking, "this is just a story about a poorly written specification for paper metadata, and about nonconformant implementations." That assessment is mainly correct. The next example is analagous – but brings the poorly conceived metadata into the professional video data stream.

Metadata Example 5: Sequence display extension

Here I describe aspects of MPEG-2's sequence display extension. Identical metadata is conveyed in H.264's Annex E, *Video usability information* (VUI).

In a manner roughly comparable with MPEG-2's RFF flag, MPEG-2's sequence display extension provides a decoder with information concerning how the image data is intended to be displayed. The standard provides (in printed form, as paper metadata) tables giving RGB primary chromaticities (*color primaries*), transfer functions (*transfer characteristics*), and luma-chroma matrices (*matrix coefficients*). The bitstream conveys enumerated codes that serve as indexes into these tables. The same scheme is adopted in H.264. The tables (simplified, and augmented with my annotations) are summarized in Tables 18.1, 18.2, and 18.3.

DeMarsh, LeRoy E. (1993), "TV display phosphors/primaries: Some history," in *SMPTE J.* **102** (12): 1095–1098.

Color primaries code 4 designates NTSC 1953 primaries. As far as I am aware, no extant recorded video material uses those primaries; they had been abandoned before the introduction of the first VTR. A bitstream containing that value is nonsensical: If the code is encountered, it ought to be ignored by all decoders. (A well-meaning technician may have set the code thinking, "I'm broadcasting NTSC; this is the only setting that says NTSC; I'd better use it.")

Code	Interpretation
0	Forbidden
1	**BT.709**
2	Unspecified
3	Reserved/future
4	BT.470-6/NTSC 1953
5	EBU Tech. 3213
6	SMPTE RP 145
7	SMPTE 240M
8	"Generic film"

Table 18.1 *Color primaries*. Entries shaded in red are obsolete; the NTSC 1953 entry is utterly obsolete. Codes 5 and 6 are unsuitable for HD. Code 8 "Generic film" (shaded in magenta) is inscrutable. No matter which code you place in the bitstream at encoding, your material will almost certainly be presented with BT.709 primaries (bolded).

Code	Interpretation
0	Forbidden
1	**BT.709**
2	Unspecified
3	Reserved/future
4	Display gamma 2.2†
5	Display gamma 2.8†
6	BT.709
7	SMPTE 240M
8	Linear
9	Log (10^2:1)
10	Log ($10^{2.5}$:1)
11	xvYCC
12	BT.1361
13 ... 255	Reserved

Table 18.2 *Transfer characteristics*. Where MPEG says *display gamma*, read *EOCF;* these entries are flagged†. All other entries define an *OECF.* Entries shaded magenta are impractical. The two codes in green-shaded rows have identical interpretations.

Code	Interpretation
0	Forbidden/GBR
1	**BT.709**
2	Unspecified
3	Reserved/future
4	BT.601
5	BT.601
6	BT.601
7	SMPTE 240M
8	$Y'C_GC_O$
9 ... 255	Reserved

Table 18.3 *Matrix coefficients*. The three enumerations in the green-shaded rows have identical interpretation. The GBR entry, in H.264's VUI, is for coding *R'G'B'* 4:4:4.

MPEG and H.264 have the pervasive conceptual model that only bitstreams and decoders are standardized. A compliant encoder emits only legal bistreams. Apart from that, no aspect of the encoder is standardized. So, *transfer characteristics* should be specified as EOCFs, not OECFs!

Concerning transfer functions (Table 18.2), MPEG-2 fails to distinguish OECF from EOCF; the table contains both. Duplicate codes are provided for BT.709. Code 5, display gamma 2.8, is never used in practice, even in Europe (where other standards mention 2.8). A linear transfer function, code 8, will give unacceptable picture quality when used with fewer than about 14 bits per component. The logarithmic encodings are unworkable: Either of these encodings would clip low-luminance colours in a manner objectionable to consumers.

Concerning the luma-chroma matrix (Table 18.3), the BT.601 setting is triplicated for no good reason.

These tables exemplify what I call the encyclopedic approach to metadata: All the possibilities are collected without regard for practical use cases; no guidance is offered concerning how to encode metadata or how to decode it.

APPLE, INC. (2011), *QuickTime File Format Specification* (July): 141.

Issues with SDE metadata must be handled by software developers. Here's what Apple says concerning the duplicate BT.709 codes in *transfer characteristics:*

> QuickTime writers should map [code] 6 to 1 when converting from *transfer_characteristics* …

MPEG cites the ITU-R document incorrectly: The cited document is a *Report* (Rep.), not a *Recommendation* (Rec.).

The MPEG-2 specification cites ITU-R Rec. BT.470-6. Concerning that reference, Apple writes,

> This information is both incomplete and obsolete.

We could add, "erroneous."

In the light of all this confusion, how should an encoder be configured?

• For SD material, set the primaries to EBU 3213 for 576*i* material and to SMPTE RP 145 for 480*i* material; set *transfer characteristics* to BT.709 and *matrix coefficients* to BT.601.

• For HD, declare BT.709 everywhere in the SDE. A problem for ATSC encoders is that North American HD material is almost all mastered with SMPTE RP 145 primaries, and you're tempted to declare that; however, ATSC specifications call for BT.709 primaries, and virtually all consumer receivers display with BT.709 primaries. My suggestion is to declare BT.709, for two reasons: to be ATSC compliant, and to prepare for the future when regional primary sets are relics of that past.

What should a decoder do?

• For SD formats, if BT.709 is declared for *color primaries,* it's probably intended and should be respected; otherwise, expect EBU 3213 for 576*i* material and SMPTE RP 145 for 480*i* material. Any other code is nonsensical and should be treated as BT.709. Treat *transfer characteristics* as BT.709 no matter what is declared. Expect *matrix coefficients* to be BT.601; BT.709 could potentially be correct but should be treated with suspicion. Any other code is almost certainly wrong.

• For HD formats, expect BT.709 across the board. Any other codes are highly suspect.

I summarize these recommendations for decoder processing in Tables 18.4, 18.5, and 18.6.

Code	Interpretation
0	Forbidden
1	**Respect for HD or SD**
2	Unspecified
3	Reserved/future
4	Suspect (Use code 1)
5	**Respect for SD**
6	**Respect for SD**
7	Suspect (Use code 1)
8	Suspect (Use code 1)

Table 18.4 *Color primaries* interpretation.

Code	Interpretation
0	Forbidden
1	**Respect**
2	Unspecified
3	Reserved/future
4	Use code 1
5	Use code 1
6	Replace with code 1
7	Suspect (Use code 1)
8	Suspect (Use code 1)
9	Suspect (Use code 1)
10	Suspect (Use code 1)
11	xvYCC: Implement
12	Suspect (Use code 1)
13 ... 255	Reserved

Table 18.5 *Transfer characteristics* interpretation. Code 11, xvYCC, might be used in future systems, but is highly unlikely to be encountered today.

Code	Interpretation
0	Forbidden/GBR
1	**Respect for HD**
2	Unspecified
3	Reserved/future
4	**Respect for SD**
5	**Respect for SD**
6	**Respect for SD**
7	Suspect (Use code 1)
8	$Y'C_GC_O$: Implement
9 ... 255	Reserved

Table 18.6 *Matrix coefficients* interpretation. Code 8 ($Y'C_GC_O$) might be used in future systems. I am unaware of any decoder today that will decode $Y'C_GC_O$ colour space, and no functional benefit is evident. It is highly unlikely to be encountered.

Conclusions

In the studio, MXF enables reliable coding, storage, and transport of metadata in files. ANC packets can convey metadata across HD-SDI streams; however, there are no common, widely used practices concerning how metadata is handled alongside video passed through processing equipment.

Apart from MXF files and HD-SDI ANC metadata, studio equipment has no reliable metadata system.

Migration to file-based workflows enables reliable metadata processing. However, the conceptual problems of metadata (evident in my examples 0 through 5 above) remain. I suggest these guidelines for implementing metadata systems:

• Devise metadata carefully. Have clear rules for what metadata to encode, and how to interpret metadata at decoding time. Don't be encyclopedic: "Make the system as simple as possible, but no simpler" [Einstein].

• Metadata should be inessential, otherwise it would be data: Design your system to work *without* metadata, then add metadata as augmentation.

• Strive for a design such that adding metadata never impairs the operation of the base system.

• If information is already available in data, don't duplicate it in metadata: To do so opens the possibility (at a later date) of conflicting information.

• If in a particular system design it is possible for essence to be separated from its metadata, the format chosen for essence must be able to serve its purpose in the absence of metadata.

Stereoscopic ("3-D") video   19

The term *S3D* ("ess-three-dee") distinguishes stereoscopic 3-D from imagery having depth cues (particularly, perspective) but only one view. Computer-generated imagery (CGI) produces images synthesized from scene geometry; CGI can relatively easily produce stereo views. Some people consider the term *S3D* to be redundant – that which is stereoscopic is necessarily 3D.

Stereoscopic 3-D (S3D) refers to acquisition, processing, storage, distribution, and display of imagery in two views, one intended for the left eye and one for the right. The views are typically acquired from cameras acquiring the same scene from positions a short lateral distance apart. Stereo viewing presents an illusion. Unlike viewing the real world, the views do not change when the viewer moves his or her head. Nonetheless, for very carefully crafted material, the effect can be convincing, and in some cases, can add to storytelling.

Acquisition

Two cameras are most often used; however, many other arrangements have been demonstrated such as one lens and two imagers, and two lenses and one imager.

To acquire images from a real scene in professional content creation, two cameras are typically used, each including an imager and signal processing. To produce "normal" stereo the optical axes of the cameras are displaced by the same distance the typical viewer's eyes are separated – the *interocular distance* (also known as *interpupillary distance*), which for adults is between about 52 mm and 75 mm, with a mean of about 63.5 mm (2.5 in). Various effects can be achieved by changing the interaxial distance of the cameras: setting a wide camera interaxial distance collapses depth, and upon display makes the scene look smaller than it is; setting a narrow camera interaxial distance expands depth and upon viewing magnifies the scene. Misaligned cameras can lead to viewer discomfort.

S3D display

S3D display can be achieved with a dedicated display for each eye, in the manner of the historical View-

Master. Many virtual reality systems from the 1990s and 2000s used the technique, sometimes in combination with head tracking; however, consumers are not comfortable with head-mounted display equipment! Viewing at a distance is a commercial necessity.

For normal television viewing distance of about 3 m, several schemes are in use that multiplex the two views at the display device and separate the views at each viewers' pair of eyes: anaglyph, temporal multiplexing, polarization, wavelength multiplexing, parallax barrier autostereoscopy, and lenticular autostereoscopy. These techniques are outlined in the sections to follow.

The techniques to be described are almost always used with a single "native" 2-D display (either direct view, or projector). In this case, all of the techniques have the disadvantage that at best 50% of the light of the native 2-D display is available (and frequently, much less). Consequently, stereo 3-D display systems tend to be dim.

Anaglyph

Associating red with left conforms to the nautical convention that red signifies the port (left) side.

Imagery is created placing the red component of the left view into the red primary, and the green and blue components of the right view, into the three components of what would otherwise be a 2-D video stream. (Clearly, several assumptions that enable chroma subsampling and MPEG or H.264 encoding are broken.)

The display presents the left-eye image using the red primary and the right-eye image using green and blue.

The viewer wears glasses having a colour filter over each eye. A red filter is placed over the left eye – the left eye only sees the red primary of the signal, containing the left image. A cyan filter is placed over the right eye – the right eye sees dichromatic combinations of the green and blue components of the right image. Full colour is not present for every pixel for each eye; nonetheless, the viewer's visual system largely compensates the loss (albeit with some discomfort). The red/cyan scheme is most common, but anaglyph display can use other combinations of colours.

Owing to the ease of recording and transmission using standard 2-D video infrastructure (admittedly outside of its usual assumptions), the anaglyph scheme was used sporadically for years in both cinema and television, but has mostly fallen into disuse and is now generally considered a novelty.

Temporal multiplexing

Two views can be multiplexed in time: The display operates at (at least) twice the frame rate of the imagery and alternately presents the left-eye image and the right.

The viewer wears active shuttered glasses, synchronized with the display such that the right eye is blocked while the left image is displayed and the left eye is blocked while the right image is displayed.

Shutter synchronization is typically achieved through an infrared (IR) light beam that is pulsed at the frame rate, flooding the viewing area. Each set of glasses includes an IR receiver. (Bluetooth radio frequency synchronization has been proposed.)

The scheme dominates 3-D consumer television, and has limited use in cinema (XPAND 3D).

Polarization

An excellent outline of the physics of polarized light is given in this book: REINHARD, ERIK et al. (2008), *Color Imaging: Fundamentals and Applications* (Wellesley, Mass.: A K Peters).

Many S3D display schemes involve polarized light. The simplest forms of polarization – those used commercially – are linear polarization (LP) and circular polarization (CP). The viewer wears passive polarized glasses; filters for two eyes have opposite polarizations.

Polarization can be time-multiplexed: The display operates at (at least) twice the frame rate of the imagery, and alternately presents the left-eye image (in one polarization) and the right-eye image (in the opposite polarization).

In the RealD system common in theatres, a "Z screen" is inserted in the light path at the projector, between the projection lens and the port glass. The Z screen is an electro-optical device that rapidly switches the polarity of circular polarization. The imager produces the left- and right-eye images time-sequentially; the Z screen is actuated in synchrony. (In the RealD system deployed in theatres as I write, there are three left-right cycles per $1/24$ s – that is, the display's modulator produces images at 144 Hz.) The technique has not been commercialized for direct-view displays.

Polarized projection can potentially produce both views at the same time – for example, by using a pair of projectors (or two image modulators sharing the same projection lens). However, such solutions are unpopular owing to their high cost. A single 4 K (4096×2160) projector can be adapted to display a 2 K (2048×1060) left image on the top and a like-sized right image on the bottom, then fitted with an optical device to oppositely polarize the two images and combine them for simultaneous display. The scheme has been commercialized for cinema by Sony.

In the system as commercialized, each image has 1060 rows, not 1080 as you might expect: 40 black rows lie between the two.

Polarized projection requires that the screen preserve polarization. Typical cinema screens depolarize, so "silver" – actually, aluminized – screens are used.

For direct-view displays, polarization can be accomplished by fabricating polarizers of opposite polarity over alternate image rows of the display. Obviously, in 3-D operation, vertical resolution is halved compared to the native display capability. Such a display can be used for normal 2-D viewing without glasses (though with at best 50% of the 2-D light available).

Opposite polarization of alternate image rows is typically achieved using a *film pattern retarder* (FPR).

A big advantage of polarized systems is the fact that the glasses are passive and inexpensive.

Wavelength multiplexing (Infitec/Dolby)

This technique was invented by Helmut Jorke at Daimler-Benz in Germany. The display operates at twice the frame rate of the imagery (or higher), and presents first the left-eye image, then the right, through different optical filters. The wavelength compositions of each pair (e.g., G_{LEFT} and G_{RIGHT}) are designed to be mostly nonoverlapping. The characteristics of the optical filters are compensated by signal processing to produce roughly metameric pairs – that is, although the wavelength composition of the pair of reds differ, the colours look roughly the same.

The viewer wears passive glasses, where each eye has a different optical filter roughly matching that of the projector. The left eye's filter rejects the wavelengths corresponding to R_{RIGHT}, G_{RIGHT}, and B_{RIGHT}; the right eye's filter rejects the wavelengths corresponding to R_{LEFT}, G_{LEFT}, and B_{LEFT}.

The wavelength multiplex scheme could simultaneously present left and right images. However, that mode hasn't been commercialized.

The Infitec scheme uses passive (albeit somewhat expensive) glasses, and does not require a polarization-preserving screen.

Dolby commercialized the scheme for 3-D cinema. It has not been commercialized for direct-view displays.

Autostereoscopic displays

Autostereoscopy refers to techniques that present stereoscopic imagery without the requirement for the viewer to wear glasses. Two techniques have received limited commercialization: the parallax barrier technique, and the lenticular technique.

Autostereoscopic displays typically create reasonable stereo across a small volume of the viewing space. The major problem is that the "sweet spot" is typically fairly small, and outside the sweet spot, the stereo effect is either dramatically reduced or vanishes entirely. Also, autostereoscopic displays sometimes have (unintended) viewing positions where the views are reversed, causing apparent depth inversion known as *pseudostereo*.

Parallax barrier display

Two views are displayed interleaved column-by-column on the same display surface. A short distance in front of the display lies a set of barriers that form slots through which, at normal viewing distance, alternate image columns can be viewed. The geometry of the barrier (pitch and position) is designed so that at a chosen optimal viewing location, one set of columns is visible to the left eye and the other is "shadowed" by the barrier; the situation is reversed for the right eye.

The technique has been commercialized in handheld devices (3-D cameras and cellphones).

Lenticular display

Two or more (N) views are interleaved on the display surface in N columns. A set of lenses is placed, one lenslet per N columns, over the display. The geometry of each lens is arranged to project the interleaved columns out into the space in front of the display. In the case of two views ($N = 2$), the left and right images lie in alternate beams.

Philips has demonstrated lenticular autostereoscopic display where several views ($N \approx 9$) are generated at the display by signal processing based upon a single 2-D image accompanied by a "depth map" (2-D + Z) that is encoded during postproduction or produced in graphics generation (for example, in PC gaming). The technique has had limited deployment in digital signage, but has not been commercialized for consumer use.

A depth map can fairly easily be created for CGI content, including computer games in consumers' premises. However, there is no widely available standard for conveying the depth map from the computer to the display. Depth map techniques do not directly deal with occlusion, so visual performance is limited.

Recording and compression

For a given image format (e.g., 1920×1080), S3D obtained through a pair of views obviously involves double the data rate of a single view. The challenges in transport and interface centre around the high data rate. Professional acquisition and postproduction usually involves doubling the data rate (and often doubling up the production equipment). For consumer recording and distribution, 3-D systems have been devised that use less than twice the data rate of 2-D imagery.

Many techniques have been devised to record S3D content and to transport S3D content through broadcasting distribution chains. Some distribution networks squeeze the left and right views 2:1 and abut them horizontally side-by-side (*SbS*) onto a single signal that can be conveyed through ordinary distribution networks.

The Blu-ray standard has been augmented with a mechanism to compress S3D content using the *stereo high profile* of H.264. The motion estimation and motion-compensated interpolation schemes of H.264 were devised to compactly code a sequence of images having a high degree of spatial correlation, where differences between the images are a consequence of elapsed time between their exposures. The left and right images of a stereo pair exhibit a high degree of spatial correlation, where differences between the images are a consequence of position shifts (*disparity*) induced by parallax. In typical SHP use, the right image is predicted by the left image after "motion" compensation by *disparity vectors* (comparable to motion vectors). Typical stereo can be coded at between about 1.3 or 1.6 times the data rate of 2-D imagery.

Consumer interface and display

Previous sections have discussed acquisition and display of S3D imagery. Here, we'll discuss interface to the consumer display.

HDMI version 1.4a has a mandatory *frame packing 3D* structure that packs left and right eye 1920×1080 images into a 1920×2205 "container" having 45 blanking (black) lines separating the images. There are progressive and interlaced versions.

HDMI 1.4a also describes an interface using a 1920×1080 container to convey a 960×1080 left eye

The stereo high profile is related to the *multiview profile* (MVP) of H.264: Both are documented in Appendix H of the current revision.

Some people might quote multiples as low as 1.2 or as high as 1.8.

Dave LeHoty describes his home HDMI system as "1.3a with a steenkin' asterisk," alluding to the wide variety of versions and options that makes system integration difficult for the expert, let alone for the average consumer.

DIGITAL VIDEO AND HD ALGORITHMS AND INTERFACES

image and a 960×1080 right eye image, both horizontally squeezed 2:1, abutted side-by-side (*SbS*). Horizontal resolution suffers.

Finally, HDMI 1.4a describes an interface using a 1920×1080 container to convey a 1920×540 left eye image and a 1920×540 right eye image, both vertically squeezed 2:1, abutted top-and-bottom (*TaB*). Vertical resolution suffers.

There are many schemes. Confusion abounds.

Ghosting

Most of the display techniques that I have described exhibit the problem that light intended for the left eye "leaks" into the right eye, and vice versa. You could call it "crosstalk." Image artifacts created by such unwanted light are called *ghosts*.

There are several reasons for ghosting. In most displays, generation of light in response to the video signal is not instantaneous. For example, the LCD material of LCD displays takes a certain time to respond to the drive signal; the phosphors of PDPs have a certain decay time. When LCD and PDP displays are used for 3-D display using temporal multiplexing, if the display is still decaying while the opposite shutter opens, ghosting will result. In polarized displays, the polarizers (at both the display and the glasses) typically have incomplete extinction. In the Infitec scheme, practical optical filters have a certain degree of unwanted spectral overlap.

Reduction of ghosting to tolerable levels involves compensating the image data prior to its reaching the display. (In cinema, the processing is called *ghost-busting*). If a bright left-eye image element is anticipated to leak into the right, light can be artificially subtracted from the corresponding spatial location in the right image. Compensation is necessarily imperfect, though: If the corresponding location in the right image is black, no light can be subtracted, and the crosstalk persists. In cinema, compensation can potentially be accomplished either in mastering or in the projector's signal processing. Movie creators don't want to create separate masters for each 3-D display technology, so the second option is now usual.

Vergence and accommodation

The region of the human retina intersected by the optical axis is the *fovea;* it is a cluster of tightly packed cone photoreceptor cells. The fovea has an angular diameter of about 1°; it covers a small fraction of the visual field – a few tenths of a percent of the area corresponding to an HD image at normal viewing distance.

The oculomotor system of the eye includes muscles attached to the eyeball. The muscles "steer" the optical axis of each eye so that the fovea images light from the region of interest in the visual field. A few times per second, the muscles operate and the gaze shifts to a new point; the movement is called a *saccade.*

Vergence movements ideally involve rotation of the eyeballs with respect to the plane that joins their centres.

In normal binocular viewing of an actual scene, eye movements are made such that the optical axes of both eyes meet at the depth of the scene element of interest. The oculomotor system's control of the distance at which the optical axes meet is known as *vergence.*

Presbyopia is age-related loss of accommodation owing to the lens becoming less pliant. Even for people having normal vision, presbyopia typically makes reading glasses necessary beyond age 50.

The lens of the human eye is enclosed in a capsule that is somewhat pliable: The lens can change shape. Within the eyeball, surrounding the lens, is a muscle – the *ciliary* muscle. When the muscle is in its relaxed state, the lens capsule is at its flattest; the focal length of the lens is at its maximum. As the ciliary muscle contracts, the lens capsule becomes more spherical; focal length decreases, focussing on nearer objects. Muscle control over the lens is called *accommodation;* it is analagous to focusing of a camera lens.

In normal human vision viewing real objects, the vergence and accommodation systems work in concert.

In a stereo display of the kinds that I have described, both the left and right images are formed on the display surface, and that surface is a fixed distance away from the viewer. To keep the images sharp requires accommodation to the distance of the display screen – not to the apparent distance of the object that is formed by the stereo display system. As apparent depth departs from the screen distance – either to longer distance ("behind" the screen) or closer distance ("in front of" the screen), conflict between vergence and accommodation (*V-A conflict*) is likely to be experienced subconsciously by the viewer. Researchers have proven that V-A conflict is a major contributor to viewer discomfort in stereo 3-D.

Part 2

Theory

20 Filtering and sampling 191

21 Resampling, interpolation, and decimation 221

22 Image digitization and reconstruction 237

23 Perception and visual acuity 247

24 Luminance and lightness 255

25 The CIE system of colorimetry 265

26 Colour science for video 287

27 Gamma 315

28 Luma and colour differences 335

Filtering and sampling 20

This chapter explains how a one-dimensional signal is filtered and sampled prior to A-to-D conversion, and how it is reconstructed following D-to-A conversion. In the following chapter, *Resampling, interpolation, and decimation,* on page 221, I extend these concepts to conversions within the digital domain. In *Image digitization and reconstruction,* on page 237, I extend these concepts to the two dimensions of an image.

When a one-dimensional signal (such as an audio signal) is digitized, each sample must encapsulate, in a single value, what might have begun as a complex analog waveform during the sample period. When a two-dimensional image is sampled, each sample encapsulates what might have begun as a potentially complex distribution of power over a small region of the image plane. In each case, a potentially large amount of information must be reduced to a single number.

Prior to sampling, detail within the sample interval must be discarded. The reduction of information prior to sampling is *prefiltering.* The challenge of sampling is to discard this information while avoiding the loss of information at scales larger than the sample pitch, all the time avoiding the introduction of artifacts. *Sampling theory* elaborates the conditions under which a signal can be sampled and accurately reconstructed, subject only to inevitable loss of detail that could not, in any event, be represented by a given number of samples in the digital domain.

Sampling theory was originally developed to describe one-dimensional signals such as audio, where the signal is a continuous function of the single dimension of

My explanation describes the original sampling of an analog signal waveform. If you are more comfortable remaining in the digital domain, consider the problem of shrinking a row of image samples by a factor of n (say, $n = 16$) to accomplish image resizing. You need to compute one output sample for each set of n input samples. This is the *resampling* problem in the digital domain. Its constraints are very similar to the constraints of original sampling of an analog signal.

time. Sampling theory has been extended to images, where an image is treated as a continuous function of two spatial coordinates (horizontal and vertical). Sampling theory can be further extended to the temporal sampling of moving images, where the third coordinate is time.

Sampling theorem

Assume that a signal to be digitized is well behaved, changing relatively slowly as a function of time. Consider the cosine signals shown in Figure 20.1 below, where the *x*-axis shows sample intervals. The top waveform is a cosine at the fraction 0.35 of the sampling rate f_S; the middle waveform is at $0.65f_S$. The bottom row shows that identical samples result from sampling either of these waveforms: Either of the waveforms can masquerade as the same sample sequence. If the middle waveform is sampled, then reconstructed conventionally, the top waveform will result. This is the phenomenon of *aliasing*.

Symbol conventions used in this figure and following figures are as follows:

$\omega = 2\pi f_S$
$[\text{rad} \cdot \text{s}^{-1}]$

$t_S = \dfrac{1}{f_S}$

$\cos \mathbf{0.35}\,\omega t$

$\cos \mathbf{0.65}\,\omega t$

sampled

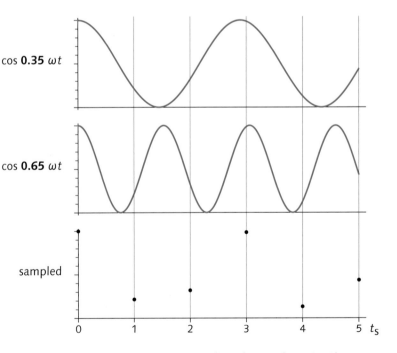

Figure 20.1 **Cosine waves less than and greater than** $0.5f_S$, in this case at the fractions 0.35 and 0.65 of the sampling rate, produce exactly the same set of sampled values when point-sampled – they *alias*.

DIGITAL VIDEO AND HD ALGORITHMS AND INTERFACES

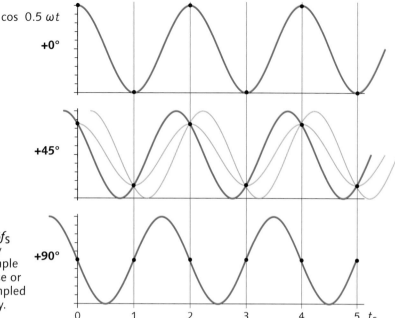

$\cos\ 0.5\,\omega t$

+0°

+45°

+90°

0   1   2   3   4   5 t_S

Figure 20.2 **Cosine waves at exactly 0.5f_S** cannot be accurately represented in a sample sequence if the phase or amplitude of the sampled waveform is arbitrary.

Nyquist essentially applied to signal processing a mathematical discovery made in 1915 by E.T. Whittaker. Later contributions were made by Claude Shannon (in the U.S.) and Aleksandr Kotelnikov (in Russia).

Sampling at exactly 0.5f_S

You might assume that a signal whose frequency is exactly half the sampling rate can be accurately represented by an alternating sequence of sample values, say, zero and one. In Figure 20.2 above, the series of samples in the top row is unambiguous (provided it is known that the amplitude of the waveform is unity). But the samples of the middle row could be generated from any of the three indicated waveforms, and the phase-shifted waveform in the bottom row has samples that are indistinguishable from a constant waveform having a value of 0.5. The inability to accurately analyze a signal at exactly half the sampling frequency leads to the strict "less-than" condition in the sampling sheorem, which I will now describe.

Harry Nyquist, at Bell Labs, published a paper in 1928 stating that to guarantee sampling of a signal without the introduction of aliases, all of the signal's frequency components must be contained strictly within half the sampling rate (now known as the *Nyquist rate*). If a signal meets this condition, it is said to satisfy the *Nyquist criterion*. The condition is usually

Figure 20.3 **Point sampling** runs the risk of choosing an extreme value that is not representative of the neighborhood surrounding the desired sample instant.

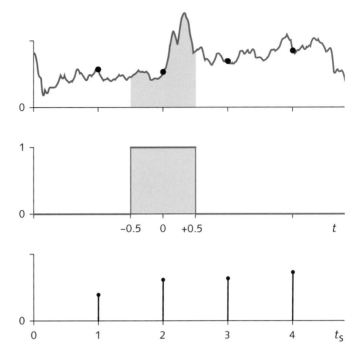

Figure 20.4 **The Box weighting function** (or "boxcar") has unity value throughout one sample interval; elsewhere, its value is zero.

Figure 20.5 **Boxcar filtering** weights the input waveform with the boxcar weighting function: Each output sample is the average across one sample interval.

imposed by analog filtering, prior to sampling, that removes frequency components at $0.5f_S$ and higher. A filter must implement some sort of integration. In the example of Figure 20.1, no filtering was performed; the waveform was simply *point-sampled*. The lack of filtering admitted aliases. Figure 20.3 represents the waveform of an actual signal; point sampling at the indicated instants yields sample values that are not representative of the local neighborhood at each sampling instant.

Perhaps the most basic way to filter a waveform is to average the waveform across each sample period. Many different integration schemes are possible; these can be represented as weighting functions plotted as a function of time. Simple averaging uses the *boxcar* weighting function sketched in Figure 20.4; its value is unity during the sample period and zero outside that interval. Filtering with this weighting function is called *boxcar* filtering, since a sequence of these functions with different amplitudes resembles the profile of a freight train. Once the weighted values are formed the signal is represented by discrete values, plotted for this example in Figure 20.5. To plot these values as

DIGITAL VIDEO AND HD ALGORITHMS AND INTERFACES

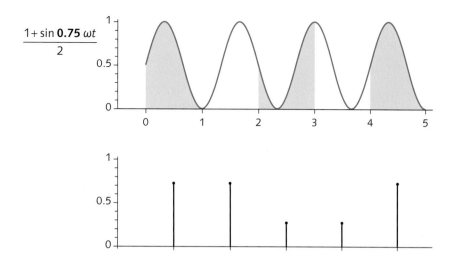

$$\frac{1+\sin \mathbf{0.75}\,\omega t}{2}$$

Figure 20.6 **Aliasing due to boxcar filtering.** The top graph shows a sine wave at $0.75f_S$. The shaded area under the curve illustrates its integral computed by a boxcar function. The bottom graph shows that the sequence of resulting sample points is dominated by an alias at $0.25f_S$.

amplitudes of a boxcar function would wrongly suggest that a boxcar function should be used as a reconstruction filter. The shading under the waveform of Figure 20.3 suggests box filtering.

A serious problem with boxcar filtering across each sample interval is evident in Figure 20.6 above. The top graph shows a sine wave at $0.75f_S$; the signal exceeds the Nyquist frequency. The shaded regions show integration over intervals of one sample period. For the sine wave at $0.75f_S$, sampled starting at zero phase, the first two integrated values are about 0.6061; the second two are about 0.3939. The dominant component of the filtered sample sequence, shown in the bottom graph, is one-quarter of the sampling frequency. Filtering using a one-sample-wide boxcar weighting function is inadequate to attenuate signal components above the Nyquist rate. An unwanted alias results.

Figure 20.6 provides another example of *aliasing:* Owing to a poor presampling filter, the sequence of sampled values exhibits a frequency component not present in the input signal. As this example shows, boxcar integration is not sufficient to prevent fairly serious aliasing.

Magnitude frequency response

To gain a general appreciation of aliasing, it is necessary to understand signals in the *frequency domain*. The previous section gave an example of inadequate filtering prior to sampling that created an unexpected alias upon sampling. You can determine whether a filter has an unexpected response at *any* frequency by presenting to the filter a signal that sweeps through all frequencies, from zero, through low frequencies, to some high frequency, plotting the response of the filter as you go. I graphed such a frequency sweep signal at the top of Figure 9.1, on page 98. The middle graph of that figure shows a response waveform typical of a low-pass filter (LPF), which attenuates high frequency signals. The magnitude response of that filter is shown in the bottom graph.

Magnitude response is the RMS average response over all phases of the input signal at each frequency. As you saw in the previous section, a filter's response can be strongly influenced by the phase of the input signal. To determine response at a particular frequency, you can test all phases at that frequency. Alternatively, provided the filter is linear, you can present just two signals – a cosine wave at the test frequency and a sine wave at the same frequency. The filter's magnitude response at any frequency is the absolute value of the vector sum of the responses to the sine and the cosine waves.

Analytic and numerical procedures called *transforms* can be used to determine frequency response. The *Laplace transform* is appropriate for continuous functions, such as signals in the analog domain. The *Fourier transform* is appropriate for signals that are sampled periodically, or for signals that are themselves periodic. A variant intended for computation on data that has been sampled is the *discrete Fourier transform* (DFT). An elegant scheme for numerical computation of the DFT is the *fast Fourier transform* (FFT). The *z-transform* is essentially a generalization of the Fourier transform. All of these transforms represent mathematical ways to determine a system's response to sine waves over a range of frequencies and phases. The result of a transform is an expression or graph in terms of frequency.

Strictly speaking, *amplitude* is an instantaneous measure that may take a positive or negative value. *Magnitude* is properly either an absolute value, or a squared or *root mean square* (RMS) value representative of amplitude over some time interval. The terms are often used interchangeably.

See *Linearity* on page 37.

Bracewell, Ronald N. (1985), *The Fourier Transform and Its Applications*, Second Edition (New York: McGraw-Hill).

DIGITAL VIDEO AND HD ALGORITHMS AND INTERFACES

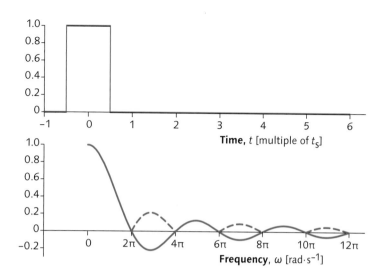

Figure 20.7 **Frequency response of a boxcar filter.** The top graph shows a boxcar weighting function, symmetrical around $t = 0$. Its frequency spectrum is a *sinc* function, shown underneath. The solid line shows that at certain frequencies, the filter causes phase inversion. Filter response is usually plotted as magnitude; phase inversion in the stopband is reflected as the absolute (magnitude) values shown in dashed lines.

$$\text{sinc } \omega = \begin{cases} 1, & \omega = 0 \\ \dfrac{\sin \pi\omega}{\pi\omega}, & \omega \neq 0 \end{cases}$$

Eq 20.1 **The sinc function** (pronounced *sink*) is defined by this equation. Its argument is in radians per second (rad·s⁻¹); here I use the conventional symbol ω for that quantity. The term (sin x)/x (pronounced *sine ecks over ecks*) is often used synonymously with sinc, without mention of the units of the argument. If applied to frequency in hertz, the function could be written (sin $2\pi f$)/$2\pi f$.

sinc is unrelated to *sync* (synchronization).

Magnitude frequency response of a boxcar

The top graph of Figure 20.7 shows the weighting function of point sampling, as a function of time (in sample intervals). The Fourier transform of the boxcar function – that is, the magnitude frequency response of a boxcar weighting function – takes the shape of (sin x)/x. The response is graphed at the bottom of Figure 20.7, with the frequency axis in units of $\omega = 2\pi f_S$. Equation 20.1 in the margin defines the function. This function is so important that it has been given the special symbol *sinc*, introduced by Phillip M. Woodward in 1952 as a contraction of *sinus cardinalis*.

A presampling filter should have fairly uniform response below half the sample rate, to provide good sharpness, and needs to severely attenuate frequencies at and above half the sample rate, to achieve low aliasing. The bottom graph of Figure 20.7 shows that this requirement is not met by a boxcar weighting function. The graph of sinc predicts frequencies where aliasing can be introduced. Figure 20.6 showed an example of a sine wave at $0.75f_S$; reading the value of sinc at 1.5 π from Figure 20.7 shows that aliasing is expected.

You can gain an intuitive understanding of the boxcar weighting function by considering that when the input frequency is such that an integer number of cycles lies under the boxcar, the response will be null. But when an integer number of cycles, plus a half-cycle, lies under the weighting function, the response will exhibit a local maximum that can admit an alias.

To obtain a presampling filter that rejects potential aliases, we need to pass low frequencies, up to almost half the sample rate, and reject frequencies above it. We need a frequency response that is constant at unity up to just below $0.5f_S$, whereupon it drops to zero. We need a filter function whose *frequency* response – not time response – resembles a boxcar.

The sinc weighting function

Remarkably, the Fourier transform possesses the mathematical property of being its own inverse (within a scale factor). In Figure 20.7, the Fourier transform of a boxcar *weighting* function produced a sinc-shaped *frequency* response. Figure 20.8 opposite shows a sinc-shaped *weighting* function; it produces a boxcar-shaped *frequency* response. So, sinc weighting gives the *ideal lowpass filter* (ILPF), and sinc is the ideal temporal weighting function for use in a presampling filter. However, there are several theoretical and practical difficulties in using sinc. In practice, we approximate it.

An analog filter's response is a function of frequency on the positive real axis. In analog signal theory, there is no upper bound on frequency. But in a digital filter the response to a test frequency f_T is identical to the response at f_T offset by any integer multiple of the sampling frequency: The frequency axis "wraps" at multiples of the sampling rate. Sampling theory also dictates "folding" around half the sample rate. Signal components having frequencies at or above the Nyquist rate cannot accurately be represented.

The temporal weighting functions used in video are usually symmetrical; nonetheless, they are usually graphed in a two-sided fashion. The frequency response of a filter suitable for real signals is symmetrical about

A near-ideal filter in analog video is sometimes called a *brick wall* filter, though there is no precise definition of this term.

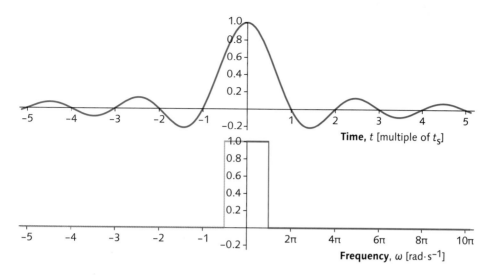

Figure 20.8 **The sinc weighting function** is shown in the top graph. Its frequency spectrum, shown underneath, has a boxcar shape: sinc weighting exhibits the ideal properties for a presampling filter. However, its infinite extent makes it physically unrealizable; also, its negative lobes make it unrealizable for transducers of light such as cameras, scanners, and displays. Many practical digital lowpass filters have coefficients that approximate samples of sinc.

zero; conventionally, frequency response is graphed in one-sided fashion starting at zero frequency ("DC"). Sometimes it is useful to consider or graph frequency response in two-sided style.

Frequency response of point sampling

The Fourier transform provides an analytical tool to examine frequency response: We can reexamine point sampling. Taking an instantaneous sample of a waveform is mathematically equivalent to using a weighting function that is unity at the sample instant, and zero everywhere else – the weighting function is an *impulse*. The Fourier transform of an impulse function is constant, unity, at all frequencies. A set of equally spaced impulses is an *impulse train;* its transform is also unity everywhere. The sampling operation is represented as multiplication by an impulse train. An unfiltered signal sampled by a set of impulses will admit aliases equally from all input frequencies.

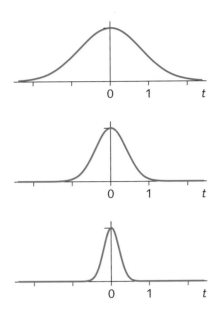

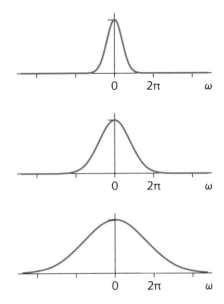

Figure 20.10 **Waveforms of three temporal extents** are shown on the left; the corresponding transforms are shown on the right. Spectral width is inversely proportional to temporal extent, not only for the Gaussians shown here, but for all waveforms.

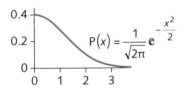

Figure 20.9 **A Gaussian function** is shown here in its one-sided form, with the scaling that is usual in statistics, where the function (augmented with mean and variance terms) is known as the *normal function*. Its integral is the *error function*, erf(x). The frequency response of cascaded Gaussian filters is Gaussian.

Fourier transform pairs

A Gaussian function – graphed in Figure 20.9 in the margin – is the identity function for the Fourier transform: It has the unique property of transforming to itself (within a scale factor). The Gaussian function has moderate spread both in the time domain and in the frequency domain; it has infinite extent, but becomes negligibly small more than a few units from the origin. The Gaussian function lies at the balance point between the distribution of power in the time domain and the distribution of power in the frequency domain.

Functions having short time durations transform to functions with widely distributed frequency components. Conversely, functions that are compact in their frequency representation transform to temporal functions with long duration. See Figure 20.10 above.

Figure 20.11 opposite shows Fourier transform pairs for several different functions. In the left column is a set of waveforms, with the Gaussian in the middle row; in the right column are the corresponding frequency spectra.

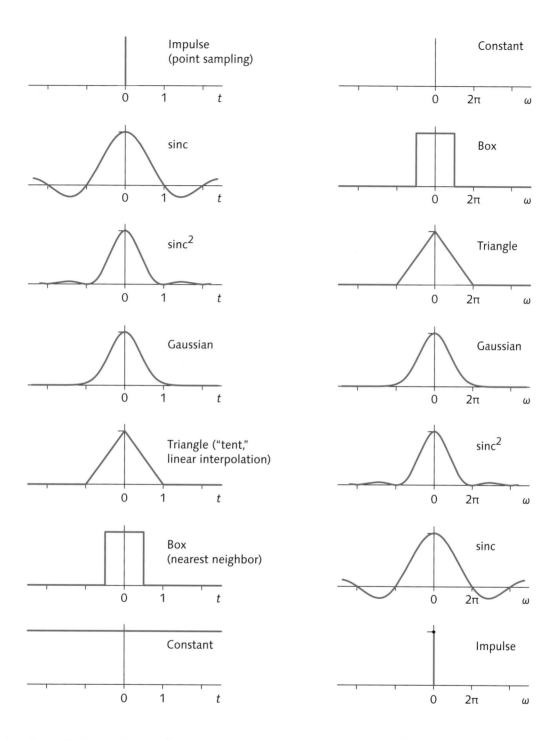

Figure 20.11 **Fourier transform pairs** for several functions are shown in these graphs. In the left column is a set of waveforms in the time domain; beside each waveform is its frequency spectrum.

Analog filters

Analog filtering is necessary prior to digitization, to bring a signal into the digital domain without aliases. I have described filtering as integration using different weighting functions; an antialiasing filter performs the integration using analog circuitry.

An analog filter performs integration by storing a magnetic field in an inductor (coil) using the electrical property of inductance (L), and/or by storing an electrical charge in a capacitor using the electrical property of capacitance (C). In low-performance filters, resistance (R) is used as well. An ordinary analog filter has an impulse response that is infinite in temporal extent.

The design of analog filters is best left to specialists.

Digital filters

Once digitized, a signal can be filtered directly in the digital domain. Design and implementation of such filters – in hardware, firmware, or software – is the domain of *digital signal processing* (DSP). Filters like the ones that I have been describing are implemented digitally by computing weighted sums of samples.

Averaging neighboring samples is the simplest form of *moving average* (MA) filter.

Perhaps the simplest digital filter is one that just sums adjacent samples; the weights in this case are [1, 1]. Figure 20.12 on the facing page shows the frequency response of such a [1, 1] filter. This filter offers minimal attenuation to very low frequencies; as signal frequency approaches half the sampling rate, the response follows a cosine curve to zero. This is a very simple, very cheap *lowpass filter* (LPF).

I have drawn in grey the filter's response from $0.5f_S$ to the sampling frequency. In a digital filter, frequencies in this region are indistinguishable from frequencies between $0.5f_S$ and 0. The gain of this filter at zero frequency (DC) is 2, the sum of its coefficients. Normally, the coefficients of such a filter are normalized to sum to unity, so that the overall DC gain of the filter is one. In this case the normalized coefficients would be [$\frac{1}{2}$, $\frac{1}{2}$]. However, it is inconvenient to call this a [$\frac{1}{2}$, $\frac{1}{2}$]-filter; colloquially, this is a [1, 1]-filter.

Digital filters can be implemented in software, firmware, or hardware. At the right side of each graph above, I show the block diagrams familiar to hardware

Figure 20.12 A [1, 1] FIR filter sums two adjacent samples; this forms a simple lowpass filter. I'll introduce the term *FIR* on page 207.

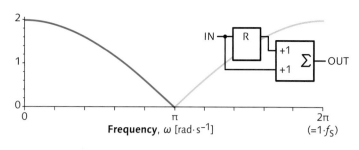

Figure 20.13 A [1, –1] FIR filter subtracts one sample from the previous sample; this forms a simple high-pass filter.

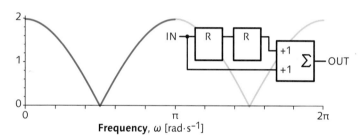

Figure 20.14 A [1, 0, 1] FIR filter averages a sample and the second preceding sample, ignoring the sample in between; this forms a bandreject ("notch," or "trap") filter at $0.25\,f_S$.

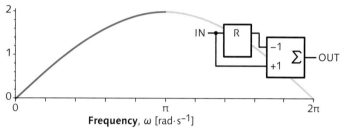

Figure 20.15 A [1, 0, –1] FIR filter subtracts one sample from the second previous sample, ignoring the sample in between; this forms a bandpass filter centered at $0.25\,f_S$.

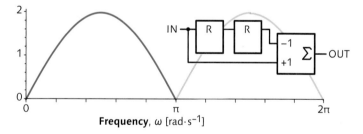

Subtracting a signal from a low-pass version of itself is equivalent to negating all of coefficients (weights) of the lowpass filter except the central coefficient, which is subtracted from unity.

designers. Each block labelled *R* designates a register; a series of these elements forms a shift register.

A simple *highpass filter* (HPF) is formed by subtracting each sample from the previous sample: This filter has weights [1, –1]. The response of this filter is graphed in Figure 20.13. In general, and in this case, a highpass filter is obtained when a lowpass-filtered version of a signal is subtracted from the unfiltered signal. The unfiltered signal can be considered as a two-tap filter having weights [1, 0]. Subtracting the weights

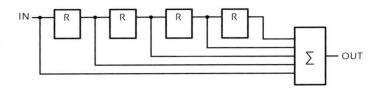

Figure 20.16 **A very simple 5-tap FIR filter** comprises four registers and an adder; five adjacent samples are summed. Prior to scaling to unity, the coefficients are [1, 1, 1, 1, 1].

A bandpass (bandstop) filter is considered *narrowband* if its passband (stopband) covers a 2:1 range of frequencies (*octave*) or less.

If a filter like that of Figure 20.16 has many taps, it needs many adders. Its arithmetic can be simplified by using an accumulator to form the running sum of input samples, another accumulator to form the running sum of outputs from the shift register, and a subtractor to take the difference of these sums. This structure is called a *cascaded integrator comb* (CIC).

[$\frac{1}{2}$, $\frac{1}{2}$] of the scaled lowpass filter from that yields the scaled weights [$\frac{1}{2}$, $-\frac{1}{2}$] of this highpass filter.

Figure 20.14 shows the response of a filter that adds a sample to the second previous sample, disregarding the central sample. The weights in this case are [1, 0, 1]. This forms a simple *bandreject filter* (BRF), also known as a *bandstop* or *notch filter,* or *trap.* Here, the response has a null at one quarter the sampling frequency. The scaled filter passes DC with no attenuation. This filter would make a mess of image data – if a picket fence whose pickets happened to lie at a frequency of $0.25f_S$ were processed through this filter, the pickets would average together and disappear! It is a bad idea to apply such a filter to image data, but this filter (and filters like it) can be very useful for signal processing functions.

Figure 20.15 shows the response of a filter that subtracts a sample from the second previous sample, disregarding the central sample. Its weights are [1, 0, –1]. This forms a simple *bandpass filter* (BPF). The weights sum to zero – this filter blocks DC. The BPF of this example is complementary to the [1, 0, 1] filter.

Figure 20.16 above shows the block diagram of a 5-tap FIR filter that sums five successive samples. As shown in the light grey curve in Figure 20.17 at the top of the facing page, this yields a lowpass filter. Its frequency response has two *zeros:* Any input signal at $0.2f_S$ or $0.4f_S$ will vanish; attenuation in the stopband reaches only about –12 dB, at $\frac{3}{10}$ of the sampling rate.

In the design of digital filters, control of frequency response is exercised in the choice of tap weights. Figure 20.18 at the bottom of the facing page shows the block diagram of a filter having fractional coefficients chosen from a Gaussian waveform. The magenta curve in Figure 20.17 shows that this set of tap weights yields a lowpass filter having a Gaussian frequency response. By using negative coefficients, low-frequency

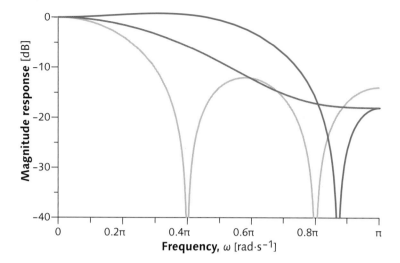

Figure 20.17 **5-tap FIR filter responses** are shown for several choices of coefficient values (tap weights).

response can be extended without deteriorating performance at high frequencies. The black curve in Figure 20.17 shows the response of a filter having coefficients [$-32/256$, $72/256$, $176/256$, $72/256$, $-32/256$]. This filter exhibits the same attenuation at high frequencies (about –18 dB) as the Gaussian, but has about twice the –6 dB frequency.

Negative coefficients, as in the last example here, potentially cause production of output samples that exceed unity. (In this example, output samples above unity are produced at input frequencies about $\omega = 0.3\pi$, $1/6$ the sampling rate). If extreme values are clipped, artifacts will result. To avoid artifacts, the signal coding range must include suitable footroom and headroom.

The operation of an FIR filter amounts to multiplying a set of input samples by a set of filter coefficients (weights), and forming the appropriate set of sums of these products. The weighting can be implemented using multipliers or using table lookup techniques. With

Figure 20.18 **A 5-tap FIR filter including multipliers** has coefficients [13, 56, 118, 56, 13], scaled by $1/256$. The coefficients approximate a Gaussian; so does the frequency response. The multipliers can be implemented by table lookup.

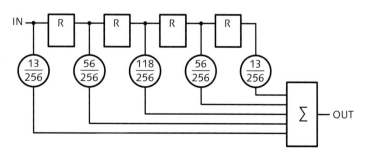

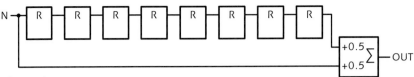

Figure 20.19 **A simple comb filter** includes several delay elements and an adder.

Figure 20.20 **The simple comb filter's response** resembles the teeth of a comb. This filter has unity response at zero frequency: It passes DC. A filter having weights [½, 0, 0, ..., 0, –½] blocks DC.

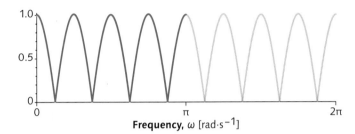

For details concerning implementation structures, see the books by Lyons and Rorabaugh cited at the end of the chapter.

respect to a complete set of input samples, this operation is called *convolution*. Ordinarily, convolution is conceptualized as taking place one multiplication at a time. An *n*-tap FIR filter can be implemented using a single multiplier-accumulator (MAC) component operating at *n* times the sample rate. A direct implementation with *n* multiplier components, or a multiplexed implementation with a single MAC, accepts input samples and delivers output samples in temporal order: Each coefficient needs to be presented to the filter *n* times. However, convolution is symmetrical with respect to input samples and coefficients: The same set of results can be produced by presenting filter coefficients one at a time to a MAC, and accumulating partial output sums for each output sample. FIR filters have many potential implementation structures.

Figure 20.19 above shows the block diagram of an FIR filter having eight taps weighted [1, 0, 0, ..., 0, 1]. The frequency response of this filter is shown in Figure 20.20. The response peaks when an exact integer number of cycles lie underneath the filter; it nulls when an integer-and-a-half number of cycles lie underneath. The peaks all have the same magnitude: The response is the same when exactly 1, 2, ..., or *n* samples are within its window. The magnitude frequency response of such a filter has a shape resembling a comb, and such a filter is called a *comb filter*.

DIGITAL VIDEO AND HD ALGORITHMS AND INTERFACES

Impulse response

I have explained filtering as weighted integration along the time axis. I coined the term *temporal weighting function* to denote the weights. I consider my explanation of filtering in terms of its operation in the temporal domain to be more intuitive to a digital technologist than a more conventional explanation that starts in the frequency domain. But my term *temporal weighting function* is nonstandard, and I must now introduce the usual but nonintuitive term *impulse response*.

An analog impulse signal has infinitesimal duration, infinite amplitude, and an integral of unity. (An analog impulse is conceptually equivalent to the Dirac or Kronecker deltas of mathematics.) A digital impulse signal is a solitary sample having unity amplitude amid a stream of zeros; The *impulse response* of a digital filter is its response to an input that is identically zero except for a solitary unity-valued sample.

Details of the relationship between the Dirac delta, the Kronecker delta, and sampling in DSP are found on page 122 of Rorabaugh's book, cited at the end of the chapter.

Finite impulse response (FIR) filters

In each of the filters that I have described so far, only a few coefficients are nonzero. When a digital impulse is presented to such a filter, the result is simply the weighting coefficients scanned out in turn. The response to an impulse is limited in duration; the examples that I have described have *finite impulse response*. They are *FIR filters*. In these filters, the impulse response is identical to the set of coefficients. The digital filters that I described on page 202 implement temporal weighting directly. The impulse responses of these filters, scaled to unity, are [$\frac{1}{2}$, $\frac{1}{2}$], [$\frac{1}{2}$, $-\frac{1}{2}$], [$\frac{1}{2}$, 0, $\frac{1}{2}$], and [$\frac{1}{2}$, 0, $-\frac{1}{2}$], respectively.

The particular set of weights in Figure 20.18 approximate a sampled Gaussian waveform; so, the frequency response of this filter is approximately Gaussian. The action of this filter can be expressed algebraically:

In Equation 20.2, g is a sequence (whose index is enclosed in square brackets), not a function (whose argument would be in parentheses); s_j is sample number j.

Eq 20.2

$$g[j] = \frac{13}{256}s_{j-2} + \frac{56}{256}s_{j-1} + \frac{118}{256}s_j + \frac{56}{256}s_{j+1} + \frac{13}{256}s_{j+2}$$

Symmetry:
$$f(x) = f(-x)$$

Antisymmetry:
$$f(x) = -f(-x)$$

I have described impulse responses that are symmetrical around an instant in time. You might think $t = 0$ should denote the beginning of time, but it is usually convenient to shift the time axis so that $t = 0$ corresponds to the central point of a filter's impulse response. An FIR (or *nonrecursive*) filter has a limited number of coefficients that are nonzero. When the input impulse lies outside this interval, the response is zero. Most digital filters used in video are FIR filters, and most have impulse responses either symmetric or antisymmetric around $t = 0$.

You can view an FIR filter as having a fixed structure, with the data shifting along underneath. Alternatively, you might think of the *data* as being fixed, and the *filter* sliding across the data. Both notions are equivalent.

Physical realizability of a filter

In order to be implemented, a digital filter must be *physically realizable:* It is a practical necessity to have a temporal weighting function (impulse response) of limited duration. An FIR filter requires storage of several input samples, and it requires several multiplication operations to be performed during each sample period. The number of input samples stored is called the *order* of the filter, or its number of *taps*. If a particular filter has fixed coefficients, then its multiplications can be performed by table lookup. A straightforward technique can be used to exploit the symmetry of the impulse response to eliminate half the multiplications; this is often advantageous!

Here I use the word *truncation* to indicate the forcing to zero of a filter's weighting function beyond a certain tap. The nonzero coefficients in a weighting function may involve theoretical values that have been quantized to a certain number of bits. This *coefficient quantization* can be accomplished by *rounding* or by *truncation*. Be careful to distinguish between truncation of impulse response and truncation of coefficients.

When a temporal weighting function is truncated past a certain point, its transform – its frequency response characteristics – will suffer. The science and craft of filter design involves carefully choosing the order of the filter – that is, the position beyond which the weighting function is forced to zero. That position needs to be far enough from the center tap that the filter's high-frequency response is small enough to be negligible for the application.

Signal processing accommodates the use of impulse responses having negative values, and negative coefficients are common in digital signal processing. But image capture and image display involve sensing and generating light, which cannot have negative power, so negative weights cannot always be realized. If you study the transform pairs on page 201 you will see that your ability to tailor the frequency response of a filter is severely limited when you cannot use negative weights.

DIGITAL VIDEO AND HD ALGORITHMS AND INTERFACES

Impulse response is generally directly evident in the design of an FIR digital filter. Although it is possible to implement a boxcar filter directly in the analog domain, analog filters rarely implement temporal weighting directly, and the implementation of an analog filter generally bears a nonobvious relationship to its impulse response. Analog filters are best described in terms of Laplace transforms, not Fourier transforms. Impulse responses of analog filters are rarely considered directly in the design process. Despite the major conceptual and implementation differences, analog filters and FIR filters – and *IIR* filters, to be described – are all characterized by their frequency response.

Phase response (group delay)

Until now I have described the magnitude frequency response of filters. *Phase frequency* response – often called phase response – is also important. Consider a symmetrical FIR filter having 15 taps. No matter what the input signal, the output will have an effective delay of 8 sample periods, corresponding to the central sample of the filter's impulse response. The time delay of an FIR filter is constant, independent of frequency.

Consider a sine wave at 1 MHz, and a second sine wave at 1 MHz but delayed 125 ns. The situation is sketched in Figure 20.21 in the margin. The 125 ns delay could be expressed as a phase shift of 45° at 1 MHz. However, if the time delay remains constant and the frequency doubles, the phase offset doubles to 90°. With constant time delay, phase offset increases in direct (linear) proportion to the increase in frequency. Since in this condition phase delay is directly proportional to frequency, its synonym is *linear phase*. A closely related condition is *constant group delay*, where the first derivative of delay is constant but a fixed time delay may be present. All FIR filters exhibit constant group delay, but only symmetric FIR filters exhibit strictly linear phase.

It is characteristic of many filters – such as IIR filters, to be described in a moment – that delay varies somewhat as a function of frequency. An image signal contains many frequencies, produced by scene elements at different scales. If the horizontal displacement of a reproduced object were dependent upon

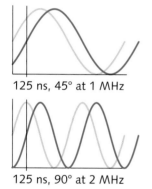

125 ns, 45° at 1 MHz

125 ns, 90° at 2 MHz

Figure 20.21 **Linear phase**

Figure 20.22 **An IIR ("recur-sive") filter** computes a weighted sum of input samples (here, just 0.25 times the current sample), and adds to this a weighted sum of previous result samples. Every IIR filter exhibits nonlinear phase response.

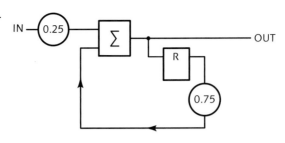

What a signal processing engineer calls an IIR filter is known in the finance and statistics communities as *autoregressive moving average* (ARMA).

frequency, objectionable artifacts would result. Symmetric FIR filters exhibit linear phase in their pass-bands, and avoid this artifact. So, in image processing and in video, FIR filters are strongly preferred over other sorts of filters: Linear phase is a highly desirable property in a video system.

Infinite impulse response (IIR) filters

The digital filters described so far have been members of the FIR class. A second class of digital filter is characterized by having a potentially *infinite impulse response* (IIR). An IIR (or *recursive*) filter computes a weighted sum of input samples – as is the case in an FIR filter – but adds to this a weighted sum of previous *output* samples.

A simple IIR is sketched in Figure 20.22: The input sample is weighted by $\frac{1}{4}$, and the previous output is weighted by $\frac{3}{4}$. These weighted values are summed to form the filter result. The filter result is then fed back to become an input to the computation of the next sample. The impulse response jumps rapidly upon the onset of the input impulse, and tails off over many samples. This is a simple one-tap lowpass filter; its time-domain response closely resembles an analog RC lowpass filter. A highpass filter is formed by taking the difference of the input sample from the previously stored filter result.

In an IIR filter having just one tap, the designer's ability to tailor frequency response is severely limited. An IIR filter can be extended by storing several previous filter results, and adding (or subtracting) a fraction of each to a fraction of the current input sample. In such a multitap IIR filter, a fine degree of control can be exercised over frequency response using just a handful of taps. Just three or four taps in an IIR filter can achieve frequency response that might take 20 taps in an FIR filter.

However, there's a catch: In an IIR filter, both attenuation and delay depend upon frequency. In the terminology of the previous section, an IIR filter exhibits nonlinear phase. Typically, low-frequency signals are delayed more than high-frequency signals. As I have explained, variation of delay as a function of frequency is potentially a very serious problem in video.

An IIR filter cannot have exactly linear phase, although a complex IIR filter can be designed to have arbitrarily small phase error. Because IIR filters usually have poor phase response, they are not ordinarily used in video. (A notable exception is the use of field- and frame-based IIR filters in temporal noise reduction, where the delay element comprises a field or frame of storage.)

Owing to the dependence of an IIR filter's result upon its previous results, an IIR filter is necessarily recursive. However, certain recursive filters have finite impulse response, so a recursive filter does *not* necessarily have infinite impulse response.

Lowpass filter

A lowpass filter lets low frequencies pass undisturbed, but attenuates high frequencies. Figure 20.23 overleaf characterizes a lowpass filter. The response has a *passband*, where the filter's response is nearly unity; a *transition band*, where the response has intermediate values; and a *stopband*, where the filter's response is nearly zero. For a lowpass filter, the *corner frequency*, ω_C – sometimes called *bandwidth*, or *cutoff frequency* – is the frequency where the magnitude response of the filter has fallen 3 dB from its magnitude at a reference frequency (usually zero, or DC). In other words, at its corner frequency, the filter's response has fallen to 0.707 of its response at DC.

The passband is characterized by the passband edge frequency ω_P and the passband ripple δ_P (sometimes denoted δ_1). The stopband is characterized by its edge frequency ω_S and ripple δ_S (sometimes denoted δ_2). The *transition band* lies between ω_P and ω_S; it has width $\Delta\omega = \omega_S - \omega_P$.

Compensation of undesired phase response in a filter is known as *equalization*. This is unrelated to the *equalization* pulses that form part of sync.

The terms *nonrecursive* and *recursive* are best used to describe filter implementation structures.

Here I represent frequency by the symbol ω, whose units are radians per second (rad·s^{-1}). A digital filter scales with its sampling frequency; using ω is convenient because the sampling frequency is always $\omega = 2\pi$ and the half-sampling (Nyquist) frequency is always π.

Some people define bandwidth differently than I do.

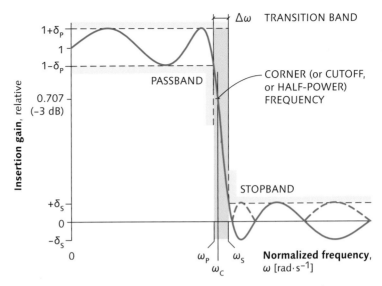

Figure 20.23 **Lowpass filter characterization.** A lowpass filter for use in video sampling or reconstruction has a corner frequency ω_C, where the attenuation is 0.707. (At the corner frequency, output power is half the input power.) In the *passband*, response is unity within δ_P, usually 1% or so. In the *stopband*, response is zero within δ_S, usually 1% or so. The *transition band* lies between the edge of the passband and the edge of the stopband; its width is $\Delta\omega$.

The complexity of a lowpass filter is roughly determined by its *normalized transition bandwidth* (or *transition ratio*) $\Delta\omega/2\pi$. The narrower the transition band, the more complex the filter. Also, the smaller the ripple in either the passband or the stopband, the more complex the filter. FIR filter tap count can be estimated by this formula, due to Bellanger:

Eq 20.3

BELLANGER, MAURICE (2000),
*Digital Processing of Signals:
Theory and Practice,* Third
Edition (Chichester, England:
Wiley): 124.

$$N_e \approx \frac{2\pi}{\Delta\omega} \cdot \frac{2}{3} \log_{10}\left(\frac{1}{10\delta_P\delta_S}\right)$$

In analog filter design, frequency response is generally graphed in log–log coordinates, with the frequency axis in units of log hertz (Hz), and magnitude response in decibels (dB). In digital filter design, frequency is usually graphed linearly from zero to half the sampling frequency. The passband and stopband response of a digital filter are usually graphed logarithmically; the passband response is often magnified to emphasize small departures from unity.

The templates standardized in BT.601 for a studio digital video presampling filter are shown in Figure 20.24 opposite. The response of a practical lowpass filter meeting this tremplate is shown in

DIGITAL VIDEO AND HD ALGORITHMS AND INTERFACES

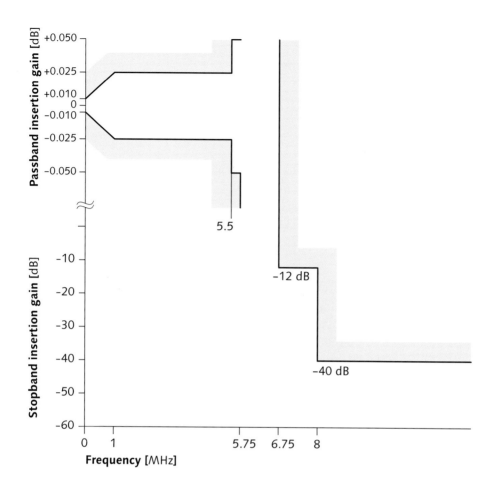

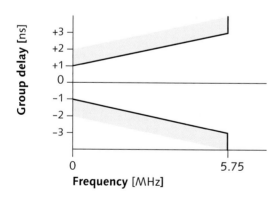

Figure 20.24 **BT.601 filter templates** are standardized for studio digital video systems in BT.601-5. The top template shows frequency response, detailing the passband (at the top) and the stopband (in the middle). The bottom template shows the group delay specification.

Figure 20.25, on page 215. This is a halfband filter, intended for use with a sampling frequency of 27 MHz; its corner frequency is $0.25f_S$. A consumer filter might have ripple two orders of magnitude worse than this.

Digital filter design

A simple way to design a digital filter is to use coefficients that comprise an appropriate number of point-samples of a theoretical impulse response. Coefficients beyond a certain point – the *order* of the filter – are simply omitted. Equation 20.4 implements a 9-tap filter that approximates a Gaussian:

I describe *risetime* on page 543. In response to a step input, a Gaussian filter has a risetime very close to $\frac{1}{3}$ of the period of one cycle at the corner frequency.

Eq 20.4
$$g[j] = \frac{1s_{j-4} + 9s_{j-3} + 43s_{j-2} + 110s_{j-1} + 150s_j + 110s_{j+1} + 43s_{j+2} + 9s_{j+3} + 1s_{j+4}}{476}$$

Omission of coefficients causes frequency response to depart from the ideal. If the omitted coefficients are much greater than zero, actual frequency response can depart significantly from the ideal.

Another approach to digital filter design starts with the ILPF. Its infinite extent can be addressed by simply truncating the weights – that is, forcing the weights to zero – outside a certain interval, say outside the region 0±4 sample periods. This will have an unfortunate effect on the frequency response, however: The frequency response will exhibit overshoot and undershoot near the transition band.

Poor spectral behavior of a truncated sinc can be mitigated by applying a weighting function that peaks at unity at the center of the filter and diminishes gently to zero at the extremities of the interval. This is referred to as applying a *windowing* function. Design of a filter using the windowing method begins with scaling of sinc along the time axis to choose the corner frequency and choosing a suitable number of taps. Each tap weight is then computed as a sinc value multiplied by the corresponding window value. A sinc can be truncated through multiplication by a rectangular window. Perhaps the simplest nontrivial window has a triangular shape; this is also called the *Bartlett* window. The *von Hann* window (often wrongly called "Hanning") has a windowing function that is a single cycle of a raised cosine. Window functions such as von Hann are fixed by the corner frequency and the number of filter taps;

We could use the term *weighting*, but sinc itself is a weighting function, so we choose a different word: *windowing*.

For details about windowing, see Lyons or Rorabaugh, at the end of the chapter, or WOLBERG, GEORGE (1990), *Digital Image Warping* (Los Alamitos, Calif.: IEEE).

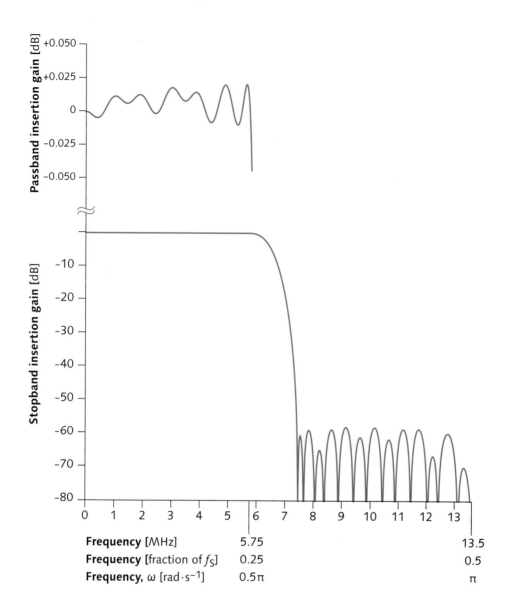

Frequency [MHz]	5.75	13.5
Frequency [fraction of f_S]	0.25	0.5
Frequency, ω [rad·s⁻¹]	0.5π	π

Figure 20.25 Halfband filter. This graph shows the frequency response of a practical filter whose corner is at one-quarter its sampling frequency of 27 MHz. The graph is linear in the abscissa (frequency) and logarithmic in the ordinate (response). The top portion shows that the passband has an overall gain of unity and a uniformity (*ripple*) of about ±0.02 dB: In the passband, its gain varies between about 0.997 and 1.003. The bottom portion shows that the stopband is rejected with an attenuation of about –60 dB: The filter has a gain of about 0.001 at these frequencies. This data, for the GF9102A halfband filter, was kindly provided by Gennum Corporation.

no control can be exercised over the width of the transition band. The *Kaiser* window has a single parameter that controls that width. For a given filter order, if the transition band is made narrower, then stopband attenuation is reduced. The Kaiser window parameter allows the designer to determine this tradeoff.

A windowed sinc filter has much better performance than a truncated sinc, and windowed design is so simple that there is no excuse to use sinc without windowing. In most engineering applications, however, filter performance is best characterized in the frequency domain, and the frequency-domain performance of windowed sinc filters is suboptimal: The performance of an *n*-tap windowed sinc filter can be bettered by an *n*-tap filter whose design has been suitably optimized.

Few closed-form methods are known to design optimum digital filters. Design of a high-performance filter usually involves successive approximation, optimizing by trading design parameters back and forth between the time and frequency domains. The classic method was published by J.H. McLellan, T.W. Parks, and L.R. Rabiner ("MPR"), based upon an algorithm developed by the Russian mathematician E.Ya. Remez. In the DSP community, the method is often called the "Remez exchange."

The coefficients of a high-quality lowpass filter for studio video are shown in Figure 20.26 in the margin.

Figure 20.26 A 25-tap lowpass FIR filter

$$
\begin{aligned}
g[i] = \ & 0.098460\, s_{i-12} \\
+ & 0.009482\, s_{i-11} \\
- & 0.013681\, s_{i-10} \\
+ & 0.020420\, s_{i-9} \\
- & 0.029197\, s_{i-8} \\
+ & 0.039309\, s_{i-7} \\
- & 0.050479\, s_{i-6} \\
+ & 0.061500\, s_{i-5} \\
- & 0.071781\, s_{i-4} \\
+ & 0.080612\, s_{i-3} \\
- & 0.087404\, s_{i-2} \\
+ & 0.091742\, s_{i-1} \\
+ & 0.906788\, s_{i} \\
+ & 0.091742\, s_{i+1} \\
- & 0.087404\, s_{i+2} \\
+ & 0.080612\, s_{i+3} \\
- & 0.071781\, s_{i+4} \\
+ & 0.061500\, s_{i+5} \\
- & 0.050479\, s_{i+6} \\
+ & 0.039309\, s_{i+7} \\
- & 0.029197\, s_{i+8} \\
+ & 0.020420\, s_{i+9} \\
- & 0.013681\, s_{i+10} \\
+ & 0.009482\, s_{i+11} \\
+ & 0.098460\, s_{i+12}
\end{aligned}
$$

Reconstruction

Digitization involves sampling and quantization; these operations are performed in an analog-to-digital converter (ADC). Whether the signal is quantized then sampled, or sampled then quantized, is relevant only within the ADC: The order of operations is immaterial outside that subsystem. Modern video ADCs quantize first, then sample.

I have explained that filtering is generally required prior to sampling in order to avoid the introduction of aliases. Avoidance of aliasing in the sampled domain has obvious importance. In order to avoid aliasing, an analog presampling filter needs to operate prior to analog-to-digital conversion. If aliasing is avoided, then the sampled signal can, according to Shannon's theorem, be reconstructed without aliases.

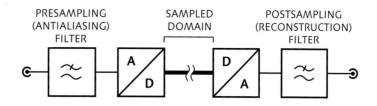

Figure 20.27 **Sampling and reconstruction**

To reconstruct an analog signal, an analog reconstruction filter is necessary following digital-to-analog (D-to-A) conversion. The overall flow is sketched in Figure 20.27 above.

Reconstruction close to 0.5f_S

Consider the example in Figure 20.28 below of a sine wave at 0.44f_S. This signal meets the sampling criterion, and can be perfectly represented in the digital domain. However, from an intuitive point of view, it is difficult to predict the underlying sinewave from samples 3, 4, 5, and 6 in the lower graph. When reconstructed using a Gaussian filter, the high-frequency signal vanishes. To be reconstructed accurately, a waveform with a significant amount of power near half the sampling rate must be reconstructed with a high-quality filter.

$$\frac{1 + \sin 0.44 \pi t}{2}$$

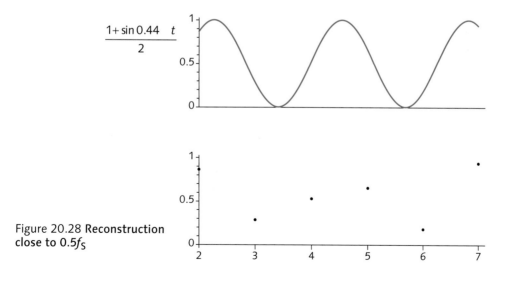

Figure 20.28 Reconstruction close to 0.5f_S

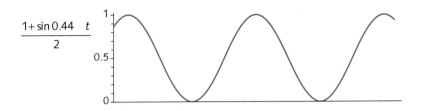

$$\frac{1+\sin 0.44 \quad t}{2}$$

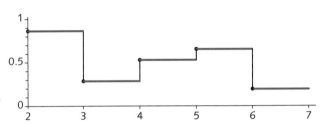

Figure 20.29 D-to-A conversion with a boxcar waveform is equivalent to a DAC producing an impulse train followed by a boxcar filter with its sinc response. Frequencies close to $0.5f_S$ are attenuated.

"(sin x)/x" correction

I place "(sin x)/x" in quotes: With the argument properly scaled it is (sin πx)/(πx), but it is almost always pronounced *sine-ecks-over-ecks*, with argument scaling implicit.

I have described how it is necessary for an analog reconstruction filter to follow digital-to-analog conversion. If the DAC produced an impulse "train" where the amplitude of each impulse was modulated by the corresponding code value, a classic lowpass filter would suffice: All would be well if the DAC output resembled my "point" graphs, with power at the sample instants and no power in between. Recall that a waveform comprising just unit impulses has uniform frequency response across the entire spectrum.

Unfortunately for analog reconstruction, a typical DAC does not produce an impulse waveform for each sample. It would be impractical to have a DAC with an impulse response, because signal power is proportional to the integral of the signal, and the amplitude of the impulses would have to be impractically high for the integral of the impulses to achieve adequate signal power. Instead, each converted sample value is held for the entire duration of the sample: A typical DAC produces a boxcar waveform. A boxcar waveform's frequency response is described by the sinc function.

You might consider a DAC's boxcar waveform to be a "sample-and-hold" operation, but that term is normally used in conjunction with an A-to-D converter, or circuitry that lies in front of an ADC.

In Figure 20.29 above, the top graph is a sine wave at $0.44f_S$; the bottom graph shows the boxcar waveform produced by a conventional DAC. Even with a high-quality reconstruction filter, whose response extends close to half the sampling rate, it is evident that

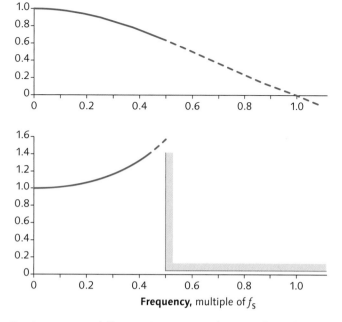

Figure 20.30 "(sin x)/x" correction is necessary following (or in principle, preceding) digital-to-analog conversion when a DAC with a typical boxcar output waveform is used. The frequency response of a boxcar-waveform DAC is shown in the upper graph. The lower graph shows the response of the "(sin x)/x" correction filter necessary to compensate its high frequency falloff.

reconstruction by a boxcar function reduces the magnitude of high-frequency components of the signal.

The DAC's holding of each sample value throughout the duration of its sample interval (*zero-order hold, ZOH*) corresponds to a filtering operation, with a frequency response of sinc. The top graph of Figure 20.30 shows the attenuation due to this phenomenon.

The effect is overcome by "(sin x)/x" correction: The frequency response of the reconstruction filter is modified to include peaking corresponding to the reciprocal of sinc. In the passband, the filter's response increases gradually to about 4 dB above its response at DC, to compensate the loss. Above the passband edge frequency, the response of the filter must decrease rapidly to produce a large attenuation near half the sampling frequency, to provide alias-free reconstruction. The bottom graph of Figure 20.30 shows the idealized response of a filter having "(sin x)/x" correction.

This chapter has detailed one-dimensional filtering. In *Image digitization and reconstruction*, I will introduce two- and three-dimensional sampling and filters.

Further reading

For an approachable introduction to the concepts, theory, and mathematics of digital signal processing (DSP), see Lyons. For an alternative point of view, see Rorabaugh's book; it includes the source code for programs to design filters – that is, to evaluate filter coefficients. For comprehensive and theoretical coverage of DSP, see Mitra and Kaiser.

LYONS, RICHARD G. (1997), *Understanding Digital Signal Processing* (Reading, Mass.: Addison Wesley).

MCCLELLAN, JAMES H. and PARKS, THOMAS W. (2005), "A personal history of the Parks-McClellan algorithm," *IEEE Signal Processing Magazine* **22** (2): 82–86.

MITRA, SANJIT K., and JAMES F. KAISER (1993), *Handbook for Digital Signal Processing* (New York: Wiley).

RORABAUGH, C. BRITTON (1999), *DSP Primer* (New York: McGraw-Hill).

Resampling, interpolation, and decimation 21

In video and audio signal processing, it is often necessary to take a set of sample values and produce another set that approximates the samples that would have resulted had the original sampling occurred at different instants – at a different rate, or at a different phase. This is called *resampling*. (In PC parlance, resampling for the purpose of picture resizing is called *scaling*.) Resampling is an essential part of video processes such as these:

- Chroma subsampling (e.g., 4:4:4 to 4:2:2)
- Downconversion (e.g., HD to SD) and upconversion (e.g., SD to HD)
- Aspect ratio conversion (e.g., 4:3 to 16:9)
- Conversion among different sample rates of digital video standards (e.g., $4f_{SC}$ to 4:2:2, 13.5 MHz)
- Picture resizing in digital video effects (DVE)

One-dimensional resampling applies directly to digital audio, in applications such as changing sample rate from 48 kHz to 44.1 kHz. In video, 1-D resampling can be applied horizontally or vertically. Resampling can be extended to a two-dimensional array of samples. Two approaches are possible. A horizontal filter, then a vertical filter, can be applied in cascade (tandem) – this is the *separable* approach. Alternatively, a direct form of 2-D spatial interpolation can be implemented.

Upsampling produces more result samples than input samples. In audio, new samples can be estimated at a higher rate than the input, for example when digital audio sampled at 44.1 kHz is converted to the 48 kHz professional rate used with video. In video, upsampling is required in the spatial upconversion from 1280×720

HD to 1920×1080 HD: 1280 samples in each input line must be converted to 1920 samples in the output, an upsampling ratio of 2:3.

One way to accomplish upsampling by an integer ratio of $1:n$ is to interpose $n-1$ zero samples between each pair of input samples. This causes the spectrum of the original signal to repeat at multiples of the original sampling rate. The repeated spectra are called "images." (This is a historical term stemming from radio; it has nothing to do with pictures!) These "images" are then eliminated (or at least attenuated) by an anti-imaging lowpass filter. In some upsampling structures, such as the Lagrange interpolator that I will describe later in this chapter, filtering and upsampling are intertwined.

Downsampling produces fewer result samples than input samples. In audio, new samples can be created at a lower rate than the input. In video, downsampling is required when converting $4f_{SC}$ NTSC digital video to BT.601 ("4:2:2") digital video: 910 samples in each input line must be converted to 858 samples in the output, a downsampling ratio of 35:33; for each 35 input samples, 33 output samples are produced.

In an original sample sequence, signal content from DC to nearly $0.5f_S$ can be represented. After downsampling, though, the new sample rate may be lower than that required by the signal bandwidth. After downsampling, meaningful signal content is limited by the Nyquist criterion at the *new* sampling rate – for example, after 4:1 downsampling, signal content is limited to $\frac{1}{8}$ of the original sampling rate. To avoid the introduction of aliases, lowpass filtering is necessary prior to, or in conjunction with, downsampling. The corner frequency depends upon the downsampling ratio; for example, a 4:1 ratio requires a corner less than $0.125f_S$. Downsampling with an integer ratio of $n:1$ can be thought of as prefiltering (antialias filtering) for the new sampling rate, followed by the discarding of $n-1$ samples between original sample pairs.

Resampling produces new samples that assume that neighbouring input samples are related by a continuous function. If the underlying function is not continuous, problems can be expected. For example, pseudocolour images are not continuous: They cannot be meaningfully resampled without creating artifacts.

Figure 21.1 **Two-times upsampling** starts by interposing zero samples between original sample pairs. This would result in the folded spectral content of the original signal appearing in-band at the new rate. These "images" are removed by a resampling filter.

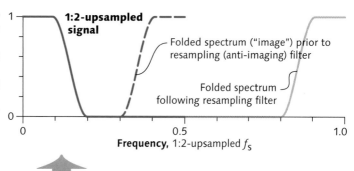

UPSAMPLING

Figure 21.2 **An original signal** exhibits folding around half the sampling frequency. This is inconsequential providing that the signal is properly reconstructed. When the signal is upsampled or downsampled, the folded portion must be handled properly or aliasing will result.

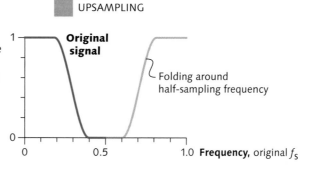

DOWNSAMPLING

Figure 21.3 **Two-to-one downsampling** requires a resampling filter to meet the Nyquist criterion at the new sampling rate. The solid green line shows the spectrum of the filtered signal; the shaded line shows its folded portion. Resampling without filtering would preserve the original baseband spectrum, but folding around the new sampling rate would cause alias products shown here in the crosshatched region.

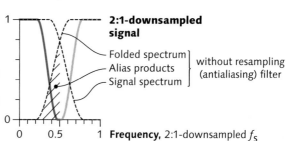

Figure 21.2, at the center above, sketches the spectrum of an original signal. Figure 21.1 shows the frequency domain considerations of upsampling; Figure 21.3 shows the frequency domain considerations of downsampling. These examples show ratios of 1:2 and 2:1; however, the concepts apply to resampling at any ratio.

2:1 downsampling

Colour video originates with $R'G'B'$ components. Transcoding to $Y'C_BC_R$ is necessary if signals are to be used in the studio. The conversion involves matrixing (to $Y'C_BC_R$ in 4:4:4 form), then chroma subsampling to 4:2:2. Chroma subsampling requires a 2:1 downsampler. If this downsampling is attempted by simply dropping alternate samples, any signal content between the original $0.25f_S$ and $0.5f_S$ will cause aliasing in the result. Rejection of signal content at and above $0.25f_S$ is required. The required filter is usually implemented as an FIR lowpass filter having its corner frequency somewhat less than one-quarter of the (original) sampling frequency. After filtering, alternate result samples can be dropped. There is no need to calculate values that will subsequently be discarded, however! Efficient chroma subsamplers take advantage of that fact, interleaving the C_B and C_R components into a single filter.

In Figure 20.12, on page 203, I presented a very simple lowpass filter that simply averages two adjacent samples. That filter has a corner frequency of $0.25f_S$. However, it makes a slow transition from passband to stopband, and it has very poor attenuation in the stopband (above $0.25f_S$). It makes a poor resampling filter. More than two taps are required to give adequate performance in studio video subsampling.

In 4:2:2 video, chroma is cosited: Each chroma sample must be located at the site of a luma sample. A symmetrical filter having an even number of (nonzero) taps does not have this property. A downsampling filter for cosited chroma must have an odd number of taps.

Oversampling

I have explained the importance of prefiltering prior to A-to-D conversion, and of postfiltering following D-to-A conversion. Historically, these filters were implemented in the analog domain, using inductors and capacitors. In discrete form, these components are bulky and expensive. It is extremely difficult to incorporate inductive and capacitive elements with suitable values and precision onto integrated circuits. However, A-to-D and D-to-A converters are operating at higher and higher rates, and digital arithmetic has become very

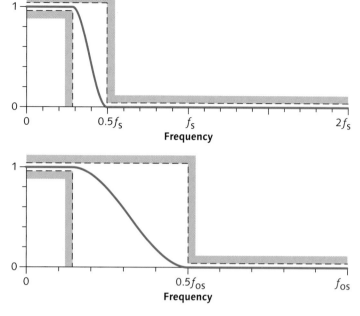

Figure 21.4 **An analog filter for direct sampling** must meet tight constraints, making it expensive.

Figure 21.5 **An analog filter for 2×-oversampling** is much less demanding than a filter for direct sampling, because the difficult part of filtering – achieving a response comparable to that of Figure 21.4 – is relegated to the digital domain.

For an explanation of transition ratio, see page 212.

inexpensive. These circumstances have led to the emergence of *oversampling* as an economical alternative to complex analog presampling ("antialiasing") and post-sampling (reconstruction) filters.

The characteristics of a conventional analog presampling filter are critical: Attenuation must be quite low up to about 0.4 times the sample rate, and quite high above that. In a presampling filter for studio video, attenuation must be less than 1 dB or so up to about 5.5 MHz, and better than 40 or 50 dB above 6.75 MHz. This is a demanding transition ratio $\Delta\omega/\omega_S$. Figure 21.4 above (top) sketches the filter template of a conventional analog presampling filter.

An oversampling A-to-D converter operates at a multiple of the ultimate sampling rate – say at 27 MHz, twice the rate of BT.601 video. The converter is preceded by a cheap analog filter that severely attenuates components at 13.5 MHz and above. However, its characteristics between 5.5 MHz and 13.5 MHz are not critical. The demanding aspects of filtering in that region are left to a digital 2:1 downsampler. The transition ratio $\Delta\omega/\omega_S$ of the analog filter is greatly relaxed compared to direct conversion. In today's technology, the cost of the digital downsampler is less than the difference in cost between excellent and mediocre analog filtering. Complexity is moved from the analog domain to the digital domain; total system cost is reduced. Figure 21.5 (on page 225) sketches the template of an analog presampling filter appropriate for use preceding a 2x oversampled A-to-D converter.

Figure 20.25, on page 215, showed the response of a 55-tap filter having a corner frequency of $0.25f_S$. This is a *halfband* filter, intended for use following a 2×-oversampled A-to-D converter.

In certain FIR filters whose corner is exactly $0.25f_S$, half the coefficients are zero. This leads to a considerable reduction in complexity.

The approach to 2×-oversampled D-to-A conversion is comparable. The D-to-A device operates at 27 MHz; it is presented with a datastream that has been upsampled by a 1:2 ratio. For each input sample, the 2×-oversampling filter computes 2 output samples. One is computed at the effective location of the input sample, and the other is computed at an effective location halfway between input samples. The filter attenuates power between 6.75 MHz and 13.5 MHz. The analog postsampling filter need only reject components at and above 13.5 MHz. As in the 2×-oversampling A-to-D conversion, its performance between 6.75 MHz and 13.5 MHz isn't critical.

Interpolation

In the common case of interpolation horizontally across an image row, the argument *x* is horizontal position. Interpolating along the time axis, as in digital audio sample rate conversion, you could use the symbol *t* to represent time.

In mathematics, *interpolation* is the process of computing the value of a function or a putative function (call it $\tilde{g}$), for an arbitrary argument (*x*), given several function argument and value pairs $[x_i,\, s_i]$. There are many methods for interpolating, and many methods for constructing functions that interpolate.

Given two sample pairs $[x_0,\, s_0]$ and $[x_1,\, s_1]$, the linear interpolation function has this form:

$$\tilde{g}(x) = s_0 + \frac{x - x_0}{x_1 - x_0}(s_1 - s_0) \qquad \text{Eq 21.1}$$

In computer graphics, the linear interpolation operation is often called *LIRP* (pronounced *lerp*).

I symbolize the interpolating function as $\tilde{g}$; the symbol f is already taken to represent frequency. I write g with a tilde ($\tilde{g}$) to emphasize that it is an approximation.

The linear interpolation function can be rewritten as a weighted sum of the neighboring samples s_0 and s_1:

$$\tilde{g}(x) = c_0(x) \cdot s_0 + c_0(x) \cdot s_1 \qquad \text{Eq 21.2}$$

The weights depend upon the x (or t) coordinate:

$$c_0(x) = \frac{x_1 - x}{x_1 - x_0}; \qquad c_1(x) = \frac{x - x_0}{x_1 - x_0} \qquad\qquad \text{Eq 21.3}$$

Lagrange interpolation

J.L. Lagrange (1736–1813) developed a method of interpolation using polynomials. A cubic interpolation function is a polynomial of this form:

$$\tilde{g}(x) = ax^3 + bx^2 + cx + d \qquad\qquad \text{Eq 21.4}$$

Julius O. Smith calls this *Waring-Lagrange* interpolation, since Waring published it 16 years before Lagrange. See Smith's *Digital Audio Resampling Home Page*, <www-ccrma.stanford.edu/~jos/resample>.

Interpolation involves choosing appropriate coefficients a, b, c, and d, based upon the given argument/value pairs [x_j, s_j]. Lagrange described a simple and elegant way of computing the coefficients.

Linear interpolation is just a special case of Lagrange interpolation of the first degree. (Directly using the value of the nearest neighbor can be considered zero-order interpolation.) There is a second-degree (quadratic) form; it is rarely used in signal processing.

In mathematics, to *interpolate* refers to the process that I have described. However, the same word is used to denote the property whereby an interpolating function produces values exactly equal to the original sample values (s_i) at the original sample coordinates (x_i). The Lagrange functions exhibit this property. You might guess that this property is a requirement of *any* interpolating function. However, in signal processing this is not a requirement – in fact, the interpolation functions used in video and audio rarely pass exactly through the original sample values. As a consequence of using the terminology of mathematics, in video we have the seemingly paradoxical situation that interpolation functions usually do not "interpolate"!

In principle, cubic interpolation could be undertaken for any argument x, even values outside the x-coordinate range of the four input samples. (Evaluation outside the interval [x_{-1}, x_2] would be called *extrapolation*.) In digital video and audio, we limit x to the range between x_0 and x_1, so as to estimate the signal in the interval between the central two samples. To evaluate outside this interval, we substitute the input sample values [s_{-1}, s_0, s_1, s_2] appropriately – for example, to

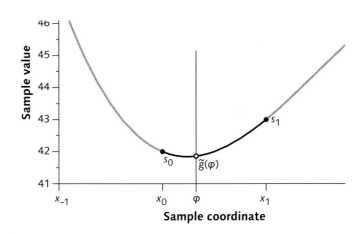

Figure 21.6 **Cubic interpolation** of a signal starts with equally spaced samples, in this example 47, 42, 43, and 46. The underlying function is estimated to be a cubic polynomial that passes through ("interpolates") all four samples. The polynomial is evaluated between the two central samples, as shown by the black segment. Here, evaluation is at phase offset φ. If the underlying function isn't a polynomial, small errors are produced.

Eq 21.5

$$\varphi = \frac{x - x_0}{x_1 - x_0}; \qquad x_0 \leq \varphi \leq x_1$$

UNSER, MICHAEL (1999), "Splines: A perfect fit for signal and image processing," *IEEE Signal Processing Magazine*: 22–38 (Nov.).

evaluate between s_1 and s_2, we shift the input sample values left one place.

With uniform sampling (as in conventional digital video), when interpolating between the two central samples the argument x can be recast as the *phase offset*, or the *fractional phase* (φ, phi), at which a new sample is required between two central samples. (See Equation 21.5.) In abstract terms, φ lies between 0 and 1; in hardware, it is implemented as a binary or a rational fraction. In video, a 1-D interpolator is usually an FIR filter whose coefficients are functions of the phase offset. The weighting coefficients (c_i) are functions of the phase offset; they can be considered as basis functions.

In signal processing, cubic (third-degree) interpolation is often used; the situation is sketched in Figure 21.6 above. In linear interpolation, one neighbor to the left and one to the right are needed. In cubic interpolation, we ordinarily interpolate in the central interval, using two original samples to the left and two to the right of the desired sample instant.

Equation 21.2 can be reformulated:

$$g(\varphi) = c_{-1}(\varphi) \cdot s_{-1} + c_0(\varphi) \cdot s_0 + c_1(\varphi) \cdot s_1 + c_2(\varphi) \cdot s_2 \qquad \text{Eq 21.6}$$

The function takes four sample values [s_{-1}, s_0, s_1, s_2] surrounding the interval of interest, and the phase offset φ between 0 and 1. The coefficients (c_i) are now functions of the argument φ; the interpolator forms a weighted sum of four sample values, where the weights are functions of the parameter φ; it returns an estimated value. (If the input samples are values of a polynomial not exceeding the third degree, then the values produced by a cubic Lagrange interpolator are exact, within roundoff error: Lagrange interpolation "interpolates"!)

If a 2-D image array is to be resampled at arbitrary x and y coordinate values, one approach is to apply a 1-D filter along one axis, then apply a 1-D filter along the other axis. This approach treats interpolation as a separable process, akin to the separable filtering that I will introduce on page 242. Surprisingly, this two-pass approach can be used to rotate an image; see Smith, cited in the margin. Alternatively, a 2×2 array (of 4 sample values) can be used for linear interpolation in 2 dimensions in one step – this is *bilinear* interpolation. A more sophisticated approach is to use a 4×4 array (of 16 sample values) as the basis for cubic interpolation in 2 dimensions – this is *bicubic* interpolation. (It is mathematically comparable to 15th-degree interpolation in one dimension.)

SMITH, ALVY RAY (1987), "Planar 2-pass texture mapping and warping," in *Computer Graphics* 21 (4): 12–19, 263–272 (July, *Proc. SIGGRAPH 87*).

Curves can be drawn in 2-space using a parameter u as the argument to each of two functions $x(u)$ and $y(u)$ that produce a 2-D coordinate pair for each value of u. Cubic polynomials can be used as $x(u)$ and $y(u)$. This approach can be extended to 3-space by adding a third function, $z(u)$. Pierre Bézier developed a method, which is now widely used, to use cubic polynomials to describe curves and surfaces. Such curves are now known as *Bézier curves* or *Bézier splines*. The method is very important in the field of computer graphics; however, Bézier splines and their relatives are infrequently used in signal processing.

BARTELS, RICHARD H., JOHN C. BEATTY, and BRIAN A. BARSKY (1989), *An Introduction to Splines for Use in Computer Graphics and Geometric Modeling* (San Francisco: Morgan Kaufmann).

Lagrange interpolation as filtering

Except for having 4 taps instead of 5, Equation 21.6 has identical form to the 5-tap Gaussian filter of Equation 20.2, on page 207! Lagrange interpolation can be viewed as a special case of FIR filtering, and can be analyzed as a filtering operation. In the previous chapter, *Filtering and sampling*, all of the examples were symmetric. Interpolation to produce samples exactly halfway between input samples, such as in a 2×-over-

Only symmetric FIR filters exhibit true linear phase. Other FIR filters exhibit very nearly linear phase, close enough to be considered to have linear phase in video and audio.

sampling DAC, is also symmetric. However, most interpolators are asymmetric.

There are four reasons why polynomial interpolation is generally unsuitable for video signals: Polynomial interpolation has unequal stopband ripple; nulls lie at fixed positions in the stopband; the interpolating function exhibits extreme behavior outside the central interval; and signals presented to the interpolator are somewhat noisy. I will address each of these issues in turn.

• Any Lagrange interpolator has a frequency response with unequal stopband ripple, sometimes highly unequal. That is generally undesirable in signal processing, and it is certainly undesirable in video.

• A Lagrange interpolator "interpolates" the original samples; this causes a magnitude frequency response that has periodic nulls ("zeros") whose frequencies are fixed by the order of the interpolator. In order for a filter designer to control stopband attenuation, he or she needs the freedom to place nulls judiciously. This freedom is not available in the design of a Lagrange interpolator.

• Conceptually, interpolation attempts to model, with a relatively simple function, the unknown function that generated the samples. The form of the function that we use should reflect the process that underlies generation of the signal. A cubic polynomial may deliver sensible interpolated values between the two central points. However, the value of any polynomial rapidly shoots off to plus or minus infinity at arguments outside the region where it is constrained by the original sample values. That property is at odds with the behavior of signals, which are constrained to lie within a limited range of values forever (say the abstract range 0 to 1 in video, or ±0.5 in audio).

• In signal processing, there is always some uncertainty in the sample values caused by noise accompanying the signal, quantization noise, and noise due to roundoff error in the calculations in the digital domain. When the source data is imperfect, it seems unreasonable to demand perfection of an interpolation function.

These four issues are addressed in signal processing by using interpolation functions that are not polynomials and that do not come from classical mathematics.

You can consider the entire stop-band of an ideal sinc filter to contain an infinity of nulls. Mathematically, the sinc function represents the limit of Lagrange interpolation as the order of the polynomial approaches infinity. See Appendix A of Smith's *Digital Audio Resampling Home Page*, cited in the margin of page 227.

Instead, we usually use interpolation functions based upon the the sinc weighting function that I introduced on page 198. In signal processing, we usually design interpolators that do not "interpolate" the original sample values.

The ideal sinc weighting function has no distinct nulls in its frequency spectrum. When sinc is truncated and optimized to obtain a physically realizable filter, the stopband has a finite number of nulls. Unlike a Lagrange interpolator, these nulls do not have to be regularly spaced. It is the filter designer's ability to choose the frequencies for the zeros that allows him or her to tailor the filter's response.

Polyphase interpolators

The 720*p*60 and 1080*i*30 standards have an identical sampling rate (74.25 MHz). In the logic design of this example, there is a single clock domain.

Some video signal processing applications require upsampling at simple ratios. For example, conversion from 1280 S_{AL} to 1920 S_{AL} in an HD format converter requires 2:3 upsampling. An output sample is computed at one of three phases: either at the site of an input sample, or $\frac{1}{3}$ or $\frac{2}{3}$ of the way between input samples. The upsampler can be implemented as an FIR filter with just three sets of coefficients; the coefficients can be accessed from a lookup table addressed by φ.

Many interpolators involve ratios more complex than the 2:3 ratio of this example. For example, in conversion from $4f_{SC}$ NTSC to BT.601 (4:2:2), 910 input samples must be converted to 858 results. This involves a downsampling ratio of 35:33. Successive output samples are computed at an increment of $1\frac{2}{33}$ input samples. Every 33rd output sample is computed at the site of an input sample (0); other output samples are computed at input sample coordinates $1\frac{2}{33}$, $2\frac{4}{33}$, ..., $16\frac{32}{33}$, $18\frac{1}{33}$, $19\frac{3}{33}$, ..., $34\frac{31}{33}$. Addressing circuitry needs to increment a sample counter by one, and a fractional numerator by 2 modulo 33 (yielding the fraction $\frac{2}{33}$), at each output sample. Overflow from the fraction counter carries into the sample counter; this accounts for the missing input sample number 17 in the sample number sequence of this example. The required interpolation phases are at fractions $\varphi = 0$, $\frac{1}{33}$, $\frac{2}{33}$, $\frac{3}{33}$, ..., $\frac{32}{33}$ between input samples.

A straightforward approach to design of this interpolator in hardware is to drive an FIR filter at the input sample rate. At each input clock, the input sample values shift across the registers. Addressing circuitry implements a modulo-33 counter to keep track of phase – a *phase accumulator*. At each clock, one of 33 different sets of coefficients is applied to the filter. Each coefficient set is designed to introduce the appropriate phase shift. In this example, only 33 result samples are required every 35 input clocks: During 2 clocks of every 35, no result is produced.

This structure is called a *polyphase filter*. This example involves 33 phases; however, the number of *taps* required is independent of the number of *phases*. A 2×-oversampled prefilter, such I described on page 224, has just two phases. The halfband filter whose response is graphed in Figure 20.25, on page 215, would be suitable for this application; that filter has 55 taps.

Polyphase taps and phases

The number of *taps* required in a filter is determined by the degree of control that the designer needs to exercise over frequency response, and by how tightly the filters in each phase need to match each other. In many cases of consumer-grade video, cubic (4-tap) interpolation is sufficient. In studio video, 8 taps or more might be necessary, depending upon the performance to be achieved.

In a direct implementation of a polyphase FIR interpolator, the number of *phases* is determined by the arithmetic that relates the sampling rates. The number of phases determines the number of coefficient sets that need to be used. Coefficient sets are typically precomputed and stored in nonvolatile memory.

On page 231, I described a polyphase resampler having 33 phases. In some applications, the number of phases is impractically large to implement directly. This is the case for the 709379:540000 ratio required to convert from $4f_{SC}$ PAL to BT.601 (4:2:2), from about 922 active samples per line to about 702. In other applications, such as digital video effects, the number of phases is variable, and unknown in advance. Applications such as these can be addressed by an interpolator having a number of phases that is a suitable power of

$$\frac{1}{512} = \frac{1}{2} \cdot \frac{1}{2^8}$$

two, such as 256 phases. Phase offsets are computed to the appropriate degree of precision, and are then approximated to a binary fraction (in this case having 8 bits) to form the phase offset φ that is presented to the interpolator.

If the interpolator implements 8 fractional bits of phase, then any computed output sample may exhibit a positional error of up to $\pm^1/_{512}$ of a sample interval. This is quite acceptable for component digital video. However, if the phase accumulator implements just 8 fractional bits, that positional error will accumulate as the incremental computation proceeds across the image row. In this example, with 922 active samples per line, the error could reach three or four sample intervals at the right-hand end of the line! This isn't tolerable. The solution is to choose a sufficient number of fractional bits in the phase accumulator to keep the cumulative error within limits. In this example, 13 bits are sufficient, but only 8 of those bits need to be presented to the interpolator.

Implementing polyphase interpolators

Polyphase interpolation is a specialization of FIR filtering; however, there are three major implementation differences. First, in a typical FIR filter, the input and output rates are the same; in a polyphase interpolator, the input and output rates are usually different. Second, FIR filters usually have fixed coefficients; in a polyphase FIR interpolator, the coefficients vary on a sample-by-sample basis. Third, typical FIR filters are symmetrical, but polyphase interpolators are not.

Generally speaking, for a small number of phases – perhaps 8 or fewer – the cost of an interpolator is dominated by the number of multiplication operations, which is proportional to the number of taps. Beyond about 8 taps, the cost of coefficient storage begins to be significant. The cost of the addressing circuitry depends only upon the number of phases.

In the 35:33 downsampler example, I discussed a hardware structure driven by the input sample rate. Suppose the hardware design requires that the interpolator be driven by the output clock. For 31 of each 33 output clocks, one input sample is consumed; however, for two clocks, two input samples are consumed. This places a constraint on memory system design: Either two paths from memory must be implemented, or the extra 44 samples per line must be accessed during the blanking interval, and be stored in a small buffer. It is easier to drive this interpolator from the input clock.

Consider a 33:35 upsampler, from BT.601 to $4f_{SC}$ NTSC. If driven from the output side, the interpolator produces one output sample per clock, and consumes at most one input sample per clock. (For 2 of the 35 output clocks, no input samples are consumed.) If driven from the input side, for 2 of the 33 input clocks, the interpolator must produce two output samples. This is likely to present problems to the design of the FIR filter and the output side memory system.

The lesson is this: The structure of a polyphase interpolator is simplified if it is driven from the high-rate side.

Decimation

In Lagrange interpolation, no account is taken of whether interpolation computes more or fewer output samples than input samples. However, in signal processing, there is a big difference between downsampling – where lowpass filtering is necessary to prevent aliasing – and upsampling, where lowpass filtering is necessary to suppress "imaging." In signal processing, the term *interpolation* generally implies upsampling, that is, resampling to any ratio of unity or greater. (The term *interpolation* also describes phase shift without sample rate change; think of this as the special case of upsampling with a ratio of 1:1.)

Taken literally, *decimation* involves a ratio of 10:9, not 10:1.

Downsampling with a ratio of 10:9 is analogous to the policy by which the Roman army dealt with treachery and mutiny among its soldiers: One in ten of the offending soldiers was put to death. Their term *decimation* has come to describe downsampling in general.

Lowpass filtering in decimation

Earlier in this chapter, I expressed chroma subsampling as 2:1 decimation. In a decimator, samples are lowpass filtered to attenuate components at and above half the *new* sampling rate; then samples are dropped. Obviously, samples that are about to be dropped need not

For details of interpolators and decimators, see CROCHIERE, RONALD E., and LAWRENCE R. RABINER (1983), *Multirate Digital Signal Processing* (New York: Prentice-Hall).

be computed! Ordinarily, the sample-dropping and filtering are incorporated into the same circuit.

In the example of halfband decimation for chroma subsampling, I explained the necessity of lowpass filtering to $0.25f_S$. In the $4f_{SC}$ NTSC to BT.601 example that I presented in *Polyphase interpolators,* on page 231, the input and output sample rates were so similar that no special attention needed to be paid to bandlimiting at the resulting sample rate. If the downsampling ratio is much greater than unity – say 5:4, or greater – then the impulse response must incorporate a lowpass filtering (prefiltering, or antialiasing) function as well as phase shift. To avoid aliasing, the lowpass corner frequency must scale with the downsampling ratio. This may necessitate several sets of filter coefficients having different corner frequencies.

Image digitization and

reconstruction   22

A sequence of still pictures captured and displayed at a sufficiently high rate – typically between 24 and 60 pictures per second – can create the illusion of motion, as I will describe further on page 51. Sampling in time, in combination with 2-D (spatial) sampling, causes digital video to be sampled in three axes – horizontal, vertical, and temporal – as sketched in Figure 22.1.

One-dimensional sampling theory was described in *Filtering and sampling,* on page 191.

One-dimensional sampling theory applies along each of the three axes. I sketch just three temporal samples, because temporal sample count is limited by the number of picture stores provided; picture stores are more expensive than linestores. I sketch five vertical samples: Each vertical sample is associated with a linestore.

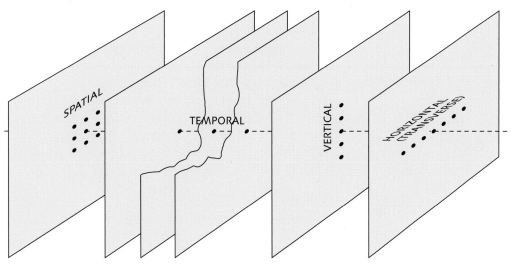

Figure 22.1 **Spatiotemporal domains**

At the far left of Figure 22.1 is a sketch of a two-dimensional *spatial* domain of a single image. Some image processing operations, such as certain kinds of filtering, can be performed separately on the horizontal and vertical axes, and have an effect in the spatial domain – these operations are called *separable*. Other processing operations cannot be separated into horizontal and vertical facets, and must be performed directly on a two-dimensional sample array. Two-dimensional sampling theory applies.

In Chapter 20, *Filtering and sampling,* on page 191, I described how to analyze a signal that is a function of the single dimension of time, such as an audio signal. Sampling theory also applies to a signal that is a function of one dimension of space, such as a single scan line (image row) of a video signal. This is the horizontal or *transverse* domain, sketched in Figure 22.2 in the margin. If an image is scanned line by line, the waveform of each line can be treated as an independent signal. The techniques of filtering and sampling in one dimension, discussed in Chapter 20, apply directly to this case.

Consider a set of points arranged vertically that originate at the same displacement along each of several successive image rows, as sketched in Figure 22.3. Those points can be considered to be sampled by the scanning process itself. Sampling theory can be used to understand the properties of these samples.

A third dimension is introduced when a succession of images is temporally sampled to represent motion. Figure 22.4 depicts samples in the same column and the same row in three successive frames.

Complex filters can act on two axes simultaneously. Figure 22.5 illustrates spatial sampling. The properties of the entire set of samples are considered all at once, and cannot necessarily be separated into independent horizontal and vertical aspects.

Spatial frequency domain

I explained in *Image structure,* on page 75, how a one-dimensional waveform in time transforms to a one-dimensional frequency spectrum. This concept can be extended to two dimensions: The two dimensions of space can be transformed into two-dimensional spatial

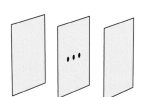

Figure 22.2 **Horizontal domain**

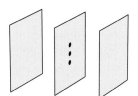

Figure 22.3 **Vertical domain**

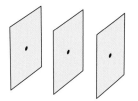

Figure 22.4 **Temporal domain**

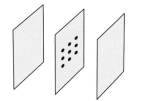

Figure 22.5 **Spatial domain**

DIGITAL VIDEO AND HD ALGORITHMS AND INTERFACES

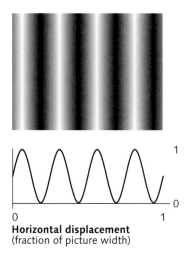

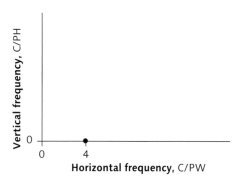

Horizontal displacement
(fraction of picture width)

Figure 22.6 Horizontal spatial frequency domain

frequency. The content of an image can be expressed as horizontal and vertical spatial frequency components. Spatial frequency is plotted using cycles per picture width (C/PW) as an *x*-coordinate, and cycles per picture height (C/PH) as a *y*-coordinate. You can gain insight into the operation of an imaging system by exploring its spatial frequency response.

In the image at the top left of Figure 22.6 above, every image row has identical content: 4 cycles of a sine wave. Underneath the image, I sketch the time domain waveform of every line. Since every line is identical, no power is present in the vertical direction. Considered in the spatial domain, this image contains power at a single horizontal spatial frequency, 4 C/PW; there is no power at any vertical spatial frequency. All of the power of this image lies at spatial frequency [4, 0].

Figure 22.7 overleaf shows an image comprising a sine wave signal in the vertical direction. The height of the picture contains 3 cycles. The spatial frequency graph, to the right, shows that all of the power of the image is contained at coordinates [0, 3] of spatial frequency. In an image where each image row takes a constant value, all of the power is located on the *y*-axis of spatial frequency.

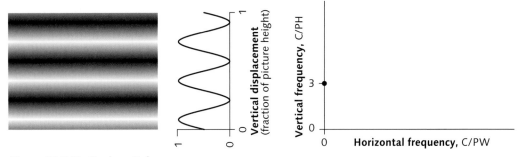

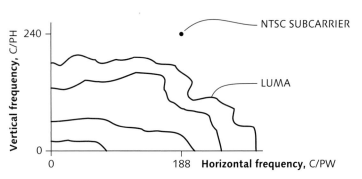

Figure 22.7 Vertical spatial frequency domain

Figure 22.8 The spatial frequency spectrum of 480*i* luma is depicted in this plot, which resembles a topographical map. If the unmodulated NTSC subcarrier were included in image data, it would take the indicated position.

When spatial frequency is determined analytically using the two-dimensional Fourier transform, the result is plotted in the manner of Figure 22.8, where low vertical frequencies – that is, low *y* values – are at the bottom. When spatial frequency is computed numerically using discrete transforms, such as the 2-D *discrete Fourier transform* (DFT), the *fast Fourier transform* (FFT), or the *discrete cosine transform* (DCT), the result is usually presented in a matrix, where low vertical frequencies are at the top.

If an image comprises rows with identical content, all of the power will be concentrated on the horizontal axis of spatial frequency. If the content of successive scans lines varies slightly, the power will spread to nonzero vertical frequencies. An image of diagonal bars would occupy a single point in spatial frequency, displaced from the *x*-axis and displaced from the *y*-axis.

The spatial frequency that corresponds to half the vertical sampling rate depends on the number of picture lines. A 480*i* system has approximately 480 picture lines: 480 samples occupy the height of the picture, and the Nyquist frequency for vertical sampling is 240 C/PH. No vertical frequency in excess of this can be represented without aliasing.

In most images, successive rows and columns of samples (of *R'*, *G'*, *B'*, or of luma) are very similar; low frequencies predominate, and image power tends to cluster toward spatial frequency coordinates [0, 0]. Figure 22.8 sketches the spatial frequency spectrum of luma in a 480*i* system. If the unmodulated NTSC colour subcarrier were an image data signal, it would take the indicated location. In composite NTSC, chroma is modulated onto the subcarrier; the resulting modulated chroma can be thought of as occupying a particular region of the spatial frequency plane, as described in *Spatial frequency spectra of NTSC,* in Chapter 6 of *Composite NTSC and PAL: Legacy Video Systems.* In NTSC encoding, modulated chroma is then summed with luma; this causes the spectra to be overlaid. If the luma and chroma spectra overlap, cross-colour and cross-luma interference artifacts can result.

In optics, the terms *magnitude frequency response* and *bandwidth* are not used. An optical component, subsystem, or system is characterized by its *modulation transfer function* (MTF), a one-dimensional plot of horizontal or vertical spatial frequency response. (*Depth of modulation* is a single point quoted from this graph.) Technically, the MTF is the Fourier transform of the point spread function (PSF) or line spread function (LSF). By definition, the MTF relates to light intensity. Since negative light power is physically unrealizable, an MTF is measured by superimposing a high-frequency sinusoidal (modulating) wave onto a constant level, then taking the ratio of output modulation to input modulation.

An *optical transfer function* (OTF) includes phase. The magnitude of an OTF is MTF; MTF disregards phase.

Comb filtering

In *Finite impulse response (FIR) filters,* on page 207, I described FIR filters operating in the single dimension of time. If the samples are from a scan line of an image, the frequency response can be considered to represent horizontal spatial frequency (in units of C/PW), instead of temporal frequency (in cycles per second, or hertz).

Consider a sample from a digital image sequence, and the sample immediately below, as sketched in Figure 22.9 in the margin. If the image has 640 active (picture) samples per line, and these two samples are presented to a comb filter like that of Figure 20.19, on page 206, but having 639 zero-samples between the two "ones," then the action of the comb filter will be identical to the action of a filter having two taps weighted [1, 1] operating in the vertical direction. In Figure 20.12, on page 203, I graphed the frequency response of a one-dimensional [1, 1] filter. The graph in

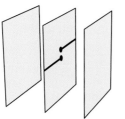

Figure 22.9 **Two samples, vertically arranged**

Figure 22.10 **The response of a [1, 1] FIR filter** operating in the vertical domain, scaled for unity gain, is shown. This is a two-line (1*H*) comb filter. Magnitude falls as cos ω.

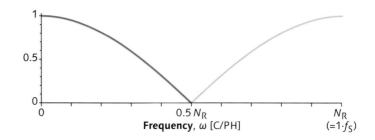

Figure 22.10 shows the response of the comb filter, expressed in terms of its response in the vertical direction. Here magnitude response is shown normalized for unity gain at DC; the filter has a response of about 0.707 (i.e., it is 3 db down) at one-quarter the vertical sampling frequency.

Spatial filtering

Placing a [1, 1] horizontal lowpass filter in tandem (cascade) with a [1, 1] vertical lowpass filter is equivalent to computing a weighted sum of spatial samples using the weights indicated in the matrix on the left in Figure 22.11. Placing a [1, 2, 1] horizontal lowpass filter in tandem with a [1, 2, 1] vertical lowpass filter is equivalent to computing a weighted sum of spatial samples using the weights indicated in the matrix on the right in Figure 22.11. These are examples of *spatial filters*. These particular spatial filters are *separable:* They can be implemented using horizontal and vertical filters in tandem.

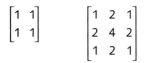

$$\begin{bmatrix} 1 & 1 \\ 1 & 1 \end{bmatrix} \qquad \begin{bmatrix} 1 & 2 & 1 \\ 2 & 4 & 2 \\ 1 & 2 & 1 \end{bmatrix}$$

Figure 22.11 **Separable spatial filter examples**

$$\begin{bmatrix} 1 & 1 & 1 \\ 1 & 1 & 1 \\ 1 & 1 & 1 \end{bmatrix} \qquad \begin{bmatrix} 0 & 0 & 1 & 0 & 0 \\ 0 & 1 & 1 & 1 & 0 \\ 1 & 1 & 1 & 1 & 1 \\ 0 & 1 & 1 & 1 & 0 \\ 0 & 0 & 1 & 0 & 0 \end{bmatrix}$$

Figure 22.12 **Inseparable spatial filter examples**

Many spatial filters are *inseparable:* Their computation must take place directly in the two-dimensional spatial domain; they cannot be implemented using cascaded one-dimensional horizontal and vertical filters. Examples of inseparable filters are given in the matrices in Figure 22.12.

Image presampling filters

In a video camera, continuous information must be subjected to a presampling ("antialiasing") filter. Aliasing is minimized by optical spatial lowpass filtering that is effected in the optical path, prior to conversion of the image signal to electronic form. MTF limitations in the lens impose some degree of filtering. An additional filter can be implemented as a discrete optical

242

element (often employing the optical property of bire-fringence). Additionally, or alternatively, some degree of filtering may be imposed by optical properties of the photosensor itself.

In resampling, signal power is not constrained to remain positive; filters having negative weights can be used. The ILPF (see page 198) and other sinc-based filters have negative weights, but those filters often ring and exhibit poor visual performance. Schreiber and Troxel found well-designed sharpened Gaussian filters with $\sigma = 0.375$ to have superior performance to the ILPF. A filter that is optimized for a particular mathematical criterion does not necessarily produce the best-looking picture!

Image reconstruction filters

On page 76, I introduced "box filter" reconstruction. This is technically known as *sample-and-hold, zero-order hold,* or *nearest-neighbor* reconstruction.

In theory, ideal image reconstruction would be obtained by using a PSF which has a two-dimensional sinc distribution. This would be a two-dimensional version of the ILPF that I described for one dimension on page 198. However, a sinc function involves negative excursions. Light power cannot be negative, so a sinc filter cannot be used for presampling at an image capture device, and cannot be used as a reconstruction filter at a display device. A box-shaped distribution of sensitivity across each element of a sensor is easily implemented, as is a box-shaped distribution of intensity across each pixel of a display. However, like the one-dimensional boxcar of Chapter 20, a box distribution has significant response at high frequencies. Used at a sensor, a box filter will permit aliasing. Used in a display, scan-line or pixel structure is likely to be visible. If an external optical element such as a lens attenuates high spatial frequencies, then a box distribution might be suitable. A simple and practical choice for either capture or reconstruction is a Gaussian having a judiciously chosen half-power width. A Gaussian is a compromise that can achieve reasonably high resolution while minimizing aliasing and minimizing the visibility of the pixel (or scan-line) structure.

SCHREIBER, WILLIAM F., and DONALD E. TROXEL (1985), "Transformations between continuous and discrete representations of images: A perceptual approach," in *IEEE Tr. on Pattern Analysis and Machine Intelligence* PAMI-7 (2): 178–186 (Mar.).

A *raised cosine* distribution is roughly similar to a Gaussian. See page 542.

Schreiber and Troxel suggest reconstruction with a sharpened Gaussian having $\sigma = 0.3$. See their paper cited in the marginal note above.

Spatial (2-D) oversampling

In image capture, as in reconstruction for image display, ideal theoretical performance would be obtained by using a PSF with a sinc distribution. However, a sinc function cannot be used directly in a transducer of light, because light power cannot be negative: Negative weights cannot be implemented. As in display reconstruction, a simple and practical choice for a direct presampling or reconstruction filter is a Gaussian having a judiciously chosen half-power width.

I have been describing direct sensors, where samples are taken directly from sensor elements, and direct displays, where samples directly energize display elements. In *Oversampling,* on page 224, I described a technique whereby a large number of directly acquired samples can be filtered to a lower sampling rate. That section discussed downsampling in one dimension, with the main goal of reducing the complexity of analog presampling or reconstruction filters. The oversampling technique can also be applied in two dimensions: A sensor can directly acquire a fairly large number of samples using a crude optical presampling filter, then use a sophisticated digital spatial filter to downsample.

The advantage of interlace – reducing scan-line visibility for a given bandwidth, spatial resolution, and flicker rate – is built upon the assumption that the sensor (camera), data transmission, and display all use identical scanning. If oversampling is feasible, the situation changes. Consider a receiver that accepts progressive image data (as in the top left of Figure 8.8, on page 91), but instead of displaying this data directly, it synthesizes data for a larger image array (as in the middle left of Figure 8.8). The synthetic data can be displayed with a spot size appropriate for the larger array, and all of the scan lines can be illuminated in each $\frac{1}{60}$ s instead of just half of them. This technique is *spatial oversampling* or *upsampling.* For a given level of scan-line visibility, this technique enables closer viewing distance than would be possible for progressive display.

Oversampling provides a mechanism for a sensor PSF or a display PSF to have negative weights, yielding a spatially "sharpened" filter. For example, a sharpened Gaussian PSF (such as anticipated by Schreiber 25 years

Oversampling to double the number of lines displayed during a frame time is called *line doubling.*

ago) can be obtained, and can achieve performance better than a Gaussian. With a sufficient degree of oversampling, using sophisticated filters having sinc-like PSFs, the interchange signal can come arbitrarily close to the Nyquist limit. However, mathematical excellence does not necessarily translate to improved visual performance. Sharp filters are liable to ring, and thereby produce objectionable artifacts.

If negative weights are permitted in a PSF, then negative signal values can potentially result. Standard studio digital interfaces provide footroom that enables conveying moderate undershoot or overshoot. Using negative weights typically improves filter performance even if negative values are clipped after downsampling.

Similarly, if a display has many elements for each digital sample, a sophisticated digital upsampler can use negative weights. Negative values resulting from the filter's operation will eventually be clipped at the display itself, but again, improved performance could result.

If oversampling had been technologically feasible in 1941, or in 1953, then the NTSC would have undoubtedly chosen a progressive transmission standard. However, oversampling was not economical for SD studio systems until about 2005, when HD production became so prevalent that HD was in essence the oversampled studio standard for SDTV. Oversampling at consumer displays was not economical until about 2005. So, until about 2005, interlace retained an economic advantage both in the studio and in consumers' premises. However, in my view this advantage has now eroded, and it is likely that all future video system standards will have progressive scanning.

Perception and
visual acuity 23

Properties of human vision are central to image system engineering. They determine how many pixels need to be provided per degree of picture angle, and how many bits are necessary to represent luminance (or tristimulus) levels. This chapter introduces the luminance discrimination and spatial properties of vision that inform image system engineering choices.

Retina

The human retina has four types of photoreceptor cells that respond to incident radiation with different spectral response curves. A retina has about 100 million *rod* cells, effective only at extremely low light levels; and about 5 million *cone* cells, of three types, that mediate colour vision. Since there is only one type of rod cell, what is loosely called *night vision* cannot discern colours.

The cone cells are sensitive to longwave, mediumwave, and shortwave light – roughly, light in the red, green, and blue portions of the spectrum. Because there are just three types of colour photoreceptors, three numerical components are necessary and sufficient to describe colour: Colour vision is inherently *trichromatic*. To arrange for three components to mimic colour vision, suitable spectral sensitivity functions must be used; this topic will be discussed in *The CIE system of colorimetry,* on page 265.

BOYNTON, ROBERT M. (1979), *Human Color Vision* (New York: Holt, Rinehart and Winston).

WANDELL, BRIAN A. (1995), *Foundations of Vision* (Sunderland, Mass.: Sinauer Associates).

Adaptation

Vision operates over a remarkable range of luminance levels – about eight orders of magnitude (decades),

Luminance of diffuse white reflector in scene [cd·m⁻²]

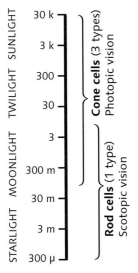

Figure 23.1 **Luminance range of vision**

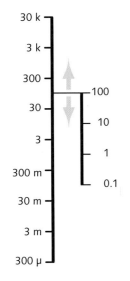

Figure 23.2 **Adaptation**

sketched in Figure 23.1. For about four decades at the low end of the range, the rods are active; vision at these light levels is called *scotopic*. For the top five or six decades, the cones are active; vision at these light levels is called *photopic*.

Mesopic vision takes place in the range of luminance levels where there is some overlap between rods and cones. Considered from the bottom of the photopic region, this is called *rod intrusion.* It is a research topic whether the rods have significance to colour image reproduction at usual luminance levels (such as in the cinema). For today's engineering purposes, the effect of rod intrusion is discounted.

During the course of the day we experience a wide range of illumination levels; adaptation adjusts accordingly, as sketched in Figure 23.2. From moonlight to sunlight, illuminance changes by a factor of about 200,000; adaptation causes the sensitivity of the visual system to reduce by about a factor of 1000. About one decade of adaptation is effected by the eye's iris – that is, by changes in pupil diameter (from about 2 mm to 8 mm). The main mechanism of adaptation is a photochemical process involving the *visual pigment* substance contained in the rods and the cones; it also involves neural mechanisms in the visual pathway.

Dark adaptation, to low luminance, is slow: Adaptation from a bright sunlit day to the darkness of a cinema can take a few minutes. Adaptation to higher luminance is rapid but can be discomforting, as you may have experienced when walking out of the cinema back into daylight.

Adaptation is a low-level phenomenon within the visual system; it is mainly controlled by total retinal illumination. Your adaptation state is closely related to the mean luminance in your field of view. In a dark viewing environment, such as a cinema, the image itself controls adaptation.

At a particular state of adaptation, vision can discern different luminances across about a 1000:1 range. When viewing a real scene, adaptation changes depending upon where in the scene your gaze is directed. In video and film, we are nearly always concerned with viewing at a known adaptation state, so a simultaneous contrast ratio of 1000:1 is adequate.

DIGITAL VIDEO AND HD ALGORITHMS AND INTERFACES

Diffuse white was described on page 117. This wide range of luminance levels is sometimes called *dynamic range*, but nothing is in motion!

For image reproduction purposes, our ability to distinguish luminance differences ordinarily extends over a ratio of luminance of about three decades – 10^3, or 1000:1 – that is, down to about 0.1% of diffuse white as portrayed on the display. Loosely speaking, luminance levels less than 0.1% of diffuse white appear just "black": Different luminances below that level are not ordinarily visually useful. Emergent *high dynamic range* (HDR) systems may increase that ratio.

Contrast sensitivity

Within the two-decade range of luminance that is useful for image reproduction, vision has a certain threshold of discrimination. It is convenient to express the discrimination capability in terms of *contrast threshold*, which is the ratio of a small test increment in luminance to the base luminance in a test stimulus having two adjacent patches of similar luminance.

Figure 23.3 below shows the pattern presented to an observer in an experiment to determine the contrast sensitivity of human vision. Most of the observer's field of vision is filled by a background luminance level, L_B, which fixes the observer's state of adaptation. In the central area of the field of vision are placed two adjacent patches having slightly different luminance levels, L and $L + \Delta L$. The experimenter presents stimuli having a wide range of test values with respect to the surround, that is, a wide range of L/L_B values. At each test luminance, the experimenter presents to the observer a range of luminance increments with respect to the test stimulus, that is, a range of $\Delta L/L$ values.

Figure 23.3 **A contrast sensitivity test pattern** is presented to an observer in an experiment to determine the contrast sensitivity of human vision. The observer is adapted to background having luminance L_B; a bipartite patch is viewed. The experimenter adjusts ΔL; the observer reports whether he or she detects a difference in lightness between the two patches.

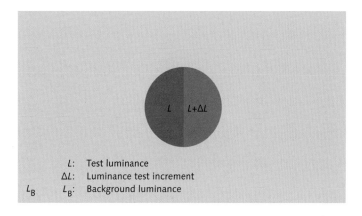

L:		Test luminance
ΔL:		Luminance test increment
L_B:		Background luminance

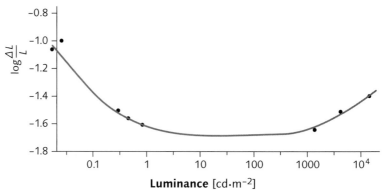

Figure 23.4 **Contrast sensitivity.** This graph is redrawn from Figure 3.4 of Schreiber's *Fundamentals of Electronic Imaging Systems.* Over a range of luminance values of about 300:1, the discrimination threshold of vision is approximately a constant ratio of luminance. The flat portion of the curve shows that the perceptual response to luminance – termed *lightness* – is approximately logarithmic. At very low luminance values, the curve departs from logarithmic behaviour and approximates a square-root; this characteristic is called the *de Vries-Rose law.*

SCHREIBER, WILLIAM F. (1993), *Fundamentals of Electronic Imaging Systems,* Third Edition (Berlin: Springer-Verlag).

$$\frac{\log 100}{\log 1.01} \approx 463; \quad 1.01^{463} \approx 100$$

$$\frac{\log 30}{\log 1.02} = 172$$

FINK, DONALD G., ed. (1955), *Color Television Standards* (New York: McGraw-Hill): 201.

When this experiment is conducted, the relationship graphed in Figure 23.4 above is found: Plotting $\log {}^{\Delta L}/_L$ as a function of $\log L$ reveals an interval of a few decades of luminance over which the discrimination capability of vision is about 1% of the test luminance level. This experiment leads to the conclusion that – for *threshold* discrimination of two adjacent patches of nearly identical luminance – the discrimination capability is roughly logarithmic.

The contrast sensitivity function begins to answer this question: What is the minimum number of discrete codes required to represent relative luminance over a particular range? In other words, what luminance codes can be thrown away without the observer noticing? On a linear luminance scale, to cover a 100:1 range with an increment of 0.01 takes ${}^{100}/_{0.01}$, or about 10,000 codes, requiring about 14 bits. If codes are spaced according to a *ratio* of 1.01, then only about 463 codes are required; codes can be represented in just 9 bits.(NTSC documents from the early 1950s used a contrast sensitivity of 2% and a contrast ratio of 30:1 to derive 172 steps; even today, 8 bits suffice for video distribution.)

The logarithmic relationship relates to contrast sensitivity *at threshold:* We are measuring the ability of the visual system to discriminate between two nearly identical luminances. If you like, call this a *just noticeable difference* (JND), defined where the difference between two stimuli is detected as often as it is undetected.

Logarithmic coding rests on the assumption that the threshold function can be extended to large luminance ratios. Experiments have shown that this assumption does not hold very well. At a given state of adaptation, the discrimination capability of vision degrades at low luminances, below several percent of diffuse white. Over a wider range of luminance, strict adherence to logarithmic coding is not justified for perceptual reasons. Coding based upon a power law is found to be a better approximation to lightness response than a logarithmic function. In video, and in computing, power functions are used instead of logarithmic functions. Incidentally, other senses behave according to power functions, as shown in Table 23.1.

STEVENS, STANLEY S. (1975), *Psychophysics* (New York: Wiley).

VAN NES, FLORIS L., and BOUMAN, MAARTEN A. (1967), "Spatial modulation transfer in the human eye," in *J. Opt. Soc. Am.* **57** (3): 401–406.

BARTEN, PETER G.J. (1999), *Contrast Sensitivity of the Human Eye and Its Effect on Image Quality* (Knegsel, Netherlands: HV Press). Also published by SPIE Press.

Contrast sensitivity function (CSF)

The contrast sensitivity of vision is about 1% – that is, vision cannot distinguish two luminance levels if the ratio between them is less than about 1.01. That threshold applies to visual features of a certain angular extent, about $1/8°$, for which vision has maximum ability to detect luminance differences. However, the contrast sensitivity of vision degrades for elements having angular subtense smaller or larger than about $1/8°$.

In vision science, rather than characterizing vision by its response to an individual small feature, we place many small elements side by side. The spacing of these elements is measured in terms of spatial frequency, in units of *cycles per degree* (CPD, or ∿/°); each cycle comprises a dark element and a white element. At the limit, a cycle comprises two samples or two pixels in adjacent columns; in the vertical dimension, the smallest cycle corresponds to two adjacent image rows.

Percept	Physical quantity	Power
Loudness	Sound pressure level	0.67
Saltiness	Sodium chloride concentration	1.4
Smell	Concentration of aromatic molecules	0.6

Table 23.1 **Power functions in perception**

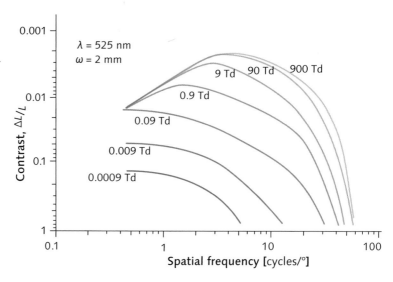

Figure 23.5 The contrast sensitivity function (CSF) of human vision varies with retinal illuminance, here shown in units of troland (Td). The curve at 9 Td, which typifies television viewing, peaks at about 4 cycles per degree (CPD, or ∿/°). Below that spatial frequency, the eye acts as a differentiator; above it, the eye acts as an integrator.

Troland [Td] is a unit of retinal illuminance equal to object luminance (in cd·m⁻²) times pupillary aperture area (in mm²).

Contrast sensitivity can also be plotted as a function of temporal modulation.

Figure 23.5 above shows a graph of the dependence of contrast sensitivity (on the *y*-axis) upon spatial frequency (on the *x*-axis, expressed in cycles per degree). Contrast sensitivity of 100 corresponds to a ratio of 1.01 (1%) being perceptible. The graph shows a family of curves, representing different adaptation levels, from very dark (0.0009 Td) to very bright (900 Td). The curve at 9 Td is typical of electronic displays.

For video engineering, three features of Figure 23.5 are important:

• First, the 90 Td curve has fallen to a contrast sensitivity of unity at about 60 cycles per degree. Vision isn't capable of perceiving spatial frequencies greater than this; a display need not reproduce detail higher than this frequency. This limit of vision sets an upper bound on the resolution (or bandwidth) that must be provided.

• Second, the peak of the 90 Td curve has a contrast sensitivity of about 1%; luminance ratios less than this need not be preserved. This limits the number of bits per pixel that must be provided.

• Third, the curve falls off at spatial frequencies below about one cycle per degree. Luminance can diminish (within limits) toward the edges of the image without the viewer's noticing; such was the case in traditional CRT consumer displays, though fall-off doesn't occur in LCD and PDP displays. Fall-off does occur in projection.

CAMPBELL, FERGUS W. and ROBSON, JOHN G. (1968), "Application of Fourier analysis to the visibility of gratings," in *J. Physiol.* (London) **197**: 551–566.

In traditional video engineering, the spatial frequency and contrast sensitivity aspects of this graph are used independently. Most video compression systems, including JPEG and MPEG, exploit the interdependence of these two aspects, as will be explained in *JPEG and motion-JPEG (M-JPEG) compression,* on page 491.

Luminance and lightness 24

Perceptual coding is essential to maximize the performance of an image coding system. In commercial imaging, we rarely use pixel values proportional to luminance; instead, we use pixel values that approximate lightness. This chapter introduces luminance and lightness.

In *Colour science for video,* on page 287, I will describe how spectral power distributions (SPDs) in the range 400 nm to 700 nm are related to colours.

Relative luminance, denoted Y, is what I call a *linear-light* quantity; it is directly proportional to physical radiance weighted by the spectral sensitivity of human vision. Luminance involves light having wavelengths in the range of about 400 nm to 700 nm. (Luminance can also be computed as a properly weighted sum of linear-light red, green, and blue tristimulus components according to the principles and standards of the CIE.)

The term *luminance* is often carelessly and incorrectly used to refer to what is now properly called *luma. See Relative luminance,* on page 258, and Appendix A, *YUV and luminance considered harmful,* on page 567.

Video signal processing equipment does not compute the linear-light luminance of colour science; nor does it compute lightness. Instead, it computes an approximation of lightness, called *luma* (denoted Y'), as a weighted sum of *nonlinear* (gamma-corrected) R', G', and B' components. Luma is only loosely related to true (CIE) luminance. In *Constant luminance,* on page 107, I explained why video systems approximate lightness instead of computing it directly. I will detail the nonlinear coding used in video in *Gamma,* on page 315. In *Luma and colour differences,* on page 335, I will outline how luma is augmented with colour information.

Radiance, intensity

Image science concerns optical power incident upon the image plane of a sensor device, and optical power emergent from the image plane of a display device.

See *Introduction to radiometry and photometry,* on page 573. Some people believe that *light* is defined by what we can see; for them, electromagnetic radiation outside the band 360 nm to 830 nm isn't light!

Radiometry concerns the measurement of radiant optical power in the electromagnetic spectrum from 3×10^{11} Hz to 3×10^{16} Hz, corresponding to wavelengths from 1 mm down to 10 nm. There are four fundamental quantities in radiometry:

- Radiant optical power, *flux*, is expressed in units of watts [W].
- Radiant flux per unit area is *irradiance;* its units are watts per meter squared [W·m^{-2}].
- Radiant flux in a certain direction – that is, radiant flux per unit of solid angle – is *radiant intensity;* its units are watts per steradian [W·sr^{-1}].
- Flux in a certain direction, per unit area, is *radiance;* its units are watts per steradian per meter squared [W·sr^{-1}·m^{-2}].

Wideband radiance is measured with an instrument called a *radiometer.* A *spectroradiometer* measures spectral radiance – that is, radiance per unit wavelength incident upon the instrument. A *spectrophotometer* incorporates a light source, and measures spectral reflectance (or for an instrument specialized for film, spectral transmittance).

Photometry is essentially radiometry as sensed by human vision: In photometry, radiometric measurements are weighted by the spectral response of human vision (to be described). This involves wavelengths (symbolized λ) between 360 nm to 830 nm, or in practical terms, 400 nm to 700 nm. Each of the four fundamental quantities of radiometry – flux, irradiance, radiant intensity, and radiance – has an analog in photometry. The photometric quantities are *luminous flux, illuminance, luminous intensity,* and (absolute) *luminance.* In video engineering, luminance is the most important of these.

The unit of luminous intensity is the candela [cd]. It is one of the seven base units in the SI system; the others are meter, kilogram, second, ampere, kelvin, and mole.

I presented a brief introduction to lightness terminology on page 27.

Luminance

The *Commission Internationale de L'Éclairage* (CIE, or International Commission on Illumination) is the international body responsible for standards in the area of colour. The CIE defines brightness as *the attribute of a visual sensation according to which an area appears to exhibit more or less light.* Brightness is, by the CIE's definition, a subjective quantity: It cannot be measured.

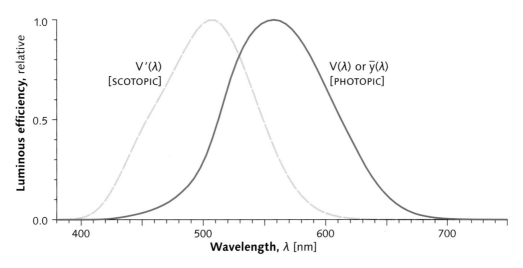

Figure 24.1 **Luminous efficiency functions.** The solid line indicates the luminance response of the cone photoreceptors – that is, the CIE *photopic* response. A monochrome scanner or camera must have this spectral response in order to correctly reproduce lightness. The peak occurs at about 555 nm, the wavelength of the brightest possible monochromatic 1 mW source. (The lightly shaded curve shows the *scotopic* response of the rod cells – loosely, the response of night vision. The increased relative luminance of shortwave light in scotopic vision is called the *Purkinje shift*.)

CIE Publication 15:2004, *Colorimetry*, 3rd Edition (Vienna, Austria: Commission Internationale de L'Éclairage).

The CIE has defined an objective quantity that is related to brightness. *Luminance* is defined as radiance weighted by the spectral sensitivity function – the sensitivity to power at different wavelengths – that is characteristic of vision. Put succinctly, brightness is apparent luminance.

The *luminous efficiency* of the CIE Standard Observer, denoted $\bar{y}(\lambda)$, is graphed as the solid line of Figure 24.1 above. The luminous efficiency function is also known as the $\bar{y}(\lambda)$ *colour-matching function* (CMF). It is defined numerically, is everywhere positive, and peaks at about 555 nm. When a spectral power distribution (SPD) is integrated using this weighting function, the result is *luminance*, symbolized L_v (or, where radiometry isn't in the context, just L). Luminance has units of candelas per meter squared, $cd \cdot m^{-2}$ (colloquially, "nits" or nt).

The y is pronounced *WYE-bar*. The luminous efficiency function is sometimes denoted V(λ), pronounced *VEE-lambda*.

In continuous terms, luminance is an integral of spectral radiance across the spectrum. It can be represented in discrete terms as a dot product. The magnitude of luminance is proportional to physical power; in that sense it resembles intensity. However, its spectral composition is intimately related to the lightness sensitivity of human vision.

You might intuitively associate pure luminance with grey, but a spectral power distribution having the shape of Figure 24.1 would *not* appear neutral grey! In fact, an SPD of that shape would appear distinctly green. As I will detail in *The CIE system of colorimetry,* on page 265, it is very important to distinguish analysis functions – called *colour-matching functions* (CMFs) of human vision, or the *spectral responsivity functions* (SRFs) of an image sensor – from synthesis functions, spectral power distributions (SPDs). The luminous efficiency function takes the role of an analysis function, not a synthesis function.

Relative luminance

In image reproduction – including photography, cinema, video, and print – we rarely, if ever, reproduce the absolute luminance of the original scene. Instead, we reproduce luminance roughly proportional to scene luminance, up to the maximum luminance available in the presentation medium. We process or record an approximation to *relative luminance*. To use the unqualified term *luminance* would suggest that we are processing or recording absolute luminance.

Luminance factor is not a synonym for relative luminance: Luminance factor refers to the reflectance – relative to a perfect diffuse reflector – of a reflective surface.

Once normalized to a specified or implied *reference white,* relative luminance is given the symbol Y; it has a purely numeric value (without units) which runs from 0 to 1 (which I prefer), or traditionally, 0 to 100. (Relative luminance is often called just "luminance.")

Relative luminance, Y, is one of three distinguished tristimulus values. The other two, X and Z, are also unitless. Various other sets of tristimulus values, such as *LMS* and *RGB*, have an implied absolute reference, come in sets of three, and also carry no units.

I will introduce *XYZ* and *LMS* in *The CIE system of colorimetry,* on page 265. I will introduce *RGB* in *Colour science for video,* on page 287.

Luminance from red, green, and blue

The luminous efficiency of vision peaks in the medium-wave region of the spectrum: If three monochromatic sources appear red, green, and blue, and have the same radiant power in the visible spectrum, then the green will appear the brightest of the three, the red will appear less bright, and the blue will be the darkest of the three. As a consequence of the luminous efficiency function, all saturated blue colours are quite dark, and all saturated yellows are quite light.

If the luminance of a scene element is to be sensed by a scanner or camera having a single spectral filter, then the spectral response of the scanner's filter must – in theory, at least – correspond to the luminous efficiency function of Figure 24.1. However, luminance can also be computed as a weighted sum of suitably chosen red, green, and blue tristimulus components. The coefficients are functions of vision, of the white reference, and of the particular red, green, and blue spectral weighting functions employed. For realistic choices of white point and primaries, the green coefficient is quite large, the blue coefficient is the smallest of the three, and the red coefficient has an intermediate value.

The primaries of contemporary video displays are standardized in BT.709. Weights computed from these primaries are appropriate to compute relative luminance from red, green, and blue tristimulus values for computer graphics, and for modern video cameras and modern displays in both SD and HD:

$$^{709}Y = 0.2126\,R + 0.7152\,G + 0.0722\,B \qquad \text{Eq 24.1}$$

My notation is outlined in Figure 28.6, on page 343. The coefficients are derived in *Colour science for video,* on page 287.

To compute luminance using $(R+G+B)/3$ is at odds with the characteristics of vision.

For BT.709 primaries, luminance comprises roughly 21% power from the red (longwave) region of the spectrum, 72% from green (mediumwave), and 7% from blue (shortwave).

Blue has a small contribution to luminance. However, vision has excellent colour discrimination among blue hues. Equation 24.1 does not give you licence to assign fewer bits to blue than to red or green – in fact, it tells you nothing whatsoever about how many bits to assign to each channel.

Lightness (CIE L^*)

Lightness is defined by the CIE as *the brightness of an area judged relative to the brightness of a similarly illuminated area that appears to be white or highly transmitting.* Lightness is most succinctly described as apparent reflectance. Vision is attuned to estimating surface reflectance factors; lightness relates to that aspect of vision. The CIE's phrase "similarly illuminated area that appears white" involves the absolute luminance by which relative luminance is normalized. In digital imaging, the reference white luminance is ordinarily

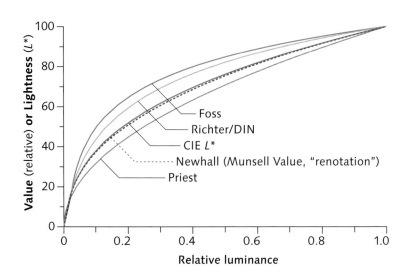

Figure 24.2 **Luminance and lightness.** The dependence of lightness (L^*) or value (V) upon relative luminance (Y) has been modeled by polynomials, power functions, and logarithms. In all of these systems, 18% "mid-grey" has lightness about halfway up the perceptual scale. This graph is adapted from Fig. 2 (6.3) in Wyszecki and Stiles, *Color Science* (cited on page 286).

The L^* symbol is pronounced *EL-star.*

closely related to the luminance of a perfectly diffusing reflector (PDR) in the scene, or the luminance at which such a scene element is presented (or will ultimately be presented) at a display.

In *Contrast sensitivity,* on page 249, I explained that vision has a nonlinear perceptual response to luminance. Vision scientists have proposed many functions that relate relative luminance to perceived lightness; several of these functions are graphed in Figure 24.2.

The computational version of lightness, denoted L^*, is defined by the CIE as a certain nonlinear function of relative luminance. In 1976, the CIE standardized *lightness,* L^* as an approximation of the lightness response of human vision. Other functions – such as *Munsell value* – specify alternate lightness scales, but the CIE L^* function is widely used and internationally standardized.

The L^* function has two segments: a linear segment near black, and a scaled and offset cube root ($1/3$-power) function everywhere else.

The 1976 version of the CIE standard expresses this definition of L^*:

Eq 24.2

$$L^*(Y) = \begin{cases} 903.3\,\dfrac{Y}{Y_N}; & \dfrac{Y}{Y_N} \leq 0.008856 \\[2ex] 116\left(\dfrac{Y}{Y_N}\right)^{\frac{1}{3}} - 16; & 0.008856 < \dfrac{Y}{Y_N} \end{cases}$$

In the 2004 version of the standard, the decimals were replaced by exact rational fractions. Today's definition is equivalent to this:

Eq 24.3

$$L^*(Y) = \begin{cases} \left(\dfrac{116}{12}\right)^3 \dfrac{Y}{Y_N}; & \dfrac{Y}{Y_N} \leq \left(\dfrac{24}{116}\right)^3 \\[2ex] 116\left(\dfrac{Y}{Y_N}\right)^{\frac{1}{3}} - 16; & \left(\dfrac{24}{116}\right)^3 < \dfrac{Y}{Y_N} \end{cases}$$

The argument Y is *relative* luminance, proportional to intensity. This quantity is already relative to some absolute white reference, typically the absolute luminance associated with a perfect (or imperfect, say 90%) diffuse reflector. The argument Y is tacitly assumed to lie on a scale whose maximum value (Y_N) is related to the viewer's adaptation state. The division by Y_N does *not* form relative luminance; rather, the normalization accommodates the tradition dating back to 1931 and earlier that tristimulus values lie on a 0 to 100 scale. For tristimulus reference range of 0 to 1, as I prefer, the division by Y_N can be omitted.

To compute L^* from optical density D in the range 0 to 2, use this relation:

$$L^* = 116 \cdot 10^{-D/3} - 16$$

The linear segment of L^* is convenient for mathematical reasons, but is not justified by visual perception: The utility of L^* is limited to a luminance ratio of about 100:1, and L^* values below 8 don't represent meaningful visual stimuli. (In graphics arts, luminance ratios up to about 300:1 are used with L^*.)

My best-fit pure power function estimate is based upon numerical (Nelder-Mead) minimization of least-squares error on L^* values 0 through 100 in steps of 10. The same result is obtained by fitting 100 samples in linear-light space.

The exponent of the power function segment of the L^* function is $\frac{1}{3}$, but the scale factor of 116 and the offset of –16 modify the pure power function such that the best-fit pure power function has an exponent of 0.42, not $\frac{1}{3}$! L^* is *based* upon a cube root, but it is not best approximated by a cube root! The best pure-power function approximation to lightness is 100 times the 0.42-power of relative luminance.

In a display system having contrast ratio of 100:1, L^* takes values between 9 and 100.

ΔL^* is pronounced *delta EL-star*.

For television viewing, we typically set Y_N to reference white at the display. In television viewing, the viewer's adaptation is controlled both by the image itself and by elements in the field of view that are outside the image. In cinema, the viewer's adaptation is controlled mainly by the image itself. In cinema, setting Y_N to reference white is not necessarily appropriate; it may be more appropriate to set Y_N to the luminance of the representation of a perfect diffuse reflector in the displayed scene.

Relative luminance of 0.01 maps to L^* of almost exactly 9. You may find it convenient to keep in mind two exact mappings of L^*: Relative luminance of $1/64$ (0.015625) corresponds to L^* of exactly 13, and relative luminance of $1/8$ (0.125) corresponds to L^* of exactly 42 (which, as Douglas Adams would tell you, is the answer to Life, the Universe, and Everything).

The difference between two L^* values, denoted ΔL^*, is a measure of perceptual "distance." In graphics arts, a difference of less than unity between two L^* values is generally considered to be imperceptible – that is, ΔL^* of unity is taken to lie at the threshold of discrimination. L^* is meaningless beyond about 200 – that is, beyond about 6.5 Y/Y_N.

In *Contrast sensitivity,* on page 249, I gave the example of logarithmic coding with a Weber contrast of 1.01. For reconstructing images for human viewing, it is never necessary to quantize relative luminance more finely than that. However, L^* suggests that a ratio of 1.01 is unnecessarily fine. The inverse L^* of 100 is unity; dividing that by the inverse L^* of 99 yields a Weber contrast of 1.025. The luminance ratio between adjacent L^* values increases as L^* falls, reaching 1.13 at L^* of 8 (at relative luminance of about 1%, corresponding to a contrast ratio of 100:1). L^* was standardized based upon estimation of lightness of diffusely reflecting surfaces; the linear segment below L^* of 8 was inserted for mathematical convenience. I consider estimating the visibility of lightness differences at luminance values less than 1% of white to be a research topic, and I recommend against using delta-L^* at such low luminances.

L^* provides one component of a *uniform colour space;* it can be described as *perceptually uniform*. Since we cannot directly measure the quantity in question, we cannot assign to it any strong properties of mathematical linearity; as far as I'm concerned, the term *perceptually linear* is not appropriate.

In Chapter 10, *Constant luminance*, I described how video systems use a luma signal (Y') that is an engineering approximation to lightness. The luma signal is only indirectly related to the relative luminance (Y) or the lightness (L^*) of colour science.

The CIE system
of colorimetry 25

The *Commission Internationale de L'Éclairage* (CIE) has defined a system that maps a *spectral power distribution* (SPD) of physics into a triple of numerical values – CIE *XYZ* tristimulus values – that form the mathematical coordinates of colour space. In this chapter, I describe the CIE system. In the following chapter, *Colour science for video*, I will explain how these *XYZ* tristimulus values are related to linear-light *RGB* values.

Figure 25.1 **Example coordinate system**

Colour coordinates are analogous to coordinates on a map (see Figure 25.1). Cartographers have different map projections for different functions: Some projections preserve areas, others show latitudes and longitudes as straight lines. No single map projection fills all the needs of all map users. Analogously, there are many "colour spaces," and as in maps, no single coordinate system fills all of the needs of users.

In Chapter 24, *Luminance and lightness*, I introduced the linear-light quantity *luminance*. To reiterate, I use the term *luminance* and the symbol Y to refer to CIE luminance. I use the term *luma* and the symbol Y' to refer to the video component that conveys an approximation to lightness. Most of the quantities in this chapter, and in the following chapter *Colour science for video*, involve "linear-light" values that are proportional to intensity. In Chapter 10, *Constant luminance*, I related the theory of colour science to the practice of video. To approximate perceptual uniformity, video uses quantities such as R', G', B', and Y' that are *not* proportional to intensity.

Fundamentals of vision

As I explained in *Retina,* on page 247, human vision involves three types of colour photoreceptor *cone* cells, which respond to incident radiation having wavelengths (λ) from about 380 nm to 750 nm. The three cell types have different spectral responses; colour is the perceptual result of their absorption of light. Normal vision involves three types of cone cells, so three numerical values are necessary and sufficient to describe a colour: Normal human colour vision is inherently *trichromatic.*

Power distributions exist in the physical world; however, colour exists only in the eye and the brain. Isaac Newton put it this way, in 1675:

"Indeed rays, properly expressed, are not coloured."

Definitions

On page 27, I outlined brightness, intensity, luminance, value, lightness, and tristimulus value. In Appendix B, *Introduction to radiometry and photometry,* on page 573, I give more rigorous definitions. In colour science, it is important to use these terms carefully. It is especially important to differentiate physical quantities (such as intensity and luminance), from perceptual quantities (such as lightness and value).

Hue is the attribute of a visual sensation according to which an area appears to be similar to one of the perceived colours, red, yellow, green, and blue, or a combination of two of them. Roughly speaking, if the dominant wavelength of a spectral power distribution shifts, the hue of the associated colour will shift.

Saturation is the colourfulness of an area, judged in proportion to its brightness. Saturation is a perceptual quantity; like brightness, it cannot be measured.

Purity is the ratio of the amount of a monochromatic stimulus to the amount of a specified achromatic stimulus which, when mixed additively, matches the colour in question. Purity is the objective correlate of saturation.

About 8% of men and 0.4% of women have deficient colour vision, called *colour blindness.* Some people have fewer than three types of cones; some people have cones with altered spectral sensitivities.

Spectral properties can be measured in electron volts (eV); the visible spectrum encompasses the range from 3.1 eV to 1.6 eV. Sometimes *wave number,* the reciprocal of wavelength is used, ordinarily expressed in cm^{-1}.

Bill Schreiber points out that the words *saturation* and *purity* are often used interchangeably, to the dismay of purists.

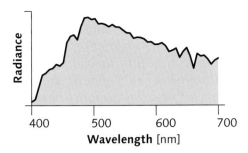

Figure 25.2 **Spectral and tristimulus colour reproduction.** A colour can be represented as a spectral power distribution (SPD), perhaps in 31 components representing power in 10 nm bands over the range 400 nm to 700 nm. However, owing to the trichromatic nature of human vision, if appropriate spectral weighting functions are used, three components suffice to represent colour. The SPD shown here is the CIE D$_{65}$ daylight illuminant.

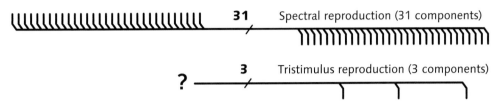

31 — Spectral reproduction (31 components)

? — 3 — Tristimulus reproduction (3 components)

Spectral power distribution (SPD) and tristimulus

The physical wavelength composition of light is expressed in a *spectral power distribution* (SPD), also known as *spectral radiance.* An SPD gives radiance [W·sr^{-1}·m^{-2}] or relative radiance as a function of wavelength, symbolized λ [nm]. An SPD representative of daylight is graphed at the upper left of Figure 25.2.

One way to reproduce a colour is to directly reproduce its spectral power distribution. This approach, termed *spectral reproduction*, is suitable for reproducing a single colour or a few colours. For example, the visible range of wavelengths from 400 nm to 700 nm could be divided into 31 bands, each 10 nm wide. However, using 31 components for each pixel is an impractical way to code an image. Owing to the trichromatic nature of vision, if suitable spectral weighting functions are used, any colour on its way to the eye can be described by just three components. This is called *tristimulus reproduction*.

The science of *colorimetry* concerns the relationship between SPDs and colour. In 1931, the Commission Internationale de L'Éclairage (CIE) standardized weighting curves for a hypothetical *Standard Observer.* These curves – graphed in Figure 25.5, on page 271 – specify how an SPD can be transformed into three *tristimulus values* that specify a colour.

The more an SPD is concentrated near one wavelength, the more saturated the associated colour will be. A colour can be desaturated by adding light with power distributed across the visible spectrum.

Strictly speaking, *colorimetry* refers to the measurement of colour. In video, *colorimetry* is taken to encompass the transfer functions used to code linear *RGB* to *R'G'B'*, and the matrix that produces luma and colour difference signals. *Colorimetry* is spelled without *u*, even in England and Canada.

Pronounced *meh-ta-MAIR-ik* and *meh-TAM-er-ism*.

To specify a colour, it is not necessary to specify its spectrum – it suffices to specify its tristimulus values. To reproduce a colour, its spectrum need not be reproduced – it suffices to reproduce its tristimulus values. This is known as a *metameric* match. *Metamerism* occurs when a pair of spectrally distinct stimuli have the same tristimulus values.

The colours produced in reflective systems – such as photography, printing, or paint – depend not only upon the colourants and the substrate (media), but also on the SPD of the illumination. To guarantee that two coloured materials will match under illuminants having different SPDs, you may have to achieve a spectral match.

Spectral constraints

The relationship between spectral distributions and the three components of a colour value is usually explained starting from the famous colour-matching experiment. I will instead explain the relationship by illustrating the practical concerns of engineering the spectral filters required by a colour scanner or camera, using Figure 25.3 opposite.

For a textbook lowpass filter – but in the signal domain – see Figure 20.23 on page 212.

The top row shows the spectral sensitivity of three wideband optical filters having uniform response across each of the longwave, mediumwave, and shortwave regions of the spectrum. Most filters, whether for electrical signals or for optical power, are designed to have responses as uniform as possible across the passband, to have transition zones as narrow as possible, and to have maximum possible attenuation in the stopbands.

At the top right of Figure 25.3, I show two monochromatic sources, which appear saturated orange and red, analyzed by "textbook" bandpass filters. These two different wavelength distributions, which are seen as different colours, report the identical *RGB* triple [1, 0, 0]. The two SPDs are perceived as having different colours; however, this filter set reports identical *RGB* values. The wideband filter set senses colour incorrectly.

At first glance it may seem that the problem with the wideband filters is insufficient wavelength discrimination. The middle row of the example attempts to solve that problem by using three narrowband filters. The narrowband set solves one problem, but creates

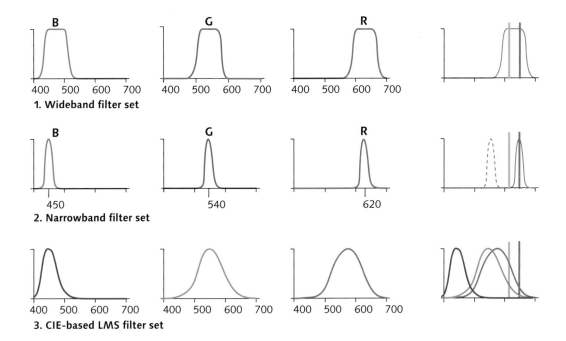

Figure 25.3 **Spectral constraints** are associated with scanners and cameras. **1. The wideband filter set** of the top row shows the spectral sensitivity of filters having uniform response across the shortwave, mediumwave, and longwave regions of the spectrum. Two monochromatic sources seen by the eye to have different colours – in this case, a saturated orange and a saturated red – cannot be distinguished by the filter set. **2. The narrowband filter set** in the middle row solves that problem, but creates another: Many monochromatic sources "fall between" the filters, and are sensed indistinguishably as black. To see colour as the eye does, the filter responses must closely relate to the colour response of the eye. **3. The CIE-based filter set** in the bottom row shows the *Hunt-Pointer-Estévez* (HPE) *colour-matching functions* (CMFs).

another: Many monochromatic sources "fall between" the filters. Here, the orange source reports an *RGB* triple of [0, 0, 0], identical to the result of scanning black.

Although my example is contrived, the problem is not. Ultimately, the test of whether a camera or scanner is successful is whether it reports distinct *RGB* triples if and only if human vision sees two SPDs as being different colours. For a scanner or a camera to see colour as the eye does, the filter sensitivity curves must be intimately related to the response of human vision – more specifically, the camera spectral sensitivities must be identical to the CIE CMFs, or a linear combination of

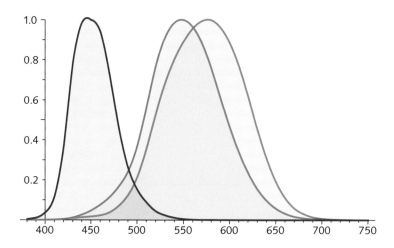

Figure 25.4 **The HPE colour-matching functions** estimate the responses of the three classes of *cone* photoreceptor cells. These are the *Hunt-Pointer-Estévez* (HPE) *colour-matching functions* (CMFs). In a practical camera, it is desirable for noise performance reasons to move the longwave ("red") response toward longer wavelengths; however, you do this, colour accuracy suffers.

What I call the *Maxwell-Ives criterion* is sometimes called *Luther-Ives*, or just *Luther*. In my view, James Clerk Maxwell and Herbert E. Ives mainly deserve the credit.

CIE 15 (2004), *Colorimetry, 3rd Edition* (Vienna, Austria: Commission Internationale de L'Éclairage).

$\bar{x}$, $\bar{y}$, and $\bar{z}$ are pronounced *ECKS-bar, WYE-bar, ZEE-bar*.

Some authors refer to CMFs as *colour mixture curves*, or CMCs. That usage is best avoided, because CMC denotes a particular colour difference formula defined in British Standard BS:6923.

them. A camera that meets this requirement is said to conform to the *Maxwell-Ives criterion.*

The famous "colour-matching experiment" was devised during the 1920s to characterize the relationship between physical spectra and perceived colour. Today, we might seek the best approximation to the spectral sensitivities of the cone photoreceptor cells. Those functions are illustrated at the bottom of Figure 25.3, and they are graphed at larger scale in Figure 25.5. Different researchers prefer slightly different versions of these functions; the ones shown here are the *Hunt-Pointer-Estévez* (HPE) *cone fundamentals.*

The CIE did not attempt to directly determine the responses of the cone cells. Instead, theirs was an indirect experiment.that measured mixtures of different spectral distributions that are required for human observers to match colours. In 1931 the CIE took data from these experiments, transformed the data according to certain mathematical principles, and standardized a set of spectral weighting functions that are related to the cone responses by a 3×3 matrix transform.

The CIE curves are called the $\bar{x}(\lambda)$, $\bar{y}(\lambda)$, and $\bar{z}(\lambda)$ *colour-matching functions* (CMFs) for the CIE Standard Observer, and are graphed in Figure 25.5. They are defined numerically; they are everywhere nonnegative.

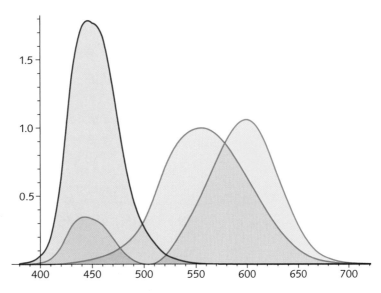

Figure 25.5 CIE 1931, 2° colour-matching functions. A sensor or camera must have these spectral response curves, or linear combinations of them, in order to capture all colours. However, practical considerations make this difficult. These are analysis functions; they are *not* comparable to spectral power distributions! The standard $\bar{y}(\lambda)$ function is scaled to unity at 560 nm. The $\bar{x}(\lambda)$ and $\bar{z}(\lambda)$ functions are scaled to match the integral of $\bar{y}(\lambda)$.

The term *sharpening* is used in the colour science community to describe certain 3×3 transforms of cone fundamentals; the "sharpening" is in the spectral domain. I consider the term to be unfortunate, because in image science, *sharpening* more sensibly refers to spatial phenomena.

The CIE 1931 functions are appropriate to estimate the visual response to stimuli subtending angles of about 2° at the eye. In 1964, the CIE standardized a set of CMFs suitable for stimuli subtending about 10°; this set is generally not appropriate for image reproduction.

The functions of the CIE Standard Observer were standardized based upon experiments with visual colour matching. Research since then revealed the spectral sensitivities of the three types of cone cells – the *cone fundamentals*. We would expect the CIE CMFs to be intimately related to the properties of the retinal photoreceptors; many experimenters have related the cone fundamentals to CIE tristimulus values through 3×3 linear matrix transforms. None of the proposed mappings is very accurate, apparently owing to the intervention of high-level visual processing. For engineering purposes, the CIE functions suffice.

The $\bar{y}(\lambda)$ and $\bar{z}(\lambda)$ CMFs each have one peak – each is "unimodal." However, the $\bar{x}(\lambda)$ CMF is bimodal, having a secondary peak between 400 nm and 500 nm. This "bump" does not directly reflect any physiological property of vision; it is best considered as a consequence of the mathematical process by which the $\bar{x}(\lambda)$, $\bar{y}(\lambda)$, and $\bar{z}(\lambda)$ curves are constructed.

CIE *XYZ* tristimulus

X, Y, and *Z* are pronounced *big-X, big-Y,* and *big-Z,* or *cap-X, cap-Y,* and *cap-Z,* to distinguish them from *little-x* and *little-y,* to be described in a moment.

Weighting an SPD under the $\bar{y}(\lambda)$ colour-matching function yields luminance (symbol *Y*), as I described on page 205. When luminance is augmented with two other values, computed in the same manner as luminance but using the $\bar{x}(\lambda)$ and $\bar{z}(\lambda)$ colour-matching functions, the resulting values are known as *XYZ tristimulus* values (denoted *X, Y,* and *Z*). *XYZ* values correlate to the spectral sensitivity of human vision. Their amplitudes – always nonnegative – are proportional to intensity.

Tristimulus values are computed from a continuous SPD by integrating the SPD under the $\bar{x}(\lambda)$, $\bar{y}(\lambda)$, and $\bar{z}(\lambda)$ colour-matching functions. In discrete form, tristimulus values are computed by a matrix multiplication, as illustrated in Figure 25.6 opposite.

Grassmann's Third Law:

Sources of the same colour produce identical effects in an additive mixture regardless of their spectral composition.

Human colour vision follows a principle of superposition known as Grassmann's Third Law: The set of tristimulus values computed from the sum of a set of SPDs is identical to the sum of the tristimulus values of each SPD. Due to this linearity of additive colour mixture, any set of three components that is a nontrivial linear combination of *X, Y,* and *Z* – such as *R, G,* and *B* – is also a set of tristimulus values. (In *Transformations between RGB and CIE XYZ,* on page 307, I will introduce related CMFs that produce *R, G,* and *B* tristimulus values.)

Luminance can be considered to be a distinguished tristimulus value that is meaningful on its own, and, exceptionally, carries units of $cd \cdot m^{-2}$. Apart from luminance, tristimuli come in sets of three, as the word suggests, and have no units.

THORNTON, WILLIAM A. (1999), "Spectral sensitivities of the normal human visual system, color-matching functions and their principles, and how and why the two sets should coincide," in *Color Research and Application* **24** (2): 139–156 (Apr.).

This chapter accepts the CIE Standard Observer rather uncritically. Although the CIE Standard Observer is very useful and widely used, some researchers believe that it exhibits some problems and ought to be improved. For one well-informed and provocative view, see Thornton.

$$
\begin{bmatrix} X \\ Y \\ Z \end{bmatrix} =
\begin{bmatrix}
0.0143 & 0.0004 & 0.0679 \\
0.0435 & 0.0012 & 0.2074 \\
0.1344 & 0.0040 & 0.6456 \\
0.2839 & 0.0116 & 1.3856 \\
0.3483 & 0.0230 & 1.7471 \\
0.3362 & 0.0380 & 1.7721 \\
0.2908 & 0.0600 & 1.6692 \\
0.1954 & 0.0910 & 1.2876 \\
0.0956 & 0.1390 & 0.8130 \\
0.0320 & 0.2080 & 0.4652 \\
0.0049 & 0.3230 & 0.2720 \\
0.0093 & 0.5030 & 0.1582 \\
0.0633 & 0.7100 & 0.0782 \\
0.1655 & 0.8620 & 0.0422 \\
0.2904 & 0.9540 & 0.0203 \\
0.4334 & 0.9950 & 0.0087 \\
0.5945 & 0.9950 & 0.0039 \\
0.7621 & 0.9520 & 0.0021 \\
0.9163 & 0.8700 & 0.0017 \\
1.0263 & 0.7570 & 0.0011 \\
1.0622 & 0.6310 & 0.0008 \\
1.0026 & 0.5030 & 0.0003 \\
0.8544 & 0.3810 & 0.0002 \\
0.6424 & 0.2650 & 0.0000 \\
0.4479 & 0.1750 & 0.0000 \\
0.2835 & 0.1070 & 0.0000 \\
0.1649 & 0.0610 & 0.0000 \\
0.0874 & 0.0320 & 0.0000 \\
0.0468 & 0.0170 & 0.0000 \\
0.0227 & 0.0082 & 0.0000 \\
0.0114 & 0.0041 & 0.0000
\end{bmatrix}^T
\bullet
\begin{bmatrix}
82.75 \\
91.49 \\
93.43 \\
86.68 \\
104.86 \\
117.01 \\
117.81 \\
114.86 \\
115.92 \\
108.81 \\
109.35 \\
107.80 \\
104.79 \\
107.69 \\
104.41 \\
104.05 \\
100.00 \\
96.33 \\
95.79 \\
88.69 \\
90.01 \\
89.60 \\
87.70 \\
83.29 \\
83.70 \\
80.03 \\
80.21 \\
82.28 \\
78.28 \\
69.72 \\
71.61
\end{bmatrix}
\begin{matrix}
\text{400 nm} \\ \\ \\ \\ \\
\text{450 nm} \\ \\ \\ \\ \\
\text{500 nm} \\ \\ \\ \\ \\
\text{550 nm} \\ \\ \\ \\ \\
\text{600 nm} \\ \\ \\ \\ \\
\text{650 nm} \\ \\ \\ \\ \\
\text{700 nm}
\end{matrix}
$$

Figure 25.6 **Calculation of tristimulus values by matrix multiplication** starts with a column vector representing the SPD. The 31-element column vector in this example is a discrete version of CIE Illuminant D_{65} sampled at 10 nm intervals. The SPD is matrix-multiplied by a discrete version of the CIE $\bar{x}(\lambda)$, $\bar{y}(\lambda)$, and $\bar{z}(\lambda)$ colour-matching functions (CMFs) of Figure 25.5, here in a 31×3 matrix (which is sometimes denoted **A**). The superscript **T** denotes the matrix transpose operation. The result of the matrix multiplication is a set of *XYZ* tristimulus components.

In the caption to Figure 25.5, I mentioned that $\bar{y}(\lambda)$ is scaled to unity at 560 nm. In the 10 nm approximation given here, the value is not exactly unity owing to the CIE's interpolation procedure.

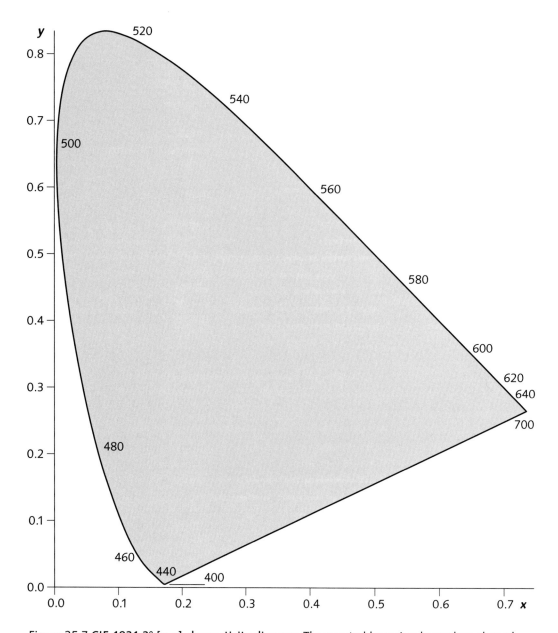

Figure 25.7 **CIE 1931 2° [x, y] chromaticity diagram.** The spectral locus is a horseshoe-shaped path swept by a monochromatic source as it is tuned from 400 nm to 700 nm. The *line of purples* traces SPDs that combine longwave and shortwave power but have no mediumwave power. All colours lie within the horseshoe-shaped region: Points outside this region are not colours.

This diagram is not a slice through $[X, Y, Z]$ space! Instead, points in $[X, Y, Z]$ project onto the plane of the diagram in a manner comparable to the perspective projection. White has $[X, Y, Z]$ values near $[1, 1, 1]$; it projects to a point near the center of the diagram, in the region of $[\frac{1}{3}, \frac{1}{3}]$. Attempting to project black, at *XYZ* coordinates $[0, 0, 0]$, would require dividing by zero in Equation 25.1: Black has no place in a chromaticity diagram.

DIGITAL VIDEO AND HD ALGORITHMS AND INTERFACES

It is convenient, for both conceptual understanding and for computation, to have a representation of "pure" colour in the absence of lightness. The CIE standardized a procedure for normalizing *XYZ* tristimulus values to obtain two *chromaticity* values x and y.

The x and y symbols are pronounced *little-x* and *little-y*.

Chromaticity values are computed by this projective transformation:

$$x = \frac{X}{X+Y+Z}; \qquad y = \frac{Y}{X+Y+Z} \qquad \text{Eq 25.1}$$

A third chromaticity coordinate, z, is defined, but is redundant since $x + y + z = 1$. The x and y chromaticity coordinates are abstract values that have no direct physical interpretation.

A colour can be specified by its chromaticity and luminance, in the form of an *xyY* triple. To recover *X* and *Z* tristimulus values from [x, y] chromaticities and luminance, use the inverse of Equation 25.1:

$$X = \frac{x}{y}Y; \qquad Z = \frac{1-x-y}{y}Y \qquad \text{Eq 25.2}$$

A colour plots as a point in an [x, y] *chromaticity diagram*, plotted in Figure 25.7 opposite.

In Figure 25.8 in the margin, I sketch several features of the [x, y] diagram. The important features lie on, or below and to the left of, the line $y = 1 - x$.

When a narrowband (monochromatic) SPD comprising power at just one wavelength is swept across the range 400 nm to 700 nm, it traces the inverted-U (or horseshoe) shaped *spectral locus* in [x, y] coordinates.

The sensation of purple cannot be produced by a single wavelength; it requires a mixture of shortwave and longwave light. The *line of purples* on a chromaticity diagram joins the chromaticity of extreme blue (violet), containing only shortwave power, to the chromaticity of extreme red, containing only longwave power.

There is no unique physical or perceptual definition of white. Many important sources of illumination are blackbody radiators, whose chromaticity coordinates lie on the *blackbody locus* (sometimes called the *Planckian*

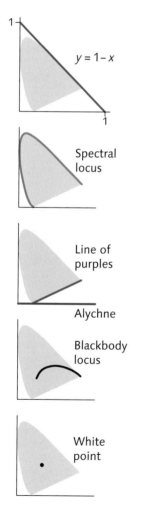

Figure 25.8 CIE [x, y] chart features.

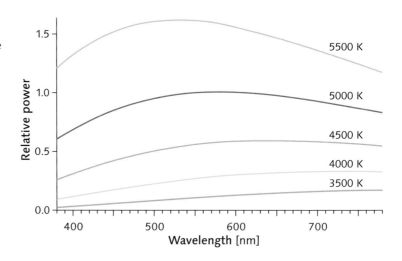

locus). Blackbody radiators will be discussed in the next section.

An SPD that appears white has CIE [*X, Y, Z*] values of about [1, 1, 1], and [*x, y*] coordinates in the region of [$\frac{1}{3}$, $\frac{1}{3}$]: White plots in the central area of the chromaticity diagram. In the section *White*, on page 278, I will describe the SPDs associated with white.

Any all-positive (*physical*, or *realizable*) SPD plots as a single point in the chromaticity diagram, within the region bounded by the spectral locus and the line of purples. All colours lie within this region; points outside this region are not associated with colours. It is silly to qualify "colour" by "visible," because colour is itself defined by vision – if it's invisible, it's not a colour!

In the projective transformation that forms *x* and *y*, any additive mixture (linear combination) of two SPDs – or two tristimulus values – plots on a straight line in the [*x, y*] plane. However, distances are not preserved, so chromaticity values do not combine linearly. Neither [*X, Y, Z*] nor [*x, y*] coordinates are perceptually uniform.

Blackbody radiation

Max Planck determined that the SPD radiated from a hot object – a *blackbody radiator* – is a function of the temperature to which the object is heated. Figure 25.9 above shows the SPDs of blackbody radiators at several temperatures. As temperature increases, the absolute

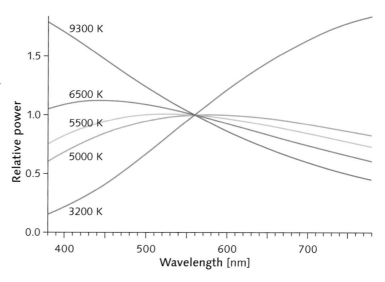

Figure 25.10 **SPDs of blackbody radiators, normalized** to equal power at 555 nm, are graphed here. The dramatically different spectral character of blackbody radiators at different temperatures is evident.

power increases and the spectral peak shifts toward shorter wavelengths. If the power of blackbody radiators is normalized at an arbitrary wavelength, dramatic differences in spectral character become evident, as illustrated in Figure 25.10 above.

Many sources of illumination have, at their core, a heated object, so it is useful to characterize an illuminant by specifying the absolute temperature (in units of kelvin, K) of a blackbody radiator having the same hue.

The *blackbody locus* is the path traced in [x, y] coordinates as the temperature of a blackbody source is raised. At low temperature, the source appears red ("red hot"). When a viewer is adapted to a white reference of CIE D$_{65}$, which I will describe in a moment, at about 2000 K, the source appears orange. Near 4000 K, it appears yellow; at about 6000 K, white. Above 10,000 K, it is blue hot.

The symbol for Kelvin is properly written K (with no degree sign).

To a colour scientist, it's paradoxical that cold water faucets are colour-coded blue and hot water faucets are colour-coded red!

Colour temperature

An illuminant may be characterized by a single colour temperature number – the temperature of a blackbody radiator that exactly matches the chromaticity of the source. If the match is approximate, the term *correlated colour temperature* (CCT) is used.

Colour temperature is sometimes augmented by a second number giving the closest distance in the deprecated CIE 1960 [u, v] coordinates of the colour

The 1960 [u, v] coordinates are described in the marginal note on page 281.

from the blackbody locus – the arcane "minimum perceptible colour difference" (MPCD) units. I consider it more sensible to specify colour temperature in kelvin for intuitive purposes, accompanied by [x, y] or [u', v'] chromaticity coordinates.

When a blackbody source's temperature sweeps from a low value (say 1000 K) to a high value (say 20,000 K), the chromaticity coordinate of the source sweeps out a path called the *blackbody locus* in the chromaticity diagram. (See Figure 25.8, on page 275.) Such a plot distributes temperatures in a highly nonuniform manner.

White

As I mentioned a moment ago, there is no unique definition of white: To achieve accurate colour, you must specify the SPD or the chromaticity of white. In additive mixture, to be detailed on page 288, the *white point* is the set of tristimulus values (or the luminance and chromaticity coordinates) of the colour reproduced by equal contributions of the red, green, and blue primaries. The colour of white is a function of the ratio – or *balance* – of power among the primary components. (In subtractive reproduction, the colour of white is determined by the SPD of the illumination, multiplied by the SPD of the uncoloured media.)

It is sometimes convenient for purposes of calculation to define white as an SPD whose power is uniform throughout the visible spectrum. This white reference is known as the *equal-energy illuminant*, denoted *CIE Illuminant E;* its CIE [x, y] coordinates are [$\frac{1}{3}$, $\frac{1}{3}$].

The CIE D illuminants are properly denoted with a two-digit subscript. CIE Illuminant D_{65} has a correlated colour temperature of about 6504 K.

A more realistic reference, approximating daylight, has been numerically specified by the CIE as Illuminant D_{65}. You should use this unless you have a good reason to use something else. The print industry commonly uses D_{50} and photography commonly uses D_{55}; these represent compromises between the conditions of indoor (tungsten) and daylight viewing. Figure 25.11 shows the SPDs of several standard illuminants; chromaticity coordinates are given in Table 25.1.

Concerning 9300 K, see page 311.

Many computer displays and many consumer television receivers have a default colour temperature setting of 9300 K. That white reference contains too much blue to achieve acceptable image reproduction in Europe or

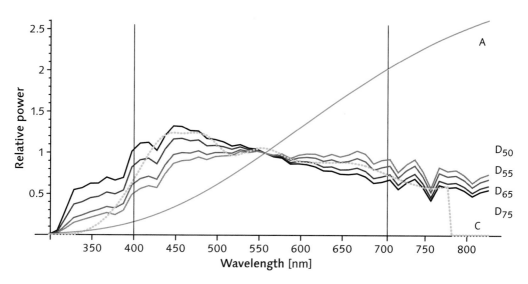

Figure 25.11 **CIE illuminants** are graphed here. Illuminant A is an obsolete standard representative of tungsten illumination; its SPD resembles the blackbody radiator at 3200 K shown in Figure 25.10, on page 277. Illuminant C was an early standard for daylight; it too is obsolete. The family of D illuminants represents daylight at several colour temperatures.

America; transform from D_{65} to 9300 K involves multiplying the BT.709 blue tristimulus value by about 1.3. However, there is a cultural preference in Asia for a more bluish reproduction than D_{65}; 9300 K is common in Asia (e.g., in studio displays in Japan).

Table 25.1 enumerates the chromaticity coordinates of several common white references:

Notation	x	y	z	u'_N	v'_N
1666.7 K (6000 mirek)	0.37683	0.38050	0.24267	0.2213	0.5027
CIE Ill. A (obsolete), ~2856 K	0.44757	0.40745	0.14498	0.2560	0.5243
CIE Ill. C (obsolete)	0.31006	0.31616	0.37378	0.2009	0.4609
CIE Ill. D_{50}	0.3457	0.3587	0.2956	0.2091	0.4882
CIE Ill. D_{55}	0.3325	0.3476	0.3199	0.2044	0.4801
CIE Ill. D_{65}, ~6504 K	0.312727	0.329024	0.358250	0.1978	0.4683
CIE Ill. E (equal-energy)	0.333334	0.333330	0.333336	0.2105	0.4737
9300 K (used in studio standards in Asia)	0.2830	0.2980	0.4190	0.1884	0.4463
∞ (0 mirek)	0.23704	0.236741	0.526219	0.1767	0.3970

Table 25.1 **White references.** The CIE D_{65} standard ubiquitous in SD and HD is highlighted.

The reciprocal of correlated colour temperature is somewhat more perceptually uniform than correlated colour temperature itself. Cinematographers use units of *mirek* (micro reciprocal kelvin [MK^{-1}]), that is, $10^{6}/_{t}$, where *t* is in units of kelvin [K]. Mirek units are more perceptually uniform than kelvin. For typical video or cinema acquisition, CCT typically ranges from 2000 K to 10,000 K; that is, from 500 to 100 mirek.

The mirek unit is sometimes called *reciprocal mega-kelvin*, and was historically called *mired* ("micro reciprocal degree") .

Chromatic adaptation

Human vision adapts to the viewing environment. An image viewed in isolation – such as a 35 mm slide, or motion picture film projected in a dark room – creates its own white reference; a viewer will be quite tolerant of variation in white point. However, if the same image is viewed alongside an external white reference, or with a second image, differences in white point can be objectionable. Complete adaptation seems to be confined to colour temperatures from about 5000 K to 6500 K. Tungsten illumination, at about 3200 K, almost always appears somewhat yellow.

Tungsten illumination can't have a colour temperature higher than tungsten's melting point, 3695 K.

Perceptually uniform colour spaces

As I outlined in *Perceptual uniformity,* on page 30, a system is perceptually uniform if a small perturbation to a component value is approximately equally percep-tible across the range of that value.

Luminance is not perceptually uniform. On page 259, I described how luminance can be transformed to light-ness, denoted L^{*}, which is nearly perceptually uniform:

$$L^{*}(Y) = \begin{cases} \left(\dfrac{116}{12}\right)^{3} \dfrac{Y}{Y_N}; & \dfrac{Y}{Y_N} \leq \left(\dfrac{24}{116}\right)^{3} \\[4mm] 116\left(\dfrac{Y}{Y_N}\right)^{\frac{1}{3}} - 16; & \left(\dfrac{24}{116}\right)^{3} < \dfrac{Y}{Y_N} \end{cases}$$

Eq 25.3

DIGITAL VIDEO AND HD ALGORITHMS AND INTERFACES

L*u*v* and L*a*b* are often written CIELUV and CIELAB; they are usually pronounced SEA-love and SEA-lab. The u* and v* quantities of colour science – and the u' and v' quantities, to be described – are unrelated to the U and V colour difference components of video.

Extending this concept to colour, *XYZ* and *RGB* tristimulus values, and *xyY* (chromaticity and luminance), are far from perceptually uniform. Finding a transformation of *XYZ* into a reasonably perceptually uniform space occupied the CIE for a decade, and in the end no single system could be agreed upon. In 1976, the CIE standardized two systems, L*u*v* and L*a*b*, which I will now describe. In both systems, perceptual difference is approximated as Euclidean distance.

CIE L*u*v*

Computation of CIE L*u*v* starts with a projective transformation of [*X, Y, Z*] into intermediate *u'* and *v'* quantities:

$$u' = \frac{4X}{X + 15Y + 3Z}; \qquad v' = \frac{9Y}{X + 15Y + 3Z} \qquad \text{Eq 25.4}$$

Equivalently, *u'* and *v'* can be computed from *x* and *y* chromaticity:

$$u' = \frac{4x}{3 - 2x + 12y}; \qquad v' = \frac{9y}{3 - 2x + 12y} \qquad \text{Eq 25.5}$$

To recover *X* and *Z* tristimulus values from *u'* and *v'*, use these relations:

$$X = \frac{9u'}{4v'}Y; \qquad Z = \frac{12 - 3u' - 20v'}{4v'}Y \qquad \text{Eq 25.6}$$

To recover *x* and *y* chromaticity from *u'* and *v'*, use these relations:

$$x = \frac{9u'}{6u' - 16v' + 12}; \qquad y = \frac{4v'}{6u' - 16v' + 12} \qquad \text{Eq 25.7}$$

The primes in the CIE 1976 *u'* and *v'* quantities denote the successor to the obsolete 1960 CIE *u* and *v* quantities. $u = u'$; $v = \frac{2}{3}v'$ – that is, the 1960 *v* quantity underestimated visual perceptibility, and was multiplied by a factor of 1.5 to form the 1976 system. (To compute 1960 *v*, replace the numerator 9*y* in Eq 25.5 by 6*y*.) The primes are not formally related to the primes in R', G', B', and Y', though all imply some degree of perceptual uniformity.

Since *u'* and *v'* are formed by a projective transformation, *u'* and *v'* coordinates are associated with a chromaticity diagram similar to the *CIE 1931 2° [x, y] chromaticity diagram* on page 274. You can use the [*u', v'*] diagram if you want to produce 2-D plots that are more suggestive of the perceptibility of colour differences than an [*x, y*] plot would be. However, [*u', v'*] are subsequently multiplied by L* (see Equation 25.8 below) to form [*u*, v**]. That multiplication effectively enlarges the perceptual increment as luminance decreases. Perceptual differences in a [*u', v'*] diagram are dependant upon luminance, but that fact is not evident from the diagram: Be careful not to draw strong conclusions from the diagram.

To compute u^* and v^*, first compute L^*. Then compute u'_N and v'_N from your reference white X_N, Y_N, and Z_N. (The subscript N suggests *normalized*.) The u'_N and v'_N coordinates for several common white points are given in Table 25.1, *White references,* on page 279. (The $[x_N, y_N]$ coordinates for a colour temperature of infinity are about [0.237, 0.237]; the $[u'_N, v'_N]$ coordinates are about [0.177, 0.397].) Finally, compute u^* and v^*:

ΔE^* is pronounced *delta E-star.*

$$u^* = 13 \cdot L^*(Y) \cdot \left(u' - u'_N \right); \qquad v^* = 13 \cdot L^*(Y) \cdot \left(v' - v'_N \right) \qquad \text{Eq 25.8}$$

Gamut refers to the range of colours available in an imaging system. For gamuts typical of image reproduction, u^* and v^* values each range approximately ±100.

Euclidean distance in $L^*u^*v^*$ – denoted ΔE^*_{uv} – estimates the perceptibility of colour differences:

$$\Delta E^*_{uv} = \sqrt{\left(L^*_2 - L^*_1 \right)^2 + \left(u^*_2 - u^*_1 \right)^2 + \left(v^*_2 - v^*_1 \right)^2} \qquad \text{Eq 25.9}$$

If ΔE^*_{uv} is unity or less, the colour difference is assumed to be imperceptible. However, $L^*u^*v^*$ does not achieve perceptual uniformity, it is merely an approximation. ΔE^*_{uv} values between about 1 and 4 may or may not be perceptible, depending upon the region of colour space being examined. ΔE^*_{uv} values greater than 4 are likely to be perceptible; whether such differences are objectionable depends upon circumstances.

A polar-coordinate version of the $[u^*, v^*]$ pair can be used to express chroma and hue:

$$C^*_{uv} = \sqrt{u^{*2} + v^{*2}}; \qquad h_{uv} = \tan^{-1} \frac{v^*}{u^*} \qquad \text{Eq 25.10}$$

In addition, there is a "psychometric saturation" term:

$$s_{uv} = \frac{C^*}{L^*} \qquad \text{Eq 25.11}$$

Chroma, hue, and saturation defined here are not directly related to saturation and hue in the *HSB, HSI, HSL, HSV,* and *IHS* systems used in computing and in digital image processing: Most of the published descriptions of these spaces, and most of the published formulæ, disregard the principles of colour science. In particular, the quantities called *lightness* and *value* are wildly inconsistent with their definitions in colour science.

CIE $L^*u^*v^*$ exhibits reasonable perceptual uniformity. $L^*u^*v^*$ has been common in video because the mapping of *XYZ*, *xyY*, and *RGB* to the $u'v'$ coordinates is projective: Straight lines in any of these spaces map to straight lines in $u'v'$. Despite the convenience and utility of $L^*u^*v^*$, colour scientists today generally agree that better perceptual performance is exhibited by $L^*a^*b^*$, which I will now describe.

CIE *L*a*b** (CIELAB)

The quantities a^* and b^* are computed as follows:

Eq 25.12

$$a^* = \frac{125}{29}\left[L^*\left(\frac{X}{X_N}\right) - L^*\left(\frac{Y}{Y_N}\right) \right]; \quad b^* = \frac{50}{29}\left[L^*\left(\frac{Y}{Y_N}\right) - L^*\left(\frac{Z}{Z_N}\right) \right]$$

The coefficients are approximately 4.310 and 1.724. My definition is written in an unusual way, using L^* instead of the traditional auxiliary function f. The definition of L^* involves a linear segment having C^1 continuity with a power function segment. That linear segment is incorporated (by way of L^*) into a^* and b^*.

The reference L^* range from black to white is zero to 100. For the BT.709 primaries typical of SD and HD, a^* and b^* are contained within the ranges [–87...+97] and [–108...+95] respectively, not including any undershoot, overshoot, or "illegal" or "invalid" $C_B C_R$ values.

As in $L^*u^*v^*$, one unit of Euclidean distance in $L^*a^*b^*$ – denoted ΔE^*_{ab} – approximates the perceptibility of colour differences:

Eq 25.13

$$\Delta E^*_{ab} = \sqrt{\left(L^*_2 - L^*_1\right)^2 + \left(a^*_2 - a^*_1\right)^2 + \left(b^*_2 - b^*_1\right)^2}$$

If ΔE^*_{ab} is unity or less, the colour difference is taken to be imperceptible. However, $L^*a^*b^*$ does not achieve perceptual uniformity: It is merely an approximation.

A polar-coordinate version of the [a*, b*] pair can be used to express chroma and hue:

Eq 25.14

$$C^*_{ab} = \sqrt{a^{*2} + b^{*2}}; \quad h_{ab} = \tan^{-1}\frac{b^*}{a^*}$$

The equations that form a* and b* coordinates are not projective transformations: Straight lines in [x, y] do not transform to straight lines in [a*, b*]. The [a*, b*] coordinates can be plotted in two dimensions, but such a plot is not a chromaticity diagram.

CIE L*u*v* and CIE L*a*b* summary

Both L*u*v* and L*a*b* improve the 80:1 or so perceptual nonuniformity of XYZ to perhaps 6:1. Both systems transform tristimulus values into a lightness component ranging from 0 to 100, and two colour components ranging approximately ±100. One unit of Euclidean distance in L*u*v* or L*a*b* corresponds roughly to a just noticeable difference (JND) of colour.

Consider that L* ranges 0 to 100, and each of u* and v* range approximately ±100. A threshold of unity ΔE^*_{uv} defines four million colours. About one million colours can be distinguished by vision, so CIE L*u*v* is somewhat conservative. A million colours – or even the four million colours identified using a ΔE^*_{uv} or ΔE^*_{ab} threshold of unity – are well within the capacity of the 16.7 million colours available in a 24-bit truecolour system that uses perceptually appropriate transfer functions, such as the function of BT.709. (However, 24 bits per pixel are far short of the number required for adequate performance with linear-light coding.)

The L*u*v* or L*a*b* systems are most useful in colour specification. Both systems demand too much computation for economical realtime video processing, although both have been successfully applied to still image coding, particularly for printing. The complexity of the CIE L*u*v* and CIE L*a*b* calculations makes these systems generally unsuitable for image coding. The nonlinear R'G'B' coding used in video is quite perceptually uniform, and has the advantage of being suitable for realtime processing. Keep in mind that R'G'B' typically incorporates significant gamut limitation, whereas L*u*v* and CIE L*a*b* represent all colours. L*a*b* is sometimes used in desktop graphics with [a*, b*] coordinates ranging from –128 to +127 (e.g., Photoshop). Even with these restrictions, CIE L*a*b* covers nearly all of the colours.

McCamy argues that under normal conditions 1,875,000 colours can be distinguished. See McCamy, Cam S. (1998), "On the number of discernible colors," in *Color Research and Application*, **23** (5): 337 (Oct.).

Colour specification and colour image coding

A colour specification system needs to be able to represent any colour with high precision. Since few colours are handled at a time, a specification system can be computationally complex. A system for colour specification must be intimately related to the CIE system. The systems useful for colour specification are CIE *XYZ* and its derivatives *xyY*, *u'v'*, *L*u*v**, and *L*a*b**.

A colour image is represented as an array of pixels, where each pixel contains three values that define a colour. As you have learned in this chapter, three components are necessary and sufficient to define any colour. (In printing it is convenient to add a fourth, black, component, giving CMYK.)

In theory, the three numerical values for image coding could be provided by a colour specification system; however, a practical image coding system needs to be computationally efficient, cannot afford unlimited precision, need not be intimately related to the CIE system, and generally needs to cover only a reasonably wide range of colours and not all possible colours. So image coding uses different systems than colour specification.

The systems useful for image coding are linear *RGB*; nonlinear *RGB* (usually denoted *R'G'B'*, with sRGB as one variant); nonlinear *CMY*; nonlinear *CMYK*; and derivatives of *R'G'B'*, such as $Y'C_BC_R$ and $Y'P_BP_R$. These systems are summarized in Figure 25.12.

If you manufacture cars, you have to match the paint on the door with the paint on the fender; colour specification will be necessary. You can afford quite a bit of computation, because there are only two coloured elements, the door and the fender. To convey a picture of the car, you may have a million coloured elements or more: Computation must be quite efficient, and an image coding system is called for.

Further reading

The bible of colorimetry is *Color Science*, by Wyszecki and Stiles. But it's daunting; it covers colour very generally, and contains no material specific to imaging.

For an approachable introduction to colour theory, accompanied by practical descriptions of image reproduction, consult Hunt's classic work.

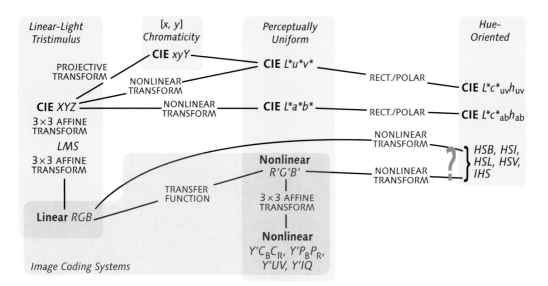

Figure 25.12 **Colour systems** are classified into four groups that are related by different kinds of transformations. Tristimulus systems, and perceptually uniform systems, are useful for image coding. (I flag *HSB, HSI, HSL, HSV*, and *IHS* with a question mark: These systems lack objective definition of colour.)

Berns' revision of the classic work by Billmeyer and Saltzman provides an excellent introduction to colour science. For an approachable, nonmathematical introduction to colour physics and perception, see Rossotti's book.

WYSZECKI, GÜNTER, and STILES, W. STANLEY (1982), *Color Science: Concepts and Methods, Quantitative Data and Formulæ,* Second Edition (New York: Wiley).

HUNT, ROBERT W. G., *The Reproduction of Colour,* Sixth Edition (Chichester, U.K.: Wiley, 2004).

HUNT, ROBERT W. G. and POINTER, MICHAEL R. (2011), *Measuring Colour,* Fourth Edition (Chichester, U.K.: Wiley).

BERNS, ROY S., (2000), *Billmeyer and Saltzman's Principles of Color Technology,* Third Edition (New York: Wiley).

ROSSOTTI, HAZEL (1983), *Colour: Why the World Isn't Grey* (Princeton, N.J.: Princeton Univ. Press).

Colour
science for video 26

Classical colour science, explained in the previous chapter, establishes the basis for numerical description of colour. However, colour science is intended for the *specification* of colour, not for image coding. Although an understanding of colour science is necessary to achieve good colour performance in video, its strict application is impractical. This chapter explains the engineering compromises necessary to make practical cameras and practical coding systems.

Video processing is generally concerned with colour represented in three components derived from the scene, usually red, green, and blue, or components computed from these. Accurate colour reproduction depends on knowing exactly how the physical spectra of the original scene are transformed into these components, and exactly how the components are transformed to physical spectra at the display. These issues are the subject of this chapter.

Once red, green, and blue components of a scene are obtained, these components are transformed into other forms optimized for processing, recording, and transmission. This will be discussed in *Component video colour coding for SD*, on page 357, and *Component video colour coding for HD*, on page 369. (Although the BT.709 primaries are now used in both SD and HD, unfortunately, other colour coding aspects differ.)

The previous chapter explained how to analyze SPDs of scene elements into *XYZ* tristimulus values representing colour. The obvious way to present those colours is to arrange for the display system to reproduce those *XYZ* values. That approach works in many applications of colour reproduction, and it's the basis for colour in video. However, in image reproduction, direct recreation of the *XYZ* values is unsuitable for perceptual reasons. Some modifications are necessary to achieve subjectively acceptable results. Those modifications were described in *Constant luminance,* on page 107.

Should you wish to skip this chapter, remember that accurate description of colours expressed in terms of *RGB* coordinates depends on the characterization of the *RGB* primaries and their power ratios (white reference). If your system is standardized to use a fixed set of primaries throughout, as in SD and HD, you need not be concerned about different "flavours" of *RGB*. However, if your images have different primary sets in different stages or production – in digital cinema, or in digital still photography – it is a vital issue.

Additive reproduction (*RGB*)

In the previous chapter, I explained how a physical SPD can be analyzed into three components that represent colour. This section explains how those components can be mixed to present ("reproduce") colour.

The simplest way to reproduce a range of colours is to mix the beams from three lights of different colours, as sketched in Figure 26.1 opposite. In physical terms, the spectra from each of the lights add together wavelength by wavelength to form the spectrum of the mixture. Physically and mathematically, the spectra add: The process is called *additive reproduction.*

I described Grassmann's Third Law on page 272: Colour vision obeys a principle of superposition, whereby the colour produced by any additive mixture of three primary SPDs can be predicted by adding the corresponding fractions of the *XYZ* tristimulus components of the primaries. The colours that can be formed from a particular set of *RGB* primaries are completely determined by the colours – tristimulus values, or luminance values and chromaticity coordinates – of the individual primaries. Subtractive reproduction, used in photography, cinema film, and commercial printing, is much more complicated: Colours in subtractive mixtures are not determined by the *colours* of the individual primaries, but by their *spectral* properties.

So-called RGB+W displays were commercialized in the in the 1990s and early 2000s, mainly in colour-sequential DLP projectors. In an RGB+W display, the luminance of white is considerably greater than the sum of the luminances of red, green, and blue: High brightness is claimed; however, such displays do *not* exhibit additive colour mixture. As I write, virtually all presentations include pictorial imagery; customers demand proper colour portrayal, and *RGB+W* projectors have consequently fallen out of favour.

If you are unfamiliar with the term *luminance*, or the symbols Y or Y', refer to *Luminance and lightness,* on page 255.

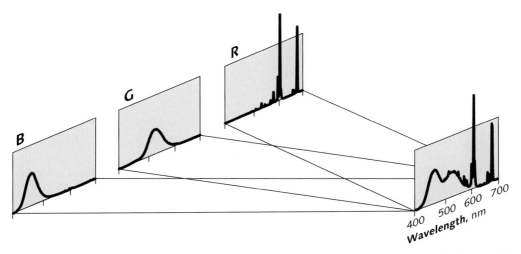

Figure 26.1 **Additive reproduction.** This diagram illustrates the physical process underlying additive colour mixture, as is used in video. Each primary has an independent, direct path to the image. The spectral power of the image is the sum of the spectra of the primaries. The colours of the mixtures are completely determined by the colours of the primaries; analysis and prediction of mixtures is reasonably simple. The SPDs shown here are those of a Sony Trinitron CRT.

Additive reproduction is employed directly in a video projector, where the spectra from a red beam, a green beam, and a blue beam are physically summed at the surface of the projection screen. Additive reproduction is also employed in a direct-view colour CRT, but through slightly indirect means. The screen of a CRT comprises small phosphor dots (triads) that, when illuminated by their respective electron beams, produce red, green, and blue light. When the screen is viewed from a sufficient distance, the spectra of these dots add in the lens and at the retina of the observer's eye.

The widest range of colours will be produced with primaries that individually appear red, green, and blue. When colour displays were exclusively CRTs, *RGB* systems were characterized by the chromaticities of their phosphors; we referred to *phosphor chromaticities*. To encompass newer devices that form colours without using phosphors, we now refer to *primary chromaticities* instead.

Three well chosen primaries can produce a large range of colours, but no finite set of primaries can cover all colours! An economic trade-off must be made that covers a wide range of colours with a very small number of primaries – preferably three.

Characterization of *RGB* primaries

An additive *RGB* system is specified by the chromaticities of its primaries and its white point. If you have an *RGB* image without information about its primary chromaticities, you cannot accurately reproduce the image. In Figure 26.2 opposite, I plot the primaries of a few *RGB* systems that I will discuss.

BT.709 specifies the primaries for HD. The BT.709 triangle is shaded in Figure 26.2.

The range of colours – or *gamut* – that can be formed from a given set of *RGB* primaries is given in the [x, y] chromaticity diagram by a triangle whose vertices are the chromaticities of the primaries. This two-dimensional plot doesn't tell the whole story, though: The range of [x, y] values that can be covered is a function of luminance. For example, BT.709's saturated blue colour at [0.15, 0.06] is only accessible at luminance below about 7% of white luminance; no chroma excursion is available at reference white! Gamut should be considered in three dimensions. I'll discuss gamut further on page 311.

In computing, the sRGB standard is now ubiquitous. The sRGB standard shares the BT.709 primaries. Many applications in desktop computing assume an sRGB interpretation unless other information accompanies the image.

The SMPTE/DCI P3 primaries that are standardized for D-cinema are overlaid on Figure 26.2.

Each of these systems will now be described in detail.

BT.709 primaries

ITU-R Rec. BT.709, *Parameter values for the HDTV standard for the studio and for international programme exchange.*

International agreement was obtained in 1990 by the former CCIR – now the ITU-R – on primaries for high-definition television (HD). The standard is formally denoted *Recommendation ITU-R BT.709* (formerly CCIR Rec. 709). I'll call it *BT.709*. Implausible though this sounds, the BT.709 chromaticities were agreed upon as the result of a political compromise that culminated in EBU red, EBU blue, and a green which is the average (rounded to 2 digits) of EBU green and SMPTE green! These primaries were adopted into the sRGB standard for computing and computer graphics. The BT.709 primaries are closely representative of contemporary displays in studio video. The chromaticities of the

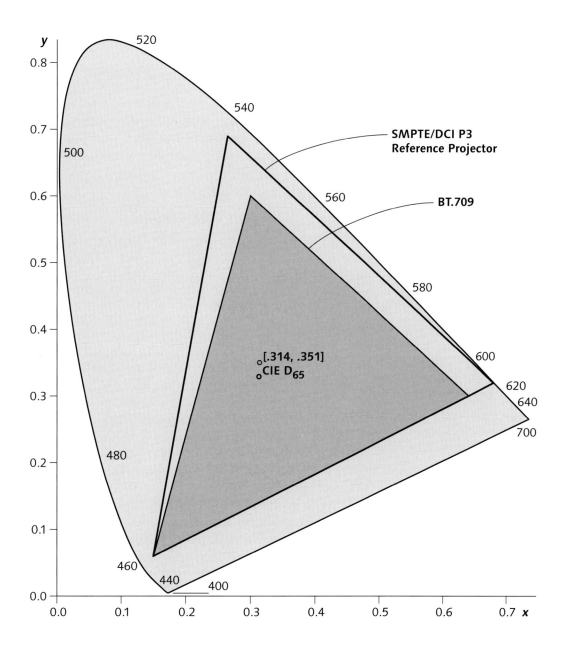

Figure 26.2 **The primaries of BT.709 and SMPTE/DCI P3** are compared. BT.709 is standard for HD worldwide, and is reasonably representative of SD; it incorporates the CIE D_{65} white point. The SMPTE/DCI P3 specification is used for D-cinema; its white point is [0.314, 0.351].

BT.709 primaries and its D_{65} white point are specified in Table 26.1:

Table 26.1 **BT.709 primaries** apply to 1280×720 and 1920×1080 HD systems; they are incorporated into the sRGB standard for desktop PCs.

	Red	Green	Blue	White, D_{65}
x	0.64	0.3	0.15	0.312727
y	0.33	0.6	0.06	0.329024
z	0.03	0.1	0.79	0.358249

Table 26.2 provides the relative luminance (*Y*) and [*x*, *y*] chromaticities of colourbars in BT.709 colour space:

	White	Yellow	Cyan	Green	Magenta	Red	Blue	Black
Y	1	0.927825	0.787327	0.715152	0.284848	0.212673	0.072175	0
x	0.312727	0.419320	0.224656	0.3	0.320938	0.64	0.15	*indeterminate*
y	0.329023	0.505246	0.328760	0.6	0.154190	0.33	0.06	*indeterminate*

Table 26.2 **Luminance and chromaticities of BT.709 colourbars**

The divisions by $X + Y + Z$ that form *x* and *y* effectively "explode" for a denominator of zero, reflected in the *indeterminate* entries for *x* and *y* of black in the table above. Black effectively covers the whole [*x*, *y*] diagram.

Video standards specify *RGB* chromaticities that are closely matched to practical displays. Physical display devices involve tolerances and uncertainties, but if you have a display that conforms to BT.709 within some tolerance, you can think of the display as being device-independent.

The importance of BT.709 as an interchange standard in studio video, broadcast television, and HD, and the firm perceptual basis of the standard, assures that its parameters will be used even by such devices as flat-panel displays that do not have the same physics as CRTs. However, there is no doubt that emerging display technologies will soon offer a wider colour gamut. SMPTE has adopted a standard for digital cinema that I will describe in a moment; that standard – SMPTE/DCI P3 – offers considerably wider gamut than BT.709. However, digital movies in their native P3 colour space are highly unlikely to be made available to consumers. IEC 61966-2-4 (xvYCC) purports to enable wide-gamut consumer video, but owing to the absence of any gamut-mapping mechanism I am highly skeptical concerning whether that claim will be realized by xvYCC.

Leggacy SD primaries

In 1953, the NTSC established primaries for emergent colour television. Those primaries were standardized by the FCC; they are now obsolete. RP 145 ("SMPTE-C") primaries have historically been used for SD in North America and Japan. EBU primaries have historically been used for SD in Europe. I detail these systems in Chapter 3, *Summary of obsolete RGB standards,* of *Composite NTSC and PAL: Legacy Video Systems.* The chromaticities of these sets of primaries are indicated below:

Table 26.3 **NTSC primaries (obsolete)** were used in 480*i* SD systems from 1953 until about 1970, when the primaries now documented in SMPTE RP 145 were adopted.

	Red	Green	Blue	White CIE III. C
x	0.67	0.21	0.14	0.310
y	0.33	0.71	0.08	0.316
z	0	0.08	0.78	0.374

Table 26.4 **EBU Tech. 3213 primaries** apply to 576*i* SD systems.

	Red	Green	Blue	White, D_{65}
x	0.640	0.290	0.150	0.3127
y	0.330	0.600	0.060	0.3290
z	0.030	0.110	0.790	0.3583

Table 26.5 **SMPTE RP 145 primaries** apply to 480*i* SD systems.

	Red	Green	Blue	White, D_{65}
x	0.630	0.310	0.155	0.3127
y	0.340	0.595	0.070	0.3290
z	0.030	0.095	0.775	0.3583

Interpreting RP 145 *RGB* values as BT.709 leads to colour errors of up to 20 ΔE, with an average error of about 14 ΔE. There are differences in primary chromaticities between the EBU standards and BT.709. Interpreting EBU *RGB* values as BT.709 leads to colour errors of up to 5 ΔE on the primaries, with an average error of about 2 ΔE.

Despite these differences between SD practice and BT.709, the BT.709 primaries are effectively being retrofitted into SD, albeit slowly.

sRGB system

IEC 61966-2-1, *Multimedia systems and equipment – Colour measurement and management – Part 2-1: Colour management – Default RGB colour space – sRGB.*

The sRGB standard is widely used in computing; the BT.709 primaries have been incorporated into sRGB. Beware that although the primary chromaticities are identical, the sRGB transfer function is somewhat different from the transfer functions standardized for studio video.

In the 1980s and 1990s, *RGB* image data in computing was commonly exchanged without information about primary chromaticities, white reference, or transfer function (to be described in *Gamma,* on page 315). If you have *RGB* image data without information about these parameters, you cannot accurately reproduce the image. The sRGB standard saw widespread deployment starting in about 2000, and today if you have an untagged RGB image it is safe to interpret the data according to sRGB.

SMPTE Free Scale (FS) primaries

SMPTE ST 2048-1, *2048×1080 and 4096×2160 Digital Cinematography Production Image Formats FS/709.* The notation *FS/709* is supposed to indicate that the standard applies either to imagery coded to FS-Gamut or to imagery coded to BT.709.

In 2011, SMPTE standardized a scheme termed *Free Scale Gamut* (FS-Gamut) that accommodates wide-gamut image data for 2 K and 4 K digital cinema production. (See *Free Scale Gamut, Free Scale Log,* on page 312.) A set of default primaries is defined. The primaries are nonphysical, so as to exceed the gamut of original camera negative film as normally processed and printed. The white point is D_{65}. The scheme is intended to encode scene-referred image data, typically using a quasilog coding specified in the same standard. The chromaticities of the default FS primaries and white are specified in Table 26.6:

Table 26.6 SMPTE "Free Scale" default primaries exceed the gamut of motion picture film as conventionally aquired, processed, and projected. Image data is scene-referred.

	Red	Green	Blue	White
x	0.7347	0.14	0.1	0.31272
y	0.2653	0.86	−0.02985	0.32903
z	0	0	0.92985	0.34065

AMPAS ACES primaries

AMPAS Specification S-2008-001, *Academy Color Encoding Specification (ACES).*

The Science and Technology Council (STC) of the Academy of Motion Picture Arts and Sciences (AMPAS) agreed upon a set of primaries for digital cinema acquisition and processing. ACES green and blue are nonphysical, so as to exceed the gamut of original

Some people will be surprised by the negative value of the ACES blue *y* coordinate: Adding ACES blue decreases luminance!

camera negative film as normally processed and printed. The standard has a white point approximating D_{60}. The system is intended to encode scene-referred image data. The chromaticities of the ACES primaries and white are specified in Table 26.7:

Table 26.7 **AMPAS ACES primaries** exceed the gamut of motion picture film as conventionally aquired, processed, and projected. ACES data is scene-referred.

	Red	Green	Blue	White
x	0.7347	0	0.0001	0.32168
y	0.2653	1	−0.0770	0.33767
z	0	0	1.0769	0.34065

SMPTE/DCI P3 primaries

SMPTE ST 428-1, *D-Cinema Distribution Master – Image Characteristics.*

Participants in the Digital Cinema Initiative (DCI) in the year 2000 achieved agreement upon primaries for a reference projector whose primaries approximately encompass the gamut of motion picture film as conventionally illuminated. Image data is display-referred. DCI's agreement has been promulgated as a SMPTE standard. The standard has a white point approximating current film practice; the tolerance on the white point specification encompasses D_{61}. The chromaticities of the DCI primaries and white are specified in Table 26.8:

Table 26.8 **SMPTE/DCI P3 primaries** approximately encompass the gamut of film, and are used for digital cinema. P3 data is display-referred.

	Red	Green	Blue	White
x	0.680	0.265	0.150	0.314
y	0.320	0.690	0.060	0.351
z	0	0.050	0.790	0.340

In establishing image data encoding standards for digital cinema, the DCI sought to make a "future-proof" standard that would accommodate wider colour gamut without the need to represent negative data values or data values above unity and without the necessity to maintain metadata. The standards adopted call for image data to be encoded in *XYZ* tristimulus values representing colours to be displayed. *XYZ* encoding amounts to using primaries having chromaticities [1, 0], [0, 1], and [0, 0], with a white reference of [$\frac{1}{3}$, $\frac{1}{3}$].

Despite DCI's adoption of *XYZ* coding, all digital cinema material mastered today is mastered to the DCI P3 gamut of the reference projector that I described above. I expect this situation to continue for the next 5 or 10 years. Issues of gamut mapping will eventually have to be addressed if new, wide-gamut material is to be sensibly displayed on legacy projectors. DCI standards are completely silent on issues of gamut mapping.

CMFs and SPDs

You might guess that you could implement a display whose primaries had spectral power distributions with the same shape as the CIE spectral analysis curves – the colour-matching functions for *XYZ*. You could make such a display, but when driven by *XYZ* tristimulus values, it would not properly reproduce colour. There are display primaries that reproduce colour accurately when driven by *XYZ* tristimuli, but the SPDs of those primaries do not have the same shape as the $\bar{x}(\lambda)$, $\bar{y}(\lambda)$, and $\bar{z}(\lambda)$ CMFs. To see why requires understanding a very subtle and important point about colour capture and reproduction.

To find a set of display primaries that reproduces colour according to *XYZ* tristimulus values would require constructing three SPDs that, when analyzed by the $\bar{x}(\lambda)$, $\bar{y}(\lambda)$, and $\bar{z}(\lambda)$ colour-matching functions, produced [1, 0, 0], [0, 1, 0], and [0, 0, 1], respectively. The $\bar{x}(\lambda)$, $\bar{y}(\lambda)$, and $\bar{z}(\lambda)$ CMFs are positive across the entire spectrum. Producing [0, 1, 0] would require positive contribution from some wavelengths in the required primary SPDs, and that we could arrange; however, there is no wavelength that contributes to *Y* that does not also contribute positively to *X* or *Z*.

The solution to this dilemma is to force the *X* and *Z* contributions to zero by making the corresponding SPDs have negative power at certain wavelengths. Although this is not a problem for mathematics, or even for signal processing, an SPD with a negative lobe is not physically realizable in a transducer for light, because light power cannot go negative. So we cannot build a real display that responds directly to *XYZ*. But as you will see, the concept of negative SPDs – and *nonphysical SPDs* or *nonrealizable primaries* – is very useful in theory and in practice.

There are many ways to choose nonphysical primary SPDs that correspond to the $\bar{x}(\lambda)$, $\bar{y}(\lambda)$, and $\bar{z}(\lambda)$ colour-matching functions. One way is to arbitrarily choose three display primaries whose power is concentrated at

To understand the mathematical details of colour transforms, described in this section, you should be familiar with linear (matrix) algebra. If you are unfamiliar with linear algebra, see STRANG, GILBERT (1998), *Introduction to Linear Algebra*, Second Edition (Boston: Wellesley-Cambridge).

DIGITAL VIDEO AND HD ALGORITHMS AND INTERFACES

three discrete wavelengths. Consider three display SPDs, each of which has some amount of power at 600 nm, 550 nm, and 470 nm. Sample the $\bar{x}(\lambda)$, $\bar{y}(\lambda)$, and $\bar{z}(\lambda)$ functions of the matrix given earlier in *Calculation of tristimulus values by matrix multiplication*, on page 273, at those three wavelengths. This yields the tristimulus values shown in Table 26.9:

Table 26.9 **Example primaries** are used to explain the necessity of signal processing in accurate colour reproduction.

	Red, 600 nm	Green, 550 nm	Blue, 470 nm
X	1.0622	0.4334	0.1954
Y	0.6310	0.9950	0.0910
Z	0.0008	0.0087	1.2876

These coefficients can be expressed as a matrix, where the column vectors give the *XYZ* tristimulus values corresponding to pure red, green, and blue at the display, that is, [1, 0, 0], [0, 1, 0], and [0, 0, 1]. It is conventional to apply a scale factor in such a matrix to cause the middle row to sum to unity, since we wish to achieve only relative matches, not absolute:

Eq 26.1 This matrix is based upon *R*, *G*, and *B* components with unusual spectral distributions. For typical *R*, *G*, and *B*, see Eq 26.8.

$$\begin{bmatrix} X \\ Y \\ Z \end{bmatrix} = \begin{bmatrix} 0.618637 & 0.252417 & 0.113803 \\ 0.367501 & 0.579499 & 0.052999 \\ 0.000466 & 0.005067 & 0.749913 \end{bmatrix} \bullet \begin{bmatrix} R_{600nm} \\ G_{550nm} \\ B_{470nm} \end{bmatrix}$$

That matrix gives the transformation from *RGB* to *XYZ*. We are interested in the inverse transform, from *XYZ* to *RGB*, so invert the matrix:

Eq 26.2

$$\begin{bmatrix} R_{600nm} \\ G_{550nm} \\ B_{470nm} \end{bmatrix} = \begin{bmatrix} 2.179151 & -0.946884 & -0.263777 \\ -1.382685 & 2.327499 & 0.045336 \\ 0.007989 & -0.015138 & 1.333346 \end{bmatrix} \bullet \begin{bmatrix} X \\ Y \\ Z \end{bmatrix}$$

The column vectors of the matrix in Equation 26.2 give, for each primary, the weights of each of the three discrete wavelengths that are required to display unit *XYZ* tristimulus values. The colour-matching functions for CIE *XYZ* are shown in Figure 26.3, *CMFs for CIE XYZ primaries*, on page 300. Opposite those functions, in Figure 26.4, is the corresponding set of primary SPDs. As expected, the display primaries have some negative spectral components: The primary SPDs are nonphysical. Any set of primaries that reproduces colour from

XYZ tristimulus values is necessarily *supersaturated*, more saturated than any realizable SPD could be.

To determine a set of physical SPDs that will reproduce colour when driven from *XYZ*, consider the problem in the other direction: Given a set of physically realizable display primaries, what CMFs are suitable to directly reproduce colour using mixtures of these primaries? In this case the matrix that relates *RGB* components to CIE *XYZ* tristimulus values is all-positive, but the CMFs required for analysis of the scene have negative portions: The analysis filters are nonrealizable.

Figure 26.6 shows a set of primary SPDs conformant to SMPTE 240M, similar to BT.709. Many different SPDs can produce an exact match to these chromaticities; the set shown is from a Sony Trinitron display. Figure 26.5 shows the corresponding colour-matching functions. As expected, the CMFs have negative lobes and are therefore not directly realizable; nonetheless, these are the idealized CMFs, or idealized *taking characterstics* – of the BT.709 primaries.

We conclude that we can use physically realizable analysis CMFs, as in the first example, where *XYZ* components are displayed directly. But this requires nonphysical display primary SPDs. Or we can use physical display primary SPDs, but this requires nonphysical analysis CMFs. As a consequence of the way colour vision works, there is no set of nonnegative display primary SPDs that corresponds to an all-positive set of analysis functions.

The escape from this conundrum is to impose a 3×3 matrix multiplication in the processing of the camera signals, instead of using the camera signals to directly drive the display. Consider these display primaries: monochromatic red at 600 nm, monochromatic green at 550 nm, and monochromatic blue at 470 nm. The 3×3 matrix of Equation 26.2 can be used to process *XYZ* values into components suitable to drive that display. Such signal processing is not just desirable; it is a necessity for achieving accurate colour reproduction!

Michael Brill and Bob Hunt agree that *R*, *G*, and *B* tristimulus values have no units. See HUNT, ROBERT W.G. (1997), "The heights of the CIE colour-matching functions," in *Color Research and Application*, **22** (5): 335–335 (Oct.).

To avoid the ambiguity of the term *pixel* – does it constitute one component or three? – I suggest that you call a sensor element a *photosite*.

In a "one-chip" camera, hardware or firmware performs spatial interpolation to reconstruct *R*, *G*, and *B* at each photosite. In a "three-chip" camera, dichroic filters are mounted on one or two glass blocks. In optical engineering, a glass block is called a prism, but it is not the prism that separates the wavelengths, it is the dichroic filters.

KUNIBA, HIDEYASU and ROY S. BERNS, (2009), "Spectral sensitivity optimization of color image sensors considering photon shot noise," in *Journal of Electronic Imaging* **18** (2): 023002-1–023002-14.

Every colour video camera or digital still camera needs to sense the image through three different spectral characteristics. Digital still cameras and consumer camcorders typically have a single area array CCD sensor ("one chip"); each 2×2 tile of the array has sensor elements covered by three different types of filter. Typically, filters appearing red, green, and blue are used; the green filter is duplicated onto two of the photosites in the 2×2 tile. This approach loses light, and therefore sensitivity. Conventional studio video cameras separate incoming light using dichroic filters operating as beam splitters; each component has a dedicated CCD sensor ("3 CCD," or "3 CMOS"). Such an optical system separates different wavelength bands without absorbing any light, achieving about a factor of two higher sensitivity than a mosaic sensor.

Figure 26.7 shows the set of spectral sensitivity functions implemented by the beam splitter and filter ("prism") assembly of an actual HD camera. The functions are positive everywhere across the spectrum, so the filters are physically realizable. However, rather poor colour reproduction will result if these signals are used directly to drive a display having BT.709 primaries. Figure 26.8 shows the same set of camera analysis functions processed through a 3×3 matrix transform. The transformed components will reproduce colour more accurately – the more closely these curves resemble the ideal BT.709 CMFs of Figure 26.5, the more accurate the camera's colour reproduction will be.

In theory, and in practice, using a linear matrix to process the camera signals can capture *all* colours correctly. However, capturing all colours is seldom necessary in practice, as I will explain in the *Gamut* section below. Also, capturing the entire range of colours would incur a noise penalty, as I will describe in *Noise due to matrixing,* on page 308.

Normalization and scaling

The $\bar{y}(\lambda)$ CMF is standardized by the CIE such that its maximum value lies at unity. For the 10 nm CIE CMFs commonly used in image science, the $\bar{y}$ curve integrates to about 10.68. The $\bar{x}(\lambda)$ and $\bar{z}(\lambda)$ CMFs are scaled such that they integrate to the same value. The CIE derived its 10 nm CMFs by interpolation from its 1 nm curves;

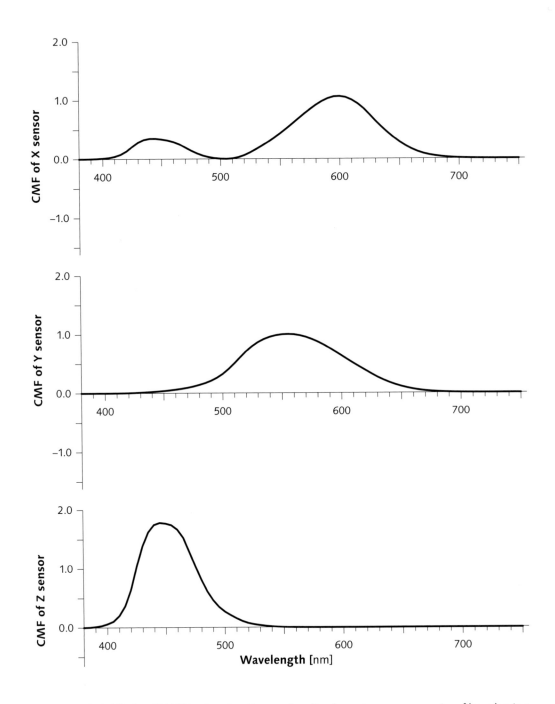

Figure 26.3 **CMFs for CIE *XYZ* primaries.** To acquire all colours in a scene requires filters having the CIE $\bar{x}(\lambda)$, $\bar{y}(\lambda)$, and $\bar{z}(\lambda)$ spectral sensitivities. The functions are nonnegative, and therefore could be realized in practice. However, these functions are seldom used in actual cameras or scanners, for various engineering reasons.

DIGITAL VIDEO AND HD ALGORITHMS AND INTERFACES

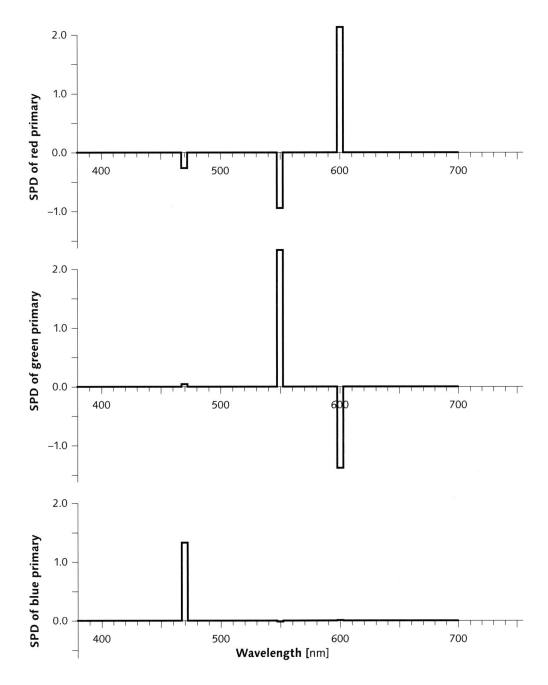

Figure 26.4 **SPDs for CIE** *XYZ* **primaries.** To directly reproduce a scene that has been analyzed using the CIE *XYZ* colour-matching functions requires *nonphysical* primaries having negative excursions, which cannot be realized in practice. Many different sets are possible. In this hypothetical example, the power in each primary is concentrated at the same three discrete wavelengths, 470, 550, and 600 nm.

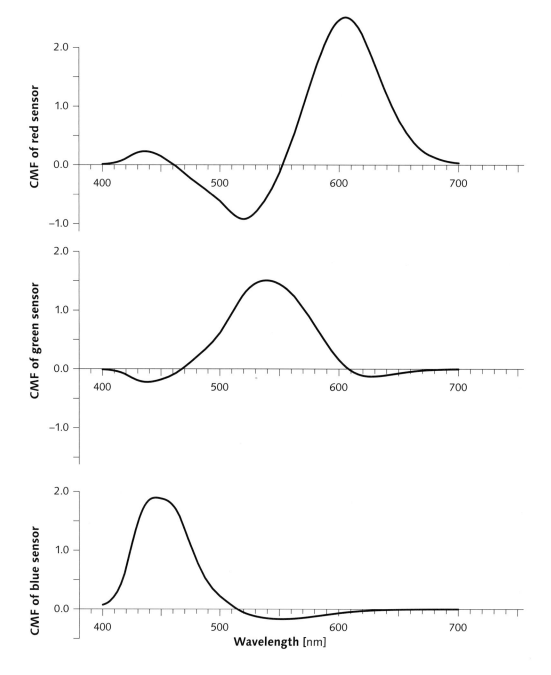

Figure 26.5 **CMFs for BT.709 primaries**. These analysis functions are theoretically correct to acquire *RGB* components for display using BT.709 primaries. The functions are not directly realizable in a camera or a scanner, due to their negative lobes; however, they can be realized by a 3×3 matrix transformation of the CIE *XYZ* colour-matching functions of Figure 26.3.

DIGITAL VIDEO AND HD ALGORITHMS AND INTERFACES

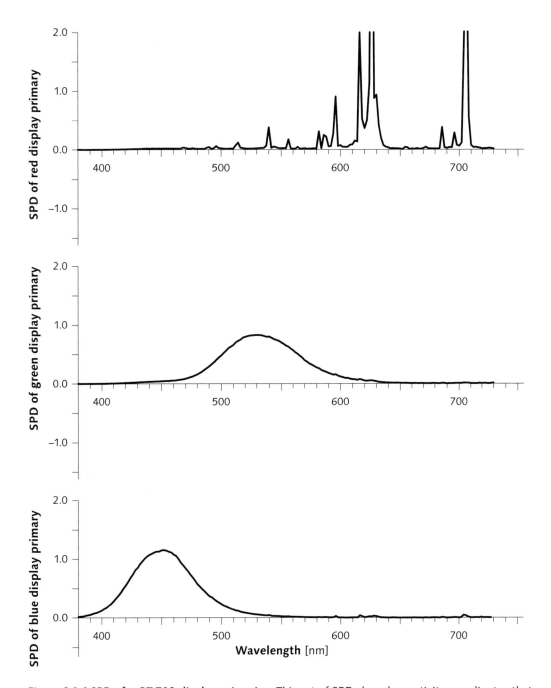

Figure 26.6 **SPDs for BT.709 display primaries.** This set of SPDs has chromaticity coordinates that conform to SMPTE RP 145, similar to BT.709. Many SPDs could produce the same chromaticity coordinates; this particular set is produced by a Sony Trinitron CRT display. The red primary uses *rare earth* phosphors that produce very narrow spectral distributions, different in character from the phosphors used for green or blue.

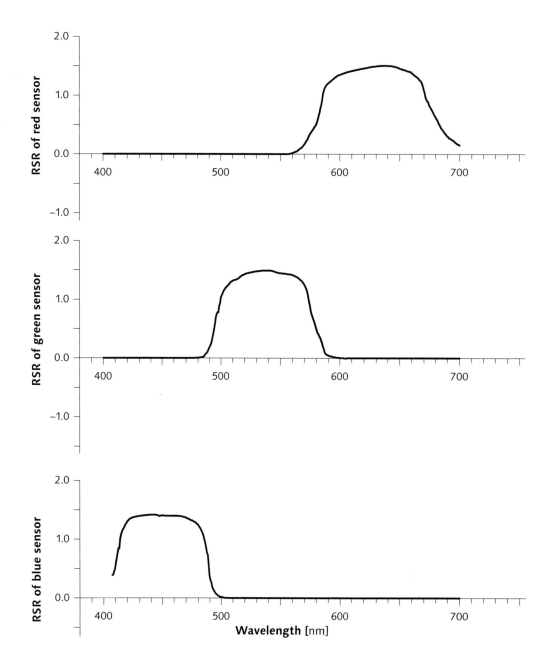

Figure 26.7 **Relative spectral responses (RSRs) for a real camera.** This set of spectral response functions is produced by the dichroic colour separation filters (*prism*) of a 2000-vintage beam-splitter CCD studio HD camera. I call these *relative spectral response* (RSR) functions.

DIGITAL VIDEO AND HD ALGORITHMS AND INTERFACES

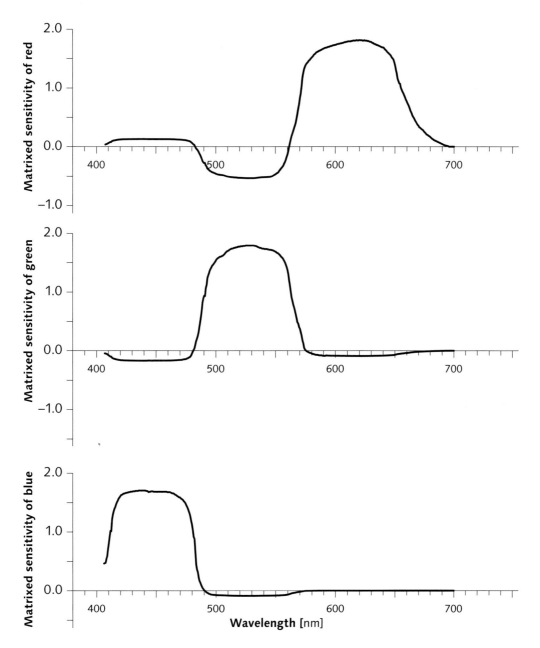

Figure 26.8 **Effective response after matrixing** for BT.709 primaries. These curves result from the analysis functions of Figure 26.7, opposite, being processed through a suitable 3×3 matrix. Colours as "seen" by this camera will be accurate to the extent that these curves match the ideal CMFs for BT.709 primaries shown in Figure 26.5.

the 10 nm $\bar{x}(\lambda)$ and $\bar{z}(\lambda)$ CMFs do not integrate to precisely the same value as $\bar{y}(\lambda)$ does.

CIE illuminants are specified scaled for unity at 560 nm. Illuminant E's SPD is represented as a vector of all ones. With the illuminant and CMF scaling specified by the CIE, Illuminant E's luminance is about 10.68.

In applying the CIE standards to imaging, I find it convenient to normalize illuminants to a luminance of unity. With spectra represented as 31-element vectors from 400 nm to 700 nm at 10 nm intervals, Illuminant E then comprises a vector all of whose elements have the value $\frac{1}{10.68}$, or about 0.0936.

In traditional practice, reference white has luminance of 100.

Luminance coefficients

Relative luminance can be formed as a properly weighted sum of *RGB* (linear-light) tristimulus components. The luminance coefficients can be computed starting with the chromaticities of the *RGB* primaries, here expressed in a matrix:

The luminance coefficients of any set of *XYZ* primary SPDs are [0, 1, 0]. Any *X* or *Z* primary is nonphysical; it has zero luminance.

$$C = \begin{bmatrix} x_R & x_G & x_B \\ y_R & y_G & y_B \\ z_R & z_G & z_B \end{bmatrix} \qquad \text{Eq 26.3}$$

Coefficients J_R, J_G, and J_B are computed from the chromaticities, and the white reference, as follows:

For the D_{65} white reference now standard in video, C^{-1} is multiplied by the vector [0.95, 1, 1.089].

$$\begin{bmatrix} J_R \\ J_G \\ J_B \end{bmatrix} = C^{-1} \cdot \begin{bmatrix} x_W \\ y_W \\ z_W \end{bmatrix} \cdot \frac{1}{y_W} \qquad \text{Eq 26.4}$$

Luminance can then be computed as follows:

$$Y = \begin{bmatrix} J_R y_R & J_G y_G & J_B y_B \end{bmatrix} \bullet \begin{bmatrix} R \\ G \\ B \end{bmatrix} \qquad \text{Eq 26.5}$$

This calculation can be extended to compute [*X*, *Y*, *Z*] from [*R*, *G*, *B*] of the specified chromaticity. First, compute a *normalized primary matrix* (NPM) denoted **T**. The NPM depends upon the primaries and the white point of the [*R*, *G*, *B*] space:

$$T = C \bullet \begin{bmatrix} J_R & 0 & 0 \\ 0 & J_G & 0 \\ 0 & 0 & J_B \end{bmatrix} \qquad \text{Eq 26.6}$$

The elements J_R, J_G, and J_B of the diagonal matrix have the effect of scaling the corresponding columns of the chromaticity matrix, balancing the primary contributions to achieve the intended chromaticity of white. CIE tristimulus values [X, Y, Z] are then computed from the specified [R, G, B] as follows:

$$\begin{bmatrix} X \\ Y \\ Z \end{bmatrix} = T \bullet \begin{bmatrix} R \\ G \\ B \end{bmatrix}$$

See *BT.601 luma* and *BT.709 luma*, on pages 346 and following.

Eq 26.7

As I explained in *Constant luminance*, on page 107, video systems compute luma as a weighted sum of *nonlinear R'G'B'* components. Although this calculation produces nonconstant-luminance (Livingston) errors, there is a second-order benefit in using the "theoretical" coefficients. The standard coefficients for SD are computed from the 1953 FCC NTSC primaries and CIE Illuminant C. The standard coefficients for HD are computed from BT.709 primaries and CIE D_{65}.

Transformations between *RGB* and CIE *XYZ*

RGB values in a particular set of primaries can be transformed to and from CIE *XYZ* by a 3×3 matrix transform. These transforms involve tristimulus values, that is, sets of three linear-light components that approximate the CIE colour-matching functions. CIE *XYZ* represents a special case of tristimulus values. In *XYZ*, any colour is represented by an all-positive set of values. SMPTE has standardized a procedure for computing these transformations.

SMPTE RP 177, *Derivation of Basic Television Color Equations*.

To transform from BT.709 *RGB* (with its D_{65} white point) into CIE *XYZ*, use the following transform:

Eq 26.8

$$\begin{bmatrix} X \\ Y \\ Z \end{bmatrix} = \begin{bmatrix} 0.412453 & 0.357580 & 0.180423 \\ 0.212671 & 0.715160 & 0.072169 \\ 0.019334 & 0.119193 & 0.950227 \end{bmatrix} \bullet \begin{bmatrix} R_{709} \\ G_{709} \\ B_{709} \end{bmatrix}$$

When constructing such a matrix for fixed-point calculation, take care when rounding to preserve the unity sum of the middle (luminance) row.

The middle row of this matrix gives the luminance coefficients of BT.709 (though BT.709 specifies four-digit values). Because white is normalized to unity, the middle row sums to unity. The column vectors are the *XYZ* tristimulus values of pure red, green, and blue. To recover primary chromaticities from such a matrix, compute *x* and *y* for each *RGB* column vector. To recover the white point, transform *RGB* = [1, 1, 1] to *XYZ*, then compute *x* and *y* according to Equation 25.1.

To transform from CIE *XYZ* into BT.709 *RGB*, invert the 3×3 matrix of Equation 26.8:

Eq 26.9

$$\begin{bmatrix} R_{709} \\ G_{709} \\ B_{709} \end{bmatrix} = \begin{bmatrix} 3.240479 & -1.537150 & -0.498535 \\ -0.969256 & 1.875992 & 0.041556 \\ 0.055648 & -0.204043 & 1.057311 \end{bmatrix} \bullet \begin{bmatrix} X \\ Y \\ Z \end{bmatrix}$$

Gamut is described on page 311.

This matrix has some negative coefficients: *XYZ* colours that are *out of gamut* for BT.709 *RGB* transform to *RGB* components where one or more components are negative or greater than unity.

Any *RGB* image data, or any matrix that purports to relate *RGB* to *XYZ*, should indicate the chromaticities of the *RGB* display primaries expected. If you encounter a matrix transform or image data without reference to any primary chromaticities, be very suspicious! Its originator may be unaware that *RGB* values must be associated with chromaticity specifications in order to have meaning for accurate colour.

Noise due to matrixing

Even if it were possible to display colours in the outer reaches of the chromaticity diagram, there would be a great practical disadvantage in doing so. Consider a camera that acquires *XYZ* tristimulus components, then transforms to BT.709 *RGB* according to Equation 26.9. The coefficient 3.240479 in the upper left-hand corner of the matrix in that equation determines the contribution from *X* at the camera into the red signal. An *X* component acquired with 4 digital codes of noise will inject 13 codes of noise into red: There is a noise penalty associated with the larger coefficients in the transform, and this penalty is quite significant in the design of a high-quality camera.

The equations below transform between systems having the same illuminant. If the illuminant differs, a chromatic adaptation transform (CAT) may be required; in that case, a suitable 3×3 matrix (such as the Bradford transform) intervenes between T_D^{-1} and T_S.

RGB values in a system employing one set of primaries can be transformed to another set by a 3×3 linear-light matrix transform. [R, G, B] tristimulus values in a source space (denoted with the subscript s) can be transformed into [R, G, B] tristimulus values in a destination space (denoted with the subscript D), using matrices T_S and T_D computed from the corresponding chromaticities and white points:

$$\begin{bmatrix} R_D \\ G_D \\ B_D \end{bmatrix} = T_D^{-1} \bullet T_S \bullet \begin{bmatrix} R_S \\ G_S \\ B_S \end{bmatrix}$$

Eq 26.10

As an example, here is the transform from SMPTE RP 145 *RGB* (e.g., SMPTE 240M) to BT.709 *RGB*:

Eq 26.11

$$\begin{bmatrix} R_{709} \\ G_{709} \\ B_{709} \end{bmatrix} = \begin{bmatrix} 0.939555 & 0.050173 & 0.010272 \\ 0.017775 & 0.965795 & 0.016430 \\ -0.001622 & -0.004371 & 1.005993 \end{bmatrix} \bullet \begin{bmatrix} R_{145} \\ G_{145} \\ B_{145} \end{bmatrix}$$

This matrix transforms EBU 3213 RGB to BT.709:

Eq 26.12

$$\begin{bmatrix} R_{709} \\ G_{709} \\ B_{709} \end{bmatrix} = \begin{bmatrix} 1.044036 & -0.044036 & 0 \\ 0 & 1 & 0 \\ 0 & 0.011797 & 0.988203 \end{bmatrix} \bullet \begin{bmatrix} R_{EBU} \\ G_{EBU} \\ B_{EBU} \end{bmatrix}$$

To transform typical Sony Trinitron *RGB*, with D_{65} white reference, to BT.709, use this transform:

Eq 26.13

$$\begin{bmatrix} R_{709} \\ G_{709} \\ B_{709} \end{bmatrix} = \begin{bmatrix} 1.068706 & -0.078595 & 0.009890 \\ 0.024110 & 0.960070 & 0.015819 \\ 0.001735 & 0.029748 & 0.968517 \end{bmatrix} \bullet \begin{bmatrix} R_{SONY} \\ G_{SONY} \\ B_{SONY} \end{bmatrix}$$

Transforming among *RGB* systems may lead to an *out of gamut RGB* result, where one or more *RGB* components are negative or greater than unity.

These transformations produce accurate results only when applied to tristimulus (linear-light) components. In principle, to transform nonlinear R'G'B' from one primary system to another requires application of the inverse transfer function to recover the tristimulus values, computation of the matrix multiplication, then reapplication of the transfer function. However, the transformation matrices of Equations 26.11, 26.12, and 26.13 are similar to the identity matrix: The diagonal terms are nearly unity, and the off-diagonal terms are nearly zero. In these cases, if the transform is computed in the nonlinear (gamma-corrected) $R'G'B'$ domain, the resulting errors will be small.

Camera white reference

There is an implicit assumption in television that the camera operates as if the scene were illuminated by a source having the chromaticity of CIE D_{65}. In practice, television studios are often lit by tungsten lamps at around 3200 K, and scene illumination is often deficient in the shortwave (blue) region of the spectrum. This situation is compensated by *white balancing* – that is, by adjusting the gain of the red, green, and blue components at the camera so that a diffuse white object reports the values that would be reported if the scene illumination had the same tristimulus values as CIE D_{65}. In studio cameras, controls for white balance are available. In consumer cameras, activating WHITE BALANCE causes the camera to integrate red, green, and blue over the picture, and to adjust the gains so as to equalize the sums. (This approach to white balancing is sometimes called *integrate to grey*.)

Display white reference

In additive mixture, the illumination of the reproduced image is generated entirely by the display device. In particular, reproduced white is determined by the characteristics of the display, and is not dependent on the environment in which the display is viewed. In a completely dark viewing environment, such as a cinema theater, this is desirable; a wide range of chromaticities is accepted as "white." However, in an environment where the viewer's field of view encompasses objects other than the display, the viewer's notion of "white" is likely to be influenced or even dominated by what he or she perceives as "white" in the ambient. To avoid subjective mismatches, the chromaticity of white reproduced by the display and the chromaticity of white in the ambient should be reasonably close. SMPTE has standardized the chromaticity of reference white in studio displays. The standard specifies that luminance for reference white be reproduced at 120 cd·m^{-2}, and surround conditions – basically, neutral grey at 10% of

SMPTE RP 166, *Critical Viewing Conditions for Evaluation of Color Television Pictures.*

EBU Tech. R23, *Procedure for the operational alignment of grade-1 colour picture monitors.*

DIGITAL VIDEO AND HD ALGORITHMS AND INTERFACES

reference white – are outlined. In Europe, reference white luminance is specified in EBU R23 as 80 cd·m^{-2}.

Modern blue CRT phosphors are more efficient with respect to human vision than red or green phosphors. Until recently, brightness was valued in computer displays more than colour accuracy. In a quest for a small brightness increment at the expense of a loss of colour accuracy, computer display manufacturers adopted a white point having a colour temperature of about 9300 K, producing a white having about 1.3 times as much blue as the standard CIE D_{65} white reference used in television. So, computer displays and computer pictures often look excessively blue. The situation can be corrected by adjusting or calibrating the display to a white reference with a lower colour temperature.

Studio video standards in Asia call for viewing with a 9300 K white reference. This practice apparently originates from a cultural preference regarding the portrayal of skin tones.

Gamut

Analyzing a scene with the CIE analysis functions produces distinct component triples for all colours. But when transformed into components suitable for a set of physical display primaries, some of those colours – those colours whose chromaticity coordinates lie outside the triangle formed by the primaries – will have negative component values. In addition, colours outside the triangle of the primaries may have one or two primary components that exceed unity. These colours cannot be correctly displayed. Display devices typically clip signals that have negative values and saturate signals whose values exceed unity. Visualized on the chromaticity diagram, a colour outside the triangle of the primaries is reproduced at a point on the boundary of the triangle.

If a camera is designed to capture all colours, its complexity is necessarily higher and its performance is necessarily worse than a camera designed to capture a smaller range of colours. Thankfully, the range of colours encountered in the natural and man-made world is a small fraction of all of the colours. Although it is necessary for an instrument such as a colorimeter to measure all colours, in an imaging system we are generally concerned with colours that occur frequently.

M.R. Pointer characterized the distribution of frequently occurring *real surface colours*. The naturally occurring colours tend to lie in the central portion of the chromaticity diagram, where they can be encompassed by a well-chosen set of physical primaries. An imaging system performs well if it can display all or most of these colours. BT.709 does reasonably well; however, many of the colours of conventional offset printing – particularly in the cyan region – are not encompassed by all-positive BT.709 *RGB*. To accommodate such colours requires wide-gamut reproduction.

POINTER, MICHAEL R. (1980), "The gamut of real surface colours," in *Color Research and Application* **5** (3): 143–155 (Fall).

Wide-gamut reproduction

For much of the history of colour television, cameras were designed to incorporate assumptions about the colour reproduction capabilities of colour CRTs. But nowadays, video production equipment is being used to originate images for a much wider range of applications than just television broadcast. The desire to make digital cameras suitable for originating images for this wider range of applications has led to proposals for video standards that accommodate a wider gamut.

POYNTON, CHARLES (2010), "Wide-gamut image capture," in *Proc. IS&T CGIV, Fourth European Conf. on Colour in Graphics and Imaging*: 471–482 (Joensuu, Finland).

The xvYCC ("x.v.Color") scheme is intended to be the basis for wide-gamut reproduction in future HD systems. The scheme is intended for use with *RGB* tristimulus values having BT.709 primaries, but with their range extended to –0.25 to +1.33, well outside the range 0 to 1. The excursions below zero and above unity allow *RGB* values to represent colours outside the triangle enclosed by the BT.709 primaries. When the extended *R'G'B'* values are matrixed, the resulting $Y'C_BC_R$ values lie within the "valid" range: Regions of $Y'C_BC_R$ space outside the "legal" *RGB* cube are exploited to convey wide-gamut colours.

Perhaps the first image coding system that accommodated linear-light (tristimulus) values below zero and above unity is described in LEVINTHAL, ADAM, and THOMAS PORTER (1984), "Chap: a SIMD graphics processor," in *Computer Graphics* **18** (3): 77–82 (July, *Proc. SIGGRAPH '84*).

Free Scale Gamut, Free Scale Log (FS-Gamut, FS-Log)

A recent SMPTE standard endorses wide-gamut imagery in production. "FS" stands for "Free Scale;" image data having arbitrary chromaticity can be conveyed. The standard uses the notation $R'_{FS}G'_{FS}B'_{FS}$ for wide-gamut colour components. The "709" component in the stan-

SMPTE ST 2048-1, *2048×1080 and 4096×2160 Digital Cinematography Production Image Formats FS/709*.

DIGITAL VIDEO AND HD ALGORITHMS AND INTERFACES

ST 2048 contains many occurrences of "tristimulus value" where "chromaticity coordinate" is meant. Expect raised eyebrows among colour and image scientists.

Color VANC is pronounced *colour-VEE-ants*. The companion standard ST 2048-2 suggests placing Color VANC in the early portion of the active interval of line 18 in 1125-line interfaces.

dard's title reflects the option to convey image data having BT.709 colorimetry. The default values for FS primaries reflect Sony "wide gamut" delivered by the F23, F35, and F65 cameras (see page 294). The standard provides no default values for the quasilog OECF.

The colour space is defined by the chromaticity coordinates of the primaries and white, and a parametricly defined quasilog OECF. Apart from toe and shoulder regions that are typically nonlinear, no provision is made for footroom or headroom. The standard does not specify how image data values are to be carried, but presumably more than 10 bits per component will be used (despite the quasilog).

The quasilog OECF is described by a set of four numerical parameters and a (fifth) "exposure" value k_{EXT}; $0 \le k_{EXT}$ indicates underexposure, $k_{EXT} = 1$ indicates correct exposure (default!), and $1 < k_{EXT}$ indicates overexposure.

The standard defines Color VANC, an ancillary data (ANC) packet carrying colour metadata – namely, the chromaticities of the primaries and reference white, the four parameters of the quasilog OECF function, k_{EXT}, and 12 numerical parameters concerned with the toe and knee (or shoulder) of the OECF. Presumably, DI ingest is expected to use the parameters carried by the Color VANC to construct a colour transform.

Further reading

For a highly readable short introduction to colour image coding, consult DeMarsh and Giorgianni. For a terse, complete technical treatment, read Schreiber.

For details of many aspects of colour imaging technology, consult either Kang (somewhat dated, now), or Sharma. For a discussion of nonlinear *RGB* in computer graphics, read Lindbloom's SIGGRAPH paper.

In a computer graphics system, once light is on its way to the eye, any tristimulus-based system can accurately represent colour. However, the interaction of light and objects involves spectra, not tristimulus values. In computer-generated imagery (CGI), the calculations actually involve sampled SPDs, even if only three samples (in this context, colour components) are used. Roy Hall discusses these issues.

DeMarsh, LeRoy E., and Edward J. Giorgianni (1989), "Color science for imaging systems," in *Physics Today:* 44–52 (Sep.).

Hall, Roy (1989), *Illumination and Color in Computer Generated Imagery* (New York: Springer).

Kang, Henry R. (1997), *Color Technology for Electronic Imaging Devices* (Bellingham, Wash.: SPIE).

Lindbloom, Bruce (1989), "Accurate color reproduction for computer graphics applications," in *Computer Graphics*, **23** (3): 117–126 (July).

Reinhard, Erik et al. (2008), *Color Imaging: Fundamentals and Applications* (Wellesley, Mass.: A K Peters).

Schreiber, William F. (1993), *Fundamentals of Electronic Imaging Systems,* Third Edition (Berlin: Springer-Verlag).

Sharma, Gaurav (2002), *Digital Color Imaging Handbook* (Boca Raton, Florida: CRC).

Gamma

In photography, video, and computer graphics, the *gamma* symbol (γ) represents a numerical parameter that estimates, in a single numerical parameter, the exponent of the assumed power function that maps from code (pixel) value to tristimulus value. Gamma is a mysterious and confusing subject, because it involves concepts from four disciplines: physics, perception, photography, and video. This chapter explains how gamma is related to each of these disciplines. Having a good understanding of the theory and practice of *gamma* will enable you to get good results when you create, process, and display pictures.

Luminance is proportional to intensity. For an introduction to the terms *brightness, intensity, luminance,* and *lightness,* see page 27. Further detail on luminance and lightness is found on page 255.

This chapter concerns the electronic display of images using video and computer graphics techniques and equipment. I deal mainly with the presentation of luminance, or, as a photographer would say, *tone scale.* Achieving good tone reproduction is one important step toward achieving good colour reproduction. (Other issues specific to colour reproduction were presented in the previous chapter, *Colour science for video.*)

A *cathode-ray tube* (CRT) is inherently nonlinear: The luminance produced at the face of the display is a nonlinear function of each (R', G', and B') voltage input. From a strictly physical point of view, *gamma correction* at the camera can be thought of as precompensation for this nonlinearity in order to achieve correct reproduction of relative luminance.

Electro-optical conversion function (EOCF) refers to the function that characterizes conversion from the electrical signal domain into light, through some combination of signal processing and intrinsic display physics.

Perceptual uniformity was introduced on page 8: Human perceptual response to luminance is quite nonuniform: The *lightness* sensation of vision is roughly the 0.42-power function of relative luminance. This nonlinearity needs to be considered if an image is to be coded to minimize the visibility of noise so as to make best perceptual use of a limited number of bits per pixel.

Combining the CRT nonlinearity (from physics), and lightness sensitivity (from perception) reveals an amazing coincidence: The nonlinearity of a CRT is remarkably similar to the *inverse* of the lightness sensitivity of human vision. Coding tristimulus value *RGB* into a gamma-corrected signal *R'G'B'* makes maximum perceptual use of each signal component. If gamma correction had not already been necessary for physical reasons at the CRT, we would have had to invent it for perceptual reasons. Modern displays such as LCDs and PDPs don't have CRT physics, but the CRT's nonlinearity has been replicated through signal processing.

I will describe how video draws aspects of its handling of gamma from all of these areas: knowledge of the CRT from physics, knowledge of the nonuniformity of vision from perception, and knowledge of viewing conditions from photography.

Gamma in CRT physics

The electron gun of a CRT involves a theoretical relationship between voltage input and light output that a physicist calls a *five-halves power law:* Luminance produced at the face of the screen is in principle proportional to voltage input raised to the $\frac{5}{2}$ power. Luminance is roughly between the square and cube of the voltage. The numerical value of the exponent of this power function is represented by the Greek letter γ (gamma). CRT displays historically had behaviour that reasonably closely approximated this power function: Studio reference display CRTs have a numerical value of gamma quite close to 2.4.

Figure 27.1 opposite is a sketch of the power function that applies to the electron gun of a greyscale CRT, or to each of the red, green, and blue electron guns of a colour CRT. The three channels exhibit very similar, but not necessarily perfectly identical, responses.

The nonlinear voltage-to-luminance function of a CRT originates with the electrostatic interaction between the cathode, the grid, and the electron beam. The function is influenced to some extent by the mechanical structure of the electron gun. Contrary to

Opto-electronic conversion function (OECF) refers to the transfer function in a scanner or camera that relates light power to signal code. In video, it's sometimes termed *opto-electronic transfer function*, OETF.

OLSON, THOR (1995), "Behind gamma's disguise," in *SMPTE Journal*, 104 (7): 452–458 (July).

DIGITAL VIDEO AND HD ALGORITHMS AND INTERFACES

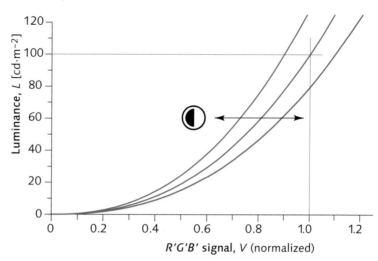

Figure 27.1 **Display electro-optical function (EOCF)** involves a nonlinear relationship between video signal and luminance, graphed here at GAIN settings of 0.9, 1.0, and 1.1 (effected by the poorly-named CONTRAST control). Luminance is approximately proportional to input signal voltage raised to the 2.4 power. The *gamma* of a display system – historically, that of a CRT – is the exponent of the assumed power function. Here the CONTRAST control is shown varying the gain of the video signal (on the *x*-axis), the way it's usually implemented; however, owing to the mathematical properties of a power function, scaling the luminance output would yield the same effect.

popular opinion, CRT phosphors themselves are quite linear, at least up to about eight-tenths of peak luminance. I denote the exponent the *decoding gamma*, γ_D.

The value of decoding gamma (γ_D) for a typical, properly adjusted CRT in a studio environment ranges from about 2.3 to 2.4. Computer graphics practitioners sometimes claim numerical values of gamma wildly different from 2.4; however, such measurements often disregard two issues. First, the largest source of variation in the nonlinearity of a display is careless setting of the BRIGHTNESS (or BLACK LEVEL) control. Before a sensible measurement of gamma can be made, this control must be adjusted, as outlined on page 56, so that black-valued pixels are correctly displayed. Second, computer systems often have lookup tables (LUTs) that effect control over transfer functions. A gamma value dramatically different from 2.4 is often due to the function loaded into the LUT. For example, Macintosh computers prior to 2009 were said to have a gamma of 1.8; however, that value was a consequence of the default Macintosh LUT, not the Macintosh display itself (which has gamma between about 2.2 and 2.4).

ROBERTS, ALAN (1993), "Measurement of display transfer characteristic (gamma, γ)," in *EBU Technical Review* 257: 32–40 (Autumn).

In Mac OS X operating system version 10.6 ("*Snow Leopard*"), released in 2009, Apple adopted a default gamma of 2.2: *R'G'B'* values presented to the graphics subsystem are now interpreted as sRGB by default.

Understanding CRT physics is an important first step toward understanding gamma, but it isn't the whole story.

The amazing coincidence!

In *Luminance and lightness,* on page 255, I described the nonlinear relationship between luminance (a physical quantity) and lightness (a perceptual quantity): Lightness is approximately luminance raised to the 0.42-power. The previous section described how the nonlinear transfer function of a CRT relates a voltage signal to luminance. Here's the surprising coincidence:

> A CRT's signal-to-luminance function is very nearly the *inverse* of the luminance-to-lightness relationship of human vision.

In analog systems, we represent lightness information as a voltage, to be transformed into luminance by a CRT's power function. Digital systems simply digitize analog voltage. To minimize the perceptibility of noise, we use a perceptually uniform code. Amazingly, the CRT function is a near-perfect inverse of vision's lightness sensitivity: CRT voltage is effectively a perceptually uniform code! In displays such as LCDs and PDPs, we impose signal processing to mimic CRT behaviour.

Gamma in video

Many video engineers are unfamiliar with colour science. They consider only the first of these two purposes, and disregard, or remain ignorant of, the great importance of perceptually uniform coding.

In a video system, "gamma correction" is applied at the camera for the dual purposes of precompensating the nonlinearity of the display's CRT and coding into perceptually uniform space. Figure 27.2 summarizes the image reproduction situation for video. At the left, gamma correction is imposed at the camera; at the right, the display imposes the inverse function. Coding into a perceptual domain was important in the early days of television because of the need to minimize the noise introduced by over-the-air analog transmission; the same considerations of noise visibility applied to analog videotape recording. These considerations also apply to the quantization error that is introduced upon digitization, when a linear-light signal is quantized to a limited number of bits. Consequently, it is universal to convey video signals in gamma-corrected form.

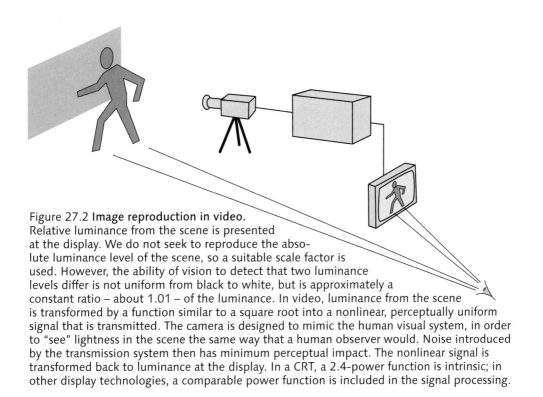

Figure 27.2 **Image reproduction in video.**
Relative luminance from the scene is presented
at the display. We do not seek to reproduce the absolute luminance level of the scene, so a suitable scale factor is
used. However, the ability of vision to detect that two luminance
levels differ is not uniform from black to white, but is approximately a
constant ratio – about 1.01 – of the luminance. In video, luminance from the scene
is transformed by a function similar to a square root into a nonlinear, perceptually uniform
signal that is transmitted. The camera is designed to mimic the human visual system, in order
to "see" lightness in the scene the same way that a human observer would. Noise introduced
by the transmission system then has minimum perceptual impact. The nonlinear signal is
transformed back to luminance at the display. In a CRT, a 2.4-power function is intrinsic; in
other display technologies, a comparable power function is included in the signal processing.

Gamma correction is ordinarily based upon a *power* function, which has the form $y = x^a$ (where a is constant). Gamma correction is sometimes incorrectly claimed to be an *exponential* function, which has the form $y = a^x$ (where a is constant).

Gamma correction is unrelated to the gamma function $\Gamma(\cdot)$ of mathematics.

The importance of picture rendering, and the consequent requirement for different exponents for encoding (γ_E) and decoding (γ_D), have been poorly recognized and poorly documented in the development of video.

In a video camera, we precompensate for the CRT's nonlinearity by processing each of the *R*, *G*, and *B* tristimulus signals through a nonlinear transfer function. This process is known as gamma correction. The function required is approximately a square root. The curve is often not precisely a power function; nonetheless, I denote the best-fit exponent the *encoding gamma*, γ_E. In video, gamma correction is accomplished by analog (or sometimes digital) circuits at the camera. In computer graphics, gamma correction is usually accomplished by incorporating the nonlinear transfer function into a framebuffer's lookup table.

As explained in *Picture rendering,* on page 115, it is important for perceptual reasons to alter the tone scale of an image presented at a luminance substantially lower than that of the original scene, presented with limited contrast ratio, or viewed in a dim surround. The dim surround condition is characteristic of television viewing. In video, the alteration is accomplished at the camera by slightly undercompensating the actual power function of the CRT, to obtain an end-to-end power

Eq 27.1
$$\gamma_E \approx 0.5; \gamma_D \approx 2.4;$$
$$\gamma_E \cdot \gamma_D \approx 1.2$$

What I call OECF, in accordance with the nomenclature of ISO 14524, is often called *opto-electronic transfer function*, OETF, in historical video literature.

BT.1361 was established by ITU-R but never deployed. It is now moribund, superseded by xvYCC.

ITU-R Rec. BT.709, *Basic parameter values for the HDTV standard for the studio and for international programme exchange.*

function whose exponent is about 1.2, as indicated in Equation 27.1 in the margin. This undercompensation achieves end-to-end reproduction that is subjectively correct (though not mathematically linear).

Opto-electronic conversion functions (OECFs)

Several different transfer functions have been standardized and are in use. In the sections to follow, I will detail these standards:

• BT.709 is an international standard that specifies the basic parameters of HD. Although intended for HD, it is representative of current SD technology, and it is being retrofitted into SD studio standards.

• The xvYCC "standard" extends $Y'C_BC_R$ and $Y'P_BP_R$ coding to accommodate a wide colour gamut. As I write, xvYCC is not deployed.

• sRGB refers to the standard transfer function of PCs.

• The transfer function of the original 1953 NTSC specification, often written $1/2.2$, has been effectively superseded by BT.1886.

• The transfer function of European standards for 576*i* is often given as $1/2.8$. Professional encoding has never expected a decoding gamma as high as 2.8. In any event, that value has been effectively superseded by BT.1886.

It is unclear from historical documents whether the classic NTSC 2.2 "gamma" and the classic EBU 2.8 "gamma" were intended to define the camera or the display! In entertainment imaging, the content creator has licence to manipulate image data at acquisition and at postproduction to yield the intended picture appearance, potentially completely independently of any standard OECF at a camera. The standard *EOCF* predominates: The EOCF establishes how image data is to be displayed in a manner faithful to the content creation process. The standard camera OECFs merely serve as engineering guidelines.

BT.709 OECF

Figure 27.3 illustrates the transfer function defined by the international BT.709 standard for high-definition television (HD). It is based upon a pure power function with an exponent of 0.45. Theoretically, a pure power function suffices for gamma correction; however, the

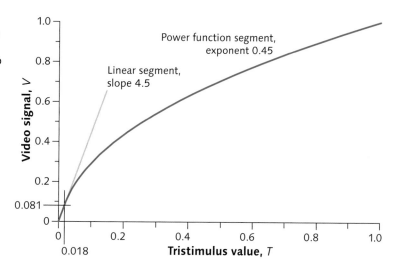

Figure 27.3 **BT.709 OECF** is standardized as the reference mapping from scene tristimulus to video code in SD and HD.

The symbol T suggests tristimulus value; the same equation applies to R, G or B. The symbol V suggests voltage, or video, or [code/pixel] value. I write this unprimed.

slope of a pure power function (whose exponent is less than unity) is infinite at zero. In a practical system such as a video camera, in order to minimize noise in dark regions of the picture it is necessary to limit the slope (gain) of the function near black. BT.709 specifies a slope of 4.5 below a tristimulus value of +0.018. The pure power function segment of the curve is scaled and offset to maintain function and tangent continuity at the breakpoint.

Reference BT.709 encoding is as follows. The tristimulus (linear light) component is denoted T, and the resulting gamma-corrected video signal – one of R', G', or B' components – is denoted with a prime symbol, V_{709}. R, G, and B are processed through identical functions to obtain R', G', and B':

$$V_{709} = \begin{cases} 4.5T; & 0 \leq T < 0.018 \\ 1.099T^{0.45} - 0.099; & 0.018 \leq T \leq 1 \end{cases} \qquad \text{Eq 27.2}$$

The reference BT.709 encoding equation includes an exponent of 0.45. I call this the "advertised" exponent. Some people describe BT.709 as having "gamma of 0.45"; broadcast video camera GAMMA controls are calibrated in terms comparable to this value. However, the effect of the scale factor and offset terms make the overall power function very similar to a square root ($\gamma_E \approx 0.5$); the *effective* power function exponent – and the value appropriate for picture rendering calculations – is 0.5.

BT.709 encoding assumes that encoded $R'G'B'$ signals will be converted to tristimulus values at a display with an EOCF close to a pure 2.4-power function:

$$T = V^{2.4}$$

Eq 27.3

The product of the effective 0.5 exponent typically used at the camera and the 2.4 exponent at the display produces an end-to-end power of about 1.2, suitable for material acquired in a bright environment for display in a typical television viewing situation, as I explained in *Picture rendering,* on page 115. In 2011, ITU-R adopted BT.1886, which specifies a 2.4-power function EOCF for HD; see *Reference display and viewing conditions,* on page 427. Unfortunately, reference white luminance and viewing conditions aren't standardized.

To recover *RGB* values proportional to scene tristimulus values, *assuming that the camera was operated with "factory"* BT.709 settings, invert Equation 27.2:

$$T = \begin{cases} \dfrac{V_{709}}{4.5}; & 0 \leq V_{709} < 0.081 \\[2em] \left(\dfrac{V_{709} + 0.099}{1.099}\right)^{\frac{1}{0.45}}; & 0.081 \leq V_{709} \leq 1 \end{cases}$$

Eq 27.4

Equation 27.4 is very similar to a square root. It does not incorporate correction for picture rendering: Recovered values are proportional to the *scene* tristimulus values, not to the intended *display* tristimulus values. BT.709 is misleading in its inclusion of this equation without discussing – or even mentioning – the issue of picture rendering.

For details of quantization to 8- or 10-bit components, see *Studio-swing (footroom and headroom),* on page 42.

SMPTE 240M OECF

SMPTE 240M, *1125-Line High-Definition Production Systems – Signal Parameters.*

SMPTE Standard 240M for 1125/60, 1035i30 HD was adopted two years before BT.709; virtually all HD equipment deployed in the decade 1988 to 1998 used the its parameters. For details, refer to the first edition of this book. The OECF specified in SMPTE 240M is intended to be used with a display EOCF comparable to that standardized (much later) in BT.1886.

sRGB transfer function

IEC 61966-2-1, *Multimedia systems and equipment – Colour measurement and management – Part 2-1: Colour management – Default RGB colour space – sRGB.*

The notation *sRGB* refers to a specification for colour image coding for personal computing, desktop graphics, and image exchange on the Internet.

The sRGB specificaton provides that a display will convert encoded *R'G'B'* signals using an EOCF that is a pure 2.2-power function.

The sRGB specification anticipates a higher ambient light level for viewing than typical broadcast studio practice associated with BT.709 encoding. Imagery originated with BT.709 encoding, displayed on a display with a 2.2-power, results in an end-to-end power of 1.1, considerably lower than the 1.2 end-to-end power produced by BT.709 encoding, but appropriate for the high display luminance, light surround, and poor contrast ratio typical of sRGB display environments.

$$\gamma_E \approx 0.45 \approx \frac{1}{2.22}$$

$$\gamma_D \approx 2.4$$

$$0.45 \cdot 2.4 \approx 1.1$$

See *Picture rendering,* on page 115.

The sRGB specification includes a function that ostensibly defines an OECF:

$$V_{sRGB} = \begin{cases} 12.92T; & 0 \leq T \leq 0.0031308 \\ 1.055T^{\left(\frac{1}{2.4}\right)} - 0.055; & 0.0031308 < T \leq 1 \end{cases} \qquad \text{Eq 27.5}$$

The standard is not explicit about the use of this function. Evidently it maps linear-light values to sRGB codes, and it includes a linear segment near black that you would expect in an OECF. The function resembles the BT.709 OECF. However, no account is taken of picture rendering. I conclude – and section 5.1 of the standard implies – that the function is intended to describe the mapping from the tristimulus values *presented on the display* to sRGB codes; in other words, sRGB coding is display referred. The encoding specified by sRGB is *inappropriate* when picture rendering is to be applied at the time of image capture – for example, when capturing a scene with a digital camera. For the latter purpose, BT.709 coding is appropriate.

Stokes, Michael, Matthew Anderson, Srinivasan Chandrasekar, and Ricardo Motta (1996), *A Standard Default Color Space for the Internet – sRGB* http://www.w3.org/Graphics/Color/ sRGB.

Although Equation 27.5 contains the exponent $^1/_{2.4}$, which suggests "gamma of 0.42," the scale factor and the offset cause the overall function to approximate a pure 0.45-power function ($\gamma_E \approx 0.45$). It is misleading to describe sRGB as having "gamma of 0.42."

It is standard to code sRGB components in 8-bit form from 0 to 255, with no footroom and no headroom.

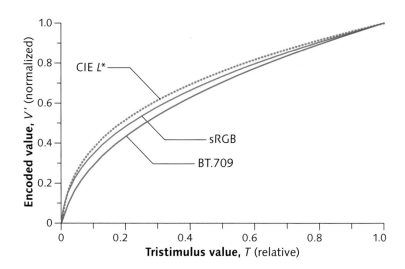

Figure 27.4 **BT.709, sRGB, and CIE L*** encoding functions are compared. They are all approximately perceptually uniform; however, they are not sufficiently close to be interchangeable.

Figure 27.4 sketches the sRGB encoding function, overlaid on the BT.709 encoding and CIE *L** functions.

Transfer functions in SD

Historically, transfer functions for SD have been very poorly specified. The FCC NTSC standard adopted in 1953 referred to a "transfer gradient (gamma exponent) of 2.2." It isn't clear whether 2.2 was intended to characterize the camera's OECF or the display's EOCF. In any event, modern CRTs have power function laws very close to 2.4! The FCC statement is widely interpreted to suggest that *encoding* should approximate a power of $\frac{1}{2.2}$; the reciprocal of $\frac{1}{2.2}$, 0.45, appears in modern standards such as BT.709. However, as I mentioned on page 321, BT.709's effective overall curve is very close to a square root. The FCC specification should not be taken seriously: Use BT.709 for encoding.

Standards for 576*i* SD also have poorly specified transfer functions. An "assumed display power function" of 2.8 is mentioned in EBUspecifications; some people interpret this as suggesting an encoding exponent of $\frac{1}{2.8}$. However, the 2.8 value is unrealistically high. In fact, European displays are comparable to displays in other parts of the world, and encoding to BT.709 is appropriate.

Surprisingly, no current standards specify viewing conditions in the studio. Only in 2011 was a standard adopted that specifies the transfer function of an idealized studio display! In the absence of a studio display EOCF, consumer display manufacturers adopted their own (nonstandard) practices, one factor leading to unpredictable image display in consumers' premises.

Bit depth requirements

In Figure 10.1 on page 108, in Chapter 10's discussion of constant luminance, I indicated that conveying relative luminance directly would require about 11 bits. That observation stems from two facts. First, studio video experience proves that 8 bits is barely sufficient to convey gamma-corrected $R'G'B'$ – that is, 2^8 (or 256) nonlinear levels are sufficient. Second, the transfer function used to derive gamma-corrected $R'G'B'$ has a certain maximum slope; a maximum slope of 4.5 is specified in BT.709. The number of codes necessary in a linear-light representation is the product of these two factors: 256 times 4.5 is 1152, which requires 11 bits.

In studio video, 8 bits per component barely suffice for distribution purposes. Some margin for roundoff error is required if the signals are subject to processing operations. For this reason, 10-bit studio video is now usual. To maintain 10-bit BT.709 accuracy in a linear-light system would require 12 bits per component. The BT.709 transfer function is suitable for video intended for display in the home, where contrast ratio is limited by the ambient environment. For higher-quality video, such as home theater, or for the adaptation of HD to digital cinema, we would like a higher maximum gain. When scaled to a lightness range of unity, CIE $L*$ has a maximum gain of 9.033; sRGB has a gain limit of 12.92. For these systems, linear-light representation requires 4 bits in excess of 10 on the nonlinear scale – that is, 14 bits per component.

If RGB or XYZ tristimulus components were conveyed directly, then 16 bits in each component would suffice for any realistic image-reproduction purpose. Linear-light 16-bit coding is now practical in high-end production, for example, scene-linear workflows using OpenEXR coding. For now, such approaches don't havve realtime hardware. In most applications, the nonlinear characteristics of perception are exploited and nonlinear image data coding is used.

In BT.601 coding with 8 bits, the black-to-white range without footroom or headroom encompasses 220 levels. For linear-light coding of this range, 10 bits suffices:

$$4.5 \cdot 220 = 990; \quad 990 < 2^{10}$$

$$4.5 \cdot 880 = 3960; \quad 3960 < 2^{12}$$

Gamma in modern display devices

Modern display devices, such as liquid crystal displays (LCDs), have transfer functions different from that of CRTs. Plasma display panels (PDPs) and Digital Light Processors (DLPs) both achieve apparent continuous tone through *pulse width modulation* (PWM): They are intrinsically linear-light devices, with straight-line transfer functions. Linear-light devices, such as PDPs and DLPs, potentially suffer from the "code 100" problem explained on page 31: In linear-light, more than 8 bits per component are necessary to achieve high quality.

No matter what transfer function characterizes the display, it is economically important to encode image data in a manner that is well matched to perceptual requirements. The BT.1886 EOCF is well matched to CRTs, but more importantly, it is well matched to perception! The performance advantage of perceptual coding, the wide deployment of equipment that expects BT.1886 decoding, and the huge amount of program material already encoded to this standard preclude any attempt to establish new standards optimized to particular devices.

A display device whose transfer function differs from a CRT must incorporate local correction, to adapt from its intrinsic transfer function to the transfer function that has been standardized for image interchange.

Estimating gamma

Knowing that a CRT is intrinsically nonlinear, and that its response is based on a power function, many researchers have attempted to summarize the nonlinearity of a CRT display in a single numerical parameter γ using this relationship, where *V* is code (or voltage) and *T* is luminance (or tristimulus value):

$$T = V^D \qquad\qquad \text{Eq 27.6}$$

The model forces zero voltage to map to zero luminance for *any* value of gamma. Owing to the model being "pegged" at zero, it cannot accommodate black-level errors: Black-level errors that displace the transfer function upward can be "fit" only by an estimate of gamma that is much smaller than 2.4. Black-level errors that displace the curve downward – saturating at zero

PDP and DLP devices are commonly described as employing PWM. However, it is not exactly the widths of the pulses that are being modulated, but the number of unit pulses per frame.

Concerning the conversion between BT.601 levels and the full-swing levels commonly used in computing, see Figure 31.3, on page 384.

over some portion of low voltages – can be "fit" only with an estimate of gamma that is much larger than 2.4. The only way the single *gamma* parameter can fit a black-level variation is to alter the curvature of the function. The apparent wide variability of gamma under this model has given gamma a bad reputation.

A much better model is obtained by fixing the exponent of the power function at 2.4, and using the single parameter to accommodate black-level error, ϵ:

$$T = (V + \epsilon)^{2.4}$$

Eq 27.7

This model fits the observed nonlinearity much better than the variable-gamma model.

A simple technique to estimate gamma uses luminance measurements for video signal codes 0.08 and 0.8. Take the $\log_{10}$ of these two luminance values. The arithmetic difference between the two logs is a decent gamma estimate. The two video signal values are one decade apart; the 0.08 video signal is high enough to avoid potential black-level issues, and the 0.8 signal is low enough to avoid CRT saturation.

Figure 27.1, on page 317, graphs several pure 2.4-power functions. Gamma is 2.4 everywhere along these curves. Consider measuring a display at $n + 1$ video signal values at equal intervals of $1/n$ between 0 and 1. (Usually ten values are used, 0.1, 0.2, ..., 0.9, 1.0.) Using L_0 to symbolize the luminance produced by zero signal value and L_N to symbolize the luminance produced by unity signal value, average gamma can be estimated as follows:

Equation 27.8 below is written with logs to base 10; however, because the ratio oof logs is taken, any base would do. In this calculation, luminance values L_1 through L_N must be strictly greater than L_0. If the video signal values are not at equal intervals, replace i/n in the denominator by V_i where each V_i is the appropriate video signal level strictly between 0 and 1.

$$\gamma = \frac{1}{9} \sum_{i=1}^{9} \frac{\log_{10} \dfrac{L\left(\frac{i}{10}\right)}{L(1)}}{\log_{10} \dfrac{i}{10}}$$

Eq 27.8

EBU Tech. 3325 (2008), *Methods for the Measurement of the performance of Studio Monitors*, Version 1.1 (Sep.).

A variant of this formulation is described in EBU Tech. 3325; it is commonly used in home theatre calibration. In my view, this formulation of average gamma gives the luminance produced at reference white video level undue influence over the estimated gamma value. If reference white luminance is depressed – as will be the case for a CRT entering saturation, or an LCD mimicking that behaviour – then all of the contributing point-gamma values will be low, and the average gamma estimate will be reduced. In some formulations (such as that of the EBU), L_i in the numerator is replaced by $L_i - L_0$, subtracting the zero-code luminance; that subtraction leads to errors.

In my view, a better way to characterize gamma is to perform a numerical fit to an appropriate model, such as the GOGO model of Berns, Mottta, and Gorzynski.

BERNS, ROY S., RICARDO J. MOTTA, and MARK E. GORZYNSKI (1993), "CRT colorimetry," in *Color Research and Application* **18**: 299–325.

Video displays have historically been aligned in the studio using the PLUGE test signal, adjusting BLACK LEVEL (BRIGHTNESS, or offset) so that 0% video and –2% video signals were just barely under the threshold of visibility. That procedure leaves video signal zero producing a small amount of light, typically between 0.01 and 0.1 nt for 100 nt reference white. For a pure 2.4-power function, the video signal corresponding to absolute, theoretical black is about –2% of the reference white signal, that is, around 10-bit interface code 32.

If you want to determine the nonlinearity of your display, consult the classic article by Cowan. In addition to describing how to measure the nonlinearity, he describes how to determine other characteristics of your display – such as the chromaticity of its white point and its primaries – that are important for accurate colour reproduction.

COWAN, WILLIAM B. (1983), "An inexpensive scheme for calibration of a colour monitor in terms of CIE standard coordinates," in *Computer Graphics* **17** (3): 315–321 (July).

Gamma in video, CGI, and Macintosh

Transfer functions in video (and PC), computer-generated imagery, and Macintosh are sketched in the rows of Figure 27.5 opposite. Each row shows four function blocks; from left to right, these are a camera or scanner LUT, an image storage device, an output LUT, and a display.

In video, sketched in the top row, the camera applies a transfer function to accomplish gamma correction. Signals are then maintained in a perceptual domain throughout the system until conversion to tristimulus values at the display. I show the output LUT with a ramp that leaves data unaltered: Video systems conventionally use no LUT, but the comparison is clarified if I portray the four rows with the same blocks.

PC graphics hardware ordinarily implements lookup tables at the output of the framestore, as I detailed in *Raster images,* on page 67. However, most PC software

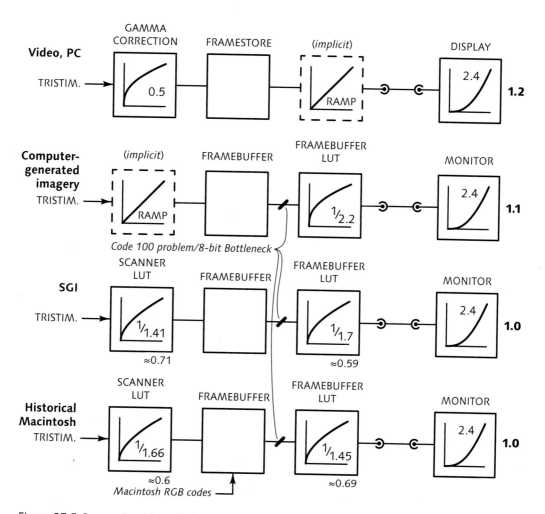

Figure 27.5 **Gamma in video, CGI, and Macintosh** are summarized in the rows of this diagram. Tristimulus signals enter from the left; the columns show the transfer functions of (respectively) a camera or scanner; the image storage device (framestore or framebuffer); output LUT; and the display.

In video, sketched in the top row, a transfer function that mimics vision is applied at the camera ("gamma correction"); the signal remains in perceptual space until the encoding is reversed by the display. (PCs have comparable signal encoding.) In computer graphics, sketched in the second row, calculations are performed in the linear-light domain, and gamma correction is applied in a LUT at the output of the framebuffer. Macintosh computers, sketched in the bottom row, take a hybrid approach: The scanner applies a $^1/_{1.66}$ power, and a $^1/_{1.45}$-power function is loaded into the LUT. Using $\gamma_E \approx {}^1/_{1.66}$ is appropriate for prerendered imagery, to produce an end-to-end exponent of 1.0.

The end-to-end power function exponent, or *picture rendering* (see page 115), is shown for each row by the number at the extreme right. This number is the product of the exponents across the system. Some people call this "system gamma," but that term is so widely misused that I reject it.

The Macintosh computer historically implemented a $^1/_{1.45}$-power function at the output LUT. John Knoll's *Gamma* Control Panel was commonly used to load the output LUT. When set to a gamma value g, the Control Panel loaded the LUT with a power function whose exponent is $^{2.61}/_g$. Strangely, gamma on Macintosh computers came to be quoted as the exponent applied prior to the framebuffer (whereas in other computers it is the exponent of the table loaded into the output LUT). So, the Mac's default gamma was said to be 1.8, not 1.45. A more reasonable value of display gamma of 2.2 results in tristimulus value proportional to code value raised to the 1.66-power (see Figure 27.6).

A Macintosh could be set to handle video (or PC) $R'G'B'$ data by loading a ramp into its output LUT. Using Knoll's control panel, this is accomplished by setting gamma to 2.61.

JPEG/JFIF files originated on Macintosh historically represented R, G, and B display tristimulus values raised to the 0.6 power (that is, about $^1/_{1.65}$).

As of Mac OS X 10.6 ("Snow Leopard"), Macintosh software has been brought into conformance with the colour properties of sRGB.

accommodates display hardware without lookup tables. When the LUT is absent, code values map directly to voltage, and the situation is equivalent to video. So, the top row in the diagram pertains to PCs.

Computer graphics systems generally store tristimulus values in the framebuffer, and use hardware LUTs, in the path to the display, to gamma-correct on the fly. This is illustrated in the second row. Typically, a $^1/_{2.2}$-power function is loaded into the output LUT; in this case, picture rendering of 1.1 is achieved.

Macintosh computers, prior to Mac OS X 10.6, used the approach shown in the bottom row. The output LUT is, by default, loaded with a $^1/_{1.45}$-power function. The combination of the default LUT and the usual 2.4-power display function results in a 1.66-power function that relates Macintosh $R'G'B'$ values (such as the values stored in a PICT file or data structure) to displayed tristimulus values.

If a desktop scanner is to produce Macintosh $R'G'B'$ values that display relative luminance correctly, then a 1.66-power function must be loaded to the scanner LUT. In the typical Macintosh situation, the $^1/_{1.66}$, $^1/_{1.45}$, and 2.4 exponents combine to achieve an end-to-end exponent of unity. This is suitable for scanning photographs or offset printed matter, where picture rendering is already incorporated into the image.

For Macintosh $R'G'B'$ values originated by application software, part of Macintosh gamma correction must be effected by application software prior to presentation of $R'G'B'$ values to the Macintosh graphics subsystem; the remainder is accomplished in the output LUTs. When scanning, part of Macintosh gamma correction is effected by the LUT in the scanner driver, and the remainder is accomplished in the output LUTs.

Halftoned printing has a builtin nonlinearity, owing to the phenomenon of dot gain. Reflectance from the printed page is approximately proportional to the 1.8-power of [1−*CMYK*] code values. Macintosh $R'G'B'$ values are not perceptually optimum; however, apparently by serendipity, Macintosh $R'G'B'$ coding is nearly perfectly matched to the dot gain of halftone printing. This led to the dominance of Macintosh computers in graphic arts and prepress, and made "gamma 1.8" image encoding a de facto standard for graphic arts.

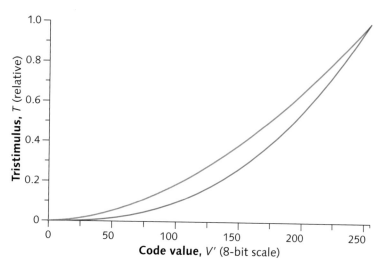

Figure 27.6 **Gamma PC and in classic Mac** are different, owing to the interpretation of *R'G'B'* code values by the display system. On a PC, the output LUT is either absent or programmed as if absent, and code values are subject to the 2.4-power function of the display (sketched in the lower curve). On a Mac prior to Mac OS X version 10.6 "Snow Leopard," the default output LUT imposes a $1/1.45$-power function on the code values, then the display imposes its usual 2.4-power function; the concatenation of these two functions results in a 1.66-power function that relates Mac code value to displayed relative luminance, as sketched in the upper curve.

At the right-hand end of each row of Figure 27.5, on page 329, I have indicated in boldface type the rendering intent usually used. In video, I have shown an end-to-end power function of 1.2. For computer-generated imagery, I have shown the typical value of 1.1. For Macintosh, I have sketched the usual situation where prerendered images are being scanned; in this case, the end-to-end power function exponent is unity.

Correct display of computer image data depends upon knowing the transfer function that is expected at the output of the graphics subsystem. If an image that originates on a PC traverses the classic $1/1.45$-power function of a pre-10.6 Macintosh LUT and a 2.4-power function display, midtones will display too light: Code 128 will produce luminance 1.5 times higher than intended. Conversely, if an image originates on a classic pre-10.6 Macintosh (where the $1/1.45$-power function is expected), but is displayed on a PC (without this function), midtones will display much too dark. The relationship between default *R'G'B'* code values and displayed luminance factors for both PC and Mac is graphed in Figure 27.6.

Gamma shift refers to an undesired alteration of effective decoding gamma that results from inadvertent application of Macintosh-related gamma correction upon import or export of video involving a Macintosh computer. Gamma shift usually involves inadvertent application of a 1.45-power function or its inverse, a 0.69-power function.

Gamma in computer graphics

Computer-generated imagery (CGI) software systems generally perform calculations for lighting, shading, depth-cueing, and antialiasing using approximations to tristimulus values, so as to model the physical mixing of light. Values stored in the framebuffer are processed by hardware lookup tables on the fly on their way to the display. If linear-light values are stored in the frame-buffer, the LUTs can accomplish gamma-correction. The power function at the CRT acts on the gamma-corrected signal voltages to display the correct luminance values at the face of the screen. Software systems usually provide a default gamma value and some method to change the default.

The BT.709 function is suitable for originating image data at high light levels (2000 lx or more) intended for viewing at about 100 nt in a dim surround. For other origination or viewing environments, see the comments on page 118.

The framebuffer's LUTs enable software to perform tricks to manipulate the appearance of the image data without changing the image data itself. To allow the user to make use of features such as accurate colour reproduction, applications should access lookup tables in the structured ways that are provided by the graphics system, and not by direct manipulation of the LUTs.

Gamma in pseudocolour

In *Pseudocolour,* on page 70, I described how the colour lookup table (CLUT) in a pseudocolour system contains values that are directly mapped to voltage at the display. It is conventional for a pseudocolour application program to provide, to a graphics system, *R'G'B'* colour values that are already gamma corrected for a typical monitor and typical viewing conditions. A pseudocolour image stored in a file is accompanied by a *colourmap* whose *R'G'B'* values are intended to be subject to an EOCF approximating a 2.4-power function at display.

Limitations of 8-bit linear coding

As mentioned in *Gamma in computer graphics,* on page 332, computer graphics systems that render synthetic imagery usually perform computations in the linear-light – or loosely, "intensity" – domain. Low-end graphics accelerators historically performed Gouraud shading in the linear-light domain, and stored 8-bit components in the framebuffer. In *The "code 100" problem and nonlinear image coding,* on page 31, I explained that linear-light representation cannot achieve high-quality images with just 8 bits per component; such images typically exhibit contouring. The visibility of contouring is enhanced by a perceptual effect called *Mach bands*; consequently, the contouring artifact is sometimes called *banding*.

High-end systems for computer-generated imagery (CGI) typically operate in the linear-light ("gamma = 1.0") domain using more than 8 bits per component (often floating point). Some systems perform gamma correction in software, then write gamma-corrected values into a limited-depth framebuffer. Other systems have "deep colour" framebuffers (having components with more than 8 bits, and often 16 bits); a unity ramp is loaded into the LUT of the framebuffer. This arrangement maximizes perceptual performance, and produces rendered imagery without the quantization artifacts of 8-bit linear-light coding.

Linear and nonlinear coding in CGI

Computer graphic standards often make no explicit mention of transfer function. Often, linear-light coding is implicit. However, in the JPEG standard there is no mention of transfer function but *nonlinear* (video-like) coding is implicit: Unacceptable results are obtained when JPEG is applied to linear-light data. All of these standards deal with *RGB* quantities; you might consider their *RGB* values to be comparable, but they're not!

Figure 27.7 **Linear and nonlinear coding in imaging standards.** In linear-light standards, code [128, 128, 128] produces luminance halfway up the *physical* scale, a relative luminance of 0.5. In video, code [128, 128, 128] produces luminance halfway up the *perceptual* scale, only about 0.18 in relative luminance. Values are denoted *RGB* in both cases; however, the values are not comparable. The discrepancy exemplifies a serious problem in the exchange of image files.

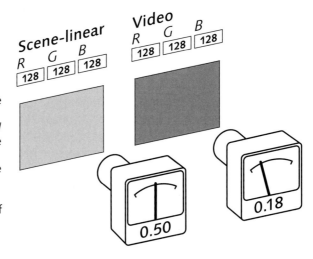

What are loosely called *JPEG files* use the *JPEG File Interchange Format* (JFIF), cited in the margin of page 502. Version 1.02 of the JFIF specification states that linear-light coding (gamma 1.0) is used. That is seldom the case in practice; instead, image data is encoded expecting a 2.2-power EOCF. See page 328.

Figure 27.7 sketches two systems displaying the same *RGB* triple, [128, 128, 128]. A photometer reading the luminance displayed by a scene-linear system is shown at the left; a photometer reading luminance displayed by a video system is shown at the right. In scene-linear, the displayed luminance is halfway up the *physical* scale, a relative luminance of 0.5. In the video case, displayed luminance is halfway up the *perceptual* scale, only about 0.18 in relative luminance. Many graphics image files do not carry any transfer function information. If you exchange *RGB* image data without regard for transfer functions, huge differences will result when image data is displayed.

The digital image-processing literature rarely discriminates between linear and nonlinear coding. Also, when *intensity* is mentioned, be suspicious: Image data may be represented in linear-light form, *proportional* to intensity. However, a pixel component value is usually associated with a small area of a sensor or a display, so its units should include a per square meter ($\cdot m^{-2}$) term, so radiance, luminance, relative luminance, or tristimulus value are technically correct. All of these quantities are *proportional* to intensity, but they do not have units of intensity and they are not properly described as intensity values.

Luma and colour differences   28

This chapter describes colour coding systems that are used to convey image data derived from additive *RGB* primaries. I outline nonlinear *R'G'B'*, explain the formation of *luma*, denoted Y', as a weighted sum of these nonlinear signals, and introduce the *colour difference* (chroma) components $[B'-Y', R'-Y']$, $[C_B, C_R]$, and $[P_B, P_R]$.

The design of a video coding system is necessarily rooted in detailed knowledge of human colour perception. However, once this knowledge is embodied in a coding system, what remains is physics, mathematics, and signal processing. This chapter concerns only the latter domains.

Colour acuity

A monochrome video system ideally senses relative luminance, described on page 256. Luminance is then transformed by the gamma correction circuitry of the camera, as described in *Gamma in video*, on page 318, into a signal that takes into account the properties of lightness perception. At the receiver, the display – historically, the CRT itself – imposes the required inverse transfer function.

A colour image is sensed in three components, red, green, and blue, as described in *Additive reproduction (RGB)*, on page 288. To minimize the visibility of noise or quantization, the *RGB* components should be coded nonlinearly.

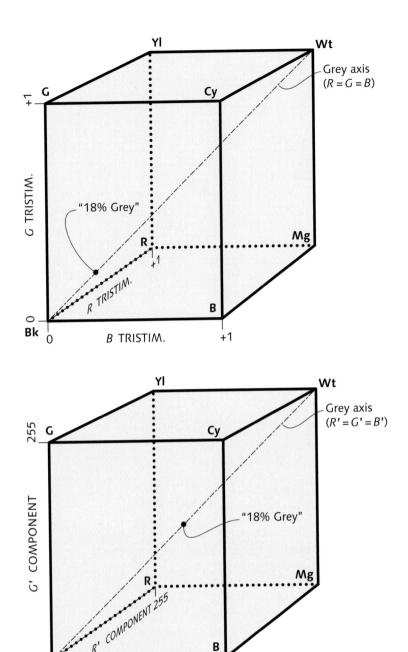

Figure 28.1 *RGB* and *R'G'B'* cubes. *RGB* components form the coordinates of a three-dimensional colour space; coordinate values between 0 and 1 define the unit cube. Linear coding, sketched at the top, has poor perceptual performance when 8 or even 10 bits are used for each component. In video, *RGB* components are subject to *gamma correction* to impose perceptual uniformity.

RGB and R'G'B' colour cubes

Red, green, and blue tristimulus (linear light) primary components, as detailed in *Colour science for video*, on page 287, can be considered to be the coordinates of a three-dimensional colour space. Coordinate values between zero and unity define the unit cube of this space, as sketched at the top of Figure 28.1 opposite. Linear-light coding is used in CGI, where physical light is simulated. However, as I explained in the previous chapter, *Gamma in video*, 8-bit linear-light coding exhibits poor perceptual performance: 12 or 14 bits per component are necessary to achieve excellent quality. The best perceptual use is made of a limited number of bits by using nonlinear coding that mimics the nonlinear lightness response of human vision. As introduced on page 27, and detailed in Chapter 27 *Gamma*, on page 315, in video, JPEG, MPEG, computing, digital still photography, and in many other domains a non-linear transfer function is applied to *RGB* tristimulus signals to give nonlinearly coded (*gamma-corrected*) components, denoted with prime symbols: *R'G'B'*. Excellent image quality is obtained with 10-bit nonlinear coding with a transfer function similar to that of BT.709 or sRGB.

In PC graphics, 8-bit nonlinear coding is common: Each of *R'*, *G'*, and *B'* ranges from 0 through 255, inclusive, following the quantizer transfer function sketched in Figure 4.1, on page 37. The resulting *R'G'B'* cube is sketched at the bottom of Figure 28.1 opposite. A total of 2^{24} colours – that is, 16,777,216 colours – are representable. Not all of them can be distinguished visually; not all are perceptually useful; but they are all colours. Studio video uses headroom and footroom, as explained in *Studio-swing (footroom and headroom)*, on page 42: 8-bit *R'G'B'* has 219 codes between black and white, for a total of 220^3 or 10,648,000 codewords.

The drawback of conveying *R'G'B'* components of an image is that each component requires relatively high spatial resolution: Transmission or storage of a colour image using *R'G'B'* components requires a capacity three times that of a greyscale image. Human vision has considerably less spatial acuity for colour information than for lightness. Owing to the poor colour acuity of vision, a colour image can be coded into a wideband

In video, *codeword* (or *codepoint*) refers to a combination of three integer values such as [*R'*, *G'*, *B'*] or [*Y'*, C_B, C_R].

monochrome component representing lightness, and two narrowband components carrying colour information, each having substantially less spatial resolution than lightness. In analog video, each colour channel has bandwidth typically one-third that of the monochrome channel. In digital video, each colour channel has half the data rate (or data capacity) of the monochrome channel, or less. There is strong evidence that the human visual system forms an achromatic channel and two chromatic colour-difference channels at the retina.

Green dominates luminance: Between 60% and 70% of luminance comprises green information. Signal-to-noise ratio is maximized if the colour signals on the other two components are chosen to be blue and red. The simplest way to "remove" lightness from blue and red is to subtract it, to form a pair of *colour difference* (or loosely, *chroma*) components.

Here the term *colour difference* refers to a signal formed as the difference of two gamma-corrected colour components. In other contexts, the term can refer to a numerical measure of the perceptual distance between two colours.

The monochrome component in colour video could have been based upon the luminance of colour science (a weighted sum of *R*, *G*, and *B*). Instead, as I explained in *Constant luminance*, on page 107, luma is formed as a weighted sum of *R'*, *G'*, and *B'*, using coefficients similar or identical to those that would be used to compute luminance. Expressed in abstract terms, luma ranges 0 to 1. Colour difference components $B'-Y'$ and $R'-Y'$ are bipolar; each ranges nearly ±1.

In component analog video, $B'-Y'$ and $R'-Y'$ are scaled to form P_B and P_R components. In abstract terms, these range ±0.5. Figure 28.2 shows the unit *R'G'B'* cube transformed into luma [*Y'*, P_B, P_R]. (Various interface standards are in use; see page 359.) In component digital video, $B'-Y'$ and $R'-Y'$ are scaled to form C_B and C_R components. In 8-bit $Y'C_BC_R$ prior to the application of the interface offset, the luma axis of Figure 28.2 would be scaled by 219, and the chroma axes by 112.

I introduced interface offsets on page 44.

Once colour difference signals have been formed, they can be subsampled to reduce bandwidth or data capacity, without the observer's noticing, as I will explain in *Chroma subsampling, revisited*, on page 347.

Figure 28.2 A $Y'P_BP_R$ cube is formed when R', G', and B' are subject to a particular 3×3 matrix transform. The *valid* $R'G'B'$ unit cube occupies about one-quarter of the volume of the $Y'P_BP_R$ unit cube. (The volume of the $Y'P_BP_R$ unit cube, the outer boundary of this sketch, is the same as the volume of the $R'G'B'$ cube in Figure 28.1 on page 336; however, the useful codes occupy only the central parallelpiped here.) Luma and colour difference coding incurs a penalty in signal-to-noise ratio, but this disadvantage is compensated by the opportunity to subsample.

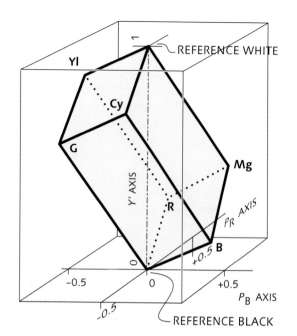

IZRAELEVITZ, DAVID, and JOSHUA L. KOSLOV (1982), "Code utilization for component-coded digital video," in *Tomorrow's Television* (Proc. 16th Annual SMPTE Television Conference): 22–30.

$$\frac{\frac{1}{4} \cdot 220 \cdot 225^2}{220^3} = \frac{2784375}{10648000}$$

$$\approx 0.261$$

It is evident from Figure 28.2 that when $R'G'B'$ signals are transformed into the $Y'P_BP_R$ space of analog video, the unit $R'G'B'$ cube occupies only part of the volume of the unit $Y'P_BP_R$ cube: Only ¼ of the $Y'P_BP_R$ volume corresponds to $R'G'B'$ values all between 0 and 1. Consequently, $Y'P_BP_R$ exhibits a loss of signal-to-noise ratio compared to $R'G'B'$. However, this disadvantage is offset by the opportunity to subsample.

In a *legal* signal, no component exceeds its reference excursion. Signal combinations that are $R'G'B'$-legal are termed *valid*. Signals within the $Y'P_BP_R$ unit cube are $Y'P_BP_R$-legal. However, about ¾ of these combinations correspond to $R'G'B'$ combinations outside the $R'G'B'$ unit cube: Although legal, these $Y'P_BP_R$ combinations are *invalid* – that is, they are $R'G'B'$-illegal.

In digital video, we refer to *codewords* instead of combinations. There are about 2.75 million valid codewords in 8-bit $Y'C_BC_R$, compared to 10.6 million in 8-bit studio $R'G'B'$. If $R'G'B'$ is transcoded to 8-bit $Y'C_BC_R$, then transcoded back to $R'G'B'$, the resulting $R'G'B'$ cannot have any more than 2.75 million colours.

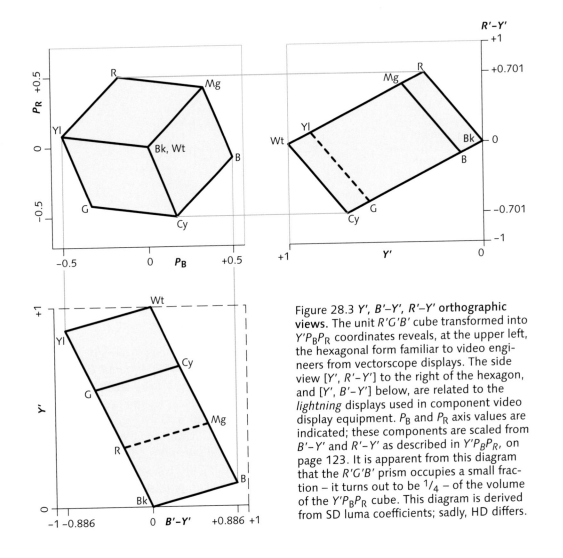

Figure 28.3 *Y′, B′–Y′, R′–Y′* **orthographic views.** The unit *R′G′B′* cube transformed into *Y′P_BP_R* coordinates reveals, at the upper left, the hexagonal form familiar to video engineers from vectorscope displays. The side view [*Y′, R′–Y′*] to the right of the hexagon, and [*Y′, B′–Y′*] below, are related to the *lightning* displays used in component video display equipment. *P_B* and *P_R* axis values are indicated; these components are scaled from *B′–Y′* and *R′–Y′* as described in *Y′P_BP_R*, on page 123. It is apparent from this diagram that the *R′G′B′* prism occupies a small fraction – it turns out to be ¹/₄ – of the volume of the *Y′P_BP_R* cube. This diagram is derived from SD luma coefficients; sadly, HD differs.

C_BC_R components are comparable to P_BP_R components, but have codeword values ranging ±112 on the 8-bit scale instead of abstract values ranging ±0.5.

In Figure 28.2, the $Y'P_BP_R$ cube is portrayed off-axis. Figure 28.3 shows three orthographic views of the $R'G'B'$ prism in $Y'P_BP_R$-space. The luma axis, denoted Y', ranges 0 to 1. The chroma axes are annotated with both [$B'-Y'$, $R'-Y'$] scaling (where the components range ±0.886 and ±0.701, respectively), and P_BP_R scaling (where the components both range ±0.5). The extent of the volume of $Y'P_BP_R$ space that lies outside the $R'G'B'$ prism is apparent. The emergent xvYCC system, to be described, uses $Y'C_BC_R$ codewords outside the unit $R'G'B'$ prism – that is, formerly "invalid" codewords – to convey wide-gamut colour.

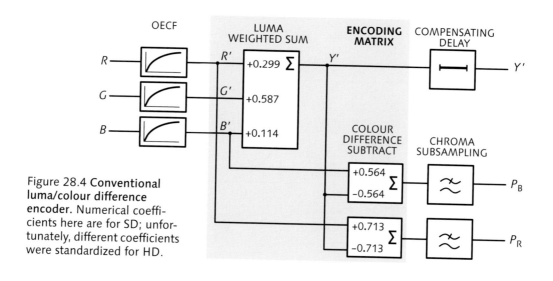

OECF · LUMA WEIGHTED SUM · **ENCODING MATRIX** · COMPENSATING DELAY

R — R' +0.299 Σ — Y' — Y'

G — G' +0.587

B — B' +0.114

COLOUR DIFFERENCE SUBTRACT · CHROMA SUBSAMPLING

+0.564 Σ / −0.564 — P_B

+0.713 Σ / −0.713 — P_R

Figure 28.4 **Conventional luma/colour difference encoder.** Numerical coefficients here are for SD; unfortunately, different coefficients were standardized for HD.

Figure 28.4 shows a time delay element in the luma path. Luma is delayed by a time interval equal to the transit delay of chroma through the chroma bandlimiting filters.

Eq 28.1 BT.601 $Y'P_BP_R$ encoding matrix (for SD)

$$P = \begin{bmatrix} 0.299 & 0.587 & 0.114 \\ -0.169 & -0.331 & 0.5 \\ 0.5 & -0.419 & -0.081 \end{bmatrix}$$

For the derivation of this matrix, and a more precise expression, see *PBPR components for SD,* on page 359.

Conventional luma/colour difference coding

I explained constant luminance on page 107. True constant luminance coding remains an intriguing possibility, but at present all video systems use nonconstant luminance coding, which I will now describe.

A conventional luma/colour difference encoder is shown in Figure 28.4 above. First, a nonlinear transfer function is applied to each of the red, green, and blue linear (tristimulus) components. Then luma is formed as a weighted sum of gamma-corrected R', G', and B' components. $B'-Y'$ and $R'-Y'$ colour difference components are formed by subtraction; in Figure 28.4, scaling to analog P_B and P_R components is indicated. Finally, the colour difference components are lowpass filtered.

The highlight rectangle in Figure 28.4 groups together the weighted adder that forms luma with the pair of colour difference subtractors; the combination is equivalent to matrix multiplication by the 3×3 matrix P shown in Equation 28.1 in the margin. The numerical values used in Equation 28.1, in Figure 28.4, and in subsequent figures in this chapter all reflect the BT.601 luma coefficients used in SD. Unfortunately, the coefficients for HD are different, as I will describe in *Component video colour coding for HD,* on page 369.

Figure 28.5 illustrates a conventional luma/colour difference decoder. In a digital decoder, the colour difference (chroma) components are horizontally (and,

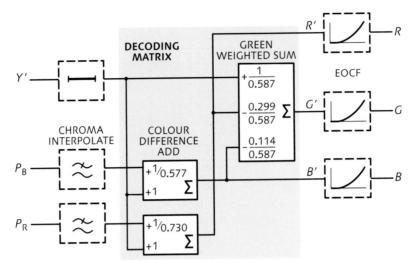

Figure 28.5 Conventional luma/colour difference decoder, Parameter values here are those of SD. In a historical analog SD television receiver, chroma interpolation is implicit, and requires no circuitry: I draw these components with dashed outlines. In a historical analog SD television receiver, the EOCF is inherent in the CRT, and similarly requires no components.

in some applications, spatially) interpolated; in an analog decoder, no circuitry is required to perform this function. Luma is added to the colour difference components to reconstruct nonlinear blue and red components. A weighted sum of luma, blue, and red is then formed to reconstruct the nonlinear green component.

The blue and red colour difference adders and the weighted adder that recovers green, all enclosed by the highlight rectangle in Figure 28.5, can be considered together as multiplication by the 3×3 matrix $\boldsymbol{P}^{-1}$ shown in Equation 28.2. These values are for SD; the matrix for HD is different.

Eq 28.2 BT.601 $Y'P_BP_R$ decoding matrix (for SD)

$$\boldsymbol{P}^{-1} = \begin{bmatrix} 1 & 0 & 1.402 \\ 1 & -0.344 & -0.714 \\ 1 & 1.772 & 0 \end{bmatrix}$$

To produce linear-light tristimulus components, all three components are subject to the inverse transfer function sketched at the right with dashed outlines. Usually, a decoder is used with a CRT that has an intrinsic 2.4-power function, or with some other display that incorporates a 2.4-power function; in either case, the transfer function need not be explicitly computed.

Luminance and luma notation

In *Luminance from red, green, and blue,* on page 258, I described how relative (linear-light) luminance, proportional to intensity, can be computed as an appropriately weighted sum of *RGB*.

In video, the luminance of colour science isn't computed. Instead, we compute a nonlinear quantity *luma* as a weighted sum of nonlinear (gamma-corrected) *R'G'B'*. The weights – or *luma coefficients* – are related to the luminance coefficients. The luma coefficients specified in BT.601 have been ubiquitous for SD, but new and different weights have been introduced in HD standards. In my opinion, the luma coefficients need not and should not have been changed for HD: Complexity is added to upconversion and downconversion in studio and consumer equipment, for no improvement in performance or quality.

Television standards documents historically used the prime symbol (') – often combined with the letter *E* for voltage – to denote a component that incorporates gamma correction. For example, E'_R historically denoted the gamma-corrected red channel. Gamma correction is nowadays so taken for granted in video that the *E* and the prime symbol are usually elided. This has led to much confusion among people attempting to utilize video technology in other domains.

See Appendix A, *YUV and luminance considered harmful*, on page 567.

The existence of several standard sets of primary chromaticities, the introduction of new coefficients, and continuing confusion between luminance and luma all beg for a notation to distinguish among the many possible combinations. In the absence of any standard notation, I was compelled to invent my own.

Figure 28.6 below sketches the notation that I use. The base symbol is *Y, R, G, or B*. The subscript denotes the standard specifying the chromaticities of the primaries

Figure 28.6 **Luminance and luma notation** is necessary because different primary chromaticity sets, different luma coefficients, and different component scale factors are in use. Unity scaling suffices for components in this chapter; in succeeding chapters, other scale factors will be introduced.

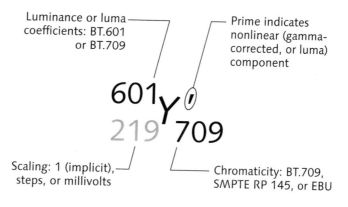

Luminance or luma coefficients: BT.601 or BT.709

Prime indicates nonlinear (gamma-corrected, or luma) component

$$601_Y'_{709} \\ 219 \quad$$

Scaling: 1 (implicit), steps, or millivolts

Chromaticity: BT.709, SMPTE RP 145, or EBU

Figure 28.7 **Typesetting** $Y'C_BC_R$ is a challenge! Luma coefficient set, scaling, and chromaticities are set out as in Figure 28.6. The prime should always be present, to distinguish *luma* from the *luminance* of colour science. *C* is appropriate for digital signals, *P* for analog. Subscripts B and R serve as tags, not variables: They should be in roman type, not italics. B comes before R.

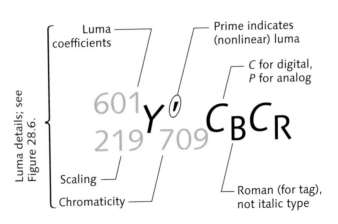

and white. An unprimed letter indicates a linear-light tristimulus component (R, G, or B), or relative luminance (Y). A prime symbol (') indicates a nonlinear (gamma-corrected) component (R', G', and B'), or luma (Y').

For luminance or luma, a leading superscript indicates the standard specifying the weights used. Historically the weights of BT.601 were implicit, but recent HD standards such as BT.709 and SMPTE ST 274 call for different weights. Finally, the leading subscript indicates the overall scaling of the signal. If omitted, an overall scaling of unity is implicit, otherwise an integer such as 219, 255, or 874 specifies the black-to-white excursion in a digital system, or a number such as 661, 700, or 714 specifies the analog excursion in millivolts.

Typesetting $Y'C_BC_R$ (or $Y'P_BP_R$) is a challenge! I illustrate the main points in Figure 28.7 above. I augment Y' with a leading superscript and subscript and a trailing subscript, according to the conventions of Figure 28.6. Without these elements, the intended colour cannot be determined with certainty. I place a single prime on the Y. Some authors prime the C_B and C_R as well, but I consider that practice to be obsessive and pedantic. Practical, deployed image coding systems are either perceptually coded in all three colour components or (rarely) fully linear-light in all three. Since there are no "hybrid" systems (linear-light luminance with nonlinear colour differences, or perceptually coded luma with linear-light colour differences), there is no need to triplicate the prime.

Nonlinear red, green, blue (R'G'B')

Video originates with approximations of linear-light (*tristimulus*) *RGB* primary components, usually represented in abstract terms in the range 0 (black) to +1 (white). In order to meaningfully determine a colour from an *RGB* triple, the colorimetric properties of the primaries and the reference white – such as their CIE [*x*, *y*] chromaticity coordinates – must be known. Colorimetric properties of *RGB* components were discussed in *Colour science for video*, on page 287. In the absence of any specific information, use the BT.709 primaries and the CIE D_{65} white point.

In *Gamma*, on page 315, I described how lightness information is coded nonlinearly, in order to achieve good perceptual performance from a limited number of bits. In a colour system, the nonlinear transfer function described in that chapter is applied individually to each of the three *RGB* tristimulus components: From the set of *RGB* tristimulus (linear-light) values, three gamma-corrected primary signals are computed; each is approximately proportional to the square-root of the corresponding scene tristimulus value.

See page 320.

BT.709 standardizes an EOCF that ostensibly should be imposed at the camera. For tristimulus values greater than a few percent, the encoding is this:

$$R'_{709} = 1.099R^{0.45} - 0.099$$
$$G'_{709} = 1.099G^{0.45} - 0.099 \qquad \text{Eq 28.3}$$
$$B'_{709} = 1.099B^{0.45} - 0.099$$

However, what is important in "BT.709" coding is that encoded image data produces the intended picture appearance on the standard display device. BT.1886 standardizes the reference EOCF for HD. Encoding should be specified in terms of the inverse EOCF.

$$R'_{709} = R^{1/2.4}$$
$$G'_{709} = G^{1/2.4} \qquad \text{Eq 28.4}$$
$$B'_{709} = B^{1/2.4}$$

To encode sRGB is similar, but using a power of $1/2.2$ instead of $1/2.4$.

BT.601 luma

The following luma equation is standardized in BT.601 for SD, and also applies to JPEG/JFIF (in computing) and Exif (in digital still photography):

$$^{601}Y' = 0.299\,R' + 0.587\,G' + 0.114\,B' \qquad \text{Eq 28.5}$$

As mentioned a moment ago, the E and prime symbols originally used for video signals have been elided over the course of time, and this has led to ambiguity of the Y symbol between colour science and television.

The coefficients in the luma equation are based upon the sensitivity of human vision to each of the *RGB* primaries standardized for the coding. The low value of the blue coefficient is a consequence of saturated blue colours having low lightness. The luma coefficients are also a function of the white point, or more properly, the *chromaticity of reference white*.

The BT.601 luma coefficients were computed using the technique that I explained in *Luminance coefficients,* on page 306, using the historical NTSC primaries and white point of 1953; see Table 3.2, on page 25 of *Composite NTSC and PAL: Legacy Video Systems.*

In principle, luma coefficients should be derived from the primary and white chromaticities. The BT.601 luma coefficients of Equation 28.5 are the same as those established in 1953 by the NTSC from the primaries and white point then in use. Primaries actually used in consumer displays changed a few years after the adoption of NTSC. The primaries in use for 480*i* SD today are approximately those specified in SMPTE RP 145; the primaries in use for 576*i* SD are approximately those specified in EBU Tech. 3213. (These primary sets are slightly different; both sets very nearly match the primaries of BT.709.) Despite the change in primaries, the luma coefficients for SD video – both 480*i* and 576*i* – have remained unchanged from the values that were established in 1953. As a consequence of the change in primaries, the luma coefficients in SD no longer theoretically match the primaries. The mismatch has little practical significance.

The mismatch between the primaries and the luma coefficients of SD has little practical significance; however, the mismatch of luma coefficients between SD and HD has great practical significance!

BT.709 luma

International agreement on BT.709 was achieved in 1990 on the basis of "theoretically correct" luma coefficients derived from the BT.709 primaries:

$$^{709}Y' = 0.2126\,R' + 0.7152\,G' + 0.0722\,B' \qquad \text{Eq 28.6}$$

Chroma subsampling, revisited

The purpose of colour difference coding is to enable subsampling. In analog video, the colour difference components are subject to bandwidth reduction through the use of analog lowpass filters; horizontal colour detail is removed. In digital video, the chroma components are subsampled, or *decimated*, by filtering followed by the discarding of samples. Figure 12.3, *Chroma subsampling*, on page 124, sketches several digital subsampling schemes. In 4:2:2 subsampling, after filtering, alternate colour difference samples are discarded at the encoder. In 4:2:0, vertical chroma detail is removed as well. At the decoder, the missing samples are approximated by interpolation.

In analog chroma bandlimiting, and in digital subsampling, some colour detail is lost. However, owing to the poor colour acuity of vision, the loss cannot be detected by a viewer *at normal viewing distance*.

Some low-end digital video systems simply drop chroma pixels at the encoder without filtering, and replicate chroma pixels at the decoder. Discarding samples can be viewed as point sampling; that operation runs the risk of introducing aliases. Proper decimation and interpolation filters should be used; these should be designed according to the principles explained in *Filtering and sampling*, on page 191.

Luma/colour difference summary

When luma and colour difference coding is used for image interchange, it is important for the characteristics of red, green, and blue to be maintained from the input of the encoder to the output of the decoder. The chromaticities of the primaries were detailed in *Colour science for video*, on page 287, and mentioned in this chapter as they pertain to the encoding and decoding of luma. I have assumed that the characteristics of the primaries match across the whole system. The primaries upon which luma and colour difference coding are based are known as the *interchange* (or *transmission*) *primaries*.

In practice, a camera sensor may produce *RGB* components whose chromaticities do not match the interchange primaries. To achieve accurate colour reproduction in such a camera, it is necessary to insert

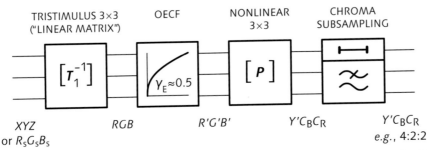

TRISTIMULUS 3×3 ("LINEAR MATRIX")   OECF   NONLINEAR 3×3   CHROMA SUBSAMPLING

$[T_1^{-1}]$ $Y_E \approx 0.5$ $[P]$ $\approx$

XYZ   RGB   R'G'B'   Y'C_BC_R   Y'C_BC_R
or $R_sG_sB_s$ e.g., 4:2:2

Figure 28.8 A luma/colour difference encoder involves the four stages summarized in this block diagram. First, linear-light (tristimulus) input signals are transformed through the "linear" matrix T_1^{-1} to produce *RGB* coded to the interchange primaries. Gamma correction is then applied. The matrix **P** then produces luma and two colour differences. The colour difference (chroma) signals are then subsampled; luma undergoes a compensating delay.

a 3×3 matrix that transforms tristimulus signals from the image capture primaries to the interchange primaries. (This is the "linear matrix" built into the camera.) Similarly, a decoder may be required to drive a display whose primaries are different from the interchange primaries; at the output of the decoder, it may be necessary to insert a 3×3 matrix that transforms from the interchange primaries to the image display primaries. (See page 309.)

Figure 28.8 above summarizes luma/colour difference encoding. If image data originated in linear *XYZ* components, a 3×3 matrix transform (T_1^{-1}) would be applied to obtain linear *RGB* having chromaticities and white reference of the interchange primaries. For BT.709 interchange primaries standard for SD and HD, the matrix would be that of Equation 26.9, on page 308. More typically, image data originates in some device-dependent space that I denote $R_1G_1B_1$, and the 3×3 "linear matrix" transform (T_1^{-1}) is determined by the camera designer. See the sequence of Figures 26.3 through 26.8, starting on page 300, and the accompanying text and captions, to gain an appreciation for how such a matrix might be crafted. Practical cameras do not have spectral sensitivities that are linear combinations of the CIE colour matching functions, so they are not properly characterized by chromaticities. Nonetheless, once a linear matrix to a set of interchange primaries has been chosen, Equation 26.10 can be used to derive equivalent sensor primaries (the "taking primaries").

I use T_1^{-1} to denote the encoding "linear matrix," to conform to the notation of *Luminance coefficients*, on page 306.

Interchange primaries are also called transmission primaries.

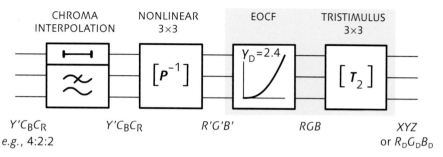

CHROMA INTERPOLATION	NONLINEAR 3×3	EOCF	TRISTIMULUS 3×3

$Y'C_BC_R$ $Y'C_BC_R$ $R'G'B'$ RGB XYZ
e.g., 4:2:2   or $R_DG_DB_D$

Figure 28.9 A luma/colour difference decoder involves the inverse of the four stages of Figure 28.8 in opposite order. First, subsampled colour difference (chroma) signals are interpolated; luma undergoes a compensating delay. The matrix P^{-1} then recovers $R'G'B'$ from luma and two colour differences. A transfer function having an exponent of about 2.4 is then applied, which produces linear-light (tristimulus) signals RGB. If the display's primaries differ from the interchange primaries, RGB are transformed through the matrix T_2 to produce appropriate $R_DG_DB_D$.

Figures 28.8 and 28.9 show 3×3 matrix transforms being used for two distinctly different tasks. When someone hands you a 3×3, you have to ascertain whether it is linearly or nonlinearly related to light power.

Once the linear matrix has been applied, each of the components is subject to a nonlinear transfer function (gamma correction) that produces nonlinear $R'G'B'$. These components are transformed through a 3×3 matrix (P), to obtain luma and colour difference components $Y'C_BC_R$ or $Y'P_BP_R$. (This matrix depends upon the luma coefficients in use, and upon colour difference scale factors.) Then, if necessary, a chroma subsampling filter is applied to obtain subsampled colour difference components; luma is subject to a compensating delay.

A decoder uses the inverse operations of the encoder, in the opposite order, as sketched in Figure 28.9. In a digital decoder, the chroma interpolation filter reconstructs missing chroma samples; in an analog decoder, no explicit operation is needed. The 3×3 colour difference matrix (P^{-1}) reconstructs nonlinear red, green, and blue primary components. The transfer functions restore the primary components to their linear-light tristimulus values. Finally, the tristimulus 3×3 matrix (T_2) transforms from the primaries of the interchange standard to the primaries implemented in the display device.

When a decoder is intimately associated with a CRT display, the decoder's transfer function is performed by the nonlinear voltage-to-luminance relationship intrinsic to the CRT: No explicit operations are required for this step. However, to exploit this transfer function, the display primaries must be the same as – or at least very similar to – the interchange primaries.

The transfer functions of the decoder (or the CRT) are intertwined with gamma correction. As explained on page 115, an end-to-end power function having an exponent of about 1.2 is appropriate for typical television acquired at studio lighting levels and viewed at 100 nt in a dim surround. The encoder of Figure 28.8 imposes a 0.5-power function; the decoder of Figure 28.9 imposes a 2.4-power function. The product of these implements the end-to-end power function. If the native EOCF of a display device differs from that of a CRT, then decoding should include a transfer function that is the composition of a 2.4-power function and the inverse transfer function of the display device.

When viewing a rather bright display (say 320 nt) in an average surround (say 20%), a 1.1 end-to-end power is appropriate; a 2.2-power EOCF (like that of sRGB) is appropriate. When viewing in a dark (0%) surround, a 1.3 end-to-end power is appropriate; a 2.6-power EOCF (like that of digital cinema) is appropriate.

If the display primaries match the interchange primaries, the decoder's 3×3 tristimulus matrix is not needed. If a display has primaries not too different from the interchange primaries, then it may be possible to compensate the primaries by applying a 3×3 matrix in the nonlinear domain. But if the primaries are quite different, it will be necessary to apply the transform between primaries in the tristimulus domain; see *Transforms among RGB systems,* on page 309.

SD and HD luma chaos

Although the concepts of $Y'P_BP_R$ and $Y'C_BC_R$ coding are identical in SD and HD, the BT.709 standard established a new set of luma coefficients for HD. That set differs dramatically from the luma coefficients for SD specified in BT.601. There are now two flavors of $Y'C_BC_R$ coding, as suggested by Figure 28.10 in the margin; I denote the flavors $^{601}Y'C_BC_R$ for SD, and $^{709}Y'C_BC_R$ for HD. Similarly, there are two flavors of $Y'P_BP_R$ for analog systems, $^{601}Y'P_BP_R$ for SD, and $^{709}Y'P_BP_R$ for HD.

In my view, it is extremely unfortunate that different coding was adopted: Image coding and decoding now depend on whether the picture is small (conventional

Owing to the dependence of the optimum end-to-end power function upon viewing conditions, there here ought to be a user control for rendering intent – perhaps even replacing BRIGHTNESS and CONTRAST – but there isn't!

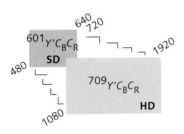

Figure 28.10 **Luma/colour difference flavors**

DIGITAL VIDEO AND HD ALGORITHMS AND INTERFACES

System	Luma coefficients	EOCF	Primary chromaticities
SD 480*i*	BT.601	*unspecified*	SMPTE RP 145
SD 576*i*	BT.601	*unspecified*	EBU Tech. 3213
HD 720*p*, 1080*i*, 1080*p*	BT.709	BT.1886	BT.709

Table 28.1 **luma coefficients, EOCF, and primary chromaticities** for video decoding and display circa 2011 are summarized. Encoding in all systems should be accomplished through forming *R'G'B'* values that yield the intended image appearance in the reference display and viewing conditions. For SD, there is no effective standard for either the reference EOCF or the viewing conditions. For HD, BT.1886 standardizes the reference EOCF, but not the viewing conditions.

video, SD) or large (HD); that dependence erodes the highly useful concept of resolution-independent production in the $Y'C_BC_R$ 4:2:2 and 4:2:0 domains. In my opinion, HD should have been standardized with the BT.601 luma coefficients. With things as they stand, the smorgasbord of colour-encoding parameters makes accurate image interchange extremely difficult. The situation is likely to get worse with time, not better.

Table 28.1 above summarizes the standards for primary chromaticities, transfer functions, and luma coefficients that are either implicit or explicit in several SD and HD standards. When video is converted among these standards, appropriate processing should be performed in order to preserve the intended colour.

The colourbar test signal is standardized in the *R'G'B'* domain, without any reference to primaries, transfer function, or luma coefficients. The colours of the bars depend upon which primary chromaticities are in use; the luma and colour difference levels of the bars depend upon which luma coefficients are in use. When colour conversions and standards conversions are properly performed, the colours and levels of the colourbar test signal will change!

It's sensible to use the term colourbar test *signal* (or *pattern*) instead of colourbar test *image,* because the signal is standardized, not the image.

Luma/colour difference component sets

These colour difference component sets, all based upon $B'-Y'$ and $R'-Y'$, are in use:

• $Y'P_BP_R$ coding is used in component analog video; P_B and P_R are scaled to have excursion nominally identical to that of luma. $Y'P_BP_R$ can be potentially based upon either BT.601 (for SD) or BT.709 (for HD). In 480i29.97 SD, three different analog interface standards are in use: EBU N10 "SMPTE," Sony, and Panasonic.

• $Y'C_BC_R$ coding is used for component digital video; C_B and C_R are scaled to have excursion $^{224}/_{219}$ that of luma. A "full-range" variant is used in JPEG/JFIF. $Y'C_BC_R$ can be potentially based upon BT.601 or BT.709 luma coefficients.

In Chapter 5, *NTSC and PAL Chroma modulation,* of *Composite NTSC and PAL: Legacy Video Systems,* I detail two additional component sets, now obsolete, whose proper use was limited to composite SD NTSC and PAL:

• $Y'UV$ components are only applicable to composite NTSC and PAL systems. $B'-Y'$ and $R'-Y'$ are scaled so as to limit the excursion of the composite (luma plus modulated chroma) signal. $Y'UV$ coding is always based upon BT.601 luma coefficients.

• $Y'IQ$ components were historically used in composite NTSC systems from 1953 to about 1970. *UV* components were rotated 33°, and axis-exchanged, to enable wideband-*I* transmission. This obsolete technique has not been practiced since about 1970. $Y'IQ$ coding was always based upon the luma coefficients now documented in BT.601.

The bewildering set of scale factors and luma coefficients in use is set out in Table 28.2A opposite for analog SD, Table 28.2B overleaf for digital SD and computing systems, and Table 28.2C for analog and digital HD. The following two chapters detail component colour coding for SD and HD, respectively.

	System	Notation	Colour difference scaling
1	Component analog video, 480*i* (EIA/CEA-770 and "SMPTE") and 576*i* EBU N10; also, 480*i* Panasonic M-II, zero setup (Japan)[a]	$^{601}_{700}Y'_{145}P_BP_R$, $^{601}_{700}Y'_{EBU}P_BP_R$	The EBU N10 standard calls for 7:3 picture-to-sync ratio, 700 mV luma excursion with zero setup. P_B and P_R components are scaled individually to range ±350 mV, an excursion identical to luma.
2	Component analog video, 480*i* Sony, 7.5% setup[a]	$^{601}_{661}Y'_{145}P_BP_R$	Sony de facto standards call for 10:4 picture-to-sync ratio, 7.5% setup, and black-to-white luma excursion of approximately 661 mV. P_B and P_R components are scaled individually to range $\frac{4}{3}$ times ±350 mV, that is, ±466$\frac{2}{3}$ mV.
3	Component analog video, 480*i* Sony, zero setup (Japan)[a]	$^{601}_{714}Y'_{145}P_BP_R$	Sony de facto standards call for 10:4 picture-to-sync ratio, zero setup, and black-to-white luma excursion of approximately 714 mV. P_B and P_R components are scaled individually to range $\frac{4}{3}$ times ±350 mV, that is, ±466$\frac{2}{3}$ mV.
4	Component analog video, 480*i* Panasonic, 7.5% setup[a]	$^{601}_{647}Y'_{145}P_BP_R$	Panasonic de facto standards call for 7:3 picture-to-sync ratio, 7.5% setup, and black-to-white luma excursion of approximately 647.5 mV. P_B and P_R components are scaled individually to range $\frac{37}{40}$ times ±350 mV, that is, ±323.75 mV.
5	Composite analog NTSC, PAL video (incl. S-video)	various, typ. $^{601}_{700}Y'_{EBU}UV$, $^{601}_{714}Y'_{145}IQ$, $^{601}_{714}Y'_{145}UV$	U and V are scaled to meet a joint constraint: Scaling is such that peak composite video – luma plus modulated chroma – is limited to $\frac{4}{3}$ of the blanking-to-white excursion. Rotation and exchange of axes (e.g., I and Q) cannot be distinguished after analog encoding. There is no standard component interface.

Table 28.2A **Colour difference systems for analog SD.** The EBU N10 levels indicated in the shaded (first) row are sensible but unpopular. Designers of 480*i* SD studio equipment were forced to implement configuration settings for three interface "standards": EBU N10 ("SMPTE"), Sony, and Panasonic.

a The component analog interface for consumer equipment (such as DVD players) is properly scaled $Y'P_BP_R$, according to EIA/CEA-770.2 (cited on page 454). Some consumer equipment was engineered and deployed with incorrect $Y'P_BP_R$ scaling. Certain consumer devices have rear-panel connectors labelled Y, $B-Y$, $R-Y$, or YUV; these designations are plainly wrong.

System	Notation	Colour difference scaling
6 Component digital video: 4:2:0, 4:1:1, BT.601 4:2:2 (incl. M-JPEG, MPEG, DVD, DVC)	$^{601}_{219}Y'_{145}C_BC_R$	BT.601 calls for luma range 0...219, offset +16 at the interface. C_B and C_R are scaled individually to range ±112, an excursion $^{224}/_{219}$ of luma, offset +128 at the interface. Codes 0 and 255 are prohibited.
7 Component digital stillframe JPEG (incl. JFIF 1.02), typical desktop publishing and the web. Transfer functions vary; see the marginal note on page 335.	$^{601}_{255}Y'_{709}C_BC_R$	There is no comprehensive standard. Luma reference range is typically 0 through 255. C_B and C_R are typically scaled individually to a "full-swing" of ±128, an excursion $^{256}/_{255}$ that of luma. C_B and C_R codes +128 are clipped; fully saturated blue and fully saturated red cannot be represented.

Table 28.2B **Colour difference systems for digital SD and computing.** The scaling indicated in the first row is recommended. For details of obsolete SD systems, see the table *Colour difference systems for analog composite SD and digital 4fSC SD*, in Chapter 14 of *Composite NTSC and PAL: Legacy Video Systems*. (Row numbering here is discontinuous so as to mesh with that table.)

System	Notation	Colour difference scaling
11 Component analog HD	$^{709}_{700}Y'_{709}P_BP_R$	7:3 picture-to-sync ratio, 700 mV luma excursion with zero setup. P_B and P_R components are scaled individually to range ±350 mV, an excursion identical to luma.
12 Component digital HD (BT.709/BT.1886)	$^{709}_{219}Y'_{709}C_BC_R$	BT.709 calls for luma range 0...219, offset +16 at the interface. C_B and C_R are scaled individually to range ±112, an excursion $^{224}/_{219}$ of luma, offset +128 at the interface. Codes 0 and 255 are prohibited.
13 Component digital HD (xvYCC)	$^{xvYCC}_{219}Y'_{709}C_BC_R$	xvYCC $Y'C_BC_R$ is identical to BT.709 $Y'C_BC_R$, except that some codewords outside the $R'G'B'$ unit cube represent wide-gamut colours.

Table 28.2C **Colour difference systems for HD.** The luma coefficient set for HD differs significantly from that of SD.

Part 3

Practical matters

29 Component video colour coding for SD 357

30 Component video colour coding for HD 369

31 Video signal processing 377

32 Frame, field, line, and sample rates 389

33 Timecode 399

34 2-3 pulldown 405

35 Deinterlacing 413

36 Colourbars 419

Various scale factors are applied to the basic colour difference components $B'-Y'$ and $R'-Y'$ for different applications. In the previous chapter, I introduced luma and colour difference coding; in this chapter, I will detail the following coding systems:

• $B'-Y'$, $R'-Y'$ components form the numerical basis for all the other component sets; otherwise, they are not directly used.

• $P_B P_R$ components are used for component analog video (including analog interfaces in devices such as DVD players and set-top boxes).

• $C_B C_R$ components as defined in BT.601 and BT.709 are used for component digital video, including studio video, DV, MPEG, and H.264.

• "Full-swing" (or "full-range") $C_B C_R$ components are used in JPEG/JFIF.

• UV components are used for composite NTSC or PAL, as described in *UV components,* in Chapter 5 of *Composite NTSC and PAL: Legacy Video Systems.*

• *IQ* components were historically used for composite NTSC until about 1970, as described in Chapter 4, *NTSC Y'IQ system,* of *Composite NTSC and PAL: Legacy Video Systems.*

Y'UV and *Y'IQ* are intermediate quantities toward the formation of composite NTSC, PAL, and S-video. Neither *Y'UV* nor *Y'IQ* has a standard component interface, and neither is appropriate when the components are kept separate. Unfortunately, the *Y'UV* nomenclature has come to be used rather loosely, and some people use *Y'UV* to denote *any* scaling of $B'-Y'$ and $R'-Y'$.

Video uses the symbols *U* and *V* to represent certain colour difference components. The CIE defines the pairs [*u, v*], [*u', v'*], and [*u*, v**]. All of these pairs represent *chromatic* or chroma information, but they are all numerically and functionally different. Video [*U, V*] components are neither directly based upon, nor superseded by, any of the CIE colour spaces.

For a discussion of primary chromaticities, see page 290.

The coding systems described in this chapter can be applied to various *RGB* primary sets – EBU 3213, SMPTE RP 145 (or potentially even BT.709). BT.601 does not specify primary chromaticities: SMPTE RP 145 primaries are implicit in 480*i* SD, and EBU 3213 primaries are implicit in 576*i* SD. However, virtually all of modern consumer receivers interpret content – whether SD or HD – according to BT.709 primaries. As I write, program content created in North America is mastered with SMPTE primaries (contrary to the spirit and letter of ITU-R, SMPTE, and ATSC standards) and content created in Europe is mastered to EBU primaries. However, all of this content is displayed in the consumer domain using BT.709 primaries. We look forward to the day when content creators actually master using the BT.709 colour space.

The equations for [Y', B'–Y', R'–Y'], $Y'P_BP_R$, and $Y'C_BC_R$ can be based upon either the BT.601 luma coefficients of SD or the BT.709 coefficients of HD. The equations and figures of this chapter are based upon the BT.601 coefficients. Unfortunately, the luma coefficients that have been standardized for HD are different from those of BT.601. Concerning the HD luma coefficients, see *BT.709 luma* on page 346; for details of HD colour difference components, see the following chapter, *Component video colour coding for HD*, on page 369.

Chroma components are properly ordered B'–Y' then R'–Y'; or P_B then P_R; or C_B then C_R. Blue associates with U, and red with V; U and V are ordered alphabetically. The subscripts in C_BC_R and P_BP_R are often written in lowercase. In my opinion, this compromises readability, so I write them in uppercase. The B in C_B serves as a tag, not a variable, so I set it in Roman type (that is, upright, not italic). Authors with great attention to detail sometimes "prime" C_BC_R and P_BP_R to indicate their nonlinear origin, but no standard or deployed image coding system has employed linear-light colour differences, nor would that be sensible for perceptual reasons, so I omit the primes.

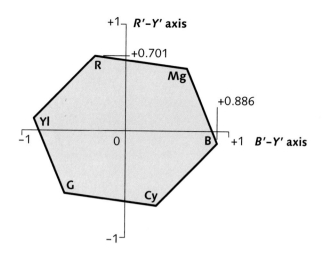

Figure 29.1 *B'–Y', R'–Y'*
components for SD

B'–Y', R'–Y' components for SD

To obtain [Y', B'–Y', R'–Y'] components from R'G'B', for BT.601 luma, use this matrix equation:

$$\begin{bmatrix} ^{601}Y' \\ B'-^{601}Y' \\ R'-^{601}Y' \end{bmatrix} = \begin{bmatrix} 0.299 & 0.587 & 0.114 \\ -0.299 & -0.587 & 0.886 \\ 0.701 & -0.587 & -0.114 \end{bmatrix} \cdot \begin{bmatrix} R' \\ G' \\ B' \end{bmatrix} \qquad \text{Eq 29.1}$$

Figure 29.1 shows a plot of the [B'–Y', R'–Y'] colour difference plane.

ITU-R Rec. BT.601-5, *Studio encoding parameters of digital television for standard 4:3 and wide-screen 16:9 aspect ratios.*

As I described on page 346, the BT.601 luma coefficients are used for SD. With these coefficients, the B'–Y' component reaches its positive maximum at pure blue (R' = 0, G' = 0, B' = 1; Y' = 0.114; B'–Y' = +0.886) and its negative maximum at pure yellow (B'–Y' = –0.886). Analogously, the extrema of R'–Y' take values ±0.701, at pure red and cyan. These are inconvenient values for both digital and analog systems. The P_BP_R, C_BC_R, and UV colour difference components all involve versions of [Y', B'–Y', R'–Y'] that are scaled to place the extrema of the component values at more convenient values.

P_BP_R components for SD

P_B and P_R denote colour difference components having excursions nominally identical to the excursion of the

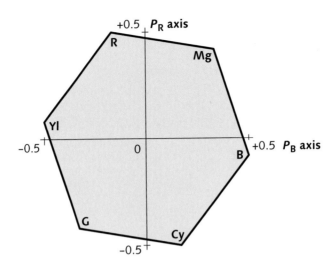

+0.5 ⊥ P_R **axis**

R

Mg

Yl

−0.5 ⊢   0   ⊢ +0.5 P_B **axis**

B

G

Cy

−0.5 ⊥

Figure 29.2 $P_B P_R$
components for SD

accompanying luma component. For BT.601 luma, the
equations are these:

Eq 29.2

$$P_B = \frac{0.5}{1-0.114}\left(B'-^{601}Y'\right) = \frac{1}{1.772}\left(B'-^{601}Y'\right) \approx 0.564\left(B'-^{601}Y'\right)$$

$$P_R = \frac{0.5}{1-0.299}\left(R'-^{601}Y'\right) = \frac{1}{1.402}\left(R'-^{601}Y'\right) \approx 0.713\left(R'-^{601}Y'\right)$$

These scale factors were chosen to limit the excursion of *each* colour difference component to the range
−0.5 to +0.5 with respect to unity luma excursion:
0.114 in the first expression above is the luma coefficient of blue, and 0.299 in the second is for red.
Figure 29.2 above shows a plot of the [P_B, P_R] plane.
    Expressed in matrix form, the $B'-Y'$ and $R'-Y'$ rows of
Equation 29.1 are scaled by $^{0.5}\!/_{0.886}$ and $^{0.5}\!/_{0.701}$.
To encode from $R'G'B'$ where reference black is zero
and reference white is unity:

Eq 29.3

$$\begin{bmatrix} ^{601}Y' \\ P_B \\ P_R \end{bmatrix} = \begin{bmatrix} 0.299 & 0.587 & 0.114 \\ -0.168736 & -0.331264 & 0.5 \\ 0.5 & -0.418688 & -0.081312 \end{bmatrix} \cdot \begin{bmatrix} R' \\ G' \\ B' \end{bmatrix}$$

The first row of Equation 29.3 comprises the luma
coefficients; these sum to unity. The second and third
rows each sum to zero, a necessity for colour difference
components. The two entries of 0.5 reflect the reference excursions of P_B and P_R, at the blue and red primaries [0, 0, 1] and [1, 0, 0]. The reference excursion is

±0.5; the peak excursion may be slightly larger, to accommodate analog undershoot and overshoot. There are no standards for how much analog footroom and headroom should be provided.

The inverse, decoding matrix is this:

$$\begin{bmatrix} R' \\ G' \\ B' \end{bmatrix} = \begin{bmatrix} 1 & 0 & 1.402 \\ 1 & -0.344136 & -0.714136 \\ 1 & 1.772 & 0 \end{bmatrix} \cdot \begin{bmatrix} {}^{601}Y' \\ P_B \\ P_R \end{bmatrix} \qquad \text{Eq 29.4}$$

See Table 28.2A on page 353; *Component analog Y'P_BP_R interface, EBU N10*, on page 453; and *Component analog Y'P_BP_R interface, industry standard*, on page 455.

$Y'P_BP_R$ is employed by 480*i* and 576*i* component analog video equipment such as that from Sony and Panasonic, where P_B and P_R are conveyed with roughly half the bandwidth of luma. Unfortunately, three different analog interface level standards are used: $Y'P_BP_R$ is ambiguous with respect to electrical interface.

P_B and P_R are properly written in that order, as I described on page 358. The *P* stands for *parallel*, stemming from a failed effort within SMPTE to standardize a parallel electrical interface for component analog video. In C_BC_R, which I will now describe, *C* stands for *chroma*. The C_BC_R notation predated P_BP_R.

C_BC_R components for SD

A straightforward scaling of $Y'P_BP_R$ components would have been suitable for digital interface. Scaling of luma to the range [0 ... 255] would have been feasible; this "full-range" scaling of luma is used in JPEG/JFIF used in computing, as I will describe on page 365. However, for studio applications it is necessary to provide signal-processing footroom and headroom to accommodate ringing from analog and digital filters, and to accommodate signals from misadjusted analog equipment.

For an 8-bit interface, luma could have been scaled to an excursion of 224; $B'-Y'$ and $R'-Y'$ could have been scaled to ±112. This would have left 32 codes of footroom and headroom for each component. Although sensible, that approach was not taken when BT.601 was adopted in 1984. Instead – and unfortunately, in my opinion – different excursions were standardized for luma and chroma. Eight-bit luma excursion was standardized at 219; chroma excursion was standardized at 224. Each colour difference component has as excursion $^{224}/_{219}$ that of luma. Since video component amplitudes are usually referenced to luma excursion, this condition is more clearly stated the opposite way: In $Y'C_BC_R$, each colour difference component has $^{224}/_{219}$ the excursion of the luma component. The notation C_BC_R distinguishes this set from P_BP_R, where the luma and chroma excursions are nominally identical: Conceptually, $Y'P_BP_R$ and $Y'C_BC_R$ differ only in scaling.

Historically, $Y'P_BP_R$ scaling was used at analog interfaces, and $Y'C_BC_R$ was used at digital interfaces. Nowadays so many different scale factors and offsets are in use in both the analog and digital domains that the dual nomenclature is more a hindrance than a help.

To provide footroom to accommodate luma signals that go slightly negative, an offset is added to luma at a $Y'C_BC_R$ interface. At an 8-bit interface, an offset of +16 is added; this places black at code 16 and white at code 235. At an 8-bit interface, codes 0 and 255 are used for synchronization purposes; these codes are prohibited from video data. Codes 1 through 15 are interpreted as signal levels $-^{15}/_{219}$ through $-^{1}/_{219}$ (respectively), relative to unity luma excursion; codes 236 through 254 are interpreted as signal levels $^{220}/_{219}$ through $^{238}/_{219}$ (respectively), relative to unity excursion. Unfortunately, luma footroom and headroom are asymmetrical.

C_BC_R colour difference components are conveyed in offset binary form: An offset of +128 is added. In studio $Y'C_BC_R$, chroma reference levels are 16 and 240, and codes 0 and 255 are prohibited from chroma data.

BT.601 provides for 10-bit components; 10-bit studio video equipment is now commonplace. At a 10-bit interface, the 8-bit interface levels and prohibited codes are maintained; extra bits are appended as least-significant bits (LSBs) to provide increased precision. The prohibited codes respect the 8-bit interface: Codes having all 8 most-significant bits either all zeros or all ones are prohibited from video data across a 10-bit interface.

For signal-processing arithmetic operations such as gain adjustment, Y', C_B, and C_R must be zero for black: The interface offsets must be removed. For 8-bit luma arithmetic, it is convenient to place reference black at code 0 and reference white at code 219. Colour difference signals are most conveniently handled in two's complement form, scaled so that reference colour

The $Y'P_BP_R$ and $Y'C_BC_R$ scaling discrepancy is unfortunate enough, but it is compounded by "full-swing" (or "full-range") $Y'C_BC_R$ used in JPEG/JFIF, scaled similarly but not identically to $Y'P_BP_R$; see page 365. Confusion is also compounded by the EBU referring in Technical Standard N10-1998 to C_BC_R analog colour difference components, when they are properly denoted P_BP_R.

Reference white and black codes of the 10-bit interface have trailing zeros "to the left" of the least significant bit of the 8-bit representation. "Widening" from 8-bit to higher precision is properly accomplished by shifting left, *not* by multiplying by $^{879}/_{219}$. "Narrowing" to 8 bits is properly accomplished by rounding then shifting right.

DIGITAL VIDEO AND HD ALGORITHMS AND INTERFACES

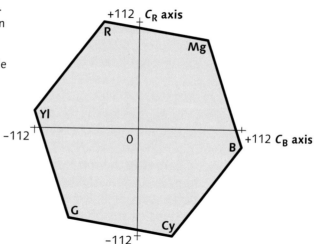

Figure 29.3 C_BC_R components for SD are shown in their mathematical form. The range outside [–112 ... +112] is available for undershoot and overshoot. At an 8-bit interface, an offset of +128 is added to each colour difference component.

difference signals (at pure yellow, cyan, red, and blue) are ±112. Figure 29.3 above shows the C_BC_R colour difference plane scaled in this manner, without offsets.

As far as I am concerned, the offsets should be treated as an interface feature. Most descriptions of $Y'C_BC_R$, though – including SMPTE and ITU standards – take the $Y'C_BC_R$ notation to include the offset. In the equations to follow, I colour the offset terms. If your goal is to compute abstract, mathematical quantities suitable for signal processing with signed numbers, omit these offset terms. If you are concerned with interfacing unsigned values, include them.

These equations form BT.601 $Y'C_BC_R$ components from [Y', $B'–Y'$, $R'–Y'$] components ranging [0 ... +1]:

The numerical values used in this equation, and in those to follow, are based on the BT.601 luma coefficients. The coefficients for HD are, unfortunately, different. See *BT.601 luma*, on page 346.

$$^{601}_{219}Y' = 16 + \left(219 \cdot {}^{601}Y'\right)$$

$$C_B = 128 + \frac{112}{0.886}\left(B' - {}^{601}Y'\right)$$

$$C_R = 128 + \frac{112}{0.701}\left(R' - {}^{601}Y'\right)$$

Eq 29.5

To extend Equation 29.5 to 10 bits, append to each of Y', C_B, and C_R two low-order bits having binary weights ½ and ¼. To extend $Y'C_BC_R$ beyond 10 bits, continue the sequence with LSBs weighted ⅛, 1⁄16, and so on. If you prefer to express these quantities as whole numbers, without fractional bits, multiply Equation 29.5 (and all of the equations to follow) by 2^{K-8}, where $8 \leq K$ denotes the bit depth.

To obtain 8-bit BT.601 $Y'C_BC_R$ from $R'G'B'$ ranging 0 to 1, scale the rows of the matrix in Equation 29.3 by the factors 219, 224, and 224, corresponding to the excursions of each of Y', C_B, and C_R, respectively:

Eq 29.6

$$\begin{bmatrix} \frac{601}{219}Y' \\ C_B \\ C_R \end{bmatrix} = \begin{bmatrix} 16 \\ 128 \\ 128 \end{bmatrix} + \begin{bmatrix} 65.481 & 128.553 & 24.966 \\ -37.797 & -74.203 & 112 \\ 112 & -93.786 & -18.214 \end{bmatrix} \cdot \begin{bmatrix} R' \\ G' \\ B' \end{bmatrix}$$

Summing the top row of this matrix yields 219, the luma excursion. The lower two rows sum to zero. The two entries of 112 reflect the positive C_B and C_R extrema, at the blue and red primaries.

To recover $R'G'B'$ in the range [0...+1] from 8-bit BT.601 $Y'C_BC_R$, invert Equation 29.6:

Eq 29.7

$$\begin{bmatrix} R' \\ G' \\ B' \end{bmatrix} = \begin{bmatrix} 0.00456621 & 0 & 0.00625893 \\ 0.00456621 & -0.00153396 & -0.00318811 \\ 0.00456621 & 0.00791071 & 0 \end{bmatrix} \cdot \left(\begin{bmatrix} \frac{601}{219}Y' \\ C_B \\ C_R \end{bmatrix} - \begin{bmatrix} 16 \\ 128 \\ 128 \end{bmatrix} \right)$$

You can determine the excursion that an encoding matrix is designed to produce – often 1, 219, 255, or 256 – by summing the coefficients in the top row. In Equation 29.8, the sum is 256. If you find an unexpected sum, suspect an error in the matrix.

This matrix contains entries larger than 256; the corresponding multipliers will need capability for more than 8 bits.

When rounding the matrix coefficients, take care to preserve the intended row sums, in this case, [1, 0, 0]. You must take care to prevent overflow due to roundoff error or other conditions: Use saturating arithmetic.

At the interface, after adding the offsets, clip all three components to the range 1 through 254 inclusive, to avoid the prohibited codes 0 and 255.

$Y'C_BC_R$ from studio RGB

In studio equipment, 8-bit $R'G'B'$ components usually have the same 219 excursion as the luma component of $Y'C_BC_R$. To encode 8-bit BT.601 $Y'C_BC_R$ from $R'G'B'$ in the range [0...219], scale the encoding matrix of Equation 29.6 by $256/219$:

Eq 29.8

$$\begin{bmatrix} \frac{601}{219}Y' \\ C_B \\ C_R \end{bmatrix} = \begin{bmatrix} 16 \\ 128 \\ 128 \end{bmatrix} + \frac{1}{256} \begin{bmatrix} 76.544 & 150.272 & 29.184 \\ -43.366 & -85.136 & 128.502 \\ 128.502 & -107.604 & -20.898 \end{bmatrix} \cdot \begin{bmatrix} 219R' \\ 219G' \\ 219B' \end{bmatrix}$$

For implementation in binary arithmetic, the multiplication by $1/256$ can be accomplished by shifting. To decode to $R'G'B'$ in the range [0...219] from 8-bit BT.601 $Y'C_BC_R$, invert Equation 29.8:

Eq 29.9

$$\begin{bmatrix} 219R' \\ 219G' \\ 219B' \end{bmatrix} = \frac{1}{256} \begin{bmatrix} 256 & 0 & 350.901 \\ 256 & -86.132 & -178.738 \\ 256 & 443.506 & 0 \end{bmatrix} \cdot \left(\begin{bmatrix} {}^{601}_{219}Y' \\ C_B \\ C_R \end{bmatrix} - \begin{bmatrix} 16 \\ 128 \\ 128 \end{bmatrix} \right)$$

The entries of 256 in this matrix indicate that the corresponding component can simply be added; there is no need for a multiplication operation. These transforms assume that the $R'G'B'$ components incorporate gamma correction, such as that specified by BT.709; see page 333.

$Y'C_BC_R$ from computer RGB

In computing it is conventional to use 8-bit $R'G'B'$ components, with no headroom and no footroom: Black is at code 0 and white is at 255. To encode 8-bit BT.601 $Y'C_BC_R$ from $R'G'B'$ in this range, scale the matrix of Equation 29.6 by $^{256}/_{255}$:

Eq 29.10

$$\begin{bmatrix} {}^{601}_{219}Y' \\ C_B \\ C_R \end{bmatrix} = \begin{bmatrix} 16 \\ 128 \\ 128 \end{bmatrix} + \frac{1}{256} \begin{bmatrix} 65.738 & 129.057 & 25.064 \\ -37.945 & -74.494 & 112.439 \\ 112.439 & -94.154 & -18.285 \end{bmatrix} \cdot \begin{bmatrix} 255R' \\ 255G' \\ 255B' \end{bmatrix}$$

To decode $R'G'B'$ in the range [0...255] from 8-bit BT.601 $Y'C_BC_R$, use the transform of Equation 29.11:

Eq 29.11

$$\begin{bmatrix} 255R' \\ 255G' \\ 255B' \end{bmatrix} = \frac{1}{256} \begin{bmatrix} 298.082 & 0 & 408.583 \\ 298.082 & -100.291 & -208.120 \\ 298.082 & 516.411 & 0 \end{bmatrix} \cdot \left(\begin{bmatrix} {}^{601}_{219}Y' \\ C_B \\ C_R \end{bmatrix} - \begin{bmatrix} 16 \\ 128 \\ 128 \end{bmatrix} \right)$$

BT.601 $Y'C_BC_R$ uses the extremes of the coding range to handle signal overshoot and undershoot. Clipping is required when decoding to an $R'G'B'$ range that has no headroom or footroom.

"Full-swing" $Y'C_BC_R$

The $Y'C_BC_R$ coding used in JPEG/JFIF stillframes in computing conventionally uses "full-swing" coding with no footroom and no headroom. Luma (Y') is scaled to an excursion of 255 and represented in 8 bits: Black is at code 0 and white is at code 255. Obviously, luma codes 0 and 255 are not prohibited! Colour difference

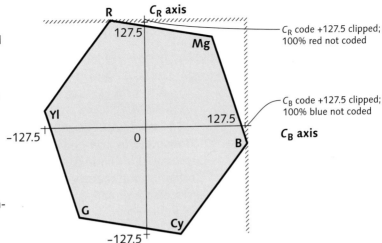

Figure 29.5 $C_B C_R$ "full-range" components used in JPEG/JFIF are shown. C_B and C_R are scaled to ±127.5; however, they are encoded into a two's complement range of –128 to +127. Chroma codes +127.5 are clipped; fully saturated blue and red cannot be preserved. No provision is made for undershoot or overshoot. The accompanying luma signal ranges 0 through 255.

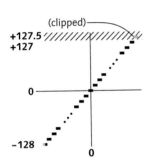

Figure 29.4 A "full-swing" $C_B C_R$ quantizer is used in JPEG/JFIF. Code +127.5 – required to represent pure blue or red – is clipped.

components are scaled to an excursion of ±127.5; each colour difference component nominally has the same excursion as luma. However, an offset of +128 is applied (instead of the +127.5 that you might expect), apparently so that pure grey has an integer code value. The +128 offset causes pure blue and pure red to take post-offset values of 255.5, which clip. Figure 29.4 shows the transfer function of the colour difference quantizer, emphasizing that pre-offset chroma code +127.5 (pure blue, or pure red) causes clipping. As a consequence, pure blue and pure red are liable to fail to make the "round-trip" accurately through JPEG/JFIF compression and decompression. Figure 29.5 above shows the full-range $C_B C_R$ colour difference plane.

To encode from $R'G'B'$ in the range [0...255] into 8-bit $Y'C_B C_R$, with luma in the range [0...255] and C_B and C_R each ranging ±128, use this transform:

Eq 29.12

$$
\begin{bmatrix} \frac{601}{255}Y' \\ C_B \\ C_R \end{bmatrix} = \frac{1}{256} \begin{bmatrix} 76.544 & 150.272 & 29.184 \\ -43.366 & -85.136 & 128.502 \\ 128.502 & -107.604 & -20.898 \end{bmatrix} \cdot \begin{bmatrix} 255 R' \\ 255 G' \\ 255 B' \end{bmatrix}
$$

To decode into $R'G'B'$ in the range [0...255] from full-range 8-bit $Y'C_B C_R$, use the transform in Equation 29.13:

Eq 29.13

$$
\begin{bmatrix} 255 R' \\ 255 G' \\ 255 B' \end{bmatrix} = \frac{1}{256} \begin{bmatrix} 256 & 0 & 357.510 \\ 256 & -87.755 & -182.105 \\ 256 & 451.860 & 0 \end{bmatrix} \cdot \begin{bmatrix} \frac{601}{255}Y' \\ C_B \\ C_R \end{bmatrix}
$$

Y'UV, Y'IQ confusion

I have detailed $Y'P_BP_R$ and $Y'C_BC_R$. These are both based on [$B'-Y'$, $R'-Y'$] components, but they have different scale factors suitable for component analog and component digital interface, respectively.

Colour differences pairs [U, V] and [I, Q] are also based on $B'-Y'$ and $R'-Y'$, but have yet another set of scale factors. *UV* scaling – or *IQ* scaling and rotation – is appropriate only when the signals are destined for composite encoding, as in NTSC or PAL.

Unfortunately, the notation *Y'UV* – or worse, *YUV* – is sometimes loosely applied to *any* form of colour difference coding based on [$B'-Y'$, $R'-Y'$]. Do not be misled by video equipment having connectors labelled *Y'UV* or *Y'*, $B'-Y'$, $R'-Y'$, or these symbols without primes, or by JPEG being described as utilizing *Y'UV* coding. In fact the analog connectors convey signals with $Y'P_BP_R$ scaling, and the JPEG standard itself specifies what I would denote $^{601}_{255}Y'C_BC_R$.

When the term *Y'UV* (or *YUV*) is encountered in a computer graphics or image-processing context, usually BT.601 $Y'C_BC_R$ is meant, but beware!

• Any image data supposedly coded to the original 1953 NTSC primaries is suspect, because it has been roughly four decades since any equipment using these primaries has been built.

• Generally no mention is made of the transfer function of the underlying $R'G'B'$ components, and no account is taken of the nonlinear formation of luma.

When the term *Y'IQ* (or *YIQ*) is encountered, beware!

• Image data supposedly coded in *Y'IQ* is suspect since no analog or digital interface for *Y'IQ* components has ever been standardized.

• NTSC encoders and decoders built since 1970 have been based upon *Y'UV* components, not *Y'IQ*. Contrary to much published information, *Y'IQ* components have not been used for "NTSC" for about 4 decades.

Component video

colour coding for HD

In the previous chapter, *Component video colour coding for SD*, I detailed various component colour coding systems that use the luma coefficients specified in BT.601. Unfortunately, for no good technical reason, BT.709 for HD standardized different luma coefficients. Deployment of HD requires upconversion and down-conversion capabilities both at the studio and at consumers' premises; this situation will persist for a few decades. Owing to this aspect of conversion between HD and SD, if you want to be an HD expert, you have to be an SD expert as well!

Today's computer imaging systems – for still frames, desktop video, and other applications – typically use the BT.601 parameters, independent of the image's pixel count ("resolution independence"). In computer systems that perform HD editing, it is highly desirable that all of the content on the same timeline uses the same colour coding, but there's no simple answer whether BT.601 or BT.709 coding should be used. Generally, it is sensible to retain the BT.601 coefficients.

In this chapter, I assume that you're familiar with the concepts of *Luma and colour differences,* described on page 335. I will detail these component sets:

- $B'-Y'$, $R'-Y'$ components, the basis for P_BP_R and C_BC_R
- P_BP_R components, used for analog interfaces
- C_BC_R components, used for digital interfaces

$B'-Y'$, $R'-Y'$ components for BT.709 HD

The $B'-Y'$ component reaches its positive maximum at blue ($R' = 0$, $G' = 0$, $B' = 1$). With BT.709 luma coefficients, the maximum of $B'-Y' = +0.9278$ occurs at

Before BT.709 was established, SMPTE 240M-1988 for 1035/30 HD standardized luma coefficients based upon the SMPTE RP 145 primaries. Equipment deployed between about 1988 and 1997 used the 240M parameters, but SMPTE 240M is now obsolete. For details, see the first edition of this book.

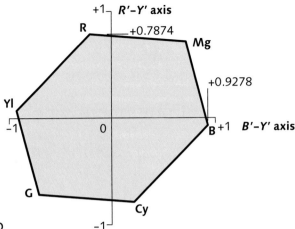

Figure 30.1 *B'–Y', R'–Y'*
components for BT.709 HD

$Y' = 0.0722$. The *B'–Y'* component reaches its negative maximum at yellow ($B'–Y' = -0.9278$). Analogously, the extrema of *R'–Y'* occur at red and cyan at values ±0.7874 (see Figure 30.1 above). These are inconvenient values for both digital and analog systems. The $^{709}Y'P_BP_R$ and $^{709}Y'C_BC_R$ systems to be described both employ versions of [*Y', B'–Y', R'–Y'*] that are scaled to place the extrema of the component values at more convenient values.

To obtain [*Y', B'–Y', R'–Y'*], from *R'G'B'*, for BT.709 luma coefficients, use this matrix equation:

$$\begin{bmatrix} ^{709}Y' \\ B'{-}^{709}Y' \\ R'{-}^{709}Y' \end{bmatrix} = \begin{bmatrix} 0.2126 & 0.7152 & 0.0722 \\ -0.2126 & -0.7152 & 0.9278 \\ 0.7874 & -0.7152 & -0.0722 \end{bmatrix} \bullet \begin{bmatrix} R' \\ G' \\ B' \end{bmatrix} \quad \text{Eq 30.1}$$

P_BP_R components for BT.709 HD

If two colour difference components are to be formed having excursions identical to luma, then P_B and P_R colour difference components are used. For BT.709 luma, the equations are these:

Eq 30.2

$$^{709}P_B = \frac{0.5}{1-0.0722}\left(B'{-}^{709}Y'\right) = \frac{1}{1.8556}\left(B'{-}^{709}Y'\right) \approx 0.5389\left(B'{-}^{709}Y'\right)$$

$$^{709}P_R = \frac{0.5}{1-0.2126}\left(R'{-}^{709}Y'\right) = \frac{1}{1.5748}\left(R'{-}^{709}Y'\right) \approx 0.6350\left(R'{-}^{709}Y'\right)$$

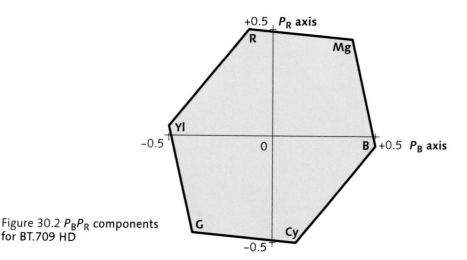

Figure 30.2 P_BP_R components for BT.709 HD

These scale factors limit the excursion of each colour difference component to the range ±0.5 with respect to unity luma excursion: 0.0722 in the first expression above is the luma coefficient of blue, and 0.2126 in the second is for red. At an HD analog interface, luma ranges from 0 mV (black) to 700 mV (white), and P_B and P_R analog components range ±350 mV. Figure 30.2 above shows a plot of the $[P_B, P_R]$ plane.

Expressed in matrix form, the $B'-Y'$ and $R'-Y'$ rows of Equation 30.1 are scaled by $^{0.5}\!/_{0.9278}$ and $^{0.5}\!/_{0.7874}$. To encode from $R'G'B'$ where reference black is zero and reference white is unity:

Eq 30.3

$$\begin{bmatrix} ^{709}Y' \\ P_B \\ P_R \end{bmatrix} = \begin{bmatrix} 0.2126 & 0.7152 & 0.0722 \\ -0.114572 & -0.385428 & 0.5 \\ 0.5 & -0.454153 & -0.045847 \end{bmatrix} \bullet \begin{bmatrix} R' \\ G' \\ B' \end{bmatrix}$$

The inverse, decoding matrix is this:

$$\begin{bmatrix} R' \\ G' \\ B' \end{bmatrix} = \begin{bmatrix} 1 & 0 & 1.5748 \\ 1 & -0.187324 & -0.468124 \\ 1 & 1.8556 & 0 \end{bmatrix} \bullet \begin{bmatrix} ^{709}Y' \\ P_B \\ P_R \end{bmatrix}$$

Eq 30.4

C_BC_R components for BT.709 HD

$^{709}Y'C_BC_R$ coding is used in component digital HD equipment. In 8-bit systems, luma has an excursion of 219. Colour differences C_B and C_R are coded in 8-bit

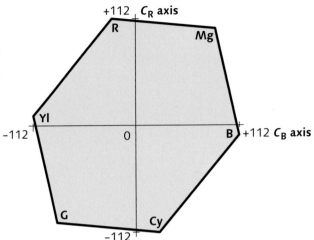

Figure 30.3 C_BC_R components for BT.709 HD are shown referenced to 8-bit processing levels. At an 8-bit interface, an offset of +128 is added to each component.

offset binary form, with excursions of ±112. The $[C_B, C_R]$ plane of HD is plotted in Figure 30.3.

In 8-bit systems, a luma offset of +16 is added at the interface, placing black at code 16 and white at code 235; an offset of +128 is added to C_B and C_R, yielding a range of 16 through 240 inclusive. (Following the convention of the previous chapter, in the equations to follow I write the offset terms in colour.) HD standards provide for 10-bit components, and 10-bit studio video equipment is commonplace. In a 10-bit interface, the 8-bit interface levels and prohibited codes are maintained; the extra two bits are appended as least-significant bits to provide increased precision.

To form $^{709}Y'C_BC_R$ from $[Y', B'-Y', R'-Y']$ components in the range [0...+1], use these equations:

Eq 30.5

$$^{709}_{219}Y' = 16 + \left(219 \cdot {}^{709}Y'\right)$$

$$C_B = 128 + \frac{112}{0.9278}\left(B' - {}^{709}Y'\right)$$

$$C_R = 128 + \frac{112}{0.7874}\left(R' - {}^{709}Y'\right)$$

To obtain $^{709}Y'C_BC_R$ from $R'G'B'$ ranging 0 to 1, scale the rows of the matrix in Equation 30.3 by the factors

[219, 224, 224], corresponding to the excursions of each of the components:

Eq 30.6

$$\begin{bmatrix} ^{709}_{219}Y' \\ C_B \\ C_R \end{bmatrix} = \begin{bmatrix} 16 \\ 128 \\ 128 \end{bmatrix} + \begin{bmatrix} 46.559 & 156.629 & 15.812 \\ -25.664 & -86.336 & 112 \\ 112 & -101.730 & -10.270 \end{bmatrix} \cdot \begin{bmatrix} R' \\ G' \\ B' \end{bmatrix}$$

Summing the first row of the matrix yields 219, the luma excursion from black to white. The two entries of 112 reflect the positive $C_B C_R$ extrema at blue and red.

To recover $R'G'B'$ in the range [0...+1] from $^{709}Y'C_B C_R$, use the inverse of Equation 30.6:

Eq 30.7

$$\begin{bmatrix} 219R' \\ 219G' \\ 219B' \end{bmatrix} = \frac{1}{256} \begin{bmatrix} 256 & 0 & 394.150 \\ 256 & -46.885 & -117.165 \\ 256 & 464.430 & 0 \end{bmatrix} \cdot \left(\begin{bmatrix} ^{709}_{219}Y' \\ C_B \\ C_R \end{bmatrix} - \begin{bmatrix} 16 \\ 128 \\ 128 \end{bmatrix} \right)$$

The $^{709}Y'C_B C_R$ components are integers in 8 bits; reconstructed $R'G'B'$ is scaled to the range [0...+1].

Figure 28.2 (on page 339) illustrated that when $R'G'B'$ components are transformed to luma and colour differences, the unit $R'G'B'$ cube occupies only a small fraction of the volume of the enclosing cube. In digital video, only about ¼ of $Y'C_B C_R$ codewords correspond to $R'G'B'$ values between zero and unity. Certain signal-processing operations (such as filtering) may produce $Y'C_B C_R$ codewords that lie outside the RGB-legal cube. These codewords cause no difficulty in the $Y'C_B C_R$ domain, but potentially present a problem when decoded to $R'G'B'$. Generally, $R'G'B'$ values are clipped between 0 and 1.

$C_B C_R$ components for xvYCC

xvYCC refers to an IEC standard. x.v.Color and x.v.Colour are Sony's trademarks for the scheme.

One method of extending the colour gamut of an $R'G'B'$ system is to allow components to excurse below zero and above unity. In *Wide-gamut reproduction,* on page 312, I explained one approach. The xvYCC scheme is based upon BT.709 primaries, but enables the RGB tristimulus components to excurse from −¼ to +⁴⁄₃.

When transformed to BT.709 $Y'C_B C_R$, all of the real surface colours documented by Pointer – that is, all the colours in Pointer's gamut – produce values that are $Y'C_B C_R$-valid. Though BT.1361 was needed to specify the $R'G'B'$ representation of wide-gamut colours, no

Concerning Pointer, see the marginal note on page 312.

special provisions are necessary to carry those colours across a $^{709}Y'C_BC_R$ interface. The notation "xvYCC $Y'C_BC_R$," or $^{xvYCC}Y'C_BC_R$, makes it explicit that code-words outside the unit $R'G'B'$ cube are to be interpreted as wide-gamut colours, instead of being treated as RGB-illegal.

There is an SD version of xvYCC, using the BT.601 luma coefficients. That scheme will almost certainly never see any deployment.

Studio equipment conforming to BT.1361 is not yet deployed, and is not anticipated for several years. Wide-gamut acquisition and production equipment will begin to replace film over the next decade or so; however, wide-gamut consumer displays are not expected in that time frame. When these begin to be deployed, it is unlikely that they will all have the same gamut; electronics associated with each display will have to process the colour signals according to the properties of each display. In the long term, gamut mapping strategies comparable to those in the desktop colour management community will have to be deployed.

$Y'C_BC_R$ from studio RGB

In studio equipment, 8-bit $R'G'B'$ components usually use the same 219 excursion as the luma component of $Y'C_BC_R$. To encode $Y'C_BC_R$ from $R'G'B'$ in the range [0...219] using 8-bit binary arithmetic, scale the encoding matrix of Equation 30.6 by $^{256}/_{219}$:

Eq 30.8
$$\begin{bmatrix} ^{709}_{219}Y' \\ C_B \\ C_R \end{bmatrix} = \begin{bmatrix} 16 \\ 128 \\ 128 \end{bmatrix} + \frac{1}{256} \begin{bmatrix} 54.426 & 183.091 & 18.483 \\ -30.000 & -100.922 & 130.922 \\ 130.922 & -118.918 & -12.005 \end{bmatrix} \cdot \begin{bmatrix} ^{219}R' \\ ^{219}G' \\ ^{219}B' \end{bmatrix}$$

To decode to $R'G'B'$ in the range [0...219] from BT.709 $Y'C_BC_R$ using 8-bit binary arithmetic:

Eq 30.9
$$\begin{bmatrix} ^{219}R' \\ ^{219}G' \\ ^{219}B' \end{bmatrix} = \frac{1}{256} \begin{bmatrix} 256 & 0 & 394.150 \\ 256 & -46.885 & -117.165 \\ 256 & 464.430 & 0 \end{bmatrix} \cdot \left(\begin{bmatrix} ^{709}_{219}Y' \\ C_B \\ C_R \end{bmatrix} - \begin{bmatrix} 16 \\ 128 \\ 128 \end{bmatrix} \right)$$

$Y'C_BC_R$ from computer RGB

In computing it is conventional to use 8-bit $R'G'B'$ components, with no headroom or footroom: Black is at code 0 and white is at 255. To encode $Y'C_BC_R$ from

R'G'B' in the range [0...255] using 8-bit binary arithmetic, the matrix of Equation 30.6 is scaled by $\frac{256}{255}$:

Eq 30.10

$$\begin{bmatrix} ^{709}_{219}Y' \\ C_B \\ C_R \end{bmatrix} = \begin{bmatrix} 16 \\ 128 \\ 128 \end{bmatrix} + \frac{1}{256} \begin{bmatrix} 46.742 & 157.243 & 15.874 \\ -25.765 & -86.674 & 112.439 \\ 112.439 & -102.129 & -10.310 \end{bmatrix} \cdot \begin{bmatrix} 255R' \\ 255G' \\ 255B' \end{bmatrix}$$

To decode R'G'B' in the range [0...255] from BT.709 Y'C_BC_R using 8-bit binary arithmetic:

Eq 30.11

$$\begin{bmatrix} 255R' \\ 255G' \\ 255B' \end{bmatrix} = \frac{1}{256} \begin{bmatrix} 298.082 & 0 & 458.942 \\ 298.082 & -54.592 & -136.425 \\ 298.082 & 540.775 & 0 \end{bmatrix} \cdot \left(\begin{bmatrix} ^{709}_{219}Y' \\ C_B \\ C_R \end{bmatrix} - \begin{bmatrix} 16 \\ 128 \\ 128 \end{bmatrix} \right)$$

Conversions between HD and SD

The differences among the EBU, SMPTE, and BT.709 primaries are negligible for practical purposes. New equipment should be designed to BT.709. Also, SD and HD have effectively converged to the transfer function specified in BT.709. Consequently, R'G'B' coding uses essentially identical parameters worldwide, for SD and HD. (The sRGB standard for desktop computing uses the primaries of BT.709, but uses a different transfer function.)

Unfortunately, as I have mentioned, the luma coefficients differ dramatically between SD and HD. This wouldn't matter if HD systems were isolated! However, in practice, SD is upconverted and HD is downconverted, both at the studio and at consumers' premises. Serious colour reproduction errors arise if differences among luma coefficients are not taken into account in conversions.

In principle, downconversion can be accomplished by decoding $^{709}Y'C_BC_R$ to R'G'B' using a suitable 3×3 matrix (such as that in Equation 30.7, on page 373), then encoding R'G'B' to $^{601}Y'C_BC_R$ using another 3×3 matrix (such as that in Equation 29.6, on page 364).

The two 3×3 matrices can be combined so that the conversion can take place in one step:

Eq 30.12

$$\begin{bmatrix} \frac{601}{219}Y' \\ C_B \\ C_R \end{bmatrix} = \begin{bmatrix} 1 & 0.099312 & 0.191700 \\ 0 & 0.989854 & -0.110653 \\ 0 & -0.072453 & 0.983398 \end{bmatrix} \cdot \begin{bmatrix} \frac{709}{219}Y' \\ C_B \\ C_R \end{bmatrix}$$

Equations 30.12 and 30.13 are written without interface offsets of +16 for luma and +128 for C_B and C_B: If the offsets are present, remove them, transform, then reapply them.

In the first row of the matrix, the coefficient 0.099312 adds about one-tenth of BT.709's C_B into BT.601's luma. This is a consequence of BT.709's blue luma coefficient being just 0.0722, compared to 0.114 for BT.601. The coefficient 0.1917 adds about one-fifth of BT.709's C_R into BT.601's luma; this is a consequence of BT.709's red luma coefficient being 0.2126, compared to 0.299 for BT.601. Clearly, failure to perform this colour transform produces large colour errors.

To convert from SD to HD, the matrix of Equation 30.12 is inverted:

Eq 30.13

$$\begin{bmatrix} \frac{709}{219}Y' \\ C_B \\ C_R \end{bmatrix} = \begin{bmatrix} 1 & -0.115550 & -0.207938 \\ 0 & 1.018640 & 0.114618 \\ 0 & 0.075049 & 1.025327 \end{bmatrix} \cdot \begin{bmatrix} \frac{601}{219}Y' \\ C_B \\ C_R \end{bmatrix}$$

Unfortunately, to upconvert or downconvert a subsampled representation such as 4:2:2 or 4:2:0 requires chroma interpolation, colour transformation, then chroma subsampling. This is computationally intensive.

Colour coding standards

ITU-R Rec. BT.709 defines $Y'P_BP_R$ for component analog HD and $Y'C_BC_R$ for component digital HD. The parameters of $Y'P_BP_R$ and $Y'C_BC_R$ for the 1280×720 and 1920×1080 systems are defined by the SMPTE standards cited below.

ITU-R Rec. BT.709, *Basic parameter values for the HDTV standard for the studio and for international programme exchange.*

SMPTE ST 274, *1920×1080 Scanning and Analog and Parallel Digital Interfaces for Multiple Picture Rates.*

SMPTE ST 296, *1280×720 Progressive Image Sample Structure – Analog and Digital Representation and Analog Interface.*

Video signal processing 31

This chapter presents several diverse topics concerning the representation and processing of video signals.

It is ubiquitous in modern computers that integer arithmetic is implemented using the two's complement representation of binary numbers. When the result of an arithmetic operation such as addition or subtraction overflows the fixed bit depth available, two's complement arithmetic ordinarily involves wrapping around – for example, in 16-bit two's complement, taking the largest positive number, 32,767 (or in hexadecimal, $7fff_h$) and adding one produces the smallest negative number, $-32,768$ (or in hexadecimal, 8000_h). It is an insidious problem with computer software implementation of video algorithms that wraparound is allowed in integer arithmetic. In video signal processing with integer values, *saturating arithmetic* must be used.

Edge treatment

If an image row of 720 samples is to be processed through a 25-tap FIR filter (such as that of Figure 20.26, on page 216) to produce 720 output samples, any output (result) sample within 12 samples of the left edge or the right edge of the image row will have nonzero filter coefficients associated with input samples beyond the edge of the image.

One approach to this problem is to produce just those output samples – 696 in this example – that can be computed from the available input samples. However, filtering operations are frequently cascaded, particularly in the studio, and it is unacceptable to repeatedly narrow the image width upon application of

Edge-replication is appropriate for motion-compensated interpolation in video compression: The replicated samples are used as predictions, and are not displayed.

a sequence of FIR filters. A strategy is necessary to deal with filtering at the edges of the image.

Many digital image-processing (DIP) textbooks suggest padding the area outside the pixel array with copies of the edge samples, replicated as many times as necessary. The assumption is unrealistic for virtually all imaging applications, because if a *small* feature happens to lie at the left edge of the image, upon replication it will effectively turn into a *large* feature and thereby exert undue influence on the filter result – that is, exert undue influence reaching into the interior of the pixel array.

Some textbooks advocate padding the image by mirroring as many left-edge samples as necessary. In the example above, padding would mirror the leftmost 12 image columns. This approach is also unrealistic: In general-purpose imaging, there is no reasonable possibility that the missing content is estimated by mirroring.

Many textbooks consider the image to wrap in a cylinder: Missing samples outside the left-hand edge of the image are copied from the *right-hand* edge of the image! This concept draws from Fourier transform theory, where a finite data set is treated as being cyclic (periodic). This assumption makes the math easy, but is not justified in practice, and the wrapping strategy is even worse than edge-pixel replication.

In video, we treat the image as lying on a field of black: Unavailable samples are taken to be black. With this strategy, repeated lowpass filtering causes the implicit black background to intrude to some extent into the image. In practice, few problems are caused by this intrusion. Video image data nearly always includes some black (or blanking) samples, as I outlined in the discussion of samples per picture width and samples per active line. (See *Scanning parameters,* on page 86.) In studio standards, a region lying within the pixel array is designated as the *clean aperture*, as sketched in Figure 8.4, on page 87. This region is supposed to remain subjectively free from artifacts that originate from filtering at the picture edges.

Transition samples

In *Scanning parameters,* on page 86, I mentioned that it is necessary to avoid an instantaneous transition from

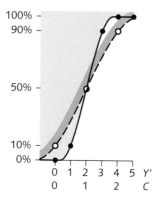

Figure 31.1 **Transition samples.**
The solid line, dots (•), and
light shading show the luma
transition; the dashed line, open
circles (o), and colour shading
show 4:2:2 chroma limits.

480*i* studio standards historically
accommodated up to 487 image
rows, as explained in *480i line
assignment,* on page 446. 576*i*
studio standards provide 574 full
lines and two halflines, as explained
in *576i line assignment,* on page 458.

blanking to picture at the start of a line. It is also necessary to avoid an instantaneous transition from picture to
blanking at the end of a line. In studio video, the first
and the last few active video samples on a line are
blanking transition samples. I recommend that the first
luma (*Y'*) sample of a line be black, and that this sample
be followed by three transition samples clipped to 10%,
50%, and 90% of the full signal amplitude. In 4:2:2,
I recommend that the first three colour difference (*C*)
samples on a line be transition samples, clipped to
10%, 50%, and 90%. Figure 31.1 sketches the transition samples. The transition values should be applied by
clipping, rather than by multiplication, to avoid
disturbing the transition samples of a signal that already
has a proper blanking transition.

Picture lines

Historically, the count of image rows in 480*i* systems
was poorly standardized. Various standards specified
between 480 and 487 "picture lines." It is pointless to
carry picture on line 21/284 or earlier, because in NTSC
transmission this line is reserved for closed caption
data: 482 full lines, plus the bottom halfline, now
suffice. With 4:2:0 chroma subsampling, as used in
JPEG, MPEG-1, and MPEG-2, a multiple of 16 picture
lines is required. DCT-based transform compression is
now so ubiquitous that a count of 480 lines has
become *de rigeur* for 480*i* MPEG video. In 576*i* scanning, a rigid standard of 576 picture lines has always
been enforced; fortuitously for MPEG in 576*i*, the
number 576 happens to be a multiple of 16.

MPEG-2 accommodates the 1920×1080 image
format; however, 1080 is not a multiple of 16. In
MPEG-2 coding, the bottom of each 1920×1080
picture is padded with eight image rows containing
black to form a 1920×1088 array that is coded. The
extra eight lines are discarded upon decoding.

Traditionally, the image array of 480*i* and 576*i*
systems had halflines, as sketched in Figures 13.3 and
13.4 on page 132: Halfline blanking was imposed on
picture information on the top and bottom lines of each
frame. Neither JPEG nor MPEG provides halfline
blanking: When halfline-blanked image data is
presented to a JPEG or MPEG compressor, the blank

image data is compressed. Thankfully, halflines have been abolished from HD.

Studio video standards have no transition samples on the vertical axis: An instantaneous transition from vertical blanking to full picture is implied. However, nonpicture vertical interval information coded like video – such as VITS or VITC – may precede the picture lines in a field or frame. Active lines comprise only picture lines (and exceptionally, in 480i systems, closed caption data). L_A excludes vertical interval lines.

Computer display interface standards, such as those from VESA, make no provision for nonpicture (vertical interval) lines other than blanking.

Choice of S_{AL} and S_{PW} parameters

In *Scanning parameters,* on page 86, I characterized two video signal parameters, *samples per active line* (S_{AL}) and *samples per picture width* (S_{PW}). Active sample counts in studio standards have been chosen for the convenience of system design; within a given scanning standard, active sample counts standardized for different sampling frequencies are not exactly proportional to the sampling frequencies.

Historically, "blanking width" was measured instead of picture width. Through the decades, there has been considerable variation in blanking width of studio standards and broadcast standards. Also, blanking width was measured at levels other than 50%, leading to an unfortunate dependency upon frequency response.

Most modern video standards do not specify picture width: It is implicit that the picture should be as wide as possible within the production aperture, subject to reasonable blanking transitions. Figure 13.1, on page 130 indicates S_{AL} values typical of studio practice.

For digital terrestrial broadcasting of 480i and 480p, the ATSC considered the coding of transition samples to be wasteful. Instead of specifying 720 S_{AL}, ATSC established 704 S_{AL}. This created an inconsistency between production standards and broadcast standards: MPEG-2 macroblocks are misaligned between the two.

Computer display interface standards, such as those from VESA, do not accommodate blanking transition samples and have no concept of clean aperture. In these standards, S_{PW} and S_{AL} are equal.

Active lines (vertically) encompass the picture height. *Active samples* (horizontally) encompass not only the picture width, but also up to about a dozen blanking transition samples.

HD standards specify that the 50%-points of picture width must lie no further than six samples inside the production aperture.

DIGITAL VIDEO AND HD ALGORITHMS AND INTERFACES

Video levels

I introduced 8-bit studio video levels on page 42. Studio video coding provides headroom and footroom. At an 8-bit interface, luma has reference black at code 16 and reference white at code 235; colour differences are coded in offset binary, with zero at code 128, the negative reference at code 16, and the positive reference at code 240. (It is a nuisance that the positive reference levels differ between luma and chroma.) I use the term *reference* instead of *peak;* the peaks of transient excursions may lie outside the reference levels. This range is known as "studio-swing."

All modern studio interfaces accommodate 10-bit signals, and most equipment today implements 10 bits. In 10-bit systems, the reference levels just mentioned are multiplied by 4; the two LSBs provide additional precision. Reference black is at code 64, and reference white at code 940.

Video levels in 480*i* systems are historically expressed in *IRE units*, sometimes simply called *units*. IRE refers to the Institute of Radio Engineers in the United States, the predecessor of the IEEE. Reference blanking level is defined as 0 IRE; reference white level is 100 IRE. The range between these values is the *picture excursion*.

In an analog interface, sync is coded at voltage level more negative than black; sync is "blacker than black." The ratio of picture excursion to sync amplitude is the *picture:sync ratio*. Two different ratios were standardized: 10:4 is predominant in 480*i* and computing; 7:3 is universal in 576*i* and HD, occasionally used in 480*i*, and rarely used in computing.

Setup (pedestal)

In 480*i* systems with setup, the term *picture excursion* refers to the range from blanking to white, even though strictly speaking the lowest level of the picture signal is 7.5 units, not 0 units.

Back porch is described in *Analog horizontal blanking interval,* in Chapter 2 of *Composite NTSC and PAL: Legacy Video Systems.*

In 480*i* composite NTSC video in North America, reference black is offset above blanking by 7.5% ($\frac{3}{40}$) of the picture excursion. *Setup* refers to this offset, expressed as a fraction or percentage of the picture excursion. In a 480*i* system with setup, there are nominally 92.5 IRE units from black to white.

Blanking level at an analog interface is established by a back porch clamp. However, in a system with setup, no signal element is present that enables a receiver to accurately recover black level. If an interface has poor

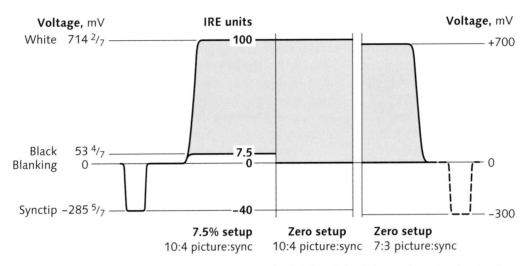

Voltage, mV
White   714 $^2/_7$

Black   53 $^4/_7$
Blanking   0

Synctip –285 $^5/_7$

IRE units
100

7.5
0

–40

Voltage, mV
+700

0

–300

7.5% setup
10:4 picture:sync

Zero setup
10:4 picture:sync

Zero setup
7:3 picture:sync

Figure 31.2 **Comparison of 7.5% and zero setup.** The left-hand third shows the video levels of composite 480*i* video, with 7.5% setup and 10:4 picture-to-sync ratio. This coding is used in some studio equipment and in most computer display interfaces. The middle third shows zero setup and 10:4 picture-to-sync, as used in 480*i* video in Japan. EBU N10 component video, 576*i* systems, and HD use zero setup, 700 mV picture, and 300 mV sync, as shown at the right.

Consumer video equipment purchased in Japan has zero setup. Some Japanese CE equipment has setup confugurable 0/7.5; sometimes the 0 setting goes by marketing terms like "enhanced black."

tolerance, calibration error, or drift, setup causes problems in maintaining accurate black-level reproduction. Consequently, setup has been abolished from modern video systems: *Zero setup* is a feature of EBU N10 component video, all variants of 576*i* video, and HD. In all of these systems, blanking level also serves as the reference level for black.

480*i* video in Japan originally used setup. However, in about 1987, zero setup was adopted; 10:4 picture-to-sync ratio was retained. Consequently, there are now three level standards for SD analog video interface. Figure 31.2 shows these variations.

The archaic EIA RS-343-A standard specified monochrome operation, 2:1 interlace with 60.00 Hz field rate, 7 µs horizontal blanking, and other parameters that have no place in modern video systems. Unfortunately, most PC graphics display standards have inherited RS-343-A's 10:4 picture-to-sync ratio and 7.5% setup. (Some high-end workstations have zero setup.)

The term *pedestal* refers to the absolute value of the offset from blanking level to black level, in IRE units or millivolts: Composite 480*i* NTSC incorporates a pedestal of 7.5 IRE. Pedestal includes any deliberate offset

DIGITAL VIDEO AND HD ALGORITHMS AND INTERFACES

added to R', G', or B' components, to luma, or to a composite video signal, to achieve a desired technical or æsthetic intent. In Europe, this is termed *lift*. (I prefer the term *black level* to either *pedestal* or *lift*.)

BT.601 to computing

The coding difference between computer graphics and studio video necessitates image data conversion at the interface. Figure 31.3 overleaf shows the transfer function that converts 8-bit BT.601 studio $R'G'B'$ into computer $R'G'B'$. The footroom and headroom regions of BT.601 are clipped, and the output signal omits 36 code values. This coding difference between computer graphics and studio video is one of many challenges in taking studio video into the computer domain.

Enhancement

This section and several subsequent sections discuss enhancement, median filtering, coring, chroma transition improvement (CTI), and scan-velocity modulation (SVM). Each of these operations superficially resembles FIR filtering: A "window" involving a small set of neighboring samples slides over the input data. For each new input sample, the filtering operation delivers one output sample that has been subject to some fixed time delay with respect to the input. Unlike FIR filtering, with the exception of the most benign forms of enhancement these operations are nonlinear. They cannot, in general, be undone.

The term "enhancement" is widely used in image processing and video. It has no precise meaning. Evidently, the goal of enhancement is to improve, in some sense, the quality of an image. In principle, this can be done only with knowledge of the process or processes that degraded the image's quality. In practice, it is extremely rare to have access to any history of the processes to which image data has been subject, so no systematic approach to enhancement is possible.

In some applications, it may be known that image data has been subject to processes that have introduced specific degradations or artifacts. In these cases, enhancement may refer to techniques designed to reduce these degradations. A common example involves degraded frequency response due to aperture

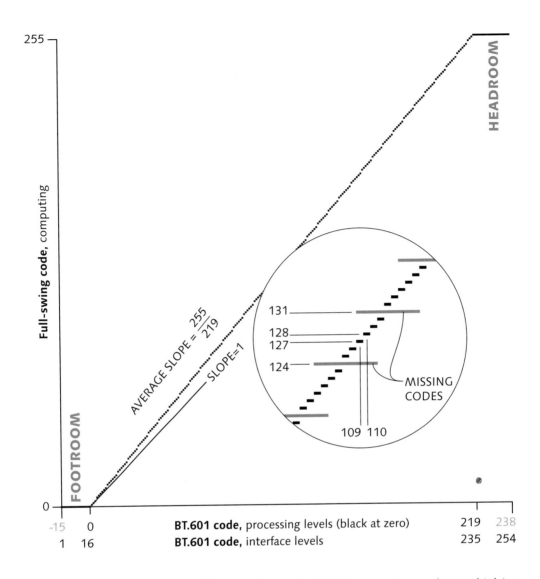

Figure 31.3 **The 8-bit BT.601 to full-range (computer)** *R'G'B'* **conversion** involves multiplying by a scale factor of $^{255}\!/_{219}$ (about 1.16), to account for the difference in range. This causes the footroom and headroom regions of the studio video signal to be clipped, and causes the output signal to be missing several code values. The detail shows the situation at mid-scale; the transfer function is symmetrically disposed around input pair [109, 110] and output pair [127, 128]. This graph shows a linear relationship from black to white. The linear relationship is suitable in computer systems where a ramp is loaded into the lookup table (LUT) between the framebuffer and the display; in that case, *R'G'B'* data is displayed on the computer display comparably to the way *R'G'B'* is displayed in video; see *Gamma*, on page 315.

effects. Enhancement in this case, also known as *aperture correction*, is accomplished by some degree of high-pass filtering, either in the horizontal direction, the vertical direction, or both. Compensation of loss of detail (MTF) should be done in the linear-light domain; however, it is sometimes done in the gamma-corrected domain. Historically, vertical aperture correction in interlaced tube cameras (vidicons and plumbicons) was done in the interlaced domain.

More generally, enhancement is liable to involve nonlinear processes that are based on some assumptions about the properties of the image data. Unless signal flow is extremely well controlled, there is a huge danger in using such operations: Upon receiving image data that has *not* been subject to the expected process, "enhancement" is liable to degrade the image, rather than improve it. For this reason, I am generally very strongly opposed to "enhancement."

The SHARPNESS control in consumer receivers effects horizontal "enhancement" on the luma signal.

Median filtering

A median filter is a nonlinear filter in which each output sample is computed as the median value of the input samples under the window – that is, the result is the middle value after the input values have been sorted. Ordinarily, an odd number of taps is used. Median filtering often involves a horizontal window with 3 taps; occasionally, 5 or even 7 taps are used. Sometimes spatial median filters are used (for example, 3×3).

In the rare case of an even-order median filter, the output is the average of the central two samples after sorting.

Any isolated extreme value, such as a large-valued sample due to impulse noise, will never appear in the output sequence of a median filter: Median filtering can be useful to reduce noise. However, a legitimate extreme value will not be included! I urge you to use great caution in imposing median filtering: If your filter is presented with image data whose statistics are not what you expect, you are very likely to degrade the image instead of improving it.

Coring

Coring is a technique widely presumed to reduce noise. The assumption (often incorrect) is made that any high-frequency signal components having low magnitude are noise. The input signal is separated into low- and high-frequency components using complementary filters. The

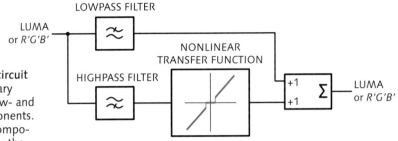

LOWPASS FILTER

LUMA
or *R'G'B'*

NONLINEAR
TRANSFER FUNCTION

HIGHPASS FILTER

+1
+1

Σ

LUMA
or *R'G'B'*

Figure 31.4 **A coring circuit** includes complementary filters that separate low- and high-frequency components. The high-frequency components are processed by the nonlinear transfer function in the sketch.

low-frequency component is passed to the output. The magnitude of the high-frequency component is estimated, and the magnitude is subject to a thresholding operation. If the magnitude is below threshold, then the high-frequency component is discarded; otherwise, it is passed to the output through summation with the low-frequency component. Coring can be implemented by the block diagram shown in Figure 31.4 above.

Like median filtering, coring depends upon the statistical properties of the image data. If the image is a flat-shaded cartoon having large areas of uniform colour with rapid transitions between them, then coring will eliminate noise below a certain magnitude. However, if the input is *not* a cartoon, you run the risk that coring will cause it to look like one! In a close-up of a face, skin texture produces a low-magnitude, high-frequency component that is *not* noise. If coring eliminates this component, the face will take on the texture of plastic.

Coring is liable to introduce spatial artifacts into an image. Consider an image containing a Persian carpet that recedes into the distance. The carpet's pattern will produce a fairly low spatial frequency in the foreground (at the bottom of the image); as the pattern recedes into the background, the spatial frequency of the pattern becomes higher and its magnitude becomes lower. If this image is subject to coring, beyond a certain distance, coring will cause the pattern to vanish. The viewer will perceive a sudden transition from the pattern of the carpet to no pattern at all. The viewer may conclude that beyond a certain distance there is a different carpet, or no carpet at all.

Chroma transition improvement (CTI)

Colour-under VCRs exhibit very poor colour difference bandwidth (evidenced as poor chroma resolution in the horizontal direction). A localized change in luma may be faithfully reproduced, but the accompanying change in colour difference components will be spread horizontally. If you assume that coloured areas tend to be uniformly coloured, one way of improving image quality is to detect localized changes in luma, and use that information to effect repositioning of colour difference information. Techniques to accomplish this are collectively known as *chroma transition improvement* (CTI).

If you use CTI, you run the risk of introducing excessive emphasis on edges. Also, CTI operates only on the horizontal dimension: Excessive CTI is liable to become visible owing to perceptible (or even objectionable) differences between the horizontal and vertical characteristics of the image. CTI works well on cartoons, and on certain other types of images. However, it should be used cautiously.

Mixing and keying

Mixing video signals together to create a transition, or a layered effect – for example, to mix or wipe – is called *compositing.* In America, a piece of equipment (with a control surface) that performs such effects is a *production switcher.* In Europe, the equipment – or the person that operates it! – is called a *vision mixer.*

Accomplishing mix, wipe, or key effects in hardware requires synchronous video signals – that is, signals whose timing matches perfectly in the vertical and horizontal domains.

Keying (or *compositing,* or *blending*) refers to superimposing a foreground (FG, or *fill video*) image over a background (BG) image. Keying is normally controlled by a *key* (or *matte*) signal, represented like luma, that indicates the opacity of the accompanying foreground image data, coded between black (0, fully transparent) and white (1, fully opaque). In computer graphics, the key signal (data) is called *alpha* (α), and the operation is called *compositing.*

The keying (or compositing) operation is performed as in Equation 31.1. Foreground image data that has been premultiplied by the key is called *shaped* in video,

PORTER, THOMAS, and TOM DUFF (1984), "Compositing digital images," in *Computer Graphics,* **18** (3): 253–259 (July, Proc. SIGGRAPH). The terms *composite* and *compositing* are overused in video!

SMPTE RP 157, *Key Signals.*

Eq 31.1

$$R = \alpha \cdot FG + (1 - \alpha) \cdot BG$$

or *associated, integral,* or *premultiplied* in computer graphics. Foreground image data that has not been premultiplied by the key is called *unshaped* in video, or *unassociated* or *nonpremultiplied* in computer graphics.

The key signal is sometimes called *linear key:* The modifier *linear* does not refer to linear light, but to a key signal representing opacity with more than just the two levels fully transparent and fully opaque. In keying or compositing, the compositing operation of Equation 31.1 is applied directly without any transfer function applied to the key signal.

Historically, keying was accomplished in the gamma domain. However, proper simulation of the physics of blending requires keying in the linear-light domain; such an approach is now widely practiced in software systems (sometimes by setting an option denoted something like "blend in gamma = 1.0 space"); an increasing number of hardware-based video switchers are now capable of linear-light blending.

The multiplication of foreground and background data in keying is equivalent to modulation: This can produce signal components above half the sampling rate, thereby producing alias components. Aliasing can be avoided by upsampling the foreground, background, and key signals; performing the keying operation at twice the video sampling rate; then suitably filtering and downsampling the result. Most keyers operate directly at the video sampling rate without upsampling or downsampling, and consequently exhibit some aliasing.

Figure 31.5 is a matte image representative of work by Yung-Yu Chuang and his colleagues at the University of Washington.

In order for a compositing operation to mimic the mixing of light in an actual scene, keying should be performed on foreground and background in the linear-light domain. However, keying in video has historically been performed in the gamma-corrected domain.

The most difficult part of keying is extracting ("pulling") the matte. For review from a computer graphics perspective, see SMITH, ALVY RAY, and JAMES F. BLINN (1996), "Blue screen matting," in *Computer Graphics* (Proc. SIGGRAPH), 259–268.

Figure 31.5 **This matte image example** shows the typical matte polarity. See CHUANG, YUNG-YU et al. (2002), "Video matting of complex scenes," in *ACM Transactions on Graphics* **21** (3) (Proc. SIGGRAPH), 243–248 (July).

Frame, field, line, and sample rates 32

This chapter outlines the field, frame, line, and sampling rates of 480i video, 576i video, and HD.

The standard sampling frequency for component SD is exactly 13.5 MHz. This rate produces an integer number of samples per line in both 480i and 576i. HD standards at integer frame rates specify multiples of 13.5 MHz: 720p, 1080i30, and 1080p30 systems sample at 74.25 MHz. HD standards also permit operation at $^{1000}/_{1001}$ times that rate.

Field rate

Television systems originated with field rates based on the local AC power line frequency: 60 Hz for North America, and 50 Hz for Europe.

In the 1940s and 1950s, coupling of the ripple of a receiver's power supply into circuitry – such as video amplifiers and high-voltage supplies – caused display luminance to pulsate. If the vertical scanning frequency was different from the power line frequency, interference caused artifacts called *hum bars*, at the difference in frequency – the beat frequency – between the two. Their visibility was minimized by choosing a field rate the same as the power line frequency, so as to make the hum bars stationary. There was no requirement to have an exact frequency match, or to lock the phase: As long as the pattern was stationary, or drifting very slowly, it was not objectionable. The power supply interactions that were once responsible for hum bars no longer exist in modern circuitry, but the vertical scan rates that were standardized remain with us.

A second reason to lock television scanning to power line frequency concerns image capture. Many light sources – for example, fluorescent lamps – flash at twice the power line frequency. If a camera operates at a picture rate unrelated to the flash rate, then the captured image is liable to contain artifacts owing to the flashing illumination. Various countermeasures can overcome these artifacts; however, the simplest approach to prevent them is to capture at a multiple or submultiple of the power line frequency.

Line rate

The total number of raster lines chosen for the 525-line television is the product of a few small integers: 525 is $7 \times 5^2 \times 3$. The choice of small integer factors arose from the use of vacuum tube divider circuits to derive the field rate from the line rate: Such dividers were stable only for small divisors. The total number of scan lines per frame is odd. Equivalently, the field rate is an odd multiple of half the line rate. The 2:1 relationship generates the 2:1 interlace that I introduced in *Interlaced format,* on page 88. These factors combined to give monochrome 525/60 television a line rate of $30 \times (7 \times 5^2 \times 3)$, or exactly 15.750 kHz.

$$\frac{525 \cdot 60}{2} = 15750$$

The flyback transformer scheme was the precursor to modern switched-mode power supplies (SMPS).

For 525-line receivers, a scheme was invented to develop high voltage for the picture tube using a transformer operating at the horizontal scanning frequency, 15.750 kHz, rather than the AC line frequency. This approach permitted a lightweight transformer, which became known as the *flyback transformer.* (The scheme is still used today; it can be considered as a precursor to the switch-mode power supply.) The flyback transformer was a complex component, and it was tuned to the horizontal frequency.

When European engineers started designing receivers, it was a practical necessity to fix the field rate at 50 Hz to match the local power line frequency. Rather than develop flyback transformers from scratch, European engineers imported them from North America! Horizontal frequency was thereby constrained to a narrow range around 15.750 kHz. The total line count was chosen as 625, that is, 5^4. Monochrome 625-line television had a line rate of 5^6, or exactly 15.625 kHz; that rate was unchanged with the addition of colour.

Sound subcarrier

In about 1941, the first NTSC recognized that visibility of sound-related patterns in the picture could be minimized by making the picture line rate and the sound subcarrier rest frequency coherent. In monochrome 525/60 television the sound subcarrier was placed at exactly $^{2000}/_7$ (i.e., $285\,^5/_7$) times the line rate – that is, at 4.5 MHz. Sound in conventional television is frequency modulated, and with an analog sound modulator even perfect silence cannot be guaranteed to generate an FM carrier of exactly 4.5 MHz. Nonetheless, making the FM sound carrier average out to 4.5 MHz was considered to have some value.

Addition of composite colour

NTSC and PAL colour coding both employ the frequency-interleaving technique to achieve compatibility with monochrome systems. With frequency interleaving, the colour subcarrier frequency is chosen to alternate phase line by line, so as to minimize the visibility of encoded colour on a monochrome receiver. The line-to-line phase relationship makes it possible to accurately separate chroma from luma in an NTSC decoder that incorporates a comb filter (although a cheaper notch filter can be used instead).

NTSC colour subcarrier

HAZELTINE CORPORATION (1956), *Principles of Color Television*, by the Hazeltine Laboratories staff, compiled and edited by KNOX MCILWAIN and CHARLES E. DEAN (New York: Wiley).

In 1953, the second NTSC decided to choose a colour subcarrier frequency of approximately 3.6 MHz. They recognized that any nonlinearity in the processing of the composite colour signal with sound – such as limiting in the *intermediate frequency* (IF) stages of a receiver – would result in intermodulation distortion between the sound subcarrier and the colour subcarrier. The difference, or *beat frequency*, between the two subcarriers, about 920 kHz, falls in the luminance bandwidth and could potentially have been quite visible.

The NTSC recognized that the visibility of this pattern could be minimized if the beat frequency was line-interlaced. Since the colour subcarrier is necessarily an odd multiple of half the line rate, the sound subcarrier had to be made an integer multiple of the line rate.

The NTSC decided that the colour subcarrier should be exactly $^{455}/_2$ times the line rate. Line interlace of the

$$f_{SC,NTSC} = \frac{455}{2} f_{H,480i}$$

beat could be achieved by increasing the sound-to-line rate ratio (previously $285\frac{5}{7}$) by the fraction $\frac{1001}{1000}$ to the next integer (286).

Setting broadcast standards in the U.S. was (and remains) the responsibility of the Federal Communications Commission. The FCC could have allowed the sound subcarrier rest frequency to be increased by the fraction $\frac{1001}{1000}$ – that is, increased by 4.5 kHz to about 4.5045 MHz. Had the FCC made this choice, the colour subcarrier in NTSC would have been exactly 3.583125 MHz; the original 525/60 line and field rates would have been unchanged; we would have retained exactly 60 frames per second – and NTSC would have no dropframes! Since sound is frequency modulated, the sound carrier was never crystal-stable at the subcarrier frequency anyway – not even during absolute silence – and the tolerance of the rest frequency was already reasonably large (±1 kHz). The deviation of the sound subcarrier was – and remains – 25 kHz, so a change of 4.5 kHz could easily have been accommodated by the intercarrier sound systems of the day.

However, the FCC refused to alter the sound subcarrier. Instead, the colour/sound constraint was met by reducing both the line rate and field rate by the fraction $\frac{1001}{1000}$, to about 15.734 kHz and 59.94 Hz. The colour subcarrier was established as $3.579\overline{45}$ MHz. What was denoted 525/60 scanning became 525/59.94, though unfortunately the 525/60 notation is still used loosely to refer to 525/59.94.

The factors of 1001 are 7, 11, and 13. This numerical relationship was known in ancient times: The book *1001 Arabian Nights* is based on it. The numbers 7, 11, and 13 are considered to be very unlucky. Unfortunately the field rate of $\frac{60}{1.001}$, about 59.94 Hz, means that 60 fields consume slightly more than one second: Counting 30 fields per second does not agree with clock time. Dropframe timecode was invented to alleviate this difficulty; see *Timecode*, on page 399.

NTSC sync generators historically used a master oscillator of $14.31818\overline{1}$ MHz. This clock was divided by 4 to obtain the colour subcarrier, and simultaneously divided by 7 to obtain a precursor of line rate.

$$525 \times \left(\frac{60}{2} \text{ Hz}\right) \times \frac{1000}{1001} \times \frac{455}{2}$$

$$= \frac{315}{88} \text{ MHz}$$

$$\approx 3.579\overline{545} \text{ MHz}$$

$$525 \times \left(\frac{60}{2} \text{ Hz}\right) \times \frac{1000}{1001} \times 455 \times 2$$

$$= \frac{315}{22} \text{ MHz}$$

$$\approx 14.31818\overline{1} \text{ MHz}$$

Prior to the emergence of framestore synchronizers in the 1980s, every major broadcast network in the United States had an atomic clock to provide 5 MHz, followed by a rate multiplier of $\frac{63}{22}$ to derive its master $14.31818\overline{1}$ MHz clock.

DIGITAL VIDEO AND HD ALGORITHMS AND INTERFACES

576*i* PAL colour subcarrier

In 576*i* PAL, the colour subcarrier frequency is based on an odd multiple of one-quarter the line rate, using the factor $^{1135}\!/_4$. The odd multiple of one-quarter, combined with the line-to-line alternation of the phase of the *V* colour difference component, causes the *U* and *V* colour components to occupy separate parts of the composite signal spectrum. This makes the PAL signal immune to the hue errors that result when an NTSC signal is subject to differential phase distortion.

$$625 \times \left(\frac{50}{2}\,\text{Hz}\right) \times \left(\frac{1135}{4} + \frac{1}{625}\right)$$
$$= 4.433618750\ \text{MHz}$$

In standard PAL-B, PAL-G, PAL-H, and PAL-I, an offset of +25 Hz is added to the basic subcarrier frequency so as to minimize the visibility of the Hanover bar effect. The 25 Hz offset means that the phase relationship of subcarrier to horizontal advances exactly +0.576° each line. Consequently, subcarrier-locked sampling in PAL is not line-locked: The subcarrier phase, modulo 90°, of vertically aligned samples is not identical! The introduction of the +25 Hz offset destroyed the simple integer ratio between subcarrier and line rate: The ratio is quite complex, as shown in the margin. The prime factor 64,489 is fairly impenetrable to digital techniques.

$$\frac{1135}{4} + \frac{1}{625} = \frac{709379}{2500}$$
$$= \frac{11 \times 64489}{2^2 \times 5^3}$$

4*f*$_{SC}$ sampling

The earliest digital television equipment sampled composite NTSC or PAL video signals. It was convenient for composite digital NTSC equipment to operate at a sampling frequency of exactly four times the colour subcarrier frequency, or about 14.318 MHz, denoted 4*f*$_{SC}$.

Any significant processing of a picture, such as repositioning, resizing, rotating, and so on, requires that the signal be represented in components. For this reason, component video equipment is preferred in production and postproduction. But 4*f*$_{SC}$ equipment has half the data rate of BT.601 equipment; 4*f*$_{SC}$ equipment is cheaper than component equipment, and dominated SD broadcast operations for many years.

Sampling NTSC at 4*f*$_{SC}$ gives 910 samples per total line (S_{TL}). A count of 768 samples (3×2^8) encompasses the active samples of a line, including the blanking transitions. A count of 512 (2^9) lines is just slightly more than the number of nonblanked lines in 480*i* scanning.

The numbers 768 and 512 were convenient for early memory systems: 512 is the ninth power of 2, and 768 is 3 times the eighth power of 2. In the early days of digital television, this combination – 768 and 512 – led to very simple memory and addressing circuits for framestores. The importance of this special combination of 768 and 512 is now irrelevant: Framestore systems today have well ovver a single frame of memory; memory devices have much higher capacities; and total memory capacity is now a more important constraint than active sample and line counts. In any case, the binary numbers 768 and 512 were never any help in the design of 576i framestores.

Common sampling rate

The designers of the NTSC and PAL systems chose video parameters based on simple integer ratios. When component digital sampling became feasible it came as a surprise that the ratio of line duration of 480i and 576i systems turned out to be the ratio of 144 to 143, derived as shown in Table 32.1.

$f_{H,480i}$	:	$f_{H,576i}$
$525 \times \dfrac{60}{2} \times \dfrac{1000}{1001}$	:	$625 \times \dfrac{50}{2}$
$7 \times 5^2 \times 3 \times \dfrac{5 \cdot 3 \cdot 2^2}{2} \times \dfrac{5^3 \cdot 2^3}{13 \cdot 11 \cdot 7}$	:	$5^4 \times \dfrac{5^2 \times 2}{2}$
$3 \times 3 \times 2^4$	:	13×11
144	:	143

Table 32.1 **Derivation of 13.5 MHz common sampling rate**

The lowest common sampling frequency corresponding to these factors is 2.25 MHz, half of the now-familiar NTSC sound subcarrier frequency of 4.5 MHz. Any multiple of 2.25 MHz could have been used as the basis for line-locked sampling of both 480i and 576i. The most practical sampling frequency is 6 times 2.25 MHz, or 13.5 MHz; this multiplier is a compromise between a rate high enough to ease the design of analog antialiasing filters and low enough to minimize data rate and memory requirements.

ITU-R Rec. BT.601-5, *Studio encoding parameters of digital television for standard 4:3 and widescreen 16:9 aspect ratios.*

At 13.5 MHz, 480*i* video has 858 samples per total line, and 576*i* video has 864 S_{TL}. The blanking tolerances between NTSC and PAL accommodated a choice of 720 samples per active line (S_{AL}) in both systems. Standardization of this number of active samples resulted in a high degree of commonality in the design of SD video processing equipment, since only the difference in active line counts needed to be accommodated to serve both 50 Hz and 60 Hz markets. Also the technically difficult problem of standards conversion was eased somewhat with a common sampling frequency, since horizontal interpolation became unnecessary. However, blanking had to be treated differently in the two systems to meet studio interchange standards.

Numerology of HD scanning

Figure 32.1 indicates 575 image rows in 625/50 systems; this constitutes 287 full lines, plus a halfline, in each field. Counting each halfline as a full line, the total is 576.

Figure 32.1 gives a graphic representation of the development of the magic numbers in HD. At the upper left is the AC power line frequency in North America, along with the factors of 525 (all small integers: $7 \cdot 5^2 \cdot 3$). Next to that is indicated the AC power frequency in Europe, and the factors of 625 (also, all small integers: 5^4).

The addition of colour to the NTSC system introduced the ratio $^{1000}\!/_{1001}$, and led to the 525/59.94 system.

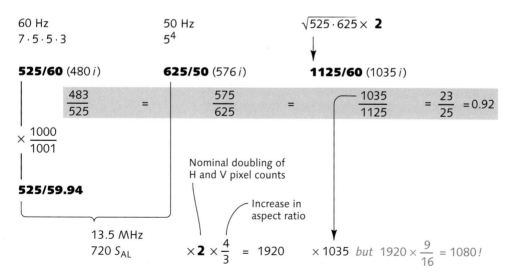

Figure 32.1 **Numerology of HD scanning**

Incidentally, $2000/_{1125}$ equals $^{16}/_9$.

HD was originally conceived at NHK as having twice the horizontal and twice the vertical resolution of conventional television: At the top right is the conceptual origin of the total number of HD scanning lines as twice the geometric mean of 525 and 625. North America would have preferred twice 525 and Europe twice 625. The designers choose a total line count of 1125 (i.e., $5^3 \times 3^2$), a compromise that was thought to be politically acceptable on both sides of the Atlantic Ocean.

Underneath the scanning designations 525/60, 625/50, and 1125/60 in Figure 32.1 is a grey bar containing the ratio of image rows to total scanning lines in each system. The count of lines per total vertical (L_T) for each of these systems is the fraction $^{23}/_{25}$ (92%) of the total. This led to NHK's original choice of 1035 image rows for 1125/60 HD.

The desire for a common sampling frequency for component digital video led to the synthesis of line rates of 480i and 576i into a common sampling frequency, 13.5 MHz, and a common count of samples per active line (S_{AL}), 720. For HD, the active pixel count was doubled to increase the horizontal resolution; then multiplied by the $^4/_3$ increase in aspect ratio (from 4:3 to 16:9), netting 1920.

An image array having dimensions 1920×1035 results from these choices, and SMPTE standardized that as 240M in 1988. However, in about 1991 it became clear that the 1920×1035 structure had a sample pitch unequal in the horizontal and vertical dimensions – nonsquare sampling. The degree of inequality was small – just 4% – but for many applications any departure from equal spacing imposes a burden. In about 1995, the standard was adapted to achieve square sampling by choosing a count of image rows $^9/_{16}$ times 1920, that is, 1080 rows. SMPTE, and subsequently ATSC, enshrined square sampling in the 1920×1080 image array. The system has about two million pixels per frame; the exact number is very slightly less than 2^{21}, a neat fit into binary-sized memory components.

NHK planned to operate the 1920×1035 system at a frame rate of exactly 30 Hz ("30.00 Hz") and early 1035i equipment operated only at that rate. However, the discrepancy of about one frame time every 33.367 seconds between 1035i30.00 and 480i29.97 is a big nuisance in standards conversion. To ease this problem, and to ease engineering difficulties associated with digital audio sample rates, 1080i HD standards accommodate both 29.97 Hz and 30 Hz frame rates.

While NHK and others were developing 1125/60 interlaced HD, progressive-scan systems having nearly identical pixel rate were being developed by other organizations, mainly in the United States. The technology of the day permitted a pixel rate of about 60 megapixels per second, whether scanning was interlace or progressive. With interlace scanning, 60 Mpx/s at 30 Hz frame rate allows a two-megapixel image structure. With progressive scanning, 60 Mpx/s at 60 Hz frame rate allows just one megapixel. Partitioning one megapixel into a square lattice yields an image structure of 1280×720; this led to the 720p family of standards.

In the mid-2000s, the digital cinema community took advantage of HD equipment and infrastructure, and adopted 1080 image rows for the "2 K" standard. However, 2048 image columns were chosen. That choice produced a new aspect ratio, about 1.896, never before used for movies. The standard 1.85 cinema aspect ratio would have been achieved with 1998 image columns, but apparently some members of the community were fearful that 1998 could not be claimed to be "2 K." The choice of a number somewhat greater than 1920 seems to be motivated by the short term desire to distinguish digital cinema from HD, politically if not technically. The 64 additional pixels on each edge can hardly be argued as increasing resolution. Super-HD has been demonstrated with 2·1920 or 3840 image rows, but "4 K" D-cinema has 4096 image columns. Ultra-HD is proposed with 4·1920 or 7680 image rows but presumably "8 K" D-cinema will offer 8192. It seems to me that the divergence of the 2^K·1920 HD-related image formats and the power-of-two D-cinema formats can't be sustained. HD formats, leveraging a connection to consumer volumes, are likely to win in the end.

Audio rates

Digital audio has two standard sample rates: 48 kHz, for professional applications, and 44.1 kHz, for consumer applications. In the standardization of digital audio, manufacturers decided to adopt two different standards in order that professional and consumer equipment could be differentiated! That goal failed miserably, and now the dichotomy in sample rates is a major nuisance in video and audio production.

The 44.1 kHz sampling rate for consumer digital audio originated from an early PCM recording system (Sony PCM-1600) that recorded three (16-bit) stereo sample pairs on 588 active lines of a 625/50 videocassette recorder. In 525/59.94 countries, the original rate was $^{44100}/_{1.001}$: Three 16-bit stereo sample pairs were recorded on each of 490 active lines per frame. Eventually, the 44.1 kHz rate was standardized worldwide. In $^{1}/_{50}$ s, there are 882 samples, an integer. In $^{1}/_{59.94}$ s, there are exactly 1471.47 samples: the noninteger ratio causes havoc.

$$3 \cdot 588 \cdot 25\,\text{Hz} = 44100\,\text{Hz}$$

$$3 \cdot 490 \cdot \frac{30\,\text{Hz}}{1.001} = \frac{44100}{1.001}\,\text{kHz}$$
$$\approx 44.056\,\text{kHz}$$

The professional audio sampling rate was chosen to be exactly 48 kHz. The time interval of one video picture at 50 fields or frames per second corresponds to exactly 960 audio samples at 48 kHz. An AES/EBU audio frame comprises 192 left/right sample pairs, with 16 bits in each sample: In 50 Hz video standards, a video frame occupies exactly the same time interval as five audio frames. In video at 59.94 fields or frames per second, the timing relationships are unfortunate. There are $1601\frac{3}{5}$ audio sample intervals in one picture time: This noninteger number is very inconvenient. The timing relationship of audio samples to video pictures aligns just once every five pictures. There are $^{1001}/_{240}$ (i.e., $4.17083\overline{3}$) AES/EBU audio frames in a video picture time.

Timecode 33

This chapter gives technical details concerning timecode, as used in video, film, audio recording, editing, and sequencing equipment.

Introduction

Timecode systems assign a number to each frame of video to allow each frame to be uniquely identified. Time data is coded in binary-coded decimal (BCD) digits in the form HH:MM:SS:FF, in the range 00:00:00:00 to 23:59:59:29. There are timecode variants for 24, 25, 29.97, and 30 frames per second. Timecode data is digitally recorded with the associated image. *Burnt-in timecode* (BITC) refers to a recording with timecode numbers keyed over the picture content (that is, embedded in the image data).

In addition to approximately 32 bits required for eight-digit time data, timecode systems accommodate an additional 32 *user bits* per frame. User bits may convey one of several types of information: a second timecode stream (such as a timecode from an original recording); a stream of ASCII/ISO characters; motion picture production data, as specified in SMPTE ST 262; auxiliary BCD numerical information, such as tape reel number; or nonstandard information. A group of 4 user bits is referred to as a *binary group*. The information portion of timecode thus totals 64 bits per frame.

A number of synchronization bits are appended to the 64 information bits of timecode in order to convey timecode through a recording channel. Sixteen synchronization bits are appended to form 80-bit *linear timecode* (LTC). Eighteen sync bits and 8 CRC bits are

SMPTE ST 262, *Binary Groups of Time and Control Codes – Storage and Transmission of Data Control Codes.*

SMPTE RP 169, *Television, Audio and Film Time and Control Code – Auxiliary Time Address Data in Binary Group – Dialect Specification of Directory Index Locations.*

appended to form 90-bit *vertical interval timecode* (VITC) that can be inserted into a video signal.

No BCD digit can contain all ones, so the all-ones code is available for other purposes. The highest possible value of certain tens digits is less than 8, so the high-order bits of certain timecode digits are available for use as flags; these flag bits are described on page 403.

The colourframe flag is asserted when the least significant bit of the timecode frame number is intentionally locked to the colourframe sequence of the associated video – in 480*i* systems, locked to Colourframes A and B of SMPTE 170M.

See *NTSC two-frame sequence*, in Chapter 7 of *Composite NTSC and PAL: Legacy Video Systems*.

Dropframe timecode

In 25 Hz video, such as in 576*i* video systems, and in 24 Hz film, there is an exact integer number of frames in each second. In these systems, timecode has an exact correspondence with clock time.

See *Frame, field, line, and sample rates*, on page 389.

During the transition from monochrome to colour television in the United States, certain interference constraints needed to be satisfied among the horizontal scanning, sound, and colour frequencies. These constraints were resolved by reducing the 60.00 Hz field rate of monochrome television by a factor of exactly $^{1000}/_{1001}$ to create the colour NTSC field rate of about 59.94 Hz. This leads to a noninteger number of frames per second in 29.97 Hz or 59.94 Hz systems. The *dropframe* (DF) mechanism can be used to compensate timecode to obtain a very close approximation to clock time. Dropframes are not required or permitted when operating at exact integer numbers of frames per second. Dropframe timecode is optional in 29.97 Hz or 59.94 Hz systems; operation with a straight counting sequence is called *nondropframe* (NDF).

In consumer 480*i*29.97 DV, dropframe timecode is mandatory.

Counting frames at the NTSC frame rate of 29.97 Hz is slower than realtime by the factor $^{1000}/_{1001}$, which – in nondropframe code – would result in an apparent cumulative error of about +3.6 seconds in an hour. To make timecode correspond to clock time, approximately once every 1000 frames a frame number is dropped – that is, omitted from the counting sequence. Of course, it is only the *number* that is dropped, not the video frame! Frame numbers are dropped in pairs in

The final field in an hour of 29.97 Hz video has DF code *hh*:59:59;29 and NDF code *hh*:59:56:23.

DIGITAL VIDEO AND HD ALGORITHMS AND INTERFACES

hh:mm: ss: ff
xx:x0:00:00
xx:x1:06:20
xx:x2:13:10
xx:x3:20:00
xx:x4:26:20
xx:x5:33:10
xx:x6:40:00
xx:x7:46:20
xx:x8:53:10

Figure 33.1
**Periodic dropped
timecode numbers**

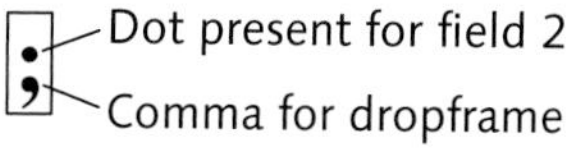

Figure 33.2 **Timecode as
displayed,** or represented in
ASCII, has the final delimiter
(separating seconds from
frames) selected from colon,
semicolon, period, or comma,
to indicate dropframe code and
field 2.

*SMPTE ST 258, Television – Transfer
of Edit Decision Lists.*

order to maintain the relationship of timecode (even or
odd frame number) to NTSC colourframe (A or B).

Dropping a pair of frames every 66 $\frac{2}{3}$ seconds – that
is, at an interval of 1 minute, 6 seconds, and
20 frames – would result in dropping the codes indicated in Figure 33.1 in the margin. Although this
sequence is not easily recognizable, it repeats after
exactly ten minutes! This is a consequence of the ratios
of the numbers: Two frames in 2000 accumulates 18
frames in 18000, and there are 18000 intervals of
$\frac{1}{30}$ second in 10 minutes (30 frames, times 60 seconds,
times 10 minutes). To produce a sequence that is easy
to compute and easy to remember, instead of dropping
numbers strictly periodically, this rule was adopted:
*Drop frame numbers 00:00 and 00:01 at the start of
every minute, except the tenth minute.* In effect,
a dropped pair that is due is delayed until the beginning of the next minute.

Figure 33.2 depicts the convention that has emerged
to represent field identification and of the use of dropframe code in timecode displays.

Dropframe does not achieve a perfect match to clock
time, just a very good match: Counting dropframe code
at $\frac{30}{1.001}$ frames per second results in timecode that is
about 86.4 ms late (slow) over 24 hours. If the residual
error were to accumulate, after 11 or 12 days timecode
would fall about one second later than clock time. If
a timecode sequence is to be maintained longer than
24 hours, timecode should be jammed daily to reference clock time at a suitable moment. No standard
recommends when this should take place; however, the
usual technique is to insert duplicate timecode numbers
00:00:00;00 and 00:00:00;01. Editing equipment treats
the duplicate codes as a timecode interruption.

Editing

Timecode is basic to video editing. An edit is denoted
by its *in point* (the timecode of the first field or frame to
be recorded) and its *out point* (the timecode of the first
field or frame beyond the recording). An edited
sequence can be described by the list of edits used to
produce it: Each entry in an *edit decision list* (EDL)
contains the in and out points of the edited material,

the in and out points of the source, and tape reel number or other source and transition identification.

An edited program is ordinarily associated with continuous "nonbroken" timecode. Editing equipment historically treated the boundary between 23:59:59:29 and 00:00:00:00 as a timecode discontinuity, and an edit at that point (such as starting a new program) was problematic. Consequently, it is conventional to start a main program segment with timecode 01:00:00:00. On videotape, it was conventional to include 1.5 minutes of "bars and tone" leader starting at timecode 00:58:30:00. (In Europe, it is common to start a program at 10:00:00:00.)

Linear timecode (LTC)

Timecode was historically recorded on studio videotape and audiotape recorders on longitudinal tracks having characteristics similar or identical to those of audio tracks. This became known as *longitudinal timecode* (LTC). The word *longitudinal* became unfashionable, and LTC was renamed *linear timecode* – thankfully, it retains its acronym. LTC was historically transported in the studio as an audio signal pair interfaced through three-pin XLR connector.s

Vertical interval timecode (VITC)

SMPTE RP 164, *Location of Vertical Interval Time Code.*

Due to the limitations of stationary head magnetic recording, longitudinal timecode from a VTR could not be read at very slow speeds or with the tape stopped. Vertical interval timecode (VITC) was coded digitally as a pulse stream onto one or two lines in the vertical interval; the scheme overcomes the disadvantage that LTC cannot be read with videotape stopped or moving slowly.

Timecode structure

Table 33.1A at the top of the facing page illustrates the structure of timecode data. The information bits include a flag bit *polarity/field* (whose function differs between LTC and VITC), and three *binary group flags* BGF_0, BGF_1, and BGF_2; they are interpreted in Table 33.1B and Table 33.1C opposite. A clumsy error was made when SMPTE standards were adapted to 25 Hz timecode: The positions of flag bits BGF_0, BGF_2, and

row	col 7	6	5	4	3	2	1	⇐ 0
0	1st binary group					Frame units 0–9		
8	2nd binary group (or character 0)				Colour frame flag	Drop-frame flag	Frame tens 0–2	
16	3rd binary group					Second units 0–9		
24	4th binary group (or character 1)				Polarity /Field {BGF$_0$}		Second tens 0–5	
32	5th binary group					Minute units 0–9		
40	6th binary group (or character 2)				BGF$_0$ {BGF$_2$}		Minute tens 0–5	
48	7th binary group					Hour units 0–9		
56	8th binary group (or character 3)				BGF$_2$ {Polarity /Field}	BGF$_1$	Hour tens 0–2	

Table 33.1A **Timecode bit assignment table.** The jumbled flag bits of 25 Hz systems are enclosed in braces.

polarity/field were jumbled. Flag bit interpretation unfortunately depends upon whether the timecode is 25 Hz-related. The timecode information bits provide no explicit indication of frame rate; frame rate must be determined after a suitable delay (e.g., 1 second), or from parameters outside timecode.

Dropframe flag	Asserted for dropframe timecode mode in 59.94 Hz systems only
Colourframe flag	Asserted when timecode is locked to the colourframe sequence of the associated video
Polarity (LTC only)	Computed such that the complete 80-bit LTC timecode for a frame contains an even number of zero bits (a.k.a. parity, or biphase mark polarity correction)
Field mark (VITC only)	Asserted for the second field

Table 33.1B **Timecode flag bits**

For details of LTC and VITC encoding, see the first edition of this book.

In LTC, the 64 bits are transmitted serially, followed by 16 LTC sync bits. In VITC, each group of 8 bits is preceded by two VITC sync bits; these ten words are followed by a final pair of VITC sync bits and a CRC.

BGF$_2$	BGF$_1$	BGF$_0$	User-bit interpretation
0	0	0	Unspecified characters or data
0	0	1	ISO 646 and ISO 2202 8-bit characters
1	0	1	SMPTE RP 136 data ("page/line")
all other combinations			Unassigned

Table 33.1C **Timecode binary group flags**

Further reading

SMPTE ST 12, *Time and Control Code*.

SMPTE RP 136, *Time and Control Codes for 24, 25 or 30 Frame-per-Second Motion-Picture Systems*.

SMPTE 266M, *4:2:2 Digital Component Systems – Digital Vertical Interval Time Code*.

SMPTE RP 196, *Transmission of LTC and VITC Data as HANC Packets in Serial Digital Television Interfaces*.

Timecode for 480*i* television is standardized in SMPTE ST 12. Timecode for 576*i* is described in IEC 60461, with additional information provided in European Broadcasting Union document EBU Tech. N12.

SMPTE RP 136 standardizes magnetic recording of timecode on motion picture film at 24, 25, 29.97, or 30 frames per second. SMPTE ST 262, cited on page 399, standardizes a method of structuring user-bit data.

SMPTE 266M standardizes a version of VITC, *Digital Vertical Interval Timecode* (DVITC), to be transported across a BT.601, 4:2:2 interface.

SMPTE RP 196 standardizes a mechanism to encode timecode data in ancillary (ANC) packets of the SDI.

2-3 pulldown 34

Motion picture film is intended for display at 24 frames per second. Many television programs, including a large number of prime-time programs, historically originated on film at this rate (or at $^{1000}/_{1001}$ of 24 Hz, that is, 23.976 Hz). This chapter discusses the conversion of film to frame rates higher than 24 Hz.

Film has historically been transferred to 29.97 frame per second video using a technique called *2-3 pulldown*, whereby successive film frames are scanned first twice then three times to produce five video fields. The process is then repeated, reversing the roles of the first and second fields. The scheme is sketched in Figure 34.1.

Except for certain very unusual film formats, motion picture film runs vertically through the camera and the projector. Be wary of anyone who presents a diagram like Figure 34.1 but rotated 90°.

Figure 34.1 "2-3 pulldown" refers to transfer of film at about 24 frames per second to video at about 60 fields per second. The first film frame is transferred to two video fields; the second frame is transferred to three. The 2-3 cycle repeats. SMPTE RP 197 denotes film frames as A, B, C, and D. The A-frame is unique in being associated with exactly two fields – first, then second – of a single video frame. ("A-frame" denotes both a film frame *and* a video frame.) According to SMPTE RP 201, the A-frame timecode's frame count should end in 0 or 5.

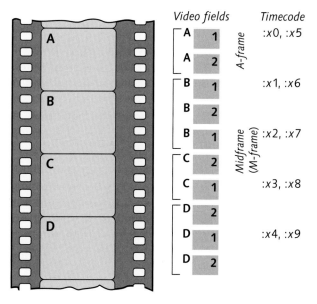

Telecine is usually pronounced *tell-e-SIN-ee.*

What I call *2-3 pulldown* was historically called *3-2 pulldown.* SMPTE standards assign letters A, B, C, and D to sets of four film frames. The A-frame is associated with the frame without a duplicate (redundant) field, so the sequence is best described as *2-3,* not *3-2.*

EBU Tech. R62, *Recommended dominant field for 625-line 50-Hz video processing.*

A piece of equipment that performs this film-to-video conversion in realtime is called a *telecine.* (The term *film scanner* ordinarily implies nonrealtime operation.)

In 29.97 Hz systems, the film is run 0.1% slow, at about 23.976 Hz, so that the $\frac{5}{2}$ ratio of 2-3 pulldown results in a field rate of exactly 59.94 Hz. Figure 34.1 sketches four film frames; beside the set of film frames is the sequence of video fields produced by 2-3 pulldown. The labels *1* and *2* at the right indicate the first and second fields in an interlaced system.

When a 2-3 sequence is associated with nondrop-frame timecode, it is standard for the A-frames to take timecode numbers ending in 0 and 5.

In a sequence containing 2-3 pulldown, *cadence* refers to the temporal regularity of the A-frames. Careful editing preserves cadence; careless editing disrupts it.

In an interlaced sequence, *field dominance* refers to the field parity (first or second) where temporal coherence is susceptible to interruption due to editing. Video edits can, in principle, be made at any field; however, it is poor practice to make edits anywhere except the beginning of the first field.

Film is transferred to 25 Hz video by the simple expedient of running the film 4% fast, scanning each film frame to two video fields. This is somewhat jokingly referred to as *2-2 pulldown.* The 0.1% speed change of 2-3 pulldown has no significant effect on the accompanying audio; however, the 4% speed change of 2-2 pulldown necessitates audio pitch correction.

I have described transfer to interlaced video. The 2-3 pulldown technique can be used to produce progressive video at 60 Hz. In this case, what I have described as first and second fields are first and second frames.

Engineers are prone to think that better-quality motion results from higher frame rates. Proposals have been made to shoot film for television – even to shoot movies – at 30 frames per second instead of 24. The 24 Hz rate is obviously the world standard for cinema, but it is also uniquely suited to conversion to both 50 Hz systems (through 2-2 pulldown, 4% fast) and 59.94 Hz systems (through 2-3 pulldown, 0.1% slow). Choosing a film frame rate other that 24 Hz would

Figure 34.2 "2-3-3-2 pull-down" is identical to 2-3 pulldown except that the eighth video field represents film frame C instead of D. The advantage over 2-3 pulldown is that film frames can be reconstructed from intact video frames; no "stitching" of fields is necessary. 35 mm motion picture film runs vertically through the camera and the projector. The scheme is also known as 24pA. It is not intended for broadcast; however, if broadcast, the motion impairment is not much worse than 2-3 pull-down.

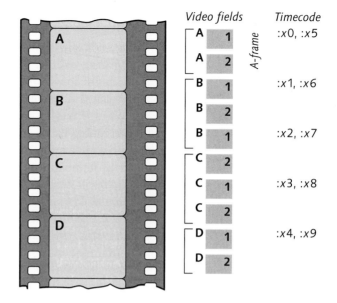

Video fields		Timecode
A 1	A-frame	:x0, :x5
A 2		
B 1		:x1, :x6
B 2		
B 1		:x2, :x7
C 2		
C 1		:x3, :x8
C 2		
D 1		:x4, :x9
D 2		

2-3-3-2 pulldown is denoted *24pA* (for *advanced*) by some manufacturers. When used with DV recording, it is an advantage of 2-3-3-2 that film frames can be reconstructed without decompressing the video bitstream.

compromise this widely accepted method of conversion, and make it difficult for film producers to access international markets.

2-3-3-2 pulldown

When film at 23.976 frames per second is subject to 2-3 pulldown, the video "midframe" (timecode x2/x7) has film frames B and C mixed; the following video frame has film frames C and D mixed. (A video frame containing elements from two film frames is sometimes called a *blur frame*.) Although film frames A, B, and D can be simply reconstructed from single video frames, there is no single video frame that contains film frame C.

This disadvantage is overcome by a minor adaptation to the pulldown sequence, denoted *2-3-3-2 pull-down*, also known as *24pA* (24-frame, progressive, advanced), diagrammed in Figure 34.2. Film frame C can now be reconstructed from the video frame having timecode ending in 3 or 8. A video sequence with 2-3-3-2 pulldown exhibits slight degradation in motion rendition compared to straight 2-3, because the 6 Hz beat frequency of 2-3-3-2 is slightly more visible than the 12 Hz of 2-3 pulldown. Nonetheless, the scheme is popular for desktop video editing.

Conversion of film to different frame rates

When an image sequence originated with 2-3 pulldown is displayed in video, motion portrayal is impaired to a certain degree. The impairment is rarely objectionable. However, if a 2-3 sequence is naively converted to a different frame rate, or if a still frame is extracted from a 2-3 sequence, the resulting impairments are liable to be objectionable. Prior to frame rate conversion from a film original, original film frames need to be reconstructed by weaving together the appropriate pair of fields in a process called *inverse telecine* or *inverse 2-3 pulldown*. Despite the fact that 2-3 pulldown has been used for half a century, no information to aid this "weaving" accompanies the video signal.

A simple method to convert from the 24 Hz film frame rate to any other rate could write successive film lines into a dual-port framebuffer at film scan rate, then read successive lines out of the buffer at video scan rate. But if a scene element is in motion with respect to the camera, this technique won't work. The right portion of Figure 34.3 opposite indicates lines scanned from film being written into a framebuffer. The slanted dashed lines intersect the video scanning; at the vertical coordinate where the lines intersect, the resulting picture switches abruptly from one field to another. This results in an output field that contains spatial discontinuities. (Although this description refers to interlaced scanning, none of these effects are directly related to interlace; exactly the same effects are found in 2-3 pulldown in progressive systems.)

Figure 34.3 shows the vertical-temporal (*V·T*) relationships of 2-3 pulldown, with time on the horizontal axis, and vertical dimension of scanning on the vertical axis. Dashed lines represent film sampling; solid lines represent video sampling. Film capture samples the entire picture at the same instant. The staggered sequence introduced by 2-3 pulldown is responsible for the irregular spacing of the film sample lines. In video, sampling is delayed as the scan proceeds down the field; this is reflected in the slant of the lines in the figure.

In deinterlacing for a dedicated display, the output frame rate can be locked to the input video field rate of 59.94 Hz or 50 Hz. But in desktop computing applica-

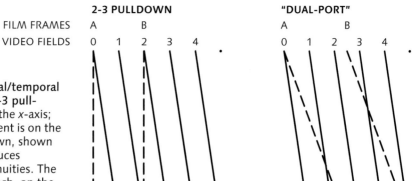

	2-3 PULLDOWN						"DUAL-PORT"				
FILM FRAMES	A	B					A	B			
VIDEO FIELDS	0	1	2	3	4		0	1	2	3	4

Figure 34.3 **Vertical/temporal relationships of 2-3 pulldown.** Time is on the *x*-axis; vertical displacement is on the *y*-axis. 2-3 pulldown, shown on the left, introduces temporal discontinuities. The "dual-port" approach, on the right, introduces spatial discontinuities.

tions of deinterlacing, the output is generally higher than 60 Hz, and asynchronous to the video rate: The output rate cannot be forced to match the native video rate. In this case, progressive reading from memory is faster than, and asynchronous to, the interlaced writing. If a single framestore is used, at some point the "fast" read pointer will cross the "slow" write pointer. If a "pointer crossing" event occurs on a scan line containing an element in motion, a spatial disturbance will be introduced into the picture. These disturbances can be prevented by using three fields of memory.

Figure 34.4 overleaf shows the effect in the spatial domain. Two intact film frames are shown at the left. The 2-3 pulldown technique introduces temporal irregularity into the video sequence, shown in the center column of five video fields, but the individual images are still intact. The result of the naive framebuffer approach is shown the right column: Spatial discontinuities are introduced into two of the five fields. With conversion from 24 Hz to 60 Hz, depending on the phase alignment of film and video, either two or three discontinuities will be evident to the viewer. With conversion from film at 24 Hz to video at 59.94 Hz, the discontinuities will drift slowly down the screen.

Using a pair of buffers – *double buffering* – and synchronizing the writing and reading of the buffers with the start of the film and video frames, keeps each frame intact and removes the spatial discontinuities. However, the delays involved in this technique reintro-

FILM   VIDEO, 2-3 PULLDOWN   VIDEO, "DUAL-PORT"

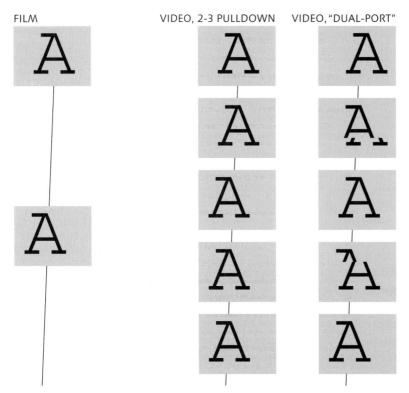

Figure 34.4 **2-3 pulldown, spatial view.** These sketches show
the effect on the picture of two schemes to transfer film frames
at 24 Hz, shown in the left column, into five video fields at
60 Hz. The center column shows the result of 2-3 pulldown.
The right column shows the naive approach of writing into
a framebuffer at film rate and reading at video rate.

duce exactly the same temporal stutter as 2-3 pulldown!

Although 2-3 pulldown introduces a temporal artifact into the video stream, acceptable motion portrayal
is obtained when the 2-3 video is displayed at video
rate. However, if the frame rate is altered a second
time, temporal artifacts of the two cascaded conversions may become objectionable, especially when the
image is displayed with a wide picture angle.

In video that carries a carefully done film transfer,
video pictures ending with timecode digits 0 or 5 correspond to A-frames of the film source. Apart from
A-frame-locked timecode, there are no standards that
convey, along with a video signal, information
concerning film origination. Absent locked timecode,

SMPTE RP 197, *Film-to-Video
Transfer List.*

SMPTE RP 201, *Encoding Film
Transfer Information Using Vertical
Interval Time Code.*

the only way to detect 2-3 pulldown is to compare data in successive fields: If two successive first fields contain luma and chroma that are identical, within a certain noise tolerance, and the repeat pattern follows the characteristic 2-3 sequence, then the material can be assumed to have originated from film. Once the original film frames have been identified, conversion to the ultimate display rate can be accomplished with minimal introduction of motion artifacts. Identifying film frames using this method is feasible for dedicated hardware, but it is difficult for today's desktop computers.

Native 24 Hz coding

Traditionally, 2-3 pulldown is imposed in the studio, at the point of transfer from film to video. The repeated fields are redundant, and consume media capacity to no good effect except compatibility with native 60 field-per-second equipment: When movies were recorded on media such as VHS tape, fully 20% of the media capacity was wasted. In the studio, it is difficult to recover original film frames from a 2-3 sequence. Information about the repeated fields is not directly available; decoding equipment typically attempts to reconstruct the sequence by comparing pixel values in successive fields.

MPEG-2 coding can handle coding of progressive material at 24 frames per second; it is inefficient to encode a sequence with 2-3 pulldown. Some MPEG-2 encoders are equipped to detect, and remove, 2-3 pulldown, so that 24 progressive frames per second are encoded. However, this process – called *inverse telecine* – is complex and trouble-prone.

Ordinarily, repeated fields in 2-3 pulldown are omitted from an MPEG-2 bitstream. However, the bitstream can include flags that indicate to the decoder that the omitted fields should be repeated at the display; with these flags, a decoder can reconstruct the 2-3 sequence for display at 59.94 Hz. Alternatively, when configured for progressive output, the decoder can reconstruct 23.976 Hz frames and present them directly to suitable display equipment, or frame-triple to 72 Hz (actually, $72/_{1.001}$ or about 71.928 Hz) at the output. All this complexity is avoided in Blu-ray, which can directly code 23.976 Hz progressive frames.

Although MPEG-2 itself permits 23.967 Hz or 24 Hz native frame rate, DVD doesn't. Film material on 480*i* DVDs must be coded as 59.94 Hz interlaced. Flags identify film frames to the decoder, which then either inserts 2-3 pulldown for 480*i*29.97 output or – if configured to do so – outputs 480*p*23.976. See *Frame rate and 2-3 pulldown in MPEG*, on page 518.

Conversion to other rates

In 2-3 pulldown from 24 Hz to 60 Hz, information from successive film frames is replicated in the fixed sequence {2, 3, 2, 3, 2, 3, …}. The frequency of the repeat pattern – the *beat frequency* – is fairly high: The {2, 3} pattern repeats 12 times per second, so the beat frequency is 12 Hz. The ratio of frame rates in this case is $\frac{5}{2}$ – the small integers in this fraction dictate the high beat frequency.

When PCs are to display 29.97 Hz video that originated on film – from sources such as DVD or digital satellite – the situation is more complicated, and motion impairments are more likely to be introduced.

In conversion to a rate that is related to 24 Hz by a ratio of larger integers, the frequency of the repeated pattern falls. For example, converting to 75 Hz involves the fraction $\frac{25}{8}$; this creates the sequence {3, 3, 3, 3, 3, 3, 3, 4}, which repeats three times per second. Converting to 76 Hz involves the fraction $\frac{17}{6}$; this creates the sequence {2, 3, 3, 3, 3, 3}, which repeats four times per second. The susceptibility of the human visual system to motion artifacts peaks between 4 and 6 beats per second; the temporal artifacts introduced upon conversion to 75 Hz or 76 Hz are likely to be quite visible. Motion estimation and motion-compensated interpolation could potentially be used to reduce the severity of these conversion artifacts, but these techniques are highly complex, and will remain out of reach for desktop computing for several years.

When 24 Hz material is to be displayed in a computing environment with wide viewing angle and good ambient conditions, the best approach to minimize motion artifacts is to choose a display rate that is an integer multiple of 24 Hz. Displaying at 60 Hz reproduces the situation with video display, and we know well that the motion portrayal is quite acceptable.

Deinterlacing 35

In *Interlaced format,* on page 88, I explained that when a scene element in motion relative to the camera is captured by an interlaced camera, the scene element appears at different positions in the two fields. Reconstruction of progressive frames is necessary for certain image-processing operations, such as upconversion, downconversion, or standards conversion. Also, computer imagery is typically represented in progressive format: Integrating video imagery into computer displays also requires deinterlacing. This chapter outlines deinterlacing techniques.

I will introduce deinterlacing in the spatial domain. Then I will describe the vertical-temporal domain, and outline practical deinterlacing algorithms.

I will discuss the problem of deinterlacing, and the algorithms, in reference to the test scene sketched in Figure 35.1. The test scene comprises a black background, partially occluded by a white disk that is in motion with respect to the camera.

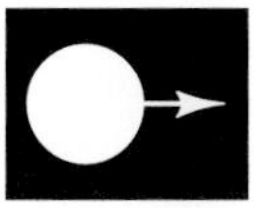

Figure 35.1 **Test scene**

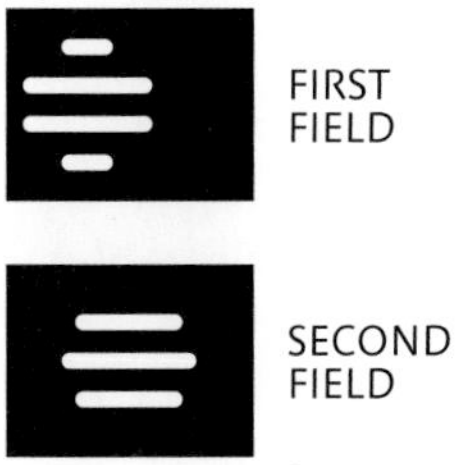

Figure 35.2 **Interlaced capture** samples the position of a football about 60 times per second; frames are produced at half that rate. (A soccer ball takes 50 positions per second.)

Spatial domain

Video captures 50 or 60 unique fields per second. If a scene contains an object in motion with respect to the camera, each field will carry half the spatial information of the object, but the information in the second field will be displaced according to the object's motion. The situation is illustrated in Figure 35.2, which shows the first and second fields, respectively. The example is typical of capture by a CCD camera set for a short exposure time; the example neglects capture blur due to nonzero exposure time at the camera. (For details of

POYNTON, CHARLES (1996), "Motion portrayal, eye tracking, and emerging display technology," in *Proc. 30th SMPTE Advanced Motion Imaging Conference*: 192-202.

temporal characteristics of image acquisition and display, see my SMPTE paper.)

You can think of an interlaced video signal as having its lines in permuted order, compared to a progressive signal. An obvious way to accomplish deinterlacing is to write into two fields of video storage – the first field, then the second – in video order, then read out the assembled frame progressively (in spatial order). This method is sometimes given the sophisticated name *field replication,* or *weave.* This method is quite suitable for a stationary scene, or a scene containing only slow-moving elements. However, image data of the second field is delayed by half the frame time (typically $\frac{1}{60}$ s or $\frac{1}{50}$ s) with respect to image data of the first field. If the scene contains an element in fairly rapid motion (such as the disk in our test scene), and image data is interpreted as belonging to the same time instant, then *field tearing* will be introduced: The scene element will be reproduced with jagged edges, either when viewed as a still frame or when viewed in motion. The effect is sketched in Figure 35.3.

Figure 35.3 **The weave technique** stitches two fields into a frame. When applied to moving objects, it produces the "field tearing," "mouse's teeth," or "zipper" artifact.

Field tearing can be avoided by *intrafield* processing, using only information from a single field of video. The simplest intrafield technique is to replicate each line upon progressive readout. A disadvantage is that this method will reproduce a stationary element with at most half of its potential vertical resolution. Also, line replication introduces a blockiness into the picture, and an apparent downward shift of one image row. The effect is sketched in Figure 35.4.

Figure 35.4 **Line replication**

The blockiness of the line replication approach can be avoided by synthesizing information that is apparently located spatially in the opposite field, but located temporally coincident with the same field. This can be accomplished by averaging vertically adjacent samples in one field, to create a synthetic intermediate line, as depicted in Figure 35.5. (In the computer industry, this is called "bob.") The averaging can be done prior to writing into the video memory, or upon reading, depending on which is more efficient for the memory system. Averaging alleviates the disadvantage of blockiness, but does not compensate the loss of vertical resolution. Nonetheless, the method performs well for VHS-grade images, which lack resolution in any case. Rather

Figure 35.5 **Interfield averaging**

DIGITAL VIDEO AND HD ALGORITHMS AND INTERFACES

For a modest improvement over 2-tap averaging, use 4 taps with coefficients [$\frac{1}{16}$, $\frac{7}{16}$, $\frac{7}{16}$, $\frac{1}{16}$].

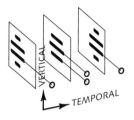

Figure 35.6 *V·T development*

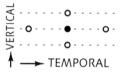

Figure 35.7 *V·T domain*

Figure 35.8 **Static lattice in the *V·T* domain** (weave)

Figure 35.9 **Interframe averaging in the *V·T* domain**

than simply averaging two lines, improved performance can be attained by using longer FIR filters with suitable tap weights; see *Filtering and sampling,* on page 191.

Vertical-temporal domain

Interlace-to-progressive conversion can be considered in the vertical-temporal (*V·T*) domain. Figure 35.6 in the margin sketches the interlaced capture fields of Figure 35.2, in a three-dimensional view. Viewed from the "side," along the axis of the scan lines, the vertical-temporal domain is projected. The temporal samples are at discrete times corresponding to the field instants; the vertical samples are at discrete intervals of space determined by the scan-line pitch. The four open disks of Figure 35.6 represent samples of original picture information that are available at a certain field instant and line number. A calculation on these samples can synthesize the missing sample value at the center of the pattern. In the diagrams to follow, the reconstructed sample will be drawn as a filled disk. (A similar calculation is performed for every sample along the scan line at the given vertical and temporal coordinate: For BT.601 digital video, the calculation is performed 720 times per scan line.)

In Figure 35.7, I sketch the vertical-temporal domain, now in a two-dimensional view. Conversion from interlace to progressive involves computing some combination of the four samples indicated by open disks, to synthesize the sample at the center of the four (indicated by the filled disk). Techniques utilizing more than these four samples are possible, but involve more complexity than is justified for desktop video.

In Figure 35.8, I sketch the field replication (or *weave*) technique in the *V·T* domain. The sample to be computed is simply copied from the previous field. The result is correct spatially, but if the corresponding area of the picture contains an element in motion, tearing will be introduced, as indicated in Figure 35.3.

Instead of copying information forward from the previous field, the previous field and the following field can be averaged. This approach is sketched in Figure 35.9. This technique also suffers from a form of field tearing, but it is useful in conjunction with an adaptive approach to be discussed in a moment.

Figure 35.10 **Line replication in the *V·T* domain** ("bob")

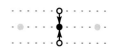

Figure 35.11 **Intrafield averaging in the *V·T* domain**

WESTON, MARTIN (1988), U.S. Patent 4,789,893, *Interpolating Lines of Video Signals*.

The line replication technique is sketched in the *V·T* domain in Figure 35.10. The central sample is simply copied from the line above. Because the copied sample is from the same field, no temporal artifacts are introduced. The line replication technique causes a downward shift of one image row. The shift is evident from Figure 35.4: The disk in the test scene is vertically centered, but in Figure 35.4 it appears off-center.

Intrafield averaging – what some people call the *bob* technique – is sketched in Figure 35.11. The central sample is computed by averaging samples from lines above and below the desired location. The information being averaged originates at the same instant in time, so no temporal artifact is introduced. Also, the one-row downward shift of line replication is avoided. However, the vertical resolution of a static scene is reduced.

Martin Weston of the BBC found that excellent deinterlacing was possible using two fields and four lines of storage, without adaptivity, using carefully chosen coefficients. His filter coefficients are shown in Table 35.1; the highlighted cell corresponds to the result:

Image row	Field $t-1$	Field t	Field $t+1$
$i-4$	32		32
$i-3$		−27	
$i-2$	−119		−119
$i-1$		539	
i	174	•	174
$i+1$		539	
$i+1$	−119		−119
$i+1$		−27	
$i+1$	32		32

Table 35.1 **Weston deinterlacer** comprises a vertical-temporal FIR filter having the indicated weights, each divided by 1024. The position marked in red is computed. No adaptivity is used.

Motion adaptivity

Analyzing the conversion in the *V·T* domain suggests that an improvement could be made by converting stationary scene elements using the static technique, but converting elements in motion using line averaging. This improvement can be implemented by detecting, for each result pixel, whether that pixel is

Figure 35.12 **Interstitial** spatial filter coefficients

Figure 35.13 **Cosited** spatial filter coefficients

likely to belong to a scene element in motion. If the element is likely to be in motion, then intrafield averaging is used (avoiding spatial artifacts). If the element is likely to be stationary, then interfield averaging is used (avoiding resolution loss).

Motion can be detected by comparing one field to a previous field. Ideally, a like field would be used – if motion is to be estimated for field 1, then the previous field 1 should be used as a point of reference. However, this approach demands that a full framestore be available for motion detection. Depending on the application, it may suffice to detect motion from the opposite field, using a single field of memory.

Whether a field or a frame of memory is used to detect motion, it is important to apply a spatial lowpass filter to the available picture information, in order to prevent small details, or noise, from causing abrupt changes in the estimated motion. Figure 35.12 shows the coefficients of a spatial lowpass filter that computes a spatial sample halfway between the scan lines. The shaded square indicates the effective location of the result. This filter requires a linestore (or a dual-ported memory). The weighted sums can be implemented by three cascaded [1, 1] sections, each of which requires a single adder.

A low-pass filtered sample cosited (spatially coincident) with a scan line can be computed using the weights indicated in Figure 35.13. Again, the shaded square indicates the central sample, whose motion is being detected. This filter can also be implemented using just linestores and cascaded [1, 1] sections. The probability of motion is estimated as the absolute value of the difference between the two spatial filter results.

The spatial filters of Figure 35.12 and Figure 35.13 incorporate transverse filters having coefficients [1, 4, 6, 4, 1]. These particular coefficients enable implementation using cascaded [1, 1]-filters. The 2-line spatial filter of Figure 35.12 can be implemented using a linestore, two [1, 4, 6, 4, 1] transverse filters, and an adder. The 3-line spatial filter of Figure 35.13 can be implemented using two linestores, three [1, 4, 6, 4, 1] transverse filters – one of them having its result doubled to implement coefficients 2, 8, 12, 8, 2 – and two adders.

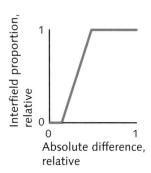

Figure 35.14 **A window function** in deinterlacing

A simple adaptive filter switches from interframe averaging to interfield averaging when the motion estimate exceeds some threshold. However, abrupt switching can result in artifacts: Two neighboring samples may have very similar values, but if one is judged to be stationary and the other judged to be in motion, the samples computed by the deinterlace filter may have dramatically different values. These differences can be visually objectionable. These artifacts can be reduced by mixing proportionally – in other words, fading – between the interframe and interfield averages instead of switching abruptly. Mixing can be controlled by a window function of the motion difference, as sketched in Figure 35.14 in the margin.

Further reading

Bellers and de Haan have written the definitive book on deinterlacing techniques. The book concentrates on techniques patented by Philips and available in VLSI from NXP. A summary of deinterlacing techniques is found in de Haan and Braspenning's chapter in Madisetti's book.

BELLERS, ERWIN B. and DE HAAN, GERARD (2000), *De-interlacing: A key technology for scan rate conversion* (Elsevier/North-Holland).

DE HAAN, GERARD and BRASPENNING, RALPH (2010), "Video Scanning Format Conversion and Motion Estimation," in MADISETTI, VIJAY K., *The digital signal processing handbook,* Second edition, Vol. 2 (Boca Raton, Fla., U.S.A.: CRC Press/Taylor & Francis).

Colourbars 36

ANSI/EIA-189-A, *Encoded Color Bar Signal* (formerly denoted EIA RS-189-A).

SMPTE EG 1, *Alignment Color Bar Test Signal for Television Picture Monitors*.

PLUGE is pronounced *ploodge*.

SD colourbars

Figure 36.1 below is a sketch of an image produced by the classic SMPTE colourbar test pattern. The upper $\frac{2}{3}$ of the image contains a 100% white bar followed by primary and secondary colours of 75% saturation. The narrow, central region contains "reverse bars"; this section enables setting composite NTSC or PAL decoder HUE and CHROMA. The bottom $\frac{1}{4}$ of the image contains subcarrier frequency at $-I$ phase, a white bar, subcarrier frequency at $+Q$ phase, and (at the right) the PLUGE element, which I will describe in a moment.

Figure 36.2 overleaf shows the $R'G'B'$ components that produce the upper $\frac{2}{3}$ of the frame of SMPTE colourbars. Each scan line is based upon a binary sequence of red, green, and blue values either zero or unity. The components are arranged in order of their contributions to luma, so that the eventual luma component decreases from left to right. (The narrow band $\frac{2}{3}$ of the way down SMPTE bars has its count

Figure 36.1 **The SMPTE EG 1 SD colourbar test signal** is represented here as an image; however, it is standardized as a signal in the $R'G'B'$ domain. Its colour interpretation depends upon the primary chromaticities in use. The corresponding $Y'C_BC_R$ or $Y'P_BP_R$ waveforms depend upon luma coefficients and scaling.

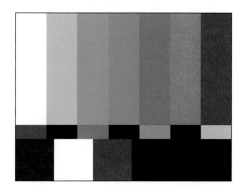

Figure 36.2 **Colourbar** *R'G'B'* **primary components** in SMPTE colourbars have amplitude of 75 IRE, denoted 75/0/75/0. A variation denoted 100/0/75/0, whose *R'*, *G'*, and *B'* waveforms are sketched here, places the white bar at 100 IRE. Other variations have different amplitudes for the uncoloured and coloured bars.

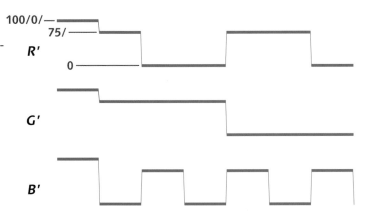

See the section *UV components* of *Composite NTSC and PAL: Legacy Video Systems.* Strictly speaking, owing to negative AM video modulation, an NTSC transmitter would *under*modulate if presented with composite video level exceeding 120%.

sequence reversed and its green component forced to zero.)

In studio equipment, in component video, and in PAL broadcast, the processing, recording, and transmission channels can accommodate all encoded signals that can be produced from mixtures of *R'G'B'* where each component is in the range 0 to 1. The *100%* colourbar signal exercises eight points at these limits.

Fully saturated yellow and fully saturated cyan cause a composite PAL signal to reach a peak value $^4/_3$ (133 $^1/_3$%) of reference white. However, an NTSC transmitter's composite signal amplitude is limited to 120% of reference white. If 100% bars were presented to an NTSC transmitter, clipping would result. To avoid clipping, *75%* bars are ordinarily used to test NTSC transmission. The white bar comprises primaries at 100%, but the other bars have their primary components reduced to 75% so as to limit their composite NTSC peak to the level of reference white. The "75% bars" convention was adopted for good reason, but analog NTSC transmitters have been decommissioned; the convention remains in use for no good reason.

R'G'B' components of 100% colourbars take *R'G'B'* (or *RGB*) values of zero or unity, independent of the chromaticity of the primaries: Owing to differences in primary chromaticities, the exact colours of the bars are not identical among SMPTE, EBU, and HD standards.

SD colourbar notation

ITU-R Rec. BT.471, *Nomenclature and description of colour bar signals.*

I have referred to 100% and 75% colourbars. Several additional variations of colourbars are in use, so many that an international standard is required to denote them. A colourbar signal is denoted by four numbers, all in units (formerly, IRE units), separated by slashes. The first pair of numbers gives the maximum and minimum values (respectively) of the primary components in uncoloured bars – that is, the black or white bars. The second pair gives the maximum and minimum primary values (respectively) in the coloured bars.

The 100% bars, described earlier, are denoted 100/0/100/0. That variation is useful in the studio, in all forms of component video, and in PAL transmission. In legacy 480*i* composite NTSC systems where 7.5% setup is used, *100% bars* refers to 100/7.5/100/7.5. That variation was once useful in the studio. However, as I explained on page 420, terrestrial analog NTSC transmission cannot handle 100% bars. NTSC transmitters are tested using 75% bars with setup, denoted 100/7.5/75/7.5. Japan uses 480*i* video with zero setup; there, 75% bars, denoted 100/0/75/0, are used.

PLUGE element

The lower-right quadrant of the colourbar pattern contains elements produced by *picture line-up generating equipment* (PLUGE); see Figure 36.3. The acronym originates with the "generating equipment," but nowadays PLUGE signifies the signal element. Superimposed on reference black are two elements, one slightly more negative than reference black, the other slightly more positive.

A display's BLACK LEVEL is adjusted so that the first (negative-going) element is just barely indistinguishable from reference black. (The second element should then be barely visible.) Details are found in *Black level setting,* on page 56. The negative-going element of PLUGE cannot be represented in positive R'G'B'.

In SD, ±4% PLUGE was standardized in the now-withdrawn SMPTE EG 1. However, SMPTE RP 219 standardizes PLUGE for HD with 8-bit interface codes 44, 64, 84, and 104 – that is, approximately –2%, +2%, and +4%.

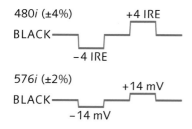

Figure 36.3 **The PLUGE element** of the colourbar signal enables accurate setting of black level. The 14 mV excursion in 576*i* PLUGE is equivalent to ±2 units.

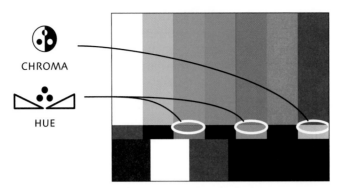

Figure 36.4 **HUE and CHROMA are adjusted** in a composite NTSC decoder using the colourbar test image, using a "blue-only" display. The controls are adjusted until the indicated transitions disappear.

Composite decoder adjustment using colourbars

When composite NTSC or PAL colourbars are decoded, the amount of blue decoded from the white, cyan, magenta, and blue bars should ideally be identical. Any chroma gain (saturation) error will affect the signal decoded from blue, but not the blue decoded from white. Chroma phase error will cause hue errors of opposite direction in the blue decoded from cyan and the blue decoded from magenta. To manually adjust a decoder's HUE and CHROMA (or TINT and COLOUR, or PHASE and SATURATION) controls involves displaying composite SMPTE colourbars, and disabling the red and green components at the decoder output. The amount of blue decoded from each of cyan and magenta is equalized by adjusting the decoder's HUE control. The amount of blue decoded from each of grey and blue is equalized by adjusting CHROMA. The comparison is facilitated by the reversed bar portion of SMPTE colourbars. Figure 36.4 shows a representation of the colourbar image, showing the bars that are visually compared while adjusting HUE and CHROMA.

If the red and green guns at the display cannot be turned off, a similar effect can be accomplished by viewing the CRT through a blue gel filter.

Adjusting HUE and CHROMA controls in this way is only meaningful to compensate errors in NTSC and PAL decoding. In component video such as $R'G'B'$ and $Y'C_BC_R$, no recording or transmission impairment rotates hue or alters chroma (saturation): Using the scheme described above is nonsensical.

−I, +Q, and PLUGE elements in SD colourbars

The −I and +Q elements correspond to $R'G'B'$ values of [−0.3824, 0.1088, 0.4427] and [0.2483, −0.2589, 0.6817], respectively; and to 10-bit $^{601}Y'C_BC_R$ values [0, 228, −244] and [0, 345, 159]. To produce RGB-legal codes having the same hue and saturation as −I and +Q, and having minimum luma, use $R'G'B'$ values [0, 0.2456, 0.412545] and [0.253605, 0, 0.470286], respectively. See SMPTE RP 219.

The lower-left quadrant of the SMPTE colourbar pattern contains subcarrier frequency components at −I and +Q phase. These elements were designed to exercise the encoding and decoding axes of the original NTSC chroma modulation method (circa 1953). Encoding and decoding on I and Q axes fell into disuse around 1970, being replaced by encoding and decoding on the $B'-Y'$ and $R'-Y'$ axes, so the utility of this portion of the signal is now lost. The historical −I and +Q elements contain high chroma resting upon black. These combinations correspond to illegal mixtures of $R'G'B'$ where one component is dramatically negative; consequently, the −I and +Q elements are not representable in the positive $R'G'B'$ domain.

The −I element, the +Q element, and the negative-going element of PLUGE are generated synthetically. None of these elements represents picture information; none is useful in evaluating pictures; and none can be generated in − or survive transit through − the positive $R'G'B'$ domain between 0 and 1 (or 0 and 255, or even 16 through 235 or 64 through 940 if footroom is clipped).

In fact, it is not just the −I, +Q, and PLUGE elements of colourbars that are synthetic: The entire signal is generated synthetically! We call it the colourbar *signal*, not the colourbar *image*, because the −I, +Q, and PLUGE elements cannot be represented in nonnegative RGB components. The colourbar signal represents values of $R'G'B'$ as if they came from a gamma-corrected camera and were inserted prior to an encoder. $R'G'B'$ values of colourbars are implicitly gamma-corrected.

HD colourbars

SMPTE RP 219, *High-Definition, Standard-Definition Compatible Color Bar Signal*.

Figure 36.1 overleaf is a sketch of an image produced by the SMPTE colourbar test pattern for HD.

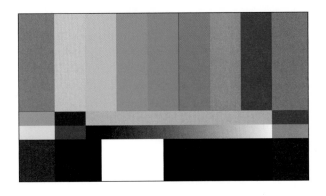

Figure 36.5 **The SMPTE RP 219 SD colourbar test signal** is used for HD.

DIGITAL VIDEO AND HD ALGORITHMS AND INTERFACES

Part 4

Studio standards

37 Reference display and viewing conditions 427

38 SDI and HD-SDI interfaces 429

39 480*i* component video 445

40 576*i* component video 457

41 1280×720 HD 467

42 1920×1080 HD 473

44 Component analog HD interface 485

43 HD videotape 481

Reference display

and viewing conditions 37

Historically, the video industry has been lax in setting standards for studio video reference displays. Over the next few years, as fixed-pixel displays (FPDs) reach studio quality levels and see deployment as reference displays, that situation has to change. As I write, standards groups within EBU, SMPTE, and ITU-R are working to remedy these deficiencies. However, given the absence today of official standards, I am writing the remainder of this chapter as if it is the missing standard. This chapter attempts to codify current practice in 2011, as exemplified by CRT "broadcast video monitors." In my view, LCDs are not yet studio-grade. Changes will be necessary to accommodate mastering of wide-gamut colour and/or high dynamic range.

Introduction

The reference display converts an $R'G'B'$ video signal to light – characterized by CIE tristimulus values according to CIE 15 – as if through an additive RGB process. (A reference display need not physically use additive mixing providing that it behaves as an additive RGB device as far as its operation is observed externally.)

Signal interface

$R'G'B'$ video signal values herein are normalized to reference black at value 0 and reference white at value 1. Signal values below 0 are clipped to 0. Signal values up to the fraction $^{955}/_{876}$ of reference white are accommodated; signal values beyond $^{955}/_{876}$ shall be clipped to $^{955}/_{876}$. (Various video standards define mappings into integers; for example, 10-bit digital video encoding according to ITU-R BT.709 includes scaling by 876 and offset of +64; reference black is represented as $R'G'B'$ signal code 64, reference white as signal code 940, and peak white as signal code 1019.)

Reference primaries, black, and white	Reference red, green, blue, black, and white tristimuli shall have the chromaticities specified by BT.709. The reference white signal [1, 1, 1] shall display luminance of 100 cd·m^{-2}. The reference black signal [0, 0, 0] shall display relative luminance denoted β preferably 0.0003 but not exceeding 0.001, of the reference white luminance. Reference white and reference black shall be measured according to ITU-R BT.815.
Reference EOCF	Across the range of each $R'G'B'$ signal component value (denoted V) from reference black to peak white, reference tristimulus value of the associated primary (denoted T), relative to reference white, computed according to SMPTE RP 177 shall be:

Eq 37.1
$$T = (1-\beta)\,(\text{MAX}[0,\ b+(1-b)\cdot V])^{2.4} + \beta,\ b \approx 0.035,\ \beta \leq 0.0003$$

The parameter b takes a value of approximately 0.035, to be determined according to operational practice of setting BLACK LEVEL. (The gain factor of $(1-\beta)$ establishes reference white at unity. Resulting peak white luminance is approximately 122 cd·m^{-2}. The power function exponent 2.4 conforms to BT.1886.)

Reference viewing conditions

The environment of the reference display – including the display surface and its surround – shall have illuminance of 2π lx (approximately 6 lx) at CIE D$_{65}$ chromaticity. The reference display shall be surrounded by approximately Lambertian neutral grey having diffuse reflectance factor of 0.5. (These conditions yield 1% very dim surround.) The surround should extend horizontally across an angle corresponding to three picture widths and vertically across an angle corresponding to three picture heights.

References

CIE 15:2004, *Colorimetry,* Third Edition (2004).

ITU-R BT.709-5, *Parameter values for the HDTV standards for production and international programme exchange* (2002).

ITU-R BT.815-1, *Specification of a signal for measurement of the contrast ratio of displays* (1994-07).

ITU-R BT.1886, *Reference electro-optical transfer function for flatpanel displays used in HDTV studio production* (2011).

SMPTE RP 177, *Derivation of Basic Television Color Equations* (1993).

Composite $4f_{SC}$ digital interfaces are obsolete. For details about them, consult the first edition of this book.

This chapter describes digital interfaces for uncompressed and compressed SD and HD. Tables 38.1 and 38.2 summarize video signal levels.

Interface	Ref. black	Ref. white
Abstract signal, mathematical	0	1
Abstract signal, units ("IRE")	0	100
Analog NTSC [mV]	$53\,^4/_7$	$714\,^2/_7$
Analog NTSC-J [mV]	0	$714\,^2/_7$
Analog PAL [mV]	0	700
Analog VGA [mV], zero setup	0	700
7.5-percent setup	$53\,^4/_7$	$714\,^2/_7$

Table 38.1 **Analog video levels** in several interfaces are summarized.

Interface	−Peak non-SDI black	−Peak SDI black	Ref. black	Ref. white	+Peak SDI white	+Peak non-SDI white
8-bit computing ("IT," e.g., sRGB)			0	255		
Studio video interface, 8-bit ("CE")	0	1	16	235	254	255
10-bit	0	4	64	940	1019	1023
Studio video processing, 8-bit	−16	−15	0	219	254	255
10-bit	−64	−60	0	876	955	959
Digital cinema interface, 12-bit	0	16[a]	0	3960[b]	3960	3960

Table 38.2 **Digital video levels** in several interfaces are summarized.

a True reference black in digital cinema cannot be conveyed across an HD-SDI interface: The minimum interface code yields black tristimulus value of $(^{16}/_{3960})^{2.6}$, or about 0.000 000 6, negligibly different from ideal black.

b Peak white code is indicated for digital cinema as 3960: This is for the coded luminance (Y') channel. The other two channels (X' and Z') have peak values 3794 and 3890 respectively.

Component digital SD interface (BT.601)

ITU-R Rec. BT.601, adopted in 1984, specifies abstract coding parameters (including 4:2:2 chroma subsampling) for 480*i*29.97 and 576*i*25 SD. Luma is sampled at 13.5 MHz; C_B and C_R colour difference components are horizontally subsampled by a factor of 2:1 with respect to luma – that is, sampled at 6.75 MHz each. Samples are multiplexed in the sequence {C_B, Y_0', C_R, Y_1'}. Sync information and optional ancillary data is multiplexed; 10-bit words at 27 MW/s are then serialized for a total bit rate of 270 Mb/s. The external interface is called the *serial digital interface* (SDI); it uses coaxial cable and BNC connectors.

Sampling at 13.5 MHz produces a whole number of samples per total line (S_{TL}) in 480*i* systems (with 858 S_{TL}) and 576*i* systems (with 864 S_{TL}). Both 480*i* and 576*i* have 720 active luma samples per line (S_{AL}). In uncompressed, 8-bit BT.601 video, the active samples consume about 20 MB/s.

The notation *4:2:2* originated as a reference to the chroma subsampling scheme that I outlined on page 124. During the 1980s, 4:2:2 denoted a specific SD component digital video interface standard incorporating 4:2:2 chroma subsampling. In the 1990s, the 4:2:2 chroma subsampling format was adopted for HD; as a result, the notation *4:2:2* came to be independent of image size.

The notations BT.601 and BT.656 have fallen into disuse in studio video. However, desktop video hardware designers often use "Rec. 601" or "BT.601" to denote a parallel interface having separate wires for vertical and horizontal sync signalling, and "Rec. 656" or "BT.656" to denote a parallel interface wherein vertical and horizontal sync are represented by embedded TRS codes.

Figure 38.1 at the top of the facing page shows the luma (or *R'*, *G'*, or *B'*) waveform of a single scan line of 480*i* component video. The time axis shows sample counts at the BT.601 rate of 13.5 MHz; divide the sample number by 13.5 to derive time in microseconds. Amplitude is shown in millivolts (according to EBU Tech. N10 levels), and in 8-bit BT.601 digital interface code values.

ITU-R Rec. BT.601-5, *Studio encoding parameters of digital television for standard 4:3 and widescreen 16:9 aspect ratios.*

BT.601 originated with 8-bit components, anticipating 10 bits.

Recall from page 124 that in 4:2:2 BT.601, C_B and C_R are *cosited* – each is centered on the same location as Y_j', where *j* is even; chroma samples are absent when *j* is odd.

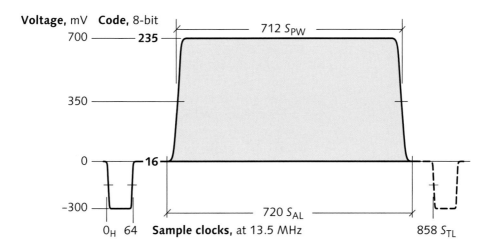

Figure 38.1 **Scan-line waveform for 480i29.97, 4:2:2 component luma.** EBU Tech. N10 analog levels are shown; however, these levels are rarely used in 480i. In analog video, sync is *blacker-than-black*, at –300 mV. (In digital video, sync is not coded as a signal level.) This sketch shows 8-bit interface levels (in bold); black is at code 16 and white is at code 235. The 720 active samples contain picture information; the remaining 138 sample intervals of the 858 comprise horizontal blanking.

Digital video interfaces convey active video framed in *timing reference signal* (TRS) sequences including *start of active video* (SAV) and *end of active video* (EAV). Ancillary data (ANC) and digitized ancillary signals are permitted in regions not occupied by active video. Figure 38.2 below shows the raster diagram of Chapter 8, augmented with EAV, SAV, and the HANC and VANC regions. Details will be presented in *SDI and HD-SDI sync, TRS, and ancillary data,* on page 433.

Figure 38.2 **The BT.656 component digital interface** uses EAV to signal the start of each horizontal blanking interval, and SAV to signal the start of active video. Between EAV and SAV, ancillary data (HANC) can be carried. In a nonpicture line, the region between SAV and EAV can carry ancillary data (VANC). Digitized ancillary signals may be carried in lines other than those that convey either VANC or analog sync.

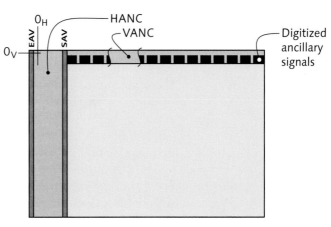

Serial digital interface (SDI)

SMPTE 259M, *10-Bit 4:2:2 Component and 4f$_{SC}$ Composite Digital Signals – Serial Digital Interface.*

Serial digital interface (SDI) refers to a family of interfaces standardized by SMPTE. The BT.601 or $4f_{SC}$ data stream is serialized, then subjected to a scrambling technique. SMPTE ST 259 standardizes several interfaces, denoted by letters A through D as follows:

• Composite $4f_{SC}$ NTSC video, about 143 Mb/s
• Composite $4f_{SC}$ PAL video, about 177 Mb/s
• BT.601 4:2:2 component video, 270 Mb/s (This interface is standardized in BT.656.)
• BT.601 4:2:2 component video sampled at 18 MHz to achieve 16:9 aspect ratio, 360 Mb/s

All but scheme C are now obsolete.

SDI is standardized for electrical transmission through coaxial cable, and for transmission through optical fiber. The SDI electrical interface uses ECL levels, 75 Ω impedance, BNC connectors, and coaxial cable. Electrical and mechanical parameters are specified in SMPTE standards and in BT.656; see *SDI coding* on page 439. Fiber-optic interfaces for digital SD, specified in SMPTE 297M, are straightforward adaptations of the serial versions of BT.656.

Component digital HD-SDI

The basic coding parameters of HD systems are standardized in BT.709. Various scanning systems are detailed in several SMPTE standards referenced in Table 15.2, on page 145.

Component SD, composite $4f_{SC}$ NTSC, and composite $4f_{SC}$ PAL all have different sample rates and different serial interface bit rates. In HD, a uniform sample rate of 74.25 MHz is adopted (modified by the ratio $1000/1001$ in applications where compatibility with 59.94 Hz frame rate is required). A serial interface bit rate of 20 times the sampling rate is used. Variations of the same standard accommodate mainstream 1080*i*30, 1080*p*24, and 720*p*60 scanning; 1080*p*30; and the obsolete 1035*i*30 system. The integer picture rates 24, 30, and 60 can be modified by the fraction $1000/1001$, giving rates of 23.976 Hz, 29.97 Hz, and 59.94 Hz.

The SDI interface at 270 Mb/s has been adapted to HD by scaling the bit rate by a factor of 5.5, yielding a fixed bit rate of 1.485 Gb/s. The sampling rate and serial bit rate for 23.976 Hz, 29.97 Hz, and 59.94 Hz

The 23.976 Hz, 29.97 Hz, and 59.94 Hz frame rates are associated with a sampling rate of:

$$\frac{74.25}{1.001} \approx 74.176 \text{ Mpx/s}$$

The corresponding HD-SDI serial interface bit rate is:

$$\frac{1.485}{1.001} \approx 1.483 \text{ Gb/s}$$

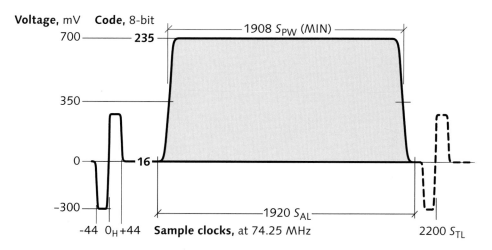

Voltage, mV   **Code,** 8-bit

Figure 38.3 **Scan-line waveform for 1080i30 HD component luma.** Analog trilevel sync is shown, excursing ±300 mV. (In digital video, sync is not coded as a signal level.) At an 8-bit interface, black is represented by code 16 and white by 235. The indicated 1920 active samples contain picture information; the remaining sample intervals of the 2200 total comprise horizontal blanking.

interfaces are indicated in the margin. This interface is standardized for $Y'C_BC_R$, subsampled 4:2:2. Dual-link HD-SDI can be used to convey R'G'B'A, 4:4:4:4.

HD-SDI accommodates 1080i25 and 1080p25 variants that might find use in Europe. This is accomplished by placing the 1920×1080 image array in a scanning system having 25 Hz rate. S_{TL} is altered from the 30 Hz standard to form an 1125/25 raster.

See Figure 15.2, on page 144.

The standard HD analog interfaces use trilevel sync, instead of the bilevel sync that is used for analog SD. Figure 38.3 above shows the scan-line waveform, including trilevel sync, for 1080i30 HD.

The HD-SDI interface is standardized in SMPTE ST 292. Fiber-optic interfaces for digital HD are also specified in SMPTE ST 292.

SMPTE ST 292, *Bit-Serial Digital Interface for High-Definition Television Systems*.

SDI and HD-SDI sync, TRS, and ancillary data

Along with picture information, a streaming interface needs to convey information about which time instants – or which digital samples – are associated with the start of each frame and the start of each line. In digital video, this information is conveyed by *timing reference signals* (TRS) that I will explain in this chapter.

SDI has the capacity to transmit ancillary (ANC) data. The *serial data transport interface* (SDTI) resembles SDI, but has no uncompressed active video – instead, the full data capacity of the link is dedicated to carrying ANC packets. Compressed digital video can be conveyed in these packets. SDTI will be described on page 441.

The IEEE 1394/DV interface, described on page 167, and the DVB-ASI interface, to be described on page 443, have no ancillary data and do not use TRS.

Standard serial interfaces transmit 10-bit samples; a transmitter must present all 10 bits at the interface (even if the two LSBs are zero).

TRS and ANC sequences are introduced by 10-bit codewords 0 and $3FF_h$. Stemming from legacy parallel interfaces such as SMPTE RP 125 and EBU Tech. 3246, a receiver must ignore the two LSBs in identifying TRS and ANC. Apart from their use to delimit TRS and ANC, codewords 0, 1, 2, 3, and $3FC_h$, $3FD_h$, $3FE_h$, and $3FF_h$ are prohibited from digital video data.

TRS in 4:2:2 SD-SDI

In *Component digital SD interface (BT.601),* on page 430, I explained that 4:2:2 samples are multiplexed in the sequence $\{C_B, Y_0', C_R, Y_1'\}$ onto the SDI. BT.601 defines the abstract signal coding parameters; BT.656 defines the interface.

Active luma samples are numbered from zero to $S_{AL}-1$; active chroma samples are numbered from zero to $(S_{AL}/2)-1$. The interface transmits two words for each luma sample clock: Even-numbered words convey chroma samples; odd-numbered words convey luma samples. The sample structure aligns with 0_H: If analog sync were digitized, a particular digitized luma sample would precisely reflect the 50% value of sync.

In 4:2:2 video, a four-word TRS sequence immediately precedes active video, indicating *start* of *active video* (SAV). SAV is followed by C_B sample zero. Immediately following the last active sample of the line is another four-word TRS sequence, *end* of *active video* (EAV). The TRS sequence comprises a word of all ones (codeword $3FF_h$), a word of all zeros, another word of all zeros, and finally a word including flag bits F (Field), V (Vertical), H (Horizontal), P_3, P_2, P_1, and P_0 (Parity). SAV is indicated by $H = 0$; EAV has $H = 1$.

Table 38.3 shows the elements of TRS.

I use the subscript h to denote a hexadecimal (base 16) integer. Sample values in this chapter are expressed in 10 bits.

The V and H bits are asserted during the corresponding blanking intervals. The F bit denotes field, not frame.

Word	Value	MSB 9	8	7	6	5	4	3	2	1	LSB 0
0	$3FF_h$	1	1	1	1	1	1	1	1	1	1
1	0	0	0	0	0	0	0	0	0	0	0
2	0	0	0	0	0	0	0	0	0	0	0
3		1	F	V	H	P_3	P_2	P_1	P_0	0	0

Table 38.3 **Timing reference sequence (TRS)** for 4:2:2 comprises 4 codewords. Start of active video (SAV) is indicated by $H = 0$; end of active video (EAV) has $H = 1$. For compatibility with 8-bit equipment, the 2 LSBs are ignored in decoding TRS.

Value		F	V	H	$P_3=$ $V{\oplus}H$	$P_2=$ $F{\oplus}H$	$P_1=$ $F{\oplus}V$	$P_0=F{\oplus}$ $V{\oplus}H$		
200_h	1	0	0	0	0	0	0	0	0	0
274_h	1	0	0	1	1	1	0	1	0	0
$2AC_h$	1	0	1	0	1	0	1	1	0	0
$2DB_h$	1	0	1	1	0	1	1	0	0	0
$31C_h$	1	1	0	0	0	1	1	1	0	0
368_h	1	1	0	1	1	0	1	0	0	0
380_h	1	1	1	0	1	1	0	0	0	0
$3C4_h$	1	1	1	1	0	0	0	1	0	0

Table 38.4 **Protection bits for SAV and EAV** are computed as the exclusive-or ($\oplus$) of various combinations of F, V, and H. The code can correct 1-bit errors, and can detect 2-bit errors. The error-correction capability was arguably useful for the parallel interface. However, it is useless for SDI, because a single-bit error in the SDI bitstream, when descrambled, corrupts up to 5 bits.

In BT.601-4 (1994) and in SMPTE RP 125-1992, in 480*i* systems, an SAV with $V=0$ could occur prior to the first active (picture) line – as early as line 10 or line 273. To be compatible with legacy equipment, do not rely upon the 1-to-0 transition of V.

The F and V bits change state in the EAV prior to the start of the associated line; rather than calling it EAV, you might call it *start of horizontal interval.* In interlaced systems, F is asserted during the second field. In 480*i* systems, F changes at lines 4 and 266; in other scanning systems, including 576*i* and HD, F changes state at line 1. In progressive systems, F is always zero (except in 483*p*59.94, where F encodes frame parity.)

The vertical blanking (V) bit is zero in every line that is defined by the associated scanning standard to contain active (picture) video; it is asserted elsewhere – that is, in the vertical interval.

The F, V, and H bits are protected by parity bits P_3, P_2, P_1, and P_0, formed as indicated in Table 38.4 by an exclusive-or across two or three of F, V, and H.

SMPTE ST 348, *High Data-Rate
Serial Data Transport Interface
(HD-SDTI).*

SMPTE standards are inconsistent in their numbering of words outside the active region. EAV functions as the start of a digital line with regard to state changes to the F and V bits, so I number words from 0 at EAV. In this scheme, SAV starts at word $S_{TL}-S_{AL}-4$. Another reason for numbering EAV as word 0 is that the proposed SMPTE standard for HD-SDTI anticipates a scheme to advance the timing of SAV codes. Word and sample numbering is strictly notational: Neither word nor sample numbers appear at the interface.

The horizontal blanking interval at the interface, from EAV to SAV, can contain ancillary data (HANC). In each active (picture) line, the interval from SAV to EAV contains active video. Outside the active picture lines, the interval between SAV and EAV can be used for ancillary data (VANC) packets. If a line outside the active picture is not carrying VANC, and the line isn't associated with analog sync elements, the interval from SAV to EAV can carry a digitized ancillary signal coded like active video. Intervals not used for EAV, SAV, active video, digitized ancillary signals, or ancillary (ANC) data are filled by alternating codes {chroma 200_h, luma 40_h}, which, in active picture, would represent blanking.

TRS in HD-SDI

HD-SDI is similar to 4:2:2 SD SDI; however, the single link carries two logical streams, one carrying chroma, the other carrying luma. Each stream has TRS sequences; independent ANC packets can be carried in each stream. The two streams are word multiplexed; the multiplexed stream is serialized and scrambled. Four words indicated in Table 38.5 at the top of the facing page are appended to each EAV. Each bit 9 is the complement of bit 8. Words 4 and 5 convey line number (LN0, LN1). Words 6 and 7 provide CRC protection for the stream's active video. Each stream has a CRC generator that implements a characteristic function $x^{18}+x^5+x^4+1$. Each generator is reset to zero immediately after SAV, and accumulates words up to and including LN1.

Word	Value	MSB 9	8	7	6	5	4	3	2	1	LSB 0
4	LN0	$\overline{L_6}$	L_6	L_5	L_4	L_3	L_2	L_1	L_0	0	0
5	LN1	1	0	0	0	L_{10}	L_9	L_8	L_7	0	0
6	CR0	$\overline{CRC_8}$	CRC_8	CRC_7	CRC_6	CRC_5	CRC_4	CRC_3	CRC_2	CRC_1	CRC_0
7	CR1	$\overline{CRC_{17}}$	CRC_{17}	CRC_{16}	CRC_{15}	CRC_{14}	CRC_{13}	CRC_{12}	CRC_{11}	CRC_{10}	CRC_9

Table 38.5 **Line number and CRC in HD-SDI** comprises four words immediately following EAV; the package is denoted EAV+LN+CRC. Bit 9 of each word is the complement of bit 8. Line number is coded in 11 bits, L_{10} through L_0, conveyed in two words. The CRC covers the first active sample through the line number. An HD-SDI interface conveys two streams, each including EAV+LN+CRC and SAV sequences; one stream carries chroma-aligned words, the other carries luma-aligned words.

Analog sync and digital/analog timing relationships

In analog interlaced video, 0_V denotes the start of either field. In digital video, 0_V for the second field is unimportant; some people use 0_V to denote the start of a frame.

In analog video, sync is conveyed by video levels "blacker than black." Line sync is achieved by associating, with every scan line, a line sync (horizontal) datum denoted 0_H (pronounced *zero-H*) defined at the midpoint of the leading (falling) edge of sync. Field and frame sync is achieved by associating, with every field, a vertical sync datum denoted 0_V (pronounced *zero-V*).

Sync separation recovers the significant timing instants associated with an analog video signal. *Genlock* reconstructs a sampling clock.

The relationship between the digital and analog domains is established by the position of 0_H with respect to some TRS element. Table 38.6 overleaf summarizes several standards for digital representation of component 4:2:2 video; the rightmost column gives the number of luma sample intervals between the first word of EAV and the 0_H sample (if it were digitized).

Ancillary data

To determine whether a line that is a candidate for a digitized ancillary signal actually contains such a signal, examine every chroma/luma pair for {200_h, 40_h}: If any pair is unequal to these values, a digitized ancillary signal is present.

In 4:2:2 SD, and in HD, ancillary data is permitted immediately after any EAV (HANC), or immediately after SAV (VANC) on a line containing neither active picture nor digitized ancillary data. (In 576*i*, ancillary data is limited to lines 20 through 22 and 333 through 335.) An ancillary packet is introduced by an ancillary data flag (ADF) comprising the three-word sequence {0, $3FF_h$, $3FF_h$}.

System	AR	Scanning	Standard	S_{TL}	S_{AL}	EAV to 0_H
483*i*29.97		525/59.94/2:1	SMPTE 125M, BT.601	858	720	12
576*i*25		625/50/2:1	EBU 3246, BT.601	864	720	16
483*i*29.97	16:9	525/59.94/2:1	SMPTE 267M, BT.601	1144	960	16
483*p*59.94	16:9	525/59.94/1:1	SMPTE 293M	1144	960	16
576*i*25	16:9	625/50/2:1	EBU 3246, BT.601	1152	960	21
720*p*60	16:9	750/60/1:1	SMPTE ST 296	1650	1280	110
1080*i*30	16:9	1125/60/2:1	SMPTE ST 274	2200	1920	88
1080*p*30	16:9	1125/30/1:1	SMPTE ST 274	2200	1920	88
1080*p*25	16:9	1125/25/1:1	SMPTE ST 274	2640	1920	192
1080*p*24	16:9	1125/24/1:1	SMPTE ST 274	2750	1920	192

Table 38.6 **Digital to analog timing relationships.** for several scanning standards are summarized. The rightmost column relates TRS to 0_H; it gives the count of luma sample intervals from EAV word 0 ($3FF_h$) to the 0_H sample (if it were digitized).

SMPTE ST 291, Ancillary Data Packet and Space Formatting.

An ANC packet must not interfere with active video, or with any TRS, SAV, or EAV. Multiple ANC packets are allowed, provided that they are contiguous. Certain ANC regions are reserved for certain purposes; consult SMPTE ST 291.

An ancillary packet comprises the three-word (4:2:2) or one-word ($4f_{SC}$) ADF, followed by these elements:

• A one-word *data ID* (DID)
• A one-word *data block number* (DBN) or *secondary DID* (SDID)
• A one-word *data count* (DC), from 0 to 255
• Zero to 255 *user data words* (UDW)
• A one-word checksum (CS)

Each header word – DID, DBN/SDID, and DC – carries an 8-bit value. Bit 8 of each header word is parity, asserted if an odd number of bits 7 through 0 is set, and deasserted if an even number of bits is set. Bit 9 is coded as the complement of bit 8. (Codewords having 8 MSBs all-zero or all-one are thereby avoided; this prevents collision with the 0_h and $3FF_h$ codes used to introduce TRS and ANC sequences.)

Two types of ANC packet are differentiated by bit 7 of the DID word. If DID_7 is asserted, the packet is Type 1; DID is followed by data block number (DBN). There are 128 DID codes available for Type 1 packets.

DIGITAL VIDEO AND HD ALGORITHMS AND INTERFACES

The DBN value indicates continuity: If zero, it is inactive; otherwise, it counts packets within each DID from 1 through 255, modulo 255.

If DID_7 is negated, the packet is Type 2: The DID is followed by a secondary data ID (SDID), giving $127 \cdot 255$ (i.e., 32,385) ID codes for Type 2 packets.

Three DID values, 004_h, 008_h, and $00C_h$ indicate a Type 2 ANC packet coded with 8-bit data; other DID values in the range 001_h through $00F_h$ are prohibited. DID 80_h marks a packet for deletion. DID 84_h marks the last ANC packet in a VANC or HANC region.

The data count (DC) word contains a value from 0 through 255 (protected by two parity bits), indicating the count of words in the user data area. The DC word spans all ten bits of the interface. Even if an 8-bit DID is indicated, SMPTE standards imply that the two least significant bits of the DC word are meaningful. (If they were not, then the count of user data words could not be uniquely determined.)

The checksum (CS) word provides integrity checking for the contents of an ancillary packet. In every word from DID through the last word of UDW, the MSB is masked out (to zero); these values are summed modulo 512. The 9-bit sum is transmitted in bits 8 through 0 of CS; bit 9 is coded as the complement of bit 8.

SDI coding

In the serial interface it is necessary for a receiver to recover the clock from the coded bitstream. The coded bitstream must therefore contain significant power at the coded bit rate. Coaxial cable attenuates high-frequency information; equalization is necessary to overcome this loss. Because equalizers involve high-frequency AC circuits, the coded bitstream should contain little power at very low frequencies: The code must be *DC-free*. To enable economical equalizers, the frequency range required for correct recovery of the signal should be as small as possible. A ratio of the highest to lowest frequency components of about 2:1 – where the coded signal is contained in one octave of bandwidth – is desirable. These considerations argue for a high clock rate. But it is obviously desirable to have

Details of the application of SDI in the studio are found in Chapter 7 of ROBIN, MICHAEL, and MICHEL POULIN (2000), *Digital Television Fundamentals: Design and Installation of Video and Audio Systems,* Second Edition (New York: McGraw-Hill).

**Figure 38.4
BNC connector**

SMPTE ST 292, *Bit-Serial Digital Interface for High-Definition Television Systems.*

a low clock rate so as to minimize cost. The choice of a clock rate is a compromise between these demands.

SDI uses scrambled coding, where the data stream is serialized, then passed through a shift register arrangement with exclusive-or taps implementing a characteristic function $x^9 + x^4 + 1$.

Scrambling techniques using a single scrambler are well known. But the SDI and HD-SDI scrambler has a second-stage scrambler, whose characteristic function is $x + 1$. The two cascaded stages offer improved performance over a conventional single-stage scrambler. The scrambling technique is self-synchronizing; there is no need for initialization.

The data rate at the interface is the word rate times the number of bits per word. It is standard to serialize 10-bit data; when coding 8-bit video, the two LSBs are forced to zero.

No provision is made to avoid data sequences that would result, after serialization and scrambling, in serial bit sequences with long runs of zeros or long runs of ones. But a long run of zeros or ones provides no signal transitions to enable a receiver to recover the clock! In practice, such *pathological sequences* are rare.

SDI is standardized for electrical transmission at ECL levels through coaxial cable, using a BNC connector as depicted in Figure 38.4. Distances between 200 m and 400 m are practical. SDI is also standardized for transmission through optical fiber. Fiber-optic interfaces for digital SD are straightforward adaptations of SDI.

HD-SDI coding

The SDI interface at 270 Mb/s was adapted to HD by scaling the bit rate by a factor of 5.5, yielding a bit rate of 1.485 Gb/s (or in 24.976, 29.97, or 59.94 Hz systems, $^{1.485}/_{1.001}$ Gb/s) – call these both "1.5 Gb/s." HD-SDI is standardized in SMPTE ST 292. The interface is modeled after SD SDI, but there are two significant changes:

• Chroma and luma are encoded in separate streams, each with its own TRS sequence. The streams are multiplexed, then scrambled.

• Coded line number and a CRC are appended to the EAV portion of the TRS sequence (giving what is called EAV+LN+CRC).

In 1080*i* and 1080*p* standards documents, samples are numbered with respect to 0$_H$ (unlike SD standards documents, where samples are numbered with respect to the zeroth active sample of the line).

Further developments doubled the data rate of the 1.5 Gb/s interface to about 3 Gb/s (sometimes termed 3G-SDI). That rate is sufficient to carry 1080*i*30 at 4:4:4:4 (that is, no chroma subsampling and an alpha component) or 1080*p*60 at 4:2:2.

Interfaces for compressed video

Compressed digital video interfaces are impractical in the studio owing to the diversity of compression systems, and because compressed interfaces would require decompression capabilities in signal processing and display equipment. Compressed 4:2:2 digital video studio equipment is usually interconnected through uncompressed SDI interfaces.

Compressed interfaces can be used to transfer video into nonlinear editing systems, and to "dub" (duplicate) between VTRs sharing the same compression system. Compressed video can be interfaced directly using *serial data transport interface* (SDTI), to be described in a moment. The DVB ASI interface is widely used to convey MPEG-2 transport streams in network or transmission applications (but not in production). The IEEE 1394/DV interface, sometimes called *FireWire* or *i.LINK*, is widely used in the consumer electronics arena, and is beginning to be deployed in broadcast applications.

SDTI

SMPTE ST 305.2, *Serial Data Transport Interface*.

SMPTE has standardized a derivative of SDI, *serial data transport interface* (SDTI), that transmits arbitrary data packets in place of uncompressed active video. SDTI can be used to transport DV25, DV50, DV100, and Sony MPEG IMX compressed datastreams. Despite DV bitstreams being standardized, different manufacturers have chosen incompatible techniques to wrap their compressed video data into SDTI streams. This renders SDTI useful only for interconnection of equipment from a single manufacturer.

Switching and mixing

Switching or editing between video sources – "cutting" – is done in the vertical interval, so that each frame of the resulting video remains intact, without any switching transients. When switching between two signals in a hardware switcher, if the output signal is to be made continuous across the instant of switching, the input signals must be synchronous – the 0_V instants of both signals must match precisely in time. To prevent switching transients from disturbing vertical sync elements, switching is done somewhat later than 0_V; see SMPTE RP 168.

Timing in digital facilities

FIFO: First in, first out.

Modern digital video equipment has, at each input, a buffer that functions as a FIFO. The buffer at each input accommodates an advance of timing at that input (with respect to reference video) of up to several line times. Timing a digital facility involves advancing each signal source so that signals from all sources arrive in time at the inputs of the facility's main switcher. This timing need not be exact; it suffices to guarantee that no buffer overruns or underruns. When a routing switcher switches among SDI streams, a timing error of several dozen samples is tolerable; downstream equipment will recover timing within one or two lines after the instant of switching.

When a studio needs to accommodate an asynchronous video input – one whose frame rate is within tolerance, but whose phase cannot be referenced to house sync, such as a satellite feed – then a *framestore synchronizer* is used. This device contains a frame of memory that functions as a FIFO buffer for video. An input signal with arbitrary timing is written into the memory with timing based upon its own sync elements. The synchronizer accepts a reference video signal; the memory is read out at rates locked to the sync elements of the reference video. (Provisions are made to adjust SYSTEM PHASE – that is, the timing of the output signal with respect to the reference video.) An asynchronous signal is thereby delayed up to one frame time, perhaps even a little more, so as to match the local reference. The signal can then be used as if it were a local source.

Studio video devices commonly incorporate framestores, and exhibit latency of a field, a frame, or more. Low-level timing of such equipment is accomplished by introducing time advance so that 0_V appears at the correct instant. However, even if video content is timed correctly with respect to 0_V, it may be late by a frame, or in a very large facility, by several frames. Attention must be paid to delaying audio by a similar time interval, to avoid lip-sync problems.

Some video switchers incorporate digital video effects (DVE) capability; a DVE unit necessarily includes a framestore.

ASI

Within a broadcast facility, an MPEG-2 transport stream can be serialized onto a dedicated *asynchronous serial interface* (ASI). A serialized ASI stream for broadcast has a payload bit rate of around 20 Mb/s; however, the ASI interface bit rate is 270 Mb/s, chosen so that SDI distribution infrastructure can be used. The ASI interface uses BNC connectors and coaxial cable. ASI is polarity sensitive (unlike SDI), though modern ASI receivers typically detect and correct polarity inversion.

ETSI EN 50083-9, *Cable networks for television signals, sound signals and interactive services – Part 9: Interfaces for CATV/SMATV headends and similar professional equipment for DVB/MPEG-2 transport streams.* Standards are not clear on whether transformer coupling is required or whether capacitive coupling suffices.

Although the SDI physical layer is used, the serialized ASI stream has no TRS codes and the interface does not use SDI scrambling. Instead, channel data is encoded according to the 8b/10b scheme borrowed from Fibre Channel standards. (ASI interface data rate is therefore at most 216 Mb/s.) An 8b/10b bitstream never has more than four consecutive 0s or 1s, so clock recovery is simple. An 8b/10b encoder minimizes low frequency ("DC") content on the media.

Some people write 8B/10B; however, the elements involved are bits, not bytes, so lowercase *b* is apt.

Since the ASI payload rate is typically far lower than the channel capacity, stuffing codes are inserted to occupy idle time. Stuffing codes – Fibre Channel *comma* codes, denoted *K28.5* – are inserted either at the earliest opportunity (bytewise, "spaced byte mode"), or at the completion of the current packet (packetwise, "burst mode"). MPEG packets are separated by at least two comma codes.

The *synchronous serial interface* (SSI) was standardized by SMPTE for the purpose of conveying MPEG transport streams between equipment, but SSI has largely fallen into disuse.

It is increasingly common to convey transport streams using IP protocols across Ethernet.

Summary of digital interfaces

Table 38.7 summarizes SD and HD digital interface standards.

ITU-R Rec. BT.656, *Interfaces for digital component video signals in 525-line and 625-line television systems operating at the 4:2:2 level of Recommendation ITU-R BT.601.*

SMPTE 125M, *Component Video Signal 4:2:2 – Bit-Parallel Digital Interface.*

SMPTE 259M, *10-Bit 4:2:2 Component and 4f_{SC} Composite Digital Signals – Serial Digital Interface.*

SMPTE 267M, *Bit-Parallel Digital Interface – Component Video Signal 4:2:2 16×9 Aspect Ratio.*

SMPTE ST 292, *Bit-Serial Digital Interface for High-Definition Television Systems.*

SMPTE ST 297, *Serial Digital Fiber Transmission System for ANSI/SMPTE 259M Signals.*

Table 38.7 **SD and HD interface standards**

480*i* component video 39

This chapter details the scanning, timing, sync structure, and picture structure of 480*i*29.97 (525/59.94/2:1) video. The scanning and timing information in this chapter applies to all variants of 480*i* video, both analog and digital. The sync information relates to component analog, composite analog, and composite digital systems.

Frame rate

$$f_{FR} = \frac{30}{1.001} \approx 29.97 \, Hz$$

480*i* video represents stationary or moving two-dimensional images sampled temporally at a constant rate of $\frac{30}{1.001}$ frames per second. For studio video, the tolerance on frame rate is normally ±10 ppm. In practice the tolerance applies to a master clock at a high frequency, but for purposes of computation and standards writing, it is convenient to reference the tolerance to the frame rate.

Interlace

$$f_H = \frac{9}{0.572} \approx 15.734 \, kHz$$

It is confusing to refer to fields as *odd* and *even*. Use *first field* and *second field* instead.

A frame is conveyed as a sequence of 525 horizontal raster lines of equal duration, uniformly scanned top to bottom and left to right. Scanning has 2:1 interlace to form a *first* field and a *second* field; scan lines in the second field are displaced vertically by half the vertical sampling pitch, and delayed temporally by half the frame time, from scanning lines in the first field. In MPEG-2 terms, the first field is the bottom field.

Lines are numbered consecutively throughout the frame, starting at 1.

Table 39.1 **480*i* line assignment**

Line number, first field (F = 0)	Line number, second field (F = 1)	V	Contents, left half	Contents, right half
	266 [3]		EQ	BR
4			BR	BR
	267 [4]		BR	BR
5			BR	BR
	268 [5]		BR	BR
6			BR	BR
	269 [6]		BR	EQ
7			EQ	EQ
	270 [7]		EQ	EQ
8			EQ	EQ
	271 [8]		EQ	EQ
9			EQ	EQ
	272 [9]		EQ	none
10–19		V = 0 §	Vertical interval video (10 lines)	
	273–282 [10–19]	V = 0 §	Vertical interval video (10 lines)	
20			Vertical interval video	
	283 [20]		Vertical interval video	
21			CC	
	284 [21]		CC	
22			Picture	
	285 [22]		Picture	
23–261		V = 0 (487 lines)	Picture (239 lines)	◊
	286–524 [23–261]		Picture (239 lines)	
262			Picture	
	525 [262]		Picture	
263			Picture	EQ
	‡1		EQ	EQ
‡264 [1]			EQ	EQ
	‡2		EQ	EQ
‡265 [2]			EQ	EQ
	‡3		EQ	EQ

EQ Equalization pulse
BR Broad pulse
CC Closed caption
[*n*] Line number relative to start of second field (deprecated)

§ *V* = 0 in RP 125-1992, and in the 480*i* version of BT.601-4 (1994); in later standards, *V* = 1 for these lines.

◊ The thick vertical bar at the right indicates lines carried in 480*i* or 480*p* MPEG-2 according to SMPTE RP 202. (The vertical center of the picture is located midway between lines 404 and 142.) Unfortunately, 480*i* DV systems digitize a range one image row up from this.

‡ In analog terminology, lines 1 through 3 are considered part of the first field; lines 264 and 265 are considered part of the second field.

Concerning closed captions, see ANSI/EIA/CEA-608-B, *Line 21 Data Services*.

For details concerning VITC line assignment, see SMPTE RP 164, *Location of Vertical Interval Timecode*.

Table 39.1 opposite shows the vertical structure of a frame in 480*i* video, and indicates the assignment of line numbers and their content.

In legacy equipment, the picture may start as early as line 20 or line 283. However, video on lines 21 and 284 is liable to be replaced by line 21 closed caption data upon NTSC transmission, so it is pointless to provide more than 483 picture lines in the studio. With the wide use of 480*i* DV and MPEG-2 systems, I argue that it is pointless to provide more than 480 lines; however, 483 lines were broadcast in analog NTSC.

Lines 10 through 21 and 273 through 284 may carry ancillary ("vertical interval") signals either related or unrelated to the picture. If *vertical interval timecode (VITC)* is used, it should be located on line 14 (277); a second, redundant copy can be placed on line 16 (279). Failing line 14, line 18 (281) is suggested. See *Vertical interval timecode (VITC)*, on page 402.

Line sync

Horizontal events are referenced to an instant in time denoted 0_H. In the analog domain, 0_H is defined by the 50%-point of the leading (negative-going) edge of each line sync pulse. In a component digital interface, the correspondence between sync and the digital information is determined by a *timing reference signal* (TRS) conveyed across the interface. (See *SDI and HD-SDI sync, TRS, and ancillary data,* on page 433.)

In an analog interface, every line commences at 0_H with the negative-going edge of a sync pulse. With the exception of vertical sync lines, which I will describe in a moment, each line commences with a *normal* sync pulse, to be described. Each line that commences with normal sync may contain video information. Every line that commences with a sync pulse other than normal sync maintains blanking level, except for the intervals occupied by sync pulses.

Field/frame sync

To define vertical sync, the frame is divided into intervals of halfline duration. Each halfline either contains no sync information or commences with the assertion of a sync pulse having one of three durations, each having a tolerance of ±0.100 μs:

EIA and FCC standards in the United States rounded the equalization pulse duration to two digits, to 2.3 µs, slightly less than the theoretical value of 2.35 µs. Equipment is usually designed to the letter of the regulation, rather than its intent.

Line 263 commences with a normal sync pulse and has an equalization pulse halfway through the line. Line 272 commences with an equalization pulse and remains at blanking with no sync pulse halfway through the line. For analog details, see Chapter 2, *Analog SD sync, genlock, and interface,* of *Composite NTSC and PAL: Legacy Video Systems.*

SMPTE RP 168, *Definition of Vertical Interval Switching Point for Synchronous Video Switching.*

• A *normal* sync pulse having a duration of 4.7 µs
• An *equalization* pulse having half the duration of a normal sync pulse
• A *broad* pulse, having a duration of half the line time less the duration of a normal sync pulse

Each set of 525 halflines in the field commences with a vertical sync sequence as follows:

• Six preequalization pulses
• Six broad pulses
• Six postequalization pulses

Vertical events are referenced to an instant in time denoted 0_V. In the analog domain, 0_V is defined by the first equalization pulse coincident with 0_H. Line number 1 is signalled by 0_V; lines count in interlaced time order (not spatial order) throughout the frame. 480*i* systems are exceptional in identifying 0_V and line 1 at the first equalization pulse: In 576*i*, and in HD, 0_V and line 1 are marked at the first broad pulse.

Historically, in the analog domain, 0_V was defined for each field by the 50%-point of the first equalization pulse; lines were numbered from 1 to 263 in the first field and from 1 to 262 in the second field. In the digital domain, the first field contains 262 lines and the second field contains 263 lines.

Figure 39.1 opposite shows details of the sync structure; this waveform diagram is the analog of Table 39.1, *480i line assignment,* on page 446.

When sync is represented in analog or digitized $4f_{SC}$ form, a raised-cosine transition having a risetime (from 10% to 90%) of 140±20 ns is imposed; the midpoint of the transition is coincident with the idealized sync.

Switching between video sources is performed in the vertical interval, to avoid disruption of sync or picture. Switching occurs 30±5 µs after 0_H of the first normal line of each field. In 480*i* systems, switching occurs midway through line 10. (If field 2 were dominant, switching would occur midway through line 273.)

R'G'B' EOCF and primaries

Picture information is referenced to linear-light primary red, green, and blue (*RGB*) tristimulus values, represented in abstract terms in the range 0 (reference black) to +1 (reference white).

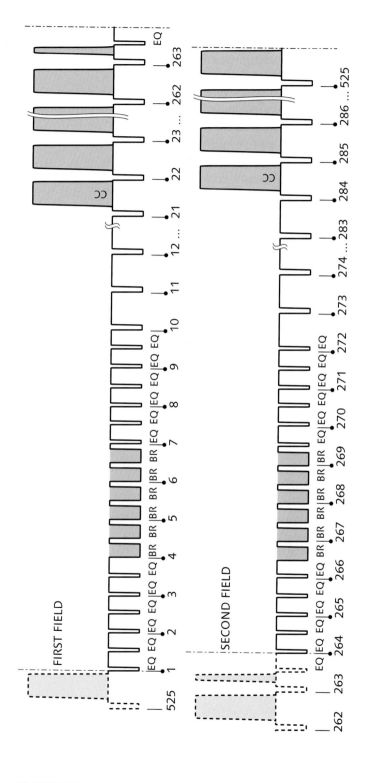

Figure 39.1 **480i raster, vertical.** This drawing shows the waveforms of the first and second fields, detailing the vertical sync intervals. CC indicates a line that may contain EIA 608 ("line 21") closed caption data.

Three nonlinear primary components R', G', and B'
are computed such that the intended image appearance is obtained on the reference display in the reference viewing conditions; see *Reference display and
viewing conditions,* on page 427.

In the default power-up state of a camera, the
nonlinear primary components are computed from the
camera's *RGB* tristimulus estimates according to the
opto-electronic conversion function of *BT.709 OECF,*
described on page 320; this process is loosely called
gamma correction.

The colorimetric properties of the display primaries
are supposed to conform to *BT.709 primaries* described
on page 290: DTV transmission standards call for
BT.709, and modern consumer displays use BT.709.
However, production and mastering of 480*i* content
historically used SMPTE primary chromaticities, not
BT.709 (see *SMPTE RP 145 primaries,* Table 26.5 on
page 293).

Luma (Y')

Luma in 480*i* systems is computed as a weighted sum
of nonlinear R', G', and B' primary components,
according to the luma coefficients of BT.601, as detailed
in *BT.601 luma,* on page 346:

$$^{601}Y' = 0.299\,R' + 0.587\,G' + 0.114\,B' \qquad \text{Eq 39.1}$$

The luma component Y', being a weighted sum of
nonlinear $R'G'B'$ components, has no simple relationship with CIE relative luminance (Y) used in colour
science. Video encoding specifications typically place
no upper bound on luma bandwidth (though transmission standards may).

Picture center, aspect ratio, and blanking

The center of the picture is located midway between
the central two of the 720 active samples of BT.601, at
the fraction $^{321}/_{572}$ between 0_H instants. Concerning
the vertical center, see Table 39.1, on page 446.

In 4:3 systems, the aspect ratio is defined to be 4:3
with respect to a *clean aperture* pixel array, 708 samples
wide at a sampling rate of 13.5 MHz, and 480 lines
high.

In *Transition samples,* on page 378, I mentioned that it is necessary to avoid, at the start of a line, an instantaneous transition from blanking to picture information. SMPTE standards call for picture information to have a risetime of 140±20 ns. For 480*i* or 576*i* video, a blanking transition is best implemented as a three-sample sequence where the video signal is limited in turn to 10%, 50%, and 90% of its full excursion.

No studio standard addresses square sampling of 480*i* video. I recommend using a sample rate of $780f_H$, that is, 12 $\overline{^{3}/_{11}}$ MHz (i.e., 12.272727 MHz). I recommend using 648 samples – or, failing that, 644 or 640 – centered as mentioned above.

SMPTE RP 202, *Video Alignment for MPEG-2 Coding.*

When MPEG-2 with 480 or 512 image rows is used in the studio, the bottom image row corresponds to line 525 (as indicated in Table 39.1). The bottom left-hand halfline (on line 263) is not among the coded image rows. Unfortunately, 480*i* DV systems digitize a range one image row up from this.

Halfline blanking

Most component video equipment treats the top and bottom lines of both fields as integral lines; blanking of halflines is assumed to be imposed at the time of conversion to analog. In composite equipment and analog equipment, halfline blanking must be imposed.

In the composite and analog domains, video information at the bottom of the picture, on the left half of line 263, should terminate 30.593 µs after 0_H. This timing is comparable to blanking at the end of a full line, but preceding the midpoint between 0_H instants instead of preceding the 0_H instant itself.

$$30.593 \approx \frac{63.55\overline{5}}{2} - \frac{732 - 716}{13.5}$$

Historically, in the composite and analog domains, a right halfline at the top of the picture – such as picture on line 284 – commenced about 41 µs after 0_H. This timing is comparable to blanking at the start of a full line, but following the midpoint between 0_H instants instead of following the 0_H instant itself. However, in NTSC broadcast, line 284 must remain available for closed captioning (along with line 21). So, it is now pointless for studio equipment to carry the traditional right-hand halfline of picture on line 284: Picture should be considered to comprise 482 full lines, plus a left-hand halfline on line 263.

$$41.259 \approx \frac{63.55\overline{5}}{2} + \frac{858 - 732 + 2}{13.5}$$

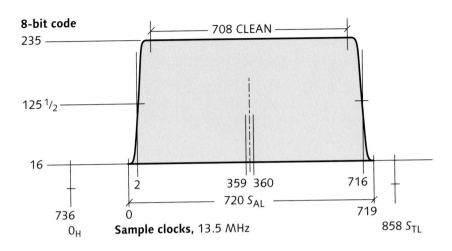

Figure 39.2 480*i* component
digital 4:2:2 luma waveform

Halfline blanking has been abolished from progressive scan video, and from JPEG, MPEG, and HD.

Component digital 4:2:2 interface

SDI was introduced on page 432. Eight-bit SD interfaces between digital ICs are often described as "601" (where horizontal and vertical sync signals are conveyed on dedicated wires) or "656" (where sync is embedded as TRS codes).

The C_B and C_R colour difference components of digital video are formed by scaling $B'-Y'$ and $R'-Y'$ components, as described in C_BC_R *components for SD* on page 361. $Y'C_BC_R$ signals are usually conveyed through the *serial digital interface* (SDI), which I introduced on page 432. $R'G'B'$ 4:4:4 (or $R'G'B'A$ 4:4:4:4) components can be conveyed across a dual-link interface using two SDI channels; alternatively, the single-link 540 Mb/s SDI interface of SMPTE 344M can be used.

In 13.5 MHz sampling of 480*i*, the sample located 16 sample clock intervals after EAV corresponds to the line sync datum (0_H): If digitized, that sample would take the 50% value of analog sync.

Figure 39.2 above shows a waveform drawing of luma in a 480*i* component digital 4:2:2 system.

Component analog R'G'B' interface

A component analog 480*i* R'G'B' interface is based on nonlinear R', G', and B' signals. Analog R',G', B' signals are conveyed as voltage, with a range of 1 V from synctip to reference white. (Transient excursions slightly above reference white are permitted.)

DIGITAL VIDEO AND HD ALGORITHMS AND INTERFACES

In studio systems, analog component $R'G'B'$ signals ideally have zero setup, so zero in Equation 39.2 corresponds to 0 V_{DC}. According to SMPTE 253M, unity corresponds to 700 mV. Sync is added to the green component according to Equation 39.2, where *sync* and *active* are taken to be unity when asserted and zero otherwise:

$$G'_{sync} = \frac{7}{10}\left(active \cdot G'\right) + \frac{3}{10}\left(-sync\right)$$

Eq 39.2

Sadly, the SMPTE $R'G'B'$ analog interface is unpopular, and "NTSC-related" levels are usually used, either with or without setup.

Some systems, such as 480i studio video in Japan, use a picture-to-sync ratio of 10:4 and zero setup. In this case, unity in Equation 39.3 corresponds to $\frac{5}{7}$ V, about 714 mV:

$$V'_{sync} = \frac{5}{7}\left(active \cdot V'\right) + \frac{2}{7}\left(-sync\right)$$

Eq 39.3

Many systems – such as computer framebuffers using the levels of the archaic EIA RS-343-A standard – code component video similarly to composite video, with 10:4 picture-to-sync ratio and 7.5% setup:

$$V'_{sync} = \frac{3}{56}\,active + \frac{37}{56}\left(active \cdot V'\right) + \frac{2}{7}\left(-sync\right)$$

Eq 39.4

Component analog $Y'P_BP_R$ interface, EBU N10

The P_B and P_R scale factors are appropriate only for component analog interfaces. For details concerning scale factors in component digital systems, see C_BC_R *components for SD*, on page 361. For details concerning scale factors in composite analog or digital NTSC or PAL, see *UV components*, in Chapter 5 of *Composite NTSC and PAL: Legacy Video Systems.*

The P_B and P_R colour difference components of analog video are formed by scaling $B'-Y'$ and $R'-Y'$ components, as described in P_BP_R *components for SD* on page 359. Wideband P_B and P_R components are theoretically possible but very rarely used; normally, P_B and P_R are lowpass filtered to half the bandwidth of luma.

Component $Y'P_BP_R$ signals in 480i are sometimes interfaced with zero setup, with levels according to the EBU Tech. N10 standard. Zero (reference blanking level) for Y', P_B, and P_R corresponds to a level of 0 V_{DC}, and unity corresponds to 700 mV. Sync is added to the luma

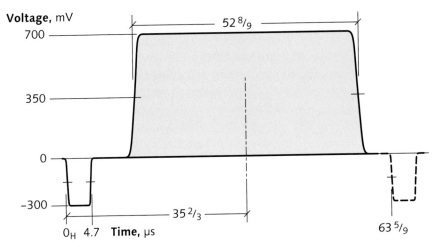

Figure 39.3 **480*i* component analog luma waveform** with SMPTE levels and zero setup.

component; *sync* is taken to be unity when asserted and zero otherwise:

$$Y'_{sync} = \frac{7}{10}Y' + \frac{3}{10}(-sync)$$

Eq 39.5

Figure 39.3 shows a waveform drawing of luma in a 480*i* component analog interface according to the EBU Tech. N10 standard. In North America, the levels of EBU N10 mysteriously became known as "SMPTE levels," or "SMPTE/EBU N10 interface," even though N10 is solely an EBU standard and SMPTE failed to standardize a component analog luma/colour difference interface.

CEA has standardized the 700 mV, zero-setup levels for use by consumer electronics devices such as DVD players and set-top boxes, for 480*i* and 480*p* formats at 4:3 and 16:9 aspect ratios.

In 2011, about a quarter of a century after the introduction of component analog video interfaces, CEA (with CEDIA, Custom Electronic Design and Installation Association) standardized the colours of the connectors to be used: green for *Y'*, blue for *C*$_B$, and red for *C*$_R$. (In the consumer domain, composite NTSC or PAL video is typically carried on a wire having yellow connectors.)

EIA/CEA-770.2, Standard Definition TV Analog Component Video Interface.

CEA/CEDIA-863-B, Connection Color Codes for Home Theater Systems.

Component analog $Y'P_BP_R$ interface, industry standard

Unfortunately, equipment from two manufacturers was deployed before SMPTE reached agreement on a standard component video analog interface for studio use. Although it is sometimes available as an option, the SMPTE standard is rarely used in 480i. Instead, two "industry" standards are in use: Sony and Panasonic. Ideally the $Y'P_BP_R$ nomenclature would signify that luma has zero setup, and that colour difference components have the same excursion (from black to white) as luma. However, both of the industry standards use setup, and neither gives the colour difference components the same excursion as luma.

Details are found in *Luma/colour difference component sets,* on page 352.

Sony SD equipment utilized 10:4 picture-to-sync ratio (roughly 714 mV luma, 286 mV sync) with 7.5% setup on luma (giving a picture excursion of $660\frac{5}{7}$ mV). Colour differences range $\frac{4}{3}$ times ±350 mV, that is, ±$466\frac{2}{3}$ mV. (75% colourbars have a P_BP_R excursion of ±350 mV.)

Panasonic SD equipment utilized 7:3 picture-to-sync ratio (exactly 700 mV luma, 300 mV sync) with 7.5% setup on luma (giving a picture excursion of 647.5 mV). Colour differences are scaled by the $\frac{37}{40}$ setup fraction, for an excursion of ±323.75 mV.

576i component video   40

This chapter details the scanning, timing, sync structure, and picture structure of 576i25 (625/50/2:1) video. The scanning and timing information here applies to all variants of 576i25 video, both analog and digital. The sync information relates to component analog, composite analog, and composite digital systems. I assume that you are familiar with 480i component video, described on page 445.

Frame rate

576i video represents stationary or moving two-dimensional images sampled temporally at a constant rate of 25 frames per second. For studio video, the tolerance on frame rate is normally ±4 ppm. In practice the tolerance applies to a master clock at a high frequency, but for purposes of computation and standards writing it is convenient to reference the tolerance to the frame rate.

Interlace

The derived line rate is 15.625 kHz.

It is confusing to refer to fields in 576i as *odd* and *even*. Use *first field* and *second field* instead.

A frame comprises a total of 625 horizontal raster lines of equal duration, uniformly scanned top to bottom and left to right with 2:1 interlace to form a *first* field and a *second* field. Scanning lines in the second field are displaced vertically by half the vertical sampling pitch, and delayed temporally by half the frame time, from scanning lines in the first field. In MPEG-2 terms, the first field is the top field.

Lines are numbered consecutively throughout the frame, starting at 1.

Table 40.1 **576i line assignment**

EQ   Equalization pulse

BR   Broad pulse

‡   Burst suppressed if −135° phase

§   Burst suppressed unconditionally

¶   In $4f_{SC}$ PAL, line recommended for 1137 S_{TL} ("reset")

†   VANC is permitted only on lines 20 through 22 and 333 through 335.

◊   The thick vertical bar at the right indicates lines carried in 576i or 576p MPEG-2 according to SMPTE RP 202. (The vertical center of the picture is located midway between lines 479 and 167.) Unfortunately, 576i DV systems digitize a range one image row up from this.

Line number, first field (F = 0)	Line number, second field (F = 1)	V	Contents, left half	Contents, right half
	¶313		EQ	BR
1			BR	BR
	314		BR	BR
2			BR	BR
	315		BR	BR
3			BR	EQ
	316		EQ	EQ
4			EQ	EQ
	317		EQ	EQ
5			EQ	EQ
	318		EQ	none
‡6			Vertical interval video	
	‡319		Vertical interval video	
7–18			Vertical interval video	
	320–331		Vertical interval video	
19			VITC	
	332		VITC	
†20			Vertical interval video	
	†333		Vertical interval video	
†21			VITC	
	†334		VITC	
†22			Quiet	
	†335		Quiet	
23			WSS	Picture ◊
	336–622	V = 0 (576 lines)	Picture (287 lines)	
24–‡310			Picture (287 lines)	
	§623		Picture	EQ
311			EQ	EQ
	624		EQ	EQ
312			EQ	EQ
	¶625		EQ	EQ

For details concerning VITC in 576*i*, see EBU Technical Standard N12, *Time-and-control codes for television recording.*

Table 40.1 opposite shows the vertical structure of a frame in 576*i* video, and indicates the assignment of line numbers and their content.

Lines 6 through 21 and 319 through 334 may carry ancillary ("vertical interval") signals either related or unrelated to the picture. If *vertical interval timecode* (VITC) is used, redundant copies should be placed on lines 19 (332) and 21 (334); see *Vertical interval timecode (VITC),* on page 402.

Line sync

Horizontal events are referenced to an instant in time denoted 0_H. In the analog domain, 0_H is defined by the 50%-point of the leading (negative-going) edge of each line sync pulse. In a component digital interface, the correspondence between sync and the digital information is determined by a *timing reference signal* (TRS) conveyed across the interface. (See *SDI and HD-SDI sync, TRS, and ancillary data,* on page 433.)

In an analog interface, every line commences at 0_H with the negative-going edge of a sync pulse. With the exception of the vertical sync lines of each field, each line commences with the assertion of a *normal* sync pulse, to be described. Each line that commences with normal sync may contain video information. Every line that commences with a sync pulse *other* than normal sync maintains blanking level, here denoted zero, except for the interval(s) occupied by sync pulses.

Analog field/frame sync

To define vertical sync, the frame is divided into intervals of halfline duration. Each halfline either contains no sync information, or commences with the assertion of a sync pulse having one of three durations, each having a tolerance of ±0.100 μs:
 • A *normal* sync pulse having a duration of 4.7 μs
 • An *equalization* pulse having half the duration of a normal sync pulse
 • A *broad* pulse having a duration of half the line time less the duration of a normal sync pulse

Each set of 625 halflines in the frame is associated with a vertical sync sequence, as follows:

Line 623 commences with a normal sync pulse and has an equalization pulse halfway through the line. Line 318 commences with an equalization pulse and remains at blanking with no sync pulse halfway through the line.

See Table 13.1, on page 132, and Figure Figure 2.2 and Figure 2.3 in Chapter 2 of *Composite NTSC and PAL: Legacy Video Systems*.

SMPTE RP 168, *Definition of Vertical Interval Switching Point for Synchronous Video Switching*.

- Five preequalization pulses
- Five broad pulses
- Five postequalization pulses

In analog sync, line 1 and 0_V are defined by the first broad pulse coincident with 0_H; see Figure 2.3 in Chapter 2 of *Composite NTSC and PAL: Legacy Video Systems*. (This differs from the 480*i* convention.)

Figure 40.1 opposite shows the vertical sync structure of 576*i* analog video. This waveform diagram is the analog of Table 40.1, *576i line assignment*, on page 458.

Sync in 576*i* systems has several differences from 480*i* sync. There are five preequalization, broad, and postequalization pulses per field (instead of six of each). The frame is defined to start with the field containing the top line of the picture, actually a right-hand halfline. (In 480*i* scanning, the first picture line of a frame is a full line, and the right-hand halfline at the top of the picture is in the second field.)

In 576*i* systems, lines are numbered starting with the first broad sync pulse: preequalization pulses are counted at the end of one field instead of the beginning of the next. This could be considered to be solely a nomenclature issue, but because line numbers are encoded in digital video interfaces, the issue is substantive. In 576*i* systems, lines are always numbered throughout the frame.

When sync is represented in analog or digitized form, a raised-cosine transition having a risetime (from 10% to 90%) of 200±20 ns is imposed, where the midpoint of the transition is coincident with the idealized sync.

Switching between video sources is performed in the vertical interval, to avoid disruption of sync or picture. Switching occurs 30±5 µs after 0_H of the first normal line of each field. In 576*i* systems, switching occurs midway through line 6. (If field 2 were dominant, switching would occur midway through line 319.)

R'G'B' EOCF and primaries

Picture information is referenced to linear-light primary red, green, and blue (*RGB*) tristimulus values, represented in abstract terms in the range 0 (reference black) to +1 (reference white).

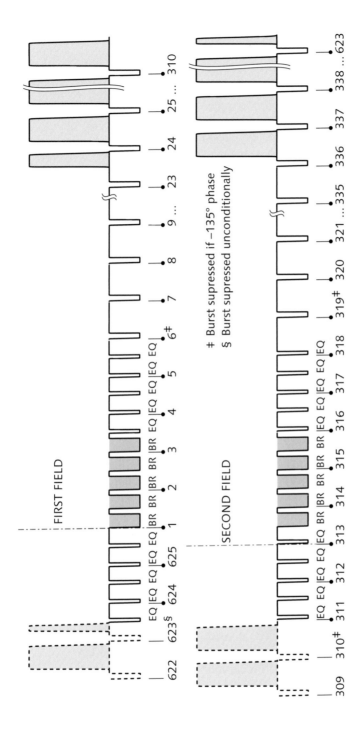

‡ Burst supressed if −135° phase
§ Burst supressed unconditionally

Figure 40.1 **576i raster, vertical.** This drawing shows the waveforms of the first and second fields, detailing vertical sync intervals. The first field comprises 312 lines, and the second field comprises 313 lines.

Historical PAL standards documents indicate a "precorrection" (OECF) with a $\frac{1}{2.8}$-power (approximately 0.36); however, that value is unrealistic. In practice, the BT.1886 EOCF value of $\frac{1}{2.4}$ is used. See *Gamma in video* on page 318.

Three nonlinear primary components R', G', and B' are computed such that the intended image appearance is obtained on the reference display in the reference viewing conditions (see *Reference display and viewing conditions,* on page 427).

In the default power-up state of a camera, the nonlinear primary components are computed from the camera's *RGB* tristimulus estimates according to the opto-electronic conversion function of the BT.709 OECF, described on page 320; this process is loosely called *gamma correction*.

The colorimetric properties of the display primaries are supposed to conform to the BT.709 primaries described on page 290: DTV transmission standards call for BT.709, and modern consumer displays use BT.709. However, production and mastering of *576i* content historically used EBU primary chromaticities, not BT.709 (see *EBU Tech. 3213 primaries,* Table 26.4 on page 293).

Luma (Y')

Luma in *576i* systems is computed as a weighted sum of nonlinear R', G', and B' primary components according to the luma coefficients of BT.601:

$$^{601}Y' = 0.299\,R' + 0.587\,G' + 0.114\,B' \qquad \text{Eq 40.1}$$

The luma component Y', being a weighted sum of nonlinear $R'G'B'$ components, has no simple relationship with the CIE relative luminance (Y) used in colour science. Video encoding specifications typically place no upper bound on luma bandwidth (though transmission standards may).

Picture center, aspect ratio, and blanking

SMPTE RP 187, *Center, Aspect Ratio and Blanking of Video Images.*

The center of the picture is located midway between the central pair of the 720 active samples of BT.601, at the fraction $^{983}/_{1728}$ between 0_H instants. Concerning the vertical center, see Table 40.1, on page 458.

Aspect ratio is defined as 4:3 with respect to a *clean aperture* pixel array, 690 samples wide at a sampling rate of 13.5 MHz, and 566 lines high. Blanking transitions should not intrude into the clean aperture.

$$\frac{S_{TL} - S_{EAV-0_H} + 0.5(S_{AL} - 1)}{S_{TL}}$$

$$= \frac{864 - 732 + 0.5(720 - 1)}{864}$$

$$= \frac{983}{1728}$$

In the composite and analog domains, video information on the left-hand halfline of line 623 terminates 30.350±0.1 µs after 0_H. Video information on the right-hand halfline of line 23 commences 42.500±0.1 µs after 0_H.

No studio standard addresses square sampling of 576*i* video. I recommend using a sample rate of $944f_H$, that is, 14.75 MHz. I recommend using 768 active samples, centered as mentioned above.

SMPTE RP 202, *Video Alignment for MPEG-2 Coding.*

When MPEG-2 with 576 or 608 image rows is used in the studio, the bottom image row corresponds to line 623 (as indicated in Table 40.1). The bottom left-hand halfline (on line 623) is among the coded image rows. The right-hand half of this line will be blank when presented to the MPEG encoder; upon decoding, it may contain artifacts. Unfortunately, 576*i* DV systems digitize a range one image row up from this.

Component digital 4:2:2 interface

The C_B and C_R colour difference components of digital video are formed by scaling *B'-Y'* and *R'-Y'* components, as described in $C_B C_R$ *components for SD* on page 361. $Y'C_B C_R$ signals were once conveyed through the parallel digital interface specified in Rec. 656 and EBU Tech. 3246; nowadays, the *serial digital interface* (SDI) is used.

SDI was introduced on page 432. Mechanical and electrical details were presented on page 439.

In 13.5 MHz sampling of 576*i*, sample 732 corresponds to the line sync datum, 0_H. If digitized, that sample would take the 50% value of analog sync. SMPTE RP 187 specifies that samples 8 and 710 correspond to the 50%-points of picture width. For flat-panel displays, EBU suggests that the central 702 samples contain active video.

The choice of 720 active samples for BT.601 accommodates the blanking requirements of both 480*i* and 576*i* analog video: 720 samples are sufficient to accommodate the necessary transition samples for either system; see page 378.

Unfortunately, the blanking tolerances between 480*i* and 576*i* do not permit a single choice of blanking transition samples: The narrowest possible picture width in 480*i* is several samples too wide to meet 576*i* tolerances.

Figure 40.2 overleaf shows a waveform drawing of luma in a 576*i* component digital 4:2:2 system.

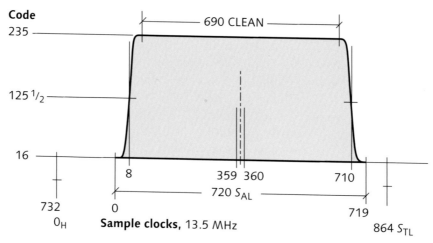

Figure 40.2 *576i* component digital 4:2:2 luma waveform

Component analog 576i interface

EBU Tech. N20, *Parallel interface for analogue component video signals in GRB form.*

A component analog *576i R'G'B'* interface is based on nonlinear *R'*, *G'*, and *B'* signals conveyed as voltage, with a range of 1 V_{PP} from synctip to reference white. Transient excursions slightly outside the reference black-to-white range are permitted. A video signal of zero – blanking level, equal to reference black – corresponds to a level of 0 V_{DC}. A video signal of unity corresponds to 700 mV.

Sync is added to the green component according to Equation 40.2, where *sync* and *active* are taken to be unity when asserted and zero otherwise:

$$G'_{sync} = \frac{7}{10}\left(active \cdot G'\right) + \frac{3}{10}\left(-sync\right)$$

Eq 40.2

The excursion of the *G'* signal from synctip to reference white is 1 V_{PP}. Levels in *576i* systems are usually specified in millivolts, not the IRE units common in *480i* systems. If IRE units were used, 1 IRE would equal 7 mV.

EBU Tech. N10, *Parallel interface for analogue component video signals.*

Analog luma (*Y'*) is carried as a voltage ranging 1 V_{PP} from synctip to reference white. Luma signal of zero – blanking level, equal to reference black – corresponds to a level of 0 V_{DC}. Luma signal of unity corresponds to

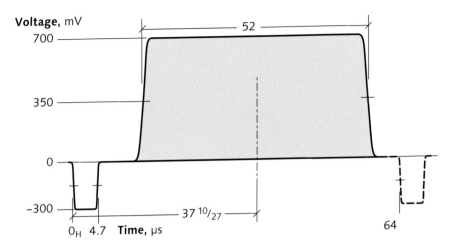

Figure 40.3 *576i* component
analog luma waveform

700 mV. Sync is added to the luma component according to Equation 40.3:

$$Y'_{sync} = \frac{7}{10}Y' + \frac{3}{10}\left(-sync\right)$$

Eq 40.3

The picture excursion of the Y' signal is 700 mV. Figure 40.3 above shows a waveform drawing of luma in a *576i* component analog interface.

The P_B and P_R colour difference components are formed by scaling $B'-Y'$ and $R'-Y'$ components, as described in *PBPR components for SD on page 359*. Although it is possible in theory to have wideband P_B and P_R components, in practice they are lowpass filtered to about half the bandwidth of luma. P_B and P_R compnents are carried as voltage with reference excursion ±350 mV.

SMPTE ST 296, 1280×720 Progressive Image Sample Structure – Analog and Digital Representation and Analog Interface.

This chapter details the scanning, timing, and sync structure of 1280×720 video, also called 720*p*. The scanning and timing information in this chapter applies to all variants of 720*p* video, both analog and digital.

Scanning

720*p* video represents stationary or moving two-dimensional images sampled temporally at a constant rate of $24/1.001$, 24, 25, $30/1.001$, 30, 50, $60/1.001$, or 60 frames per second. The sampling rate is 74.25 MHz (modified by the ratio $1000/1001$ in 720*p* 59.94, 720*p* 29.97, and 720*p* 23.976). All of these systems have 750 total lines (L_T). The number of samples per total line (S_{TL}) is adapted to achieve the desired frame rate. Table 41.1 below summarizes the scanning parameters.

$$\frac{24}{1.001} \approx 23.976$$

$$\frac{30}{1.001} \approx 29.97$$

$$\frac{60}{1.001} \approx 59.94$$

A frame comprises a total of 750 horizontal raster lines of equal duration, uniformly progressively scanned top to bottom and left to right, numbered consecutively

System	f_S [MHz]	S_{TL}
720*p*60	74.25	1650
720*p*59.94	$74.25/1.001$	1650
720*p*50	74.25	1980
720*p*30	74.25	3300
720*p*29.97	$74.25/1.001$	3300
720*p*25	74.25	3960
720*p*24	74.25	4125
720*p*23.976	$74.25/1.001$	4125

Table 41.1 **720*p* scanning parameters** are summarized.

Line number	Contents
1–5	tri/BR (5 lines)
6	Blanking
7–25 (19 lines)	Blanking/Ancillary
26–745 (720 lines)	Picture [Clean aperture 702 lines]
746–750 (5 lines)	Blanking

Table 41.2 **1280×720 line assignment**

tri Trilevel pulse

BR Broad pulse

The vertical center of the picture is located midway between lines 385 and 386.

starting at 1. Of the 750 total lines, 720 contain picture. Table 41.2 above shows the assignment of line numbers and their content.

For studio video, the tolerance on frame rate is normally ±10 ppm. In practice the tolerance applies to a master clock at a high frequency, but for purposes of computation and standards writing it is convenient to reference the tolerance to the frame rate.

At a digital interface, video information is identified by a *timing reference signal* (TRS) conveyed across the interface. (See *SDI and HD-SDI sync, TRS, and ancillary data*, on page 433.) The last active line of a frame is terminated by EAV where the *V*-bit becomes asserted. That EAV marks the start of line 746; line 1 of the next frame starts on the fifth following EAV.

Analog sync

0_H precedes the first word of SAV by 256 clocks.

0_H follows the first word of EAV by $S_{TL} - 1280 - 260$ clocks.

Horizontal events are referenced to 0_H, defined by the zero-crossing of trilevel sync. Digital samples and analog timing are related such that the first (zeroth) sample of active video follows the 0_H instant by 260 reference clock intervals.

At an analog interface, each line commences with a trilevel sync pulse. Trilevel sync comprises a negative portion asserted to −300±6 mV during the 40 reference clock intervals preceding 0_H, and a positive portion asserted to +300±6 mV during the 40 reference clock intervals after 0_H. The risetime of each transition is 4±1.5 reference clock intervals.

Vertical sync in the analog domain is signaled by *broad pulses*, one each on lines 1 through 5. Each broad pulse is asserted to –300±6 mV, with timing identical to active video – that is, to the production aperture's picture width. The risetime of each transition is 4±1.5 reference clock intervals. Line 1 can be detected as the first broad pulse of a frame – that is, by a line without a broad pulse followed by a line with one.

Lines 7 through 25 do not convey picture information. They may convey ancillary or other signals either related or unrelated to the picture.

Analog signal timing is defined by the digital standard; the digital sampling frequency defines reference time intervals used to define analog timing.

Figure 41.1 overleaf shows details of the sync structure; this waveform diagram is the analog of Table 41.2.

Picture center, aspect ratio, and blanking

The center of the picture is located midway between the central two of the 1280 active samples – that is, between samples 639 and 640 – and midway between the central two 720 picture lines – that is, between lines 385 and 386.

The aspect ratio is defined to be 16:9 with respect to the production aperture of 1280×720.

In *Transition samples,* on page 378, I mentioned that it is necessary to avoid, at the start of a line, an instantaneous transition from blanking to picture information. A *clean aperture* pixel array 1248 samples wide and 702 lines high, centered on the production aperture, should remain subjectively uncontaminated by edge transients.

R'G'B' EOCF and primaries

Picture information is referenced to linear-light primary red, green, and blue (*RGB*) tristimulus values, represented in abstract terms in the range 0 (reference black) to +1 (reference white).

Three nonlinear primary components *R'*, *G'*, and *B'* are computed such that the intended image appearance is obtained on the reference display in the reference viewing conditions; see *Reference display and viewing conditions,* on page 427.

In the default power-up state of a camera, the nonlinear primary components are computed according to the opto-electronic conversion function of *BT.709*

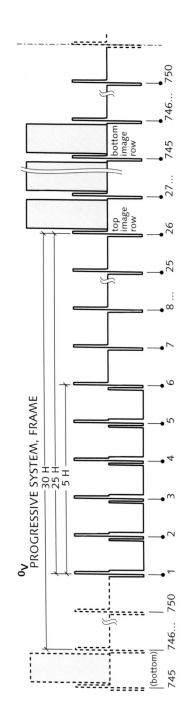

Figure 41.1 **720p raster, vertical**

OECF, described on page 320; this process is loosely called *gamma correction*.

The colorimetric properties of the primary estimates are supposed to conform to *BT.709 primaries* described on page 290: DTV transmission standards call for BT.709, and modern consumer displays use BT.709. However, as I write in 2011, nearly all 50 Hz program material is created and mastered using EBU primaries (see *EBU Tech. 3213 primaries*, Table 26.4 on page 293), and nearly all 60 Hz program material is created and mastered using SMPTE primaries (see *SMPTE RP 145 primaries*, Table 26.5 on page 293). I expect the situation in mastering to change upon the introduction of new studio display technologies such as OLEDs – but among content creators and broadcasters, old habits die hard.

Luma (Y')

Luma is a weighted sum of nonlinear *R'*, *G'*, and *B'* components according to the BT.709 luma coefficients:

$$^{709}Y' = 0.2126\,R' + 0.7152\,G' + 0.0722\,B' \qquad \text{Eq 41.1}$$

The luma component *Y'*, being a weighted sum of nonlinear *R'G'B'* components, has no simple relationship with the CIE relative luminance (*Y*) used in colour science. The formulation of luma in HD differs from that of SD; see *SD and HD luma chaos*, on page 350. Video encoding specifications typically place no upper bound on luma bandwidth. Video encoding specifications typically place no upper bound on luma bandwidth.

Component digital 4:2:2 interface

For details of the analog inter-face, see *Component analog HD interface*, on page 485.

$Y'C_BC_R$ components are formed by scaling *Y'*, *B'–Y'*, and *R'–Y'* components, as described in C_BC_R *components for BT.709 HD* on page 371. TRS is inserted as described in *SDI and HD-SDI sync, TRS, and ancillary data* on page 433. The HD-SDI interface is described in *HD-SDI coding*, on page 440. It is standard to subsample according to the 4:2:2 scheme (sketched in the third column of Figure 12.1, on page 124). Image quality wouldn't suffer if subsampling were 4:2:0 – that is, if colour differences were subsampled vertically as well as horizontally – but this would be inconvenient for hardware design and interface.

1920×1080 HD 42

SMPTE ST 274, *1920×1080 Scanning and Analog and Parallel Digital Interfaces for Multiple Picture Rates.*

HD equipment based on 1125/60 scanning and 1920×1035 image format, with nonsquare sampling, according to SMPTE 240M, was deployed for several years. That system is obsolete. (It can now be considered as a 1035*i* variant of 1080*i*30 or 1080*i*29.94 having 1035 picture lines instead of 1080, nonsquare sampling, and slightly different colorimetry.)

$$\frac{24}{1.001} \approx 23.976$$

$$\frac{30}{1.001} \approx 29.97$$

$$\frac{60}{1.001} \approx 59.94$$

This chapter details a family of high-definition television systems standardized in SMPTE ST 274. The systems have an image format of 1920×1080, an aspect ratio of 16:9, and square sampling.

SMPTE ST 274 represents agreement on colorimetry according to the international standard BT.709. Previous revisions of SMPTE ST 274 allowed use of 240M colour and luma parameters on an "interim" basis. It will take some time for manufacturers and users to complete the transition to the new standard.

Scanning

1920×1080 video represents stationary or moving two-dimensional images sampled temporally at a constant rate of $^{24}/_{1.001}$, 24, 25, $^{30}/_{1.001}$, 30, 50, $^{60}/_{1.001}$, or 60 frames per second. The base sampling rate is 74.25 MHz; this rate is modified by the ratio $^{1000}/_{1001}$ for systems having noninteger frame rate, and doubled to 148.5 MHz (possibly times $^{1000}/_{1001}$) for progressive systems at frame rates higher than 30 Hz. All of these systems have 1125 total lines (L_T); the number of samples per total line (S_{TL}) is adapted to achieve the desired frame rate. Table 42.1 above summarizes the scanning parameters.

For studio video, the tolerance on frame rate is normally ±10 ppm. In practice the tolerance applies to a master clock at a high frequency, but for purposes of computation and standards writing it is convenient to reference the tolerance to the frame rate.

A frame comprises a total of 1125 horizontal raster lines of equal duration, uniformly scanned top to

System	f_S [MHz]	S_{TL}
1080p60¶	148.5	2200
1080p59.94¶	$148.5/1.001$	2200
1080p50¶	148.5	2640
1080i30	74.25	2200
1080i29.97	$74.25/1.001$	2200
1080i25	74.25	2640
1080p30	74.25	2200
1080p29.97	$74.25/1.001$	2200
1080p25	74.25	2640
1080p24	74.25	2750
1080p23.976	$74.25/1.001$	2750

Table 42.1 **1920×1080 scanning parameters** are summarized. 1080p systems, marked ¶, are not allowed for ATSC broadcast.

bottom and left to right, numbered consecutively starting at 1. Of the 1125 total lines, 1080 contain picture. Table 42.2 opposite indicates the assignment of line numbers and their content.

A progressive system conveys 1080 active picture lines per frame in order top to bottom.

An interlaced system scans a frame as a *first* field then a *second* field. The scan lines of each field have half the vertical spatial sampling density of the frame. Scanning lines in the second field are displaced vertically by the vertical sampling pitch, and delayed temporally by half the frame time, from scanning lines in the first field. The first field conveys 540 active picture lines, starting with the top picture line of the frame. The second field conveys 540 active picture lines, ending with the bottom picture line of the frame.

At a digital interface, video information is identified by a *timing reference signal* (TRS) conveyed across the interface. (See *SDI and HD-SDI sync, TRS, and ancillary data*, on page 433.) In progressive systems, the last active line of a frame is terminated by EAV where the V-bit becomes asserted. That EAV marks the start of line 1122; line 1 of the next frame starts on the fourth following EAV. In interlaced systems, the last active line of a field is terminated by EAV where the V-bit becomes asserted. In the first field, that EAV marks the

Line number, progressive	Line number, first field (F = 0)	Line number, second field (F = 1)	V	Contents, left half	Contents, right half
		563			
1	1				
		564			
2	2				
		565			
3	3				
		566			
4	4				
		567			
5	5				
		568			
6	6				
7–41 (35 lines)	7–20 (14 lines)				vertical interval video
		569–583 (15 lines)			vertical interval video
	21–560 (540 lines)				picture
42–1121 (1080 lines)			V = 0 (1080 lines)		
		584–1123 (540 lines)			picture
1122–1125 (4 lines)	561–562 (2 lines)	1124–1125 (2 lines)			

Table 42.2 1080*i* and 1080*p* line assignment

start of line 561. In the second field, that EAV marks the start of line 1124; line 1 of the next frame starts on the second following EAV.

Analog sync

At an analog interface, each line commences with a tri-level sync pulse. The zero-crossing of trilevel sync defines the line sync datum 0_H, to which horizontal events are referenced. Digital samples and analog timing are related such that the first (zeroth) sample of

0_H precedes the first word of SAV by 192 clocks.

0_H follows the first word of EAV by S_{TL} – 1920 –192 clocks.

active video follows the 0_H instant by 192 reference clock intervals.

Trilevel sync comprises a negative portion asserted to –300±6 mV during the 44 reference clock intervals preceding 0_H, and a positive portion asserted to +300±6 mV during the 44 reference clock intervals after 0_H. The risetime of each transition is 4±1.5 reference clock intervals.

Details of horizontal timing are shown in Figure 42.1 opposite.

Vertical sync in the analog domain is signaled by *broad pulses,* whose structure differs between progressive and interlaced systems.

A progressive system has five broad pulses per frame, one each on lines 1 through 5. Each broad pulse is asserted to –300±6 mV, 132 reference clock intervals after 0_H, and deasserted 2112 reference clock intervals after 0_H. (Deassertion coincides with the end of active video – that is, with the right-hand edge of the production aperture.) The risetime of each transition is 4±1.5 reference clock intervals. Line 1 is defined by the first broad pulse of a frame – that is, by a line with a broad pulse preceded by a line without one. Line 6 has a second trilevel pulse whose zero-crossing is $S_{TL}/2$ reference clock intervals after 0_H. This pulse is reminiscent of an equalization pulse in analog SD.

In an interlaced system, several lines in the vertical interval have a second trilevel sync pulse whose zero-crossing is at $S_{TL}/2$ reference clock intervals after 0_H. An interlaced system has ten broad pulses per field, in the arrangement indicated in Table 42.2. Each broad pulse is asserted to –300±6 mV, 132 reference clock intervals after the zero-crossing of the immediately preceding trilevel sync, and is deasserted 880 reference clock intervals later. The risetime at each transition is 4±1.5 reference clock intervals. Line 1 can be decoded as the first broad pulse in a left-hand halfline – that is, by detecting a normal line (with no broad pulse and no mid-line trilevel sync) followed by a broad pulse immediately after 0_H. Each broad pulse is preceded by a trilevel pulse whose zero-crossing is either at 0_H or delayed $S_{TL}/2$ reference clock intervals from 0_H.

DIGITAL VIDEO AND HD ALGORITHMS AND INTERFACES

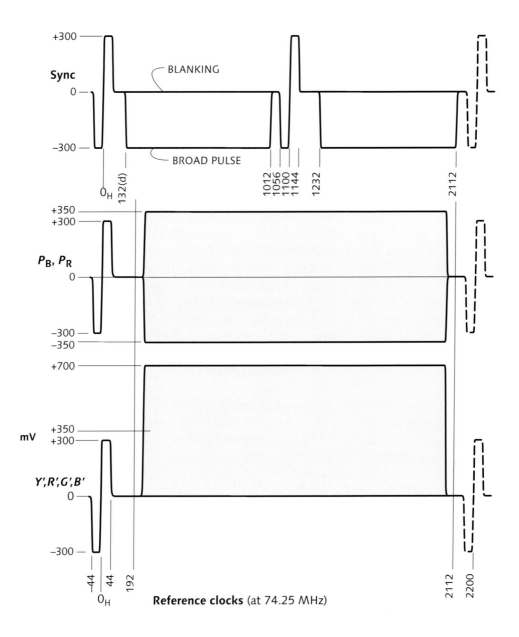

Figure 42.1 **1080i30 analog line details.** Time intervals are shown as intervals of a reference clock at 74.25 MHz, with reference clock zero defined at 0_H. To obtain sample numbers relative to the zeroth sample of active video, add $S_{AL} + 88$ (modulo S_{TL}) to these counts.

Vertical interval video lines do not convey picture information. They may convey ancillary or other signals either related or unrelated to the picture.

Analog signal timing is defined by the digital standard; the digital sampling frequency defines reference time intervals used to define analog timing.

Figure 42.2 shows details of the vertical sync structure; this waveform diagram is the analog of Table 42.2, on page 475.

Picture center, aspect ratio, and blanking

The center of the picture is located midway between the central two of the 1920 active samples (between samples 959 and 960), and midway between the central two 1080 picture lines (between lines 581 and 582 in a progressive system, and between lines 290 and 853 in an interlaced system).

The aspect ratio is defined to be 16:9 with respect to the production aperture of 1920×1080.

In *Transition samples*, on page 378, I mentioned that it is necessary to avoid, at the start of a line, an instantaneous transition from blanking to picture information. A *clean aperture* pixel array 1888 samples wide and 1062 lines high, centered on the production aperture, should remain subjectively uncontaminated by edge transients.

R'G'B' EOCF and primaries

Picture information is referenced to linear-light primary red, green, and blue (*RGB*) tristimulus values, represented in abstract terms in the range 0 (reference black) to +1 (reference white).

Three nonlinear primary components *R'*, *G'*, and *B'* are computed such that the intended image appearance is obtained on the reference display in the reference viewing conditions; see *Reference display and viewing conditions*, on page 427.

In the default power-up state of a camera, the nonlinear primary components are computed according to the opto-electronic conversion function of *BT.709 OECF*, described on page 320; this process is loosely called *gamma correction*.

The colorimetric properties of the display primaries are supposed to conform to *BT.709 primaries* described

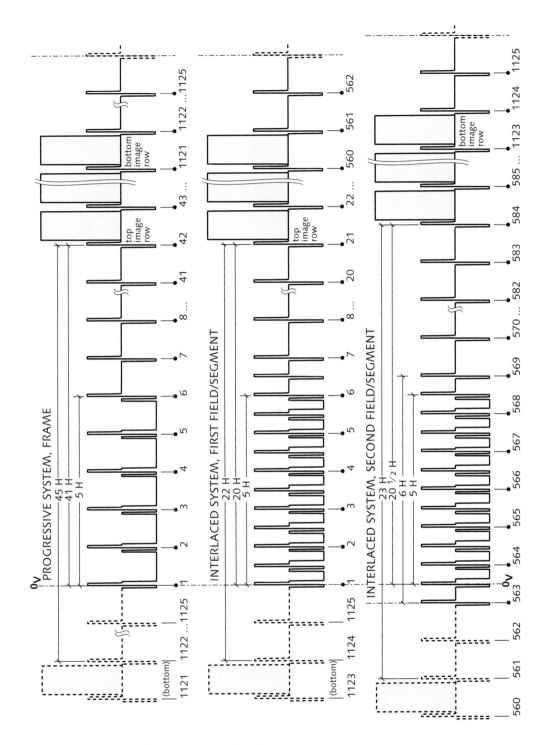

Figure 42.2 1080*i* and 1080*p* vertical blanking interval

on page 290: DTV transmission standards call for BT.709, and modern consumer displays use BT.709. However, as I write in 2011, nearly all 50 Hz program material is created and mastered using EBU primaries (see *EBU Tech. 3213 primaries*, Table 26.4 on page 293), and nearly all 60 Hz program material is created and mastered using SMPTE primaries (see *SMPTE RP 145 primaries*, Table 26.5 on page 293). I expect the situation in mastering to change upon the introduction of new studio display technologies such as OLEDs – but among content creators and broadcasters, old habits die hard.

Luma (Y')

Luma is computed as a weighted sum of nonlinear R', G', and B' primary components according to the luma coefficients introduced in *BT.709 luma*, on page 346:

$$^{709}Y' = 0.2126\,R' + 0.7152\,G' + 0.0722\,B' \qquad \text{Eq 42.1}$$

The luma component Y', being a weighted sum of nonlinear $R'G'B'$ components, has no simple relationship with the CIE relative luminance (Y) used in colour science. The formulation of luma in HD differs from that of SD; see *SD and HD luma chaos*, on page 350. Video encoding specifications typically place no upper bound on luma bandwidth.

Component digital 4:2:2 interface

For details of the analog interface, see *Component analog HD interface*, on page 485.

$Y'C_BC_R$ components are formed by scaling $B'-Y'$ and $R'-Y'$ components, as described in *C_BC_R components for BT.709 HD* on page 371. The HD-SDI interface is described *HD-SDI coding*, on page 440.

HD videotape   43

For SD, refer to *Composite NTSC and PAL: Legacy Video Systems.*

Since publication of the first edition of this book there has been a dramatic decline in the use of videotape. Much legacy SD videotape equipment is still in use, but SD requirements are now fairly easily met by hard drive and flash media. Videotape is still in fairly wide use for HD, and still retains a few advantages over hard drive and flash media. Also, several compression systems originally devised for videotape have successfully made the transition into hard drive and flash media.

Table 43.1 summarizes digital videotape formats for HD.

Notation	Method	Tape	Data rate [Mb/s]	Notes
D-5 HD (HD-D5, D-15)	Component compressed, 4:2:2 HD	12.65 mm (½ inch, VHS-derived)	270	(Panasonic)
D-6	Uncompressed 4:2:2 HD	19 mm	1188	
HDCAM (D-11)	Component compressed, M-JPEG-like, 1440×1080, 3:1:1 HD	12.7 mm (Beta-derived)	135	(Sony)
DVCPRO HD (D-12)	Component compressed, DV100, 1280×1080 (or 960×720), 4:2:2 HD	6.35 mm	100	DV100
HDCAM SR (D-16)	Component compressed, MPEG-4 SStP, 1920×1080, 4:2:2 (Lite), 4:2:2 (SQ), 4:4:4 (HQ)	12.65 mm (Beta-derived)	220 440 880	(Sony)

Table 43.1 **Digital videotape formats for HD.** The D-6 format is "uncompressed" (although subject to chroma subsampling); all of the other formats use compression.

D-5 HD (HD-D5, D-15)

The SMPTE D-5 standard defined recording of uncompressed SD at 270 Mb/s. Panasonic adapted the D-5 format to HD by equipping it with a motion-JPEG codec having a compression ratio of about 5:1; the coding is quite similar to that of DV. This variant of the D-5 VTR is denoted D-5 HD or HD-D5; after its introduction, it was standardized by SMPTE as D-15.

The D-5 HD system records 720*p* or 1080*i* video at either 59.94 Hz or 60.00 Hz, with 4:2:2 chroma subsampling.

MALVAR, HENRIQUE S. (1992), *Signal Processing with Lapped Transforms* (Norwood, Mass.: Artech House).

One difference from DV is that D-5 HD compression uses a lapped (overlapped) transform, where the rightmost column of samples in an 8×8 block overlaps the leftmost column of the next block to the right. Upon decoding, the redundantly coded columns are reconstructed by averaging appropriate samples from two neighboring blocks. This scheme reduces blocking artifacts compared to the nonlapped transform used in DV.

D-6

SMPTE D-6 defined a videotape format for uncompressed, 8-bit, 4:2:2 HD, at a bit rate of 1.188 Gb/s. This equipment had superb performance and was very expensive; it is now obsolete.

HDCAM (D-11)

Downsampling of 1920×1080 to 1440×1080 means that luma sample aspect ratio is effectively $\frac{4}{3}$ (and chroma subsampling is equivalent to 4:1:1) relative to the original luma array.

HDCAM was developed and commercialized by Sony. Interlaced or progressive HD video at any of several frame rates is downsampled to 1440×1080 image format and subject to 3:1:1 chroma subsampling. Compression is M-JPEG-style, comparable to that of DV, using a lapped (overlapped) transform (like D-5 HD), coded at about 135 Mb/s. HDCAM uses a tape cassette derived from Betacam, with ½-inch tape. The videotape recording scheme was standardized as SMPTE D-11.

DVCPRO HD (D-12)

Downsampling of 1920×1080 to 1280×1080 means that luma sample aspect ratio is effectively $\frac{3}{2}$ (and chroma subsampling is equivalent to 3:1:1) relative to the original 1920×1080 luma array.

The DV25/DV50 standards were adapted to 100 Mb/s to accommodate 1080*i*30 HD signals downsampled to 1280×1080 image format (or 720*p*60 downsampled to 960×720), with 4:2:2 chroma subsampling in the downsampled domain. The compression scheme is denoted DV100. The compression scheme is sometimes called DVCPRO100; digital videotape recorders were introduced by Panasonic as DVCPRO HD, sharing many of the mechanical and signal processing elements of the DV25 and DV50 DVTRs. The videotape recording scheme was later standardized as SMPTE D-12.

HDCAM SR (D-16)

HDCAM SR compression conforms to MPEG-4 Part 2 *simple studio profile* (SStP). HDCAM SR records 1920×1080, either $Y'C_BC_R$ 4:2:2 at 440 Mb/s (SQ mode), or $R'G'B'$ 4:4:4 at 880 Mb/s (HQ mode). HDCAM SR equipment can also record or play two independent $Y'C_BC_R$ 4:2:2 streams in 880 Mb/s mode. An additional mode, SR Lite, was added having a data rate of 220 Mb/s. ("Lite" refers to the data rate requirement; the compression is heavy.)

Component
analog HD interface 44

Component analog HD signals are interfaced in the analog domain as $Y'P_BP_R$ signals conveyed as voltage. Luma ranges 1 V_{PP} from synctip to reference white. A luma signal of zero – blanking level, equal to reference black – corresponds to a level of 0 V_{DC}. A luma signal of unity corresponds to 700 mV. Transient excursions slightly outside the reference black-to-white range are permitted.

Sync is added to luma according to Equation 44.1, where *sync* and *active* are taken to be unity when asserted and zero otherwise:

$$Y'_{sync} = \frac{7}{10}Y' + \frac{3}{10}\left(-sync\right)$$

Eq 44.1

The excursion of the Y' signal from synctip to reference white is 1 V_{PP}. One IRE unit corresponds to 7 mV.

Figure 44.1 overleaf shows a waveform drawing of luma in a 720*p*60 component analog interface; Figure 44.2 overleaf shows a waveform drawing of luma in 1080*i*30.

P_B and P_R colour difference components are formed by scaling $B'-Y'$ and $R'-Y'$ components, as described in *P_BP_R components for BT.709 HD* on page 370. Although it is possible in theory to have wideband P_B and P_R components, in practice they are lowpass filtered to about half the bandwidth of luma. P_B and P_R components are carried as voltage with reference excursion ±350 mV.

SMPTE standards do not specify tolerances on time-coincidence of R', G', and B' components at an analog interface. I recommend that the components be time-

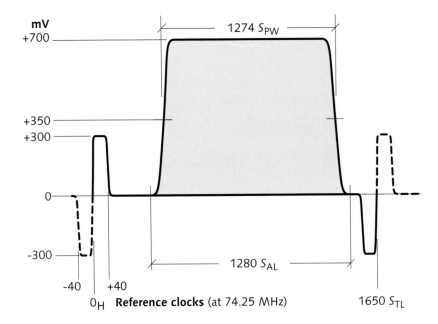

Figure 44.1 **720*p*60 component analog luma waveform**. Time intervals are shown as intervals of a reference clock at 74.25 MHz.

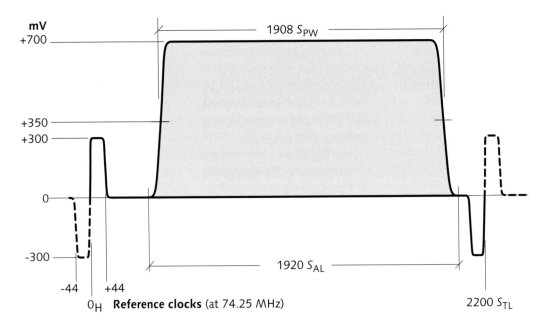

Figure 44.2 **1080*i*30/1080*p*30 component analog luma waveform**. Time intervals are shown as intervals of a reference clock at 74.25 MHz.

DIGITAL VIDEO AND HD ALGORITHMS AND INTERFACES

coincident with each other, and with sync, within ¼ of a sample clock – for 720p60 and 1080i30, time-coincident within ±3.4 ns.

EIA/CEA-770.3, *High Definition TV Analog Component Video Interface*.

EIA/CEA has standardized the 720p60 and 1080i30 systems as described here, including these $Y'P_BP_R$ levels, for use in consumer HD electronics devices.

Pre- and postfiltering characteristics

Component Y', R', G', or B' signals in 720p59.94 or 720p60 – and for that mattter, 1080i30 – have a nominal passband of 30 MHz; colour difference components have a nominal passband of 15 MHz.

Figure 44.3 overleaf, *Filter template for Y' and R'G'B' components*, depicts filter characteristics for pre- and postfiltering of R', G', B', and Y' component signals. Analog P_B and P_R colour difference component signals are pre- and postfiltered using the same template scaled by a factor of two on the frequency axis. The characteristics are frequency-scaled from the template included in BT.601, with a few modifications.

Amplitude ripple tolerance in the passband is ±0.05 dB with respect to insertion loss at 100 kHz. Insertion loss is 6 dB or more at half the sampling rate of the Y', R', G', and B' components.

SMPTE ST 274 includes luma and colour difference templates in "Annex B (Informative)." In standards lingo, the word *informative* signals that the information is distributed with the standard, but compliance with the annex is not required to claim conformance with the standard.

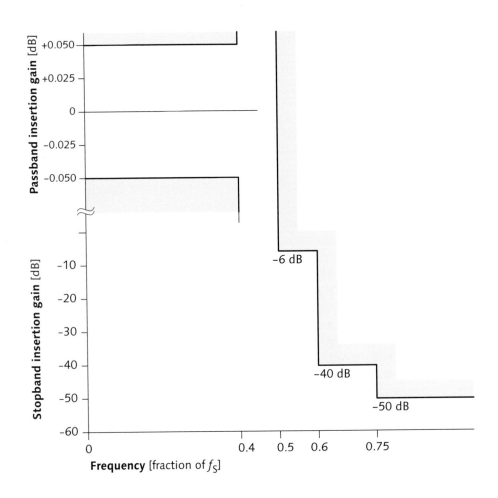

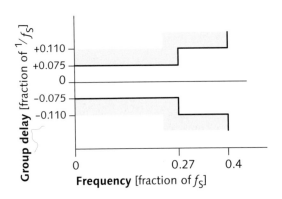

Figure 44.3 Filter template for *Y'* and *R'G'B'* components

Part 5

Video compression

45   JPEG and motion-JPEG (M-JPEG) compression   491

46   DV compression   505

47   MPEG-2 video compression   513

48   H.264 video compression   537

49   VP8 compression   549

JPEG and motion-JPEG (M-JPEG) compression   45

This chapter describes *JPEG*, a standard for lossy compression of still images. JPEG is based upon the discrete cosine transform (DCT). JPEG is rarely used directly in video, but it forms the basis of M-JPEG (used in desktop video editing) and DV compression. Also, JPEG techniques form the core of MPEG.

Motion-JPEG (M-JPEG) refers to the use of a JPEG-like algorithm to compress each field or frame in a sequence of video fields or frames. M-JPEG systems use the methods of JPEG, but rarely (if ever) conform to the ISO/IEC JPEG standard. DV is a specific type of M-JPEG, which is well standardized; it is described in the following chapter, *DV compression,* on page 505. The *I-frame-only* variant of MPEG-2 is conceptually equivalent to M-JPEG, but again has a well-respected standard; see *MPEG-2 video compression,* on page 513.

ISO/IEC 10918, *Information Technology – Digital compression and coding of continuous-tone still images.*

The JPEG standard, cited in the margin, defines four modes: *sequential, hierarchical, progressive,* and *lossless.* The JPEG standard accommodates DCT coefficients having from 2 to 16 bits, and accommodates two different entropy coders (*Huffman* and *arithmetic*). *Baseline* refers to a defined subset of JPEG's sequential mode that is restricted to 8-bit coefficients and restricted to Huffman coding. Only baseline JPEG is commercially important; JPEG's other modes are mainly of academic interest, and won't be discussed here.

Figure 45.1 **A JPEG 4:2:0 minimum coded unit** (MCU) comprises six 8×8 blocks: four luma blocks, a block of C_B, and a block of C_R. The six constituent blocks result from nonlinear *R'G'B'* data being matrixed to $Y'C_BC_R$, then subsampled according to the 4:2:0 scheme; chroma subsampling is effectively the first stage of compression. The blocks are processed independently.

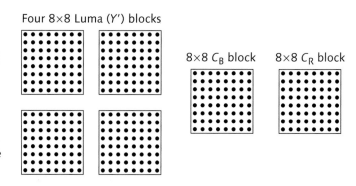

Four 8×8 Luma (*Y'*) blocks

8×8 C_B block   8×8 C_R block

In MPEG, a *macroblock* is the area covered by a 16×16 array of luma samples. In DV, a macroblock comprises the Y', C_B, and C_R blocks covered by an 8×8 array (block) of chroma samples. In JPEG, an MCU comprises those blocks covered by the minimum-sized tiling of Y', C_B, and C_R blocks. For 4:2:0 subsampling, all of these definitions are equivalent; they differ for 4:1:1 and 4:2:2 (or for JPEG's other rarely used patterns).

In desktop graphics, saving JPEG at high quality may cause individual *R'G'B'* channels (components) to be compressed without subsampling.

Quantizer matrices and VLE tables will be described in the example starting on page 496.

I use zero-origin array indexing.

JPEG blocks and MCUs

An 8×8 array of sample data is known in JPEG terminology as a *block*. Prior to JPEG compression of a colour image, normally the nonlinear *R'G'B'* data is matrixed to $Y'C_BC_R$, then subsampled 4:2:0. According to the JPEG standard (and the JFIF standard, to be described), other colour subsampling schemes are possible; strangely, different subsampling ratios are permitted for C_B and C_R. However, only 4:2:0 is widely deployed, and the remainder of this discussion assumes 4:2:0. Four 8×8 luma blocks, an 8×8 block of C_B, and an 8×8 block of C_R are known in JPEG terminology as a *minimum coded unit* (MCU); this corresponds to a *macroblock* in DV or MPEG terminology. The 4:2:0 macroblock arrangement is shown in Figure 45.1 above.

The luma and colour difference blocks are processed independently by JPEG, using virtually the identical algorithm. The only significant difference is that the quantizer matrix and the VLE tables used for chroma blocks are usually different from the quantizer matrix and VLE tables used for luma blocks.

As explained in *Spatial frequency domain* on page 238, typical images are dominated by power at low spatial frequencies. In Figure 45.4, on page 496, I present an example 8×8 array of luma samples from an image. In Figure 45.2 at the top of the facing page, I show an 8×8 array of the spatial frequencies computed from this luma array through the DCT. The [0, 0] entry (the *DC term*), at the upper left-hand corner of that array represents power at zero frequency. That entry typically contains quite a large value; it is not

Figure 45.2 **The DCT concentrates image power** at low spatial frequencies. In Figure 45.4, on page 496, I give an example 8×8 array of luma samples from an image. The magnitudes of the spatial frequency coefficients after the DCT transform are shown in this plot. Most of the image power is collected in the [0, 0] (DC) coefficient, whose value is so large that it is omitted from this plot. Only a handful of other (AC) coefficients are much greater than zero.

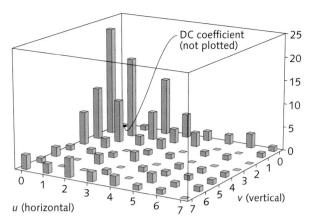

plotted here. Coefficients near that one tend to have fairly high values; coefficients tend to decrease in value further away from [0, 0]. Depending upon the image data, a few isolated high-frequency coefficients may have high values.

This typical distribution of image power, in the spatial frequency domain, represents the redundancy present in the image. The redundancy is reduced by coding the image in that domain, instead of coding the sample values of the image directly.

In addition to its benefit of removing redundancy from typical image data, representation in spatial frequency has another advantage. The lightness sensitivity of the visual system depends upon spatial frequency: We are more sensitive to low spatial frequencies than high, as can be seen from the graph in Figure 23.5, on page 252. Information at high spatial frequencies can be degraded to a large degree, without having any objectionable (or perhaps even perceptible) effect on image quality. Once image data is transformed by the DCT, high-order coefficients can be approximated – that is, coarsely quantized – to discard data corresponding to spatial frequency components that have little contribution to the perceived quality of the image.

In principle, the DCT algorithm could be applied to any block size, from 2×2 up to the size of the whole image, perhaps 512×512. (DCT is most efficient when applied to a matrix whose dimensions are powers of

Figure 45.3 **The JPEG block diagram** shows the encoder (at the top), which performs the *discrete cosine transform* (DCT). The DCT is followed by a *quantizer* (Q), then a *variable-length encoder* (VLE). The decoder (at the bottom) performs the inverse of each of these operations, in reverse order.

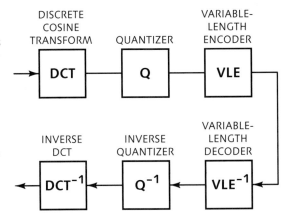

two.) The choice of 8×8 blocks of luma for the application of DCT in video represents a compromise between a block size small enough to minimize storage and processing overheads, but large enough to effectively exploit image redundancy.

The DCT operation discards picture information to which vision is insensitive. Surprisingly, though, the JPEG standard itself makes no reference to perceptual uniformity. Because JPEG's goal is to represent visually important information, it is important that so-called *RGB* values presented to the JPEG algorithm are first subject to a nonlinear transform such as that outlined in *Perceptual uniformity,* on page 8, that mimics vision.

JPEG block diagram

The JPEG block diagram in Figure 45.3 shows, at the top, the three main blocks of a JPEG encoder: the *discrete cosine transform* (DCT) computation (sometimes called *forward DCT,* FDCT), *quantization* (Q), and *variable-length encoding* (VLE). The decoder (at the bottom of Figure 45.3) performs the inverse of each of these operations, in reverse order. The inverse DCT is sometimes denoted *IDCT*; inverse quantization is sometimes called *dequantization,* and sometimes denoted *IQ*.

Inverse quantization (IQ) has no relation to the historical NTSC *IQ* colour difference components.

Owing to the eight-line-high vertical transform, eight lines of image memory are required in the DCT subsystem of the encoder, and in the IDCT (DCT^{-1}) subsystem of the decoder. When the DCT is implemented in separable form, as is almost always the case, this is called *transpose* memory.

Level shifting

The DCT formulation in JPEG is intended for signed sample values. In ordinary hardware or firmware, the DCT is implemented in fixed-point, two's complement arithmetic. Standard video interfaces use offset binary representation, so each luma or colour difference sample is *level shifted* prior to DCT by subtracting 2^{k-1}, where k is the number of bits in use.

Discrete cosine transform (DCT)

The 8×8 forward DCT (FDCT) takes an 8×8 array of 64 sample values (denoted f, whose elements are $f_{i,j}$), and produces an 8×8 array of 64 transform coefficients (denoted F, whose elements are $F_{u,v}$). The FDCT is expressed by this equation:

Eq 45.1

$$F_{u,v} = \frac{1}{4} C(u) C(v) \sum_{i=0}^{7} \sum_{j=0}^{7} f_{i,j} \cos\left[\frac{(2i+1)u\pi}{16}\right] \cos\left[\frac{(2j+1)v\pi}{16}\right];$$

$$C(w) = \begin{cases} \frac{1}{\sqrt{2}}; & w = 0 \\ 1; & w = 1, 2, \ldots, 7 \end{cases}$$

The cosine terms need not be computed on-the-fly; they can be precomputed and stored in tables.

The inverse transform – the IDCT, or DCT^{-1} – is this:

Eq 45.2

$$f_{i,j} = \frac{1}{4} \sum_{u=0}^{7} \sum_{v=0}^{7} C(u) C(v) F_{u,v} \cos\left[\frac{(2i+1)u\pi}{16}\right] \cos\left[\frac{(2j+1)v\pi}{16}\right]$$

The forward and inverse transforms involve nearly identical arithmetic: The complexity of encoding and decoding is very similar. The DCT is its own inverse (within a scale factor), so performing the DCT on the transform coefficients would perfectly reconstruct the original samples, subject only to the roundoff error in the DCT and IDCT.

If implemented directly according to these equations, an 8×8 DCT requires 64 multiply operations (and 49 additions) for each of the 64 result coefficients, for a total of 4096 multiplies, an average of 8 multiplication operations per pixel. However, the DCT is *separable:* an 8×8 DCT can be computed as eight 8×1 horizontal transforms followed by eight 1×8 vertical transforms. This optimization, combined with other optimizations comparable to those of the fast Fourier transform (FFT), greatly reduces computational complexity: A fully optimized 8×8 DCT requires as few as 11 multiplies for each 8 samples (or in an IDCT, transform coefficients).

JPEG encoding example

I will illustrate JPEG encoding by walking through a numerical example. Figure 45.4 represents an 8×8 array of luma samples from an image, prior to level shifting:

Figure 45.4 **An 8×8 array of luma samples** from an image is shown. This 8×8 array is known in JPEG terminology as a *block*.

$$f = \begin{bmatrix} 139 & 144 & 149 & 153 & 155 & 155 & 155 & 155 \\ 144 & 151 & 153 & 156 & 159 & 156 & 156 & 156 \\ 150 & 155 & 160 & 163 & 158 & 156 & 156 & 156 \\ 159 & 161 & 162 & 160 & 160 & 159 & 159 & 159 \\ 159 & 160 & 161 & 162 & 162 & 155 & 155 & 155 \\ 161 & 161 & 161 & 161 & 160 & 157 & 157 & 157 \\ 162 & 162 & 161 & 163 & 162 & 157 & 157 & 157 \\ 162 & 162 & 161 & 161 & 163 & 158 & 158 & 158 \end{bmatrix}$$

The result of computing the DCT, rounded to integers, is shown in Figure 45.5:

Figure 45.5 **The DCT tends to concentrate** the power of the image block into low-frequency DCT coefficients (those in the upper left-hand corner of the matrix). No information is lost at this stage. The DCT is its own inverse, within a scale factor, so performing the DCT on these transform coefficients would reconstruct the original samples (subject only to roundoff error).

$$F = \begin{bmatrix} 1260 & -1 & -12 & -5 & 2 & -2 & -3 & 1 \\ -23 & -17 & -6 & -3 & -3 & 0 & 0 & 1 \\ -11 & -9 & -2 & 2 & 0 & -1 & -1 & 0 \\ -7 & -2 & 0 & 1 & 1 & 0 & 0 & 0 \\ -1 & -1 & 1 & 2 & 0 & -1 & 1 & 1 \\ 2 & 0 & 2 & 0 & -1 & 1 & 1 & -1 \\ -1 & 0 & 0 & -1 & 0 & 2 & 1 & -1 \\ -3 & 2 & -4 & -2 & 2 & 1 & -1 & 0 \end{bmatrix}$$

This example shows that image power is concentrated into low-frequency transform coefficients – that is, those coefficients in the upper left-hand corner of the DCT matrix. No information is lost at this stage. The DCT is its own inverse, so performing the DCT a second time would perfectly reconstruct the original samples, subject only to the roundoff error in the DCT and IDCT.

As expressed in Equation 45.1, the arithmetic of an 8×8 DCT effectively causes the coefficient values to be multiplied by a factor of 8 relative to the orig-

In MPEG-2, DC terms can be coded with 8, 9, or 10 bits – or, in 4:2:2 profile, 11 bits – of precision.

$$Q = \begin{bmatrix} 16 & 11 & 10 & 16 & 24 & 40 & 51 & 61 \\ 12 & 12 & 14 & 19 & 26 & 58 & 60 & 55 \\ 14 & 13 & 16 & 24 & 40 & 57 & 69 & 56 \\ 14 & 17 & 22 & 29 & 51 & 87 & 80 & 62 \\ 18 & 22 & 37 & 56 & 68 & 109 & 103 & 77 \\ 24 & 35 & 55 & 64 & 81 & 104 & 113 & 92 \\ 49 & 64 & 78 & 87 & 103 & 121 & 120 & 101 \\ 72 & 92 & 95 & 98 & 112 & 100 & 103 & 99 \end{bmatrix}$$

Figure 45.6 **A typical JPEG quantizer matrix** reflects the visual system's poor sensitivity to high spatial frequencies. Transform coefficients can be approximated, to some degree, without introducing noticeable impairments. The quantizer matrix codes a step size for each spatial frequency. Each transform coefficient is divided by the corresponding quantizer value; the remainder (or fraction) is discarded. Discarding the fraction is what makes JPEG lossy.

inal sample values. The value 1260 in the [0, 0] entry – the *DC* coefficient, or term – is $\frac{1}{8}$ of the sum of the original sample values. (All of the other coefficients are referred to as *AC*.)

The human visual system is not very sensitive to information at high spatial frequencies. Information at high spatial frequencies can be discarded, to some degree, without introducing noticeable impairments. JPEG uses a *quantizer matrix* (**Q**), which codes a step size for each of the 64 spatial frequencies. In the quantization step of compression, each transform coefficient is divided by the corresponding quantizer value (step size) entry in the **Q** matrix. The remainder (fraction) after division is discarded.

It is not the DCT itself, but the discarding of the fraction after quantization of the transform coefficients, that makes JPEG lossy!

JPEG has no standard or default quantizer matrix; however, sample matrices given in a nonnormative appendix are often used. Typically, there are two matrices, one for luma and one for colour differences.

An example **Q** matrix is shown in Figure 45.6 above. Its entries form a radially symmetric version of Figure 23.5, on page 252. The [0, 0] entry in the quantizer matrix is relatively small (here, 16), so the DC term

In MPEG, default quantizer matrices are standardized, but they can be overridden by matrices conveyed in the bitstream.

is finely quantized. Further from [0, 0], the entries get larger, and the quantization becomes more coarse. Owing to the large step sizes associated with the high-order coefficients, they can be represented by fewer bits.

In the JPEG and MPEG standards, and in most JPEG-like schemes, each entry in the quantizer matrix takes a value between 1 and 255.

At first glance, the large step size associated with the DC coefficient (here, $Q_{0,0} = 16$) looks worrisome: With 8-bit data ranging from –127 to +128, owing to the divisor of 16, you might expect this quantized coefficient to be be represented with just 4 bits. However, as mentioned earlier, the arithmetic of Equation 45.1 scales the coefficients by 8 with respect to the sample values, so a quantizer value of 16 corresponds to 7 bits of precision when referenced to the sample values.

DCT coefficients after quantization, and after discarding the quotient fractions, are shown in Figure 45.7:

Figure 45.7 **DCT coefficients after quantization** are shown. Most of the high-frequency information in this block – DCT entries at the right and the bottom of the matrix – are quantized to zero. The nonzero coefficients have small magnitudes.

$$F^* = \begin{bmatrix} 79 & 0 & -1 & 0 & 0 & 0 & 0 & 0 \\ -2 & -1 & 0 & 0 & 0 & 0 & 0 & 0 \\ -1 & -1 & 0 & 0 & 0 & 0 & 0 & 0 \\ 0 & 0 & 0 & 0 & 0 & 0 & 0 & 0 \\ 0 & 0 & 0 & 0 & 0 & 0 & 0 & 0 \\ 0 & 0 & 0 & 0 & 0 & 0 & 0 & 0 \\ 0 & 0 & 0 & 0 & 0 & 0 & 0 & 0 \\ 0 & 0 & 0 & 0 & 0 & 0 & 0 & 0 \end{bmatrix}$$

Most of the high-frequency information in this block – the DCT entries at the right and the bottom of the matrix – are quantized to zero. Apart from the DC term, the nonzero coefficients have small magnitudes.

Following quantization, the quantized coefficients are rearranged according to the likely distribution of image power in the block. This is accomplished by *zigzag scanning*, sketched in Figure 45.8 at the top of the facing page.

Once rearranged, the quantized coefficients are represented in a one-dimensional string; an *end of block* (EOB) code marks the location in the string where all

Figure 45.8 **Zigzag scanning** is used to rearrange quantized coefficients according to the likely distribution of image power in the block.

$$F^* = \begin{bmatrix} 79 & 0 & -1 & 0 & 0 & 0 & 0 & 0 \\ -2 & -1 & 0 & 0 & 0 & 0 & 0 & 0 \\ -1 & -1 & 0 & 0 & 0 & 0 & 0 & 0 \\ 0 & 0 & 0 & 0 & 0 & 0 & 0 & 0 \\ 0 & 0 & 0 & 0 & 0 & 0 & 0 & 0 \\ 0 & 0 & 0 & 0 & 0 & 0 & 0 & 0 \\ 0 & 0 & 0 & 0 & 0 & 0 & 0 & 0 \\ 0 & 0 & 0 & 0 & 0 & 0 & 0 & 0 \end{bmatrix}$$

succeeding coefficients are zero, as sketched in Figure 45.9:

79	0	−2	−1	−1	−1	0	0	−1	EOB

Figure 45.9 **Zigzag-scanned coefficient string**

In the usual case that just a few high-order quantized coefficients are nonzero, zigzag reordering tends to produce strings of repeating zeros. Additional compression can be accomplished by using *variable-length encoding* (VLE, also known as *Huffman* coding). Variable-length encoding is a lossless process that takes advantage of the statistics of the "run length" (the count of zero codes) and the "level" (absolute value, or magnitude) of the following transform coefficient.

In JPEG and MPEG terminology, the magnitude (absolute value) of a coefficient is called its *level*.

The DC term is treated specially: It is differentially coded. The first DC term is coded directly (using a DC VLE table), but successive DC terms are coded as differences from that. In essence, the previous DC term is used as a predictor for the current term. Separate predictors are maintained for Y', C_B, and C_R.

Zero AC coefficients are collapsed, and the string is represented in {run length, level} pairs, as shown in Figure 45.10:

{1: −2}, {0: −1}, {0: −1}, {0: −1}, {2: −1}, EOB

Figure 45.10 **VLE {run length, level} pairs**

A JPEG encoder has one or more VLE tables that map the set of {run length, level} pairs to variable-length bitstrings; pairs with high probability are assigned short bitstrings. JPEG has no standard VLE tables; however, sample tables given in a nonnormative appendix are often used. Typically, there are two tables, one for luma and one for colour differences. The tables used for an

MPEG's VLE tables are standardized; they do not need to be transmitted with each sequence or each picture.

image are included at the head of the JPEG bitstream, and thereby conveyed to the decoder.

JPEG decoding

Decompression is achieved by performing the inverse of the encoder operations, in reverse order. Figure 45.11 shows the matrix of differences between original sample values and reconstructed sample values for this example – the reconstruction error. As is typical of JPEG, the original sample values are not perfectly reconstructed. However, discarding information according to the spatial frequency response of human vision ensures that the errors introduced during compression will not be too perceptible.

JPEG performance is loosely characterized by the error between the original image data and the reconstructed data. Metrics such as mean-squared error (MSE) are used to objectify this measure; however, MSE (and other engineering and mathematical measures) don't necessarily correlate well with subjective performance. In practice, we take care to choose quantizer matrices according to the properties of perception. Imperfect recovery of the original image data after JPEG decompression effectively adds noise to the image. Imperfect reconstruction of the DC term can lead to JPEG's 8×8 blocks becoming visible – the JPEG *blocking artifact*.

The lossiness of JPEG, and its compression, come almost entirely from the quantizer step. The DCT itself may introduce a small amount of roundoff error; the inverse DCT may also introduce a slight roundoff error. The variable-length encoding and decoding processes are perfectly lossless.

Figure 45.11 **Reconstruction error** is shown in this matrix of differences between original sample values and reconstructed sample values. Original sample values are not perfectly reconstructed, but discarding information according to the spatial frequency response of human vision ensures that the errors will not be too perceptible.

$$
\varepsilon = \begin{bmatrix}
-5 & -2 & 0 & 1 & 1 & -1 & -1 & -1 \\
-4 & 1 & 1 & 2 & 3 & 0 & 0 & 0 \\
-5 & -1 & 3 & 5 & 0 & -1 & 0 & 1 \\
-1 & 0 & 1 & -2 & -1 & 0 & 2 & 4 \\
-4 & -3 & -3 & -1 & 0 & -5 & -3 & -1 \\
-2 & -2 & -3 & -3 & -2 & -3 & -1 & 0 \\
2 & 1 & -1 & 1 & 0 & -4 & -2 & -1 \\
4 & 3 & 0 & 0 & 1 & -3 & -1 & 0
\end{bmatrix}
$$

DIGITAL VIDEO AND HD ALGORITHMS AND INTERFACES

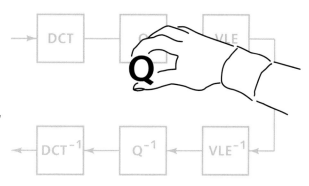

Figure 45.12 **Compression ratio control in JPEG** is effected by altering the quantizer matrix: The larger the entries in the quantizer matrix, the higher the compression ratio. The higher the compression ratio, the higher the reconstruction error. At some point, compression artifacts will become visible.

In ISO JPEG, the quantizer matrix is directly conveyed in the bitstream. In the DV adaptation of JPEG, several quantizer matrices are defined in the standard; the bitstream indicates which one to use.

Compression ratio control

The larger the entries in the quantizer matrix, the higher the compression ratio. Compression ratio control in JPEG can be achieved by altering the quantizer matrix, as suggested by the manual control sketched in Figure 45.12. Larger step sizes give higher compression ratios, but image quality is liable to suffer if the step sizes get too big. Smaller step sizes give better quality, at the expense of poorer compression ratio. There is no easy way to predict, in advance of actually performing the compression, how many bytes of compressed data will result from a particular image.

The quantizer matrix could, in principle, be chosen adaptively to maximize the performance for a particular image. However, this isn't practical. JPEG encoders for still images generally offer a choice of several compression settings, each associated with a fixed quantizer that is chosen by the system designer.

Because different quantizer matrices may be associated with different images, the quantizer matrix must be conveyed to the decoder, as sketched in Figure 45.13, either as part of the file, or through a side channel. In colour images, separate quantizers are typically used for the luma and chroma components. In stillframe applications, the overhead of this operation is small. In a realtime system, the overhead of conveying quantizer matrices with every frame, or even within a frame, is a burden.

A modified approach to compression ratio control is adopted in many forms of M-JPEG (and also, as you will see in the next chapter, in MPEG): Reference luma and chroma quantizer matrices are established, and all of

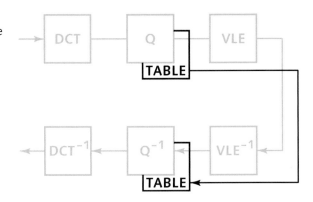

Figure 45.13 **Because the quantizer is adjustable,** the quantizer matrix must be conveyed through a side channel to the decoder. In colour images, separate quantizers are used for the luma and chroma components.

The notation *mquant* is found in the ITU-T H.261 standard for teleconferencing; *mquant* (or *MQUANT*) is not found in JPEG or MPEG documents, but is used informally.

their entries are scaled up and down by a single numerical parameter, the *quantizer scale factor* (QSF, sometimes denoted *Mquant*). QSF can be varied to accomplish rate control.

As mentioned earlier, JPEG ordinarily uses luma/chroma coding with 4:2:0 chroma subsampling. However, the JPEG standard accommodates *R'G'B'* image data without subsampling, and also accommodates four-channel image data (such as CMYK, used in print) without subsampling. These schemes are inapplicable to video.

JPEG/JFIF

The ISO/IEC standard for JPEG defines a bitstream, consistent with the original expectation that JPEG would be used across communication links. To apply the JPEG technique to computer files, a small amount of supplementary information is required; in addition, it is necessary to encode the ISO/IEC *bit*stream into a *byte*stream. The de facto standard for single-image JPEG files is the *JPEG File Interchange Format* (JFIF), adopted by an industry group led by C-Cube. A JFIF file encapsulates a JPEG bitstream, along with a small amount of supplementary data. If you are presented with an image data file described as JPEG, it is almost certainly an ISO/IEC JPEG bitstream in a JFIF wrapper.

HAMILTON, ERIC (1992), *JPEG File Interchange Format*, Version 1.02 (Milpitas, Calif.: C-Cube Microsystems). This informal document was endorsed by ECMA and was published in June 2009 as ECMA TR/98 having the same title.

The JPEG standard itself implies that JPEG could be applied to linear-light *RGB* data. However, JPEG has poor visual performance unless applied to perceptually coded image data, that is, to gamma-corrected *R'G'B'*.

The ISO/IEC JPEG standard itself seems to suggest that the technique can be applied to arbitrary *RGB* data. The standard itself fails to mention primary chromaticities, white point, transfer function, or gamma correction. If accurate colour is to be achieved, then means outside the standard must be employed to convey these parameters. Prior to Mac OS X 10.6, there were two classes of JPEG/JFIF files, PC and Macintosh. Files that were created on classic Macintosh conformed to the default Macintosh coding, where *R'G'B'* codes were expected to be raised to the 1.52 power to produce display tristimulus. There was no reliable way to distinguish the two classes of files. Files created on PCs, and modern Macs, are interpreted in sRGB coding.

Motion-JPEG (M-JPEG)

Motion-JPEG (M-JPEG) refers to the use of a JPEG-like algorithm to compress every picture in a sequence of video fields or frames. I say "JPEG-like": The algorithms used have all of the general features of the algorithm standardized by JPEG, including DCT, quantization, zig-zag scanning, and variable-length encoding. However, ISO JPEG bitstreams are not typically produced, and some systems add algorithmic features outside of the JPEG standard. Various M-JPEG systems are widely used in desktop video editing; however, there are no well established standards, and compressed video files typically cannot be interchanged between M-JPEG systems.

In studio applications, file interchange is a practical necessity, and two approaches have emerged. Both are functionally equivalent to M-JPEG, but have firm standards.

The first approach is DV compression, developed for consumer digital recording on videotape, but also used in desktop video editing. DV compression is described in the following chapter.

The second approach is MPEG-2 video compression, described in Chapter 47, on page 513. MPEG-2 was developed to exploit interframe coherence to achieve much higher compression ratios than M-JPEG, and is intended mainly for video distribution. However, the I-picture-only variant of MPEG-2 (sometimes called *I-frame-only*) is functionally equivalent to M-JPEG, and is being used for studio editing.

A few studio DVTR formats, such as Digital Betacam and HD-D5, use M-JPEG-style compression, but are not intimately related to any of JPEG, DV, or MPEG.

Further reading

Clarke describes the theory of transform coding of stilll images. Rabbani and Jones have written an excellent introduction to the mathematics of still image compression. Symes provides an approachable introduction to video compression.

CLARKE, R.J. (1985), *Transform Coding of Images* (Boston: Academic Press).

RABBANI, MAJID, and PAUL W. JONES (1991), *Digital Image Compression Techniques* (Bellingham, Wash.: SPIE).

SYMES, PETER (2003), *Digital Video Compression* (New York: McGraw-Hill).

DV compression 46

DV denotes the compression and data packing scheme introduced for consumer *digital video cassette* (DVC) recorders and later adapted for professional use. DV compression uses discrete cosine transform (DCT), quantization, and variable-length encoding (VLE) comparable to JPEG; however, DV does not *conform* to the JPEG standard: Optimizations have been made to accommodate interlaced scanning, constant bit-rate (CBR) operation, and other features related to video-tape recording. Interlace is handled by allowing the encoder to dynamically choose between frame and field modes. Constant bit-rate is achieved by dynamically altering the quantization matrices to avoid exceeding the available capacity.

Concerning DVC recording of SD, see *DV recording*, in Chapter 9 of *Composite NTSC and PAL: Legacy Video Systems*. DVCPRO and DVCPRO 50 have been standardized as SMPTE D-7. JVC's Digital-S was standardized as D-9. See *Professional DV variants*, on page 512.

Consumer DVC has a data rate of 25 Mb/s. I call this *DV25*. DV25 coding was adopted for studio use in D-7 (DVCPRO) and DVCAM; it was extended to 50 Mb/s (*DV50*), used in the DVCPRO50 and D-9 systems, and then to 100 Mb/s (*DV100*), used in D-11 (DVCPRO HD).

DV25 and DV50 compress either 480*i*29.97 or 576*i*25 SD video according to BT.601. DV100 compresses HD video according to BT.709. Chroma subsampling in DV is a smorgasbord; see Table 46.1.

	480*i*	576*i*	HD
DV25 (consumer, DVCAM)	4:1:1	4:2:0	
DV25 (DVCPRO, D-7)	4:1:1	4:1:1	
DV50 (DVCPRO50, D-9)	4:2:2	4:2:2	
DV100 (DVCPRO HD, D-12)			4:2:2

Table 46.1 **DV chroma subsampling**

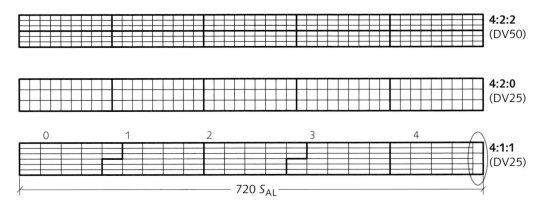

Figure 46.1 **DV superblocks** are shown for three chroma subsampling schemes – 4:2:2 (top), 4:2:0 (middle), and 4:1:1 (bottom). Thin lines enclose *macroblocks.* Each macroblock contains an 8×8 block of C_B, an 8×8 block of C_R, and two or more 8×8 blocks of luma. Thick lines enclose *superblocks;* each superblock comprises 27 macroblocks. A 4:1:1 macroblock is about four times wider than it is tall.

DV chroma subsampling

Different versions of DV use different subsampling schemes: 4:2:2, 4:1:1, 4:2:0, and even 3:1:1 and 3:1:0! In DV, a macroblock comprises an 8×8 block of C_B samples, an 8×8 block of C_R samples, and the requisite number and arrangement of 8×8 blocks of luma samples.

SMPTE 314M declares that in subsampling 4:2:2 to 4:1:1, "every other pixel is discarded." Obviously, high image quality requires that proper filtering be performed before discarding samples. In DV, C_B and C_R samples coincide with luma both horizontally and vertically. However, in the 4:2:0 scheme used in 576*i* consumer equipment, C_R samples are not sited at the same locations as C_B samples. Instead, C_B and C_R samples are sited in line-alternate vertical positions throughout each field: Each C_B sample is centered two image rows below an associated C_R sample.

The DV format originated for consumer applications. Consumer DV25 aggregates 27 macroblocks into a *superblock* (SB), covering 48 image rows, whose arrangement is depicted in Figure 46.1 above. In 480*i*29.97 DV25, there are 50 superblocks per frame; in 576*i*25 DV25, there are 60 superblocks per frame.

SMPTE 314M defines DV25 and DV50 for studio use. The Blue Book, and IEC standards, use the word *decimated* instead of *discarded.* IEC 61834-1, cited in Chapter 9, *Videotape recording,* of *Composite NTSC and PAL: Legacy Video Systems,* prescribes the subsampling schemes for consumer DV.

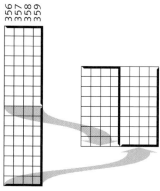

356 357 358 359

Figure 46.2 **Chroma samples in 4:1:1 DV** require special treatment at the right-hand edge of the picture, in the region circled in Figure 46.1. Here I show chroma as if square-sampled; actually, each 4:1:1 chroma sample is about four times wider than tall.

For consumer 576*i*25 DV25, and the 576*i*25 variant of DVCAM, 4:2:0 chroma subsampling was chosen, allegedly to offer some compatibility with DVB. The 4:2:0 superblock structure is shown in the middle sketch of Figure 46.1; in 4:2:0, each superblock comprises a regular array of 9×3 macroblocks.

For consumer 480*i*29.97 DV25, 4:1:1 subsampling was chosen. This was sufficient to achieve NTSC chroma bandwidth, and avoided conflict between subsampling and interlace. BT.601 video adapted to 4:1:1 subsampling has 180 active chroma samples per line; however, 180 isn't divisible by 8, so a regular superblock structure wasn't possible. To form 8×8 chroma blocks, C_B and C_R samples at the right-hand edge of the image are treated strangely, as detailed in Figure 46.2 in the margin: Pairs of vertically adjacent 4×8 arrays of chroma samples from the right end of each line are abutted horizontally to form 8×8 blocks.

The studio version of DV25 (used in D-7) uses 4:1:1 chroma subsampling in both 480*i*29.97 and 576*i*25; the strange 4:1:1 superblock structure is used.

DV50 has twice the data rate of DV25. DV50 uses 4:2:2 chroma subsampling for both 480*i*29.97 and 576*i*25. Owing to 4:2:2 subsampling, each macroblock has four blocks (instead of the six blocks of either 4:1:1 or 4:2:0); a frame has twice as many macroblocks as DV25, and twice as many superblocks. The 4:2:2 super-block structure is depicted in the top sketch of Figure 46.1. Today's DV50 recorders are implemented using two DV25 encoders, processing alternate 24-row bands of the image; they record the resulting two channels to parallel tracks.

DV frame/field modes

ISO JPEG assumes a progressive source image: All image rows are processed in spatial order. In video, the two fields of an interlaced frame can be woven together and processed as if progressive, where every 8×8 block has alternate rows taken from opposite fields. Providing interfield motion is limited, this scheme works well. In the presence of interfield motion, though, the high vertical frequency AC coefficients produced by the DCT will have high magnitude. This produces low quality for a given data rate. Higher quality can be obtained if the

See *weave*, on page 414.

This scheme involves two 8×4 DCTs; it should be called *2-8-4-DCT!* MPEG-2 has a similar scheme: An encoder can choose *frame DCT coding* or *field DCT coding* for each macroblock in an interlaced MPEG-2 sequence.

fields are coded separately. DV dynamically adapts to the degree of interfield motion by allowing the compressor to choose, on a block-by-block basis, whether to use *8-8-DCT mode* or *2-4-8-DCT mode.*

In 8-8-DCT ("frame") mode, opposite fields are woven together and subject to a single DCT as an 8×8 block.

In 2-4-8-DCT ("field") mode, two 8×4 arrays of samples from like fields are formed. The element-by-element sums of the two 8×4 arrays, and their element-by-element differences, are subject to separate DCTs. The sum matrix is associated with a DC term; the difference array has only AC terms. Each of the sum and difference DCT arrays is zigzag scanned, and the coefficients are alternated for joint VLE encoding.

DV standards do not dictate how an encoder is to choose between 8-8-DCT and 2-4-8-DCT modes. Typically, luma differences are analyzed in the spatial domain to detect interfield motion, and 2-4-8-DCT mode is chosen if interfield motion is significant.

Picture-in-shuttle in DV

It is a practical necessity that a VCR recover a usable picture in fast forward and rewind ("shuttle"). When a digital VCR is operating in shuttle mode, isolated sync blocks are read from the tape. In DV, recovering a usable picture in shuttle mode is made possible by having each sync block correspond to one *coded macroblock* (CM); an entire macroblock can thereby be reconstructed individually from an isolated sync block. This scheme precludes predictive coding of the DCT's DC terms: DC terms are represented directly in each CM.

The correspondence of sync blocks with coded macroblocks seems to require that *every* macroblock be coded into a fixed number of bits. In the DV system, every macroblock is associated with a 77-byte coded macroblock, and a sync block contains one CM. Each CM contains the DC term, and several AC terms, of each block's DCT. However, that's not the whole story.

DV overflow scheme

When a portion of an image is devoid of detail, a few low-frequency AC coefficients of its DCT may have significant magnitude, but nearly all high-frequency AC terms will have very small magnitude. When a portion of an image has a lot of fine detail, many high-frequency AC terms will have large magnitude. To reproduce the image accurately requires that these terms be recorded. Generally, increasing amounts of detail require increased data capacity.

It is unusual for an image to contain detail everywhere; typically, complexity is spatially concentrated in an image. A compression algorithm should adapt to the spatial distribution of image detail, by allocating bits where they are needed. If fine detail is distributed throughout an image – in a full-frame image of the leaves of a tree, perhaps – then even quite large reconstruction errors are likely to be imperceptible.

The requirement for picture-in-shuttle seems to preclude allocation of data capacity to the regions where more bits are required. However, DV implements an overflow scheme whereby the bits resulting from compression of a handful of macroblocks are shared among a handful of CMs. Should the VLE-coded AC coefficients for a complex block (augmented by a 4-bit EOB) require more bits than the fixed capacity assigned to that block in the CM, the overflow bits "spill" into other blocks whose capacity was not filled. Overflow data first spills into space that might remain in other blocks of the same CM; any remaining bits spill into available space in any of four other CMs associated with diverse regions of the image. The set of five coded macroblocks that share overflow space is called a *segment;* a segment has a fixed capacity of 385 bytes. The macroblocks of a segment are spatially distributed throughout the frame: No two macroblocks are taken from the same row or the same column of superblocks. This distribution exploits the statistical likelihood that only one or two of the macroblocks will be complex.

When a DV VCR is in shuttle mode, it is likely that a single CM will be recovered individually, without any of the other four CMs of its segment. Overflow data for the macroblock is quite likely to be missing. However, overflow data is limited to high-frequency AC coefficients. In shuttle playback, missing overflow coefficients are replaced by zero. This causes loss of picture detail in the reconstructed picture; however, the absence of these coefficients does not seriously degrade picture

CMs in a segment are denoted *a* through *e*.

quality, and in any event users do not expect the same picture quality in shuttle mode as in normal playback.

DV quantization

The main challenge of DV encoding is to determine suitable quantization matrices for a segment's AC coefficients, such that when all of the quantized coefficients are subject to variable-length encoding, the VLE-coded coefficients just neatly fit in the available space. The goal is to quantize the AC terms as finely as possible, without exceeding the capacity of a segment. In essence, this is a form of rate control. Quantization of a segment takes place after the DCT, using this algorithm:

• First, each block in the segment is assigned to a *class* from 0 (fine) to 3 (coarse), representing the block's spatial complexity. DV standards provide a table that suggests how an encoder can assign a class number according to the magnitude of the largest AC term of a block; however, use of that table is not mandatory.

What DV standards call *level* is the magnitude – that is, the absolute value – of the AC coefficient. Sign is coded separately.

• Then, up to 15 trial quantization passes are made, to determine a *quantization number* (QNO) from 0 (coarse) to 15 (fine). Class number and quantization number are combined to determine a quantization matrix according to tables in the standard. For each trial QNO, DCT coefficients are quantized and zigzag scanned. Nonzero AC coefficient are identified; {run length, level} pairs are computed for each nonzero coefficient; and the required number of variable-length-encoded bits is accumulated. Quantization is eased by the fact that the entries in the quantization matrices are all powers of two (1, 2, 4, 8, 16); each coefficient quantization operation is merely a binary shift. The lookup and assembly of VLE-coded bitstream need not be performed at this stage; it suffices for now to accumulate the bit count.

For a more elaborate description, and the quantization tables, see Symes, cited on page 535.

The final QNO for the segment is the one that produces the largest number of bits not exceeding the capacity of the segment – for DV25, 500 bits for luma AC coefficients (including four 4-bit EOBs), and 340 bits for chroma AC coefficients (including two 4-bit EOBs).

Once the segment's QNO is determined, VLE coding takes place, and the CMs of the segment are assembled. Each CM starts with one byte containing its QNO and error concealment *status* (STA) bits. Each block

This scheme is described as *three-pass*; however, the first pass is trivial

includes its DC coefficient, its mode (8-8-DCT or 2-4-8-DCT), and its class. Finally, the VLE-coded AC coefficients are distributed in a deterministic three-pass algorithm – first to the associated block, then to unused space in other blocks of the same CM (if space is available), and finally to unused space in other CMs of the segment. QNO has been chosen such that sufficient space for all coefficients is guaranteed to be available: Every bit of every coefficient will be stored somewhere within the segment.

Each CM comprises 77 bytes, including by a 1-byte header. In DV25, a CM includes four coded luma blocks and two coded chroma blocks:

• A coded luma block totals 14 bytes, and includes a 9-bit DC term, one mode bit, and a 2-bit class number. One hundred bits are available for AC coefficients.

• A coded chroma block totals 10 bytes, and includes a 9-bit DC term, one mode bit, and a 2-bit class number. Sixty-eight bits are available for AC coefficients.

For 4:2:2 subsampling in DV50, a CM has four blocks, not six; space that in 4:1:1 or 4:2:0 would be allocated to luma blocks is available for overflow data. For 3:1:0 subsampling (used in SDL, to be described in a moment), a CM has eight blocks, not six: Each luma block has 10 bytes; each chroma block has 8 bytes.

DV digital interface (DIF)

The superblocks that I have mentioned form the basis for digital interface of DV bitstreams. A 3-byte ID is prepended to each 77-byte coded macroblock to form an 80-byte *digital interface* (DIF) *block*.

A coded DV25 superblock is represented by 135 video DIF blocks. That is augmented with several nonvideo DIF blocks to form a *DIF sequence* of 150 DIF blocks:

• 1 header DIF block
• 2 subcode DIF blocks
• 3 VAUX DIF blocks
• 9 audio DIF blocks
• 135 video DIF blocks

Realtime DV25 video requires 10 or 12 DIF sequences – that is, about 1500 or 1800 DIF blocks – per second. DV50, and DV100 systems have comparable structures, but different data rates.

Once packaged in DIF sequences, DV bitstreams can be conveyed across the IEEE 1394 interface, also known as *FireWire* and *i.LINK*, that I described on page 167. IEEE 1394 is suitable for consumer use, and is widely used in desktop video. For professional applications, DIF sequence bitstreams can be transported across various interfaces including the SDTI interface that I introduced on page 441. (The 3-byte ID is unused in DV-over-SDTI.) DIF sequences can be stored in files – for example, QuickTime or MXF files.

Consumer DV recording

DV25 was widely adopted for consumer SD recording on MiniDV cassettes. Several schemes to extend DV to HD were described in the first edition of this book; none of these were commercialized. Consumer HD recording on MiniDV uses the HDV system, outlined on page 161.

Professional DV variants

DVCPRO and DVCAM data rate is 25 Mb/s, identical to consumer DV; however, the physical magnetic tape is more robust and more suitable for professional use.

DV technology was introduced for consumer videotape recording, and was widely deployed in consumer camcorders and desktop video editing systems. DV videotape technology was adapted to professional videotape recorders – first for SD as DVCPRO (D-7) and DVCAM, then for HD as DVCPRO HD (D-12). The DV compression system made the transition into products using hard disk drive and flash media.

DVCPRO50 DVTRs are standardized in SMPTE's D-7 series; DV50 SD bitstreams are recorded onto 6 mm tape in DVC-style cassettes.

DV50, also for SD, has twice the data rate, twice as many macroblocks per second (or per frame), and twice as many superblocks per second (or per frame) as DV25. DV50 uses 4:2:2 subsampling; a CM contains just two luma blocks instead of four. Space that in DV25 would have been allocated to AC terms of the other two luma blocks is available for overflow AC terms. The corresponding DC terms, mode bits, and class bits are reserved. In DV50, the first four bits of DV25's AC coefficient spaces are filled with EOB symbols.

Panasonic introduced the DVCPRO HD DVTR format, which was subsequently standardized as SMPTE D-12. See page 482.

DV100 doubles the DV50 data rate to 100 Mb/s, and accommodates HD image formats and 4:2:2 chroma subsampling: 1280×1080 downsampled from 1080*i* or 1080*p*, or 960×720 downsampled from 720*p*.

MPEG-2 video compression   47

I assume that you are familiar with *Introduction to video compression,* on page 147, and with JPEG, M-JPEG, and DV, described in the preceding two chapters.

The DCT-based intrafield or intraframe compression at the heart of M-JPEG is suitable for video production; however, for distribution, dramatically higher compression ratios can be obtained by using interframe coding. MPEG-2 video compression exploits temporal coherence – the statistical likelihood that successive pictures in a video sequence are very similar. MPEG-2's intended application ranges from below SD to beyond HD; the intended bit rate ranges from about 1.5 Mb/s to well over 20 Mb/s. MPEG-2 also defines audio compression, and provides for the transport of video with associated audio.

ISO/IEC 13818-1, *Generic coding of moving pictures and associated audio information: Systems* [MPEG-2], also published as ITU-T H.220.0.

ISO/IEC 13818-2, *Generic coding of moving pictures and associated audio information: Video* [MPEG-2], also published as ITU-T H.262.

MPEG-2 refers to a suite of standards, promulgated jointly by ISO/IEC and ITU-T. The suite starts with Part 1: *Systems* and Part 2: *Video,* cited in the margin, which are jointly published by ISO, IEC, and ITU-T. Six other parts are jointly published by ISO and IEC – Part 3: *Audio;* Part 4: *Conformance testing;* Part 5: *Software simulation;* Part 6: *Extensions for DSM-CC;* Part 7: *Advanced Audio Coding* (AAC); Part 9: *Extension for real time interface for systems decoders;* and Part 10: *Conformance extensions for Digital Storage Media Command and Control* (DSM-CC). The projected Part 8, for 10-bit video, was discontinued. MPEG-2 standards were first issued in 1996; subsequently, several corrigenda and amendments have been issued.

MPEG-2 specifies exactly what constitutes a legal bitstream: A legal ("conformant") encoder generates only legal bitstreams; a legal decoder correctly decodes any legal bitstream. MPEG-2 does *not* standardize how an encoder accomplishes compression!

The MPEG-2 standard implicitly defines exactly how a decoder reconstructs pictures data from a coded bitstream, without dictating the implementation of the decoder. MPEG-2 explicitly avoids specifying what it calls the "display process" – how reconstructed pictures are displayed. Most MPEG-2 decoder implementations have flexible output formats; however, MPEG-2 decoder equipment is ordinarily designed to output a specific raster standard.

An MPEG-2 bitstream may represent interlaced or progressive pictures. Typical decoder equipment outputs either interlace or progressive signals. Certain decoder equipment has the capability to switch between the two output formats. Because interlaced scanning remains dominant in consumer electronics – both in SD and in HD – a decoder system must be capable of producing an interlaced signal from a progressive sequence. Also, it is a practical necessity for an MPEG-2 decoder to have spatial resampling capability: If an HD MPEG-2 decoder is presented with an SD sequence, consumers would complain if reconstructed pictures were not upconverted for display in HD.

MPEG-2 profiles and levels

An MPEG-2 bitstream can potentially invoke many algorithmic features – some practitioners call them "tools" – at a decoder. Also, a bitstream can reflect many possible parameter values. The MPEG-2 standard classifies bitstreams and decoders in a matrix of *profiles* and *levels*.

Profiles constrain the algorithmic features potentially used by an encoder, present in a bitstream, or implemented in a decoder. The higher the profile, the more complexity is required of the decoder. MPEG-2 defines six profiles: *Simple* (SP), *Main* (MP), *4:2:2* (422P), *SNR*, *Spatial* (Spt), *High* (HP), and *Multiview* (MVP).

Levels place restrictions on parameter values used by an encoder or decoder. The higher the level, the more memory or data throughput is required of a decoder. MPEG-2 defines four levels: *Low* (LL), *Main* (ML), *High-1440* (H14), and *High* (HL).

A profile and level combination is indicated by profile and level separated by an at sign – for example, MP@ML or MP@HL. The SNR, Spatial, High, and

MPEG-2 specifies several algorithmic features – such as arbitrary frame rate, and 4:4:4 chroma subsampling – that are not permitted in any standard profile. These features are unlikely to see commercialization.

Profile @Level	MPEG-1 CPB	Simple (no B pictures)	Main (MP)	4:2:2 (422P)
High (HL)			1920×1152 60 Hz 80 Mb/s	1920×1088 60 Hz 300 Mb/s
High-1440 (H14)			1440×1152 60 Hz 47 Mb/s	
Main (ML)		720×576 30 Hz 15 Mb/s	720×576 30 Hz 15 Mb/s	720×608 30 Hz 50 Mb/s
Low (LL)			352×288 30 Hz 4 Mb/s	
MPEG-1 CPB †max 99 Kpx	768×576† 30 Hz 1.856 Mb/s			

Table 47.1 MPEG-2 profiles, here arranged in columns, specify algorithmic features. (I exclude SNR, Spt, HP, and MVP.) MPEG-2 levels, here arranged in rows, constrain parameter values. Each entry gives maximum picture size, frame rate, and bit rate. The two shaded entries are commercially dominant: Main profile at main level (MP@ML) is used for SD distribution; main profile at high level (MP@HL) is used for HD distribution. SMPTE 308M places constraints on GoP structure for 422P@HL. Any compliant MPEG-2 decoder must decode an MPEG-1 *constrained-parameters bitstream* (CPB); the constrained parameters effectively constitute a profile/level combination.

Multiview profiles have no relevance to video production or distribution, and are unlikely to see commercial deployment. I won't discuss them further.

The profile and level combinations defined by MPEG-2 – excluding SNR, Spt, HP, and MVP – are summarized in Table 47.1 above. Excepting 422P, the combinations have a hierarchical relationship: A decoder claiming conformance to any profile must be capable of decoding all profiles to its left in Table 47.1; also, a decoder claiming conformance to any level must be capable of decoding all lower levels. Exceptionally, a simple profile at main level (SP@ML) decoder must be capable of decoding main profile at low level (MP@LL).

Every compliant MPEG-2 decoder must be capable of decoding an MPEG-1 *constrained-parameters bitstream* (CPB). I include MPEG-1 CPB at the lower left of Table 47.1, as if it were both a profile and a level, to emphasize this MPEG-2 conformance requirement.

Profile@Level	Image columns (N_C)	Image rows (N_R)	Frame rate, Hz	Luma rate [samples/s]	Bit rate [Mb/s]	VBV size [KBytes]
422P@HL	1920	1088	60	62,668,800	300	5,760
MP@HL	1920	1088	60	62,668,800	80	1,194
MP@H-14	1440	1088	60	47,001,600	60	896
422P@ML	720	608	60	11,059,200	50	1,152
MP@ML	720	576	30	10,368,000	15	224
MP@LL	352	288	30	3,041,280	4	58

Table 47.2 **MPEG-2 main and 4:2:2 profiles** are summarized. MP@ML and MP@HL are shaded to emphasize their commercial significance. The DVD-video specification requires MP@ML compliance, and imposes additional constraints. ATSC standards for 720*p*, 1080*p*, and 1080*i* HD require MP@HL compliance, and impose additional constraints.

The simple profile has no B-pictures. Prohibition of B-pictures minimizes encoding latency, and minimizes buffer storage at the decoder. However, the simple profile lacks the compression efficiency of B-pictures.

Of the eight combinations in Table 47.1, only two are commercially important to television. MP@ML is used for SD distribution, and for DVD, at rates from about 2 Mb/s to about 6 Mb/s. MP@HL is used for HD distribution, usually between 10 Mb/s and 20 Mb/s.

422P@ML allows 608 lines at 25 Hz frame rate, but is limited to 512 lines at 29.97 and 30 Hz frame rates.

The 4:2:2 profile allows 4:2:2 chroma subsampling; it is intended for use in television production. The major reason for a separate 4:2:2 profile is that main profile *disallows* 4:2:2 chroma subsampling. MPEG-2's high profile allows 4:2:2 subsampling, but to require high-profile conformance would oblige a decoder to handle SNR and spatial scalability. 422P@ML is used in the studio, as Sony MPEG IMX, at bit rates between 30 Mb/s and 50 Mb/s. Some numerical parameter limits of main and 4:2:2 profiles are presented in Table 47.2 above.

SMPTE 308M, *Television – MPEG-2 4:2:2 Profile at High Level*.

MPEG-2 defines 4:2:2 profile at high level (422P@HL). In addition to MPEG-2's requirements for 422P@HL, SMPTE 308M imposes these restrictions on

GoP structures permitted at high data rates, as shown in Table 47.3:

Bit rate	Interlace?	GoP structure allowed
0 to 175	any	any
175 to 230	any	I-only, IP, or IB
230 to 300 {	interlaced	I-only
	progressive	I-only, IP, or IB

Table 47.3 **GoP restrictions in SMPTE 308M**

I have presented the profile and level constraints of MPEG-2 itself. Certain applications of MPEG-2 – such as ATSC broadcasting, and DVD – impose restrictions beyond those of MPEG's profiles and levels. For example, MPEG-2 allows a frame rate of 24 Hz, but that rate is disallowed for DVD. (Movies originating at 24 frames per second are ordinarily coded onto 480*i* DVD at 29.97 Hz, but signalling 2-3 pulldown.)

Picture structure

Concerning the distinction between luminance and luma, see Appendix A, on page 567.

Each frame in MPEG-2 is coded with a fixed number of image columns (S_{AL}, called *horizontal size* in MPEG) and image rows (L_A, called *vertical size*) of luma samples. I use the term *luma;* MPEG documents use *luminance,* but that term is technically incorrect in MPEG's context.

A frame in MPEG-2 has either square sampling, or 4:3, 16:9, or 2.21:1 picture aspect ratio – that is, nonsquare sampling is permitted only at 4:3, 16:9, or 2.21:1. (MPEG writes aspect ratio unconventionally, as as *height:width.*) Table 47.4 presents MPEG-2's *aspect ratio information* field. The 2.21:1 value is not permitted in any defined profile.

MPEG-2 accommodates both progressive and interlaced material. An image having N_C columns and N_R rows of luma samples can be coded directly as a *frame-structured* picture, as depicted at the left of Figure 47.1 overleaf. In a frame-structured picture, all of the luma and chroma samples of a frame are taken to originate at the same time, and are intended for display at the same time. A flag *progressive sequence* asserts that a sequence contains only frame-structured pictures.

Alternatively, a video frame (typically originated from an interlaced source) may be coded as a pair of *field-structured* pictures – a *top-field* picture and a *bottom-*

Code	Aspect ratio
0000	Forbidden
0001	Square sampling
0010	4:3
0011	16:9
0100	2.21:1
0101 ... 1111	Reserved

Table 47.4 **MPEG-2 *aspect ratio information*.** The 2.21:1 aspect ratio is not permitted in any defined profile.

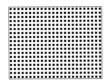

Figure 47.1 **An MPEG-2 frame picture** contains an array of luma samples N_C columns by N_R rows. It is implicit that an MPEG-2 frame picture occupies the entire frame time.

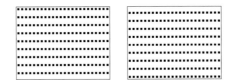

Figure 47.2 **An MPEG-2 field picture pair** contains a *top-field* picture and a *bottom-field* picture, each N_C columns by $N_R/2$ rows. The samples are vertically offset. Here I show a pair ordered {top, bottom}; alternatively, it could be {bottom, top}. Concerning the relation between top and bottom fields and video standards, see *Interlacing in MPEG-2*, on page 132.

field picture – each having N_C columns and $N_R/2$ rows as depicted by Figure 47.2. The two fields are time-offset by half the frame time, and are intended for interlaced display. Field pictures always come in pairs having opposite parity (top/bottom). Both pictures in a field pair must have the same *picture coding type* (I, P, or B), except that an I-field may be followed by a P-field (in which case the pair functions as an I-frame, and may be termed an *IP-frame*).

I, P, and B picture coding types were introduced on page 153.

Frame rate and 2-3 pulldown in MPEG

The defined profiles of MPEG-2 provide for the display frame rates shown in Table 47.5 in the margin. Frame rate is constant within a video *sequence* (to be defined on page 533). Unfortunately, it is unspecified how long a decoder may take to adapt to a change in frame rate.

In a sequence of frame-structured pictures, provisions are made to include, in the MPEG-2 bitstream, information to enable the display process to impose 2-3 pulldown upon display. Frames in such a sequence are coded as frame-structured pictures; in each frame, both fields are associated with the same instant in time. The flag *repeat first field* may accompany a picture; if that flag is set, then an interlaced display is expected to display the first field, the second field, and then the first field again – that is, to impose 2-3 pulldown. The frame rate in the bitstream specifies the display rate after 2-3 processing. I sketched a 2-3 sequence of four film frames in Figure 34.1, on page 405; on DVD, that sequence would be coded as the set of four progressive MPEG-2 frames flagged as indicated in Table 47.6 at the top of the facing page.

Code	Frame rate
0000	Forbidden
0001	$24/1.001$
0010	24
0011	25
0100	$30/1.001$
0101	30
0110	50
0111	$60/1.001$
1000	60
1001 ... 1111	Reserved

Table 47.5 **MPEG-2 frame rate code**

A frame-coded picture can code a top/bottom pair or a bottom/top pair – that is, a frame picture may correspond to a video frame, or may straddle two video frames. The latter case accommodates M-frames in 2-3 pulldown.

Film frame	Top first field (TFF)	Repeat first field (RFF)
A	0	0
B	0	1
C	1	0
D	1	1

Table 47.6 **2-3 pulldown sequence in MPEG-2.** For the definitions of film frames A through D, see *2-3 pulldown,* on page 405.

Luma and chroma sampling structures

MPEG-2 accommodates 4:2:2 chroma subsampling, suitable for studio applications, and 4:2:0 chroma subsampling, suitable for video distribution. Unlike DV, C_B and C_R sample pairs are spatially coincident. The MPEG-2 standard includes 4:4:4 chroma format, but it isn't permitted in any defined profile, so is highly unlikely to be commercialized.

There is no vertical subsampling in 4:2:2 – in this case, subsampling and interlace do not interact. 4:2:2 chroma for both frame-structured and field-structured pictures is depicted in the third (BT.601) column of Figure 12.1, on page 124.

4:2:0 chroma subsampling in a frame-structured picture is depicted in the rightmost column of Figure 12.1; C_B and C_R samples are centered vertically midway between luma samples in the frame, and are cosited horizontally.

4:2:0 chroma subsampling in a field-structured picture is depicted in Figure 47.3 in the margin. In the top field, chroma samples are centered $\frac{1}{4}$ of the way vertically between a luma sample in the field and the luma sample immediately below in the same field. (In this example, C_{B0-3} is centered $\frac{1}{4}$ of the way down from Y'_0 to Y'_2.) In the bottom field, chroma samples are centered $\frac{3}{4}$ of the way vertically between a luma sample in the field and the luma sample immediately below in the same field. (In this example, C_{B4-7} is centered $\frac{3}{4}$ of the way down from Y'_4 to Y'_6.) This scheme centers chroma samples at the same locations that they would take in a frame-structured picture; however, alternate rows of chroma samples in the frame are time-offset by half the frame time.

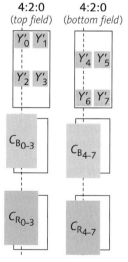

Figure 47.3 **Chroma subsampling in field-structured pictures**

Macroblocks

If *horizontal size* or *vertical size* is not divisible by 16, then the encoder pads the image with a suitable number of black "overhang" samples at the right edge or bottom edge. For example, when coding HD at 1920×1080, an encoder appends 8 rows of black pixels to the image array, to make the row count 1088. Upon decoding, these samples are cropped prior to display. The overhang regions are retained in the reference framestores.

At the core of MPEG compression is the DCT coding of 8×8 blocks of sample values (in I-pictures, as in JPEG), or 8×8 blocks of prediction errors – *residuals,* or *residues* (in P- and B-pictures). To simplify the implementation of subsampled chroma, the same DCT and block coding scheme is used for both luma and chroma. When combined with 4:2:0 chroma subsampling, two 8×8 block of chroma samples are associated with a 16×16 block of luma. This leads to the tiling of a field or frame into units of 16×16 luma samples. Each such unit is a *macroblock* (MB). Macroblocks lie a on 16×16 grid aligned with the upper-left luma sample of the image.

Each macroblock comprises four 8×8 luma blocks, accompanied by the requisite number and arrangement of 8×8 C_B blocks and 8×8 C_R blocks, depending upon *chroma format.* In the usual 4:2:0 chroma format, a macroblock comprises six blocks: four luma blocks, a C_B block, and a C_R block. In the 4:2:2 chroma format, a macroblock comprises eight blocks: four luma blocks, two blocks of C_B, and two blocks of C_R.

Picture coding types – I, P, B

MPEG-2 and H.264 use the term *reference picture*. Some people say *anchor picture*.

I-pictures, P-pictures, and B-pictures were introduced on page 152. Coded I-picture and P-picture data are used to reconstruct *reference pictures* – fields or frames that are available for constructing predictions. An MPEG decoder maintains two reference framestores, one past and one future. An encoder also maintains two reference framestores, reconstructed as if by a decoder; these track the contents of the decoder's reference framestores. The simple profile has no B-pictures; a single reference framestore suffices.

Each I-picture is coded independently of any other picture. When an I-picture is reconstructed by a decoder, it is displayed. Additionally, it is stored as a reference frame so as to be available as a predictor. I-pictures are compressed using a JPEG-like algorithm, using perceptually based quantization matrices.

Each P-picture is coded using the past reference picture as a predictor. Residuals are compressed using the same JPEG-like algorithm that is used for I-pictures, but typically with quite different quantization matrices.

When a decoder reconstructs a P-picture, it is displayed; additionally, the picture is written into a reference frame so as to be available for subsequent predictions.

Each B-picture contains elements that are *bipredicted* from one or both reference frames. The encoder computes, compresses, and transmits residuals. The decoder reconstructs a B-picture, displays it, then discards it: No B-picture is used for prediction.

Each reference picture is associated with a full frame of storage. When a decoder reconstructs a reference *field* (an I-field or a P-field), half the lines of the reference framestore are written; the other half retains the contents of the previous reference field. After the first field of a field pair has been reconstructed, it is available as a predictor for the second field. (The first field of the previous reference frame is no longer available.)

Prediction

In Figure 16.1, on page 152, I sketched a naïve interpicture coding scheme. For any scene element that moves more than few pixels from one video frame to the next, the naïve scheme is liable to produce large interpicture difference values. Motion can be more effectively coded by having the encoder form motion-compensated predictions. The encoder also produces motion vectors; these are used to displace a region of a reference picture to improve the prediction of the current picture relative to an undisplaced prediction. The residuals are then compressed using DCT, quantized, and VLE-encoded.

At a decoder, predictions are formed from the reference picture(s), based upon the transmitted motion vectors and prediction modes. Residuals are recovered from the bitstream by VLE decoding, inverse quantization, and inverse DCT. Finally, the decoded residual is added to the prediction to form the reconstructed picture. If the decoder is reconstructing an I-picture or a P-picture, the reconstructed picture is written to the appropriate portion (or the entirety) of a reference frame.

The obvious way for an encoder to form forward interpicture differences is to subtract the current source picture from the reference picture. (The reference

Inverse quantization is sometimes denoted *IQ*, not to be confused with *IQ* colour difference components.

picture would have been subject to motion-compensated interpolation, according to the encoder's motion estimate.) Starting from an intra coded picture, the decoder would then accumulate interpicture differences. However, MPEG involves lossy compression: Both the I-picture starting point of a GoP and each set of decoded interpicture differences are subject to reconstruction errors. With the naïve scheme of computing interpicture differences, reconstruction errors would accumulate at the decoder. To alleviate this potential source of decoder error, the encoder incorporates a decoder. The interpicture difference is formed by subtracting the current source picture from the previous reference picture *as a decoder will reconstruct it.* Reconstruction errors are thereby brought "inside the loop," and are prevented from accumulating.

The prediction model used by MPEG-2 is blockwise translation of 16×16 blocks of luma samples (along with the associated chroma samples): A macroblock of the current picture is predicted from a like-sized region of a reconstructed reference picture. The choice of 16×16 region size was a compromise between the desire for a large region (to effectively exploit spatial coherence, and to amortize motion vector overhead across a fairly large number of samples), and a small region (to efficiently code small scene elements in motion).

Macroblocks in a P-picture are typically forward-predicted. However, an encoder can decide that a particular macroblock is best intracoded (that is, not predicted at all). Macroblocks in a B-picture are typically predicted as averages of motion-compensated past and future reference pictures – that is, they are ordinarily bidirectionally predicted. However, an encoder can decide that a particular macroblock in a B-picture is best intracoded, or unidirectionally predicted using either forward or backward prediction. Table 47.7 at the top of the facing page indicates the four macroblock types. The macroblock types allowed in any picture are restricted by the declared picture type, as indicated in Table 47.8.

Each nonintra macroblock in an interlaced sequence can be predicted either by frame prediction (typically chosen by the encoder when there is little motion

A prediction region in a reference frame is rarely aligned to a 16-luma-sample macroblock grid; it is not properly referred to as a *macroblock*. Some authors fail to make the distinction between macroblocks and prediction regions; other authors use the term *prediction macroblocks* for prediction regions.

In a *closed GoP*, no B-picture is permitted to use forward prediction to the I-picture that starts the next GoP. See the caption to Figure 16.5, on page 155.

DIGITAL VIDEO AND HD ALGORITHMS AND INTERFACES

Table 47.7 MPEG macroblock types		Prediction	Typ. quantizer matrix
Intra		None – the macroblock is self-contained	Perceptual
Inter (Nonintra)	Backward predictive-coded	Predicts from the future reference picture	Flat
	Forward predictive-coded	Predicts from the past reference picture	Flat
	Bipredictive-coded	Averages predictions from past and future reference pictures	Flat

Table 47.8 MPEG picture coding types	Binary code	Reference picture?	Permitted macroblock types
I-picture	001	Yes	Intra
P-picture	010	Yes	Intra
			Forward predictive-coded
B-picture	011	No	Intra
			Forward predictive-coded
			Backward predictive-coded
			Bipredictive-coded

Table 47.9 MPEG-2 prediction modes	For	Description	Max. MVs back.	fwd.
Frame prediction	(P, B)-pictures	Predictions are made for the frame, using data from one or two previously reconstructed frames.	1	1
Field prediction	(P, B)-pictures, (P, B)-fields	Predictions are made independently for each field, using data from one or two previously reconstructed fields.	1	1
16×8 motion compensation (16×8 MC)	(P, B)-fields	The upper 16×8 and lower 16×8 regions of the macroblock are predicted separately. (This is completely unrelated to top and bottom fields.)	2	2
Dual prime	P-fields with no intervening B-pictures	Two motion vectors are derived from the transmitted vector and a small differential motion vector (DMV, –1, 0, or +1); these are used to form predictions from two reference fields (one top, one bottom), which are averaged to form the predictor.	1	1
Dual prime	P-pictures with no intervening B-pictures	As in dual prime for P-fields (above), but repeated for 2 fields; 4 predictions are made and averaged.	1	1

between the fields), or by field prediction (typically chosen by the encoder when there is significant inter-field motion). This is comparable to field/frame coding in DV, which I described on page 507. Predictors for a field picture must be field predictors. However, predictors for a frame picture may be chosen on a macroblock-by-macroblock basis to be either field predictors or frame predictors. MPEG-2 defines several additional prediction modes, which can be selected on a macroblock-by-macroblock basis. MPEG-2's prediction modes are summarized in Table 47.9.

Motion vectors (MVs)

A *motion vector* identifies a region of 16×16 luma samples in a reference picture that are to be used for prediction. A motion vector refers to a prediction region that is potentially quite distant (spatially) from the region being coded – that is, the motion vector range can be quite large. Even in field pictures, motion vectors are specified in units of frame luma samples. A motion vector can specify integer pixel coordinates, in which case forming the 16×16 prediction is accomplished by merely copying pixels. However, in MPEG, a motion vector can be specified to half-sample precision: If the fractional bit of a motion vector is set, then the prediction is formed by averaging sample values at the neighboring integer coordinates – that is, by linear interpolation. Transmitted motion vector values are halved for use with subsampled chroma. All defined profiles require that no motion vector refers to any sample outside the bounds of the reference frame.

Each macroblock's header contains a count of motion vectors. Motion vectors are themselves predicted! An initial MV is established at the start of a *slice* (see page 534); the motion vector for each successive nonintra macroblock is differentially coded with respect to the previous macroblock in raster-scan order.

Motion vectors are variable-length encoded, so that short vectors – the most likely ones in large areas of translational motion or no motion – are coded compactly. Zero-valued motion vectors are quite likely, so provision is made for compact coding of them.

Intra macroblocks are not predicted, so motion vectors are not necessary for them. However, in certain circumstances *concealment motion vectors* (CMVs) are allowed: If a macroblock is lost owing to transmission error, CMVs allow a decoder to use its prediction facilities to synthesize picture information to conceal the erred macroblock. A CMV would be useless if it were contained in its own macroblock! So, a CMV is associated with the macroblock immediately below.

Coding of a block

Each macroblock is accompanied by a small amount of prediction mode information; zero, one, or more *motion vectors* (MVs); and DCT-coded residuals.

A perverse encoder could use an intra quantizer matrix that isn't perceptually coded.

Each block of an intra macroblock is coded similarly to a block in JPEG. Transform coefficients are quantized with a quantizer matrix that is (ordinarily) perceptually weighted. Provision is made for 8-, 9-, and 10-bit DC coefficients. (In the 422 profile [422P], 11-bit DC coefficients are permitted.) DC coefficients are differentially coded within a slice (to be described on page 534).

In an I-picture, DC terms of the DCT are differentially coded: The DC term for each luma block is used as a predictor for the corresponding DC term of the following macroblock. DC terms for C_B and C_R blocks are similarly predicted.

In principle, residuals in a nonintra macroblock could be encoded directly. In MPEG, they are coded using DCT, for two reasons. First, DCT coding exploits any spatial coherence that may be present in the residual. Second, DCT coding allows use of the same rate control (based upon quantization) and VLE encoding that are already in place for intra macroblocks. The residuals for a nonintra block are dequantized, then added to the motion-compensated values from the reference frame. Because the dequantized transform coefficients are not directly viewed, it is not appropriate to use a perceptually weighted quantizer matrix. By default, the quantizer matrix for nonintra blocks is *flat* – that is, it contains the same value in all entries.

A perverse encoder could use a nonintra quantizer matrix that isn't flat. Separate nonintra quantizer matrices can be provided for luma and chroma.

Frame and field DCT types

Luma in a macroblock is partitioned into four blocks according to one of two schemes, *frame DCT coding* or *field DCT coding*. I will describe three cases where frame

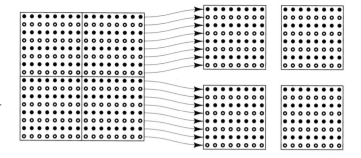

Figure 47.4 **The frame DCT type** involves straightforward partitioning of luma samples of each 16×16 macroblock into four 8×8 blocks. This is most efficient for macroblocks of field pictures, native progressive frame pictures, and frame-structured pictures having little interfield motion.

At first glance it is a paradox that *field*-structured pictures must use *frame* DCT coding!

DCT coding is appropriate, and then introduce field DCT coding.

• In a frame-structured picture that originated from a native-progressive source, every macroblock is best predicted by a spatially contiguous 16×16 region of a reference frame. This is *frame DCT coding:* Luma samples of a macroblock are partitioned into 8×8 luma blocks as depicted in Figure 47.4 above.

• In a field-structured picture, alternate image rows of each source frame have been unwoven by the encoder into two fields, each of which is free from interlace effects. Every macroblock in such a picture is best predicted from a spatially contiguous 16×16 region of a reference field (or, if you prefer to think of it this way, from alternate lines of a 16×32 region of a reference frame). This is also frame DCT coding.

• In a frame-structured picture from an interlaced source, a macroblock that contains no scene element in motion is ordinarily best predicted by frame DCT coding.

An alternate approach is necessary in a frame-structured picture from an interlaced source where a macroblock contains a scene element in motion. Such a scene element will take different positions in the first and second fields: A spatially contiguous 16×16 region of a reference picture will form a poor predictor. MPEG-2 provides a way to efficiently code such a macroblock. The scheme involves an alternate partitioning of luma into 8×8 blocks: Luma blocks are formed by collecting alternate rows of the reference frame. The scheme is called *field DCT coding;* it is depicted in Figure 47.5 at the top of the facing page.

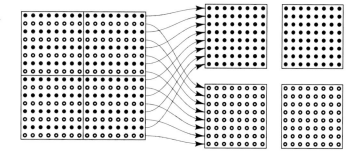

Figure 47.5 **The field DCT type** creates four 8×8 luma blocks by collecting alternate image rows. This allows efficient coding of a frame-structured picture from an interlaced source, where there is significant interfield motion. (Comparable unweaving is already implicit in field-structured pictures.)

You might think it a good idea to handle chroma samples in interlaced frame pictures the same way that luma is handled. However, with 4:2:0 subsampling, that would force having either 8×4 chroma blocks or 16×32 macroblocks. Neither of these options is desirable; so, in a frame-structured picture with interfield motion, chroma blocks are generally poorly predicted. Owing to the absence of vertical subsampling in the 4:2:2 chroma format, 4:2:2 sequences are inherently free from such poor chroma prediction.

Zigzag and VLE

Once DCT coefficients are quantized, an encoder scans them in zigzag order. I sketched zigzag scanning in JPEG in Figure 45.8, on page 499. This scan order, depicted in Figure 47.6 overleaf, is also used in MPEG-1.

In addition to the JPEG/MPEG-1 scan order, MPEG-2 provides an alternate scan order optimized for frame-structured pictures from interlaced sources. The alternate scan, sketched in Figure 47.7 overleaf, can be chosen by an encoder on a picture-by-picture basis.

After zigzag scanning, zero-valued AC coefficients are identified, then {run-length, level} pairs are formed and variable-length encoded. For intra macroblocks, MPEG-2 allows an encoder to choose between two VLE schemes: the scheme first standardized in MPEG-1, and an alternate scheme more suitable for frame-structured pictures with interfield motion.

Block diagrams of an MPEG-2 encoder and decoder system are sketched in Figure 47.8 overleaf.

In MPEG terminology, the absolute value of an AC coefficient is its *level*. I prefer to call it *amplitude*. Sign is coded separately.

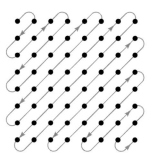

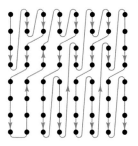

Figure 47.6 Zigzag *scan*[0] denotes the scan order used in JPEG and MPEG-1, and available in MPEG-2.

Figure 47.7 Zigzag *scan*[1] may be chosen by an MPEG-2 encoder on a picture-by-picture basis.

Refresh

Occasional insertion of I-macroblocks is necessary for three main reasons: to establish a reference picture upon channel acquisition; to limit the duration of artifacts introduced by uncorrectable transmission errors; and to limit *drift* (that is, divergence of encoder and decoder predictors due to mistracking between the encoder's IDCT and the decoder's IDCT). MPEG-2 mandates that every macroblock in the frame be refreshed by an intra macroblock before the 132nd P-macroblock. Encoders usually meet this requirement by periodically or intermittently inserting I-pictures. However, I-pictures are not a strict requirement of MPEG-2, and *distributed refresh* – where I-macroblocks are used for refresh, instead of I-pictures – is occasionally used, especially for direct broadcast from satellite (DBS).

A sophisticated encoder examines the source video to detect scene cuts, and adapts its sequence of picture types according to picture content.

Distributed refresh does not guarantee a deterministic time to complete refresh. See Lookabaugh, cited at the end of this chapter.

Motion estimation

A motion vector must do more than cover motion from one frame to the next: With B-pictures, a motion vector must describe motion from one *reference* frame to the next – that is, from an I-picture or P-picture to the following I-picture or P-picture. As the number of interposed B-pictures increases – as page 155's *M* value increases – motion vector range must increase. The cost

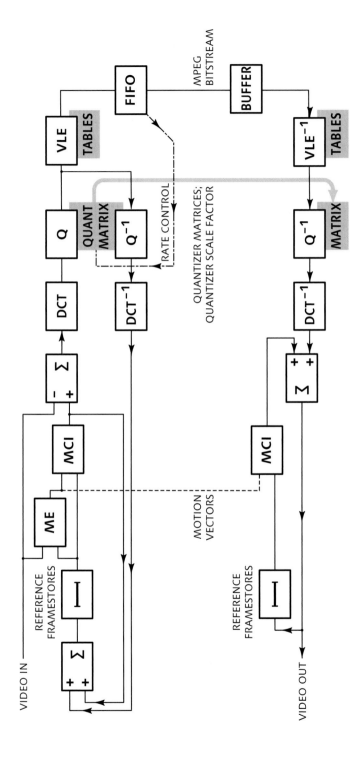

Figure 47.8 **MPEG encoder and decoder** block diagrams are sketched here. The encoder includes a motion estimator (ME); this involves huge computational complexity. Motion vectors (MVs) are incorporated into the bitstream and thereby conveyed to the decoder; the decoder does not need to estimate motion. The encoder effectively contains a copy of the decoder; the encoder's picture difference calculations are based upon reconstructed picture information that will be available at the decoder.

and complexity of motion estimation increases dramatically as search range increases.

The burden of *motion estimation* (ME) falls on the encoder. Motion estimation is very complex and computationally intensive. MPEG-2 allows a huge motion vector range: For MP@ML frame-structured pictures, the 16×16 prediction region can potentially lie anywhere within [–1024...+1023$\frac{1}{2}$] luma samples horizontally and [–128...+127$\frac{1}{2}$] luma samples vertically from the macroblock being decoded. Elements in the picture header (*f code*) specify the motion vector range used in each picture; this limits the number of bits that need to be allocated to motion vectors for that picture.

Whether an encoder actually searches this extent is not standardized!

The purpose of the motion estimation in MPEG is not exactly to estimate motion in regions of the picture – rather, it is to access a prediction region that minimizes the amount of prediction error (residual) information that needs to be coded. Usually this goal will be achieved by using the best estimate of average motion in the 16×16 macroblock, but not always. I make this distinction because some video processing algorithms need accurate motion vectors, where the estimated motion is a good match to motion as perceived by a human observer. In many video processing algorithms, such as in temporal resampling used in standards converters, or in deinterlacing, a motion vector is needed for every luma sample, or every few samples. In MPEG, only one or two vectors are needed to predict a macroblock from a 16×16 region in one or two reference pictures.

If the fraction bit of a motion vector is set, then predictions are formed by averaging sample values from neighboring pixels (at integer coordinates). This is straightforward for a decoder. However, for an encoder to *produce* $\frac{1}{2}$-luma-sample motion vectors in both horizontal and vertical axes requires quadruple the computational effort of producing full-sample vectors.

There are three major methods of motion estimation:
• *Block matching*, also called *full search*, involves an exhaustive search for the best match of the target macroblock through some two-dimensional extent of

the reference frame. For the large ranges of MPEG-2, full block matching is impractical.

• *Pixel-recursive* (or *pel-recursive*) methods start with a small number of initial guesses at motion, based upon motion estimates from previous frames. The corresponding coordinates in the reference frame are searched, and each guess is refined. The best guess is taken as the final motion vector.

• *Pyramidal* methods form spatial lowpass-filtered versions of the target macroblock, and of the reference frames; block matches are performed at low resolution. Surrounding the coordinates of the most promising candidates at one resolution level, less severely filtered versions of the reference picture regions are formed, and block matches are performed on those. Successive refinement produces the final motion vector. This technique tends to produce smooth motion-vector fields.

Rate control and buffer management

A typical video sequence, encoded by a typical MPEG-2 encoder, produces I-, P-, and B-pictures that consume bits roughly in the ratio 60:30:10. An I-picture requires perhaps six times the number of bits as two B-pictures.

Many applications of MPEG-2, such as DTV, involve a transmission channel with a fixed data rate. This calls for *constant bit rate* (CBR) operation. Other applications of MPEG-2, such as DVD, involve a channel having variable (but limited) data rate. Such applications call for *variable bit rate* (VBR) operation, where the instantaneous bit rate is varied to achieve the desired picture quality for each frame, maximizing storage utilization.

The larger the decoder's buffer size, the more flexibility is available to the encoder to allocate bits among pictures. However, a large buffer is expensive. Each profile/level combination dictates the minimum buffer size that a decoder must implement.

An encoder effects *rate control* by altering the quantization matrices – the perceptually weighted matrix used for intra macroblocks, and the flat matrix used for nonintra macroblocks. MPEG-2 allows quantizer matrices to be included in the bitstream. Additionally, and more importantly, a *quantizer scale code* is transmitted at the slice level, and may be updated at the

This method is sometimes called "logarithmic," which I consider to be a very poor term in this context.

The fractions 0.6, 0.3, and 0.1 are comparable to the SD luma coefficients of green, red, and blue; so, I use green, red, and blue to designate I-picture, P-picture, and B-picture data respectively in Figures 16.2, 16.3, and 16.4 (page 153).

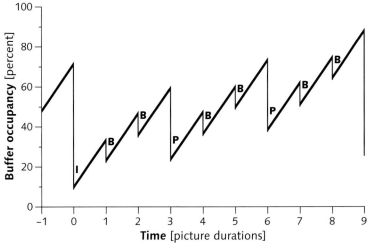

macroblock level. This code determines an overall scale factor that is applied to the quantizer matrices. The encoder quantizes more or less severely to achieve the required bit rate; the quantizer scale code is conveyed to the decoder so that it dequantizes accordingly.

Video display requires a constant number of frames per second. Because an I-picture has a relatively large number of bits, during decoding and display of an I-picture in all but degenerate cases, the decoder's net buffer occupancy decreases. During decoding and display of a B-picture, net buffer occupancy increases. Figure 47.9 shows typical buffer occupancy at the start of a sequence, for a duration of about one GoP.

An MPEG bitstream must be constructed such that the decoder's buffer doesn't overflow: If it did, bits would be lost. The bitstream must also be constructed so that the buffer doesn't underflow: If it did, a picture to be displayed would not be available at the required time.

Buffer management in MPEG-2 is based upon an idealized model of the decoder's buffer: All of the bits associated with each picture are deemed to be extracted from the decoder's buffer at a certain precisely defined instant in time with respect to the bitstream. Every encoder implements a *video buffering verifier* (VBV) that tracks the state of this idealized buffer. Each picture header contains a *VBV delay* field that declares the fullness of the buffer at the start of that picture. After channel acquisition, a decoder waits a corresponding amount of time before starting decoding. (If the decoder did not wait, buffer underflow could result.)

Bitstream syntax

The end product of MPEG-2 video compression is a bitstream partitioned into what MPEG calls a *syntactic hierarchy* having six layers: *sequence, GoP, picture, slice, macroblock,* and *block*. Except for the video sequence layer, which has a *sequence end* element, each syntactic element has a header and no trailer. The sequence, GoP, picture, and slice elements each begin with a 24-bit *start code prefix* comprising 23 zero bits followed by a one bit. A start code establishes byte alignment, and may be preceded by an arbitrary number of zero-stuffing bits. All other datastream elements are constructed so as to avoid the possibility of 23 or more consecutive zero bits.

Video sequence layer

The top layer of the MPEG syntax is the *video sequence*. The sequence header specifies high-level parameters such as bit rate, picture rate, picture size, picture aspect ratio, profile, level, progressive/interlace, and chroma format. The *VBV buffer size* parameter declares the maximum buffer size required within the sequence. The sequence header may specify quantizer matrices. At the encoder's discretion, the sequence header may be retransmitted intermittently or periodically throughout the sequence, to enable rapid channel acquisition by decoders.

The start of each interlaced video sequence establishes an immutable sequence of field pairs, ordered either {top, bottom, ...}, typical of 480*i*, or {bottom, top, ...}, typical of 576*i* and 1080*i*. Within a sequence, any individual field may be field-coded, and any two adjacent fields may be frame-coded; however, field parity must alternate in strict sequence.

Group of pictures (GoP header)

The GoP is MPEG's unit of random access. The GoP layer is optional in MPEG-2; however, it is a practical necessity for most applications. A GoP starts with an I-picture. (Additional I-pictures are allowed.) The GoP header contains SMPTE timecode, and *closed GoP* and *broken link* flags.

A GoP header contains 23 bits of coded SMPTE timecode. If present, this applies to the first frame of the GoP (in display order). It is unused within MPEG.

If a GoP is *closed,* no coded B-picture in the GoP may reference the first I-picture of the following GoP. This is inefficient, because the following I-picture ordinarily contains useful prediction information. If a GoP is *open,* or the GoP header is absent, then B-pictures in the GoP may reference the first I-picture of the following GoP. To allow editing of an MPEG bitstream, GoPs must be closed.

A device that splices bitstreams at GoP boundaries can set *broken link;* this signals a decoder to invalidate B-pictures immediately following the GoP's first I-picture.

Picture layer

The picture header specifies picture structure (frame, top field, or bottom field), and picture coding type (I, P, or B). The picture header can specify quantizer matrices and *quantizer scale type.* The *VBV delay* parameter is used for buffer management.

Slice layer

A slice aggregates macroblocks in raster order, left to right and top to bottom. No slice crosses the edge of the picture. All defined profiles have "restricted slice structure," where slices cover the picture with no gaps or overlaps. The slice header contains the *quantizer scale code.* The slice serves several purposes. First, the slice is the smallest unit of resynchronization in case of uncorrected data transmission error. Second, the slice is the unit of differential coding of intra-macroblock DC terms. Third, the slice is the unit for differential coding of nonintra motion vectors: The first macroblock of a slice has motion vectors coded absolutely, and motion vectors for subsequent macroblocks are coded in terms of successive differences from that.

Macroblock layer

The macroblock is MPEG's unit of motion prediction. Coded macroblock data contains an indication of the macroblock type (intra, forward predicted, backward predicted, or bipredicted); a *quantizer scale code;* 0, 1, or 2 forward motion vectors; and 0, 1, or 2 backward motion vectors. The *coded block pattern* flags provide a compact way to represent blocks that are not coded (owing to being adequately predicted without the need for residuals).

Block layer   Each block is represented in the bitstream by VLE-coded DCT coefficients – a differentially encoded DC coefficient, and zero or more AC coefficients. Each coded block's data is terminated by a 4-bit *end of block* (EOB).

Transport

Various syntax elements of MPEG video or audio are serialized to form an *elementary stream* (ES). MPEG-2 defines a mechanism to divide an ES into packets, forming a *packetized elementary stream* (PES). Each PES pack header contains system-level clock information, packet priority, packet sequence numbering, and (optionally) encryption information. If an MPEG-2 PES is stored in a file, the file conventionally has the extension *m2v;* however, a video PES can't contain audio! More commonly, though, MPEG-2 video and audio are multiplexed, then stored or transported, using *program streams* or *transport streams,* to be discussed in the chapter *MPEG-2 storage and transport,* on page 555.

Further reading

GIBSON, JERRY D., TOBY BERGER, TOM LOOKABAUGH, DAVID LINDBERGH, and RICHARD L. BAKER (1998), *Digital Compression for Multimedia* (San Francisco: Morgan Kaufmann). Lookabaugh's chapter provides an excellent 55-page description of MPEG-2. His chapter also covers MPEG audio.

HASKELL, BARRY G., ATUL PURI, and ARUN N. NETRAVALI (1997), *Digital Video: An Introduction to MPEG-2* (New York: Chapman & Hall). This book fails to distinguish luminance and luma; both are called *luminance* and given the symbol *Y.* See Appendix A, *YUV and luminance considered harmful,* on page 567 of the present book.

MITCHELL, JOAN L., WILLIAM B. PENNEBAKER, CHAD E. FOGG, and DIDIER J. LEGALL (1997), *MPEG Video Compression Standard* (New York: Chapman & Hall). This book concentrates on MPEG-1. Egregiously incorrect information appears concerning chroma subsampling.

SYMES, PETER (2003), *Digital Video Compression* (New York: McGraw-Hill).

WATKINSON, JOHN (1999), *MPEG-2* (Oxford: Focal Press).

H.264 video compression   48

ITU-T H.264, *Advanced Video Coding for Generic Audiovisual Services – Coding of Moving Video*, also published as ISO/IEC 14496-10 (MPEG-4 Part 10), *Advanced Video Coding.*

H.264 is usually pronounced *H-*dot*-TWO-SIX-FOUR*.

Compounding 1.06 twelve times yields a factor of two:

$$1.06^{12} \approx 2$$

H.264 denotes a codec standardized by ITU-T (under the designation *H.264*) and by ISO/IEC (under the designation *MPEG-4 Part 10*). The Simple Studio Profile (SStP) of MPEG-4 Part 2 is used in HDCAM. That aspect of Part 2, and all of Part 10, are applicable to broadcast-quality video; other than those cases, MPEG-4 is generally not applicable to broadcast-quality video. H.264 was developed by the *Joint Video Team* (JVT), where it was referred to as *Advanced Video Coding* (AVC); its ITU-T nomenclature during development was H.26L. All of these terms were once used to denote what is now, after adoption of the standard, best called H.264.

H.264 is broadly similar to MPEG-2, but the "low fruit" had been taken. Compression improvements in H.264 are obtained by a dozen or so techniques, each having perhaps 6% improvement in coding efficiency – but a dozen of those cascaded yields twice the efficiency of MPEG-2. (Practitioners claim efficiency as low as 1.5 and as high as 3 times that of MPEG-2.) H.264 spans a wide range of applications, from surveillance video, to video conferencing, to mobile devices, to internet video streaming, to HDTV broadcasting.

H.264 is complicated. The standard (in its 2010-03 edition) comprises 669 pages of very dense description. Implementing an encoder or decoder takes many man-years. Software, firmware, and hardware implementations are commercially available. Even hardware implementations require embedded firmware: H.264 VLSI solutions typically involve one or more embedded RISC processors and quite a bit of associated firmware.

The H.264 features that extend MPEG-2 are described in the remaining sections of this chapter. I assume that you are familiar with *Introduction to video compression,* on page 147, and with JPEG, M-JPEG, DV, and MPEG-2, described in the preceding three chapters.

Like MPEG-2, H.264 specifies exactly what constitutes a conformant bitstream: A conformant ("legal") encoder generates only conformant bitstreams; a legal decoder correctly decodes any conformant bitstream. H.264 effectively standardizes the behaviour of a *decoder,* but does *not* standardize the encoder!

The goal of compression is to reduce data rate while minimizing the visibility of artifacts. The best way – most experts say, the only way – to establish the performance of an encoder is to visually assess the result of compressing and decompressing video streams.

H.264 is covered by hundreds of patents. Implementors, manufacturers, users, and/or others may or may not be required to take out a licence to the "patent pool" administered by MPEG LA.

Not all features of H.264 are expected to be implemented in every decoder; for example, B-slices (comparable to MPEG-2 B-pictures) are prohibited in the baseline profile. Applications have various bit rates, and decoders can have various levels of resources (e.g., memory); like MPEG-2, a system of profiles and levels determines the minimum requirements.

MPEG LA, L.L.C. is not affiliated with MPEG (the standards group). LA apparently stands for *Licensing Administration.* The organization is based in Denver, not Los Angeles.

Algorithmic features, profiles, and levels

Table 48.1 opposite summarizes the algorithmic features of H.264 beyond MPEG-2. The features in the top section are available in all profiles; features in the sections below are profile-dependent.

The features available in the baseline and extended profiles concern robust handling of data conveyed across unreliable channels. These features (and profiles) are generally not of interest for professional video, and they are not permitted in the main and high profiles.

The features of the extended, main, and high profiles offer improved coding efficiency. CABAC improves the performance of variable-length entropy coding.

Fidelity range extensions (FRExt) refers to several algorithmic features incorporated into the high profiles – HiP, Hi10P, Hi422P, and Hi444P – to enable

Algorithmic feature ("tool")	Profile	Baseline (BP)	Extended (XP)	Main (MP)	High (HiP)
Features in all profiles					
Multiple reference pictures		·	·	·	·
Flexible motion compensation		·	·	·	·
I-slices and P-slices		·	·	·	·
$1/4$-pel motion-comp. interpolation		·	·	·	·
16-bit exact-match integer transform		·	·	·	·
Unified variable-length coding (UVLC/Exp-Golomb)		·	·	·	·
CAVLC		·	·	·	·
Deblocking filter in-the-loop		·	·	·	·
Set 1					
Flexible macroblock ordering (FMO)		•	•		
Arbitrary slice order (ASO)		•	•		
Redundant slices (RS)		•	•		
Set 2					
Data partitioning			•		
SI & SP slices			•		
Set 3					
B-slices			•	•	•
Interlaced coding (PicAFF, MBAFF)			•	•	•
Weighted and offset MC prediction			•	•	•
Set 4					
CABAC entropy coding				•	•
FRExt					
8×8 luma intra prediction					•
Increased sample depth					•
4:4:4 and 4:2:2 chroma subsampling					•
Inter-picture lossless coding					•
8×8/4×4 transform adaptivity					•
Quantization scaling matrices					•
Separate C_B and C_R QP control					•
Monochrome (4:0:0)					•

Table 48.1 **H.264 features** are arranged in rows; the columns indicate presence of features in the commercially important profiles.

higher quality video. Hi10P allows 10-bit video; Hi422P permits 4:2:2 chroma subsampling, and Hi444P permits 4:4:4, 12-bit video, and several other features.

Four of H.264's profiles are commercially important: baseline, extended, main, and high. The main and high profiles are relevant to professional video. H.264 has fifteen levels, accommodating images ranging from 176×144 (coded at rates as low as 64 kb/s) to 4 K×2 K (coded at rates as high as 240 Mb/s). Profile and level combinations important to professional video are summarized in Table 48.2 overleaf.

Level	Typ. image format	Typ. frame rate [Hz]	Max. bit rate [b/s]
L1	176×144	15	64 k
L1b	176×144	15	128 k
L1.1	352×288 or 176×144	7.5 or 30	192 k
L1.2	352×288	15	384 k
L1.3	352×288	30	768 k
L2	352×288	30	2 M
L2.1	352×480 or 352×576	30 or 25	4 M
L2.2	SD	15	4 M
L3.0	SD	30 or 50	10 M
L3.1	1280×720	30	14 M
L3.2	1280×720	60	20 M
L4.0	1920×1080	30	20 M
L4.1	1920×1080	30	50 M
L4.2	1920×1080	60	50 M
L5	2048×1024	72 or 30	135 M
L5.1	4096×2048	30	240 M

Table 48.2 **H.264 levels** are summarized.

Baseline and extended profiles

You might imagine a *baseline* profile to be decodable by every decoder. That is not the case in H.264. The baseline profile is intended to address low bit-rate applications that suffer from poor quality transmission. The flexible macroblock ordering (FMO), arbitrary slice order (ASO), and redundant slices (RS) features all contribute to robustness. Other features – in particular, B-slices – are excluded from the baseline profile, so as to achieve low computational complexity. The baseline profile is rarely used (if used at all) in professional video.

You might imagine an *extended* profile to have features beyond those of the main profile. That is not the case in H.264. The extended profile extends the robustness features of the *baseline* profile by including two additional features, data partitioning and SI and SP slices. Two additional features improve coding efficiency: B-slices, and interlaced coding (PicAFF, MBAFF). The extended profile is rarely used in professional video.

High profiles

The original H.264 features were augmented by the Fidelity range extensions (FRExt), which are available in the high profiles.

Ten bit sample depth is available in Hi10P and Hi422P; fourteen bit sample depth is available in Hi444P.

Hi444PP stands for *High 4:4:4 predictive profile.*

Hi422P and Hi444P offer 4:2:2 chroma subsampling: $Y'C_BC_R$ 4:2:2 (loosely, *Y'UV* 4:2:2) can be coded. Hi444P offers 4:4:4 "chroma subsampling" – that is, no subsampling at all.

Hierarchy

The syntax elements in an H.264 bitstream have a hierarchical structure like that of MPEG-2. The bitstream hierarchy of H.264 – the *syntax* hierarchy – is as follows:

- sequence
- picture
- slice
- macroblock
- macroblock partition
- sub-macroblock partition
- block
- sample

The *video coding layer* (VCL) comprises elements at the slice level and below. A *network abstraction layer* (NAL) defines *NAL units* to convey coded data. Information at layers above the VCL – that is, at the sequence and picture levels – is conveyed in *non-VCL NAL units*. The two types of NAL units (VCL and non-VCL) can be transmitted in different streams, for example to achieve higher network robustness, though specification of such transmission mechanisms is outside the scope of H.264.

Supplemental enhancement information (SEI) and *video usability information* (VUI) are "messages" inserted into non-VCL NAL units of the coded bitstream. SEI comprises sequence and picture parameter sets (SPS and PPS). VUI conveys information comparable to the contents of the sequence display extension of MPEG-2.

Multiple reference pictures

VP8 has three reference frames.

MPEG-2 has two reference frames: one in the past, and one in the "future." The "future" frame is available to predict B-pictures that lie earlier in display order.

In H.264, multiple reference pictures are allowed – between 4 and 13, depending upon level. If the material being coded has a quick cut to a reverse shot, the encoder can instruct the decoder to retain the picture at the end of the first shot, and use it to predict the picture upon return from the reverse shot. Reference pictures can be addressed in arbitrary order.

Slices

Slices offer a decoder the option of parallelism: No intra prediction crosses a slice boundary. Decoder state effectively resets on slice boundaries, so slices limit the spatial extent of transmission-induced impairments. Slices can be coded redundantly to further mitigate against transmission error.

Spatial intra prediction

In MPEG-2, a macroblock may be coded entirely independently as an I-macroblock, or may exploit temporal prediction and be coded as a P-macroblock. In the development of H.264 it was realized that decoded intra macroblocks above the current one, and those to the left in the same slice, have prediction value in the spatial domain. H.264 implements intra prediction based upon that data, where image data above or to the left is copied directionally in several modes. The prediction can then be refined by transform-coded quantized residuals in the usual way. Intra prediction uses only information from intra-coded macroblocks.

There is also an intra-PCM mode, where I-macroblock pixel data is directly coded, bypassing the transform. The mode is potentially useful at very high data rates.

Flexible motion compensation

In MPEG-2, motion prediction is accomplished in units of 16×16 blocks of luma pixels – that is, macroblocks. The encoder tries to find a 16×16 region of a reference picture that forms a good predictor, then codes the relative coordinates of that block into the data stream as a motion vector.

In H.264, a macroblock can be partitioned into several shapes and sizes for prediction from different regions of a reference picture, even prediction from different reference pictures. An entire macroblock can be predicted from one 16×16 source; alternatively, the macroblock can be partitioned into two 8×16 macroblock partitions, two 16×8 macroblock partitions, or four 8×8 macroblock partitions, all predicted independently. In high profiles, if a macroblock is partitioned into four 8×8 macroblock partitions, each of those can be partitioned into two 4×8 sub-macroblock partitions, two 8×4 sub-macroblock partitions, or four 4×4 sub-macroblock partitions, again all predicted independently. A macroblock can be associated with up to 16 motion vectors.

Quarter-pel motion-compensated interpolation

In the margin:

What is $1/4$-pel for luma is $1/8$-pel for 4:2:0 chroma.

In MPEG-2, motion vectors can have $1/2$-pixel precision with respect to luma samples. In H.264, motion-compensated interpolation can be performed to quarter-pel precision – that is, motion vectors can be encoded in units of $1/4$-pel (sometimes called *quarter-pel,* or *Qpel*). The interpolation operation uses simple 6-tap FIR filters, and has the beneficial effect of lowpass-filtering the prediction signal in addition to delivering it at an optimal spatial position.

Weighting and offsetting of MC prediction

MPEG-2 behaves poorly in fades from one picture to another and in fades to black – or, in the case of *Six Feet Under,* fades to white. The DC terms of the transform coefficients are coded reasonably well, but in fade to black all of the AC terms scale down together; that stresses the quantizer. H.264 implements weighting and offsetting of MC prediction, to improve performance in fades and certain other circumstances.

16-bit integer transform

MPEG-2 followed JPEG in using the 8×8 DCT, virtually always implemented in binary fixed-point arithmetic. The theoretical DCT matrix contains irrational numbers; encoders and decoders approximate them in fixed-point binary integers, usually 16-bit. Neither the JPEG nor MPEG-2 standards specify the accuracy of the DCT. The encoder includes a simulation of the decoding process, but owing to different roundoff error in different implementations, the encoder's DCT may not match the decoder's DCT. When a decoded block is used as a prediction, the prediction formed at the decoder may not exactly match the prediction expected by the encoder. We assume that the encoder has more computational resources that the decoder, and is likely to have more accuracy, so we term the problem – perhaps unfairly to the decoder – as *decoder drift.*

In H.264, decoder drift is eliminated through use of a transform defined by a matrix of simple binary fractions whose inverse also comprises simple binary fractions. With 8-bit residuals and 16-bit arithmetic, no roundoff error occurs, so no drift occurs.

Quantizer

In MPEG-2, the transform coefficient quantizer levels are uniformly spaced. In H.264, the quantizer has 52 steps that are exponentially spaced: Each step increases the step size by a ratio of 1.122, that is, six steps double the step size. (As a rough guide, increasing quantizer step size by +1 decreases bit rate by about 10%, and doubling halves the bit rate. This heuristic can be used for rate control at an encoder.)

Variable-length coding

Symbol	Scheme F	Scheme V
A	00	0
B	01	10
C	10	110
D	11	111

Table 48.3 **Two hypothetical coding schemes** mapping symbols (A through D) into a bitstream are sketched. Scheme F allocates a fixed number of bits to each symbol; Scheme V allocates a variable number of bits to symbols.

Suppose you're given sequences of four symbols (A, B, C, and D) to encode into a bitstream. Consider two simple coding schemes set out in Table 48.3 in the margin. Scheme F uses two bits for any of the four symbols. Scheme V uses one, two, or three bits, depending upon the symbol being coded. Both schemes faithfully encode *any* input sequence that is presented – that is, both encodings are lossless. However, if the input contains a lot of As, scheme V emits fewer bits than scheme F. Scheme V exemplifies the basic notion of variable-length coding: It's advantageous to have an encoding that reflects the probabilities of the symbols being coded. In this example, scheme F is well adapted to inputs where A, B, C, and D have equal probabilities. Scheme V is well adapted to probabilities [$\frac{1}{2}$, $\frac{1}{4}$, $\frac{1}{8}$, $\frac{1}{8}$] respectively.

In MPEG-2, a few dozen VLC coding schemes were devised for various syntax elements. H.264 required many additional syntax elements, and the developers got tired of constructing *ad hoc* tables. A systematic method, *universal variable-length coding* (UVLC) was

POS	INT	Coded bitstream
1	0	**1**
2	+1	0**1**0
3	-1	0**1**1
4	+2	00**1**00
5	-2	00**1**01
6	+3	00**1**10
7	-3	00**1**11
8	+4	0001**000**
9	-4	0001**001**
10	+5	0001**010**
11	-5	0001**011**

Table 48.4 **An example of exponential Golomb coding** of positive numbers 1 through 11 or integers ranging ±5 is shown.

The POS example of Table 48.4 is constructed for ease of explanation; H.264's *unsigned integer* (ue) codes are the indicated numbers less one. The INT example of Table 48.4 corresponds to H.264's *signed integer* (se) codes.

INT	Coded bitstream
0	**1**
±1	0**1**s
±2...±3	00**1**xs
±4...±7	000**1**xxs
±8...±15	0000**1**xxxs
±16...±31	00000**1**xxxxs
±32...±63	000000**1**xxxxxs
±64...±127	0000000**1**xxxxxxs

Table 48.5 **Exp-Golomb coding can be generalized** to signed integers represented in 1 bit, 2 bits, 3 bits, 4 bits, and more, indefinitely. The scheme favours inputs where small numbers are most likely: If inputs ±127 were equally likely, then fixed-length 8-bit two's complement coding would be more efficient.

adopted. It is based upon the *exponential Golomb* scheme, an example of which is sketched in Table 48.4.

Decoding of the positive number (POS) symbols of the example proceeds as follows: If the datastream bit is **1**, the coded value is 1. Otherwise, count leading zero bits, denoting the count N. Consider the following $N+1$ bits (including the leading **1** bit) to be the binary-coded positive number, most-significant bit first.

When used for signed integers (the INT symbols of the example), decode as follows: If the datastream bit is **1**, the coded value is 0. Otherwise, count leading zero bits, denoting the count N. Consider the following N bits (including the leading **1** bit) to be the absolute value of the coded number, expressed in binary, most-significant bit first. The trailing $(N+1)^{th}$ bit is the sign.

The INT example in Table 48.4 encodes signed integers such as those encountered in motion vector displacements. The code is easily adapted to nonnumeric symbols by simply assigning the required values or symbols to the appropriate number. Table 48.5 shows how the coding extends to arbitrarily large numbers (or to a set of symbols of arbitrary size).

In H.264, UVLC is used at syntax levels above the transform coefficients, for data such as prediction modes and motion vectors. The UVLC scheme is not used for transform coefficients: either CAVLC or CABAC is used for those.

Context adaptivity

The MPEG-2 designers used their judgement and experience, and the results of many experiments, to set up MPEG-2's VLC tables. However, those tables are static.

Usage of VLC entries by particular source material can be considered as a statistical distribution – that is, VLC table usage depends upon history, upon *context.*

Context adaptivity refers to an encoder dynamically keeping track of the use of table entries, estimating the probability of their use, and changing VLC mapping so that the coded bitstream has a compact representation for the symbols that are likely to be encountered.

Context adaptivity leads to increased complexity at both the encoder and the decoder. In H.264, the basic form of context adaptivity is *context-adaptive variable-length coding* (CAVLC), used at slice level and below.

CABAC

VLC (and its relative, CAVLC) as outlined above are optimal when coding symbols whose probabilities can be expressed as binary fractions, for example, if in the Scheme V example of Table 48.3 the probabilities of [A, B, C, and D] were [$1/2$, $1/4$, $1/8$, $1/8$]. In general, symbols being coded don't have probabilities that all lie close to binary fractions. For example, your task may be to code three symbols having probabilities [$1/3$, $1/3$, $1/3$].

A technique called *arithmetic coding* can be used to efficiently encode distributions where individual symbols occupy the equivalent of fractions of a bit. A potentially large group of symbols is collected, then coded into what amounts to a single number, where the range of the number is divided into subranges corresponding to the probabilities of the individual symbols.

Like VLC, arithmetic coding can be made context adaptive – hence, *CABAC: context-adaptive binary arithmetic coding.* If that sounds complicated, it is. CABAC can yield 10% or so bit rate improvement; however, it adds complexity to both the encoder and the decoder and it consumes processing and memory resources. CABAC is available in H.264's main and high profiles.

Deblocking filter

In MPEG-2, it is a problem that the inverse transform tends to produce discontinuities – blocking artifacts –

noun, *ah-RITH-meh-tik;*
adjective, *are-ith-MEH-tik.*

CABAC is part of the main and high profiles of H.264; however, its use may be gated by concerns outside H.264 proper. For example, CABAC is allowed in AVC-Intra 50, but prohibited in AVC-Intra 100.

DIGITAL VIDEO AND HD ALGORITHMS AND INTERFACES

where two 8×8 blocks abut. Many MPEG-2 decoders include post-processing to mitigate the effects of blocking artifacts, but treatment after the fact ("out of the loop") is invisible to the encoder.

H.264 standardizes an adaptive, in the loop deblocking filter. The filter adapts to picture content, such as edges (which typically cause the worst artifacts). Deblocking is standardized, and it takes place within the encoder's prediction loop.

Buffer control

In MPEG-2, a *video buffer verification* (VBV) value is transmitted from the encoder to the decoder, to ensure that the decoder's buffer tracks that of the encoder without underflowing or overflowing.

In H.264 it's more complicated. Memory occupancy is tracked at both the encoder and the decoder for two hypothetical buffers: the *coded picture buffer* (CPB), representing pictures in the coded bitstream; and the *decoded picture buffer* (DPB), representing pictures after decoding.

Scalable video coding (SVC)

Scalable video coding – defined in Annex G of H.264 – allows conveyance of information structured in a hierarchical manner to allow portions of the bitstream to be extracted at lower bit rate than the complete sequence to enable decoding of pictures with multiple image structures (for sequences encoded with spatial scalability), pictures at multiple picture rates (for sequences encoded with temporal scalability), and/or pictures with multiple levels of image quality (for sequences encoded with SNR/quality scalability).

In a single bitstream, a decoder having limited computational resources can extract the base bitstream to decode a low-level representation. (No data rate advantage accrues in this case.)

Different layers can be separated into different bitstreams. All decoders access the base stream; more capable decoders can access enhancement streams. However, for some applications – like HTTP live streaming – it may be more efficient to encode a single program at several different rates, each in a self-

Profile @Level	High 10 Intra (Hi10Intra)
L3.2	AVC-Intra 50: CABAC, 4:2:2, 1280×720p downsampled to 960×720
L4.0	AVC-Intra 50: CABAC, 4:2:2, 1920×1080 downsampled to 1440×1080
L4.1	AVC-Intra 100: CAVLC, 4:2:2, native 1280×720p and 1920×1080

Table 48.6 AVC-Intra profile/level combinations are summarized.

contained stream, so that a decoder can simply access a single stream at a suitable rate.

Multiview video coding (MVC)

Multiview video coding – Annex H of H.264 – standardizes features to efficiently code two (or potentially more than two) pictures that are highly spatially correlated. The common application is to code the left and right images of a stereo pair.

MVC adds two new profiles, *multiview high profile* (MHP) and *stereo high profile* (SHP). Video encoded with either of these profiles is backward compatible with H.264 high profile; the decoder sees just the base view. (In the case of SHP, this is typically the left eye.)

AVC-Intra

AVC-Intra is Panasonic's notation for studio-quality H.264 using Hi10Intra profile. Video in 720p, 1080i, or 1080p format at various frame rates is represented in 10-bit $Y'C_BC_R$ 4:2:2 components. In *AVC-Intra 50*, 720p, 1080i, and 1080p video is downsampled and compressed to 50 Mb/s. In *AVC-Intra 100*, 720p, 1080i, and 1080p video at native pixel count are compressed to 100 Mb/s. Table 48.6 summarizes.

Further reading

RICHARDSON, IAIN E.G. (2010), *The H.264 Advanced Video Compression Standard* (Chichester, U.K.: Wiley).

SULLIVAN, GARY J., PANKAJ N. TOPIWALA, and AJAY LUTHRA (2004), "The H.264/AVC advanced video coding standard: Overview and introduction to the fidelity range extensions," in *Proc. SPIE* **5558**: 454–474.

SULLIVAN, GARY J. and THOMAS WIEGAND (2005), "Video compression – From concepts to the H.264/AVC standard," in *Proc. IEEE* **93** (1): 18–31.

VP3, a distant predecessor to VP8, was made available by On2 as open source. VP3 subsequently developed into *Theora*. On2 licensed VP6 and VP7 to Adobe as the basis for Flash 8 video; subsequently, H.264 was incorporated into Flash 9. On2 licensed VP7 to Skype.

In 2010, Google acquired a company called On2 that had, over a decade or more, developed a series of proprietary software-based codecs for video distribution. Google made the VP8 codec open-source and used it as the basis for a proposal called *WebM* for web (IP-based) distribution of video to consumers. WebM comprises video encoded by the VP8 codec and audio encoded by the *Vorbis* codec, both wrapped in the *Matroska* file wrapper.

The VP8 codec is broadly based upon the principles of MPEG-2 and H.264 discussed in earlier chapters, although Google intends VP8 to be unencumbered by MPEG-2 and H.264 intellectual property rights (IPR, in this case, patent rights). Patents on elements of VP8 were issued to On2; Google permits their royalty-free use. Google's license to VP8 requires that the user not litigate any IP that addresses VP8 ("mutual nonassert"). There's no guarantee or indemnity that Google's VP8 implementation does not infringe patents not controlled by Google – perhaps even patents in the MPEG-2 or H.264 pools.

IP-based means based upon internet (TCP/IP) protocols. *H.264 IP* means intellectual property (patent) rights associated with H.264.

It is a technical and commercial problem with VP8 that the descriptive standard is not comprehensive: The definitive specification of VP8 is effectively its reference code. In places, there is opaque code that raises the question, should the VP8 "standard" be defined by what was apparently intended, or by what is executed by the code? In the absence of a written standard, implementors are forced to treat the reference code as definitive, even if performance or interoperability suffer.

Algorithmic features

As mentioned earlier, the VP8 codec is broadly based upon the principles of MPEG-2 and H.264. To make the most of what follows, you should be familiar with *Introduction to video compression* (on page 147), and with JPEG/M-JPEG, DV, MPEG-2, and H.264, described in the preceding four chapters.

VP8 codes only progressive, 8-bit, 4:2:0 $Y'C_BC_R$ video. No provision is made for interlace.

VP8 has what it calls *key-frames* (comparable to MPEG-2 I-frames), and *inter-frames* (like MPEG-2 P-frames). VP8 has no B-frames: All decoded frames are potentially available for predictions. A VP8 decoder has three reference frames: the *golden* frame, the *previous* frame, and the *altref* ("alternate reference") frame.

The bitstream is partitioned into *segments.* Within a segment there is a 4-byte frame header, and between one and nine *partitions* denoted I, II, III, and so on. A partition is a sequence of bytes representing aspects of video (akin to the separation of VCL NAL units and non-VCL NAL units in H.264). Partition I conveys prediction modes and motion vectors, per macroblock, in raster order. Partitions beyond I convey quantized transform coefficients (in VP8, sometimes termed *texture*). Macroblock rows can be mapped to a single partition, or to 2, 4, or 8 partitions each of which can be processed in parallel. (Entropy contexts, to be described, are shared among partitions; binary arithmetic *decoding* can be parallelized to some extent, but encoding can't be.)

VP8 subdivides 16×16 macroblocks into *subblocks* of 4×4 pixels. There are 24 subblocks in each $Y'C_BC_R$ 4:2:0 macroblock. Unlike H.264, VP8 has no 8x8 luma blocks. Chroma prediction is performed on 8×8 chroma blocks.

VP8 has two luma intra prediction modes – *i16x16* and *i4x4* – which reference previously decoded pixels in the same frame. Using intra prediction precludes parallelism.

The bitstream identifies one of four methods through which the intra prediction for each block can be obtained:

• *V_PRED:* Prediction values are replicated down the block from the row above.

Google documents refer to $Y'C_BC_R$ as *YUV.*

Every picture is accompanied by a 1-bit flag *show_frame*, signalling whether to display the frame. That flag can cause a decoded frame to be placed into one of the reference frames but not displayed. Under unusual circumstances, using this mechanism can simulate a B-frame.

VP8 has no 8×8 intra luma prediction.

DIGITAL VIDEO AND HD ALGORITHMS AND INTERFACES

- *H_PRED:* Prediction values are replicated across the block from the column to the left.
- *DC_PRED:* Prediction values are all set to the average value of the row above and the column to the left; this is called "DC" chroma prediction.
- *TM_PRED:* Prediction values are extrapolated from the row above and the column to the left using (fixed) second differences from the upper-left corner. (This mode is roughly comparable to H.264's planar prediction.)

VP8's core transform is a 4×4 DCT approximated by 16-bit integer coefficients. The decoder uses exact 16-bit arithmetic; there is no decoder drift.

For the 16×16 luma prediction mode, luma processing involves a second level (Y2) transform: After the 16 luma subblocks have been transformed by the DCT, the 16 DC coefficients are collected and a (twenty-fifth) 4×4 transform is performed on those coefficients. The second-level transform is not a DCT, but a Walsh-Hadamard transform (WHT).

Every entry in a Walsh-Hadamard matrix is either +1 or −1.

There are six quantizers, each with its own levels. Which quantizer is used depends upon the "plane" (first-order luma, second-order [Y2] luma, or chroma), and whether the coefficient is DC or AC.

Quantizer level is a 7-bit number that indexes an entry in one of the quantization tables. Quantization is potentially region-adaptive: The encoder associates each macroblock with one of four classes; each class has a different quantization parameter set.

VP8 implements a sophisticated arithmetic coding scheme, simpler than CABAC, but having comparable performance and lighter processing load. The encoder constructs estimates of probabilities of various syntax elements and parameter values. A default baseline parameter set is maintained; upon the occurrence of a keyframe, probability distributions are reset to the baseline. Probabilities are updated as each frame is processed; the encoder signals whether upon completion of decoding the updated set is to become the new baseline ("persistent") or is to be discarded ("one-time").

VP8 has an adaptive in-loop deblocking filter having quality and complexity roughly comparable to that of H.264's deblocking filter.

Further reading

BANKOSKI, JIM, PAUL WILKINS, and YAOWU XU (2011), "Technical overview of VP8, an open source video codec for the web," in *Multimedia and Expo (ICME), 2011 IEEE International Conf.*: 1–6.

BANKOSKI, JIM, PAUL WILKINS, and YAOWU XU (2011), *VP8 Data Format and Decoding Guide*, IETF Informational RFC. This information is available in a more readable form as GOOGLE ON2 (2011), *VP8 Data Format and Decoding Guide* (revised 2011-02-04).

FELLER, CHRISTIAN, JUERGEN WUENSCHMANN, THORSTEN ROLL, and ALBRECHT ROTHERMEL (2011), "The VP8 video codec – overview and comparison to H.264/AVC," in *Consumer Electronics – Berlin (ICCE-Berlin), IEEE International Conf.*: 57–61.

Part 6

Distribution standards

50 MPEG-2 storage and transport 555
51 Digital television broadcasting 559

MPEG-2 storage and transport   50

Multimedia encompasses video and audio, potentially accompanied by other elements such as subtitles, coded in a manner suitable for synchronous presentation to the viewer. Many video compression systems are in use; for consumer use, MPEG-2 and H.264 are widely used. Many audio compression systems are in use; in the consumer domain, Dolby Digital (AC-3) and MPEG-1 Level III (MP3) are widely used.

Multimedia broadcasting or distribution requires that the various elements – *essences,* in the lingo of multimedia – are multiplexed into a single file or stream where the video and audio elements can subsequently be synchronized so as to be presented simultaneously.

In multimedia computing, multiplexing is accomplished by structuring the various components into a *container file*. Microsoft's AVI, Apple's QuickTime, and *Matroska* (used in WebM) are examples. Such container formats are fairly well suited for computers, but not usually well suited to broadcast and sometimes even not very well suited to dedicated, high-performance playback from media such as DVD and Blu-ray disc.

The *Systems* part of the MPEG-1 standard from 1992 established a multiplexing structure. That scheme was extended in MPEG-2, and the MPEG-2 scheme is now widely used in computing, in broadcasting, and in consumer video applications (including consumer camcorders using hard drive or flash media). MPEG-2 Part 1, *Systems,* defines two multiplexing mechanisms, the *program stream* (PS) and the *transport stream* (TS). Both can be regarded as MPEG "containers," whose structure is the subject of the remainder of this chapter.

Some multimedia formats used in PCs use multiple files – for example, one file for video and another for audio. Such schemes effectively push the multiplexing operation to the player software. Such schemes are prone to failure to play one kind of essence, or to have essences fall out of sync.

In the section *MPEG-4,* on page 159, I briefly discussed the *ISO Base Media File Format.* That format serves as a container format for MPEG-4 Part 2/ASP video. That format is generally agreed to be inapplicable to professional video.

Elementary stream (ES)

A coder – audio or video – produces a stream of bytes known as an *elementary stream.* The previous chapter outlines the information that is encoded into a video elementary stream. (Audio encoding is outside the scope of this book.)

An elementary stream can contain private streams.

Packetized elementary stream (PES)

An elementary stream is packetized into packets of 188 bytes, the first byte being MPEG's sync byte valued 47_h. Some systems construct 204 byte packets, expecting the channel coder to overwrite the final 16 bytes of each packet; in this case the sync byte will be $B8_h$.

MPEG-2 program stream

An MPEG-2 *program stream* (PS) a relatively simple mechanism to multiplex video and audio of a single program for storage or transmission on relatively error-free media such as computer disks or digital optical media. PS packets are variable-length; packets of 1 KByte or 2 KBytes are typical, though a packet can be as long as 64 KBytes. MPEG-2 program streams are used in applications such as these:

• DVD media uses a strict subset of MPEG-2 program stream encoding; the associated file extension is *vob*.

MOD is reported to stand for *MPEG on disk*.

• The MOD consumer video format is essentially an MPEG-2 MP@ML SD program stream according to DVD conventions. On a computer, such files typically have extensions *mpg* or *mpeg*.

MPEG-2 transport stream

An MPEG-2 *transport stream* (TS) is a part of the MPEG-2 suite of standards that specifies a relatively complex mechanism of multiplexing video and audio for one or more programs into a data stream, typically having short packets, suitable for transmission through error-prone media where relatively powerful forward error-correction (FEC) is required. A transport stream is suitable for applications where a player connects to a transmission in progress (like television), as opposed to reading a file from its beginning. For terrestrial over-the-air (OTA) or cable television, TS packets are expected to be suitably protected; however specification of the FEC and channel coding lies outside the MPEG standards and ordinarily lies within the realm of digital television standards (for example, ATSC standards in North America, and DVB standards in Europe).

A *transport stream packet* (TSP) comprises 188 bytes – a 4-byte header (whose first byte has the value 47_h), including a 13-bit *packet identifier* (PID), and 184 bytes of payload. Packet size was designed with ATM in mind: One TS packet fits into four ATM cells (48 bytes each). Owing to a lack of external interfaces for program streams, a *single program transport stream* (SPTS) may be used to carry one program. For some applications, a *multiple program transport stream* (MPTS) is used.

Transport stream packets with PID 0 contain the *program association table* (PAT), repeated a few times per second. The PAT lists one or more PIDs of subsequent packets containing *program map tables* (PMTs). A PMT lists PIDs of video and audio elementary streams associated with a single program.

An ATSC DTV transport stream contains a set of packets implementing the *program and system information protocol* (PSIP). PSIP identifies channels and programs, and conveys time-of-day and station callsign information. PSIP enables a receiver to provide an electronic program guide (EPG).

On a computer, 188-byte transport stream packets typically have a 4-byte timecode appended (resulting in 192-byte packets); a file comprising a sequence of such packets typically has the extension *m2t, m2ts,* or just *ts*.

MPEG-2 transport streams are used in applications such as these:
• The TOD consumer video format (essentially an MPEG-2 MP@HL HD transport stream)
• The BDAV container of Blu-ray
• H.264 compressed video
• AVCHD compressed video (in computing, the file extension *mts* is usual)

System clock

Synchronization in MPEG is achieved through a *system clock reference* (SCR). The lowest common multiple of 25 Hz and 29.97 Hz is 30 kHz; In MPEG-2, 90 kHz was

ATM: Asynchronous transfer mode, a protocol for high performance networking.

ATSC Standard A/65, *Program and System Information Protocol*.

TOD is reported to stand for *transport stream on disk*.

I write 29.97 Hz; expressed exactly, it's $30/1.001$.

chosen as the basis for the *program clock reference* (PCR). A program clock value is represented in 33 bits, sufficient to provide unique PCR values over 24 hours.

MPEG system timing is based upon a 27 MHz reference clock, expressed by augmenting the PCR by a nine-bit field taking a value from 0 through 299. Table 50.1 in the margin enumerates the number of PCR counts per frame at various frame rates.

Each program stream has a single reference clock. Different programs in an MPTS can have different program clocks, so provision is made for a transport stream to carry multiple independent PCRs.

27 MHz divided by 90 kHz is 300.

Frame rate [Hz]	PCR counts per frame
30	3000
29.97	3003
25	3600
24	3750

Table 50.1 MPEG-2 PCR counts per frame

Further reading

CHEN, XUEMIN (2002), *Digital Video Transport System* (Springer).

WHITAKER, JERRY C. (2003), "DTV Service Multiplex and Transport Systems," Chapter 13.2 in *Standard Handbook of Video and Television Engineering*, Fourth Edition (McGraw-Hill).

WHITAKER, JERRY C. (2003), "DTV Program and System Information Protocol," Chapter 13.4 in *Standard Handbook of Video and Television Engineering*, Fourth Edition (McGraw-Hill).

Digital television broadcasting 51

This chapter briefly summarizes digital television broadcasting. Most digital broadcast systems that have been standardized are based upon MPEG-2 compression, described in *MPEG-2 video compression* on page 513. Some cable and satellite systems use H.264.

HDTV transmission systems were conceived to deliver images of about twice the vertical and twice the horizontal resolution of SDTV – that is, about 2 megapixels – in a 6 MHz analog channel. MPEG-2 can compress 2 megapixel images at 30 frames per second to about 20 Mb/s. Modern digital modulation schemes suitable for terrestrial RF transmission have a payload of about 3.5 bits per hertz of channel bandwidth. Combining these numbers, you can see that one HDTV digital signal can be transmitted in the spectrum formerly occupied by one analog NTSC 6 MHz channel.

The basic RF parameters of the 525-line, 60-field-per-second interlaced transmission scheme are basically unchanged since the introduction of black-and-white television in 1941! The modulation scheme requires that potential channels at many locations remain unused, owing to potential interference into other channels. The unused channels were called *taboo*. Digital television transmission takes advantage of half a century of technological improvements in modulation systems. The modulation system chosen allows very low power. This low power has two major consequences: It minimizes interference from digital transmitters into NTSC or PAL, and it allows use, for digital television transmission, of the channels that were formerly taboo. Digital television service is thus overlaid on top of analog service. (In early deployment of HDTV, program material was simulcast on a conventional analog transmitter.)

Japan

NHK SCIENCE AND TECHNICAL RESEARCH LABORATORIES (1993), *High Definition Television: Hi-Vision Technology* (New York: Van Nostrand Reinhold).

HDTV broadcasting based on 1035*i*30.00 scanning and MUSE compression was deployed in Japan in the early 1990s; the system is called *Hi-Vision*. MUSE is a hybrid analog/digital system optimized for direct broadcast from satellite (DBS); it is documented in the book from NHK Labs. MUSE predates the MPEG standards; nowadays, it is generally agreed that Japan adopted analog HDTV transmission standards prematurely.

In 2003, MUSE was superseded by ISDB-T, a terrestrial broadcasting system based upon MPEG-2 video coding and OFDM transmission.

United States

HDTV developers in the United States planned for broadcasters to gradually replace analog SDTV transmission with digital HDTV transmission. Partway through the development of HDTV, it became clear that the same compression and transmission technology that would allow one HDTV channel to be coded and transmitted at about 20 Mb/s would be equally suited to allow five SDTV channels to be coded, multiplexed, and transmitted at 4 Mb/s each! So, what began as high-definition television evolved into digital television (DTV), which encompasses both SDTV and HDTV. Compression is in accordance with MPEG-2 MP@ML for SD and MP@HL for HD, with restrictions specified in ATSC A/53.

ATSC A/53, *Digital Television Standard*.

DTV standards in the United States were developed by the Advanced Television Systems Committee (ATSC). Those standards were adopted by the Federal Communications Commission (FCC), with one significant change: The FCC rejected the set of 18 formats documented in Table 3 of ATSC Standard A/53 (presented as my Table 15.1, on page 143). Bowing to pressure from the computer industry, the FCC deleted that table, but left the rest of the ATSC standards intact. The fact that Table 3 is absent from FCC standards has virtually no practical import: In practice, consumer receivers are obliged to decode the Table 3 formats; they cannot be depended upon to decode anything else.

The FCC's deletion of Table 3 supposedly left the choice of raster standards to the marketplace: In principle, any format compliant with MPEG-2 MP@HL could be used. In practice, no U.S. broadcaster has chosen, and no consumer equipment is guaranteed to implement, any format outside ATSC's Table 3. In practice, DTV decoders conform to MPEG standards, and additionally conform to the restrictions imposed by the ATSC standards.

In the United States, DTV audio is standardized with Dolby Digital audio coding (also known as AC-3), a coding scheme not specified in the MPEG-2 standard. Dolby Digital is capable of "5.1" channels: left and right (stereo) channels, a front center channel, left and right surround channels, and a low-frequency effects (LFE) channel (the ".1" in the notation) intended for connection to a "subwoofer." ATSC audio consumes a maximum of 512 kb/s.

EIA-708-B standardizes a method for conveying closed caption data (DTVCC).

One or more MPEG-2 program streams, the associated audio streams, ancillary data, and other data is multiplexed into a transport stream with a bit rate of about 19.28 Mb/s. The transport stream is augmented by Reed-Solomon forward error correction: Each 188-byte transport packet is augmented by 16 FEC bytes, resulting in 204-byte packets that are presented to the modulator.

ATSC modulation

The ATSC standardized 8-level digital vestigial sideband (8-VSB) modulation, transmitting about 10.762 million 3-bit symbols per second. To enable the receiver to overcome errors introduced in transmission, two forward error-correction (FEC) schemes are concatenated: The outer code is Reed-Solomon (R-S), and the inner code is a simple $^3/_2$ trellis code. Between the R-S and trellis coding stages, data is interleaved. Synchronization information comprising segment and field syncs is added after interleaving and coding. A low-level pilot carrier is inserted 310 kHz above the lower band edge

MPEG-2 specifies upper bounds for picture size at various levels. Surprisingly, ATSC A/53 specifies exact values. MPEG-2 MP@ML allows 720 image columns, but ATSC A/53 does not.

EIA-708-B, *Digital Television (DTV) Closed Captioning.*

$$4.5 \frac{684}{286} \approx 10.762$$

to aid in carrier recovery. Analog techniques are used to upconvert to the UHF broadcast channel.

At a receiver, analog techniques downconvert the UHF broadcast to intermediate frequency (IF), typically 44 MHz. Demodulation is then accomplished digitally. Typically, an analog frequency and phase-locked loop (FPLL) recovers the carrier frequency based upon the pilot carrier. A quadrature demodulator then recovers *I* and *Q* components. The *I* component is converted from analog to digital at 10.76 MHz to recover the bitstream; the *Q* component is processed to effect phase control. The bitstream is then subject to trellis decoding, deinterleaving, R-S decoding, and MPEG-2 demultiplexing.

It is a challenge to design a demodulator that is immune to transmission impairments such as multipath distortion and co-channel interference from NTSC transmitters. An interference rejection filter – a variation of a comb filter – is built into the demodulator; it attenuates the video, chroma, and audio carriers of a potentially interfering NTSC signal. An adaptive equalizer built into the demodulator alleviates the effects of multipath distortion; the field sync component of the signal serves as its reference signal. An adaptive equalizer is typically implemented as an FIR filter whose coefficients are updated dynamically as a function of estimated channel parameters.

Cable television has very different channel characteristics than terrestrial broadcast. DTV over cable typically does not use 8-VSB modulation: Quadrature amplitude modulation (QAM) is used instead, with either 64 or 256 levels (64-QAM or 256-QAM).

For DBS, quadrature phase-shift keying (QPSK) is generally used.

Consumer receivers in the United States must accept the diversity of frame rates and raster standards in ATSC's Table 3 (my Table 15.1 on page 143). Although multiscan displays are ubiquitous in computing, both price and performance suffer when a display has to accommodate multiple rates. Most consumer HDTV receivers are designed with displays that operate over a limited range of scanning standards; the wide range of ATSC Table 3 is accommodated by digital resampling. In early deployment of HDTV, many receivers used

1366×768 displays, upconverting 720*p* or downconverting 1080*i* to that format. Today, most consumer HDTV receivers are 1080*i*-native, and convert other formats to 1080*i*.

Europe

In Europe, huge efforts were made in the 1980s and 1990s to develop an HDTV broadcasting system using 1250/50 scanning and a transmission system built upon the MAC transmission technology originally designed for 576*i*. MAC failed in the marketplace. HD-MAC failed also; this was partially a consequence of the commercial failure of MAC, partially because of technical weaknesses of HD-MAC, and partially because HD-MAC did not address worldwide markets.

DVB standards are promulgated by ETSI [www.etsi.org].

HDTV broadcasting in Europe was late, but digital broadcasting of SD is deployed based upon MPEG-2 MP@ML, with 720×576 image structure. The Digital Video Broadcasting (DVB) organization has created a comprehensive set of standards for cable (DVB-C), satellite (DVB-S), and terrestrial (DVB-T) broadcasting. DVB audio conforms to MPEG-2 audio. These standards are promulgated by ETSI.

The RF modulation system chosen for DVB-T is coded orthogonal frequency division multiplexing (COFDM). COFDM uses a large number of subcarriers to spread the information content of a signal evenly across a channel. The subcarriers of COFDM are individually modulated, typically using QPSK or QAM. COFDM exhibits greatly improved immunity to multipath distortion compared to 8-VSB. Also, COFDM accommodates transmission using single-frequency networks (SFNs) where the same bitstream is transmitted from multiple transmitters at different locations but operating on the same frequency.

Further reading

ADAMS, MICHAEL, (2000), *Opencable Architecture* (Indianapolis, Indiana, U.S.A.: Cisco Press).

ATSC A/54A, (2006), *Recommended Practice: Guide to the Use of the ATSC Digital Television Standard, including Corrigendum No. 1* (Dec.)

CICIORA, WALTER, JAMES FARMER, DAVID LARGE, and MICHAEL ADAMS (2004), *Modern Cable Television Technology,* Second Edition (San Francisco: Morgan Kaufmann).

COLLINS, GERALD W. (2001), *Fundamentals of Digital Television Transmission* (New York: Wiley).

DAMBACHER, PAUL (1998), *Digital Terrestrial Television Broadcasting* (Berlin: Springer).

FISCHER, WALTER (2008), *Digital Video and Audio Broadcasting Technology: A Practical Engineering Guide*, Second Edition (Berlin: Springer).

REIMERS, ULRICH, ed. (2005), *DVB: The Family of International Standards for Digital Video Broadcasting* (Berlin: Springer).

WEISS, S. MERRILL (1997), *Issues in Advanced Television Technology* (Boston: Focal Press).

WHITAKER, JERRY C. (2003), "The ATSC DTV system," Chapter 13.1 in *Standard Handbook of Video and Television Engineering*, Fourth Edition (McGraw-Hill).

Appendices

A *YUV* and *luminance* considered harmful   567
B Introduction to radiometry and photometry   573

YUV and *luminance*

considered harmful   A

This is a plea for precise terminology. The notation *YUV*, and the term *luminance*, are widespread in digital video, computer graphics, and digital image processing. Actually, digital video almost never uses $Y'UV$ colour difference components, and never directly represents the *luminance* of colour science. The common terms are almost always wrong. This note explains why. I urge video engineers and computer graphics specialists to use the correct terms, almost always $Y'C_BC_R$ and *luma*.

Cement *vs.* concrete

I'll demonstrate by analogy why it is important to use correct terms. Next time you're waiting in line for a bus, ask the person next to you in line what building material is used to construct a sidewalk. Chances are that person will answer, "cement."

The correct answer is *concrete*. Cement is calcined lime and clay, in the form of a fine, grey powder. Cement is one ingredient of concrete; the other ingredients are sand, gravel, and water.

In an everyday situation, you need not be precise about which of these terms are used: If you refer to a sidewalk as being constructed of "cement," people will know what you mean. Laypeople are not confused by the term *cement*. Interestingly, experts are not confused either. If a construction superintendent yells out to his foreman, "Get me 50 pounds of cement!" the foreman understands immediately from context whether the superintendent actually wants concrete. However, if you phone your local building material supplier and order 50 pounds of cement, you will certainly not receive 50 pounds of concrete! Laypeople have no trouble with the loose nomenclature, and the experts have little trouble. It is the people in the middle who are liable to become confused. Worse still, they are liable to use a term without realizing that it is ambiguous or wrong!

True CIE luminance

Absolute luminance – symbolized *L*, and having units of $cd \cdot m^{-2}$, colloquially *nit* – is rarely used in video. We ordinarily use an approximation to *relative* luminance, symbolized *Y*.

The principles of colour science dictate that true CIE relative luminance – denoted *Y* – is formed as a weighted sum of linear (tristimulus) *RGB* components. If CIE luminance were transmitted in a video system, the system would conform to the *Principle of Constant Luminance*. But in video we implement an engineering approximation that departs from this principle. It was standardized for NTSC in 1953, and remains standard for all contemporary video systems (both SD and HD), to form *luma*, denoted *Y'*, as a weighted sum of *nonlinear* (gamma-corrected) *R'G'B'* components:

$$^{601}Y' = 0.299\,R' + 0.587\,G' + 0.114\,B' \qquad \text{Eq A.1}$$

The nonlinear transfer function usually used is roughly comparable to a square root. We use the theoretical coefficients of colour science, but we use them in a block diagram different from the one prescribed by colour science: Gamma correction is applied *before* forming the weighted sum, not after. The "order of operations" is reversed from what you might expect from colour science.

The misinterpretation of luminance

Video engineers in the 1950s recognized that the video quantity *Y'* was very different from CIE luminance, and that it needed to be distinguished from luminance. They described it by the phrase *the quantity representative of luminance* or *the luminance signal*. They used the symbol *Y*, but augmented it with a prime to denote the nonlinearity: *Y'*. Obviously the qualifier "quantity representative of" was cumbersome, and over the decades, it was elided. And over time, the prime symbol was elided as well.

Unfortunately, no new word was invented to supplement *luminance*, to reinforce the distinction between

DIGITAL VIDEO AND HD ALGORITHMS AND INTERFACES

Pritchard, Dalton H. (1977), "U.S. color television fundamentals – A review," in *SMPTE Journal*, **86** (11): 819–828 (Nov.).

Smith, Alvy Ray (1978), "Color gamut transform pairs," in *Computer Graphics* **12** (2): 12–19 (Aug., Proc. SIGGRAPH).

Foley, James D., and Andries van Dam (1984), *Fundamentals of Interactive Computer Graphics* (Reading, Mass.: Addison-Wesley).

Foley, James D., Andries van Dam, Steven Feiner, and John Hughes (1990), *Computer Graphics: Principles and Practice*, Second Edition (Reading, Mass.: Addison-Wesley). 589 (Section 13.3.3).

Widespread use of incorrect terminology is not a new phenomenon. The indigenous people of North America were, for many centuries, referred to as "Indians." Why? After his long voyage across what we now call the Atlantic Ocean, when Christopher Columbus finally saw land, he thought it was India.

the colour science quantity and the video quantity. Most video engineers nowadays are unfamiliar with colour science, and most do not understand the distinction. Engineers today often carelessly use the word *luminance*, and the symbol Y, to refer to the weighted sum of nonlinear (gamma-corrected) $R'G'B'$ components.

The sloppy nomenclature made its way into ostensibly authoritative video references, such as Pritchard's influential SMPTE paper published in 1977.

The computer graphics pioneer Alvy Ray Smith encountered the word *luminance* in his quest to adapt video principles to computer graphics. Smith apparently correlated the use of the term *luminance* with his knowledge of colour science, and understandably – though wrongly – concluded that video "luminance" and colour science luminance were identical. Consequently, video $Y'IQ$ was introduced to computer graphics, having its Y component alleged to be identical to CIE luminance.

That incorrect interpretation propagated into authoritative computer graphics textbooks. *Computer Graphics: Principles and Practice*, Second Edition, in the section entitled *The YIQ Color Model*, includes this sentence:

> The Y component of YIQ is not yellow but luminance, and is defined to be the same as the CIE **Y** primary.

The emphasis is in the original. "Yellow" refers to *CMY*; printing inks were mentioned in the immediately preceding section. "CIE **Y** primary" would be more accurately denoted "CIE Y component."

Contrary to the quoted paragraph, the so-called Y component of video – more properly designated with a prime symbol, Y' – is *not* the same as CIE luminance. Video Y' cannot even be computed from CIE Y, unless two other colour components (typically colour difference components based upon $B'-Y'$ and $R'-Y'$) are also available. The quoted passage is quite wrong. Apparently, hundreds of thousands of copies of various editions and adaptations of this book have been printed. Confusion is rampant.

PRATT, WILLIAM K. (1991),
Digital Image Processing, Second
Edition (New York: Wiley), 64.
The error is corrected in the third
[2001] and fourth [2007] editions.

The error propagated into the digital image-processing community. Pratt's textbook states:

> N.T.S.C. formulated a color coordinate system for transmission composed of three tristimulus values YIQ. The Y tristimulus value is the luminance of a color.

The video quantities are certainly *not* tristimulus values, which are, by CIE's definition, proportional to intensity.

Loose nomenclature on the part of video engineers has misled a generation of digital image processing, computer software, and computer hardware engineers.

The enshrining of luma

The term *luma* was used in video for a long time, without having had a precise interpretation. I campaigned among video engineers, and among computer graphics experts, for adoption of the term *luma* to designate the nonlinear video quantity. The term offers no impediment to video engineers – in fact, it slides off the tongue more easily than *luminance*. By virtue of its being a different word from *luminance*, the word *luma* invites readers from other domains to investigate fully before drawing conclusions about its relationship with luminance.

SMPTE EG 28, *Annotated
Glossary of Essential Terms for
Electronic Production*.

With the help of Fred Kolb, my campaign succeeded: In 1993, SMPTE adopted Engineering Guideline EG 28, *Annotated Glossary of Essential Terms for Electronic Production*. EG 28 defines the term *luma*, and clarifies the two conflicting interpretations of the term *luminance*. While a SMPTE EG is not quite a SMPTE "Standard," at long last the term has received official recognition. There's no longer any excuse for sloppy use of the term *luminance* by the authors of video engineering papers and books. Had the term *luma* been widespread 20 years ago when A.R. Smith was writing about *YIQ*, or when Foley and van Dam were preparing *Computer Graphics: Principles and Practice*, this whole mess would have been avoided. But EG 28 was unavailable at the time.

It is a shame that today's SMPTE, ISO/IEC, ITU-R, and ITU-T standards persist in using the incorrect word *luminance,* without ever mentioning the ambiguity – even conflict – with the CIE standards of colour science.

Colour difference scale factors

To represent colour, luma is accompanied by two *colour difference* – or *chroma* – components, universally based on *blue minus luma* and *red minus luma*, where blue, red, and luma have all been subject to gamma correction: $B'-Y'$ and $R'-Y'$. Different scale factors are applied to the basic $B'-Y'$ and $R'-Y'$ components for different applications. $Y'P_BP_R$ scale factors are optimized for component analog video. $Y'C_BC_R$ scale factors are optimized for component digital video, such as 4:2:2 studio video, JPEG, and MPEG. Correct use of the $Y'UV$ and $Y'IQ$ scale factors is limited to the formation of composite NTSC and PAL video.

$Y'C_BC_R$ scaling as defined by BT.601 is appropriate for component digital video. $Y'C_BC_R$ chroma is almost always subsampled using one of three schemes: 4:2:2, or 4:2:0, or 4:1:1.

$Y'UV$ scaling is properly used only as an intermediate step in the formation of composite NTSC or PAL video signals. $Y'UV$ scaling is not appropriate when the components are kept separate. However, the $Y'UV$ nomenclature is now used rather loosely, and sometimes – particularly in computing – it denotes *any* scaling of $B'-Y'$ and $R'-Y'$.

In about 1991, digital disk recorders (DDRs) were introduced that were able to transfer files across Ethernet using IP protocols. Abekas introduced the extension *yuv* for these files. But the scale factors typically used (then and now) actually correspond to $Y'C_BC_R$. Use of the *yuv* extension reinforced the misleading *YUV* nomenclature.

Subsampling is a digital technique, properly performed only on component digital video – that is, on $Y'C_BC_R$. Subsampling is inappropriate for $Y'UV$ in all but very specialized applications (namely, digital encoding of $4f_{SC}$ NTSC or PAL composite video). If you see a system described as $Y'UV$ 4:2:2, you have a dilemma. Perhaps the person who wrote the description is unfamiliar with the principles of component video, and the scale factors actually implemented in the equipment (or the software) are correct. But you must allow for the possibility that the engineers who designed or implemented the system used the wrong scale factors! If the

When I say *NTSC* and *PAL*, I refer to colour encoding, not scanning. I do not mean 480*i* and 576*i*, or 525/59.94 and 625/50!

ITU-R Rec. BT.601-5, *Studio encoding parameters of digital television for standard 4:3 and widescreen 16:9 aspect ratios*.

Chroma components are properly ordered $B'-Y'$ then $R'-Y'$, or C_B then C_R. Blue associates with U, and red with V; U and V are in alphabetic order.

HAMILTON, ERIC (1992), *JPEG File Interchange Format*, Version 1.02 (Milpitas, Calif.: C-Cube Microsystems).

wrong equations were used, then colour accuracy will suffer; however, this can be difficult to diagnose.

Proper $Y'C_BC_R$ scaling is usual in Motion-JPEG, and in MPEG. However, the $Y'C_BC_R$ scaling used in still-frame JPEG/JFIF in computer applications usually uses full-range luma and chroma excursions, without any headroom or footroom. The chroma excursion is $256/255$ of the luma excursion. The scaling is almost exactly that of $Y'P_BP_R$, but is unfortunately described as $Y'C_BC_R$: Now even $Y'C_BC_R$ is ambiguous! It is far too late for proper $Y'C_BC_R$ scaling to be incorporated into JFIF; compressed stillframe and motion imagery in computing is bound to suffer a conversion process.

$Y'IQ$ coding has been obsolete in studio practice for at least three decades. It should now be banished in favour of $Y'C_BC_R$.

Conclusion: A plea

Using the term *luminance* for video Y' is tantamount to using the word *cement* instead of *concrete* to describe the primary construction material of a sidewalk. Lay people don't care, and experts can live with it, but people in the middle – in this case, the programmers and engineers who are reimplementing video technology in the computer domain – are liable to draw the wrong conclusions from careless use of terms, and thereby make inaccurate colour. The accurate exchange of images is compromised, and users suffer.

I urge video engineers and computer graphics specialists to avoid the terms *YUV, Y'UV, YIQ, Y'IQ,* and *luminance,* except in the highly specialized situations where those terms are technically correct. The appropriate terms are almost always $Y'C_BC_R$ and *luma*.

Introduction to radiometry
and photometry
B

The domain of *radiometry* involves optical power and its spatial and angular distributions. *Photometry* is, in essence, radiometry weighted by the spectral response of vision. These fields involve several subtle concepts, masked by a bewildering array of symbols and units. I strive to sort out some of the confusion, and make some suggestions concerning units and nomenclature.

ANSI/IESNA RP-16, *Nomenclature and Definitions for Illuminating Engineering*.
CIE Nº 17.4 (E-1.1) (1987), *International Lighting Vocabulary*, 4th Edition (Vienna, Austria: Commission Internationale de L'Éclairage).

Table B.1 below summarizes radiometric quantities, symbols, and units (in the left columns) and the corresponding photometric quantities, symbols, and units (to the right). The symbol for a photometric quantity is just the symbol for the corresponding radiometric quantity, with the addition of the subscript v (for *visual*). Some people add the subscript e to the radiometric symbols.

Differentiate flux with respect to	Radiometric (Radiant)		Photometric (Luminous)	
	Quantity (Symbol)	Unit	Quantity (Symbol)	Unit
–	**radiant flux, power** (Φ, F, P)	watt [W]	**luminous flux** (Φ_v, F_v, P_v)	lumen [lm]
area	**irradiance** (E), **radiant exitance** (M)	$W \cdot m^{-2}$	**illuminance** (E_v), **luminous exitance** (M_v)	$lm \cdot m^{-2}$ = lux [lx]
solid angle	**radiant intensity** (I)	$W \cdot sr^{-1}$	**luminous intensity** (I_v)	$lm \cdot sr^{-1}$ = candela [cd]
area *and* solid angle	**radiance** (L)	$W \cdot sr^{-1} \cdot m^{-2}$	**luminance** (L_v)	$cd \cdot m^{-2}$ = nit [nt]

Table B.1 **Quantities, symbols, and units of radiometry and photometry.** The symbol L_v (or L) is used for absolute luminance (e.g., in photometry). The symbol Y is used for relative luminance (e.g., in colour science and in video).

Radiometry and photometry involve light, in space. No surface is necessary! Light properties may be described *at* a real or imaginary surface; however, they are not properties *of* a surface. Absorptance (*a*), reflectance (*ρ*), and transmittance (*τ*) are intrinsic properties of surfaces, not properties of light.

In what follows, I use the usual physics convention of writing letter symbols in italics and units in Roman type.

Radiometry

Radiometry starts with energy (symbolized *Q*) at wavelengths between about 100 nm and 1 mm. Energy is expressed in units of joules [J]. A photon's energy (Q_p) is related to its wavelength (*λ*), here given in meters:

Eq B.1

$$Q_p = h\frac{c}{\lambda}; \quad \begin{matrix} h \approx 6.6260755 \cdot 10^{-34} \text{ J·s (Planck's constant)} \\ c \equiv 299792458 \text{ m·s}^{-1} \text{ (speed of light)} \end{matrix}$$

The rate of flow – or formally, the time-derivative – of radiant energy is power (*P*), also known as radiant flux (*F*, or preferably, *Φ*), expressed in units of watts [W].

Radiant flux per unit area – that is, flux density – arriving at a point, throughout all directions in a hemisphere, is *irradiance* (*E*). Irradiance is expressed in units of watts per meter squared [W·m^{-2} or W/m^2]. Solar irradiance (*insolation*) at noon is about 1 kW·m^{-2}.

Radiant flux per unit area leaving a point, in all directions, is *radiant exitance* (*M*). Formally, this is the derivative of radiant flux with respect to area. Radiant exitance is expressed in units of watts per meter squared [W·m^{-2}]. Radiant exitance from a nonemissive surface is simply its irradiance times its reflectance.

Radiant flux in a specified direction – formally, radiant flux per unit solid angle – is *radiant intensity* (*I*); its SI unit is watts per steradian [W·sr^{-1} or W/sr]. Intensity must be specified in a particular direction. Intensity is a property of a point-like source; it is independent of distance to the observer or measurement device. Intensity does not follow the inverse square law! Intensity has many other meanings in physics, with the most common being power per unit area, but the unambiguous term for that quantity is *irradiance.*

The late James M. Palmer pointed out that the term *intensity* is widely misused, for no good reason, because it is one of the seven base units of the SI system!

Radiant exitance sums emitted and reflected light. The former term *emittance* excludes reflected light.

Some thermal engineers use the term *radiosity* for radiant exitance. In computer graphics, *radiosity* refers to a specialized technique to compute illumination; it does not refer to any particular quantity.

In photography, the symbol *I* is often used for irradiance or illuminance, instead of intensity. Beware that *sound* intensity is conceptually unlike light intensity: Sound intensity has dimensions of power per unit area, comparable to irradiance of light.

PALMER, JAMES M. (1993), "Getting intense on intensity," in *Metrologia* **30** (4): 371–372.

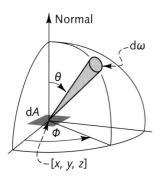

Figure B.1 **Geometry associated with the definition of radiance** The quantity d*A* represents unit area; the quantity dω represents unit solid angle. Projected area falls off as cos θ.

Beware so-called intensity expressed in units other than watts per steradian, $W \cdot sr^{-1}$. Some authors in thermal engineering, and some authors in the computer graphics field of radiosity, use the term *radiant intensity* for what I call *radiance*, which I will now describe.

Radiant flux density in a specified direction is *radiance* (symbol *L*). Formally, radiance is radiant flux differentiated with respect to both solid angle and projected area; the geometry of this definition is depicted in Figure B.1. Radiance is expressed in units of watts per steradian per meter squared [$W/sr/m^2$, or preferably, $W \cdot sr^{-1} \cdot m^{-2}$]. For a large, nonpoint source, radiance is independent of distance.

Confusingly, radiance is often called *intensity* in some domains, especially heat transfer, astrophysics, and astronomy. Also, what is today called radiance was once called *radiometric brightness,* or just *brightness.* The term *brightness* remains in use in astronomy, but it is deprecated for image and colour science.

Radiance can be considered to be the fundamental quantity of radiometry: All other radiometric quantities can be computed from it. You might find it intuitive to start with radiance, and then consider the following:
• Radiant intensity is radiance integrated across an area.
• Irradiance is radiance integrated through solid angle, that is, integrated across all directions in a hemisphere.
• Flux is irradiance integrated across area, or equivalently, radiant intensity integrated through solid angle.

All of these radiometric terms relate to a broad spectrum of wavelengths. Any of these terms may be limited to a narrow spectrum by prepending *spectral* to the term, subscripting the letter symbol with λ, and appending *per nanometer* ($\cdot nm^{-1}$) to the units.

Photometry

So far, I have discussed the physical quantities of radiometry. Photometry is entirely analogous, except that the spectral composition of each quantity is weighted by the spectral sensitivity of human vision, standardized as the luminous efficiency of the CIE Standard Observer (graphed in Figure 20.1 on page 205).

Radiometry and photometry are linked by the definition of the candela: One candela [cd] is the luminous
intensity of a monochromatic 540 THz source having
a radiant intensity of $\frac{1}{683}$ W·sr^{-1}. Once this definition
is established, the remaining photometric quantities
and units parallel those of radiometry. The relationships
are sketched in Figure B.2 opposite.

The photometric analog of radiant flux is luminous
flux (ϕ_v). To quote James Palmer, luminous flux is what
you want when you buy a light bulb. Its brightness is
lumens, the photometric analog of watts; its efficacy is
measured in lumens per watt. One lumen appears
equally bright regardless of its spectral composition.

Luminous flux per unit area – that is, luminous flux
density – arriving at point is *illuminance* (E_v), having SI
units of lux [lx]. One lux is defined as 1 lm·m^{-2}. Illuminance is the photometric analog of irradiance; it is the
quantity measured by an incident light meter. Luminous
flux per unit area leaving a point is *luminous exitance*
(M_v). One lux equals 1 lm·m^{-2}, whether the light is
coming or going; however, traditionalists often state
luminous exitance in units of lm·m^{-2}. Luminous
exitance from a nonemissive surface is its illuminance
times its reflectance.

Luminous flux in a particular, specified direction is
luminous intensity (I_v), expressed in units of lm·sr^{-1}, or
candela [cd]. The candela is the modern equivalent of
the old *candle* (colloquially, candlepower). Intensity is
independent of distance: A candle has a luminous
intensity of about 1 cd, at any viewing distance.

The unit of luminous energy is the *talbot* [T].
A talbot is a lumen-second.

Luminous flux density in a particular direction is
luminance (L_v). Formally, luminance is luminous flux
differentiated with respect to both solid angle and
projected area. Luminance is the photometric analog of
radiance; it is expressed in units of cd·m^{-2}, or collo-
qially, *nit* [nt]. Luminance is an important and useful
measure, because it is invariant under transformation by
a lens. Luminance of 1 cd·m^{-2} corresponds to roughly
a million photons at 560 nm, per square degree, per
second. Brightness is the perceptual correlate of luminance; however, brightness perception is very complex

DIGITAL VIDEO AND HD ALGORITHMS AND INTERFACES

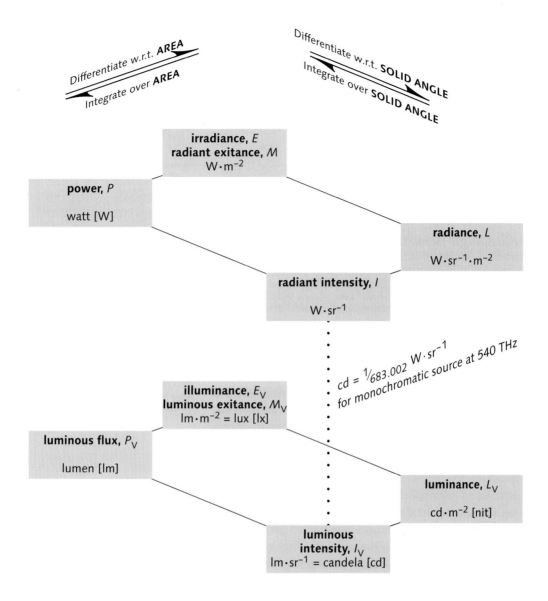

Figure B.2 **Radiometric and photometric quantities** and units are related in this diagram. The top quad shows radiometric quantities – radiant flux, irradiance, radiant intensity, and radiance. At the bottom are photometric quantities – luminous flux, illuminance, luminous intensity, and luminance. The systems are linked by the definition of the candela in terms of radiant intensity.

and highly nonlinear. By CIE's definition, brightness is a subjective quantity that can't be measured.

A perfect Lambertian (diffuse) reflector exhibits luminance [in $cd \cdot m^{-2}$, nt] of $1/\pi$ times its illuminance [in lux].

Light level examples

The following table gives examples of light levels that are encountered in everyday life.

Situation	Illuminance [lx]	Luminance of 90% diffuse reflector [nt]	Luminance of 18% diffuse reflector [nt]
Clear, bright sunlight at noon	100 000	30 000	6 000
Typical daylight	10 000	3 000	600
Overcast daylight sky; TV studio	1 000	300	60
Very dark overcast sky; living room	100	30	6
Twilight; candle at 33 cm	10	3	0.6
Deep twilight; candle at 1 m	1	0.3	0.06
Full moon overhead, clear sky	0.1	0.03	0.006
Half moon overhead, clear sky	0.01	0.003	0.000 6
Starlight + airglow	0.002		
Total starlight, overcast night	0.000 1		
Sirius (m_V = –1.47)	0.000 01		
Vega (m_V = 0)	0.000 003		

Table B.2 **Light level examples**

Image science

Absolute luminance has units of cd·m^{-2}, colloquially called nits [nt]. In image science, luminance is usually normalized to a range of 100 (or as I prefer, 1) with respect to a specified or implied white reference, and expressed without units. So normalized, its symbol is Y. The term *luminance* is often used as shorthand to refer to this pure quantity; however, it is properly called *relative luminance*. The term *luminance factor* should be avoided for this quantity, since the latter term refers to a property of a surface or material: *Luminance factor* is the ratio of luminance of a surface, under specified conditions of light source, incidence, and observation, to the luminance of a perfectly diffusing ("Lambertian") surface, under the same conditions.

Relative luminance (Y) is one of three distinguished *tristimulus values* standardized by the CIE; the other two distinguished tristimulus values are X and Z. Other tristimulus values such as [R, G, B] are related to CIE [X, Y, Z] values by a 3×3 linear matrix product. Relative luminance (Y) and other tristimulus values such as X, Z, R, G, or B are pure numbers.

Michael Brill and Bob Hunt agree that R, G, and B tristimulus values have no units. See HUNT, R.W.G. (1997), "The heights of the CIE colour-matching functions," in *Color Research and Application*, **22** (5): 337 (Oct.).

Units

Many bizarre units have been used for illuminance and luminance. I urge you to abandon these, and to adopt the standard SI units. Radiometry and photometry are sufficiently difficult without having to deal with a plethora of arcane units. If radiometry and photometry are new to you, I believe that your understanding will come more rapidly if you ignore the traditional units – which were deprecated by the scientific community 40 years ago – and adopt the SI units. If you are a practitioner who learned the science and the craft using the traditional Imperial units, please don't stubbornly stick to them: According to the *CIA World Factbook*, only three countries – Burma, Liberia, and the United States – have not adopted International System of Units (SI, or metric system) as their official system of weights and measures. I urge you to use SI units. Simply learn to multiply footlamberts by 3.4 to get candelas per meter squared. A movie screen has a typical white luminance of about 14 fL; call this 48 nits. A studio reference display in North America typically has a reference white luminance of about 100 nits (about 33 fL).

To convert illuminance into lux [lx], use Table B.3:

It was inconsistent mixture of US customary (*Imperial!*) units and SI units that led to the 1998 crash of NASA's Mars Climate Orbiter. American cinema experts often express luminance in footlamberts; why then do they refer to cinema film as 35 mm instead of 1 3/8-inch?

$$\frac{10^6}{25.4^2 \cdot 12^2} = \frac{1}{0.3048^2} \approx 10.764$$

To obtain lm·m^{-2} [lx], multiply unit below	by	numerically
lm·ft^{-2}, footcandle, fc	10.764	10.764
metercandle	1	1

Table B.3 **Conversion of illuminance into lux**

To convert luminance into candelas per meter squared, use Table B.4:

To obtain cd·m^{-2} [nit, nt], multiply unit below	by	numerically
lambert, L	$10\,000/\pi$	3183.1
millilambert, mL	$10/\pi$	3.1831
cd·ft^{-2}	10.764	10.764
footlambert, fL	$10.764/\pi$	3.4263

Table B.4 **Conversion of luminance into cd·m^{-2}**

Further reading

Chapter 1 of Ian Ashdown's book presents a very approachable introduction to measuring light. (The remainder of the book details the computer graphics technique called *radiosity*.) A version of that chapter is available on the web.

D. Allan Roberts offers a terse summary of the basic quantities of radiometry and photometry, and describes the confusing units. (It is worth seeking out the 1994 edition; sadly, the description of radiometry in the 2006 edition of this handbook is not nearly as lucid.)

ASHDOWN, IAN (1994), *Radiosity: A Programmer's Perspective* (New York: Wiley).

ASHDOWN, IAN (2002), *Photometry and Radiometry – A Tour Guide for Computer Graphics Enthusiasts,* <http://www.helios32.com/Measuring%20Light.pdf>.

ROBERTS, D. ALLAN (1994), "A Guide to Speaking the Language of Radiometry and Photometry," in *Photonics Design and Applications Handbook*, 1994 edition, vol. **3**, pages H-70 to H-73 (Pittsfield, Mass.: Laurin Publications).

Glossary

a–ω 0–9 A B C D E F G H I J K L M N O P Q R S T U V W X Y Z

This glossary supplements the main text of *Digital Video and HD Algorithms and Interfaces*. This glossary is self-contained; it contains no references to the main text, and it is not indexed. For discussion in the main text concerning any term herein, consult the index. I spell colour with a *u*.

For the purpose of collating, we place Greek letters first, then numbers, then alphabetic entries. Adjacent letters form units separated by spaces, hyphens, and other symbols; numbers (including decimal point) are also units. Sorting is by unit, so *A/VC* and *AVC* lie several pages apart, and C_B lies with C/PH, not next to CC. Sorting of numbers is by increasing numeric value (considering any decimal fraction). Entries for values between 0 and 9 come first, then 10 to 99, then three-digit numbers, then four – for example, 0_H, 1-bit, 2-2 pulldown, 3:1:1, 3.58 MHz, $4f_{SC}$, 7.5-percent setup, 8 VSB, 10-bit, 18%, 24*p*, 109%, 525/59.94, 601, 1080*i*, 9300 K.

Terms specific to legacy analog NTSC and PAL are not included here. For those terms, see the *Glossary of legacy video signal terms* in the book *Composite NTSC and PAL: Legacy Video Systems*.

α (alpha)

1 In optics, absorptance, the fraction of light absorbed – that is, neither reflected nor transmitted.

2 For computer graphics usage, see *alpha, ·,* on page 591.

γ (gamma)

See several entries for *gamma,* starting on page 621.

0_H datum

In a video stream, the reference point of horizontal (line) sync. In bilevel sync, the 50%-point of the leading edge of the transition to synctip level. In trilevel sync, the zero-crossing between the negative and positive pulses.

0_V datum

In a video stream, the reference point of vertical sync; the start of line 1.

0–255

The standard range of 8-bit pixel values (*R'*, *G'*, *B'*, or *Y'*) from reference black to reference white according to the sRGB standard IEC 61966-2-1 and common computer graphics practice.

1:1 pixel mapping	A system or subsystem that maps video samples to display pixels without any image resampling.
1-chip	A camera having a single image sensor. In the usual case of a colour camera, a 1-chip sensor incorporates mosaic colour separation filters. Compare to *3-CCD, 3-CMOS, 3-chip*, below.
1-D LUT	A LUT (see page 637) that enumerates the scalar results of a function over a range of whole numbers, typically 0 to $2^N - 1$. Useful in greyscale imaging, and useful component-wise in colour imaging exhibiting additive colour mixture.
1 GbE	Informal designation for 1 Gb/s Ethernet; formally *1000BASE-T* and informally also *GigE*.
2-2 pulldown	A process whereby a picture sequence originated at 24 frames per second (cinema or 24*p* digital material) is transferred to video at a field (or, in progressive scanning, frame) rate of 50 Hz. Each 24*p* frame is scanned twice; once to produce the first field (or frame), and once again to produce the second field (or frame). Synonymous with *24 @ 25*, but different from *24 @ 25 pulldown*! See *24 @ 25 pulldown* and *2-3 pulldown*.
2-2-2-4 pulldown	A deprecated process whereby a picture sequence originated at 23.976 fps [or 24 fps] (motion picture film, or 23.976*p* or 24*p* digital material) is transferred to video at a field (or, in progressive scanning, frame) rate of 59.94 Hz [or 60 Hz]. Groups of four film frames are scanned two, two, two, then four times to form successive video pictures. When such material is viewed directly, the process yields severe stutter.
2-3 pulldown	A process whereby a picture sequence originated at 23.976 fps [or 24 fps] (motion picture film, or 23.976*p* or 24*p* digital material) is transferred to video at a field (or, in progressive scanning, frame) rate of 59.94 Hz [or 60 Hz]. Alternate film frames are scanned first two then three times to form successive video pictures.
2-3-3-2 pulldown	A process whereby a picture sequence originated at 23.976 fps [or 24 fps] (motion picture film, or 23.976*p* or 24*p* digital material) is transferred to video at a field (or, in progressive scanning, frame) rate of 59.94 Hz or 60 Hz. Alternate film frames are scanned two, three, three, then two times to form successive video pictures. The advantage over classic 2-3 pulldown is that when interlaced video is produced, every video frame contains two fields from a single film frame; the disadvantage is that such material viewed directly exhibits somewhat more stutter than 2:3 pulldown.
2.0	Two-channel (stereophonic) sound, contrasted with 5.1.
2:1 interlace	See *interlace*, on page 628.
2 K	Relating to image representations having 2048 image columns (samples per picture width), such as 2048×1080; particularly

the system for digital cinema devised by the DCI and standardized by SMPTE. Use of 2048 image columns instead of 1920 reflects an industry differentiation rather than a technical advantage; however, 2 K image data is normally represented in a colour space that mimics cinema, not the BT.709 colour space that characterizes HD.

2-pop	A 1 kHz audio tone burst at –20 dB_{FS} occupying exactly one frame interval ending exactly 2 seconds (or in 25 fps systems, 1.92 s) prior to the first frame of action of a program. In cinema, the 2-pop is synchronized with the leader frame that displays the digit "2."
2.4:1	The "CinemaScope" aspect ratio commonly used for movies.
3-CCD, 3-CMOS, 3-chip	A camera having three optically aligned image sensors, achieving colour separation through an optical beamsplitter ("prism"). Compare to *1-chip,* above.
3:1:1	Component digital video wherein each C_B and C_R component is horizontally subsampled by a factor of 3 with respect to luma, and not subsampled vertically. Not widely used.
3-2 pulldown	See *2-3 pulldown,* above. The notation *3-2 pulldown* is inaccurate because SMPTE standards denote as the *A-frame* the first 24*p* frame in the four-frame sequence; that frame is associated with two fields (the first and second) of one picture, which is scanned twice (not three times).
3 dB	Three decibels: half power, equivalent to 0.707 signal amplitude. Relative amplitude at a filter's corner frequency.
3-D	**1** Relating to imaging in general, stereoscopic: A system that acquires, processes, records, transmits, and/or displays two views of the same scene from slightly different positions, one destined for the viewer's left eye and the other for the right.
	2 Relating to colour processing, techniques – ordinarily involving lookup tables – that process three components in conjunction using nonlinear operations instead of processing components separately or combining them in linear manner.
3-D LUT	A LUT (see page 637) that enumerates the three-dimensional vector results of a function over three-dimensional vector arguments. Arguments and results are typically whole numbers 0 to $2^N - 1$. Useful in colour imaging exhibiting nonadditive colour mixture (that is, exhibiting nonlinear colour crosstalk).
3-D LUT interpolation	A process using a 3-D LUT (see above) that includes an algorithm that rather coarsely quantizes argument values (perhaps to 17 or 33 levels) and interpolates between result values.
3G-SDI	A serial digital interface (SDI) having a data rate of either $^{2.97}/_{1.001}$ Gb/s or 2.97 Gb/s, commonly used to transport 1080*p*30, 4:4:4 video and also capable of 1080*p*60, 4:2:2.

3 K	**1** Relating to image representations having roughly 3000 image columns (samples per picture width), such as 2880×2160 (i.e., 1.5 times 1920×1080) or 3072×1728 (i.e., $3 \cdot 1024 \times {}^9\!/_{16} \cdot 3 \cdot 1024$); particularly systems intended for digital cinema acquisition. 3 K image data is normally represented in a colour space that mimics cinema. The notation 3 K is ambiguous with respect to whether a pixel comprises one or three colour components; see *4 K,* on page 584.
	2 The approximate temperature, in units of kelvin, of the cosmic background radiation, the discovery of which earned the Nobel prize in physics for Arno Penzias and Robert Wilson.
3-way colour correction	Colour correction of video-coded image data whereby the colour balance of shadow tones, midtones, and light tones is adjusted separately. The "thresholds" defining the transition points between these regions (in terms of luma) can typically be adjusted. Often presented as a set of three colour wheels. Not to be confused with *lift-gamma-gain*.
3.58 MHz	More precisely, 3.579545 MHz, or exactly, $5 \times {}^{63}\!/_{88}$ MHz: the colour subcarrier frequency of 480*i* NTSC video.
$4f_{SC}$	Obsolete composite digital video using a sampling frequency of 4 times the colour subcarrier frequency. There were 480*i* NTSC and 576*i* PAL versions of $4f_{SC}$.
4 K	Relating to image formats having 4096 image columns (samples per picture width), such as 4096×2160; particularly the system for digital cinema devised by the DCI and standardized by SMPTE. 4 K imagery is normally represented in a colour space that mimics cinema.
	The notation *4 K* is ambiguous. When used to characterize a digital cinema camera, the each of the 4096×2160 "pixels" typically comprise a single colour component (red, green, *or* blue, or perhaps another green). When used to characterize a digital cinema film scanner, or a projector, each of the 4096×2160 pixels typically comprises three colour components – red, green, *and* blue.
4:0:0	Greyscale video (sometimes confusingly called *monochrome*).
4:1:1	Chroma subsampling wherein C_B and C_R components are horizontally subsampled by a factor of 4 with respect to luma, and not subsampled vertically.
4:2:0	This confusing notation denotes chroma subsampling wherein C_B and C_R chroma components are subsampled both vertically and horizontally by a factor of 2, with respect to luma. There are two variants of 4:2:0 chroma: *interstitial* 4:2:0, used in JPEG/JFIF, H.261, and MPEG-1; and *cosited* 4:2:0, used in MPEG-2.

4:2:2	**1** Chroma subsampling wherein each C_B and C_R component is horizontally subsampled by a factor of 2 with respect to luma, and not subsampled vertically.
	2 An SD component digital video coding or interface standard, based upon BT.601, using 4:2:2 chroma subsampling, having versions for both 480*i* or 576*i* scanning. The corresponding 19 mm videotape format is denoted D-1.
4:2:2:4	A 4:2:2 system, as in 4:2:2 above (2), augmented by an opacity (or *alpha*, or *key*) component sampled at the same rate as the luma component. See *alpha, α,* on page 591.
4:3	The standard aspect ratio of SD.
4:4:4	Component digital video where *R′G′B′* (or rarely, $Y'C_BC_R$) components are conveyed with equal data rate.
4:4:4:4	A 4:4:4 system, as above, augmented by a transparency (also known as *alpha*, or *key*) component sampled at the same rate as the *R′ or Y′* component. See *alpha, α,* on page 591.
4.43 MHz	Expressed exactly, 4.433618750 MHz: the colour subcarrier frequency of 576*i* PAL-B/G/H/I video.
5-5-5	A 15 bit per pixel image format, used in low-end computer graphics, having 5 bits for each component of a pixel (i.e., red, green, and blue). Historically called *Hi-color* [sic].
5-6-5	A 16 bit per pixel image format, used in low-end computer graphics, having 5, 6, and 5 bits per component of red, green, and blue, respectively. Historically called *Hi-color* [sic].
5.1	Notation invented by Tom Holman for surround sound having five channels (front left, centre, and right; back left and right; and *low frequency effects* (LFE), the .1 in the notation.
6-way	**1** Video colour adjustment whereby hue and chroma (and possibly luminance or luma) of red, green, blue, cyan, magenta, and yellow are individually controlled. Additive colour mixing properties are easily broken. Also called *6-axis*.
	2 Video colour adjustment whereby the off-diagonal elements of a linear-light 3×3 matrix in *RGB* are altered in a linear manner.
7.5% setup	See *setup*, on page 657.
8-VSB	See *VSB*, on page 664.
10-bit Cineon/DPX	A data value, or a file containing image data values, where transmittance of exposed and developed camera negative film is transformed logarithmically to a quantity proportional to optical density, then digitized and encoded into integers ranging 0…1023. (For transport across HD-SDI, codes 0…3

and 1020…1023 are excluded.) Data encoding is usually in accordance with SMPTE ST 268 ("DPX") *printing density.*

10-bit log	**1** 10-bit log *RGB:* Estimated *RGB* tristimulus values, transformed approximately logarithmically, then digitized and encoded into integers ranging 0…1023. See *log RGB,* on page 635.
	2 10-bit Cineon/DPX, see above.
10 GbE	10 Gb/s Ethernet; formally, 10GBASE-T.
13.5 MHz	The standard luma sampling rate for SD.
14:9	A compromise aspect ratio used in Europe during the transition to HD. Programming at 16:9 was created "14:9-safe" to allow cropping to 14:9 without harm. On 4:3 receivers, narrow top and bottom bars (less objectionable than wide bars) are displayed.
16:9	The standard aspect ratio of HD.
16–235	The standard range of 8-bit video code interface values (*R'*, *G'*, *B'*, or *Y'*) from reference black to reference white according to BT.601 and BT.709. Code values 0 and 255 are reserved for sync; 1–15 and 236–254 are permitted for transient elements.
16-way	Video colour adjustment whereby hue and chroma (and possibly luminance or luma) at 16 different hue angles are individually controlled. Additive colour mixing properties are easily broken.
18%	Reflectance factor (in the linear-light domain, relative to a perfect diffuse Lambertian reflector) of a "mid grey" test card.
23.976 Hz	A common frame rate for cinema production involving interface to SD or HD video. Expressed exactly, $^{24}/_{1.001}$.
24 Hz	The standard frame rate for cinema production and exhibition.
24 @ 25	A process whereby pictures (motion picture film, or 24*p* digital material) originated at 24 frames per second is run 4% fast and transferred to progressive video at 50 Hz frame rate (or interlaced video at 50 Hz field rate). Each film frame is scanned twice. (In interlace, one scan produces the first field and the next produces the second field.) Synonymous with *2-2 pulldown.*
24 @ 25 pulldown	The process of converting motion picture film or 24*p* digital material at 24 frames per second into a 50 picture per second video representation (e.g., 576*i*50), wherein exactly 24 frames per second are conveyed, but pictures having original 24*p* timecodes :11 and :23 are replicated. The result could be described as 2:2:2:2:2:2:2:2:2:2:2:3:2:2:2:2:2:2:2:2:2:2:2:3 pulldown; such material is unsuitable for direct viewing but is fairly easily processed.

DIGITAL VIDEO AND HD ALGORITHMS AND INTERFACES

24*a*	24 frames per second, progressive "advanced," whereby 24 fps progressive frames are subject to 2:3 pulldown in the camera for recording in 59.94 Hz or 60 Hz interlaced form, and each recording starts on an A-frame.
24*p*	24 frames per second, progressive. Preferably written *p*24 to correspond to notations such as 720*p*24 and 1080*p*24.
24*p*A	24 frames per second, progressive "advanced," carried across a 29.97 Hz video stream. See *2-3-3-2 pulldown*, on page 582.
24PsF	24 frames per second, progressive segmented-frame. The image format is typically 1920×1080. See *PsF*, on page 648.
25 Hz	The usual frame rate for interlaced video production in Europe and Oceana.
29.94 Hz	The usual frame rate for interlaced video production in North America and Japan. Expressed exactly, $^{30}/_{1.001}$.
50 Hz	The usual frame rate for interlaced video production in Europe and Oceana.
59.94 Hz	The usual frame rate for interlaced video production in North America and Japan. Expressed exactly, $^{60}/_{1.001}$.
64–940	The standard range of 10-bit video code interface values (R', G', B', or Y') from reference black to reference white according to BT.601 and BT.709. Code values 0–4 and 1020–1023 are reserved for sync; 4–63 and 941–1019 are permitted for transient values outside the reference range.
74.176 MHz	The standard luma sampling rate (rounded to three decimal places) for HD at picture rates altered by the ratio $^{1000}/_{1001}$.
74.25 MHz	The standard luma sampling rate for HD at integer picture rates.
90%	Reflectance factor – in the linear-light domain, and relative to a perfect diffuse Lambertian reflector – of a typical white test card. (Some people prefer 89.1%, representing an optical density of 0.05 relative to a perfect diffuse reflector.)
109%	Encoded Y', R', G', or B' signal level – in the gamma-corrected, perceptual domain – at the peak white level defined in BT.601 or BT.709. Expressed exactly, $^{238}/_{2.19}$.
360*p*	A progressive video standard having image structure of 480×360; suitable for square-sampled SD content at 16:9 aspect ratio.
422P	The 4:2:2 profile of MPEG-2. (The colons are elided; the P is written in Roman uppercase.)

480*i*, 480*i*29.97	An interlaced scanning standard or image format for SD used primarily in North America, Japan, Korea, and Taiwan, having 525 total lines per frame, approximately 480 image rows (usually in an image structure of 704×480 or 720×480), and 29.97 frames per second. The notation 480*i*29.97 does not specify colour coding; colour in 480*i*29.97 systems is conveyed in the studio using $R'G'B'$, $Y'C_BC_R$, or $Y'P_BP_R$ components, and was historically encoded for transmission using composite NTSC. Historically denoted 525/59.94 (see below), or *ITU-R System M*. Often loosely referred to as *525/60*. Often incorrectly called *NTSC*, which properly refers to a colour-encoding standard, not a scanning standard.
525/59.94	Archaic notation for what is now called 480*i*29.97; see above.
540*p*	A progressive image format having an image structure of 960×540. A variant deployed by Apple is denoted *iFrame;* its frame rate (written after the *p*) is not publicly documented, but is reported to be 29.97 Hz. (I-frame compression is apparently used for this image format.)
555 format	See *5-5-5*, on page 585.
565 format	See *5-6-5*, on page 585.
576*i*, 576*i*25	An interlaced scanning standard or image format for SD used primarily in Europe, Australia, and parts of Asia, having 625 total lines per frame, 576 image rows (usually in an image structure of 720×576), and 25 frames per second. A raster notation such as 576*i*25 does not specify colour coding; colour in 576*i*25 systems is commonly conveyed in the studio using $R'G'B'$, $Y'C_BC_R$, or $Y'P_BP_R$ components, and typically conveyed through analog distribution by composite PAL. Historically denoted 625/50. Often incorrectly called *PAL*, which properly refers to a colour-encoding standard, not a scanning standard. Sometimes inaccurately called *CCIR*.
601	See *BT.601*, on page 597.
625/50	Archaic notation for what is now called 576*i*25; see above.
656	See *BT.656*, on page 598.
709	See *BT.709*, on page 598.
720*p*	A progressive image format for HD, having an image structure of 1280×720, and any of several frame rates including 23.976, 24, 29.97, 30, 59.94, or 60 Hz (or rarely, 50 Hz).
1035*i*	A developmental interlaced image format for HD, now obsolete, having an image structure of 1920×1035, a frame rate (written after the *i*) of 30.00 Hz, and nonsquare sampling.

1080*i*	An interlaced image format for HD having an image structure of 1920×1080 and a frame rate (written after the *i*) of 29.97 Hz or 30.00 Hz (or rarely, 25 Hz).
1080*p*	A progressive image format for HD, having an image structure of 1920×1080, and any of several frame rates (written after the *p*) including 23.976, 24, 25, 29.97, or 30.00 Hz, and potentially 50, 59.94, or 60.00 Hz.
1125/59.94/2:1	An interlaced scanning standard for HD, having a field rate of 59.94 Hz, and 1125 total lines per frame (of which formerly 1035, and now 1080, contain picture). The standard system with 1080 lines is now denoted 1080*i*29.97.
1125/60/2:1	An interlaced scanning standard for HD, having a field rate of 60 Hz, and 1125 total lines per frame (of which formerly 1035, and now 1080, contain picture). The standard system with 1080 lines is now denoted 1080*i*30.
1280×720	A standard image array for HD. (Aspect ratio is 16:9, 1.78:1.)
1556*p*24	A progressive image format compatible with film having an image structure of 2048×1556 and frame rate of 24 Hz or 23.976 Hz (though the latter should be written 1556*p*23.976). The count of 1556 image rows is suitable for "open gate"; 1536 image rows suffices for exact 4:3 aspect ratio ("Academy aperture").
1920×1080	A standard image array for HD. (Aspect ratio is 16:9, 1.78:1.)
1998×1080	An image array, having the 1.85:1 aspect ratio of typical movies, commonly used for 2 K digital cinema.
2048×1080	An image array, having aspect ratio of about 1.9:1, commonly used for 2 K digital cinema.
2048×858	An image array, having aspect ratio 2.4:1 (*CinemaScope*), commonly used for 2 K digital cinema.
4096×2160	An image array, having aspect ratio of about 1.9:1, commonly used for 4 K digital cinema.
6500 K	In colour science generally, and in video and computer graphics, a white reference corresponding to CIE Illuminant D_{65}, whose correlated colour temperature is approximately 6504 K.
9300 K	In computer graphics, and in studio video in Asia, a white reference whose correlated colour temperature is 9300 K.
A-frame	In 2-3 pulldown, the first 24*p* frame in a sequence of four frames A, B, C, and D, or the corresponding video frame. The A-frame is scanned twice, to produce a first field then a second field. If nondropframe timecode HH:MM:SS:F*u* is coherent with 24*p* scanning, the A-frame produces first and second fields

where $u=0$; the B-frame produces first and second fields where $u=1$, then a first field where $u=2$; the C-frame produces a second field with $u=2$ and a first field with $u=3$; and finally, the D-frame produces a second field where $u=3$, then first and second fields where $u=4$. The sequence continues with A (5), B (6, 7), C (7, 8), then D (8, 9).

A/VC	In IEEE 1394, audio/video control. A mechanism to control audio and video devices across an IEEE 1394 interface. Sometimes written AV/C. Not to be confused with AVC (see below).
AAC	Advanced audio coding: A lossy audio compression system defined in MPEG-2 Part 7.
ABL	Automatic brightness limiter: In a PDP display, signal processing circuitry that reduces display R, G, and B tristimulus values uniformly for any image where the sum of the input signal tristimuli exceeds about 25% of the peak relative luminance of the panel. For example, the luminance of a full white signal is reduced when it occupies more than about 25% of the image area. The limitation is imposed to avoid excessive power dissipation in the panel. See *power loading*, on page 648.
ABR, adaptive bit rate	Schemes capable of varying transmission bit rate depending upon available data capacity. Contrast *CBR, constant bit rate*, on page 599, and *VBR, variable bit rate*, on page 663. VBR ordinarily applies to storage media, and ABR to network delivery.
AC	**1** Alternating current: Historically, an electrical current or voltage that reverses in polarity periodically – that is, whose sign alternates periodically between positive and negative.
	2 In modern usage, a signal whose value varies periodically. Distinguished from *DC, direct current;* see page 611.
	3 In JPEG and MPEG, any or all DCT coefficients in an 8×8 block apart from the DC coefficient.
AC-3	Originally, *Audio Coding 3:* Dolby Labs' designation of a digital audio compression standard incorporated into the ATSC HDTV system. AC-3 is now called *Dolby Digital*.
Academy	Academy of Motion Picture Arts and Sciences (AMPAS).
Academy aperture	1.375:1 aspect ratio, standardized by the Academy in 1932.
accuracy	The degree of closeness of a measurement to a true value. Distinguished from *precision* (page 648).
ACES	Academy Color Encoding Specification.
achromatic	Without hue: In digital imagery, lightness-related information (or component) only.

active	**1** Historically, a signal element (sample, or image row, or in analog systems, scan line) defined by an image representation or scanning standard to contain part of the picture or its associated blanking transition. In a digital representation (such as 1920×1080), all of the indicated image matrix elements are "active." The term *visible picture element* is an oxymoron: If an element is in the picture, it's intended to be visible! (Exceptionally, in 480*i*29.97, line 21 closed caption data is considered to be active, despite the fact that it does not contain picture.)
	2 In the context of *active format description* (AFD, see below), *active* refers to portion of the pixel array that contains the image intended to be viewed by the consumer, not including any fixed content surrounding the picture that is necessary to meet the aspect ratio requirements of the container.
Adobe RGB (1998)	A colour exchange standard promulgated by Adobe and used in graphic arts and professional digital photography, having wider gamut than BT.709.
ADU	Analog-to-digital unit: The digital number produced by analog-to-digital conversion of an sensor signal. Sometimes denoted DN (digital number) or DCV (digital code value). For a conventional linear sensor such as a CCD, ADU and DN are linear-light measures; DCV may incorporate nonlinear coding.
AES3	An interface, for professional use, for uncompressed digital audio, standardized for several physical interfaces including balanced twisted-pair, unbalanced coax, and optical fibre. Standardized in IEC 60958 Part 4.
AFD, active format description	Metadata (defined in SMPTE ST 2016) accompanying video to indicate the portion of the raster that contains the image intended to be viewed by the consumer.
albedo	In physics, average diffuse reflectance across the visible spectrum (and perhaps extending into the infrared and ultraviolet).
alpha, α	In computer graphics, a component of a pixel indicating the opacity – conventionally between black (0, fully transparent) and white (1, fully opaque) – of the pixel's colour components. Colour component values ($R'G'B'$, $Y'P_BP_R$, or $Y'C_BC_R$) may have been premultiplied by the value of a corresponding alpha value; this is sometimes called *shaped video*. Colour component values that have not been so premultiplied are *unassociated* (or *unshaped*, or *nonpremultiplied*). See also *key*, on page 631.
alychne	"Absence of lightness line": In a chromaticity diagram, the locus of coordinates having zero luminance. In the CIE [*x, y*] diagram, the *x*-axis.
anamorphic	A subsidiary format (or its associated lens) standing in relation to a base format having relatively narrow aspect ratio, wherein the horizontal dimension of a widescreen image is squeezed by

some factor with respect to the horizontal dimension of the base format. In cinema, the widescreen (anamorphic) image conventionally has 2.4:1 aspect ratio and the squeeze is by a factor of 2. In video, the widescreen (anamorphic) image has 16:9 aspect ratio, and the squeeze is typically by a factor $\frac{4}{3}$.

ANC	In SDI and HD-SDI, ancillary (nonessence) information typically conveyed during vertical and horizontal blanking intervals.
anchor picture	See *reference picture,* on page 651.
ANSI lumens	Total light output of a projector measured in accordance with ANSI/NAPM IT7.228 (withdrawn in 2003). To achieve 48 nt white on a perfect unity-gain screen, luminous flux of $48 \cdot \pi$ lumens is required for each square meter of screen area.
APC	Automatic power control: A signal processing mechanism common in plasma display panels whereby the video level is reduced in order to limit total power to the display surface. See *loading, luminance,* on page 635.
APL, average picture level	A historical term, now ambiguous:

    1 Traditionally in video, APL is equivalent to average pixel level, see below.

    2 Average relative luminance. This is a linear-light measure unlike average pixel level. Properly termed *average relative luminance* (ARL).

APL, average pixel level	The average of luma (Y') throughout the image area of a frame, sequence, scene, or program. Average *pixel* level is preferred to the historical term *average picture level* for disambiguation, to make clear that it is gamma-corrected pixel values (not their luminance or tristimulus equivalents) that are averaged.
ARL, average relative luminance	The average of luminance (Y) throughout the entire image area of a frame, sequence, scene, or program. ARL is a linear-light measure (unlike average pixel level).
ARS, adaptive rate streaming	Streaming (network) delivery wherein bit rate potentially varies depending upon network loading. See also *ABR, adaptive bit rate,* on page 590.
ASI	Asynchronous serial interface: An industry standard electrical interface, standardized by DVB, used to convey an MPEG-2 transport stream.
aspect ratio	The ratio of the width of an image to its height. (Some authors, such as MPEG, write this improperly as height:width.)
aspect ratio, sample (or pixel)	The ratio of horizontal sample pitch to vertical sample pitch.
ATSC	Advanced Television Systems Committee: A U.S.-based organization that standardizes and promotes digital SDTV and HDTV

broadcasting. ATSC advocates MPEG-2 video compression and Dolby Digital (AC-3) audio compression, supplemented by ATSC terrestrial broadcasting transmission standards. Note that *Systems* is plural (contrary to the singular *System* in NTSC).

AV	Audiovisual: Electronic technology to capture, process, record, transmit, and/or present moving pictures along with associated sound.
AVC	Originally, advanced video compression: The effort within IEC, ISO, and ITU-T that produced the H.264 standard (see page 623). Now more clearly expressed as *H.264.*
AVC-Intra	A subset of H.264 video coding (see page 623) for professional applications, using I-frame only compression of 720*p*,1080*i*, or 1080*p* video, typically at data rates of 50 Mb/s (using the Hi10PIntra profile) or 100 Mb/s (using the Hi422PIntra profile).
AVCHD	A consumer HD system for 720*p*, 1080*i*, and 1080*p*24, adapted for professional use, typically using 12 cm DVD-R media, SDHC flash memory cards, or hard disk drive recording, using long-GoP H.264 video coding, Dolby Digital audio coding, and having a bit rate between about 6 Mb/s and 18 Mb/s.
AVCCAM	Panasonic's adaptation of AVCHD (see above) to professional markets.
average luminance	The mean (CIE, linear-light) luminance across the image area of a frame, sequence, scene, or program. The term is often used to refer to what is more properly called average *relative* luminance, that is, computed relative to the luminance of reference white. Not to be confused with *APL* (see above), which averages a gamma-corrected (perceptually uniform) signal.
average pixel level	See *APL, average pixel level,* on page 592.
AVS	Audio and Video coding Standard: A collection of standards of the People's Republic of China (PRC) relating to compression of audio and video. The standards specify a system comparable to H.264 but generally avoid its intellectual property.
AWGN, additive white Gaussian noise	Noise that is additive (i.e., has the same amplitude across the whole range of values of the associated signal), white in the frequency sense (that is, having power uniformly distributed across the frequency spectrum), and Gaussian (i.e., has a probability distribution function that follows the statistical "normal" curve). Some kinds of noise are well characterized as AWGN (e.g., sensor read noise); other kinds are not (e.g., photon shot noise).
b, bit	Binary digit: The elemental unit of information, valued either 0 or 1 (sometimes interpreted as false/true, no/yes, off/on, etc.).
B, byte	Byte: An ordered collection of eight bits, capable of representing whole numbers 0 through 255 (i.e., 0 through 2^8-1),

B-field	In MPEG, a field-coded B-picture. B-fields come in pairs (either top then bottom, or bottom then top). See *B-picture,* below.
B-frame	In MPEG and related standards, either a frame-coded B-picture, or a pair of B-fields (one top field and one bottom field, in either order). See *B-picture,* below.
B-picture	In MPEG, a bidirectionally predictive-coded picture: A picture, or coded picture information, in which one or more macroblocks involve prediction from a preceding or a following anchor picture. B-pictures exploit temporal coherence. They are computed and displayed, but do not form the basis for any subsequent predictions.
b/s	Bits per second; the *b* is preferably set in lowercase.
B/s	Bytes per second; the *B* is preferably set in uppercase.
B'–Y', R'–Y'	A pair of colour difference components, *B'* minus luma and *R'* minus luma. Following decoding of *Y', B'–Y',* and *R'–Y',* the resulting red, green, and blue components (*R'G'B'*) are subject to an EOCF to produce tristimulus (linear-light). *B'–Y',* and *R'–Y'* colour differences may be scaled to form C_B and C_R for component digital systems, scaled to form P_B and P_R for component analog systems, or scaled to form *U* and *V* (or, in specialized forms of NTSC, *I* and *Q*) for composite encoding.
band-interleaved by line (BIL)	A method of storing pixels whereby like components of an image row occupy adjacent storage locations. A 3×2 8-bit *RGB* image could be stored in the order RRRGGGBBBRRRGGGBBB. See also *interleaved, component interleaved,* on page 628, and *planar,* on page 647.
bandwidth	**1** Technically, the frequency or frequency range where an analog or digital signal's power has fallen 3 dB – that is, to 0.707 – from its value at a reference frequency (usually zero frequency, *DC*). Equivalently, the frequency or frequency range where an analog or digital signal's amplitude has fallen 3 dB – that is, to 0.707 – from its value at a reference frequency.
	2 In common language, *data rate;* see page 610.
Bayer pattern	The mosaic pattern (see page 639), named for Kodak researcher Bryce E.Bayer, comprising a 2×2 arrangement of photosites or pixel components representing red, green, green, and blue.
BD	Blu-ray disc.
BER	Bit error ratio: The probability that recording or transmission in an error-prone medium corrupts any single bit recorded or transmitted. Sometimes incorrectly expressed as bit error *rate,*

integers from –128 to +127 in two's complement form, other number systems, or characters in a variety of encodings.

DIGITAL VIDEO AND HD ALGORITHMS AND INTERFACES

which properly refers to the *rate* of occurrence of erroneous bits.

Betacam — Sony's trademarked term for a professional component analog videotape format for 480*i* or 576*i* on ½-inch tape. The successor system, with higher bandwidth, is denoted Betacam SP. See also *Digital Betacam, Digital-β,* on page 612.

bias — **1** In signal processing in general, an additive term contributing to a signal value; offset.

2 In display systems, a low-level adjustment – traditionally necessary for CRT displays owing to analog drift, and now thoughtlessly replicated in many fixed-pixel displays – to set *RGB* biases individually on a component-by-component basis. (BLACK LEVEL or BRIGHTNESS sets bias on all components together.) Sometimes called CUTOFF or OFFSET; in the home theatre community, sometimes called *RGB*-LOW. See also *drive* (**2**) on page 614.

3 In the home theatre community, surround lighting.

bias light — **1** An obsolete scheme used in certain tube-type video cameras and telecines to uniformly illuminate the sensor with a low level of illumination to ameliorate lag.

2 In the home theatre community, surround lighting.

bilevel — A system where each pixel contains one bit representing either full black or full white; no shades of grey are possible. In computer graphics, such imagery or equipment is traditionally called *monochrome,* but that usage is misleading because it conflicts with the colour science definition of *monochrome.*

bilevel sync — Analog sync information conveyed through a single pulse having a transition from blanking level to a level more negative than blanking (synctip level), then a transition back to blanking level. In analog systems, synctip level is either $-285\tfrac{5}{7}$ mV or -300 mV. Bilevel sync is used in SD; distinguished from trilevel sync (see page 662), standardized for HD.

bit error rate — See *BER,* above.

bit splitting — In a pulse-duration modulated display such as a PDP or DLP, video codes are converted to tristimuli (linear-light) values, thence to pulses of light having durations that are small multiples (typically $\tfrac{1}{1000}$ or less) of the frame time. Bit splitting refers to the assignment of linear-light values to time intervals.

BITC — Burnt-in timecode: Timecode in visual form overlaid (keyed) onto picture content, so as to be human readable (but contaminating the picture, and not ordinarily machine readable).

black level — The level representing black: nominally 7.5 units for analog System M outside Japan and zero in other systems. See also *pedestal,* on page 645, and *reference black,* on page 651.

BLACK LEVEL	User-accessible means to adjust black level, traditionally by imposing the same additive offset to each of the gamma-corrected $R'G'B'$ components. The term BLACK LEVEL is preferred to BRIGHTNESS.
black-to-white excursion	The excursion from reference black to reference white. Conventionally 92.5 units ($^{37}/_{56}$ V, approximately 660 mV) for System M, 100 units ($^5/_7$ V, approximately 714 mV) in NTSC-J, 700 mV in other analog systems, and codes 16 through 235 at an 8-bit component (BT.601 or BT.709) digital interface.
blanking interval	The time interval – in the vertical domain, the horizontal domain, or both – during which a video signal is defined by an interface standard not to contain picture. Ancillary signals such as VITC may be conveyed during blanking.
blanking level	Zero level; 0 units by definition. Identical to reference black level (see page 651) except in System M with setup.
block	In JPEG, M-JPEG, and MPEG, an 8×8 array of samples, or coded information representing them.
Blu-ray	A set of standards for data recording on and playback from optical media, typically HD, using shortwave (blue light) laser.
BNC	Bayonet Neill-Concelman (contrary to the entry in the *IEEE Standard Dictionary of Electrical and Electronics Terms*): A coaxial connector, now standardized in IEC 169-8, used in video. Paul Neill, working at Bell Telephone Laboratories, developed a threaded connector adopted by the U.S. Navy and named the N connector, after him. Carl Concelman, working at Amphenol, came up with a bayonet version (slide on and twist), called the C connector. The two collaborated on a miniature version, which became the BNC. A screw-on relative, the threaded Neill-Concelman connector, is the TNC. [Mark Schubin/*Videography*]
BOB	Break-out box: A panel of connectors remote from the associated equipment, ordinarily attached with a proprietary cable.
bob	A deinterlacing technique, common in PC video, where vertically adjacent samples in a single field are averaged to create synthetic intermediate image rows, effecting a crude form of interlace-to-progressive conversion. See also *weave* (sense **2**), on page 665.
bottom field	In MPEG, the field that contains the bottom coded image row of a frame; typically the first field in 480*i* and the second field in 576*i*.
bpc, bits per component (or bits per channel)	The number of bits allocated to each colour component (channel) of an image – that is, the "bit depth" per colour component (or sample). It is implicit that all colour components have the same number of bits. An image may comprise more than three components.

bpp, bits per pixel	The number of bits allocated to each pixel; in an uncompressed representation, the "bit depth" of the pixel. It is implicit that each pixel contains a complete set of colour components: The term is not directly applicable to chroma-subsampled representations, although it is used sometimes to give the effective (average) number of bits. A pixel may have more than three components.
BRCR	Bright room contrast ratio: Contrast ratio measured under relatively high ambient illuminance, higher than about 100 lx. Compare *DRCR,* on page 614.
brightness	*The attribute of a visual sensation according to which an area appears to emit more or less light* [CIE]. Brightness is, by definition, subjective: It cannot be measured or quantified, and so is inappropriate to describe pixel values. *Luminance* (see page 636) is a related objective quantity; loosely speaking, brightness is apparent luminance. Brightness is absolute, not relative; unlike *lightness* (see page 633), it is not expressed relative to any reference level.
BRIGHTNESS	User-accessible means to adjust *black level* (page 595). The term BLACK LEVEL is preferred to BRIGHTNESS. (See also *brightness,* above.)
brightness, photometric	Archaic, deprecated term for luminance (see page 636).
brightness, radiometric	Archaic, deprecated term for radiance (see page 650).
broad pulse	In analog video, a pulse – part of the vertical sync sequence – that remains at sync level for substantially longer than normal line sync and indicates vertical sync.
BT.601	**1** Formally, ITU-R Recommendation BT.601: The international standard for studio digital video sampling for SD. BT.601 specifies a sampling frequency of 13.5 MHz (for both 480*i*29.97 and 576*i*25 SD), $Y'C_B C_R$ coding, and this luma equation:

$$^{601}Y'= 0.299\,R'+0.587\,G'+0.114\,B'$$

BT.601 is silent concerning *RGB* chromaticities. It is implicit that 480*i* systems use SMPTE RP 145 primaries, and that 576*i* systems use EBU Tech. 3213 primaries. BT.601 is silent concerning encoding gamma. BT.601 specifies "studio swing"; see page 659.

2 Loosely, in computer graphics, an interface for BT.601-style digital SD video stream where synchronization is accomplished using separate horizontal and vertical drive logic signals.

The notations "ITU 601" and "Rec. 601" are ambiguous – and should be avoided – because ITU-T has an unrelated recommendation G.601 that could be called ITU 601 or Rec. 601.

BT.656	**1** Formally, *ITU-R Recommendation BT.656*. The international standard for parallel or serial interface of BT.601 digital video SD signals.

2 Loosely, in computer graphics, an interface for BT.601-style digital SD video stream where synchronization is accomplished with TRS (SAV and EAV) sequences embedded in video data.

BT.709   Formally, *ITU-R Recommendation BT.709:* The international standard for studio digital video sampling and colour encoding for HD. Chromaticity and transfer function parameters of BT.709 have been introduced into modern studio standards for 480*i* and 576*i*. BT.709 specifies this luma equation (whose coefficients are unfortunately different from the BT.601 coefficients of SD):

$$^{709}Y' = 0.2126\,R' + 0.7152\,G' + 0.0722\,B'$$

The notations "ITU 709" and "Rec. 709" are ambiguous, and should be avoided, because ITU-T has an unrelated recommendation G.709 that could be called ITU 709 or Rec. 709.

BT.1886   Formally, *ITU-R Recommendation BT.1886*. The international standard defining the EOCF of studio reference displays for HD.

BTB   Blacker than black. See *superblack,* on page 659.

BTW   Black-to-white: A nonstandard measure of the transition time ("response time") of a display (often an LCD) from black level to white level. See also, *GTG,* on page 623.

burn, burn-in   **1** To impose permanently upon image data – for example, by keying – auxiliary information such as timecode.

2 To manipulate image data values so as to permanently impose a colour interpretation. Also known as *bake.*

3 Permanent aging (evident as loss of brightness) in certain types of display (e.g., PDP) when stationary bright or colourful elements are displayed for a long time (days or weeks).

4 Significant alteration of performance observed in the first few hours, days, or weeks of operation of a new device, or the act of operating a new device for such a period of time.

burst   A brief sample of eight to ten cycles of unmodulated colour subcarrier inserted by an NTSC or PAL encoder onto the back porch of a composite video signal. Burst enables a decoder to regenerate the continuous-wave colour subcarrier.

C_B, C_R **1** Versions of colour difference components $B'-Y'$ and $R'-Y'$, scaled and offset with "studio swing" for digital component transmission. At an 8-bit interface, C_B and C_R have excursion 16 through 240. See also $[B'-Y', R'-Y']$, $[P_B, P_R]$, $[U, V]$, and $[I, Q]$. In systems using BT.601 luma, such as 480*i* and 576*i*, it is standard to apply these scale factors (and interface offsets, shown below in grey) to $B'-Y'$ and $R'-Y'$:

$$C_B = 128 + 112\frac{1}{0.886}(B'-Y'); \quad C_R = 128 + 112\frac{1}{0.701}(R'-Y')$$

In HD systems using BT.709 luma, such as 1280×720 and 1920×1080, it is standard to apply the following scale factors (and offsets) to $B'-Y'$ and $R'-Y'$:

$$C_B = 128 + 112\frac{1}{0.9278}(B'-Y'); \quad C_R = 128 + 112\frac{1}{0.7874}(R'-Y')$$

2 Versions of colour difference components $B'-Y'$ and $R'-Y'$, scaled to "full-swing" or "full-range" (±128, with code +128 clipped) for use in stillframe JPEG/JFIF. It is usual to apply the following scale factors (and offsets) to $B'-Y'$ and $R'-Y'$:

$$C_B = 128 + 128\frac{1}{0.886}(B'-Y'); \quad C_R = 128 + 128\frac{1}{0.701}(R'-Y')$$

C/PH	Cycles per picture height: A unit of resolution corresponding to a cycle (a black and a white element, comparable to a line pair) across the height of the picture.
C/PW	Cycles per picture width: A unit of resolution corresponding to a cycle (a black and a white element, comparable to a line pair) across the width of the picture.
cadence	In a motion image sequence having 2-3 pulldown (or some variant thereof), the property of having strictly periodic A-frames. Careful editing preserves continuous cadence; careless editing disrupts it.
calibration (colour)	Modification of the colour reproduction parameters of a particular device – effected either within the device itself, or within associated equipment – to bring the device into conformance with an absolute reference associated with a standard or exemplified by a reference device. Distinguished from *characterization (colour)* (see page 601), which is passive with respect to the device.
candela [cd]	The SI unit for luminous intensity; one of the seven base SI units. See *intensity* (**1**, on page 628).
CBR, constant bit rate	Any compression format in which the bit (or byte) count of compressed data is the same from one second to the next.
CC	**1** Colour correction; see page 604.
	2 Closed caption; see page 603.
CCA	Means for a display user (or technician) to alter the effective chromaticity of red, green, and blue by building the appropriate 3×3 matrix on the fly. The term *CCA* refers to various approaches offered by various manufacturers. *Comprehensive*

Color Adjustment (CCA), is trademarked by Christie Digital, but other vendors use terms such as *Color Coordinate Adjustment*.

CCD	Charge-coupled device. In modern use of the term, a micro-electronic image sensor constructed using MOS technology. A CCD converts incident photons to electrons; the electrons are collected and then transported to an on-chip converter and amplifier then output from the device.

CCIR

1 *Comité Consultatif Internationale des Radiocommunications* (International Radio Consultative Committee): A treaty organization, as of 1993 renamed ITU-R.

2 Sometimes incorrectly used to denote 576*i* scanning.

CCIR Rec. 601, Rec. 709

Obsolete designations, now properly referred to as ITU-R Rec. BT.601 (colloquially, BT.601), or ITU-R Rec. BT.709 (colloquially, BT.709). See *BT.601* and *BT.709*, on page 598.

CCO

Centre cut-out, see below.

CCT

Correlated colour temperature: The temperature (in units of kelvin, K) of the point on the blackbody radiator's locus where a line drawn on a CIE 1960 [*u*, *v*] diagram from a colour stimulus intersects the blackbody curve perpendicularly. If that sounds obscure, it is: If a source's chromaticity lies near the blackbody curve, then CCT gives a reasonable expression of its chromaticity, but ordinarily chromaticity coordinates should be used instead.

CCTV

1 Closed circuit television. An archaic term denoting video systems used in nonbroadcast applications such as security.

2 China Central Television (in the Peoples' Republic of China).

CCU

Camera control unit: A device that enables remote control of the iris of a camera lens and basic camera settings, most importantly gain, white balance, and pedestal.

$cd \cdot m^{-2}$

Candela per meter squared: the SI unit for absolute luminance.

CE

Consumer electronics.

centre-cut, centre cut-out

A widescreen image that has been cropped to 4:3 aspect ratio.

CFA

Colour filter array. A regular arrangement of coloured filters placed over neighbouring photosites in an image sensor. The Bayer structure (see page 594) is commonly used, but other structures (such as interleaved red, green, and blue vertical stripes placed over successive photosite columns) are also used.

CGI

Computer-generated imagery: Synthetic image data, generated by computation (as opposed to being acquired from a physical scene by a camera).

　　　　DIGITAL VIDEO AND HD ALGORITHMS AND INTERFACES

characterization (colour)	Modelling, measurement, and/or estimation of colour parameters of a particular device, class of devices, or subsystem. Distinguished from *calibration (colour)* (see page 599).
chroma	**1** In colour science, *colourfulness of an area judged in proportion to the brightness of a similarly illuminated area that appears to be white or highly transmitting* [CIE].
	2 Generally, a component or set of components such as [C_B, C_R] that conveys colour independent of luma or luminance.
	3 In component video, colour independent of (or accompanied by) luma, conveyed as a pair of colour difference signals such as [C_B, C_R], or [P_B, P_R].
	4 In composite video, colour subcarrier modulated using the NTSC or PAL technique by two colour difference components [U, V] to form a *modulated chroma* signal, C.
	5 In video, the polar-coordinate modulus (radius) of a colour difference pair in C_B, C_R coordinates for component digital video or P_B, P_R coordinates for component analog video.
	6 User-accessible means to adjust colour *saturation* (**5,** on page 655), sometimes called CHROMA GAIN. This adjustment is often called COLOUR; however, that term fails to make clear whether *which* colour (i.e., hue) or the *amount* of the colour (i.e., chroma) is affected. To avoid ambiguity, use HUE for the former and CHROMA for the latter.
CHROMA GAIN	User-accessible means to adjust colour *saturation* (**5**); preferably called CHROMA.
CHROMA PHASE	**1** Phase of modulated NTSC or PAL chroma.
	2 User adjustment of *chroma phase* (**1**); preferably called HUE, see *hue* (**4**).
chromakey	An archaic technique of matte extraction based upon *hue* (**3,** on page 626) – and possibly *chroma* (**5,** on page 601) – of foreground video, followed by keying.
chromaticity	**1** Specification of colour in terms of CIE [x, y] or [u', v'] coordinates – that is, in terms of a projective transform of tristimuli.
	2 Loosely, the *chromaticity* (**1**) of the red, green, and blue primaries, and the chromaticity of the white reference, of a video system.
chrominance	**1** Formally, the colour of a scene element or image element independent of its luminance; usually expressed in the form of CIE [x, y] chromaticity.
	2 Loosely, *chroma;* see above.

CIE	*Commission Internationale de L'Éclairage* (International Commission on Illumination): The international standards organization that sets colorimetry standards.
CIE D$_{65}$	The standard spectral radiance (SPD) or chromaticity of white, representative of northern daylight and having a colour temperature of approximately 6504 K. See *reference white,* on page 651.
CIE luminance, CIE *Y*	See *luminance (page 636).* A qualifier *CIE* or *linear-light* is sometimes used to emphasize that the associated quantity is representative of tristimulus value proportional to intensity, as opposed to the nonlinear, gamma-corrected quantity *luma.*
CIF, common image format	**1** Historically, the elusive goal of a single (common) worldwide standard pixel array for digital video, perhaps at different frame rates, not achieved in SD standardization, but achieved for HD as 1920×1080. Confusingly, the acronym collides with *CIF, common intermediate format (see below).*
	2 In MPEG-2 or other video compression systems excepting those for videoconferencing, an image format of either 720×480 or 720×576. The term is an oxymoron, since for SD there is not a single ("common") format, but rather two different formats. (In the deliberations that led to digital SD studio standards, agreement was not reached upon a common image format!)
CIF, common intermediate format	In ITU-T Rec. H.261 and related standards, a progressive 352×288 image format with 4:2:0 chroma subsampling, a frame rate of 29.97 Hz, and a sample aspect ratio of 12:11 (width:height). CIF image data is ordinarily subsampled from SD. The format is a compromise derived from the image structure of 576*i*25 and the frame rate of 480*i*29.97. Distinguished from *CIF, common image format,* above. See also *QCIF,* on page 649.
CinemaScope	Material intended for display at 2.4:1 aspect ratio.
Cineon	A project and set of products from Kodak, discontinued in 1994, that started the digital cinema revolution. The legacy of the project lives on in *Cineon printing density, CPD (see below).*
Cineon printing density, CPD	Colour data metric representing optical density values measured from (or approximating) exposed and developed colour-negative photographic film as 10-bit log data.
clamp (*v.*)	**1** Imposition (by addition or subtraction) of a DC offset (bias) onto a signal, so as to place a certain signal feature (such as back porch) at a specific level (such as blanking level, 0 IRE).
	2 Commonly but incorrectly used to indicate *clip;* see below.

clean aperture	The specified or standardized rectangular portion of the pixel array that remains subjectively free from intrusion of artifacts resulting from filtering of the picture edges.
clip (*v.*)	A process of forcing a signal not to exceed a certain maximum level (or not to fall below a certain minimum level).
clipped (*adj.*)	A signal that has been limited to a certain maximum (or minimum) level.
clone (*n.* or *v.*)	Digital copy with no degradation from a master. See also *dub.*
closed caption (CC)	Digital data conveying textual information that can be decoded and displayed for the benefit of hearing-impaired viewers. In 480*i* NTSC analog video, closed caption data is inserted into line 21. (Unlike other vertical interval signals, NTSC line 21 is classified as active picture video.)
CLUT	Colour lookup table: A LUT (see page 637) that maps from a set of integer pixel values (often 0 through 255) to *R'G'B'* triplets (encoded red, green, and blue component values). Each *R'G'B'* value (typically 8 bits) is proportional to the $1/2.2$-power of the associated display tristimulus value. See *pseudocolour.*
CM	In DV compression, a coded (compressed) macroblock.
CMF	See *colour matching functions,* on page 605.
CMOS	Complementary-symmetry metal-oxide-semiconductor (pronounced *see-moss*): The most common type of analog or digital microelectronic semiconductor technology.
CMOS image sensor	An image sensor constructed using CMOS technology. Each photosite has a photodiode that converts incident photons to electrons, and a small number of transistors (typically 3 or 4) that amplify and gate the corresponding voltage to an amplifier and/or analog-to-digital converter for subsequent transmission off-chip.
CMY[K]	Cyan, magenta, yellow: The traditional primaries in subtractive colour reproduction. For halftone printing, CMY are usually augmented by K (historically, *key;* in modern terms, black).
codec	Coder/decoder: Hardware circuitry, firmware, software, or equipment to encode or decode data between two formats (perhaps between analog and digital, or between two digital formats), often including signal compression or decompression.
coherence, frequency	The property whereby two or more periodic signals are phase-locked to a common reference frequency. The unmodulated colour subcarrier of a studio-quality NTSC or PAL composite video signal is coherent with its sync.

coherence, spatial	In a single image, the property whereby adjacent samples have values that are correlated.
coherence, temporal	In a motion image sequence, the property whereby corresponding samples in successive images, perhaps subject to spatial displacement of moving image elements, are correlated.
COFDM	Coded orthogonal frequency-division multiplexing: An RF modulation system using a large number of subcarriers to spread the information content of a signal evenly across a transmission channel. The subcarriers of COFDM are individually modulated, typically using QPSK or QAM. COFDM is used in DVB-T.
COLOR/COLOUR	User-accessible means to adjust *chroma* (**5**). The term COLOUR fails to make clear whether *which* colour (i.e., hue) or the *amount* of the colour (i.e., chroma) is affected. To avoid ambiguity, use HUE for the former and CHROMA for the latter.

colorimetry

1 Formally, the science of measuring colour, especially as standardized by the CIE. Even Canadians spell this word without *u*.

2 In video, *colorimetry* (**1**) as above, augmented by concerns outside the domain of classical colorimetry, including some or all of the following: the parameters of the opto-electronic conversion function (OECF) applied to the linear-light (tristimulus) *RGB* components of classical colorimetry to form *R′G′B′*; the parameters of the 3×3 matrix transform applied to *R′G′B′* to form luma and two colour difference components; the inverse of that matrix; and the parameters of the electro-optical conversion function (EOCF) applied to *R′G′B′* signals to form linear-light *RGB* (tristimulus) values at the display.

colourburst	See *burst,* on page 598.
colour correction	This term can refer to either of two processes which are, in a well-designed imaging system, separate. If the first process is omitted (owing to being absent from the camera design, or having been disabled by the camera operator), done poorly by the camera manufacturer, or done poorly owing to misadjustment by the camera operator, then the second will be difficult:

1 The process – ordinarily included in an SD or HD camera where it is called *linear matrixing,* but potentially implemented in postproduction or DI – by which linear-light sensor signals are processed by a 3×3 linear matrix having coefficients carefully chosen such that the resulting signals have a specific colorimetric interpretation (for example as additive *RGB* with a specific set of primaries and a specific reference white chromaticity).

2 The process, ordinarily carried out in postproduction by a skilled person called a *colourist,* of altering image colour component values in order to implement the visual æsthetic goals of a program intended to be coded into a standard colour

image interchange space and subsequently viewed on a standardized display (ordinarily characterized as additive *RGB* with a specific set of primaries, a specific reference white chromaticity, and a standard EOCF) in a known environment.

colour correction, primary	Colour correction (**2**), where colour alterations are effected uniformly across all pixels in the image ("globally"), and where the alteration is limited to adjustment – either to all components at once ("master"), or to individual *RGB* components – of black level, power function exponent (gamma), and gain. (These three controls are often called "lift, gamma, and gain.")
colour correction, secondary	Colour correction (**2**), where colours are altered selectively by luminance or luma range, by colour range, by spatial extent, or by any combination of these.

colour difference

1 A numerical measure of the perceptual distance between two colours; for example, CIE ΔE_{uv}^* ("delta-*E*").

2 A signal that vanishes – that is, becomes identically zero – for pure luma without colour. A video system conveys a colour image using a set of three signals: a luma signal (Y') and a pair of colour difference signals. Spatial filtering may be applied to reduce the information rate of the colour difference components without perceptible degradation. The usual colour-difference pairs are $[B'-Y', R'-Y']$, $[C_B, C_R]$, $[P_B, P_R]$, and $[U, V]$.

colour fulness

The attribute of a visual sensation according to which an area appears to exhibit more or less of its own hue [CIE].

colour management

1 Generally, and specifically in graphics arts and desktop publishing, techniques that use colour profiles to quantify the colour reproduction characteristics of colour devices, and facilities to impose colour transforms based upon the profiles with the goal of achieving predictable colour.

2 In home theatre displays, facilities to adjust chromaticity, luma, and/or luminance of primary colours (red, green, and blue) and secondary colours (cyan, magenta, and yellow) independently. If a display correctly implements additive colour reproduction, so-called colour management is antagonistic to accurate display. If a display does not correctly implement additive colour reproduction, there is no assurance that colour management facilities can be used to bring it into conformance.

colour matching functions

A set of three functions across the wavelength interval 380 nm to 780 nm, closely associated with the CIE Standard Observer, that weights a spectral power distribution (see page 658) and yields a 3-vector comprising tristimulus values (see page 662).

colour saturation

The colourfulness of an area judged in proportion to its brightness [CIE]. Subjective, by definition. Saturation runs from neutral grey through pastel to saturated colours. Roughly speaking, the more an SPD is concentrated at one wavelength, the more saturated the associated colour becomes. A colour can be desaturated by adding light that contains power distributed across a wide range of wavelengths.

COLOUR SATURATION

User-accessible means to adjust colour saturation. Preferably called CHROMA; see *chroma* (**6,** on page 601).

colour standard

The parameters associated with encoding of colour information – for example, *R'G'B'* or *Y'C$_B$C$_R$ component* video standards, or historical NTSC or PAL *composite* video standards. Distinguished from *scanning standard* (see page 656).

colour subcarrier

1 A continuous sinewave signal at about 3.58 MHz or 4.43 MHz used as the basis for quadrature modulation or demodulation of *chroma* (**2,** on page 601) in an NTSC or PAL composite video system. See also *burst,* on page 598.

2 Colour subcarrier (see above), onto which two colour difference signals have been imposed by quadrature modulation. Properly, modulated chroma.

colour temperature

1 Characterization of an illuminant or a white reference in terms of the absolute temperature (in units of kelvin) of a blackbody radiator having the same chromaticity (in 1960 [*u, v*] coordinates).

2 User- or technician-accessible adjustment of *colour temperature* (**1**), by which *RGB* gains are adjusted to achieve the intended chromaticity of reference white.

comb filter

1 Generally, a filter having magnitude frequency response with periodic equal-magnitude maxima and equal-magnitude minima.

2 In video, a *comb filter* (**1**) incorporating delay elements with line, field, or frame time duration.

3 In a composite NTSC video decoder, circuitry incorporating one or more line delay elements (linestores) to exploit the frequency interleaving of modulated chroma to separate chroma from luma. A comb filter provides better separation than a notch filter, owing to its suppression of *cross-colour* and *cross-luma* artifacts. A *3-D comb filter* incorporates at least one fieldstore.

4 In a composite PAL video decoder, circuitry incorporating a line delay element (linestore) to separate the modulated *U* chroma component from the modulated *V* chroma component.

component (*adj.*)

In video, a system that conveys three colour values or signals independently, free from mutual interference. Examples are *R'G'B'* and *Y'C$_B$C$_R$*. Distinguished from *composite (adj.),* below.

component (*n.*)

1 Generally, a device or a piece of equipment.

2 In mathematics or signal processing, one element of a vector.

3 One value or signal from the set of three necessary to completely specify a colour.

4 A value, channel, or signal – such as transparency or depth – that is spatially associated with image data, or temporally associated with an image in a sequence, that does not contribute to the specification of colour.

component analog	An analog video system (as opposed to digital) using $R'G'B'$ or $Y'P_BP_R$ component colour coding (as opposed to using composite colour coding such as NTSC or PAL).
component digital	A digital video system (as opposed to analog), using $R'G'B'$ or $Y'C_BC_R$ component colour coding (as opposed to using composite colour coding such as NTSC or PAL). Component digital SD systems are sometimes called "4:2:2," though the latter notation strictly refers to just the colour subsampling, not any of the other encoding parameters.
composite (*adj.*)	Combined, as in combined vertical and horizontal sync elements [see *composite sync*, below]; combined luma and chroma [see *composite video (1)*, below]; or combined video and sync [see *composite video (2)*, below].
composite (*v.*)	To combine images by layering, keying, matting, or a similar process usually performed as $R = \alpha \cdot FG + (1-\alpha) \cdot BG$, where FG represents foreground (*fill*) image or video data and BG represents background. Foreground image data that has been premultiplied by the key is called *shaped* in video (or *associated*, or, in computer graphics, *premultiplied*). Foreground image data that has not been premultiplied by the key is called *unshaped* in video (or *unassociated,* or, in computer graphics, *nonpremultiplied*). Image data may be represented in linear-light form (typical of D-cinema DI and postproduction) or in gamma-corrected form (typical of studio video).
composite digital	A digital video system (as opposed to analog), using composite colour coding such as NTSC or PAL (as opposed to using component colour coding such as $Y'C_BC_R$). All standard composite systems sample at four times the colour subcarrier frequency, so composite digital video is also known as $4f_{SC}$.
composite sync	A deprecated term meaning *sync*. The word *sync* alone implies both horizontal and vertical elements, so *composite* is redundant. The adjective *composite* more meaningfully applies to *video* or *colour*, so its use with *sync* is confusing.
composite video	**1** A video system in which three colour components are simultaneously present in a single signal. Examples are NTSC and PAL, which use the *frequency-interleaving* principle to encode (combine) luma and chroma. SECAM is another form of composite video. Distinguished from *component (adj.)*, above.
	2 A *composite video (1)* signal, including luma, sync, chroma, and burst components; called *CVBS* in Europe.

concatenated	In compression, two or more compression systems in series. Also known as *tandem codecs*.
constant luminance	In a colour video system that dedicates one component to greyscale-related information, the property that true (CIE) relative luminance reproduced at the display is unaffected by the values of the other two components. All standard video systems, including NTSC, PAL, $Y'C_BC_R$, HD, JPEG, MPEG, and H.264 approximate constant luminance operation; however, because luma in these systems represents a weighted sum of nonlinear primary components ($R'G'B'$), "true" constant luminance operation is not achieved: A certain amount of (CIE) luminance "leaks" into the colour difference components and induces second-order artifacts (*Livingston errors*).
contrast, ANSI	Contrast ratio (see below) of a display (typically a projector) measured in accordance with ANSI/NAPM IT7.228 (withdrawn in 2003): Contrast ratio derived from an illuminance measurement taken by averaging black and white rectangles of a 4×4 "checkerboard" pattern without considering any effect of the screen or the viewing environment.
contrast	**1** Generally, a large or small difference in luminance or colour.
	2 *contrast ratio;* see below.
CONTRAST	User-accessible means to adjust the luminance of reference white (sometimes incidentally changing the luminance of reference black as well). In video processing equipment, preferably called VIDEO GAIN; in consumer display equipment, preferably called PICTURE or WHITE LEVEL.
contrast ratio	The ratio between specified light and dark luminances, typically the luminance associated with the peak white or reference white of a display system and the luminance associated with reference black. *Inter-image* (or *on/off,* or *sequential*) contrast ratio is measured between separate full-screen white and black images. *Intra-image* (or *simultaneous*) contrast ratio is specified with respect to white and black measurements from a single test image such as that specified by ANSI ("checkerboard") or ITU-R BT.815. Different results are obtained if ambient light is present or absent in the measurement. Display manufacturers routinely exclude ambient light from contrast ratio measurements; however, estimating visual performance requires that ambient light be included.
corner frequency	The frequency at which the output power of a lowpass or highpass filter or subsystem has fallen to 0.707 of its value at a reference frequency, typically DC. (For a digital or constant-impedance system, this is equivalent to the frequency at which the output magnitude has been attenuated 3 dB.)
cosited	Chroma subsampling in which each subsampled chroma sample is located at the same horizontal position as a luma sample. BT.601, BT.709, and MPEG-2 standards specify cosited chroma

DIGITAL VIDEO AND HD ALGORITHMS AND INTERFACES

subsampling. (MPEG-2, 4:2:0 chroma subsampling places chroma samples interstitially in the vertical domain.)

CSC

Colour space conversion, typically in gamma-corrected colour space, typically $Y'C_BC_R$ to $R'G'B'$ or $R'G'B'$ to $Y'C_BC_R$, but potentially including 3×3 processing in the linear-light domain.

CRC

Cyclic redundancy check (code). Information inserted prior to recording or transmission that allows playback or receiver equipment to determine whether errors were introduced. A CRC with a small number of bits provides error-detection capability; a CRC with a large number of bits provides error-correction capability. CRC codes involve multiplying and dividing polynomials whose coefficients are chosen from the set {0, 1}. Similar capability can be achieved using codes based upon mathematical principles other than CRC; see *ECC,* on page 616.

CRF

Camera response function. Synonym used in the computer vision community for OECF (see page 643). See also *RSR,* on page 653.

cross-colour

An artifact of composite (NTSC or PAL) video encoding and/or decoding that involves the erroneous interpretation of luma information as colour. The cross-colour artifact appears frequently when luma information having a frequency near that of the colour subcarrier appears as a swirling colour rainbow pattern.

cross-luma

An artifact of composite video encoding and/or decoding involving erroneous interpretation of colour signals as luma. Cross-luma frequently appears as *dot crawl* or *hanging dots*.

crossover (bar/chip)

In an optical greyscale step (chip) chart having an odd number of chips (often 9 or 11), the chip in the middle. (That chip conventionally has relative luminance of about 18%.)

CRT

Cathode-ray tube.

CRU

A dockable hard disk drive carrier, commonly used in digital cinema, manufactured by the company CRU-DataPort.

CUE

Chroma upsampling error: An implementation error in tens of millions of DVD players whereby subsampled chroma was reconstructed with incorrect position.

cutoff (*n.*)

1 The phenomenon (particularly in a vacuum tube such as a CRT) where for a sufficiently low input signal the electron current (and in a CRT, emitted light) drops to essentially zero.

2 See *bias* (**2**) on page 595.

cutoff frequency

See *corner frequency,* on page 608.

cuts	In home theatre terminology, individual red, green, and blue cutoff adjustments; see *bias* (**2**) on page 595.
CVBS	Composite video with burst and syncs: A European term for *composite video* (**2**).
D-5 HD (*HD-D5*)	A component HD digital videotape format utilizing $1/2$-inch tape cassettes and recording BT.709 Y'CBCR signals, based upon either 720*p*60 or 1080*i*30, mildly compressed to about 270 Mb/s using motion-JPEG. Also known as *HD-D5*.
D-6	A SMPTE-standard component HD digital videotape format utilizing $1/2$-inch tape in cassettes, recording uncompressed BT.709 Y'CBCR signals, subsampled 4:2:2, at about 1.5 Gb/s.
D-7 (*DVCPRO/DVCPRO50*)	The SMPTE-standard SD compression and recording scheme introduced by Panasonic as *DVCPRO* (at 25 Mb/s) or *DVCPRO50* (at 50 Mb/s). See *DVCPRO,* on page 615.
D-9 (*Digital-S*)	SMPTE designation for JVC's obsolete Digital-S; see page 613.
D-10 (*MPEG IMX*)	SMPTE standard designation of Sony's *MPEG IMX;* see page 641.
D-11 (*HDCAM*)	SMPTE standard designation for Sony's *HDCAM;* see page 624.
D-12 (*DVCPRO HD*)	SMPTE designation for Panasonic's *DVCPRO HD;* see page 615.
D_{65}	See *reference white,* on page 651; and *CIE D_{65},* on page 602.
D-cinema	Digital cinema: relating to the production, postproduction, distribution, and exhibition of movies using digital technology instead of photochemical film. See also *E-cinema,* on page 616. (E-cinema refers to distribution of movie-like material using HD technology.)
D-SLR	Digital single-lens reflex. A type of digital camera incorporating a swinging mirror that normally admits light to an optical viewfinder, but can be repositioned to admit light to a sensor.
dailies	Image sequences delivered to a set or location to enable production staff to quickly decide whether shots have been adequately captured from that set or that location. Dailies were historically film prints from developed camera negative film; now SD or HD video media or QuickTime files are typical. The term *dailies* originated when film processing imposed a latency of $1/2$ a day or so, perhaps overnight. The term *rushes* is synonymous.
data rate	Information rate of digital transmission, in bits per second (b/s) or bytes per second (B/s). Colloquially (and incorrectly) called *bandwidth* (see page 594).
datum	See 0_H *datum* and 0_V *datum,* on page 581.

dB, decibel	**1** Twenty times the logarithm (to base 10) of the ratio of a signal level (e.g., voltage, or digital code value) to a reference signal level.
	2 Ten times the logarithm (to base 10) of the ratio of a power to a reference power. Exceptionally, in video, HD, digital cinema, and still cameras, when optical power is being characterized, the $20 \cdot \log_{10}$ convention (of sense **1**) is used even though the $10 \cdot \log_{10}$ convention is strictly correct.
DC, direct current	**1** Historically, an electrical current or voltage having no periodic reversal in polarity.
	2 In modern usage, having zero frequency.
	3 In video, a signal having frequency substantially lower than the frame rate.
	4 In JPEG and MPEG, that spatial frequency component having uniform response over an 8×8 block. Distinguished from *AC* (**3**), on page 590.
DC, dynamic contrast	Mechanisms separate from the main light modulator – such as backlight control in an LCD, or mechanical iris in a projector – that reduce light output for dark images or scenes.
DCI P3	A set of *RGB* chromaticities and a white reference, standardized by the Digital Cinema Initiative (DCI) and in SMPTE ST 431, for use in digital cinema projectors.
DC restoration	In analog video, *clamp (v.)* (**1**) at blanking level (or in low-quality systems, at synctip level).
DCT	Discrete cosine transform: In image and video compression, the mathematics at the heart of the JPEG and MPEG algorithms.
DCV	Digital code value: A pixel component value, ordinarily a whole number representable in 8, 10, or 12 bits. The term is applicable to any image coding scheme (linear-light, gamma-corrected, pseudolog, etc.). See *ADU,* on page 591.
DCT	Discrete cosine transform.
DDC	Display data channel: A scheme standardized by VESA to convey display parameters upstream to a graphics subsystem.
DDL	Digital drive level: A pixel component data value that crosses an interface – typically DVI, HDMI, or DisplayPort – and drives display equipment. For "full-range" data, each component value is interpreted as an integer $0 \ldots 2^{\kappa}-1$ (where κ is the bit depth at the interface); DDL 0 produces minimum tristimulus value, and DDL $2^{\kappa}-1$ produces maximum.
DDWG	Digital Display Working Group, the now-defunct organization that developed and promulgated the DVI interface.

decade	Factor of 10: one $\log_{10}$ unit; almost exactly (or some would say, exactly) $3\,^1/_3$ stops.
decimation	Producing fewer output samples per unit time than input samples. Decimation could involve just dropping samples; if proper filtering is used, the term *downsampling* is preferred.
decoding	**1** Generally, converting one or more coded signals into uncompressed form, reversing a previous encoding operation that was applied to reduce data rate for transmission or recording. **2** In traditional video usage, taking NTSC or PAL composite video, performing luma/chroma separation and chroma demodulation, then producing component video output such as $Y'C_BC_R$ or $R'G'B'$. **3** In modern video usage, taking coded picture information (such as a JPEG, M-JPEG, or MPEG compressed bitstream) and recovering uncompressed $Y'C_BC_R$ or $R'G'B'$ picture data.
deep colour	Pixels having more than 8 bits per colour component, particularly when conveyed across a display interface.
degamma	See *inverse gamma correction,* on page 629.
deinterlace	A process of spatiotemporal upsampling that produces estimated progressive image data from interlaced image data. Also known as *I-P* (interlace-to-progressive) conversion.
demosaic	The process of processing spatially multiplexed colour samples, as produced by a CFA sensor (see page 600) to create three spatially coincident colour samples (typically three samples per photosite). Also called *deBayer,* which strictly applies only to Bayer-pattern sensors (see *Bayer pattern,* on page 594).
DF	dropframe; see page 614.
DFC, dynamic false contouring	An artifact of pulse-width modulated displays (such as PDP and DLP) whereby the time course of pulse modulation interacts with the viewers' eye-tracking of image elements in motion to create spatiotemporal artifacts.
DI	Digital intermediate. Historically, digital image data comprising the entirety of a movie, where the data originated with scanning cinema camera negative film, and was destined to be recorded onto cinema print film. In modern usage, image data typically originates from a digital cinema or HD camera, and data is typically destined for digital cinema release.
DIF	Digital interface standardized for DV bitstreams.
Digital Betacam, Digital-β	Sony's trademarked term for a component SD digital videotape format for professional use, utilizing $\frac{1}{2}$-inch tape and recording BT.601 $Y'C_BC_R$ signals, based upon either $480i$ or

576*i* scanning, mildly compressed using M-JPEG to about 90 Mb/s.

Digital-S	An obsolete SD digital videotape format for professional use, utilizing $\frac{1}{2}$-inch tape in VHS-type cassettes and recording BT.601 $Y'C_BC_R$ signals based upon either 480*i* or 576*i* scanning, mildly compressed to about 50 Mb/s using the DV motion-JPEG technique (DV50). Standardized as SMPTE D-9.
Dirac, Basic	A long-GoP motion-compensated wavelet codec developed by the BBC and released as open source.
Dirac PRO	A standard initially developed by BBC and subsequently standardized as SMPTE ST 2047-1 (VC-2), for the lossy mezzanine-level compression of 1080*p* HD video using intraframe wavelet compression at high bit rates. An open-source implementation (*Schrödinger*) is available.
disc	Rotating optical media, for example, Blu-ray disc.
disk	Rotating magnetic media, for example, hard disk.
display-referred	Image signal values (e.g., *R'G'B'*) having a well-defined mapping to tristimulus values and absolute luminance at an intended display in a specified viewing condition.
DisplayPort	A display interface promulgated by VESA.
DivX5	An implementation of MPEG-4 ASP.
DLP	Digital light processing: A trademark of Texas Instruments referring to projection displays based upon an array of digital micromirrors fabricated on silicon using MEMS techniques.
DN	Digital number. See *ADU,* on page 591.
DNxHD	A standard, developed and deployed by Avid for use in post-production, subsequently standardized as SMPTE ST 2042-1 (VC-3), for the lossy compression of digital motion images at bit rates between about 60 Mb/s and 220 Mb/s. DNxHD data is typically conveyed in MXF files.
Dolby Digital	Trademark term designating a digital audio compression standard incorporated into ATSC's DTV system; formerly, *AC-3*.
dominant field	See *field dominance,* on page 619.
dot crawl	A cross-luma artifact that results from a notch filter decoder, appearing as fine luma detail crawling up a vertical edge in a picture that contains a saturated colour transition.
dot-by-dot (dot-for-dot)	**1** In video, a system or subsystem that maps video samples directly to display pixels without image resampling.

2 In printing technology, mapping halftone dots without descreening.

downconversion	In video, conversion to a scanning standard at the same frame rate having substantially lower pixel count (e.g., HD to SD).
downsampling	Resampling that produces fewer output samples than the number of input samples provided. (*Downsampling* does *not* properly describe rounding or truncating to shallower bit depth.)
digital picture exchange, DPX	An image file format standardized in SMPTE ST 268 that accommodates image data with a variety of bit depths and coding metrics. Commonly used to convey three 10-bit components according to the Cineon printing density (CPD) metric.
DRCR	Dark room contrast ratio: Contrast ratio measured under relatively high ambient illuminance, exceeding about 100 lx. Compare *BRCR,* on page 597.

drive (*n.*)

1 A periodic pulse signal, now rarely used, that conveys either horizontal or vertical synchronization information.

2 A low-level adjustment (DRIVE) – traditionally necessary for CRT displays owing to analog drift, and now thoughtlessly replicated in many fixed-pixel displays – to set *RGB* gain individually on a component-by-component basis. See *gain* (**2**).

dropframe

A timecode stream associated with scanning at a field or frame rate of 59.94 Hz, wherein timecodes of the form *HH:Tu*:00:00 and *HH:Tu*:00:01 are omitted from the count sequence whenever *u* (the units digit of minutes) is nonzero; counting frames in this manner obtains a very close approximation to clock time. This adjustment almost exactly compensates for the field or frame rate being a factor of exactly $^{1000}/_{1001}$ slower than 60 Hz.

DTIM	See *DCI P3, on page 611.*
DTV	Digital television: A generic term including digital SDTV and digital HDTV. Generally, broadcast is implied.
dual-link HD-SDI	Dual-link high-definition serial digital interface: A SMPTE-standard interface using a pair of HD-SDI links to transmit 4:4:4:4 HD.
dub (*n.* or *v.*)	Copy, typically degraded slightly from a master. (A digital copy with no degradation is a *clone.*)

DV

1 Generally, digital video.

2 A specific motion-JPEG compression technique, videotape recording format, and/or digital interface (DIF) bitstream, for $Y'C_BC_R$ digital video. See *DV25, DV50,* and *DV100,* below.

DV25	DV (see above), coded at 25 Mb/s. DV25 is widely implemented in consumer DVC and Digital8 equipment, and in professional D-7 (DVCPRO) and DVCAM equipment.
DV50	DV (see above), coded at 50 Mb/s. DV50 is used in professional D-7 (DVCPRO50), D-9 (Digital-S), DVCAM, and DVCPRO50 equipment.
DV100	DV (see above), coded at 100 Mb/s. DV100 is used in DVCPRO HD equipment.
DVB	Digital Video Broadcasting: An organization that standardizes and promotes DTV broadcasting. or the suite of standards promulgated by this organization. DVB advocates MPEG-2 video and audio compression, supplemented by DVB transmission standards for cable (DVB-C), satellite (DVB-S), and terrestrial (DVB-T) broadcasting (for which DVB-T specifies COFDM transmission).
DVC	Digital video cassette: A component SD digital videotape format for consumer use, taking BT.601 $Y'C_BC_R$ video having either 480i or 576i scanning, compressing to about 25 Mb/s using the DV motion-JPEG technique (DV25), and recording on 6.35 mm tape encased in a cassette of one of two sizes – small ("MiniDV") or large.
DVCAM	Sony's trademarked term for a component SD digital videotape format for professional use, utilizing 6.35 mm tape cassettes and recording BT.601 $Y'C_BC_R$ video having either 480i or 576i scanning, compressed to about 25 Mb/s using the DV motion-JPEG technique.
DVCPRO	Digital video cassette, professional version: A component SD digital videotape format for professional use, utilizing 6.35 mm tape encased in a cassette of one of three sizes (small, medium, or large), recording BT.601 $Y'C_BC_R$ signals, based upon either 480i or 576i scanning, compressed using the DV motion-JPEG technique to about 25 Mb/s. Standardized as SMPTE D-7.
DVCPRO50	Digital video cassette, professional version, 50 megabits per second: A component SD digital videotape format for professional use, utilizing 6.35 mm tape encased in a cassette of one of three sizes (small, medium, or large), recording BT.601 $Y'C_BC_R$ signals, based upon either 480i or 576i scanning, compressed using the DV motion-JPEG technique to about 50 Mb/s. Standardized as SMPTE D-7.
DVCPRO HD (*DVCPRO100*)	Digital video cassette, professional version, high-definition: A component HD digital videotape format utilizing 6.35 mm tape encased in a cassette of one of three sizes (small, medium, or large), recording 720p, 1080i, or 1080p, 4:2:2 signals, compressed to about 100 Mb/s using the DV motion-JPEG technique (DV100). Standardized as SMPTE D-12.

DVI	Digital Visual Interface: An interface established in 1999 and promulgated by the now-defunct Digital Display Working Group (DDWG) for the connection from a PC to a display.
DVTR	Digital videotape recorder. See *VTR, on page 665.*
DWT	Discrete wavelet transform: In image compression, the mathematical technique at the heart of the JPEG 2000 algorithm.
dynamic range	The ratio of physical quantities associated with the maximum and minimum meaningful or usable values, usually expressed as decibels (dB) using the $20 \cdot \log_{10}$ convention. For an image sensor, dynamic range is the ratio between the saturation-equivalent exposure and the noise-equivalent exposure.
EAV	End of active video: A sequence of four words inserted into a component digital video data stream, marking the end of picture samples on a line. See also *SAV, on page 655,* and *TRS, on page 662.*
EBU	**1** European Broadcasting Union: An organization mainly comprising European state broadcasters.
	2 In the context of colour standards: EBU Tech. 3213, which defines the chromaticities historically used in 576*i* video.
ECC	Error checking and correction: A method of inserting redundant information prior to digital storage, recording or transmission, and processing that information upon subsequent playback or reception, so that recording or transmission errors can be detected (and in some cases, perfectly corrected). ECC systems can perfectly correct errors having certain statistical properties. Synonymous with EDC.
E-cinema	Electronic cinema: relating to the distribution and exhibition of movies using HD technology instead of photochemical film. See also *D-cinema, on page 610.* (D-cinema applies to the entire cinema chain starting at production, and is not limited to HD technology. The term *E-cinema* generally implies use of video equipment and lower quality than cinema film or D-cinema.)
EDC	Error detection and correction: A synonym for ECC; see above.
EDH	Error detection and handling: A system standardized by SMPTE for encoding transmission error status into data conveyed across a series of SDI interfaces.
EDID	Extended Display Identification Data: A VESA standard specifying data to be conveyed from a display to a host graphics subsystem (across a display interface such as DVI, HDMI, or DisplayPort), giving display parameters such as raster timing and colour space.

encoding	**1** Generally, the process of converting one or more signals into a more complex representation, with the goal of reducing data rate for transmission or recording.
	2 In traditional video usage, the process of taking component video input (e.g., $Y'C_BC_R$ or $R'G'B'$), performing chroma modulation and luma/chroma summation, and producing composite video (e.g., NTSC or PAL).
	3 In modern video usage, the processing of uncompressed image data to produce a compressed bitstream (such as in JPEG, M-JPEG, MPEG, or H.264 compression).
ENOB	Effective number of bits (of an analog-to-digital converter). See IEEE Standard 1241.
EOCF	Electro-optical conversion function. The function that maps an $R'G'B'$ video component signal value to a tristimulus value at the display. Typical EOCFs approximate power functions having exponents between 2.2 and 2.6. EOCFs are standardized for graphics arts and for digital cinema; as I write, there is no standard EOCF for studio video. See also *gamma, decoding* (γ_D), on page 621.
EOTF	Electro-optical transfer function. See *EOCF*. The acronym EOCF is preferred owing to its use in ISO standards such as ISO 22028.
equalization	**1** The correction of undesired frequency or phase response. Coaxial cable introduces a high-frequency rolloff that is dependent upon cable length and proportional to $\frac{1}{\sqrt{f}}$ (pronounced *one over root f*); this is corrected by a subsystem called an *equalizer*. A naively designed analog lowpass filter, or a simple digital IIR filter, has poor phase response; this can be corrected by an *equalizer* filter section.
	2 equalization pulse; see below.
equalization pulse	In analog SD sync, a pulse, part of vertical sync, that has approximately half the duration of a normal sync and occurs at 0_H or halfway between two 0_H instants.
error concealment	Masking, by playback or receiver circuits, of errors introduced in recording or transmission. Concealment is enabled by the playback or receiver circuits' detection of errors by using ECC codes. Concealment is accomplished by replacing errored samples by interpolated (estimated) signal information.
error correction	Perfect correction, by playback or receiver circuits, of errors introduced in recording or transmission. Correction is effected by the decoder using the redundant ECC information inserted by the recorder or transmitter to perfectly reconstruct the errored bits.

ETTR, expose to the right	Methodology for setting camera exposure that chooses exposure as high as possible just short of saturation – that is, without clipping highlights. The term derives from placement of image data on a histogram display. The technique maximizes photon shot noise performance.
essence	Data representing the sampled, quantized, and possibly compressed representations of continuous sound and/or image signals. Distinguished from metadata.
even field	Historically, in 480*i* (interlaced) scanning, the field whose first broad pulse starts halfway between two line syncs. Compare *odd field,* on page 643. The terms *odd* and *even* should be avoided, and *first* and *second* used instead.
excursion	The amplitude difference between two widely separated levels. Unless otherwise noted, reference excursion.
exponential function	A function of the form $y = b^x$, where b (the *base*) is constant. Exponential functions are rarely used in video. Gamma correction, and the EOCFs of typical displays, are approximate *power* functions, not exponential functions (as is frequently claimed).
exposure latitude	The range of camera exposures, typically expressed in stops with respect to ideal exposure, over which image quality is not significantly degraded. The term latitude is sometimes used to describe the maximum and minimum exposures for which the recorded image exhibits measurable contrast variation; however, *dynamic range* is preferred for the latter usage. The term *latitude* is sometimes used to describe the ratio (typically in number of stops) between the exposure associated with sensor saturation and the exposure associated with a PDR in the scene; however, *headroom* is preferred for that usage.
extended range	See *full-range, full-swing,* on page 620.
f-stop	**1** Diameter of the optical aperture, assumed circular, of a lens relative to the focal length (denoted f) of the lens.
	2 Particular *f*-stop (**1**) settings (see above) in a $2^{-0.5k}$ sequence (e.g., *f*/1.4, *f*/2, *f*/2.8,*f*/ 4, *f*/5.6, etc.), where each step is associated with approximately a factor of 2 (one $\log_2$ unit) of light power, radiance, luminance, or tristimulus value.
FEC	Forward error correction: A synonym for ECC (see page 616), particularly when used in transmission or video recording systems.
FHA	Full-height anamorphic: Imagery occupying the full height of the format used for transport. (The image carried is spatially distorted with respect to the transport standard.)
field	In interlaced scanning, the smallest time interval that contains a set of scanning lines covering the height of the entire picture, along with all associated preceding sync elements. Fields were

once denoted *odd* and *even;* these terms should be avoided, and *first* and *second* (as appropriate) used instead.

field dominance

In an interlaced motion image sequence, the field (first or second) immediately prior to which temporal coherence is susceptible to interruption due to editing. In principle, video edits can be made at any field, but good practice calls for edits in the vertical interval prior to the first field – that is, first field dominant. Good practice also calls for editing on frame *pairs,* in the vertical interval prior to even timecode numbers.

field merging

A deinterlacing technique, also knows as *weave,* that merges fields together, without interpolation, to form a frame. The technique is suitable for deinterlacing field pairs (or regions) that exhibit minimal motion; however, in the presence of significant motion, the zipper or sawtooth artifact will result.

field sync

In interlaced scanning, the analog sync pulse pattern that defines the start of a field. Field sync contains the 0_V datum. In 480*i* and 576*i* systems, field sync is a sequence comprising preequalization pulses, broad pulses, and postequalization pulses. In 480*i* systems there are six of each; in 576*i* systems there are five.

first field

In interlaced scanning, the first field of the pair of fields comprising a frame. In analog 480*i*, the field whose first equalization pulse starts coincident with 0_H. In analog 576*i*, the field whose first broad pulse starts coincident with 0_H. (See also *field dominance,* above, and *second field,* on page 657.)

first frame of action, FFoA

The first picture (frame) of a program, excluding leader.

fL,
footlambert

Deprecated unit for luminance. Multiply by $^{10.764}/_\pi$, about 3.4263, to obtain $cd \cdot m^{-2}$ [nit, or nt]. See *cd·m-2,* on page 600.

flare

Light, associated with a region of an image or an entire image, that is reflected and diffused in a manner that interferes with another part (or the entirety) of the image, either at a camera or a display. Flare is image-related: The unwanted light is modulated by image content. (See also *glare,* which is unmodulated. Both terms are sometimes used in a manner that fails to distinguish image-related and non-image-related sources.)

footprint, NTSC;
footprint, PAL

The first time that the NTSC or PAL luma and modulated chroma components of an image are added together into a single composite signal, cross-luma and cross-colour artifacts become permanently embedded: Subsequent decoding and reencoding cannot remove them. The permanence of these artifacts is referred to as the *NTSC footprint* or the *PAL footprint.*

format conversion

An ambiguous term. See *transcoding,* on page 661, *scan conversion,* on page 656, *downconversion,* on page 614, *upconversion,* on page 663, and *standards conversion,* on page 658.

fourcc	Four-character code: A scheme to select among a potentially large number of options or formats – for example, to choose a video data structure – by indexing with a 32-bit field that contains four bytes coded in ASCII, for example, "YUV2", "YV12", or "r408".
FPD	Fixed-pixel display (or, flat-panel display): A direct-view display (not a projector) having a flat display surface and discrete individually addressable light-emitting or light-modulating elements.
fps	Frames per second. Alternatively, express frame rate in hertz.
frame	The time interval or set of data that contains all of the elements of one picture, complete with all of the associated preceding sync elements. In analog systems, the frame occupies the interval between 0_V instants; in digital systems, the frame occupies the interval between the EAVs preceding line 1. In an interlaced system, a frame comprises two fields, *first* and *second*, which normally exhibit temporal coherence; each field contains half the image rows of the frame.
frame A	Deprecated. See *A-frame,* on page 589.
frequency interleaving	Modulation of chroma, and summation with luma, such that the modulated chroma signal occupies frequencies disjoint from the integer multiples of the line rate (at and near which the luma signal is concentrated).
FTA	Free-to-air: Terrestrial broadcasting, implicitly including content that has been or will be relayed by cable or satellite TV.
full HD	Generally, 1920×1080 HD, as opposed to subsampled variants such as 1366×768 or 1440×1080*i*.
full-range, full-swing	**1** In computing, an R', G', B', or Y' signal where reference black is at code 0, and reference white is at the largest possible code value in the code range available (e.g., 255 in an 8-bit system). In a full-swing $Y'C_BC_R$ system, C_BC_R are typically scaled to have $256/255$ the excursion of Y'. Full-swing $Y'C_BC_R$ coding is rarely used in video systems having more than 8 bits per component, though it is sometimes used in digital cinema. Preferably called *full-swing.* Contrast with *studio-swing,* on page 659.
	2 In a 10-bit studio HD or digital cinema interface, coding where reference black is well below 10-bit interface code 64 (and typically code 0 or code 4), or reference white is well above interface code 940 (typically code 1019 or 1023), or both. Contrast with *studio-swing,* on page 659. Sometimes misleadingly called *extended range.*
full width half maximum, FWHM	The duration or spatial extent of a pulse, assumed to be symmetric, measured between the 50% points of amplitude.

G'B'R'	Green, blue, and red. An alternate notation for *R'G'B'*, with the components reordered to associate with [*Y'*, C_B, C_R], respectively (or with [*Y'*, P_B, P_R], respectively). *G'* associates with *Y'* because green dominates luma. Properly written with primes, but sometimes sloppily written *GBR*.
gain	**1** In signal processing, multiplying signal amplitude by a given factor (sometimes adjustable). In video, gain control ordinarily applies to *Y'* or to *R'G'B'* components; the zero reference for gain adjustment is ordinarily taken at reference black level.
	2 In displays, individual *R'*, *G'*, and *B'* gain control; sometimes called *drive*. (CONTRAST sets gain on all components together.) A closely related adjustment is *colour temperature* (**2**). In home theatre terminology, individual *R'G'B'* gain adjustments are sometimes called *RGB-HIGH*. Distinguished from *bias* (**2**) on page 595.
gamma	A numerical parameter giving the exponent of a power function assumed to approximate the relationship between a signal quantity (such as video signal code) and light power. See *gamma, decoding* (γ_D), *gamma, encoding* (γ_E), and *gamma, system* below.
	The term *gamma* is so overloaded and so confused that it is best avoided. Use OECF (page 643) and EOCF (page 617) where possible. Certain relationships between applied signal and light power are not well approximated by a single-parameter power function; for example, the native electro-optical response of an LCD often takes an S-curve shape, which is not a power function. In such cases, *gamma* is not appropriate.
gamma = 1.0	A subsystem whose output values are linear with respect to its input values – that is, the subsystem has no net nonlinear transform (such as an OECF or EOCF). Sometimes used to indicate blending in the linear-light domain.
gamma, decoding (γ_D)	The exponent (greater than unity) of a power function taking the form V^{γ_D} that characterizes an EOCF (see page 617). The parameter γ_D is the exponent to which a video component signal *R'*, *G'*, or *B'* is raised to obtain a linear-light (luminance or tristimulus) value. In practical displays for electronic imaging, the value of decoding gamma is typically between 2.2 and 2.6. (For HD studio video, BT.1886 standardizes the value at 2.4.) Gamma characterizes a *display*, and is critical to achieving perceptually uniform coding. See *EOCF*, on page 617.
gamma, encoding (γ_E)	The exponent, less than 1, of a power function of the form L^{γ_E} that approximates, in a single parameter, an OECF (see page 643). A linear-light signal (for example, a relative luminance or tristimulus estimate) is transformed through the OECF to obtain a video signal *R'*, *G'*, or *B'*. (Subsequently, luma, *Y'*, is computed.) Encoding gamma today typically has a value between approximately 0.4 and 0.5. Historical NTSC and FCC standards for SD mention 2.2, but do not state whether this value relates to encoding or decoding. Standards for *576i*

systems mention display (decoding) gamma of 2.8; however, such a high value is never found in practice. For television, encoding gamma is typically about 1.2 times the reciprocal of the decoding (display) gamma; for modern systems, it is about 0.5. See *picture rendering,* on page 646. Encoding gamma properly has a value less than unity, though sometimes its reciprocal is quoted. See also *OECF,* on page 643.

gamma, system	The product of all of the power function exponents to which image data is subjected as it traverses a set of subsystems, starting from linear-light components captured from a scene by a camera (or from linear-light components captured from a previously reproduced image by a scanner), and ending with linear-light components reproduced at an image display. The term is best avoided owing to the difficulty of identifying exactly what constitutes the "system," and because it is used so widely without any consideration of picture rendering.
gamma-corrected	Image data to which gamma correction has been applied – that is, a signal that is intended to be converted to tristimulus through a power function (*OECF;* see page 643) having an exponent between about 2.0 and 2.6. Because gamma correction produces a video signal that mimics the lightness sensitivity of human vision, a gamma-corrected signal exhibits good perceptual uniformity: Noise or quantization error introduced into the signal is approximately equally perceptible across the tone range of the system from black to white.
gamma correction	The process by which a quantity proportional to intensity, such as an estimate of CIE luminance or some other tristimulus signal, is transformed into a signal intended for display through a power function having an exponent in the range roughly 2.0 to 2.6. See *OECF,* on page 643. In video, gamma correction is ordinarily performed at a video camera or its control unit.
gamma shift	Undesired alteration of effective gamma that results from inadvertent application of Macintosh-related gamma upon import or export of video involving a Macintosh computer. Gamma shift usually involves inadvertent application of a 1.45-power function or its inverse, a $1/1.45$ (i.e., 0.69) power function.
gamut	Generally, the largest possible set of colours of a particular device or circumstance.

1 Of a display device, the set of colours that can be produced in a particular viewing condition.

2 Of a colour interchange space, the set of colours that can be represented across all permitted codeword combinations – for example, $R'G'B'$ video signals each ranging from reference black to peak white – when displayed as intended and analysed colorimetrically in a particular viewing condition.

3 Of a camera whose output is characterized colorimetrically, the set of colours represented across all possible output codeword

DIGITAL VIDEO AND HD ALGORITHMS AND INTERFACES

combinations, displayed as intended and analysed colorimetrically in a particular viewing condition. (A camera whose output is not characterized colorimetrically, for example, a camera delivering "camera raw" data, has no defined gamut.)

gamut alarm	A studio device that warns of $R'G'B'$ codewords outside the permitted set (for example, in narrow-gamut colour, codewords outside the $R'G'B'$ unit cube. See *legal,* on page 632).
GbE	Gigabit [per second] Ethernet: A set of standards relating to conveying of data across shielded or unshielded twisted pair ("copper") wire, or optical fibre, at the rate indicated (typically either 1 Gb/s [implicit if no number is shown] or 10 Gb/s).
genlock (*v.*)	[Sync] generator lock: Synchronization, to a video source, of the scan timing of video origination or processing equipment.
glare	Light from the ambient environment (or potentially other sources) that interferes with an image. Glare sources are not image-related. (See also *flare,* which is modulated by image-related light. Both terms are sometimes used in a manner that fails to distinguish image-related and non-image-related light.)
global shutter	In an image sensor, operation (or resulting data) wherein exposure of all image rows starts at the same instant of time. (Opposed to *rolling shutter;* see page 653.)
GoP	Group of pictures: In MPEG or H.264, a set of consecutive pictures starting with a coded I-picture. A GoP typically extends to (but does not include) the following I-picture; however, a GoP may contain more than one I-picture. A short GoP has roughly 6 or fewer pictures; a long GoP, 15 or more.
grading	In the context of cinema, *colour correction* (**2**).
greyscale	**1** Generally, the range of achromatic values – that is, tones devoid of colour – from black to white.
	2 In video or computer graphics, the achromatic (or black and white, or lightness) component of image data.
GTG	Grey-to-grey: A nonstandard measure of the transition time ("response time") of a display (often an LCD) from one grey level to another. See also, *BTW,* on page 598.
H.264	Formally, ITU-T H.264, also published as ISO/IEC 14496-10 and known as MPEG-4 Part 10: A standard, jointly developed by ISO, IEC, and ITU-T, for the lossy compression of digital motion images and associated audio. The H.264 algorithm is based upon the basic principles of MPEG-2, but has many additional features that offer improved bit rate for the same performance (at the expense of additional encoder and/or decoder complexity). H.264 is sometimes loosely referred to as *MPEG-4;* however, that term does not uniquely identify H.264 because MPEG-4 Part 2 defines unrelated (SP/ASP and SStP) codecs.

HANC	Horizontal interval ancillary data: Ancillary data multiplexed into the horizontal blanking interval of an SDI or HD-SDI interface.
hanging dots	A cross-luma artifact appearing as a fine alternating pattern of dark and light dots along a horizontal edge in a picture having a saturated vertical colour transition, when decoded by a comb filter. Hanging dots are particularly evident when viewing the SMPTE colourbar test signal.
HD	**1** High-definition (video): There is no official definition; generally, a video system having aspect ratio of 16:9, frame rate of 23.976 Hz or higher, image data comprising 729 Kpixels (about ³⁄₄-million pixels) or more, and at least two channels of digital audio. Commonly either 720*p* (see page 588) or 1080*i* or 1080*p* (see page 589). Appending the letters TV (*HDTV*) implies entertainment programming. **2** Hard disk; to avoid ambiguity, use *hard disk drive, HDD.*
HD-CIF	ITU-R term referring to HD common image format – that is, 1920×1080.
HD-D5	See *D-5 HD,* on page 610.
HD-SDI	High-definition serial digital interface: A SMPTE-standard interface with a data rate of about 1.485 Gb/s or 2.97 Gb/s ("3G"), typically for uncompressed 4:2:2 studio-quality HD though other variants are accommodated.
HD-SLR	A D-SLR camera (see *D-SLR,* on page 610) adapted to record HD (often 1080*p*) video.
HDCAM	A component HD digital videotape format for professional use, utilizing ¹⁄₂-inch tape in Beta-type cassettes and recording $Y'C_BC_R$ signals based upon a 1440×1080 image structure, scanned progressive or interlaced at any of several frame rates, chroma subsampled 3:1:1, and mildly compressed to about 50 Mb/s using a motion-JPEG technique. Standardized by SMPTE as D-11.
HDCP	High-bandwidth Digital Content Protection: A scheme, promulgated by Digital Content Protection LLC, for encrypting uncompressed AV content conveyed across consumer digital interfaces (such as DVI, HDMI, and DisplayPort).
HDMI	High-Definition Multimedia Interface: An interface, promulgated by HDMI Licensing, LLC, to convey uncompressed audio-visual data.
HDTV	High-definition television: HD (see above); the *TV* suffix implies recording or transmission of entertainment programming.
HDV	A consumer HD system introduced by Canon, JVC, Sharp, and Sony, for 720*p* and 1080*i* (and in some systems,1080*p*), using

long-GoP MPEG-2 MP@H-14 video compressed to a bit rate between about 19 Mb/s and 25 Mb/s and recording to DV tape, hard drive, or flash media.

HEVC	High Efficiency Video Coding: A compression scheme in development by the Joint Collaborative Team on Video Coding (JCTVC) of ITU-T VCEG and ISO/IEC MPEG, intended to compress video up to UHD to bit rate roughly half that of H.264.
HHR	Half horizontal resolution. An image format related to a base format (usually 704×480 or 704×576) by 2:1 horizontal down-sampling.
Hi-color	A degenerate form of *truecolour* (page 662), now largely obsolete, wherein a pixel comprises 5 bits each of *R'*, *G'*, and *B'*. (Some Hi-color systems use 6 bits for green.) Not to be confused with *High Color* (see below).
Hi-Vision	NHK's term for 1080*i*29.97 HD.
hidef, high def	Slang term for *high-definition* (HD). I suggest that you avoid these terms: *def* suggests lack of hearing, but HD comes with sound.
High Color	Microsoft's term (in Windows 7) for pixel representations having 30 or 48 bits per pixel. Not to be confused with Hi-color (see above).
HLS	**1** Hue, lightness, saturation: Three basic perceptual attributes of human colour vision.
	2 http live streaming, HLS, see below.
hold-type	A display wherein a newly written pixel value is converted to light that is sustained for more than about half the frame time. Such a display is expected to exhibit motion blur induced by the viewers' eye-tracking of image elements in motion with respect to the frame.
horizontal blanking	The time interval – usually expressed in microseconds or sample counts, or sometimes the fraction of line time – between the end (or right edge) of picture information on one line and the start (or left edge) of picture information on the following picture line.
HomePNA, HPNA	HomePNA Alliance, formerly the Home Phoneline Networking Alliance: An organization promulgating standards for consumer IPTV. Its standards have been adopted by ITU-T (e.g., G.9954).
HSDL	High-speed data link. An adaptation of HD-SDI to convey 10-bit image data (typically *R'G'B'*) having image structure 2048×1556, typically scanned from film slower than realtime (at about 15 fps). Obsolete.

HTiB	Home theatre in a box. The notion that a consumer is sufficiently skillful to install a surround sound system.
http live streaming, HLS	Technology introduced by Apple to stream video across an IP network using just http (web) protocols. The stream is broken into components transferred across http as files.
HTVL	*Horizontal* resolution, expressed in units of *TVL*/PH: A unit of horizontal resolution used in CCTV and video security systems.

hue

1 *The attribute of a visual sensation according to which an area appears to be similar to one of the perceived colours, red, yellow, green and blue, or a combination of two of them* [CIE]. Roughly speaking, if the dominant wavelength of an SPD shifts, the hue of the associated colour will shift.

2 In colour science, h^*_{uv} or h^*_{ab}, the polar-coordinate angle of a colour difference value in CIE $L^*u^*v^*$ or CIE $L^*a^*b^*$ components.

3 In video, the polar-coordinate angle of a colour difference value as displayed on a vectorscope, in C_B, C_R coordinates for component digital video or P_B, P_R coordinates for component analog video.

4 User-accessible means to adjust *hue* (**3**), sometimes confusingly called TINT or PHASE.

HVS

1 Human visual system.

2 Hue, value, and saturation: Three basic perceptual attributes of human colour vision.

I-field

In MPEG, a field-coded I-picture. I-fields come in pairs, either top then bottom, or bottom then top. See *I-picture*, below.

I-frame

In MPEG, either (i) a frame-coded I-picture, or (ii) a field-coded I-picture [either top or bottom] followed by a field-coded I-picture or P-picture [of opposite parity]. In the second case, the two fields form what is sometimes called an *IP-frame;* the P-field may involve prediction from the I-field. See *I-picture*, below.

I-frame-only

More generally, I-*picture*-only: A compression system that performs only *intra* compression – that is, compresses individual pictures (fields or frames) without exploiting coherence between frames.

I-P conversion

Interlace-to-progressive conversion: an alternate term for *deinterlace;* see page 612.

I-picture

In MPEG, an intraframe picture (field or frame): A picture, or coded picture information, that makes no reference to preceding or following pictures. An I-picture makes no use of temporal coherence.

DIGITAL VIDEO AND HD ALGORITHMS AND INTERFACES

I, Q	In-phase and Quadrature colour difference components of NTSC: *U* and *V* components rotated +33° and then axis-exchanged. When NTSC was established in 1953, modulated chroma was based on *I* and *Q* colour differences; *I* had considerably more bandwidth than *Q*. Since about 1970, NTSC colour modulation has been performed on equiband *U* and *V* components. When *I* and *Q* components are explained in a contemporary publication in any context other than purely historical, the presence of such an explanation signals that the author is uninformed about video practice during the last four decades.
IAR, image aspect ratio	See *aspect ratio,* on page 592.
IBP	See *long GoP,* on page 635.
IDCT	**1** In image compression, inverse discrete cosine transform.
	2 In scene-linear workflow, input device calibration transform.
ICT	In JPEG2000, irreversible colour transform: A mapping producing $Y'C_BC_R$ from $R'G'B'$ using BT.601 luma coefficients [0.299, 0.587, 0.114]. When inverted with fixed-point binary arithmetic, roundoff error results, so the transform is not perfectly reversible. Compare *RCT,* on page 651.
iFrame	Apple designation for a progressive video format having an image structure of 960×540 at aspect ratio 16:9, typically having a frame rate of 29.97 or 30 Hz – i.e., 540p30. (Apple apparently uses I-frame-only compression for this format.)
illegal	Not *legal* (page 632), each of the 3 senses.
image	A two-dimensional distribution of numerical values representing light levels associated with pictorial information.
image array	A two-dimensional array of sets of numerical values (picture elements, usually in a matrix) representing pictorial information.
image column	A column of the image matrix. (An image column corresponds to the "active" region of a historical analog scan line.)
image matrix	R', G', B', or Y' (luma) samples of a frame (or in an interlaced system, a field), considered as image rows and columns.
image row	A row of the image matrix. (An image row corresponds to an "active" historical scan line.)
image sequence	A set of images, conventionally uncompressed, stored in separate files (often TIFF or DPX) whose filenames incorporate sequence numbers or timecode that allows files in the set to be played out in order to present motion.
impulsive noise	**1** In analog transmission, noise where the signal is contaminated by very brief pulses. Limited channel bandwidth typically

causes impulsive noise to be distributed across a few pixels once sampled.

2 In digital transmission, noise where individual, isolated digital sample values are corrupted (often to full black or full white, in which case the noise is sometimes referred to as "salt and pepper"). True impulsive noise is rare to nonexistent today. In uncompressed digital video, almost all useful channel coding methods implement error checking or correction. In compressed digital video, an individual pixel has no direct counterpart in the data stream, consequently pixels cannot be corrupted individually.

IMX   See *MPEG IMX,* on page 641.

intensity

1 Of light, the amount of radiant or luminant flux (often radiated from or incident onto a surface), in a specified direction (that is, per unit solid angle). Intensity is a linear-light measure properly expressed in radiometric units such as watts per steradian [$W \cdot sr^{-1}$] or in photometric units such as candela [cd]. Image scientists and video engineers are usually interested in luminous intensity *per unit projected area* – that is, they are usually interested not in intensity but *luminance;* see page 636.

2 Of sound, power per unit area (in SI units, $W \cdot m^{-2}$). Intensity of sound is comparable to irradiance or illuminance of light.

3 In computer graphics, video, and digital image processing, often used carelessly. The intensity produced by an image display subsystem is ordinarily *not* proportional to the applied signal, but is proportional to approximately the 2.4-power of the signal. Instead of *intensity* or *pixel intensity,* use *pixel value.*

intensity level   See *intensity* (**3**), above.

interlace   A scanning standard or image format in which alternate raster lines of a frame are displaced vertically by half the scan-line pitch and displaced temporally by half the frame time to form a *first field* and a *second field.* Examples are 480*i*29.97, 576*i*25, and 1080*i*30. Modern usage of the term *interlace* implies 2:1 interlace. See also *field,* on page 618.

interlace factor   The ratio between the number of picture lines in a reference progressive system and the number of picture lines necessary to defeat twitter in an interlaced system having equivalent spatial resolution. Distinguished from, but often mistakenly described as, *Kell factor, k.*

interleaved, component interleaved   A method of storing pixels whereby all components of a pixel occupy adjacent storage locations. A 3×2 image matrix of 8-bit *RGB* data could be stored as bytes in the order RGBRGBRGB RGBRGBRGB. Also known as *band-interleaved by pixel* (BIP), *chunky, packed pixel,* or *pixel interleaved.* See also *planar,* on page 647, and *band-interleaved by line (BIL),* on page 594.

interpolation	Resampling that produces more output samples than original samples (synonymous with *upsampling*), or that produces the same number of output samples as input samples (phase shifting).
interstitial	**1** Chroma subsampling wherein each subsampled chroma sample is effectively horizontally positioned halfway between adjacent luma samples. Interstitial 4:2:0 chroma subsampling is implicit in the JPEG/JFIF, H.261, and MPEG-1 standards.
	2 In television programming, a short element such as a commercial inserted into or between programs.
intra	A compression system that compresses individual pictures (fields or frames) without exploiting interpicture coherence.
inverse gamma correction	The process by which a video component signal value is transformed by an EOCF (resembling a power function having an exponent in the range roughly 2.0 to 2.6) to produce a tristimulus signal proportional to intended light power output at a display. See *EOCF,* on page 617. Inverse gamma correction is ordinarily performed as part of display processing.
inverse telecine	A process of taking interlaced video at 59.94 fps (or rarely, 60 fps) that has been subject to 2:3 pulldown, and recovering noninterlaced images corresponding to the original 23.976 Hz (or 24*p*) frames. In the studio, inverse telecine is trivially simple if the video is locked to an available timecode stream and cadence has been maintained. In consumer equipment, all bets are off, and inverse telecine usually involves comparison and analysis of several video fields.
IP	**1** Internet protocol: The foundation standards of the internet.
	2 Intellectual property: Copyright, patents, and trademarks.
	3 Intellectual property in the form of trade secrets incorporated into electronic subsystems (typically expressed in hardware description language such as Verilog or VHDL) known as *cores*.
IPR	Intellectual property rights: The right of a patent holder to control (and gain revenue from) deployment of a technology.
IPTV	Internet protocol television: Distribution of compressed digital video and associated audio over TCP/IP networks.
IRD	Integrated receiver-decoder: A device that receives an RF signal carrying digital television, and produces an uncompressed video signal. An IRD performs demodulation, demultiplexing, and MPEG-2 decoding. An IRD is typically a set-top device (*set-top box*, or STB).
IRE	*Institute of Radio Engineers,* the predecessor of the IEEE.

IRE unit	A historical unit of video signal amplitude adopted by the IRE (see above): In modern video systems having zero setup (including all forms of HD), one-hundredth of the excursion from reference black level (0 IRE) to reference white level (100 IRE). Today, *unit* or *video level* is preferred (see page 664).
IT	Information technology: Computer technology (or in one aspect, personal computing).
ITU-R	*International Telecommunications Union, Radiocommunications Sector;* successor to the *Comité Consultatif Internationale des Radiocommunications* (CCIR, International Radio Consultative Committee): A treaty organization that obtains international agreement on standards for radio and television broadcasting. The ITU-R BT (Broadcast Technology) series of Recommendations and Reports deals with radio and television. Although studio standards do not strictly involve radio frequency transmission, they are used in the international exchange of programs, so they fall under the jurisdiction of ITU-R.
ITU-R Rec. BT. 601, 709	Colloquially, *BT.601* and *BT.709* (or *Rec. 601* and *Rec. 709*); see *BT.601* and *BT.709*, on page 598.
ISO	International Standards Organization.
iso	Isolated. Referring to one camera of several that are recorded simultaneously to enable editing between shots in post-production; contrasted with *film style,* where a single camera is used to acquire several viewpoints of the same action shot multiple times.
ISP, image signal processor	A series of processing stages (a "pipeline") that receives digital signals (usually in mosaic colour form, commonly in a "Bayer" pattern) from an image sensor, and delivers processed image data with spatially coincident colour components.
JFIF	JPEG file interchange format. A file format, adopted in 1992 by an industry group led by C-Cube, that encapsulates a JPEG-compressed image, along with a small amount of supplementary data. If you are presented with an image data file described as JPEG, in all likelihood it is JFIF internally.
JND, just noticeable difference	The magnitude of change in a perceptually relevant physical stimulus that produces a 75:25 proportion of correct and incorrect responses in a two-alternative, forced-choice (2AFC) experiment. Observers are asked if they can detect a difference; the 75:25 proportion results from a stimulus that produces a 50% correct response rate; the remaining responses are guesses, half of which are correct by chance.
JPEG	**1** Joint Photographic Experts Group: A standards committee constituted jointly by the ISO and IEC and formally denoted ISO/IEC JTC1.

2 A standard, formally denoted ISO/IEC 10918, adopted by *JPEG* (**1**) for the lossy compression of digital still images (either colour or greyscale).

judder See *stutter,* on page 659.

JustScan See *1:1 pixel mapping,* on page 582.

KB Kilobyte: 2^{10} (or 1 024) bytes.

K Unit of absolute temperature, kelvin. Properly written with no degree sign. In colour science, commonly used to quantify correlated colour temperature.

K-factor, *K*-rating A numerical characterization of frequency response characteristics as evidenced by pulse fidelity, obtained by measuring the tightest fit of a specific time-domain envelope to a raised cosine test pulse. Distinguished from *Kell factor, k,* below.

Kell effect In a video system – including sensor, signal processing, and display – *Kell effect* refers to the loss of vertical resolution, compared to the Nyquist limit, caused by the spatial dispersion of light power. Some dispersion is necessary to avoid aliasing upon capture, and to avoid objectionable scan line (or pixel) structure at display.

Kell factor, *k* Historically, the ratio between effective vertical resolution and theoretically obtainable vertical resolution for a given number of picture lines. Generally between 0.7 and 0.9. Now deprecated. Distinguished from *interlace factor (page 628);* also distinguished from *K-factor, K-rating* (above).

kelvin Unit of absolute temperature; its unit symbol is K, written with no degree sign. In colour science, commonly used to quantify colour temperature. See also *mirek,* MK^{-1}, on page 639.

key **1** A component signal indicating opacity of the accompanying foreground image data, coded between black (0, fully transparent) and white (1, fully opaque). In computer graphics, called *alpha,* · (see page 591). See *composite (v.)* on page 607.

2 The key component of KLV, see below.

KLV Key, length, value: A data encoding defined in SMPTE ST 336 used to embed structured information in files (e.g., MXF).

knee That portion of a video camera's OECF, or a comparable transfer function used in postproduction, that lies above a diffuse scene reflectance of about 90%. Video cameras are usually adjusted to compress (highlight) information beyond the knee.

L Symbol for absolute luminance, having SI units $cd \cdot m^{-2}$, "nit."

L_A, active lines	The count of scan lines containing the picture. L_A for a frame is equivalent to the number of rows of image samples. In modern terminology, the count of image rows (N_R).
L_T, total lines	In raster scanning, the count of total scan lines in a frame.
L_V, luminance (visual)	Absolute (linear-light) luminance, preferably in SI units of $cd \cdot m^{-2}$, or informally, *nit* [nt]. See *luminance, absolute* on page 636.
latitude	See *exposure latitude,* on page 618.
LB	Letterbox, see below.
LCD	Liquid crystal display. Most commonly direct view, but LCD technology (usually, LCoS) is used in projectors.
LCoS	Liquid crystal on silicon. A reflective type of LCD microdisplay structure used in projectors. (Pronounced *EL-koss*.)
leader	Film or tape media preceding and following program content, historically used for threading cameras, recorders, and projectors; by extension, digital imagery outside the bounds of a program. (Pronounced *LEED-er*.)
LED	Light-emitting diode, a solid-state semiconductor light source. LEDs are often used to backlight LCD displays.
legal	**1** In component video processing or transmission, the condition where each signal of a component set does not exceed its reference range: In an *R'G'B'*-legal combination, none of *R'*, *G'*, and *B'* exceed their reference ranges except perhaps for brief transients. (See also *valid,* on page 663.)
	2 In NTSC and PAL processing or transmission, compliance of the composite NTSC or PAL signal (or its luma and chroma components) with broadcast standards. NTSC analog broadcast transmission has a 120 unit amplitude limit that requires limiting the chroma at hue values near yellow and cyan.
	3 In JPEG, MPEG, or H.264, a bitstream that is compliant with standards, an encoder that produces only compliant bitstreams, or a decoder that correctly decodes any compliant bitstream.
legalizer	A studio device operating on *R'G'B'* or *Y'C_BC_R* video, warning of excursions outside the unit *R'G'B'* cube and/or clipping to the *R'G'B'* unit cube. A legalizer is incompatible with wide-gamut xyYCC.
letterbox	A widescreen image (such as 16:9 aspect ratio) conveyed or presented in a format having a narrower aspect ratio (such as 4:3), using the full width of the narrower format but not using the full height.

DIGITAL VIDEO AND HD ALGORITHMS AND INTERFACES

level	**1** In video, generally, the amplitude of a video signal, or one of its components, expressed on an abstract scale having reference values 0 and 1, or in volts, millivolts, IRE units, or digital code values.
	2 In JPEG, MPEG, and DV compression, the magnitude (i.e., absolute value) of a DCT coefficient.
level shifting	In JPEG, MPEG, and similar transform-based compression systems, the process effected prior to encoding of subtracting from each $Y'C_BC_R$ component half of its maximum excursion, so as to form a signed number that is subject to the transform mathematics (e.g., DCT). The process is reversed at decoding.
lift	**1** European term for *pedestal* (both senses); see page 645.
	2 A user control (LIFT) that introduces black-level offset, but changes gain correspondingly so as to maintain white level.
lift/gamma/gain	Three basic controls for colour correction of video-coded image data, often controlled by a set of three trackballs. See *lift* (above), and several entries for *gamma,* starting on page 621. *Gain* refers simply to a multiplicative scale factor applied to pixel values. (The scheme is generally inappropriate for image data in CPD or quasilog coding.)
lightness	**1** *The brightness of an area judged relative to the brightness of a similarly illuminated area that appears to be white or highly transmitting* [CIE]. Loosely, lightness is apparent reflectance. Lightness is expressed relative to some reference luminance or reflectance.
	2 CIE *L*:* An objective quantity defined by the CIE, approximately the 0.42-power of relative luminance.
limited range	HDMI term for *studio-swing,* on page 659.
line, active; line, picture	A scanning line – or in modern terms, image row – that is specified by a scanning standard to contain picture. (Exceptionally, in 480*i* systems, closed caption lines are considered to be "active.") In modern terms, image row.
line doubling	A special case of image resampling that produces an image having exactly twice the number of image rows as the source.
line frequency	**1** In video, the frequency of horizontal scanning; about 15.7 kHz for SD, and 33.7 kHz or higher for HD.
	2 AC power line (mains) frequency, typically 50 Hz or 60 Hz, usually similar to the field rate of video.
	The term *line frequency* should be used with care in video because it may refer to the frequency of *horizontal* scanning, or to AC power (mains) frequency, which is usually similar or identical to the frequency of *vertical* scanning.

line-locked	**1** In digital video, having an integer number of samples per total line: If 0_H were digitized, it would take the same value every line. A line-locked system has coherent sampling and line frequencies, as in BT.601 or $4f_{SC}$ NTSC. Owing to the +25 Hz offset of the PAL subcarrier in PAL-B/G/H/I and PAL-N, PAL sampled at $4f_{SC}$ is not line-locked.
	2 In CCTV, industrial, or security video, having vertical scan frequency locked to the AC power line (mains) frequency.
line sync	The sync signal pulse that defines the start of a scan line. In 480*i* and 576*i* systems, line sync may be the start of a normal sync or the start of certain equalization or broad pulses. See also *0_H datum,* on page 581.
line time	The time interval from the 0_H datum of one line to the 0_H datum of the next. In a digital system, from EAV to EAV.
linear (*adj.*)	A dangerously ambiguous term:

1 In mathematics, actual or presumed adherence to this equation:

$$g\left(a \cdot x + b \cdot y\right) \equiv a \cdot g\left(x\right) + b \cdot g\left(y\right) \qquad \text{[for scalar } a, b\text{]}$$

In digital image and video processing, the quantities *x* and *y* in this equation are the "signals"; *a* and *b* are "constants." The assertion that a process is linear offers no information concerning the nature of *x* and *y*.

2 *linear-light (adj.),* see below.

3 Often confusingly used by digital imaging technicians (DITs) to denote video acquisition (e.g., BT.709), which is *not* linear-light, contradicting sense **2**.

4 Storage or processing of audio or video where the arrangement of data on the media is in direct correspondence to the timeline. Magnetic tape is sometimes referred to as "linear" media; hard drive media is sometimes called "nonlinear."

linear colour space, linear image data	Colour data wherein each component value, over nearly all of its range, is proportional to light power – that is, proportional to radiance, intensity, luminance, or tristimulus value.
linear-light (*adj.*)	Pertaining to a radiometrically linear signal – that is, proportional to radiance, intensity, luminance, or tristimulus value, or an estimate of one of these.

Video signals are *not* encoded in linear-light form. Instead, individual *R'G'B'* values are *gamma-corrected,* that is, proportional to a power function (typically having an exponent between $^1/_{2.2}$ and $^1/_{2.6}$) of intended display luminance. Other forms of linear-light coding may be used to encode approximations of luminance in the original scene (*scene-referred* coding).

lines	**1** In raster scanning, the total number of lines per frame, L_T.
	2 In an image format, active lines, L_A: image rows.
	3 A unit of resolution; properly, *TV lines per picture height*, *TVL/PH* (see page 662).
loading, luminance	In PDP displays, sometimes used inaccurately to refer to *power loading;* see page 648.
log	**1** (*n.*) A recording of a series of events; (*v.*) to make a recording of a series of events.
	2 Abbreviation of *logarithm.*
log colour space	Colour data wherein each component value, over much of its range, is proportional to the logarithm of light power – that is, proportional to the logarithm of radiance, intensity, luminance, or tristimulus value. See *log neg* and *log RGB*, below.
log neg	Image coding conveying integer codes representative of optical density values measured from (or approximating) exposed and developed colour-negative photographic film. *Cineon printing density* (CPD) is a widely used example of log neg coding.
log *RGB*	Image coding whereby scene-linear *RGB* values are mapped into integer codes through an approximately logarithmic OECF. It is usual to avoid the logarithm's singularity at zero by imposing an additive offset to a linear-light signal prior to taking the logarithm, so log *RGB* coding is usually more accurately called *quasilog.*
long GoP	Long group of pictures. Literally, a group of pictures (see *GoP*, on page 623) comprising more than about 10 pictures. Figuratively, an MPEG-, H.264-, or VC-1-class video compression system operating in non-intra mode using long GoPs.
LP/mm	Line pairs per millimeter: A unit of absolute resolution corresponding to a cycle (a black and a white element, comparable to a line pair) across one millimeter of physical distance.
LP/PH	Line pairs per picture height: A unit of resolution corresponding to a cycle (a black and a white element, comparable to a line pair) across the height of the picture.
LP/PW	Line pairs per picture width: A unit of resolution corresponding to a cycle (a black and a white element, comparable to a line pair) across the width of the picture.
luma	A video signal component representative of the greyscale component of an image, computed as a suitably weighted sum of nonlinear primary components (*R'G'B'*). At decoding, luma is combined with colour differences to produce *R'G'B'*, each of which is subjected to an EOCF in the conversion to tristimulus values at a display. A luma signal is approximately perceptually

uniform across the range from black to white. Luma is symbolized Y'. For SD, BT.601 standardizes these coefficients:

$$^{601}Y' = 0.299\,R' + 0.587\,G' + 0.114\,B'$$

For HD, BT.709 standardizes these coefficients:

$$^{709}Y' = 0.2126\,R' + 0.7152\,G' + 0.0722\,B'$$

Luma is nonlinearly related to relative luminance; luma alone is not sufficient to determine relative luminance.

luma coefficients

The coefficients of nonlinear (gamma-corrected) $R'G'B'$ in the weighted sum that represents luma. Luma coefficients differ between SD and HD; see *luma*, above.

luminance

Properly, either *luminance, absolute* (see below) or *luminance, relative* (see below). The term *luminance* is often carelessly used in video engineering to refer to *luma;* see above.

In video, and computer graphics, much confusion surrounds the term *luminance*. In colour science and physics, *luminance* is proportional to intensity ("linear-light" light power). Absolute luminance has the symbol L or L_V and SI units of $cd \cdot m^{-2}$ (or informally, *nit* [nt]). Relative luminance has the symbol Y, and is a dimensionless quantity typically between 0 and 1 (or 0 and 100); it can be computed as a properly weighted sum of *RGB* tristimulus values. In video, *luma* represents a weighted sum of nonlinear (gamma-corrected) $R'G'B'$ components, and is properly denoted Y'. Confusion is heightened because luma coefficients are typically similar to or identical to the coefficients for relative luminance. The term *luma*, and the primed symbol Y', denote the nonlinear quantity in a manner that avoids ambiguity. However, the term *luminance* is often sloppily used for this quantity, and the prime on the symbol is often omitted. Sloppy use of the word *luminance* and omission of the prime renders both the term *luminance* and the symbol Y ambiguous: Whether the associated quantity is CIE luminance (linear) or video luma (nonlinear) must then be determined from context.

luminance, absolute (*L*)

Luminous flux density (i.e., power per unit projected area) in a particular direction (i.e., per unit solid angle): The spectral radiance of a scene, in a particular direction (that is, per unit solid angle), weighted by the luminous efficiency function $\bar{y}(\lambda)$ of the CIE Standard Observer. Denoted L_V; properly expressed in SI units of $cd \cdot m^{-2}$ (or informally, *nit* [nt]). Luminance is the photometric analog of radiance; it is the objective correlate of brightness. If that sounds complex, it is. Briefly and informally, absolute luminance is the physical linear-light quantity that is associated with the lightness sensation of human vision.

luminance, relative (*Y*)

1 Absolute luminance (see above), relative to a certain absolute white luminance (often a perfect diffuse reflector, or its depiction on a display). Relative luminance is symbolized Y; it is a dimensionless quantity having no units, and typically has a reference value of 1 or 100. In video, absolute reproduction of luminance is unnecessary; video normally involves an estimate of relative luminance.

2 An estimate of relative luminance (**1**) obtained from a camera or scanner whose spectral sensitivities cannot be linearly combined to exactly match the CIE $\bar{y}(\lambda)$ function.

luminance coefficients	The coefficients of linear-light (tristimulus) *RGB* in the weighted sum that forms luminance. For the primaries of BT.709 – the primary set of HD and sRGB, also representative of modern SD – the luminance coefficients are 0.2126, 0.7152, and 0.0722.
luminance loading	In PDP displays, sometimes used inaccurately to refer to *power loading;* see page 648.
luminosity	Historically, the ratio of luminous flux to total radiant flux (over a wide range of wavelengths). Now deprecated. Used widely and incorrectly by Adobe to refer to (BT.601) luma.
LUT	Lookup table: A table enumerating the scalar or low-dimensional vector results of a function over a scalar or low-dimensional vector argument. The argument and result components are typically whole numbers in the range 0 to $2^K - 1$.
M-JPEG	A technique or file format using *JPEG* (**2**), or a JPEG-like algorithm, to individually compress each field or frame in a motion image sequence, without exploiting interfield or interframe coherence. M-JPEG is not standardized.
M/NTSC	See *NTSC, National Television System Committee (3)*, on page 642. The *M* is an archaic reference to the nomenclature of ITU-R Rep. 470.
M-frame, midframe	In 2:3 pulldown to 29.97 Hz interlaced video, the video frame – unique in the 5-frame sequence – comprising a first field from one 24*p* frame (conventionally frame B) and a second field from another 24*p* frame (conventionally 24*p* frame C). An edit in the 24*p sequence* could intervene. See *2-2 pulldown,* on page 582 and *A-frame,* on page 589.
.m2ts	File extension commonly used for an MPEG-2 transport stream (including the Blu-ray container format).

macroblock

1 In MPEG, image data comprising, or coded picture information representing, one of the 16×16 arrays of luma samples that tile the image, accompanied by the requisite number and arrangement of associated blocks of C_B and C_R. In the common MPEG-2 case of 4:2:0 chroma subsampling, four 8×8 luma blocks are accompanied by an 8×8 block of C_B and an 8×8 block of C_R; in this case, a macroblock comprises six blocks.

2 In DV, image data comprising – or coded picture information representing – an 8×8 block of C_B, an 8×8 block of C_R, and the associated two (4:2:2), three (3:1:1), four (4:1:1 or 4:2:0), or six (3:1:0) 8×8 blocks of luma.

3 In JPEG, an MCU (minimum coded unit; see page 638).

MADI	Motion-adaptive deinterlacing.
MAE	Mean absolute error: Sum of absolute differences (see *SAD,* on page 654), divided by the number of samples considered.
Matroska	An open-source container format used in Google's WebM project.
mb	See *macroblock,* above. It's sensible to write the abbreviation in lowercase, to disambiguate from megabyte; in compressed video there are both megabytes per second (MB/s) and macro-blocks per second (mb/s).
Mb	Megabit: 2^{20} (or 1,048,576) bits; 131,072 bytes, or 128 KB.

MB

1 Megabyte: 2^{20} (or 1,048,576) bytes, or in disk storage, $2^{10} \cdot 10^3$ (or 1,024,000) bytes.

2 In MPEG and associated standards, macroblock.

MCU, minimum coded unit

In JPEG without subsampling, image data comprising, or coded picture information representing, a set of 8×8 blocks of image data, one per component. In $Y'C_BC_R$ JPEG, with 4:2:0 subsampling, image data comprising, or coded picture information representing, an 8×8 block of C_B, the corresponding 8×8 block of C_R, and the four associated 8×8 luma blocks.

median filter

A nonlinear "rank order" filter whose output is the middle value of the input samples, sorted by amplitude (in the case of image data, sorted by pixel value). (If an even number of input samples are provided, the output is the average of the two middle values.)

mesopic

Pertaining to vision at adaptation levels between about 0.1 nt and 3 nt, where the retina's rod cells and code cells are both active ("mez-*AH*-pick"). See mesopic, scotopic.

metadata

Generally, data about data. *Structural metadata* describes how essence is stored. *Descriptive metadata* describes the content of the essence.

metamerism

1 In colour science, the condition that two different spectral power distributions, when weighted according to the CMFs (spectral response curves) of the CIE Standard Observer, produce identical tristimulus values – that is, appear to a colour-normal observer as the same colour. Metamerism frequently holds for spectra that are markedly different.

2 In a camera or scanner, the condition that two objects that are metameric with respect to the CIE Standard Observer produce different sets of *RGB* components, owing to the spectral response of the device departing from the CIE curves. A camera or scanner has metamerism errors when it "sees" colour differently from a colour-normal human observer.

mezzanine Pertaining to "light" compression for use in applications intermediate between acquisition/postproduction (where a high data rate is important to maintain image quality) and distribution (where a low data rate is important for economy).

midgrey,
midscale,
midtone Reflectance in a scene, or the corresponding image data value carried in a film or video system, that represents diffuse scene reflectance of roughly 18% of a perfect diffuse reflector.

MiniDV The small cassette size variant of DVC. (See page 615.)

mirek, MK^{-1} Reciprocal megakelvin: a unit of correlated colour temperature, $10^6/_t$, where t is CCT in kelvin [K]. Formerly, *mired.*

modulated chroma In NTSC and PAL, a colour subcarrier (**1**) onto which two colour difference signals (typically U and V) have been imposed by quadrature modulation.

monochrome,
monochromatic **1** In colour science, shades and tones of a single hue: A colour stimulus having a single (usually narrowband) spectral peak.

2 In video, the greyscale (or achromatic, or black and white, or lightness) component of image data. This usage of *monochrome* is confusing because it contradicts sense **1**; to avoid confusion, use *greyscale* (page 623) or *achromatic* (page 590).

3 In computing, image data having one bit per pixel, representing either full black or full white. This usage is confusing because it contradicts sense **2**; also, the suffix *-chrome* suggests colour, but in computer terminology a so-called monochrome image has no colour. A colour scientist would describe a sodium vapour streetlamp as *monochrome,* but its light is coloured! Use *bilevel* (page 595) to describe image data with one bit per pixel.

MOS **1** Metal-oxide-semiconductor (pronounced *moss*): The layers in a certain type of semiconductor structure widely used in integrated circuits (e.g., CMOS).

2 In cinema acquisition, without sound; pronounced *em-oh-ess.* Some people believe the acronym to originate from *minus optical stripe*, referring to the optical sound track on a print. However, the term is associated with image capture where the sound is not recorded on film. The Hollywood legend is probably correct that the term arose from the famous German director Otto Preminger, who in frustration with the noisy cameras of his day is reported to have shouted, "Mit out sound!" indicating that shooting should commence immediately without concern for ambient noise, where the intended audio would be created later in postproduction.

mosaic See *CFA,* on page 600.

mosquito noise	Visual noise having very high spatial frequency produced by motion-compensated transform coding (such as MPEG and H.264) using aggressive compression. Such noise is typically incoherent picture-to-picture, and can appear like buzzing mosquitoes surrounding pronounced edges in an image.
motion-JPEG	See *M-JPEG*, on page 637.
motion compensated interpolation, MCI	A technique of using one or more motion vectors to compute spatially displaced image information representing a certain time instant, derived from one or more pictures sampled at different time instants.
motion detection, MD	A technique of estimating, for a certain pixel or a certain block of pixels, whether an underlying scene is in motion (with respect to the picture boundary) at a speed greater than a certain number of pixels per picture time.
motion estimation, ME	A technique of estimating, for a certain pixel or a certain block of pixels, the speed and direction of motion (with respect to the picture boundary) of assumed underlying scene elements.
motion vector, MV	A vector, associated with a pixel or a block of pixels, that estimates the displacement (horizontally and vertically) of an assumed scene element from its position in a previous or future picture.
movie mode	In consumer television displays, a setting that typically disables proprietary signal processing features believed by the manufacturer to "enhance" or "improve" the picture. Such circuitry distorts material that is presented to the display in pristine form; *movie mode* defeats the "enhancement."
MP3 (.mp3)	Formally, MPEG-1 Audio Layer III: An audio compression standard, defined in MPEG-1 and MPEG-2, that is widely used for music distribution. Sometimes incorrectly called MPEG-3.
MP4 (.mp4)	A container (file) format used in MPEG-4 Parts 1 and 14 (not Part 10/AVC) that is based upon the container format used in Apple's QuickTime system.
MPD	Motion-picture disturbance (or moving pixel distortion): See *DFC, dynamic false contouring*, on page 612.
MPEG	Moving (not Motion!) Picture Experts Group: A standards committee, jointly constituted by ISO/IEC and ITU-T, that develops standards for the lossy compression of digital motion images and associated audio. The MPEG algorithms exploit the temporal coherence found in video and audio data (and the spatial coherence found in video data). The MPEG-2 standard (see below) is of interest to digital video and HD. Its predecessor, now denoted MPEG-1, offers VHS-quality. Other MPEG standards, such as MPEG-7, and MPEG-21, are for applications other than broadcast television.

MPEG-1	A standard, adopted by MPEG (see above), formally denoted ISO/IEC 11172, optimized for SD video data rates of about 1.5 Mb/s and having approximately VHS quality.
MPEG-2	A standard, adopted by MPEG (see above), co-published as ISO/IEC 13818 and ITU-T standard Rec. H.262), optimized for SD and HD at data rates of 4 Mb/s and higher.
MPEG-3	There is no MPEG-3. The term is sometimes mistakenly applied to MPEG Audio Layer III; see *MP3 (.mp3),* above.
MPEG-4	A set of standards promulgated by ISO and ITU-T MPEG; however, as commonly used, MPEG-4 is an ambiguous term:

1 MPEG-4 Part 2, formally known as ISO/IEC 14496-2 ("Part 2"), and informally known as SP/ASP; intended for low bit rate applications such as mobile and handheld broadcasting, but largely superseded in commercial applications by H.264.

2 MPEG-4 Part 10, formally known as ISO/IEC 14496-10 ("Part 10") defines a video compression scheme used for broadcast. To avoid confusion with MPEG-4 Part 2 (SP/ASP), MPEG-4 Part 10 is better denoted by its ITU-T designation, H.264; see *H.264,* on page 623.

MPEG-4 Part 2 ASP	Formally, ISO/IEC 14496-2 ("Part 2"): A standard for video compression intended for low bit rate applications such as mobile and handheld broadcasting; it has been largely superseded commercially by H.264.
MPEG IMX	A component SD digital videotape format introduced by Sony for professional use, utilizing $\frac{1}{2}$-inch tape in Beta-type cassettes and recording BT.601 $Y'C_BC_R$, 4:2:2 signals based upon either 480i or 576i scanning, mildly compressed to between about 30 Mb/s and 50 Mb/s using MPEG-2, I-frame-only video compression and conveying eight 24-bit uncompressed digital audio streams. Standardized as SMPTE D-10.
MVC	Multiview Video Coding: A mechanism standardized in Annex H of H.264 to efficiently code two or more pictures that are temporally coincident and highly spatially correlated, usually the left and right images of a stereo pair.
MXF	Material eXchange Format: A container or "wrapper" file format for exchange of professional digital video and audio media ("essence") and associated metadata, defined by SMPTE ST 377 and related standards.
ND	Neutral density: an optical filter having uniform transmittance across the visible spectrum.
NDF	Nondropframe. See *dropframe,* on page 614.
NG	No good. Common Japanese technical acronym; opposite of OK.

NHK 日本放送協会	Nippon Hoso Kyokai (Japan Broadcasting Corporation): The organization that invented HDTV.
nit [nt]	Colloquial term – derived from the Latin *nitere,* to shine – for the SI unit for luminance, $cd \cdot m^{-2}$. See $cd \cdot m^{-2}$, on page 600.
nonlinear	**1** A process that does not exhibit mathematical linearity; see *linear (adj.),* on page 634.
	2 Storage or processing of audio or video where the arrangement of data on the media is *not* in direct correspondence to the timeline. Magnetic tape is sometimes referred to as "linear" media; hard drive media is sometimes called "nonlinear."
normal line sync	In analog SD, a line sync pulse that remains at sync level for about 4.7 μs. In interlaced systems, the leading edge of equalization and broad pulses are utilized as line syncs.
notch filter	In a composite video decoder, circuitry that separates chroma from a composite signal using a simple bandpass filter centered at the colour subcarrier frequency. A notch filter introduces dot crawl artifacts into any picture that has luma detail at frequencies near the colour subcarrier.
NPM	Normalized primary matrix: A 3×3 matrix which, when matrix-multiplied by a linear-light *RGB* column vector on the right, produces an *XYZ* column vector. The middle row of an NPM gives the luminance coefficients for a set of display primaries. Owing to normalization, the middle row sums to unity.
nt	Abbreviation for *nit [nt]*, see above.
NTSC, National Television System Committee	**1** The group, now referred to as *NTSC-I*, that in 1941 standardized 525-line, 60.00 Hz field rate, interlaced monochrome television in the United States.
	2 The group, formally referred to as *NTSC-II*, that in 1953 standardized 525-line, 59.94 Hz field rate, interlaced colour television in the United States. NTSC-II introduced the composite video technique.
	3 A method of composite video encoding based on quadrature modulation of *I* and *Q* (or *U* and *V*) colour difference components onto a colour subcarrier, then summing the resulting chroma signal with luma. Used only with 480*i* scanning, with a subcarrier frequency nominally $\frac{455}{2}$ times the horizontal line rate (i.e., a subcarrier frequency of about 3.579545 MHz).
	4 Often imprecisely used to denote 480*i*29.97 (525/59.94) scanning or 480*i*29.97 image format.
NTSC-J	NTSC as practiced in Japan: NTSC **(3)** with zero setup (and luma and chroma levels modified accordingly).

NTSC-legal	The condition where an NTSC signal is *R'G'B'*-legal and additionally has no chroma content that would cause the composite signal to exceed +120 units.
octave	Factor of 2, one $\log_2$ unit. Usually applied to frequency. [A factor of 2 in amplitude is a *stop (f-stop, T-stop)*; see page 659.]
odd field	In 480*i* (interlaced) scanning, the field whose first broad pulse is coincident with line sync. Compare *even field,* on page 618. The terms *odd* and *even* should be avoided, and *first* and *second* used instead as appropriate.
OECF	Opto-electronic conversion function. The function that maps estimated tristimulus value in a scene into an *R'G'B'* video component signal value. A typical OECF resembles a power function whose exponent lies between 0.4 and 0.5; however, OECF is routinely subject to various creative manipulations that cause it to diverge from a power function. Standards such as BT.709 and SMPTE 274M purport to standardize OECF, but those standards are useful only for engineering purposes and not for video production. See also *gamma, encoding* (γ_E), on page 621.
OETF	Opto-electronic transfer function. See *OECF (above).* The acronym OECF is preferred owing to its being firmly established in ISO standards such as ISO 22028.
OFDM	Orthogonal frequency-division multiplexing. In video transmission, OFDM is always applied to digital data, and referred to as *coded;* see *COFDM* on page 604.
offset sampling	A digital image format in which samples of one image row are offset horizontally by one-half the sample pitch from samples of the previous image row. Also known as *quincunx sampling.* Contrasted with *orthogonal sampling,* which is now ubiquitous.
OP-Atom	In MXF (see page 641), an operational pattern wherein video and audio tracks are stored in separate files. See SMPTE ST 390. Used in Panasonic's P2.
OP1a	In MXF (see page 641), a simple operational pattern in which video and associated audio are interleaved and stored in one file; typically, audio data is stored nearby the associated video. Used in Sony's XDCAM. OP1a is sometimes described as having "self-contained essence."
open (caption, subtitle, etc.)	*Open,* in the context of auxiliary information for the consumer that originates from nonimage sources, refers to information that is composited onto the image at some point in the production or distribution chain. (Contrasted with *closed,* referring to information embedded in metadata and only available to viewers having suitable, enabled decoding equipment.) Technical information that is composited onto the image but which is not intended for consumers is called *burnt-in.*

optical density	The base-10 logarithm of the reciprocal of transmission through partially absorbing optical material (in cinema, either negative or positive film). Various spectral weightings are used.
Opto-electronic conversion function	See *OECF,* above.
orthogonal sampling	A digital image format in which samples of one image row are vertically aligned with samples of the previous line of the field (or frame). Contrasted with offset sampling (see above).
OTA	Over-the-air: Terrestrial UHF broadcasting (implicitly DTV).
OTT	Over-the-top: Any system for video delivery that bypasses the traditional OTA, cable, and satellite providers.
overscan	The unfortunate practice, common in consumer electronics, of signal processing that crops some number of image rows at the top and bottom edges and some number of image columns at the left and right edges, then spatially expands by a factor slightly greater than 1. Overscan between about 3% and 5% is common in consumer HD equipment. If a source having 1920×1080 structure is displayed on a native 1920×1080 display, then overscan is unnecessary. If overscan is used, picture elements will be lost and scaling artifacts are likely.
P-field	In MPEG, a field-coded P-picture. P-fields come in pairs (either top then bottom, or bottom then top). See *P-picture,* below.
P-frame	In MPEG, either a frame-coded P-picture, or a pair of P-fields (one top field and one bottom field, in either order). See *P-picture,* below.
P-picture	In MPEG, a predictive-coded picture: A picture, or coded picture information, in which one or more macroblocks are predicted from a preceding anchor picture, and which may itself be used as the basis of subsequent predictions. P-pictures exploit temporal coherence.
P2	Panasonic flash-memory video storage media, based upon the 32-bit PCMCIA/Cardbus interface.
P3	See *DCI P3, on page 611.*
packed, packed pixel	In the context of storage of pixels in memory, see *interleaved, component interleaved,* on page 628.
paint, painting (*v.*)	With respect to camera signal processing, the act of adjusting gain, black level ("pedestal"), OECF ("gamma"), and other parameters in order to overcome technical deficiencies and/or to achieve a desired æsthetic effect. See also *shading,* on page 657.
PAL (phase alternate line, or phase alternation line)	**1** A composite video standard comparable to NTSC, except that the modulated *V* colour difference component inverts phase on

alternate scan lines, and burst meander is applied. Usually used in 576*i* systems with a subcarrier frequency of 4.433618750 MHz, but also used with subcarriers of about 3.58 MHz in PAL-N and PAL-M analog broadcasting.

2 Often incorrectly used to denote 576*i* (625/50) scanning.

PAR, pixel aspect ratio	Properly, *SAR, sample aspect ratio*; see page 655.
parade	Presentation of three signal components (usually red, green, and blue) in sequential order on a waveform display.
pathological sequence	In SDI or HD-SDI, an encoded bit-serial sequence (or the pixel values causing such a sequence) that presents a long string of consecutive like-valued bits in the channel (many 0s or many 1s), potentially leading to PLL stress or equalizer stress.
P_B, P_R	Scaled colour difference components, blue and red, used in component analog video: Versions of B' minus luma ($B'-Y'$) and R' minus luma ($R'-Y'$) scaled for excursion nominally identical to luma for component analog transmission. P_B and P_R in the range ±0.5 according to the EBU N10 standard are equivalent to C_B and C_R scaled by the factor $1/224$; however, various different industry standards are in wide use for 480*i*. See also C_B, C_R, on page 598, and *U, V,* on page 662.
PDP	Plasma display panel.
PDR, perfect diffuse reflector	A perfectly Lambertian diffuse (nonspecular) 100% reflector. A PDR is well approximated by pressed titanium dioxide or magnesium oxide powder.
peak white	The maximum value of absolute luminance, relative luminance, or luma. Distinguished from *reference white:* Studio video systems typically allow signals to excurse to a peak somewhat above reference white – for BT.601 and BT.709, peak white luma, R', G', or B' lies at $^{238}/_{219}$ of the reference black to reference white excursion; with 2.4-gamma, peak white luminance is about 1.23 times reference white luminance.
pedestal	**1** black level (see page 595) expressed as an offset in voltage or units relative to blanking level. Conventionally 7.5 units (about 54 mV) in 480*i* SD and zero in all other systems (where blanking level and black level are identical). Pedestal is properly an offset or a level; it is incorrect to express pedestal as a percentage. See also *setup,* on page 657.
	2 In camera or processing equipment, adjustment of *pedestal* (**1**). In a camera, provision may be made for operator adjustment of pedestal in the linear-light domain (i.e., prior to application of the opto-electronic transfer function, OECF).
percent	In general, one hundredth. In video and digital cinema, some uses (e.g., 18%) refer to relative luminance (in the linear-light domain). Other uses (e.g., 109%) refer to the encoded Y', R',

	G', or *B'* signal (in the gamma-corrected, perceptual domain); in that case, *IRE* and/or *unit* are synonymous.
PH	Picture height, the basis for a relative measure of viewing distance.
PHASE	Means accessible to the studio technician to adjust composite NTSC or PAL subcarrier phase. The associated consumer control is preferably called HUE – see *hue* (**4**, on page 626).
photometric *(adj.)*	Relating to a quantity of light, proportional to power or energy, that has been weighted spectrally by a function similar or identical to the CIE luminous efficiency function [denoted $V(\lambda)$ or $\bar{y}(\lambda)$]. See also *radiometric (adj.),* on page 651.
photopic	Pertaining to vision at adaptation levels above about 3 nt, where the retina's rod cells are inactive ("pho-*TAH*-pick").
picture	An ordered set of image rows (or historically, scan lines) covering the height of the picture. In a progressive system, the whole frame; in an interlaced system, either a top field or a bottom field.
picture excursion	The excursion from blanking to reference white. In 480*i*, 100 units by definition. In analog System M, $\frac{5}{7}$ V (about 714 mV); in other systems, particularly 576*i* and HD, 700 mV. Confusingly, in 480*i* systems having setup, *picture* in this term includes blanking (nonpicture information) occupying levels from 0 units to 7.5 units.
picture rendering	Encoding and subsequent decoding of estimated relative luminance – or, in a colour system, estimated tristimulus values – incorporating correction for effects owing to display characteristics and viewing environment characteristics so that colour appearance is correctly presented. In video, picture rendering is imposed by the combination of encoding to approximately the 0.5-power of scene tristimulus value, and decoding with a 2.4-power function; an end-to-end power function exponent of approximately 1.2 results.
pillarbox	An image, with an aspect ratio such as 4:3, conveyed or presented at correct aspect ratio in a format having a wider aspect ratio (such as 16:9), using the full height of the widescreen format but not using the full width. The term echoes *letterbox;* in common language in the U.K., a pillarbox is a tall postbox.
pixel	Picture element. Unfortunately, a deeply ambiguous term:

1 Historically, in greyscale digital imaging in general, and greyscale ("monochrome") video in particular, the quantized sample value specific to a single spatial sampling site in an image.

2 Historically, in colour digital imaging in general and colour video in particular, and in modern systems that accomplish colour separation or recombination using optical superposition, a set of three spatially coincident colour component samples; perhaps augmented by spatially coincident data such as opacity (*alpha* or *key*) data. Even in its historical interpretation, the term *pixel* is ambiguous when chroma subsampling is involved.

3 In the terminology of digital still cameras – and, by extension, in mosaic-sensor-based digital cinema cameras – any single colour component sample.

To resolve the ambiguity, I suggest using the term *triplet* to refer to a set of three spatially coincident colour samples, and the term *photosite* to refer to an image sensor element.

pixel intensity	See *intensity* (**3**, on page 628). Because imaging systems are rarely designed to have pixel values proportional to (physical) intensity, the term *pixel value* (see below) is preferred.
pixel-by-pixel, pixel-mapped,	A system or subsystem that maps optical samples to pixels (or pixels to optical samples) without the necessity for image data resampling. Sometimes called *dot-by-dot;* sometimes known by trade names such as *Just Scan.*
pixel value, PV	The numerical value of a component of a pixel, ordinarily a whole number representable in 8, 10, 12, 16, or some other number of bits, in certain cases represented in floating point form (e.g., OpenEXR).
PJ	Abbreviation, commonly used in Japanese, for projector.
PLUGE	*Picture line-up generator:* Originally, equipment, but now a test signal, that produces video signal elements slightly below reference black, exactly reference black, and slightly above reference black, to aid a technician in setting display equipment BLACK LEVEL. Modern standards for PLUGE call for 8-bit interface codes 12, 16, 20, and 24 (about –2%, 0%, +2%, and +4%).
planar	A method of storing pixels whereby like components of an image occupy adjacent storage locations. A 3×2 8-bit *RGB* image could be stored in the order RRRRRRGGGGGGBBBBBB. Also known as *band sequential* (BSQ), *plane interleaved,* or (confusingly, in Photoshop) *per channel.* Distinguished from *interleaved, component interleaved* (page 628), and *band-interleaved by line (BIL)* (page 594).
PNM	Pulse number modulation: A process that produces apparently continuous sample values by altering the number of pulses present per frame time. Each pulse is typically much shorter than a frame time. Sometimes loosely called PWM; see page 649.
postage stamp	When an image at 16:9 aspect ratio is padded with bars top and bottom for conveyance in a 4:3 container, then subsequently the 4:3 container is padded out to 16:9 format by the

power function	A function of the form $y = x^a$ (where a is constant). Distinguished from *exponential function*, which has the form $y = a^x$ (where a is constant). Gamma correction in video is often approximated as a power function $V = L^{\gamma_E}$, where γ_E (the *encoding gamma*) symbolizes a numerical parameter typically having a value between about 0.4 and 0.5.
power loading	A phenomenon of PDP signal processing whereby above a certain requested tristimulus value (R, G, or B) the displayed value is reduced from that requested. The power limit is imposed to prevent excessive heating of the panel. See *ABL*, on page 590. Sometimes inaccurately called *luminance loading*.
precision	The degree to which repeated measurements under unchanged conditions show the same results. Distinguished from *accuracy* (page 590).
proc amp	Processing amplifier: A unit of processing equipment that has at least GAIN and OFFSET (BLACK LEVEL) controls, and if intended for composite video, CHROMA GAIN and CHROMA PHASE controls.
production aperture	The active samples of a video format: The pixel array, comprising S_{AL} image columns and L_A image rows.
progressive	A scanning standard or image format in which spatially adjacent picture lines are associated with consecutive periodic (or identical) instants in time. Examples are 1080*p*24 and 720*p*60. Distinguished from *interlace*. See also *PsF*, below.
ProRes	A family of proprietary intraframe codecs developed by Apple, compressing 10-bit video to data rates between about 82 Mb/s and 264 Mb/s.
proxy	A subsampled (relatively low pixel-count) image, or sequence of images, used to represent an image or a sequence that would require substantial storage, network, or compute resources if represented directly.
pseudocolour	Image data wherein each pixel (typically 8 bits) represents a scalar colour index value. Pseudocolour image data is accompanied by a CLUT (see page 603) that maps each possible index value to an $R'G'B'$ triplet. Each encoded data value is a whole number (typically 0 ... 255) proportional to the $^1/_{2.2}$-power of the associated additive *RGB* display tristimulus value.
PsF	Progressive segmented frame: A transport scheme for progressive imagery whereby image rows are rearranged to resemble an interlaced scheme for transmission or recording. Unlike interlace, the first and second fields of the transmission format are temporally coincident and are properly displayed during the

DIGITAL VIDEO AND HD ALGORITHMS AND INTERFACES

same time interval. No vertical filtering is necessary at origination. Correct reconstruction is achieved by simply weaving the transmission fields back into a frame. The technique is ordinarily used at 24 fps; see *24PsF*, on page 587.

PSF

Point spread function.

PSNR

Peak (to peak) signal to noise ratio. The ratio – ordinarily expressed in decibels, computed as 20 times the base-10 log of the arithmetic ratio – of peak-to-peak signal to RMS noise. PSNR can apply to a physically related quantity such as luminance, but is usually applied to a nonlinearly coded quantity such as luma or *R'G'B'*.

pulldown

The term is ambiguous, potentially referring to two different processes used individually or in combination:

1 2-3 pulldown: The process of converting 24 fps material to 60 fps, or 23.976 fps material to 59.94 fps, by repeating first 2 pictures then 3 pictures. See *2-3 pulldown*, on page 582.

2 Alteration of the picture rate of video or the sampling rate of digital audio by the factor $^{1000}/_{1001}$ (about –0.1%), by reclocking without altering any sample values; for example, to represent 30.00 fps video at 29.97 fps, or audio recorded at 48.048 kHz at 48 kHz.

pullup

Alteration of the picture rate of video or the sampling rate of digital audio by the factor $^{1001}/_{1000}$ (about +0.1%), by simply reclocking without altering any sample values; for example, to represent video recorded at 29.97 fps at 30.00 fps.

PW, peak white

See peak white, on page 645.

PWM

Historically, pulse width modulation: A process that produces apparently continuous sample values by altering the width of each pulse in a train of binary (off/on) pulses occurring at a fixed, high rate. Strictly speaking, modern displays such as PDP and DLP do not use PWM; see *PNM*, on page 647.

QAM

Quadrature amplitude modulation: A modulation system wherein two information signals independently modulate two subcarriers that are in *quadrature* (that is, offset in phase by 90°), which are then summed to form the modulated subcarrier. An analog version of QAM, usually called just *quadrature modulation*, combines two colour difference components onto a colour subcarrier in NTSC and PAL composite video. A digital version of QAM is used for RF modulation in some digital television transmission systems (e.g., 16-QAM, 64-QAM), particularly for cable television.

QCIF

Quarter common intermediate format: In ITU-T standards for videoconferencing (e.g., H.261), a progressively scanned raster with 4:2:0 chroma subsampling having 176×144 luma samples at 29.97 frames per second. QCIF image data is ordinarily subsampled from SD. See *CIF, common intermediate format,* on page 602.

QPSK

Quadrature phase-shift keying: A modulation system wherein the modulating signal alters the phase of a carrier (or subcarrier). In video, digital QPSK is used for RF modulation.

Quad-HD

Video systems having 3840×2160 image format, comparable to 4 K.

quantization

The process of assigning a discrete, numbered level to each of two or more intervals of amplitude of a data value. (In video or audio, there are typically hundreds or thousands of intervals.) In the usual *uniform quantization,* the *steps* between levels have equal amplitude. Quantization can be performed upon sample values in the time domain (e.g., audio), upon sample values in the spatial domain (e.g., images or video), or upon transform coefficients (e.g., in DCT or wavelet-based compression algorithms).

quasi-interlace

Term in consumer electronics denoting progressive segmented frame; see *PsF,* on page 648.

quasilog

Partially log. Typical "log *RGB*" image coding is usually more accurately called quasilog because a small offset (often about $^1/_{60}$ or $^1/_{90}$ of the reference black-to-white range in the linear-light scale) is introduced prior to taking the logarithm.

QuickTime

1 Apple's trademark identifying a system for encoding, recording, decoding, and playing back realtime media on computers.

2 A proxy represented in a QuickTime format.

quincunx sampling

Synonymous with *offset sampling;* see page 643. The term became obsolete in the early 1990s, but was resurrected around 2008 for stereoscopic video. The term stems from the arrangement of club, diamond, heart, or spade symbols on a playing card of value five. The term is misleading: There is nothing special about the eponymous geometrical arrangement of five samples, and it would be nonsensical to tile an image array with that pattern.

R'G'B'

Red, green, and blue nonlinear primary components. The prime symbol makes gamma correction explicit: *R', G',* and *B'* denote *RGB* tristimulus signals that are intended to be converted to tristimulus through a power function *EOCF* (page 617) having an exponent between about 2.0 and 2.6. The precise colour interpretation of *RGB* values depends on the characteristics of the *RGB* primaries; see *RGB,* below.

R'–Y'

See *B'-Y', R'-Y',* on page 594.

radiance

Radiant flux per unit projected area.

raw	Image data encoding wherein no picture rendering and no chroma subsampling has taken place. Usually, image data is in scene-referred, linear-light form (though some systems use nonlinear conversion functions); usually, no compression has been applied (though some systems use wavelet or other compression schemes).
radiometric *(adj.)*	Relating to a quantity of light, proportional to power or energy, that has been weighted uniformly across some (wide) region of the spectrum. Distinguished from *photometric (adj.)* (page 646).
RCT	In JPEG2000, reversible colour transform: A mapping producing $Y'C_BC_R$ from $R'G'B'$ using simple binary integer luma coefficients $[^1/_4, \ ^1/_2, \ ^1/_4]$. Called "reversible" because it is perfectly invertible in fixed-point binary arithmetic without roundoff error. Compare *ICT*, on page 627.
Rec. 601	See *BT.601*, on page 597.
Rec. 709	See *BT.709*, on page 598.
raster	The pattern of parallel horizontal scan lines that paints out a picture in a system that uses scanning. The raster is the static spatial pattern that is refreshed with successive frames of video. Historically relates to an entire scanning pattern (including blanking intervals); in modern usage, may relate to image alone.
reference black	The reference level for abstract video signal value 0. In an 8-bit system, code 16; in a 10-bit system, code 64; historically, in 480*i*, 7.5 units; in all other systems, 0 units. The absolute luminance displayed for reference black in the studio depends upon the studio technician's setting of BLACK LEVEL (using PLUGE); for 100 nt white, it is typically between 0.01 nt and 0.1 nt.
reference picture	In interframe compression, a picture, or coded picture information that is available as the basis for prediction of a subsequent picture in transmission order. (It is misleading to refer to an reference *frame*, because when MPEG-2 or H.264 is used with interlaced video, a picture may comprise a single field.) Also called *anchor picture*.
reference white	The video signal level corresponding to white (100 units by definition), or the corresponding relative or absolute luminance. In video, it is standard for reference white to have the colorimetric properties of CIE Illuminant D_{65} (except in Japan and in certain other Asian regions where the standard white reference is 9300 K). As I write, there is no effective standard for the luminance of white, but most studios use about 100 nt.
relative luminance	See *luminance, relative*, on page 636.
rendering	**1** Depiction of a scene, usually involving an æsthetic treatment.

2 A software process to convert a synthetic scene described in geometric primitives into a raster image, or a sequence of raster images. The process is usually slower than realtime.

3 (picture rendering) Application of algorithmic processes to raster image data to impose the appearance associated with a particular display and/or viewing condition.

reordering

In compression systems such as MPEG-2 and H.264, when B-pictures are used they are reconstructed at the decoder from reference pictures that must already be present at the decoder. Transmission order is therefore different from display order.

resampling

The process of estimating, from a given set of samples, the samples that would have been produced had sampling taken place at different instants or at different positions.

resolution

A heavily overloaded term that, strictly speaking, refers to spatial or temporal properties of a bandlimited continuous analog signal or its sampled digital representation:

1 Generally, a measure of the ability of an imaging system or component, or of human vision, to delineate picture detail.

2 In image science, horizontal resolution in cycles per picture width [C/PW] is the maximum number of line pairs (where each "pair" comprises a black line and a white line) that can be visually discriminated from a test chart containing vertically disposed alternating black and white lines (square wave).

3 In image science, vertical resolution in cycles per picture height [C/PH] is the maximum number of cycles that can be visually discriminated per picture height from a test chart containing horizontally disposed alternating black and white lines.

4 Traditionally, in analog video, if unqualified by *horizontal* or *vertical*, horizontal resolution: twice the number of vertical black and white pairs (cycles) that can be visually discerned across a horizontal distance equal to the picture height, expressed in TVL/PH or colloquially, "*TV lines*" (see page 662). Horizontal resolution in video is sometimes expressed in units of megahertz. Also known casually as *limiting resolution;* see IEEE Std. 208.

5 In computing, *resolution* usually refers to pixel count, the count of image columns and image rows of a device or an image (that is, the number or columns and rows in the pixel array), without regard to the amount of picture detail carried or displayed.

6 Often improperly used to refer to the number of quantization levels (or bits per sample).

7 Often improperly used to express what is properly called sample density, for example in "dots per inch" [dpi].

reverse telecine	See *inverse telecine*, on page 629.
RF modulation	In video, a composite video signal that has been modulated onto a *radio frequency* (VHF or UHF) carrier in the range 50 MHz to 1 GHz. RF-modulated video in electrical form is usually conveyed with coaxial cable using Type-F (cable TV) connectors. Historically, NTSC consumer video signals conveyed from a video source to a receiver are often RF modulated onto channel 3 or channel 4 (both VHF).
RFF, repeat first field	In a compressed video bitstream (such as MPEG-2 or H.264) conveying an interlaced picture, a bit that asserts that the first field should be repeated to reconstruct a display at 2.5 times the frame rate represented in the compressed sequence. RFF enables the decoder to reconstruct the intended 2:3 pulldown.
RGB	**1** Strictly, red, green, and blue tristimulus components (linear-light). The precise colour interpretation of *RGB* values depends on the *chromaticity coordinates* of the primaries and the chromaticity coordinates of reference white. Different primary chromaticities are specified by the FCC 1953 NTSC standard (obsolete), SMPTE RP 145, EBU Tech. 3213, and BT.709; however, BT.709 is ubiquitous today in the consumer domain.
	2 Loosely, red, green, and blue nonlinear primary components, properly denoted *R'G'B'* (page 650).
RGBA	**1** In video and computing, red, green, blue, and alpha (key).
	2 In LEDs, red, green, blue, and amber.
RMS	Root-mean-square: A set of numbers, individually squared, then arithmetically averaged (to form the mean value), then square-rooted. (The order of operations is right-to-left: *square*, then *mean*, then *root*.) Equivalent to Euclidean distance.
rolling shutter	In an image sensor, operation (or resulting data) wherein exposure of successive image rows is delayed by a certain fixed time interval from the previous row. The last image row is exposed a significant fraction of the frame time later than the first row. (Opposed to *global shutter*; see page 623.)
RSR	Relative spectral response: The response of one colour channel of a sensor or camera to an elemental band of wavelength, in arbitrary units having dimensions of flux per unit wavelength.
RTP	Realtime Transport Protocol: A set of IP protocols for realtime streaming (typically, of video) defined by RFC 3550.
rushes	Synonym for *dailies* (see page 610).
S-HD, S-HDTV	Super high-definition [television]: Experimental video systems with a 3840×2160 image format (frame rate is undecided).

S-video	An analog interface conveying luma (Y') and quadrature-modulated chroma (C) separately on a specific four-pin mini-DIN connector. S-video is not exactly component video, and not exactly composite video. There are three types of S-video: *S-video-525*, *S-video-525-J* (used in Japan), and *S-video-625*. S-video uses quadrature modulation. If a VCR has an S-video interface, its S-video signal almost certainly does not exhibit frequency interleaving – the colour subcarrier is likely incoherent.
S_{AL}, samples per active line	The count of luma samples in a scan line that are permitted by a scanning standard to convey picture (and the associated blanking transitions). Digital video systems typically store just active samples. In modern terms, the number of columns of image samples (N_C).
S_{PW}, samples per picture width	The number of samples in a scan line corresponding to the width of the picture, measured at the 50% points of a white flatfield. In modern terminology, the count of image columns.
S_{TL}, samples per total line	The number of sample intervals between consecutive 0_H instants in a scanning standard.
S/PDIF	Sony/Philips digital interface: An interface specified in IEC 60958 (formerly IEC 958) for uncompressed consumer digital audio.
S3D	Stereoscopic, 3-dimensional: Imagery created, acquired, processed, or displayed with a pair of views, one intended for the viewer's left eye and the other for the right. The term *S3D* distinguishes stereoscopic imagery from planar raster images created from 3D models (e.g., computer-generated imagery).
SAD	Sum of absolute differences. A particular similarity metric commonly used in algorithms for motion estimation whereby pixel values of a reference macroblock are subtracted from pixel values from a displaced target macroblock, absolute values of the differences are formed, then the sum is computed. The task is computationally intensive. See also *MAE,* on page 638.
sample	**1** The value of a bandlimited, continuous signal at an instant of time and/or space. Usually, but not necessarily, quantized.
	2 Component; see page 606.
	See also S_{PW}, *samples per picture width* and S_{TL}, *samples per total line,* on page 654.
sampling, 1-D	The process of forming, from a continuous bandlimited one-dimensional function of time, a series of discrete values, each of which is a function of the distribution of intensity across a small time interval. *Uniform sampling*, where the time intervals are of equal duration, is nearly always used.

sampling, 2-D	The process of assigning, to each element of a sampling grid (or lattice), a value that is a function of the distribution of intensity over the corresponding small area of the image plane. In digital video and in conventional image processing, the samples lie on a regular, rectangular grid.
SAR, sample aspect ratio	The ratio of horizontal distance between luma (or RGB) samples to vertical distance between samples. HD standards have square sampling (where SAR is unity).
saturation	**1** The condition that a signal has reached the maximum value that can be carried on the circuit or channel on which it is being carried. More accurately called *clipping* (see *clip*, on page 603).
	2 The condition that exposure to a high light level in a scene has caused an image sensor (or channel) to reach *saturation* (**1**).
	3 In colour science, colour saturation: *The colourfulness of an area judged in proportion to its brightness* [CIE]. Subjective, by definition. Saturation runs from neutral grey through pastel to saturated colours. Roughly speaking, the more an SPD is concentrated at one wavelength, the more saturated the associated colour becomes. A colour can be desaturated by adding light that contains power distributed across a wide range of wavelengths.
	4 The radius of a colour difference value as displayed on a vectorscope (in polar coordinates), ordinarily in C_B, C_R coordinates for component digital video (or historically in P_B, P_R coordinates for component analog video or *U, V* coordinates for composite video). Loosely, chroma.
	5 SATURATION: User-accessible means to adjust colour *saturation* (**4**), typically implemented by altering chroma (C_B, C_R) gain; preferably labelled CHROMA.
SAV	Start of active video: A sequence of four words inserted into a 4:2:2 component digital video data stream, marking the start of active samples on a line. See also *EAV, TRS*.
sawtooth artifact	See *zipper artifact*.
SbS	Side-by-side: A frame-packing scheme for stereo 3-D whereby left and right images are subsampled 2:1 horizontally then assembled horizontally into one picture for transmission.
scaling (*v.*)	**1** Generally, and in mathematics, multiplying by a constant factor.
	2 With respect to image data samples, the process of multiplying by a constant factor (for example, to effect video gain).
	3 Term used in desktop computing and consumer electronics referring to the process of resizing – by the same factor, and without temporal filtering – every image in an image sequence.

Scaling converts from one image format to another having different spatial structure (image row and column counts), interpolating to increase pixel count or decimating to decrease pixel count. Also called *upconversion* or *downconversion;* historically, *scan conversion.*

scaler

A subsystem to accomplish *scaling* (3). Not to be confused with *scalar.*

scan conversion

Conversion, without temporal filtering, between video signals having different sampling structures.

scanning standard

The set of parameters of raster scanning of video equipment or a video signal. Historically, a scanning standard was denoted by its total line count and its field rate (in hertz), separated by a virgule (slash); for example, 525/59.94, 625/50, or 1125/60. Interlace was implicit. Modern preference is to provide image format notation, comprising the count of picture lines, *p* for progressive or *i* for interlace, and the frame rate; for example, 480*i*29.97, 576*i*25, 720*p*60, 1080*i*30, or 1080*p*60.

scene-linear

An image signal whose pixel component values are proportional to tristimulus values (or estimates of them) in the scene.

scene-referred

An image signal that has a well-defined mapping (such as a quasi-power function, or a quasilog function) to tristimulus values (or estimates of them) in the scene.

scotopic

Pertaining to vision adapted to very low light levels, below about 0.1 nt, where only the retina's rod cells are active.

screen (*n.*)

1 Generally, a surface upon which a display image is formed.

2 An archaic term; see *bias* (**2**).

SD

Standard definition (video). There is no official definition, but generally, a video system having frame rate 23.976 Hz or greater whose digital image comprises fewer than about $^3/_4$ million pixels. The most widely deployed SD studio and broadcasting systems are 480*i* (see page 588) and 576*i* (see page 588). See also SDTV, below. The term *SDTV* implies transmission or recording of entertainment programming.

SDI

Serial digital interface: A SMPTE-standard studio video interface having data rate between 143 Mb/s and 360 Mb/s (usually 270 Mb/s). Usually, uncompressed SD video is conveyed, though the SDTI variant may be used to wrap compressed data (such as from D-7). See also *HD-SDI,* on page 624.

SDI-safe

A signal that excludes codes 0 and 255 (in 8-bit code) or 0–3 and 1020–1023 (in 10-bit code), avoiding the TRS codes required for synchronization across an SDI or HD-SDI interface.

SDTI	Serial data transmission interface: A SMPTE-standard variant of SDI used to convey arbitrary data (or compressed video data) instead of uncompressed digital video.
SDTV	Standard-definition television. See SD, above. *SDTV* implies transmission or recording of entertainment programming.
SECAM	*Séquential couleur avec mémoire:* An obsolete *composite video (1)* system based on line-alternate B'–Y' and R'–Y' colour difference signals, frequency modulated onto a subcarrier, then summed with luma. Neither quadrature modulation nor frequency interleaving was used. SECAM was used for broadcast in certain countries with 576*i* scanning (e.g., France and Russia). There was no SECAM production equipment: 576*i* component equipment or PAL composite equipment was used instead; signals were transcoded to SECAM at transmission.
second field	In interlaced scanning, the second field of the pair of fields comprising a frame. In analog 480*i*, the field containing the top image row (whose first equalization pulse starts midline). In analog 576*i*, the field whose first broad pulse starts at midline. (See also *field dominance*, and *first field, on page 619*.)
serration	**1** In bilevel analog sync, the interval between the end of a broad pulse and the start of the following sync pulse. This term refers to the absence of a pulse rather than the presence of one, and is deprecated in favor of the terms *equalization, broad,* and *normal* sync pulses.
	2 See *zipper artifact*.
setup	Reference black level expressed as a percentage of the blanking-to-reference-white excursion. In modern video systems, blanking level and black level are identical, so setup is zero. Setup is 7.5% in 480*i* SD in North America. Setup is properly expressed as a percentage: It is incorrect to express setup in voltage, level, or units. See also *pedestal, on page 645*. Confusion notwithstanding, PAL has always had zero setup, and setup has never been present in digital video or HD.
shading (*v.*)	With respect to camera signal processing, the act of imposing position-dependent R, G, and B gain alteration in order to overcome technical deficiencies of a camera optical system. See also *paint, painting (v.), on page 644*.
SHV	Super Hi-Vision; see *Super Hi-Vision* (page 659).
shoulder	That portion of the response of photochemical film at relatively high exposure where the slope of the transfer function decreases significantly compared to the slope at midscale. In camera negative film, scene highlights are exposed on the shoulder. (Video uses the term *knee*.)
sidebar format	An image with an aspect ratio such as 4:3 conveyed or presented in a format having a wider aspect ratio (such as

	16:9), using the full height of the widescreen format but not using the full width. Synonymous with *pillarbox* (see page 646).
sinc	*Sinus cardinalis,* the function $^{(\sin \pi x)}/_{\pi x}$. An argument of 1 corresponds to the sampling frequency. Loosely known as "sine *x* over *x*," see below.
sine *x* over *x*	Colloquial expression for *sinc;* see above (but here π is absent).
SMPTE	**1** Society of Motion Picture and Television Engineers: A professional society and ANSI-accredited standards-writing organization.
	2 In the context of colour standards: SMPTE RP 145, which defines the chromaticities historically used in 480*i* video.
SMPTE 170M	The defining standard for 480*i* 29.97 (525/59.94) NTSC studio video.
SNR	Signal to noise ratio. The ratio – ordinarily expressed in decibels, computed as 20 times the base-10 log of the arithmetic ratio – of peak-to-peak signal to RMS noise. SNR can apply to a physically related quantity such as luminance, or to a nonlinearly coded quantity such as luma. See also *PSNR* (page 649).
SPD	Spectral power distribution: The amount of power (or more usually, radiance) per unit wavelength (in SI units, per nanometer).
SPTS	Single program transport stream: In MPEG-2, a transport stream that contains a single program.
square sampling ("square pixel")	Image sampling wherein horizontal sample pitch is identical to vertical sample pitch. Use *square sampling* instead of "square pixel": The latter term offers the possibility of round pixels.
sRGB	Formally, IEC 61966-2-1: An international standard for *R'G'B'* colour image coding; sRGB incorporates BT.709 primary chromaticities, is display-referred, and has a 2.2-power EOCF.
SStP	Simple Studio Profile: A profile defined in MPEG-4 Part 2. SStP is used by Sony in HDCAM SR.
standards conversion	Conversion, including temporal filtering, of a video input signal having one scanning standard into an output signal having a different image format and a different frame rate. Historically, the output signal had similar pixel count to the input, for example, a 480*i*-to-576*i* standards converter (loosely known as an NTSC-to-PAL standards converter), though today "standards conversion" may incorporate upconversion or downconversion. See *scanning standard,* on page 656. See also *transcoding, scan conversion, downconversion,* and *upconversion.*

stereoscopic	A system that acquires, processes, records, transmits, and/or displays two separate views of a (possibly synthetic) scene, one destined for the viewer's left eye and another for the right.
stop (*f*-stop, *T*-stop)	Factor of 2 (or $10^{0.3}$) of light power, radiance, luminance, tristimulus value, or other amplitude value.
studio-swing	An R', G', B', or Y' signal having reference black-to-white excursion of $219 \cdot 2^{k-8}$, where k ($8 \le k$) is the number of bits in the representation. It is standard to add an offset of $+16 \cdot 2^{k-8}$ at a digital video interface, so the studio-swing range is 16 to 235 at an 8-bit interface and 64 to 940 at a 10-bit interface. In a $Y'C_BC_R$ system, C_BC_R are scaled to have $^{224}/_{219}$ the excursion of Y'. Distinguished from *full-swing* (see page 620).
stutter	A motion artifact whereby image elements in motion appear to move intermittently instead of smoothly, typically caused by temporal disturbances at frequencies of 10 Hz or lower.
subfield, subframe	In a pulse-duration modulated display such as a PDP or DLP, temporal repeating or upsampling of the video signal such that the information is dispersed temporally so as to be relatively uniformly distributed across the frame time. In 2011 it is typical to have between 8 and 12 subframes per frame at 60 Hz. (See also *bit splitting* on page 595.)
subpixel	**1** In a fixed-pixel sensor or display using spatial multiplexing of colour, a colour component of a pixel. A pixel typically comprises red, green, and blue subpixels.
	2 In spatial resampling, the number of potential interpolated (synthetic) positions between two original samples.
Super Hi-Vision	NHK's term for Ultra-HDTV (U-HD, U-HDTV) experimental equipment with an image format of about 7680×4320 ("8 K").
superblack	The condition where an $R'G'B'$ component signal or a luma signal within a picture is intentionally sustained below reference black level for more than a few sample intervals. In studio video, the practice has historically been discouraged.
superwhite	The condition where an $R'G'B'$ component signal or a luma signal within a picture is intentionally sustained above reference white level for more than a few sample intervals. Specular highlights commonly excurse briefly into the headroom region; the term *superwhite* generally relates to content other than speculars. In some consumer gear (e.g., PS3), *SuperWhite* is an option that enables the interface to carry footroom and headroom codes; when not set, interface codes are clipped.
SVC	Scalable video coding: In H.264, A mechanism standardized in Annex G to convey information structured in a hierarchical manner to allow of portions of the bitstream at lower bit rate than the complete sequence to be extracted to enable decoding of pictures with multiple image structures (for

sequences encoded with spatial scalability), pictures at multiple picture rates (for sequences encoded with temporal scalability), and/or pictures with multiple levels of image quality (for sequences encoded with quality scalability).

SxS   Sony flash-memory storage media (pronounced *ess-by-ess*); based upon ExpressCard/34 (not to be confused with CardBus, although both were developed by the PCMCIA organization).

sync (*n*.)   **1** A signal comprising solely the horizontal and vertical timing elements necessary to accomplish synchronization.

2 The component of a video signal that conveys horizontal and vertical synchronization information.

3 *sync level;* see below.

sync (*v*.)   Synchronization, to a video source, of the scan timing of receiving, processing, or display equipment. See also *genlock,* on page 623.

sync level   The analog level of synctip. Conventionally –40 units (–285$\frac{5}{7}$ mV) in System M, and –300 mV in other systems.

System M   Formerly CCIR System M; now properly referred to as ITU-R System M: An archaic designation specifying 480*i* scanning along with certain analog and RF transmission parameters.

TaB   Top-and-bottom: A frame-packing scheme for stereo 3-D whereby left and right images are subsampled 2:1 vertically, then assembled vertically into one picture for transmission.

tandem   Two or more systems or subsystems that are cascaded in series.

telecine   Equipment to scan motion picture film in realtime to produce video or HD. Distinguished from *film scanner,* which typically is slower than realtime. Pronounced *tell-e-SIN-eee.*

theatre black   Luminance (relative or absolute) of a cinema screen when the projector is commanded to produce no light.

timecode   A number of the form *HH:MM:SS:FF* (hours, minutes, seconds, frames) that designates a single frame in a video or cinema motion image sequence.

timing   See *grading,* on page 623. The term *timing,* now obsolete, originated with control of exposure time in photographic printing.

TINT   User-accessible means to adjust hue. Artists use the term "tint" to refer to adding white to a colour, thereby decreasing chroma, so it isn't clear whether TINT is related to hue or to chroma. To avoid ambiguity, this control should be called HUE. (In composite NTSC studio equipment, often called PHASE.)

toe	**1** In photochemical film, that portion of the response at relatively low exposure where the slope of the transfer function in log-log coordinates is significantly less than its slope at midtone exposure. See also *shoulder,* on page 657.
	2 In video, that portion of the camera's OECF that lies within about 2% of optical black. See also *knee,* on page 631.
top field	The field that contains the uppermost coded image row of a frame; typically the second field in 480*i* and 1080*i* and the first field in 576*i*.
TFF, top field first	In a compressed video bitstream (such as MPEG-2 or H.264) conveying an interlaced picture, a bit that asserts that the field containing the uppermost image row should be displayed first in temporal order. Typically negated for 480*i* and HD and asserted for other formats.
transcoding	**1** Traditionally, converting a video signal having one colour-encoding method into a signal having a different colour-encoding method, without altering the scanning standard; for example, 576*i* PAL to 576*i* SECAM.
	2 In compressed digital video distribution, various methods of recoding a compressed bitstream, or decompressing then recompressing.
transition sample	An image data value near the left or right edge of the picture whose amplitude is reduced or forced to blanking level so as to limit the high-frequency content of the video signal at the picture edges.
TRC	Tone reproduction curve, or tone response curve: A (generally nonlinear) function that relates a greyscale or colour signal value to a physical characteristic such as reflectance or relative luminance. The term is common in graphics arts.
triad	In image science, a set of three discrete colour emitting or modulating elements – almost always red, green, and blue – that form an elemental colour picture element. Triads regularly tile the display surface. In an *FPD* (page 620), triads are individually addressable.
trichromaticity	The property of human vision whereby additive mixtures of exactly three properly chosen primary components are necessary and sufficient to match a wide range of colours. That such matching is possible is surprising considering that physical spectra are infinitely variable; but not surprising considering that the human retina contains just three types of colour-sensitive photoreceptor (cone) cells.
trick mode	Achieving usable image display when modes such as pause, fast-forward, rewind, and slow-motion are used in video playback (particularly from videotape).

trilevel sync	Analog HD sync information conveyed by a pulse having a transition from blanking level to +300 mV, then a transition from +300 mV to –300 mV, then a final transition back to blanking level. Standard for HD. Distinguished from *bilevel sync*, used in SD.
tristimulus	One of a set of three component values that together represent relative spectral radiance weighted by a spectral sensitivity function having significance with respect to the trichromaticity of human vision (see *trichromaticity*, above). Tristimulus values (such as L, M, S; R, G, B; or X, Y, Z) are proportional to intensity. *RGB* signals are typically subject to *gamma correction*, forming $R'G'B'$, as part of their conversion into video signals.
TRS	**1** Timing reference signal: A sequence of four words across an SDI or HD-SDI interface that signals sync. See *EAV, on page 616*, and *SAV, on page 655*. **2** Tip, ring, sleeve: A connector – ordinarily 6.35 mm ($1/_4$-inch) in diameter – typically used for unbalanced analog stereo audio.
truecolour	Image data containing encoded values of independent additive components red, green, and blue (symbolized $R'G'B'$); typically, each encoded data value is an 8-bit quantity proportional to the $1/_{2.2}$-power of the associated display tristimulus value.
TrueHD, True 24*p*, etc.	"Truth is relative. It is only a matter of opinion." [Pythagoras] Truth is probabilistic, dependent upon speaker and listener, and upon historical, cultural, social, and technical context. TrueHD, True 24*p* – or "true" anything else – must be qualified by context in order to be meaningful. Be suspicious when a provider of information finds it necessary to tag it with "truth" (or related terms like *fact* or *myth*). For further enlightenment on this subject, consult a Zen master.
TV lines per picture height, TVL/PH	A unit of resolution – in the horizontal, vertical, diagonal, or any other direction – equivalent to half of a cycle spanning the picture height. If a fine vertical pattern of 400 dark/light line pairs (cycles) can just barely be discriminated in a system having 4:3 aspect ratio, then resolution is $3/_4 \cdot 2 \cdot 400$ or 600 TVL/PH. One TV line corresponds to a pixel, or half a cycle; or in film, one line width or half a line pair. C/PH is preferred; see page 599; C/PW may also be used. See also *resolution, on page 652*.
U, V	**1** Historically, colour difference components, blue minus luma $[B'-Y']$ and red minus luma $[R'-Y']$, scaled by the factors 0.492111 and 0.877283, respectively, such that after quadrature modulation the reference excursion of the composite video signal is contained within the range $-1/_3$ ($-33\,1/_3$ units) to $+4/_3$ ($+133\,1/_3$ units). See also $[C_B, C_R]$; $[I, Q]$; $[P_B, P_R]$. **2** In modern usage, the symbols U and V refer to unscaled $B'-Y'$ and $R'-Y'$ components; to C_B and C_R components scaled for component digital transmission; or (most commonly) to P_B and

	P_R components scaled ±0.5 – that is, having the same reference excursion as luma (Y'). (There are many exceptions and errors in the scale factors.)
Ultra-HDTV (U-HD, U-HDTV)	Ultra high-definition [television]: Experimental video systems with a 7680×4320 image structure (frame rate is undecided). Also known as *Super Hi-Vision*.
uncompressed	In video, signal recording or transmission without using JPEG, M-JPEG, MPEG, or wavelet techniques. (Chroma subsampling effects lossy compression with a ratio of about 1.5:1 or 2:1; however, video with chroma subsampling is deemed *uncompressed;* in video, the term *compression* is reserved for transform techniques.)
unit	Loosely, video level expressed in percentage: one-hundredth of the excursion from reference black level (0 units) to reference white level (100 Iunits). Historically, *IRE unit*; see page 630.
upconversion	In video, conversion to an image format, usually at the same frame rate, having substantially higher pixel count (e.g., SD to HD).
upsampling	Resampling where more output samples are produced than the number of input samples provided.
V	See *U, V,* on page 662.
VANC	Vertical interval ancillary data: Ancillary data multiplexed into the vertical blanking interval of an SDI or HD-SDI interface.
valid	The condition where a video signal is *R'G'B'*-legal (see page 632) – that is, where none of the corresponding *R', G',* and *B'* signals exceeds its reference range except perhaps for brief transients.
value	In colour science, measures of lightness apart from CIE *L** (typically expressed in the range 0 to 10).
VBI	See *vertical blanking interval (VBI),* below.
VBR, variable bit rate	Pertaining to a compression format wherein data rate (bit or byte count per second) may vary from one frame to the next.
VC-1	A standard, developed and deployed by Microsoft as part of Windows Media 9, subsequently standardized as SMPTE 421M, for the lossy compression of digital motion images and associated audio. The VC-1 algorithm shares the basic principles of H.264, but differs in many details. VC-1 decoding is mandated in the Blu-ray disc specification.
VC-2	See *Dirac PRO,* on page 613.
VC-3	See *DNxHD,* on page 613.

VCR	Videocassette recorder. Implicitly, consumer-grade: In professional usage, VTR (with *T* for *tape*) is used even if the tape medium is encased in a cassette.
veiling glare	Light from the viewing environment reflected from a display surface, producing unwanted luminance.
vertical blanking interval (VBI)	Those scan lines of a field (or frame) that are precluded by an interface standard from containing picture. The vertical interval may contain nonpicture video, audio, or ancillary information.
vertical frequency	**1** The vertical component of spatial frequency.
	2 In interlaced scanning, field rate; in progressive scanning, frame rate.
vertical interval	Vertical blanking interval (VBI); see above.
vertical sync	Those nonpicture elements of a video signal that delimit the boundary between fields or frames.
video level	*R'G'B'* or *Y'* signal level, in digital video typically expressed as a percentage where 0 corresponds to reference black and 100 corresponds to reference white, or expressed as 8-bit or 10-bit digital interface code values (where the reference range is 16 through 235 or 64 through 940, respectively). Modest excursions outside the reference levels are permitted, generally just for transient content.
visual density	**1** For partially absorbing optical material (such as photochemical film), the base-10 logarithm of the reciprocal of transmission weighted by the CIE luminous efficiency function.
	2 For a light emitting, transmitting, or reflecting element, the base-10 logarithm of the reciprocal of relative luminance.
VITC	Vertical interval timecode: Timecode data encoded in an analog representation and conveyed in the VBI.
VLI	Video line index; see SMPTE RP 186.
VOB	Video object: A container file format used in DVD comprising a restricted MPEG-2 program stream with the addition of private streams specifying elements such as menus and subtitles. (All VOB files are MPEG-2 program streams, but not all MPEG-2 program streams are DVD compliant.) A VOB file contains 2^{20} bytes (1 GiB) or less.
Vorbis (Ogg Vorbis)	An open-source audio compression system; part of WebM.
VP8	An open-source video compression system, originally designed and implemented by On2; part of WebM.
VSB	Vestigial sideband: An RF modulation system. Analog VSB is used in the NTSC and PAL standards for terrestrial television.

DIGITAL VIDEO AND HD ALGORITHMS AND INTERFACES

A form of digital VSB (namely, *8-VSB*) is used in the ATSC standard for terrestrial digital television.

VTR

Videotape recorder. Implies professional: *T* for *tape* is used even if the tape medium is encased in a cassette.

VTVL

Vertical resolution, expressed in units of *TVL*/PH: A unit of vertical resolution used in CCTV and video security systems.

wave number

Reciprocal of wavelength, usually expressed in units of cm^{-1}.

weave

1 In motion picture film, or video originated from film, erratic side-to-side motion of the image owing to imperfect registration of the sprocket holes to the film gate.

2 A deinterlacing technique, common in PC graphics, that merges two fields together, irrespective of interfield motion, to form a frame. Also known as *field merging*. See also *bob*, on page 596. (The terms "bob" and "weave" are said to originate from the sport of boxing.)

WebM

An open-source project sponsored by Google, or the associated video/audio files, based upon the Matroska container format, Vorbis audio compression, and VP8 video compression.

white

See *reference white*, on page 651.

window

1 In general, a rectangular region in an image.

2 A rectangular region – often square and at the centre of an image – occupying about 10% of the total image area, filled with a uniform colour (often white).

working space

In colour management, the colour image encoding space in which the arithmetic of image manipulation is performed.

WTW

Whiter than white. See *superwhite*, on page 659.

WSS

Widescreen signalling: A mechanism implemented in analog transmission of 576*i*25 to signal widescreen image data.

x.v.Color, x.v.Colour

Sony's trademarked terms for xvYCC (see below).

XDCAM

Various systems commercialized by Sony to record and play SD and HD content from optical disc and SxS flash media using various image formats and various compression systems.

XLR3

A connector typically used for audio (either monophonic analog audio, typically about 770 mV RMS into 600 Ω impedance in balanced mode, or stereo digital according to AES3-4, in balanced mode).

xvYCC

A colour coding scheme defined in IEC 61966-2-4, purported to extend $Y'C_BC_R$ to allow chroma excursions outside the $R'G'B'$-legal range to represent wide-gamut colours. SD and HD versions, corresponding to BT.601 and BT.709, are defined. (The acronym is said to represent *extended video, Y'C̲_BC̲_R*.)

XYZ	A particular set of CIE tristimuli: linear-light quantities, where *Y* is luminance relative to a specified white reference.

X'Y'Z' Nonlinear *XYZ* encoded for digital cinema: CIE *XYZ* tristimuli at the reference display, relative to reference white of 48 nt, each subject to a $1/2.6$-power function (inverse EOCF).

Y

1 In physics and colour science, and when used carefully in video and computer graphics, the symbol for the CIE relative luminance tristimulus component, relative to an absolute reference white luminance. See *luminance, relative,* on page 636.

2 In video, in digital image processing, and in computer graphics, the symbol *Y* is often carelessly used to denote *luma* (properly symbolized *Y'*); see *Y'*, below.

Y'

In video, the symbol for luma: A quantity representing nonlinear *R'G'B'* primary components, each weighted by its luma coefficient. Luma may be associated with SD (BT.601) luma coefficients, or HD (BT.709) luma coefficients. *R'G'B'* components are intended to be converted to tristimulus through a power function (*OECF;* see page 643) having an exponent between about 2.0 and 2.6. *Y'* is distinguished from luminance, *Y,* which represents a weighted sum of linear-light (tristimulus) red, green, and blue primary components. Historically, the *Y* symbol in video was *primed* (*Y'*), but in modern times the prime is often carelessly elided, leading to widespread confusion with luminance.

Y'/C,
Y'/C 3.58,
Y'/C 4.43

Analog luma, *Y'* (not luminance), accompanied by a modulated chroma signal, *C,* quadrature modulated at approximately the subcarrier frequency indicated in megahertz. Preferably denoted S-video, S-video-525 (or in Japan, S-video-525-J), and S-video-625, respectively. May have stable or unstable timebase; may have coherent or incoherent colour subcarrier.

$Y'C_1C_2$

Luma, *Y'* (not luminance), accompanied by two colour difference signals, where the components C_1 and C_2 are specified (or evident from context) and may or may not be any of the common pairs [*B'–Y', R'–Y'*], [P_B, P_R], [C_B, C_R], or [*U, V*].

$Y'C_BC_R$

1 In video, MPEG, and M-JPEG, luma, *Y'* (*not* luminance) accompanied by two colour difference components scaled independently to have a peak-to-peak excursion $224/219$ that of the luma excursion. In processing, reference black is at code 0 and reference white is at code 219, both referenced to 8-bit signals. At an 8-bit interface, luma has reference black code 16 and reference white code 235 ("studio-swing" or "normal-range"). C_B and C_R are scaled to a reference excursion of ±112; an offset of +128 is added. For processing or interfacing with more than 8 bits, additional bits provide additional precision but do not change the scaling. See *luma,* on page 635; and C_B, C_R (**1**) on page 598. Beware that BT.601 (SD) $Y'C_BC_R$ is coded differently than BT.709 (HD) $Y'C_BC_R$: The luma coefficients differ.

2 In JPEG/JFIF as used in computing, luma, Y' (*not* luminance) having "full-swing" or "full-range" excursion 0 through 255, accompanied by two colour difference components scaled independently to have 128±128 peak-to-peak excursion, $256/255$ that of the luma excursion; pure blue and pure red are clipped. See *luma,* on page 635; and *CB, CR* (**2**) on page 599. Full-swing $Y'C_BC_R$ is ordinarily coded according to BT.601 (SD) luma coefficients, independent of pixel count.

$Y'C_XC_Z$ A colour encoding space sometimes used for interfacing between a digital cinema server and a 48 Hz or stereo/3D projector, comprising $X'Y'Z'$ (see above) processed through the JPEG 2000 ICT matrix (a matrix identical to the BT.601 luma/chroma encoding); see *ICT,* on page 627.

$Y'P_BP_R$ 1 Historically, luma, Y' (not luminance) accompanied by analog $[P_B, P_R]$ colour difference components. P historically stood for *parallel.* The EBU N10 standard specifies luma excursion of 700 mV and P_BP_R excursion of ±350 mV. This standard is used in 576*i* and in HD; however, various industry standard analog interfaces have been used for 480*i*. See *luma,* on page 635, and P_B, P_R, on page 645.

2 In modern usage, luma, Y' (not luminance) having reference excursion 0 to 1, accompanied by $[P_B, P_R]$ colour difference components having reference excursion ±0.5 (that is, the same reference amplitude as luma).

$Y'UV$ 1 Historically, luma, Y' (not luminance) accompanied by two colour difference components $[U, V]$ scaled for subsequent encoding into a composite video signal such as NTSC or PAL. For component analog video, $[U, V]$ components are inappropriate, and $[P_B, P_R]$ should be used. For component digital video, $[U, V]$ components are inappropriate, and $[C_B, C_R]$ should be used. See *luma,* on page 635; and *U, V,* on page 662.

2 In modern usage, the notation $Y'UV$ – or, carelessly written, *YUV* – is often used to denote any component system employing luma, Y' (not luminance), accompanied by two colour difference components derived from B'–Y' and R'–Y' such that U and V range ±0.5. (There are many exceptions and errors in the scale factors.)

YCM   The traditional term in the motion picture industry for a set of three black-and-white ("silver") cinema films recording the yellow, cyan, and magenta transmittances of a movie release print, for archiving purposes.

zap delay   The delay (latency) associated with displaying newly acquired video upon changing channels.

zebra
A pattern of moving dashed diagonal lines overlaying an image indicating where image data occupies a certain range of code values, for example to indicate high exposure.

zipper artifact
An artifact associated with deinterlacing (particularly, field merging of field pairs) of source material containing rapid horizontal motion, where alternate image rows of the resulting frame contain horizontally displaced scene elements. Also called *sawtooth artifact* or *serration*.

ZOH
Zero-order hold: Retaining a sampled value for the whole duration of the sampling interval.

Index

α–ω 0–9 A B C D E F G H I J K L M N O P Q R S T U V W X Y Z

α, alpha (absorptance)   574
α, alpha (opacity component)   387
ΔE^* (delta E)   283
ΔL^* (delta L)   262
γ (gamma)   see gamma
λ (lambda, wavelength)   574
φ (flux, radiant)   256, 574, 577
$φ_V$ (flux, luminous)   576
ρ, rho (reflectance)   574
τ, tau (transmittance)   574
~/° (cycles per degree)   252
μ-law   38

0

0_H (line sync datum)   437
    in 1080i, 1080p 475
    in 480i 447
    in 576i 459
    in 720p 468
    in 1080i, 1080p 475
0_V (vertical sync datum)   90 (sketch), 448
1.33:1 aspect ratio   see 4:3 aspect ratio
1.66:1 aspect ratio   5
1.78:1 aspect ratio   see 16:9 aspect ratio
1.85:1 aspect ratio   5
1.896:1 aspect ratio   397
2×-oversampling   226
2's complement   see two's complement
2 K   397
2:1 downsampling   224
2:1 interlace   see interlace
2-2 pulldown   94, 406
2-3 pulldown   93, 405–411
    in MPEG-2   518

2-3-3-2 pulldown   407
2-4-8-DCT (in DV)   508
2.4-power function EOCF   428
2.4:1 aspect ratio   5
3 CCD   299
3-pass algorithm (in DV)   511
3G-SDI   441
3:1:0 chroma subsampling   511
3:1:1 chroma subsampling   482, 512
3-2 pulldown   see 2-3 pulldown
3.58 MHz   130, 137, 392
3-pass algorithm (in DV)   511
$4f_{SC}$ 128
    in 576i PAL   131
    to BT.601 (4:2:2) conversion   231
    interface   429
    sampling rate   393
    and square sampling   133
4:1:1 chroma subsampling   124
    in DV   506 (sketch)
4:2:0 chroma subsampling   125
    in DV   506 (sketch)
    in MPEG-2 field pictures   519 (sketch)
4:2:2 chroma subsampling   124
    in DV   506 (sketch)
4:2:2 component digital   430
    13.5 MHz common sampling rate   130, 394, 430
    in HD
        1080i, 1080p interface   480
    in SD
        480i interface   452
        576i interface   463
4:2:2 profile (MPEG-2)   514, 516

4:3 aspect ratio   5
   compared to 16:9   14
   in 480*i*   450
   in 576*i*   462
   in MPEG-2   517
4:4:4 sampling   452
   in MPEG-24:4:4 sampling   519
4.43 MHz   130, 137
4 K   397
5.1 channel audio   561
5:3 aspect ratio, in 1035*i* HD   141
8b/10b encoding   166, 443
8 K   397
8-8-DCT (in DV)   508
8-VSB   561
13.5 MHz sampling rate   130, 394, 430
   in 480*i*   452
   in 576*i*   463
14.318$\overline{18}$1 MHz   392
15.734 kHz   392
16:9 aspect ratio   5
   in 720*p*   469
   in 1080*i*, 1080*p*   478
   compared to 4:3   14
   in HD   13, 396
   in MPEG-2   517
   in widescreen SD   432
18 MHz sampling rate   432
24*p*A   407
24PsF   94
+25 Hz offset, in PAL   393
32-bit colour   70
50%-point
   of analog sync   434
   of sync   452
      in 480*i*   447
      in 576*i*   459, 463
   of picture width   380
59.94 Hz   392
64-QAM   562
74.25 MHz sampling rate   432
   in 720*p*   467
   in 1080*i*, 1080*p*   473
100/0/100/0 colourbars   421
100/7.5/100/7.5 colourbars   421
143 Mb/s   432
177 Mb/s   432
256-QAM   562
270 Mb/s   432
360 Mb/s   432
422P (4:2:2 profile of MPEG-2)   516

480*i*   93
   notation   93
   2-D frequency spectrum   240 (sketch)
   component video   445–455
   line assignment   446 (table)
   scanning   129, 445–448
   switch, vertical interval   442, 448
480*p*, 483*p*
   notation   93
525/59.94/2:1 scanning
   notation   92
   see 480*i*
525/60 scanning (obsolete)   390, 392
   used loosely to refer to 480*i*
576*i*
   notation   93
   component video   457–465
   line assignment   458 (table)
   scanning   129, 457
   switch, vertical interval   460
576*p*
   notation   93
601 interface   452
601, Rec.   *see* BT.601
625/50/2:1 scanning
   see 576*i*
   notation   92
640×480   92
656 interface   452
709, Rec.   *see* BT.709
720*p*   141–145, 467–485
   notation   93
   interface   432
   line assignment   468 (table)
   see also 1280×720
750/60/1:1 scanning   145
   see also 720*p*
800×600   92
1001 Arabian Nights   392
1024×768   92
1035*i*   141, 396, 473
   interface   432
1080*i*   141–145, 433
   notation   93
   interface   432
   line assignment   475 (table)
   see also 1920×1080
1080*i*   473
   picture centre   478
1080*p*   141–145, 473
   notation   93
   1080*p*24   144

1080*p* (continued)
    1080*p*60   145
    interface   432
    line assignment   475 (table)
    picture centre   478
    see also 1920×1080
1125/60 HD   141, 396
1250-line scanning   563
1280×720   141–145, 467–485
    image format   142
    picture centre   468
1280×1024   92
1366×768   563
1440×1080   482, 512
1600×1200   92
1920×1035   396
1920×1080   92, 141–145, 473–485
    image format   142
2048×1536   92
3200 K (colour temperature)   280
5000 K (colour temperature)   280
5500 K (colour temperature)   280
6504 K (colour temperature)   279
9300 K (colour temperature)   311

A

A-frame (in 2-3 pulldown)   406
A-law   38
AAC (advanced audio coding)   513
Abekas   173, 571
AC
    DCT coefficient   493 (sketch), 497
        in DV   507, 510–511
        in DV50   512
        in JPEG   499
        in MPEG-2   527, 535
    power (mains) frequency   389
AC-3   561
accumulator
    multiplier (MAC)   206
    phase   232
ACES
    primary chromaticities   294
active
    line time   85
        see also horizontal extent
    lines (L_A)   4, 86, 379
        in HD   145 (table)
        in MPEG-2   517
        see also image rows (N_R)
acuity, visual   77, 99
    for colour   335

Adams, Douglas   262
Adams, Michael   563
adaptation   116, 247, 280
ADC (analog-to-digital converter)   216
additive mixture of colour   288–289
ADF (ancillary data flag)   437
Adobe
    Flash   162
    Photoshop   62, 72
advanced audio coding (AAC)   513
advanced simple profile (ASP)   159
advanced video coding (AVC)   160, 537
alias   192–199
    owing to boxcar filtering   195 (sketch)
    and chroma subsampling   127, 347
    and downsampling   224
    and interlace   90
    and Kell effect   102, 631
    and keying   388
    and reconstruction   219
    in resampling   134, 222–223
    spatial   79–81, 240, 242
    see also antialiasing
alpha (*α*), absorptance   574
alpha (*α*), opacity component   387
amazing coincidence   34–35, 318
ambient illumination   56, 83
    and 24 Hz material   412
    in cinema   248
    and contrast ratio   29
    in desktop computing   119, 325
    and reference white   310
    and sRGB   323
AMPAS ACES   *see* ACES
analog
    component interface
        480*i*   453
        HD   485–487
    filter   198, 202, 225
analog-to-digital converter (ADC)   216
anamorphic   5
    lens   5
ANC (ancillary data)   433, 437–439
    colour VANC   313
    and timecode   404
ancillary
    data (ANC)   433, 437–439
        and timecode   404
    data flag (ADF)   437
    digitized ancillary signal   436
Anderson, Matthew   323

angle
    angular discrimination of vision   99
    picture   101 (sketch)
    viewing   80, 84, 133
ANSI/EIA   *see* EIA
antialiasing   202, 225, 242, 332
    in CGI   332
    in image capture   242
    in downsampling   235
    see also alias; reconstruction; sampling
        theorem
antisymmetry   207
aperture
    clean   87 (sketch), 378
        in 1080*i*, 1080*p* HD   478
        in 480*i*   450
        in 576*i*   462
        in 720*p* HD   469
    correction   385
    effect   383
    production   86–87 (sketch), 380
    pupillary   252
    sampling   78
APL (average pixel level), in Photoshop   64
Apple   178
    iTunes store   xxxv
    ProRes   151
    QuickDraw   330
    see also Macintosh
Applebaum, Sidney   108
AR   *see* aspect ratio
Arabian Nights (1001)   392
Argentina   130
arithmetic
    two's complement   46, 377, 495
ARMA (autoregressive moving average)   210
artifact   40
    banding, contouring   32, 333
    blocking
        in D-11 (HDCAM) and HD-D5   482
        in deinterlacing   414
        in JPEG   500
    coring   386
    cross-colour, cross-luma   136–137
    enhancement   383
    field tearing   414
    Hanover bar (PAL)   393
    hum bar   389
    Mach bands   333
    Moiré   78 (sketch)

artifact   *(continued)*
    motion   412
        beat frequency   412
        field tearing, in interlaced scanning
            414
        in interlaced scanning   92
    ringing   87, 361
Ashdown, Ian   72, 580
ASI (asynchronous serial interface)   443
ASP (advanced simple profile)   159
aspect ratio   4
    1.33:1 aspect ratio   *see* 4:3 aspect ratio
    1.66:1 aspect ratio   5
    1.78:1 aspect ratio   *see* 16:9 aspect ratio
    1.85:1 aspect ratio   5
    1.896:1 aspect ratio   397
    4:3
        in 480*i*   450
        in 576*i*   462
        in MPEG-2   517
        pillarbox format   17
    16:9
        in 1080*i*, 1080*p*   478
        in 720*p*   469
        in HD   13, 141, 396
        in MPEG-2   517
        widescreen SD version of BT.601
            133, 432
    cinema   5
    comparison, 4:3 and 16:9   14
    display (DAR)   4
    in MPEG-2   517
    picture (PAR)   5
    pixel, sample   134
    sample (SAR)   14
    see also letterbox format; widescreen
associated foreground   388
astronomers' rule of thumb   99
asynchronous serial interface (ASI)   443
Atlantic Ocean   396, 569
ATM, in MPEG-2   557
atomic clock   392
ATSC   380, 560
    A/53   143, 560
    bitstream   562
    and square sampling   133
    transport stream   557
attenuation
    of high frequencies in cable   39, 439
    owing to (sin *x*)/*x* phenomenon   219
audio
    compact audio disc (CD)   38

audio   *(continued)*
    digital telephony   38
    during digital video blanking   86
    for DTV   561
    taper, in volume control   8
AVC (advanced video coding)   160, 537
AVCHD   162
AVC-Intra   160
average pixel level (APL), in Photoshop   64
AVI   555
Avid
    DNxHD   151
axis
    exchange, from *UV* to *IQ*   123
    horizontal/vertical/temporal
        237 (sketch)

B

B (bel)   *see* decibel
B-picture   153, 520–524
B/PAL   393
    see also PAL
back porch
    clamp   381
    and setup   381
background (BG)   387
    and edge of picture   378
Baker, Richard L.   535
banding artifact   32, 333
bandlimiting   *see* bandwidth
bandreject filter (BRF)   203
bandstop filter   204
bandwidth   99
    defined   211
    distinguished from data rate   99
    for NTSC and PAL broadcast   135
    of lowpass filter   211
Bankoski, Jim   552
Barsky, Brian A.   229
Bartels, Richard H.   229
Barten, Peter G.J.   251
Bartlett window   214
BBC   324
    deinterlacer   416
    and Dirac basic   162
    and Dirac PRO   151
BCD (binary-coded decimal)   399
BDAV, container in Blu-ray   557
beat frequency
    AC power into picture   389
    colour subcarrier into sound   391

    motion artifact   412
Beatty, John C.   229
Bedford, A.V.   102
Beethoven, Ludwig van   171
Beethoven's Ninth Symphony   171
Bell, Alexander Graham   38
Bellamy, John C.   38
Bellanger, M.   212
Bellers, Erwin B.   418
Berger, Toby   535
Berns, Roy S.   286, 299, 328
Bézier spline (or curve)   229
Bézier, Pierre   229
BG (background)   387
BGF_0, BGF_1, BGF_2 flags   402
bias, and BRIGHTNESS   48, 53
bicubic interpolation   229
bilevel image   68
bilinear interpolation   229
binary group flags (in timecode)   402
binary-coded decimal (BCD)   399
bit depth   4, 45
BITC (burnt-in timecode)   399
bits per channel/component (bpc)   7, 69
bits per pixel (bpp)   7
bitstream
    ATSC   562
    constrained parameters (CPB)   515
    DV   441, 511
    JPEG   500, 502
    MPEG-2   514, 532
        legal   513, 538
        splicing   534
        syntax   533
    SDI   439
black
    and white
        television receivers   135
        see also greyscale
    BLACK LEVEL control
        in BT.1886   428
        and monitor nonlinearity   317
    "enhanced"   382
    level   383
        error   60, 326–327, 382
    reference   42
    slope of transfer function near   321
blackbody radiator   276–277
    SPD   276 (graph)–277 (graph)
blacker-than-black (BTB)   44
    combined sync   90

blanking 85–86
    halfline 132, 379
        in 480*i* 451
        in 576*i* 462
        abolished in HD 380
    horizontal 86
    transition samples 87, 451
    vertical interval (VBI) 85
    width 380
Blinn, James F. 388
block
    2×2, in chroma subsampling 127
    8×8
        in DV 507
        in JPEG 492
        in MPEG-2 520
    coding of
        in DV 511
        in MPEG-2 525, 535
    digital interface (DIF), in DV 511
    end of (EOB)
        in DV 509–510, 512
        in JPEG 498
        in MPEG-2 535
    matching, in MPEG-2 encoding 530
    sync, in VTR 508
    see also macroblock (MB); superblock (SB)
blocking artifact
    in D-11 (HDCAM) and HD-D5 482
    in deinterlacing 414
    in JPEG 500
blue
    always appears dark 258
    "Blue Book" 506
    and colour temperature 277
    contribution to luminance 258
    efficiency of modern CRT phosphors
        311
    excess in typical computer monitor 311
    gel filter 422
    in chromaticity diagram 275
    maximum excursion of $B'–Y'$
        in HD 369
        in SD 359
    minus luma *see $B'–Y'$, $R'–Y'$ colour*
        difference components
    screen 388
blur frame 407
Blu-ray
    BDAV container 557

bob (technique for deinterlacing) 414,
    416 (sketch)
bottom field, in MPEG-2 132, 517
Bouman, Maarten A. 251
box distribution 80
boxcar filter 194–198
    D-to-A conversion 218
    image reconstruction using 77 (figure)
Boynton, Robert M. 247
bpc (bits per channel/component) 7, 69
bpp (bits per pixel) 7
Bracewell, Ronald N. 196
Bradford transform 309
Braspenning, Ralph 418
Brazil 130
BRF (bandreject filter) 203
brick wall filter 198
brightness 27, 256
    BRIGHTNESS control 47–64
        and display power function 118
Brill, Michael 298, 578
Bringhurst, Robert xxxvii
British Standard BS:6923 270
broadcast wave format (BWF) 172
browser safe CLUT/palette 71
BT.601 131, 395, 430
    4:2:2 chroma subsampling 124
    digital to analog timing 438
    luma coefficients 122, 346, 359
    transform from $R'G'B'$ 359, 370
    widescreen 16:9 aspect ratio 133, 438
BT.709 290, 427–428
    luma coefficients 346
    luminance coefficients 307
    OECF 320
    primary chromaticities 290
    white reference 290
BT.815 428
BTB (blacker-than-black) 44
    combined sync 90
buffer
    management, in MPEG-2 531
    overflow/underflow, in MPEG-2 532
    see also framebuffer
burnt-in timecode (BITC) 399
burst 138
BWF (broadcast wave format) 172
$B'–Y'$, $R'–Y'$ colour difference components
    114, 123, 135, 335–341
    for HD 369
    for SD 359

c

C_BC_R components   11, 94
    in HD   371
    in JPEG/JFIF   365
    not ordered C_RC_B 358
    in SD   361
    xvYCC   373
    see also $Y'C_BC_R$
C/PW (cycles per picture width)   104, 239
cable
    coaxial   38, 430, 432, 439
    delay
        and equalization   211, 439
    television   562
cadence   406
camera
    CCD (charge coupled device)   8, 299,
        304, 413
    twitter, with interlace   89
    white reference   310
Campbell, Fergus W.   253
candela (cd)   576–577
candela per meter squared [cd·m^{-2}]   27, 576
candle (obsolete)   576
candlepower   576
cartoon   386–387
cascaded integrator comb (CIC)   204
CAT (chromatic adaptation transform)   309
cathode-ray tube   *see* CRT
CBR (constant bit-rate)   505, 531
CC (closed caption)   379, 446
    DTVCC   561
CCD (charge coupled device)   8, 299, 304,
    413
CCIR   *superseded by* ITU-R
    incorrectly used to refer to 576*i* (625/50)
        scanning   129
CCO, *see* centre-cut
CCT (correlated colour temperature)   277
cd (candela)   576–577
CD (compact audio disc)   38
cd·m^{-2}, candela per meter squared   27, 576
CD-DA (compact disc-digital audio)   172
CDDB   172
CE (consumer electronics)   17
CEA/CEDIA-863-B   454
CEA-770.2   454
CEDIA   454
cement   567
centre
    centre-cut (centre cut-out)   16

centre   *(continued)*
    channel, in "5.1" sound   561
    of C_B and C_R samples   127
        in MPEG-2   519
    of picture
        in 1080*i*, 1080*p*   478
        in 480*i*   450
        in 576*i*   462
        in 720*p*   469
CGI (computer-generated imagery)   333
    and gamma   332
    limitations of 8-bit intensity   333
    and tristimulus values   313
    and twitter   89
Chandrasekar, Srinivasan   323
chaos
    colour difference scale factors   352
    SD and HD luma   350
checkerboard   76
checksum, in ANC   438
Chen, Xuemin   558
chroma
    gain error   422
    modulation   128, 137
        quadrature   137
        wideband *I*, in NTSC   352
    phase   138
    subsampling   11, 109, 112,
        124 (sketch)–127, 224, 234, 347
        notation   125
        3:1:0   511
        3:1:1   482, 512
        4:1:1   124
        4:2:0   125
        4:2:2   124
        3:1:1   125, 482
        4:4:4   124
        in DV   506
        in DV50   511
        in JPEG   492, 502
        in MPEG-2   516, 519, 527
            field pictures   519 (sketch)
        not considered compression   150
    transition improvement (CTI)   383, 387
control
    and colourbars   137, 422
chromatic adaptation transform (CAT)   309
chromaticity
    ACES   294
    BT.709   290
    CIE [*x, y*]   275–276
    in JPEG   503

chromaticity   (continued)
    of primaries   290
      in colourbars   420
    SMPTE/DCI P3   295
chrominance   128
    see also chroma
Chuang, Yung-Yu   388
CIC (cascaded integrator comb)   204
Ciciora, Walter S.   563
CIE   122, 256, 265, 267
    chromaticity   275–276
    CIELAB   *see* CIE $L*a*b*$
    CIELUV   *see* CIE $L*u*v*$
    Illuminant C (obsolete)   279, 293
    Illuminant D_{65} 267 (graph), 273 (table)
      in EBU Tech. 3213   279, 293
      in BT.709   292
      in SMPTE RP 145   293
      white adaptation   277
    Illuminant E   278
    $L*$ (lightness)   259
    $L*a*b*$ 283–284
    $L*u*v*$ 281, 284
    luminance (Y)   27, 256–259
    luminous efficiency function   257 (graph)
    Standard Observer   270
    tristimulus   272
    $u'v'$ 282
    uv (1960, obsolete)   281
    [x, y] chromaticity   275–276
      see also chromaticity
    XYZ tristimulus   272
      poor perceptual uniformity   284
      see also tristimulus
CIELAB   *see* CIE $L*a*b*$
CIELUV   *see* CIE $L*u*v*$
CineForm   151
cinema
    ambient illumination   248
    aspect ratio   5
    digital   *see* D-cinema
    frame rate   84, 406
    luminance levels   30, 248, 258
    rendering intent   116
    transfer function   119, 325
    see also film
CinemaScope   5
clamp
    back porch   381
Clarke, R.J.   504
class, in DV   510

clean aperture   87 (sketch), 378
    in 1080i, 1080p HD   478
    in 480i 450
    in 576i 462
    in 720p HD   469
clipping
    of extreme values
      in filtering   205, 245
    in BRIGHTNESS or CONTRAST adjustment
      61–62
    in conversion of BT.601 to computing
      $R'G'B'$ 383–384 (sketch)
    in CRT   56
    in NTSC transmission   420
    of C_B and C_R, in JPEG/JFIF   354,
      366 (sketch)
    of negative signals, in display devices
      311
    of transition samples   379
clock
    atomic   392
    system, in MPEG-2   557
closed caption (CC)   379–380, 446–447
    DTVCC   561
closed GoP   155 (sketch), 522, 533
CLUT (colour lookup table)   70
    browser-safe   71
    see also LUT
CM (coded macroblock)   508
CMC (term best avoided)   270
CMF   270
    of CIE Standard Observer   271 (graph)
    for BT.709 primaries   302 (graph)
    for CIE XYZ primaries   300 (graph)
    Hunt-Pointer-Estévez (HPE)   270 (graph)
    and SPD   296
CMV (concealment motion vector)   525
CMYK   330
coaxial cable   *see* cable, coaxial
code 100 problem   31 (sketch)–32
    in truecolour   69
coded macroblock (CM), in DV   508
codepoint   337
codeword   337
coefficient
    DCT
      AC
        in DV   507–511
        in DV50   512
        in JPEG   493 (sketch), 497
        in MPEG-2   527, 535

coefficient *(continued)*
  DCT *(continued)*
    DC
      in DV 508, 511
      in JPEG 492, 497, 499
      in MPEG-2 525, 534
    in digital filter 202–208
    interlace 103
    luma (*Y*′) 122, 338, 342–351, 358
    luminance 259, 306
    spatial filter 417
COFDM 563
coherence
  frequency, of line rate with subcarrier
    139
  spatial 239, 522, 525
  temporal 150, 513
coincidence
  amazing 34–35, 318
  of C_B and C_R samples
    spatial 124
      in MPEG-2 519
  time, of *R*′*G*′*B*′
    in 720*p* 485
color *see* colour
colorimetry 265–286
colour
  acuity of vision 335
  adaptation 116, 247
    and colour temperature 280
  additive mixture 288–289
  bars 419–423
  blindness 266
  coding, component video
    in HD 369–376
    in SD 357–367
  colourbars 419–423
  colourmap 70, 333
    see also CLUT; pseudocolour
  components
    B′–*Y*′, *R*′–*Y*′ 114, 123, 135, 335–
      341
      for HD 369
      for SD 359
    $C_B C_R$ 11
      in HD 371
      in JPEG/JFIF 365
      in SD 361
      xvYCC 373
    CIE *u*′*v*′ 282
    CIE *uv* (1960, obsolete) 281
    IQ 123

colour *(continued)*
  components *(continued)*
    $P_B P_R$ 11, 94, 339
      for HD 370
      for SD 359
    XYZ tristimulus 272
  COLOUR control, *see* CHROMA [GAIN]
    control
  cube, *Y*′$P_B P_R$ 339 (sketch)
  deficient vision 266
  difference
    coding 123
    decoder 342 (block diagram)
    encoder 341 (block diagram)
    lowpass filter 347
    and luma 335–352
    scale factor chaos 352
    terminology 338
    see also chroma
  gamut 282, 290, 311
  image coding 285
  lookup table *see* CLUT; LUT
  matching
    experiment 268
    functions *see* CMF
  noise due to matrixing 308
  palette *see* CLUT
  perceptual uniformity 280–284
  RGB and *R*′*G*′*B*′ cubes 336 (sketch)
  saturation 113, 266
    and colourbars 419
    in NTSC and PAL coding 138
    psychometric 282
  science 265–286
    for video 287–312
  specification 285
  subsampling *see* chroma subsampling
  systems 286 (sketch)
  temperature 277–280
    9300 K 311
  transform
    among *RGB* systems 309
    between *RGB* and CIE *XYZ* 307
  truecolour 68
  uniform colour space 280
  vision, principle of superposition 288
COLOUR control, *see* CHROMA [GAIN] control
colour VANC 313
colourbars 419–423
  notation 421
  and colour saturation 419
  and hanging dot artifact 421, 423

colourbars   *(continued)*
    IQ components   423
    and luma coefficients   351
    and primary chromaticities   351
colourframe
    and timecode   400–401, 403
colourmap   70, 333
    see also CLUT
Columbus, Christopher   569
column, image columns (N_C)   87 (diagram)
comb filter   206 (graph), 241
    in ATSC DTV   562
    in NTSC and PAL decoding   137, 139
combined sync   90
Commission Internationale de L'Éclairage
    see CIE
compact disc-digital audio (CD-DA)   172
component
    4:2:2
        480*i* interface   452
        576*i* interface   463
    480*i* video   445–455
    576*i* video   457–465
    720*p* video   467–485
    1080*i*, 1080*p* video   473–485
    analog interface
        480*i*   453
        HD   485–487
    colour coding
        in HD   369–376
        in SD   357–367
    digital
        720*p* interface   471
        1080*i*, 1080*p* interface   480
        see also colour components
composite
    digital 4f_{SC} 131, 429
        chroma   128
    mix/wipe   387
    NTSC and PAL   128–139
    sync   90
        see also sync
    video, addition of colour   391
    see also keying
compression   147–162
    DV   505
    H.264   537–548
    JPEG   491–503
    lossless   148
    lossy   148
    motion-JPEG (M-JPEG)   503

compression   *(continued)*
    MPEG
        MPEG-2   513
        MPEG-2   555
        MPEG-4 Part 10 *see* H.264
    ratio   501
computer-generated imagery   *see* CGI
concealment motion vector (CMV)   525
Concelman, Carl   596
concrete   567
cone
    cells   247, 266
    fundamentals   271
confusion
    colour difference (chroma) components
        362
    luma and luminance   122
    power function and exponential
        function   319
    scanning notation (field rate and frame
        rate)   92
    UV, u*v*, and *u'v'* components   357
    Y'UV and *Y'IQ*   367, 571
connector
    XLR   402
constant bit-rate (CBR)   505, 531
constant luminance   107–114
    error   114
constrained-parameters bitstream (CPB)   515
consumer electronics (CE)   17
continuous-tone (contone)   68, 76
contone (continuous-tone)   68, 76
contouring artifact   32, 333
contrast
    CONTRAST control   47–64
        and CRT transfer function   317
    overloaded term   28
    in photography   29
    ratio
        defined   29
        inter-image   29
        intra-image   29
        simultaneous, *see* contrast ratio,
          simultaneous
    sensitivity   249–251
        test pattern   249 (sketch)
    simultaneous   116
    Weber   48
control
    BRIGHTNESS   47–64
        and display power function   118

control   *(continued)*
    CONTRAST   47–64
       and CRT transfer function   317
    GAIN   50
    PICTURE   50
    rate
       in DV   510
       in MPEG-2   531
    SATURATION (or COLOUR)   422
    SHARPNESS   385
    VOLUME   8
conversion
    among types of raster images   72
    analog to digital   216
    scan   95
    standards   96
    transcode   95, 130
conversion function
    OECF   316
convolution   206
coring   383, 385–386 (block diagram)
corner frequency, of filter   211
correction
    aperture   385
    gamma   28, 315
    $(\sin x)/x$ 218
correlated colour temperature (CCT)   277
cosine transform, discrete (DCT)
    see transform, DCT
cositing (of $C_B C_R$ samples)   124, 127
Cowan, William B.   328
CPB (constrained-parameters bitstream)   515
CPD (cycles per degree)   252
CPH (cycles per picture height)   *see* C/PH
CPW (cycles per picture width)   *see* C/PW
C_R *see* $C_B C_R$ component
CRC (cyclic redundancy check)
    in HD-SDI   436–437
Crochiere, Ronald E.   235
cross-chroma   *see* cross-colour
cross-colour, cross-luma artifacts   136–137
CRT (cathode-ray tube)   33
    see also display   310
    blanking   85
    Gaussian spot profile   76, 81
    grid   316
    nonlinearity   315
    phosphor   317
       efficiency of blue   311
    SPD, typical   303 (graph)
CTI (chroma transition improvement)   383,
    387

cubic interpolation   228
curve, Bézier   229
cutoff frequency, of filter   211
cyan
    negative excursion of *R'-Y'*   359, 370
    out of gamut for video   312
cycles per degree (CPD)   252
cycles per picture height (C/PH)   104, 239
cycles per picture width (C/PW)   104, 239
cyclic redundancy check (CRC)
    in HD-SDI   436–437

D

D-cinema   9, 144, 397
D-to-A   *see* digital-to-analog converter
D-5 HD VTR   481–482
    compression   482
D-6 VTR   481–482
D-7 VTR   150
D-9 VTR   150
D-11 VTR   481–482
D-12 VTR   481–482
    compression   482
D-12 HD VTR
    compression   482
D-15 VTR   481–482
D-16 VTR   481, 483
D_{50}, D_{55}, D_{65} *see* illuminant
DAC (digital-to-analog converter)
    in computing   68
    and CRT   35
    in pseudocolour   70
    and reconstruction   217
    and $(\sin x)/x$ correction   218 (graph)
    in truecolour   69
    in video   70
Dambacher, Paul   564
DAR (display aspect ratio)   4
DASH (dynamic adaptive streaming over
    http)   169
data
    block number (DBN), in ANC   438
    compression   147
    count (DC), in ANC   438
    ID (DID), in ANC   438
dB (decibel)   38
DBN (data block number)   438
DBS (direct broadcast satellite)
    and MPEG-2   528
    for ATSC DTV   562
    MUSE, in Japan   560

DC
    DCT coefficient
        in DV   508, 511
        in JPEG   492, 497, 499
        in MPEG-2   525, 534
DC (data count), in ANC   438
DCI (Digital Cinema Initiative)   295
    P3   *see* SMPTE/DCI P3
DCT (discrete cosine transform)   147
    2-4-8 (in DV)   508
    8-8 (in DV)   508
    coding, in MPEG-2   525
    DCT type, in MPEG-2   525
    and vision   497
    see also transform, DCT
DCT^{-1} 495
de Haan, Gerard   418
de Vries-Rose law   250
Dean, Charles E.   391
decade   39
decibel (dB)   38
decimation   221–235
decoder, conventional luma/colour
    difference   342 (block diagram)
decoding gamma (γ_D)   317
delay
    audio/video   443
    element
        in digital filter   206
        in luma/chroma encoder   341, 349
    encoding, in MPEG-2   156
    of filter   209
    group   209
    phase   209
    of second field, in interlaced video   88
delta *E**   282–283
delta *L**   262
DeMarsh, LeRoy E.   116, 176, 314
demodulation, in ATSC DTV   562
demosaicking   4
depth of modulation   241
dequantization   494
DF (dropframe timecode)   400
DFT (discrete Fourier transform)   240
DI (digital intermediate)   23
DID (data ID)   438
difference
    colour   335–352
        in HD   369–376
        in SD   357–367
    interpicture   152 (sketch)
    just-noticeable (JND)   31, 250, 284

differential
    coding of DC coefficient, in JPEG   499
    phase (DP)
        hue shift immunity of PAL   393
diffuse white   115, 117, 249
digital
    to analog converter   *see* DAC
    Digital Light Processor (DLP)   326
    filter
        design of   214
        see FIR filter; filter, IIR
    interface (DIF), in DV   511
    still camera
        nonlinear coding   34
        pixel count   4
    video effects (DVE)   221, 443
Digital Cinema Initiative (DCI)   295
digital cinema   *see* D-cinema
digital driving level (DDL)   51
    normalized   51
digital image processing (DIP)   378
digital intermediate (DI)   23
Digital Light Processor (DLP)   326
Digital Natural Image engine (DNIe)   26
Digital Reality Creation (DRC)   26
digital video cassette (DVC)   150, 505
Digital-S   150
digitization   7
    of images   237–243
    see also quantization; sampling
Dirac
    basic   162
    delta   207
    PRO   151
direct broadcast satellite (DBS)
    and MPEG-2   528
    for ATSC DTV   562
    MUSE, in Japan   560
discrete cosine transform (DCT)   147
discrete wavelet transform (DWT)   147
display
    aspect ratio (DAR)   4
    reference   427–428
    white reference   310
display referred image state   21
DisplayPort   51, 166
    Mini DisplayPort   167
distance
    between colours   262, 276, 281–282
    Euclidean   281–282
    intensity, independent of   576

distance   *(continued)*
     video interface
         SDI   440
     viewing   100–101 (sketch), 104–106
         and chroma subsampling   347
         and oversampling   244
distortion   40
     multipath   562–563
DivX   159
DLP   288
DLP (Digital Light Processor)   326
DNIe (Digital Natural Image engine)   26
DNxHD   151
Dolby
     AC-3   561
     Dolby Digital   561
dominance, field   406
dot
     per inch (dpi)   72–73
downconvert   96
downsampling   222–223 (sketch)
     2:1   224
     and 3:1:1, in HDCAM   482
     in $4f_{SC}$ to BT.601 (4:2:2) conversion
         231
     and keying   388
     see also decimation   234
dpi (dots per inch)   72–73
DRC (Digital Reality Creation)   26
drive
     horizontal pulse (HD)   90
     vertical pulse (VD)   90
dropframe timecode   392, 400
DSC   *see* digital still camera
DSM-CC   513
DTV (digital television)   143, 560
DTVCC   561
dual link
     for HD-SDI   433
dub (duplicate)   441
Duff, Tom   387
DV   168, 505
     DV25   168, 506
     DV50   507
     DV100   168, 483
     DV-over-1394   168
     DV-over-SDTI   512
DVB   563
     ASI   *see* ASI
     DVB-C, DVB-S, DVB-T   563
DVC (digital video cassette)   150, 505
DVCAM   150

DVCPRO   150
     DVCPRO HD   481–483, 512
         compression   482
     DVCPRO50   150
DVCPRO100   483
DVD   531, 556
DVE (digital video effects)   221, 443
DVI   51, 166
DVITC   404
DWT (discrete wavelet transform)   147

E

E (irradiance)   256, 574, 577
E_v (illuminance)   256, 576–577
EAV (end of active video)   431 (sketch), 434
     EAV+LN+CRC   440
EBU
     green   290
     Tech. 3213   293
     Tech. 3246   434, 438
     Tech. N10   362, 430–431, 453, 464
     Tech. N12   404
     Tech. N20   464
     Tech. R62   310–311, 406
edge
     frequency, of filter   211
     of picture   451
         in MPEG-2   520
     sync   437
edit decision list (EDL)   401
effect, aperture (in camera)   383
EG (Engineering Guideline)   *see* SMPTE EG
EIA
     EIA/CEA-770.2   454
     EIA/CEA-770.3   487
     EIA-189-A   419
     EIA-608   447
     EIA-708-B   561
     equalization pulse in NTSC   448
     RS-343-A (obsolete)   382, 453
Einstein, Albert   179
electron volt [eV]   266
electronic program guide (EPG)   557
electro-optical conversion function (EOCF)   9
     CRT   33
electro-optical transfer function (EOTF)   315
elementary stream (ES)   535, 556
Elvis   77
emittance, radiant (deprecated)   574
encoder   95
     conventional luma/colour difference
         341 (block diagram)

encoding gamma (γ_E)   319
end of active video (EAV)   431 (sketch), 434
end of block (EOB)
    in DV   509–510, 512
    in JPEG   498
    in MPEG-2   535
energy (Q)   574
"enhanced" black   382
enhancement   383
EOB (end of block)
    in DV   509–510, 512
    in JPEG   498
    in MPEG-2   535
EOCF (electro-optical conversion function)   9
    in 480i 448
    in 576i 460
    in 720p 469
    in 1920×1080   478
    BT.1886   322, 428
    and headroom   43
EOTF (electro-optical transfer function),   *see*
    EOCF
equal-energy illuminant   278
equalization
    in cable   211, 439
    in filter   211
    pulse   132
        in 480i 448
        in 576i 459
E_R' 343
erf(x), error function   200
error
    black level   60, 382
    chroma
        gain   422
        phase   422
    concealment
        status (STA), in DV   510
    constant luminance   114
    cross-colour, cross-luma   136
    differential
        phase (DP)
            hue shift immunity of PAL   393
    function, erf(x)   200
    hue   422
    Livingston   114
    phase
        differential (DP)
            hue shift immunity of PAL   393
        in IIR filter   211
    position, in interpolation   233
    prediction, in MPEG   520–530

error   *(continued)*
    quantization   40
    reconstruction, in JPEG   500
    roundoff
        in 8-bit interface   45, 325
        in computing *RGB*   364
        in DCT/IDCT   495–496, 500
    saturation   422
    timebase   139
    timecode   400
ES (elementary stream)   535, 556
    packetized   556
ETSI   563
Euclidean distance   281–282
eV (electron volt)   266
even/odd (fields)   88, 132
excursion   41
    of $B'–Y'$ and $R'–Y'$
        in HD   369
        in SD   359
    of chroma and luma
        in $Y'C_BC_R$ 362, 365, 371
        in $Y'P_BP_R$ 360, 371
    in colour difference encoding matrix
        364
    peak   361, 381
    picture   381
Exif   34, 346
exitance
    luminous (M_v)   576
    radiant (M)   574
exponential function, distinguished from
    power function   319
extended range   44
extrapolation   227
eye   7, 248
    tracking   93
    see also vision

F

f code, in MPEG   530
F flag bit (in TRS)   434
F23   313
F35   313
F65   313
factor
    interlace   103
    Kell   102
    luminance   578
Fairchild, Mark D.   118
Farmer, James   563
Farrell, Joyce E.   84

fast forward   *see* shuttle
fax   67
    and compression   148
FCC (Federal Communications Commission)
    392, 448, 560
FDCT (forward DCT)   495
FEC (forward error-correction)   561
    and MPEG-2   556
Feiner, Steven   569
Feller, Christian   552
FFT (fast Fourier transform)   240
FG (foreground)   387
fidelity range extensions (FRExt)   538, 541
field
    bottom   132, 517
    DCT coding, in MPEG-2   525
    dominance   406
    even/odd   88, 132
    F flag bit, in TRS   434
    field-structured picture, in MPEG-2   517
    in MPEG-2   132
    mode, in DV   508
    parity (odd/even, first/second,
        top/bottom)   132
    rate   389–395
    sync datum (0_V)   90 (sketch)
    tearing artifact   414
    top/bottom   88, 517
        in MPEG-2   132
field/frame sync
    in 480*i*   447
    in 576*i*   459
FIFO (first-in, first-out)   442
file extension
    .m2t   557
    .m2ts   557
    .m2v   535
    .mod   556
    .mp4   159
    .mpeg   556
    .mpg   556
    .mts   557
    .tod   557
    .ts   557
    .vob   556
    .yuv   571
    .m3u   168
files   163–169
fill video   387
film
    anamorphic lens   5
    aspect ratio   5

film   *(continued)*
    compensation of dark surround   118
    flat (1.85:1 aspect ratio)   5
    film pattern retarder (FPR)   184
    "scope" (2.4 aspect ratio)   5
    spherical (1.85:1 aspect ratio)   5
    transfer function ("gamma")   119
    see also cinema
filter
    [1, 0, 1] filter   203
    [1, 0, –1] filter   203
    [1, 1] filter   203
    [1, –1] filter   203
    2-D (spatial)   242
    analog   198, 202, 225
    bandreject (BRF)   203
    bandstop   204
    bandwidth   99, 211
    blue gel   422
    boxcar   194–198
        and D-to-A conversion   218
        image reconstruction using
            77 (figure)
    brick wall   198
    BT.601 template   213
    chroma subsampling   127
    coefficient quantization   208
    colour difference lowpass   347
    comb   *see* comb filter
    corner frequency   211
    cutoff frequency   211
    digital
        design   214
        see also FIR filter; filter, IIR
    equalization   211
    finite impulse response   *see* FIR filter
    flicker   *see* filter, twitter
    Gaussian   200, 204, 207, 214
        in image reconstruction   77 (figure)
        risetime of   214
        sharpened   243–244
    halfband   226
    highpass (HPF)   203
    IIR (infinite impulse response)   210
    impulse response   207
    infinite impulse response (IIR)   210
    lowpass (LPF)
        characterization   211
        template   212 (sketch)
    median   383, 385
    moving average (MA)   202, 210
    narrowband   204

filter   *(continued)*

     nonrecursive   *see* FIR filter

     notch   203–204

     optical   242, 269

     physical realizability of   208

     polyphase   232

     recursive   *see* IIR filter

     ringing   87, 361

     and sampling   191–220

     spatial   242, 417

         median   385

     template

         for BT.601 SD   213

         for HD   488

         for oversampling filter   225

     trap   203–204

     twitter   89

     vertical   241

     zero, of   204

finite impulse response *see* FIR filter

Fink, Donald G.   49, 250

FIR filter   207–208

     [1, 0, 1] filter   203

     [1, 0, –1] filter   203

     [1, 1] filter   203

     [1, –1] filter   203

     comb filter   206 (graph)

     and edge of picture   378

     vertical   241

FireWire   167, 512

first/second (fields)   88, 132

Fischer, Walter   564

five-halves power law   316

fixed-point   45

     and DCT   495

     linear-light coding   31 (sketch)

     and matrix transforms   307

flag

     ancillary data (ADF)   437

     binary group (BGF, in timecode)   402

     broken link, in MPEG-2   533

     closed GoP, in MPEG-2   533

     coded block pattern, in MPEG-2   534

     colourframe   400

     dropframe (in timecode)   403

     F, V, H (in TRS)   434

     in timecode   403

     P_0, P_1, P_2, P_3 (in TRS)   434

     polarity/field (in timecode)   402

     progressive sequence, in MPEG-2   517

     repeat first field (RFF), in MPEG-2   518

     top field first (in MPEG-2)   132

flare   116

flat

     1.85:1 aspect ratio   5

     flatfield   100

     flat-panel display (FPD)

         active area in 576*i*   463

         colour primaries   292

         MPEG-2 nonintra quantizer matrix   523, 525, 531

flicker   83

     filter   *see* twitter filter

     and interlace   105, 142, 244

     interline   *see* twitter

     and motion portrayal   93

flux

     luminous (φ_v)   576

     radiant (φ)   256, 574, 577

flyback transformer   390

Fogg, Chad E.   535

folding, of frequency   198

Foley, James D.   569–570

footcandle   576

footroom   42, 365, 374

     and clipping   423

     in *R'G'B'*   365, 383

     in $Y'C_BC_R$ 361, 381

foreground (FG)   387

forward DCT (FDCT)   495

forward error-correction (FEC)   561

     and MPEG-2   556

Fourier transform   196

     discrete (DFT)   240

     and edge of picture   378

     fast (FFT)   196, 240

     pairs   200

     self inverse   198

foveal vision   84

FPD (flat-panel display)

     active area in 576*i*   463

     colour primaries   292

FPR (film pattern retarder)   184

frame   4

     blur   407

     DCT coding, in MPEG-2   525

     frame-structured picture, in MPEG-2   517

     mode

         in DV compression   508

     parity (in 483*p*59.94)   435

frame   *(continued)*
     rate   83, 389–395
         in 480*i*   445
         in 576*i*   457
         in cinema   84, 406
         in MPEG-2   518
     segmented progressive (24PsF)   94
framebuffer   4
framestore   4
France   130
Fredendall, G.L.   102
Free Scale Gamut (FS-Gamut)   312
Free Scale Log (FS-Log)   312
frequency
     beat
         AC power into picture   389
         colour subcarrier into sound   391
         motion artifact   412
     corner, of lowpass filter   211
     cutoff, of lowpass filter   211
     folding (in sampled systems)   198
     interleaving   137
     intermediate (IF)   391, 562
     Nyquist *see* Nyquist rate
     response   99
         of a filter   196
         of point sampling   199
     spatial frequency domain   238,
         493 (sketch)
         480*i* luma   240 (sketch)
     sweep   98
     wrapping (in sampled systems)   198
FRExt (fidelity range extensions)   538, 541
FS-Gamut (Free Scale Gamut)   312
FS-log (Free Scale Log)   312
Fujio, Takashi   141
Fukuda, Tadahiko   83
full search   530
full-swing   41
     in JPEG/JFIF   362
full-swing (in JPEG/JFIF)   365–366
fundamentals, cone   271

G

G/PAL   393
     see also PAL
CHROMA   137, 422
COLOUR control, see CHROMA
gain
     chroma
         error   422
     and CONTRAST   48, 53

GAIN control   50
gamma (γ)   28, 315–334
     1.45, in Macintosh   330
     1.8, in Macintosh   330
     2.2
         in 480*i*   320, 324
         in CGI   330
     2.8, in 576*i*   320, 324
     in computer graphics   329 (sketch), 332–
         333
     correction   28, 121, 315
         and constant luminance   114
         indicated by prime symbol   343
     decoding (γ_D)   317
     encoding (γ_E)   319
     in film   119
     in JFIF (JPEG file interchange format)
         334, 503
     Macintosh   329 (sketch)
     in physics   316–318
     and picture rendering   117
     and pseudocolour   332
     shift, in Macintosh   332
     system   329
     in video   318–322, 329 (sketch)
gamma function Γ(·), of mathematics   319
gamut   282, 290, 311
     mapping, in digital cinema   296
     wide-gamut reproduction   312
Gaussian
     filter
         FIR   204, 207, 214
         risetime of   214
         sharpened   243–244
     function   200
     image reconstruction   77 (figure)
     problem with reconstruction   217
     spot profile   102
         of CRT   76, 81
Gennum   215
Gibson, Jerry D.   535
Giorgianni, Edward J.   20, 115–116, 314
global shutter (GS)   94
GOP (group of pictures)   517
GoP (group of pictures)   153–154, 156, 517,
     533, 623
     closed   155 (sketch), 522, 533
     open   155 (sketch)
GoPro   151
Gorzynski, Mark E.   328
Gouraud shading   333
Gracenote   172

Grassmann's third law   272
green   258
    contribution to luminance   258
    EBU   290
    SMPTE   290
grey   258
    integrate to   310
greyscale   68
    see also gamma
grid   655
    of CRT electron gun   316
    macroblock, in MPEG-2   520
    sampling   78
group delay   209
    of BT.601 filter   213
group of pictures, *see* GoP
GS (global shutter)   94

H

H/PAL
    see also PAL
h (subscript), hexadecimal   46
H flag bit (in TRS)   434
H.261   124–125, 127
H.264   160, 537–548
    video usability information (VUI)   176
H/PAL   393
H14L (high-1440 level), in MPEG-2   514
halfband filter   226
halfline
    blanking   379
        abolished in HD   380
        in 480*i*   451
        in 576*i*   462
    offset, in interlaced scanning   90
Hall, Roy   314
Hamilton, Eric   175, 502, 572
HANC   431 (sketch), 437
"Hanning" window   214
Hanover bar artifact (in PAL)   393
Haskell, Barry G.   535
Hazeltine Corporation   391
HCT, in H.264   544
HD (high definition)   141
    1080*i*, 1080*p*   473–485
    720*p*   467–485
    component colour coding   369–376
    halflines (abolished)   380
    scanning   141
        notation   93
        interlace and progressive   89, 397
        numerology   395

HD   *(continued)*
    and SD luma chaos   350
    viewing angle, distance   101
HD (horizontal drive)   90
HDCAM   125, 481–482
HDCAM SR   481
HD-D5   482
    compression   482
    see also D-5 HD VTR
HD-MAC   563
HDMI   51, 166
HD-SDI   166
HD-SDI (high definition serial digital
        interface)   432–433
    coding   440
    and TRS   436
HDV   161
headroom   42, 365, 374
    in $R'G'B'$ 365, 383
    in $Y'C_BC_R$ 361, 381
height, picture (PH)   100
hexadecimal   46
Heynderickx, Ingrid   47
Hi-Vision   560
hicolour   68
hierarchy, syntactic, of MPEG-2   533
high definition   *see* HD
high level (HL), in MPEG-2   514
high profile (HP), in MPEG-2   514
high-1440 level (H14L), in MPEG-2   514
highpass filter (HPF)   203
HL (high level), in MPEG-2   514
horizontal
    axis   237 (sketch)–238 (sketch)
    blanking   85–86
    datum (0_H) *see* 0_H
    DCT transform   495
    domain   237 (sketch)–238 (sketch)
    drive pulse (HD)   90
    H flag bit (in TRS)   434
    resampling   134
    resolution   104
        of HD   141
    size, in MPEG-2   517
HP (high profile), in MPEG-2   514
HPE (Hunt-Pointer-Estévez)   270
HPF (highpass filter)   203
HSB, HSI, HSL, HSV   28
Hsu, Stephen C.   102
hue
    defined   266
    error   422

HUE control   137
    and colourbars   422
Huffman coding   499
Hughes, John   569
Hulu   xxxv, 165
hum bar artifact   389
Hunt, Robert W.G.   286, 298, 578
Hunt-Pointer-Estévez (HPE)   270
    colour matching functions   270 (graph)
hyperspectral imaging   10

I

I-macroblock (intra macroblock)   156, 528
I-only MPEG-2   503, 517
I-picture   153, 520–524, 528
I (radiant intensity)   256, 574, 577
I_v (luminous intensity)   256, 576–577
i.LINK   167, 512
I/PAL   393
    see also PAL
IDCT   495
ideal lowpass filter (ILPF)   198, 243
IEC
    10918 (JPEG)   491, 502
    11172-1 (MPEG-1)   157
    13818 (MPEG-2)   513
    14496 (MPEG-4 Part 10)   537
    14496-12 (ISO Base Media File Format)
        159
    15938 (MPEG-7)   158
    21000 (MPEG-21)   158
    60461   404
    60966-2-1   294, 323
    61834-1   506
    61883-1   168
IEEE 1394   167, 512
IF (intermediate frequency)   391, 562
IIR (infinite impulse response)   210
ILFP (ideal lowpass filter)   243
illegal   see legal
illuminance
    in reference HD viewing   428
illuminance (E_v)   256, 576–577
illuminant
    CIE A (obsolete)   279
    CIE C (obsolete)   279, 293
    CIE D_{50}, D_{55} 278
    CIE D_{65} 267 (graph), 273 (table)
        in EBU Tech. 3213   279, 293
        in SMPTE RP 145   293
        and white adaptation   277
        in BT.709   292

illuminant   (continued)
    CIE E, equal-energy   278
    SPD of various   279 (graph)
illumination
    ambient   56, 83
        and 24 Hz material   412
        and contrast ratio   29
        in desktop computing   119, 325
        and reference white   310
        and sRGB   323
    SPD   278
    tungsten   280
    usage as quantity, deprecated   576
ILPF (ideal lowpass filter)   198, 243
image   7, 65, 68
    1280×720 format   142
    1920×1080 format   142
    bilevel   68
    coding of colour images   285
    columns (N_C)   86–87 (diagram)
    compression   65, 148
        lossless   148
        lossy   148, 497
    digitization   237–243
    greyscale raster   68
    plane   7
    pseudocolour   70
    raster   130 (sketch)
        conversion among types   72
        in computing   65–73
    reconstruction   237–243
    repeated spectra, in filtering   222–
        223 (sketch)
    rows (N_R)   86–87 (diagram)
        and viewing distance   100
    structure   75–103
    symbolic description   65–66
    truecolour   68
    vector   3
image state   21
impedance   432
impulse
    Dirac   207
    Kronecker   207
    response   207
        finite (FIR)   207
        infinite (IIR)   210
    train   199, 218
infinite impulse response (IIR)   210
inhibition, lateral   116
insolation   574
integral α (alpha)   388

integrate to grey   310
intensity   27
   and CRT   35 (figure)
   defined   255
   luminous (I_v)   256, 576–577
   and pixel component values   334
   radiant (I)   256, 574, 577
   of sound   38
interchange primaries   348, 350
interface
   4:2:2 digital
      480*i*   452
      576*i*   463
   720*p*   471
   1080*i*, 1080*p*   480
   analog
      SD   452
   digital interface (DIF), in DV   511
   digital video   429, 433–441
   offset   44
   serial digital
      for HD   *see* HD-SDI
      for SD   *see* SDI
   S-video   137
interfield
   averaging, in deinterlacing   414 (sketch),
      416 (sketch)–417
   motion
      in deinterlacing   414
      in DV   507
      in MPEG-2   524, 527
   see also interpicture coding
interframe
   averaging, in deinterlacing   415 (sketch)
   see also interpicture coding
inter-image contrast ratio   29
interlace   88
   in 480*i*   445
   in 576*i*   457
   coefficient   103
   factor   103
   quasi-interlace   94
intermediate frequency (IF)   391, 562
International Commission on Illumination
      see CIE
Internet-protocol television (IPTV)   165
interpicture
   coding   152 (sketch)
      in MPEG   513
interpolation   221–235
   bicubic   229
   bilinear   229

interpolation   *(continued)*
   cubic   228
   Lagrange   227
   linear   226
      in MPEG-2   524
   nearest-neighbor   227
   polyphase   231
interstitial siting (of C_BC_R samples)   124, 127
intersymbol interference (ISI)   99
intra
   macroblock (I-macroblock)   156, 528
   picture   *see* I-picture
   prediction mode, in VP8   550
intrafield processing, in deinterlacing   414,
      416
intrafield/intraframe/intrapicture
      compression   150, 513
inverse
   2-3 pulldown   408
   DCT   495
   quantization   494
   telecine   408
inverse telecine   411
IP-frame   518
IPTV (Internet-protocol television)   165
IQ components   123
   and colourbars   423
IQ (inverse quantization)   494
IRE unit   381
irradiance (*E*)   256, 574, 577
Ishida, J.   141
ISI (intersymbol interference)   99
ISO
   646   404
   2202   404
   10918 (JPEG)   491, 502
   11172-1 (MPEG-1)   157
   13818 (MPEG-2)   513
   14496-10   537
   14496-12 (ISO Base Media File Format)
      159
   14524   320
   15938 (MPEG-7)   158
   21000 (MPEG-21)   158
   Base Media File Format
      (ISO/IEC 14496-12)   159
   JPEG   502
iTunes store   xxxv
ITU-R
   BT.471   421
   former CCIR   131
   see also BT.601, BT.709

ITU-T
   former CCITT   148
   H.220.0 (MPEG-2 Systems)   513
   H.261   124–125, 127
   H.262 (MPEG-2 Video)   513
   H.264   160, 537
   H.26L   537
Ives, Herbert E.   270
Izraelevitz, David   339

J

Jackson distance   105
Jackson, Richard   105
jaggies   77
   see also alias, spatial
James, T.H.   118
Japan   560
JFIF (JPEG file interchange format)   175, 334, 502, 572
   and "full-range" $C_B C_R$ 357, 572
   and luma   346
JND (just-noticeable difference)   31, 250, 284
Joint Video Team (JVT)   537
Jones, Paul W.   504
Jorke, Helmut   184
JPEG   491–503
   file interchange format (JFIF)   175, 334, 502, 572
     and "full-range" $C_B C_R$ 357
     and luma   346
   gamma   175, 334, 502–503
   and linear/nonlinear coding   36
   luma   346
just-noticeable difference (JND)   31, 250, 284
JVT (Joint Video Team)   160, 537

K

K (kelvin), unit of temperature   277
Kaiser window   216
Kaiser, James F.   220
Kallmann, Heinz. E.   49
Kan, Ti   172
Kang, Henry R.   314
Kell effect   102
Kell factor   102
Kell, Ray D.   102
key   387
   linear   388
   in photography   29

keying   387
Knoll, John   330
Kolb, Fred   570
Komoto, T.   141
Koslov, Joshua L.   339
Kotelnikov, Aleksandr   193
Kronecker delta   207
Kuniba, Hideyasu   299

L

L_A (active lines)   4, 86, 379
   in HD   145 (table)
   in MPEG-2   517
$L*a*b*$ 283–284
$L*$ (CIE lightness)   260
L (radiance)   255–256, 575, 577
L_T (total lines)   86
   in HD   145 (table)
$L*u*v*$ 281, 284
L, L_v (absolute luminance)   576–577
   see also luminance, relative (Y)
L, L_v (luminance, absolute)   256
L_A (active lines)   86
LAB   *see* CIE $L*a*b*$
Lagrange interpolation   227
Lagrange, Joseph Louis   227
lambda (λ, wavelength)   574
Langendijk, Erno   47
Laplace transform   196
lapped transform   482
Large, David   563
lateral inhibition   116
lattice   655
layer, in MPEG-2   533–535
layering   *see* keying
LCD (liquid crystal display)   73, 76, 326
   controls   62
Lechner distance   105
Lechner, Bernard   105
legal   339
   MPEG-2 bitstream   513, 538
   RGB-legal   373
     and wide gamut   312, 374
     in colourbars   423
LeGall, Didier J.   535
LeHoty, Dave   186
Lempel-Ziv-Welch (LZW)   148
lens   7
   anamorphic   5
lerp   226
letterbox format   17

level
>   black   383
>   in MPEG-2   514–517, 540 (table),
>   548 (table)
>   of AC coefficient
>   in DV   510
>   in JPEG   499
>   in MPEG-2   527
>   in quantization   37
>   shifting, in DCT/JPEG   495
>   video   381
>   *see also* IRE unit

level shifting
>   in JPEG   495

Levinthal, Adam   312

LFE (low frequency effects)   561

lift   383
>   *see also* pedestal

lightness   27
>   CIE L^* 259–260
>   and luminance   27–28, 255–263
>   sensitivity   249–251

limiting resolution   98–99

Lindbergh, David   535

Lindbloom, Bruce   314

line
>   AC power   389
>   active (L_A)   4, 86, 379
>   in HD   145 (table)
>   in MPEG-2   517
>   assignment
>   in 1080i, 1080p 475 (table)
>   in 480i 446 (table)
>   in 576i 458 (table)
>   in 720p 468 (table)
>   overloaded term   85
>   picture   379
>   of purples   275
>   rate   389–395
>   samples per active line (S_{AL})   4, 86, 131,
>   380, 395, 438 (table)
>   in HD   145 (table)
>   in MPEG-2   517
>   samples per picture width (S_{PW})
>   87 (diagram), 380
>   samples per total line (S_{TL})   86–
>   87 (diagram), 130 (diagram)–131,
>   393, 395, 438 (table)
>   in HD   145 (table)
>   scan line   83
>   spread function (LSF)   241

line   *(continued)*
>   sync
>   in 480i 447
>   in 576i 459
>   in 720p 468
>   in 1080i and 1080p 475
>   sync datum (0_H)   437
>   time   85
>   *see also* horizontal extent
>   total (L_T)   86
>   in HD   145 (table)
>   TV line (TVL/PH)   104

linear
>   interpolation   226
>   in MPEG-2   524
>   key   388
>   light   28
>   linear-light   27–36
>   and 8-bit coding   333
>   and bit depth   325
>   in computing   64–65, 69
>   and constant luminance   108
>   and luminance   255
>   and *RGB* tristimulus components
>   307, 312
>   matrix, in a video camera   348
>   and nonlinear coding   31
>   in JPEG   494, 502
>   phase   209
>   timecode (LTC)   399, 402

linearity   37
>   CRT phosphors   317
>   linear-light coding   31 (sketch)
>   in optical and electrical domains   36
>   phase linearity, in filter   209
>   principle of   37
>   *see also* linear

linear-light   27–36

lip-sync   443

liquid crystal display (LCD)   73, 76, 326
>   CONTRAST and BRIGHTNESS controls   62

LIRP (linear interpolation)   226

Livingston error   114

Livingston, Donald C.   114

LL (low level), in MPEG-2   514

lm (lumen)   576

locus, spectral   275

logarithm
>   in contrast sensitivity   250
>   in decibel and SNR calculations   38
>   in filter specification   212
>   in lightness sensitivity   33

logarithm (continued)
    in loudness perception 8
    "logarithmic" search, in MPEG 531
longitudinal timecode 399, 402
Lookabaugh, Tom 535
lookup table (LUT) see CLUT; LUT
lossless compression 148
lossy compression 148, 497
loudness 8, 251
low level (LL), in MPEG-2 514
lowpass filter (LPF)
    characterization 211
    optical 242
LSF (line spread function) 241
LTC (linear timecode) 399, 402
luma (Y') 28, 121, 335–352
    notation 342, 567
    in 480i 450
    in 576i 462
    in 720p 471
    in 1080i, 1080p 480
    BT.601 346
    BT.709 346
    coefficients 28, 122, 338, 342–351, 358
        and colourbars 351
    SD and HD chaos 350
    SMPTE 240M 369
lumen (lm) 576
luminance 27, 256–259
    absolute (L, L_v)
        defined 256, 576
    absolute (L, L_v)
        defined 577
    coefficients 259, 306
    constant luminance 107–114, 341
    defined 257
    factor 578
    and lightness 27–28
    nonconstant 341
    from red, green and blue 258
    relative (Y) 258, 578
        defined 258
        tristimulus component 272
    unfortunate use of term in video 122
luminance factor 258
luminance
    notation 567
luminance (Y)
    and lightness 255–263

luminous
    efficiency function 257, 270–271 (graph), 273 (table), 296
    exitance (M_v) 576
    flux (Φ_v) 576
    intensity (I_v) 256, 576–577
LUT (lookup table) 328, 330, 332
    see also CLUT
Luthra, Ajay 548
LUV see CIE $L*u*v*$
lux (lx) 576, 579
Lyons, Richard G. 220
LZW (Lempel-Ziv-Welch) 148

M

M-frame 518
M-JPEG (motion JPEG) 503
M (radiant exitance) 574
M_v (luminous exitance) 576
M/PAL 130
    see also PAL
.m2t (file extension) 557
.m2ts (file extension) 557
.m2v (file extension) 535
.m3u (file extension) 168
MA (moving average) 202, 210
MAC (multiplexed analog components) 563
MAC (multiplier-accumulator) 206
Mac OS X 10.6 317, 330
Mach bands 333
Macintosh 70
    gamma 317, 328
        in pseudocolour 70
        in truecolour 69
    JPEG/JFIF 503
    QuickDraw 330
    transfer function (gamma) 64, 328–329 (sketch)
macroblock
    in DV 506
macroblock (16×16) 492
    coded (CM), in DV 508
    in VP8 550
    in JPEG see MCU
    misalignment 380
    in MPEG-2 156, 520, 523 (table), 534
    see also block
Madden, Thomas E. 20, 115
Madisetti, Vijay K. 418
main level (ML), in MPEG-2 514
main profile (MP), in MPEG-2 514
Malvar, Henrique S. 482

Marcellin, Michael W.   150
mark   68
material exchange format (MXF)   151, 165
matrix
    linear, in a video camera   348
    multiplication, to calculate tristimulus
        273
    noise due to colour   308
    quantization
        in JPEG   497
        in MPEG-2   525
    transform
        among *RGB* systems   309
        between *RGB* and CIE *XYZ*   307
        to compute colour difference   359,
            370
Matroska   555
matte   387–388
Maxwell, James Clerk   270
McCamy, Cam S.   284
McClellan, James H.   220
McIlwain, Knox   391
McLellan, J.H.   216
MCP (motion-compensated prediction)   153
MCU (minimum coded unit), in JPEG   492
ME (motion estimator)   528–529
mean-squared error (MSE)   500
median filtering   383, 385
Meier, Hans Eduard   712
metadata   158
metamerism   268
metercandle   576
mid-tread quantization   46 (sketch)
Mini DisplayPort   167
minimum coded unit (MCU), in JPEG   492
minimum perceptible colour difference
    (MPCD)   278
mired   *see* mirek
mirek (reciprocal megakelvin, MK^{-1})   280
mistracking   528
Mitchell, Joan L.   535
Mitra, Sanjit K.   220
Mitsuhashi, Tetsuo   103
mix   387
mixture, additive   288–289
MJPEG (motion JPEG)   503
MK^{-1} (reciprocal megakelvin)   280
ML (main level), in MPEG-2   514
MOD file   556
.mod (file extension)   556

modulation
    8-VSB   561
    256-QAM   562
    64-QAM   562
    chroma   128
        in NTSC   352
    COFDM   563
    depth of   241
    noise   41
    QPSK   562
    quadrature
        in ATSC DTV   562
        chroma   137
    transfer function (MTF)   241
Moiré pattern   78 (sketch)
display
monitor, *see* CRT
monochrome   68, 337
    see also greyscale
moon, angular subtense   99
motion
    artifact   412
        beat frequency   412
        in interlaced scanning   92
            field tearing   414
    detection
        in DV   508
    estimator/estimation (ME)   528–529
    JPEG (M-JPEG)   503
    portrayal   84, 93
    vector (MV)   524
motion-compensated prediction (MCP)   153
Motta, Ricardo J.   323, 328
movie
    see also cinema
moving average (MA)   202, 210
MP (main profile), in MPEG-2   514
    MP@HL (main profile at high level)   514
    MP@LL (main profile at low level)   515
    MP@ML (main profile at main level)
        514
MP3   172
.mp4 (file extension)   159
MPCD (minimum perceptible colour
    difference)   278
MPEG
    MPEG-1   157
    MPEG-2   555
        4:2:0 chroma subsampling   127
        and interlace   132
        macroblock   520
            misalignment   380

MPEG (continued)
   MPEG-3 (abandoned) 158
   MPEG-4 159
      Part 2 159
      Part 10 160, 537
         see also H.264
      Part 12 (ISO Base Media File
         Format) 159
   MPEG-7 158
   MPEG-21 158
.mpeg (file extension) 556
MPEG IMX see Sony, MPEG IMX 158
MPEG-2 513
.mpg (file extension) 556
MPM (normalized primary matrix) 306
MPR (McLellan, Parks, Rabiner) 216
MPTS (multiple program transport stream)
   557
Mpx (megapixels) 4
Mquant 502
MSE (mean-squared error) 500
MTF (modulation transfer function) 105,
   241
   and "enhancement" 385
.mts (file extension) 557
multipath distortion 562–563
multiple program transport stream (MPTS)
   557
multiplier-accumulator (MAC) 206
multiprimary 10
multispectral imaging 10
multiview profile (MVP), in MPEG-2 514
Munsell value 260
Murray, James D. 66
MUSE 560
MV (motion vector) 524
MVP (multiview profile), in MPEG-2 514
MXF (material exchange format) 151, 165

N

N_C (image columns) 87 (diagram)
N_R (image rows) 87 (diagram)
N/PAL 130
   see also PAL
N10 see EBU Tech. N10
narrowband 204
   filter, optical 269
N_C (image columns) 86
NDF (nondropframe) 400
nearest-neighbor 227, 243

negative
   camera film 119
   excursion of $B'-Y'$ and $R'-Y'$
      in HD 370
      in SD 359
   lobe (in CMF) 298, 302 (graph)
   $R'G'B'$ values 423
   RGB values 309, 311
   SPD 296–297
   sync voltage, in analog sync 381
   weights
      in filtering 204, 208, 243
      in linear (colour) matrix 308
      in PSF 244
      in sinc 199, 243
      in upsampling 245
   $Y'C_BC_R$ values 362
Neill, Paul 596
NetFlix xxxv
Netflix 165
Netravali, Arun N. 535
Newton, Isaac 266
NHK (Nippon Hoso Kyokai) 141, 396–397,
   560
night vision 10, 247, 257
Nippon Hoso Kyokai (NHK) 141, 396, 560
Nishizawa, Taiji 141
nit (nt) 27, 257, 576
noise 40–41
   due to colour matrixing 308
   modulation 41
   quantization see error, quantization
nonconstant luminance 341
noninterlaced scanning see progressive
   scanning
nonlinear
   and "enhancement" 383
   and linear coding 31
      in JPEG 494, 502
nonlinearity
   indicated by prime symbol 343
nonphysical, nonrealizable primaries, SPDs
   296
nonpremultiplied foreground 388
nonrecursive filter see FIR filter
normal function 200
normalized primary matrix (NPM) 306
notation
   4:1:1, 4:2:0, 4:2:2, etc. 125
   4:2:2 interface 430
   480*i*29.97, 576*i*25, etc. 92
   1280×720, 1920×1080, etc. 92

notation   (continued)
    CCIR   129
    chroma subsampling   125
    colour matching functions, e.g., $\bar{x}(\lambda)$,
        $X(\lambda)$ 270
    colourbars   421
    fields (in interlaced scanning)   88
    h (subscript), hexadecimal   46, 434
    luminance and luma   122, 342, 567–
        572
    prime ('), for nonlinearity   28, 122, 344
    scanning   92
    xvYCC$Y'C_BC_R$, xvYCC   374
    $Y'C_BC_R$, $Y'P_BP_R$ 344, 353, 361
    $Y'UV$, $Y'IQ$ 367, 567–572
notch filter   203–204
N_R (image rows)   86
    and viewing distance   100
nt (nit)   27, 257, 576
NTSC   94–95, 129–130, 135–139
    composite   128
    incorrectly used to refer to 480*i*
        (525/59.94) scanning   136
    scanning   see 480*i*
    sound subcarrier   391
    subcarrier frequency, choice of   391
Nyquist
    criterion   193
        in resampling   222
    frequency see Nyquist rate
    rate   193
Nyquist, Harry   78, 193

O

Ocean, Atlantic   396
OCR (optical character recognition)   67
octave   39
odd/even (fields)   88, 132
OECF
    quasilog, in FS-Log   313
OECF (opto-electronic conversion function)
    33, 316, 320
    BT.709   320
OETF (opto-electronic transfer function)
    see OECF
offset
    +25 Hz, in PAL   393
    and BRIGHTNESS   48, 53
    interface   44
Oliver, B.M.   49
Olson, Thor   316
On2   162

one-chip (1 CCD)   299
on-off contrast ratio   see contrast ratio, inter-
    image   29
opacity   70, 388
open GOP   534
open GoP   155 (sketch)
optical
    character recognition (OCR)   67
    domain, linearity in   36
    filter   269
    transfer function (OTF)   241
opto-electronic conversion function (OECF)
    33, 320
opto-electronic conversion function, see OECF
OTF (optical transfer function)   241
overflow
    AC coefficients, in DV   508
    buffer, in MPEG-2   532
    computing in *RGB*   364
    in phase accumulator   231
oversampling   224
    2×-oversampling   226
overshoot   365

P

P_BP_R components   11, 94, 339
    for HD   370
    for SD   359
    see also $Y'P_BP_R$
P-picture   153, 520–524
P (power)   574
P_0, P_1, P_2, P_3 flag bits (in TRS)   434
packetized elementary stream (PES)   535,
    556
PAL   94–95, 129–130, 135–139
    +25 Hz offset   393
    composite   128
    incorrectly used to refer to 576*i* (625/50)
        scanning   136
    PAL-B   393
    PAL-G   393
    PAL-H   393
    PAL-I   393
    PAL-M   130
    PAL-N   130
    scanning   see 576*i*
    subcarrier frequency, choice of   393
palette   see CLUT
Palmer, James M.   574, 576
pan-and-scan   16
Panasonic   455
PAR (picture aspect ratio)   5

parallelpiped 339
parity
    in ANC 438–439
    field (odd/even, first/second,
        top/bottom) 132
        in MPEG-2 158, 518
    frame (in 483p59.94) 435
    in LTC timecode 403
    field (odd/even, first/second, top/bottom)
        in 2-3 pulldown 406
    P_0, P_1, P_2, P_3, in TRS 434
    in TRS 435
Parks, T.W. 216
Parks, Thomas W. 220
passband 211
PAT (program association table) 557
pathological sequence (in SDI) 440
PCM-1600 398
PCR (program clock reference) 558
PDP (plasma display panel)
    and gamma 326
    and "resolution" 73
    controls 62
PDR (perfect diffuse reflector) 30
peak
    excursion 361, 381
    peak-to-peak 40
    white 42
pedestal 381–383
pel (picture element)
    pel-recursive motion estimation 531
    see also pixel
Pennebaker, William B. 535
perceptual uniformity 8, 27–36
    and colour 280–284
    in DCT/JPEG 494, 502
    in MPEG-2 525
    in video 318, 322
perfect diffuse reflector (PDR) 30
PES (packetized elementary stream) 535,
  556
phase
    accumulator 232
    alternate line see PAL
    error
        in IIR filter 211
    linearity 209
    offset 228
    response
        in BT.601 213
        of filter 209
PHASE control, see HUE control

Philips
    compact disc-digital audio (CD-DA) 172
phosphor
    CRT 317
    rare earth 303
photometry 573–580
photoreceptor 7, 247, 266
    cone cells 247, 266
Photoshop 62, 72
    BRIGHTNESS and CONTRAST 62–64
photosite 299
physical realizability
    of filter 208
    of SPD 296
PICT 330
picture
    anchor, in MPEG-2 see picture,
      reference, in MPEG-2
    angle 101 (sketch)
    centre
        in 480i 446
        in 576i 458
        in 720p 468
        in 1080i, 1080p 478
        in 480i 450
        in 576i 462
        in 720p 469
    edge 87, 377, 451
        in MPEG-2 520
    element see pixel
    excursion 381
    header, in MPEG-2 530
    height (PH) 100
    layer, in MPEG-2 534
    lines 379
    line-up generating equipment (PLUGE)
      421
    picture:sync ratio 132, 381
    reference, in MPEG-2 152–522
    samples per picture width (S_{PW}) 87
    in shuttle see shuttle
picture aspect ratio (PAR) 5
PICTURE control 50
picture rendering 115–120
    and constant luminance 112
pillarbox format 17
pixel 3
    aspect ratio 134
    bilevel 68
    greyscale 68
    pseudocolour 70
    recursive motion estimation 531

pixel   *(continued)*
   round   14
   square   *see* sampling, square
   truecolour   68
   see also dot
pixels per inch (ppi)   7, 72–73, 100
Planck, Max   276
plasma display panel (PDP)
   and gamma   326
   and "resolution"   73
   CONTRAST and BRIGHTNESS controls   62
Pleasantville   21
PLUGE   421
   and footroom   43
PMT (program map table)   557
point   73
   sampling   79
      frequency response of   199
   spread function (PSF)   75, 241
point spread function (PSF)   105
Pointer, Michael R.   312
polyphase interpolator   231
Porter, Thomas   312, 387
position
   centre of picture   *see* picture centre
   error, in interpolation   233
PostScript   67
Poulin, Michel   440
power   38
   AC mains frequency   389
   half-power   99
   optical   255, 277, 573
   switched-mode power supply (SMPS)
      390
power function   33, 251, 319
   five-halves law   316
power (*P*)   574
Powers, Kerns   5
Poynton, Charles   52, 70, 93, 312, 414
   Fourth Law   60
ppi (pixels per inch)   7, 72–73, 100
Pratt, William K.   570
prediction
   in MPEG   521
      error   520, 525, 530
   of DC term, in JPEG   499
premultiplied foreground   387–388
primaries
   ACES, chromaticities   294

primaries   *(continued)*
   BT.709
      chromaticities   290
      CMFs   302 (graph)
      SPDs   303 (graph)
   camera, typical effective spectral
      responses   305 (graph)
   characterization of *RGB*   290–292
   chromaticities   290
   chromaticity
      and colourbars   351, 420
   CIE *XYZ*
      CMFs   300 (graph)
      SPDs   301 (graph)
   in computing   290
   EBU Tech. 3213   293
   interchange   348, 350
   in JPEG   503
   nonphysical, nonrealizable   296
   SMPTE/DCI P3
      chromaticities   295
   taking   348
   transmission   *see* primaries, interchange
   triangle of *RGB*   290
   of video standards   291 (graph)
prime symbol
   in CIE *u'* and *v'*   281
   signifies nonlinearity   343, 568
Pritchard, Dalton H.   569
production aperture   86–87 (sketch), 380
profile, in MPEG-2   514–517
profile, spot   75
program and system information protocol
   (PSIP)   557
program association table (PAT)   557
program map table (PMT)   557
program stream (PS)   167, 556
progressive
   scanning   86
   segmented-frame, progressive (24PsF)
      94
   sequence, in MPEG-2   517
prohibited codes   43
   in D-cinema   44
projective transformation   276
ProRes   151
PS (program stream)   167, 556
PS3 and superblack/superwhite   44
pseudocolour   70
   and gamma   332
   raster image   70

PSF (point spread function)   75, 105, 241
    and negative weights   245
PsF (progressive segmented-frame)   94
PSIP (program and system information
        protocol)   557
PSNR (peak signal to RMS noise ratio)   40
psychometric saturation   282
pulse
    equalization
        in 480*i*   448
        in 576*i*   459
    horizontal drive (HD)   90
    vertical drive (VD)   90
    see also sync
pulse width modulation (PWM)   326
pupil   248
    pupillary aperture   252
Puri, Atul   535
purity   266
Purkinje shift   257
purple
    line of   275
    see also magenta
PWM (pulse width modulation)   326
pyramidal motion estimation   531

Q

Q (energy)   574
QNO (quantization number)   510
QPSK   562
QSF (quantizer scale factor)   502
quadrature modulation   128
    in ATSC DTV   562
    chroma   137
quantization   37–46, 494
    in DV   510
    error   40
    of filter coefficients   208
    matrix
        in JPEG   497
        in MPEG-2   525
    mid-tread   46 (sketch)
    of DCT coefficients   493
quantization number (QNO)   510
quantizer scale
    code, in MPEG-2   531
    factor (QSF)   502
quasi-interlace   94
quasilog OECF   313
QuickDraw   330
QuickTime   512, 555
QXGA   92

R

R'–Y'   *see B'–Y', R'–Y'*
R-S coding (Reed-Solomon)   561
Rabbani, Majid   504
Rabiner, Lawrence R.   216, 235
radiance (*L*)   255–256, 575, 577
radiance, spectral (SPD)   267
radiant
    emittance (deprecated)   574
    exitance (*M*)   574
    flux (*Φ*)   256, 574, 577
    intensity (*I*)   256, 574, 577
radiometer   256
radiometry   573–580
radiosity   574
ramp
    in LUT   69
rare earth phosphor   303
raster   83–86
    digital video   130 (sketch)
    image
        in computing   65–73
        processing (RIP)   67
    locked   76
raster-locked   76
rate
    480*i* and 576*i*, common sampling   394
    control
        in DV   510
        in MPEG-2   525, 531
    frame   83
        in 480*i*   445
        in 576*i*   457
        in cinema   84, 406
        in MPEG-2   518
    Nyquist   193
    refresh   83
    sampling, 13.5 MHz   130, 394, 430
        in 480*i*   452
        in 576*i*   463
    sampling, 74.25 MHz (in HD)   141, 432
        1080*i*, 1080*p*   473
        720*p*   467
RCA   102
realizability, physical
    of filter   208
    of SPD   296
RealPlayer   162
Rec. 601   *see* BT.601
Rec. 709   *see* BT.709
Rec. 815   *see* BT.815

receiver
    colour temperature   278
    HDTV   142, 562
    introduction of colour   135
    scanning standards   129
reciprocal megakelvin (MK^{-1})   280
reconstruction   216–217
    at $0.45f_S$ 217 (graph)
    close to $0.5f_S$ 217
    error, in JPEG   500
    of images   237–243
    sampling and   217 (block diagram)
rectangular window   214
recursive
    filter   *see* IIR filter
    motion estimation   531
red
    contribution to luminance   258
    in chromaticity diagram   275
    maximum excursion of $R'-Y'$ 359, 370
    minus luma   *see* $B'-Y'$, $R'-Y'$ colour
        difference components
    rare earth phosphor   303
Red Book (compact disc-digital audio)   172
RedCode   151
Reed-Solomon coding (R-S)   561
reference
    black   42
    display   427–428
    white   42
        in camera   310
reference picture, in MPEG-2   152–522
reflectance (ρ)   574
refresh
    in MPEG-2   528
    rate   83
Reimers, Ulrich   564
Reinhard, Erik   314
relative luminance   258, 578
relative spectral response (RSR)   304
Remez exchange   216
Remez, E.Ya.   216
rendering
    in computer graphics   67
    viewing
        and gamma   322, 330
repeat first field (RFF), in MPEG-2   518
repeat first field (RFF, in MPEG-2)   174
resampling   191, 221–235
residual   152
residual (in MPEG-2)   *see* prediction error
residual, in MPEG-2   *see* prediction error

residue (in MPEG-2)   *see* prediction error
resolution   97–106
    limiting   98–99
retina   7, 289
retrace   85
rewind   *see* shuttle
RFF (repeat first field), in MPEG-2   518
RFF (repeat first field, in MPEG-2)   174
R'G'B'
    colour cubes   336 (sketch)
    components
        in 480*i*   452
        in 576*i*   464
    EOCF
        in 480*i*   448
        in 576*i*   460
        in 720*p*   469
        in 1920×1080   478
    footroom, headroom   365, 383
    nonlinear transfer function   315–334,
        345
    transform to BT.601 luma   359, 370
RGB
    colour cubes   336 (sketch)
    primary components
        in 480*i*   450
        in 576*i*   462
        in 720*p*   450, 462, 471, 478
    RGB-legal   373
        and wide gamut   312, 374
        in colourbars   423
    transforms to and from CIE *XYZ*   307
RGB+W   288
rho (ρ), reflectance   574
Richardson, Iain E.G.   548
ringing   87, 361
RIP (raster image processing)   67
ripple, in filter   215
risetime
    of Gaussian LPF   214
RLE (run-length encoding)   148
    in DV   510
    in JPEG   499
    in MPEG-2   527
RMS (root mean square)   40, 196
Roberts, Alan   317
Roberts, D. Allan   580
Roberts, Lawrence G.   41
Robin, Michael   440
Robson, John G.   253
Roll, Thorsten   552
rolling shutter (RS)   94

root mean square (RMS)   40, 196
Rorabaugh, C. Britton   220
Rossotti, Hazel   286
rotation
    of an image   229
    of bitmapped image   79
    of *UV* into *IQ*   123, 352
Rothermel, Albrecht   552
rounding
    of filter coefficients   208
    of matrix coefficients   364
roundoff error
    in 8-bit interface   45, 325
    in computing *RGB*   364
    in DCT/IDCT   495–496, 500
row, image rows (N_R)   87 (diagram)
RP (Recommended Practice) *see* SMPTE RP
RS (rolling shutter)   94
RS-343 (obsolete)   382, 453
RSR (relative spectral response)   304
rule of thumb
    astronomers'   100
    data rate and storage capacity   147
run-length encoding (RLE)   148
    in DV   510
    in JPEG   499
    in MPEG-2   527
Russia   130

s

S_{AL} (samples per active line)   4, 86, 131,
        380, 395, 438 (table)
    in ATSC A/53   143, 380
    common between 480*i* and 576*i*   395
    in HD   145 (table)
    in MPEG-2   517
S_{PW} (samples per picture width)   87, 380
S_{TL} (samples per total line)   86–87 (diagram),
        130 (diagram)–131, 393, 395,
        438 (table)
    in HD   145 (table)
S-video   137
Salomon, David   148
sample
    aspect ratio (SAR)   14, 134
    per active line (S_{AL})   4, 86, 131, 380,
        395, 438 (table)
        common between 480*i* and 576*i*
            395
        in ATSC A/53   143, 380
        in HD   145 (table)
        in MPEG-2   517

sample   *(continued)*
    per picture width (S_{PW})   87, 380
    per total line (S_{TL})   86–87 (diagram),
        130 (diagram)–131, 393, 395,
        438 (table)
        in HD   145 (table)
    sample-and-hold   218, 243
    transition   87, 378–379, 388
sampling   237
    1-D   8
    2-D   8
    4:4:4   124
    $4f_{SC}$ 128, 131, 133, 393
    aperture   78
    chroma subsampling   124–127
    at exactly $0.5f_S$ 193
    and filtering   191–220
    grid   78, 655
    horizontal/vertical/temporal   237
    lattice   655
    Nyquist criterion   193
    point sampling   79
    rate   389–395
        13.5 MHz, common 480*i* and 576*i*
            394
        18 MHz   432
        74.25 MHz   141, 432
        in resampling   222
    and reconstruction   217 (block diagram)
    resampling   191
    square   14, 133, 396, 451, 463
        in MPEG-2   517
    theorem   192–194
    see also chroma subsampling;
            quantization; resampling; sample
            rate
SAR (sample aspect ratio)   14
saturation   266
    and colourbars   419
    and constant luminance   113
    error   422
    in NTSC and PAL coding   138
    psychometric   282
    SATURATION decoder control
        adjustment   422
SATURATION control, see CHROMA [GAIN]
    control
SAV (start of active video)   431 (sketch), 434
Sayood, Khalid   148
SB (superblock)   506
scaling (in PC parlance)   95

scan
    conversion   95
    line   83
    see also scanning
scanner
    and rendering intent   120
    spectral constraints   268
scanning
    notation   92
    480*i*   129, 445–448
    525/59.94/2:1
        notation   92
        see 480*i*
    525/60 (obsolete)   390, 392,
        395 (diagram)
        used loosely to refer to 480*i*
    576*i*   129, 457–460
    625/50/1:1   *see* 576*p*
    625/50/2:1
        notation   92
        see 576*i*
    720*p*   467
    750/60/1:1   145
        see also 720*p*
    1125-line HD   141
    1250-line   563
    interlaced   88
    progressive   86
scan-velocity modulation (SVM)   383
scene referred image state   21
Scherf, Steve   172
Schreiber, William F.   41, 243, 250, 266, 314
Schubin, Mark   5
"scope" (2.4 aspect ratio)   5
scotopic vision   10
SCR (system clock reference)   557
scrambling, in SDI and HD-SDI   440
SD (standard definition)   129–134
    and HD
        luma chaos   350
    component colour coding   357–367
    viewing angle, distance   101
    widescreen   133
    see also 480*i*
SDI   166
SDI (serial digital interface)   432
    coding   439
    and timing   442
SDTI   164, 433, 441, 512
SECAM   128, 130
segment (in DV)   509
segmented-frame (24PsF)   94

sensitivity   40
    contrast   249–251
    lightness   249–251
separability   221, 229, 238, 242, 494
sequence
    layer, in MPEG-2   533
    pathological (in SDI)   440
sequential contrast ratio   *see* contrast ratio,
        inter-image   29
sequential scanning   *see* progressive scanning
serial digital interface
    for HD   *see* HD-SDI
    for SD   *see* SDI
setup   381–383
    abolished in modern systems   382
    comparison of zero and 7.5 percent
        382 (sketch)
    zero   382
SFN (single-frequency network)   563
Shannon, Claude   193
shaped foreground video   387
Sharma, Gaurav   314
sharpened Gaussian   243–244
sharpening   271
SHARPNESS control   385
sharpness, and contrast ratio   30
shielded twisted pair (STP)   167
shutter
    in film projector   84
    global (GS)   94
    rolling (RS)   94
shuttle
    and digital VCR   508
sidebar format   *see* pillarbox format
signal-to-noise ratio (SNR)   40
simple profile (SP), in MPEG-2   514, 516
simple studio profile (SStP)   159
simultaneous contrast   116
$(\sin x)/x$ 197, 199 (graph)
    also known as sinc
    correction   218–219 (graph)
sinc function   198–199 (graph)
    also known as $(\sin x)/x$
single program transport stream (SPTS)   557
siting
    cositing (of $C_B C_R$ samples)   124, 127
    interstitial (of $C_B C_R$ samples)   124, 127
skipped macroblock   156
slice, in MPEG-2   524, 531, 534
Smith, Alvy Ray   388, 569–570
Smith, Julius O.   227, 231
SMPS (switched-mode power supply)   390

SMPTE
    standards notation   xxxvi
    125M   438, 444
    240M   141
        luma coefficients   369
        OECF   322
    ST 240M   396
    253M   453
    259M   432, 444
    266M   404
    267M   438, 444
    293M   438
    308M   516
    344M   452
    421M   160
    274M
        see also BT.709
    SMPTE-C   293
        see also SMPTE RP 145
    D-6   481–482
    D-7   150
    D-9   150
    D-11   481–482
    D-12   481–482
    D-15   481–482
    D-16   481, 483
    EG 1   419
    EG 28   570
    FS/709   294, 312
    green   290
    HD-SDI   *see* HD-SDI
    SMPTE/EBU N10   454
    RP 125   434
    RP 136   404
    RP 145   293, 303
    RP 157   387
    RP 164   402, 447
    RP 166   310
    RP 167   56
    RP 168   442, 448, 460
    RP 169   399
    RP 177   307, 428
    RP 187   450, 462–463
    RP 196   404
    RP 197   93, 405, 410
    RP 201   405, 410
    RP 202   451, 463
    RP 219   423
    RP 227   160
    RP 228   160
    SDI   *see* SDI
    SDTI   433, 441

SMPTE/DCI P3   290–291
SMPTE/EBU N10 component analog
    interface   454
    see also SMPTE 253M
ST 12   404
ST 258   401
ST 262   399
ST 266   404
ST 274   145, 376, 438
    OECF   33
ST 274M   473
ST 291   438
ST 292   433, 440
ST 292M   444
ST 296   145, 376, 438, 467
ST 305.2   441
ST 348M   436
ST 428   295
ST 428-1   295
ST 2042   151
ST 2048-1   294, 312
SMPTE/DCI P3
    primary chromaticities   295
    white reference   295
Snow Leopard,   *see* Mac OS X 10.6
SNR (signal-to-noise ratio)   40
    profile, in MPEG-2   514
Sony   125, 455
    compact disc-digital audio (CD-DA)   172
    F23   313
    F35   313
    F65   313
    MPEG IMX   158, 167
        and SDTI   441
    PS3, and superblack/superwhite   44
    XDCAM   159
sound
    subcarrier   391
    see also audio
South America   130
SP (simple profile), in MPEG-2   514, 516
    SP@ML (simple profile at main level)
        515
spatial
    alias   79–81, 240, 242
    coherence   239, 522, 525
    discontinuity, in 2-3 pulldown   408
    domain   238 (sketch)
        and deinterlacing   413
    filter   242, 417
        median   385

spatial   *(continued)*
    frequency   251, 493 (sketch)
        domain   239 (sketch)–240 (sketch)
        spectrum
            480i luma   240 (sketch)
    profile (Spt), in MPEG-2   514
    resampling, in MPEG-2   514
SPD   265
    blackbody radiator   276 (graph)–
        277 (graph)
    BT.709   303 (graph)
    and CMF   296
    for CIE *XYZ* primaries   301 (graph)
    luminous efficiency function   257
    nonphysical, nonrealizable   296
    tristimulus   267
spectral
    locus   275
    power distribution   *see* SPD
    radiance (SPD)   267
    response
        relative (RSR)   304
        typical camera   305 (graph)
    sensitivity, of camera or scanner   268
spectroradiometer   256
spectrum, frequency
    2-D, of 480i luma   240 (sketch)
spherical (1.85:1 aspect ratio)   5
SPL (sound pressure level)   38
splicing, of MPEG-2 bitstreams   534
spline, Bézier   229
spot
    profile   75
        Gaussian   81, 102
    size   73, 81, 100, 244
        and interlaced scanning   106
        in interlaced scanning   88
        and Kell effect   102
spot profile, Gaussian   76
Spt (spatial profile), in MPEG-2   514
SPTS (single program transport stream)   557
square
    pixels   *see* sampling, square
    sampling   *see* sampling, square
sRGB
    BT.709 primaries in   294
    and EOCF   51
    and JPEG/JFIF   503
    picture rendering in   120
    rendering intent in   30, 119
    transfer function in   323
SStP (simple studio profile)   159

STA (error concealment status), in DV   510
Standard Observer, CIE   270
    CMFs of   271 (graph)
    luminous efficiency function of   257,
        270–271 (graph), 273 (table), 296
standards conversion   96
start code prefix   533
start of active video (SAV)   431 (sketch), 434
Stevens, Stanley S.   251
Stiles, W. Stanley   286
Stokes, Michael   323
stop (in photography)   39
stopband   211
STP (shielded twisted pair)   167
Strang, Gilbert   296
stream   163–169
    program stream (PS)   167
    transport stream (TS)   167
    see also bitstream
subblock (4×4)
    in VP8   550
subcarrier
    +25 Hz offset, in PAL   393
    choice of frequency
        in NTSC   391
        in PAL   393
    sound, in 480i 391
subsampling
    chroma   11, 109, 112, 124 (sketch)–
        127, 224, 234, 347
        in DV   506
        in DV50   511
        in JPEG   492, 502
        in MPEG-2   519, 527
        not considered compression   150
    colour differences   347
    see also decimation
subwoofer   561
Sullivan, Gary J.   548
superblack   44
superblock (SB)   506
    see also block
Super-HD   397
superposition
    in colour vision   288
    principle of   *see* linearity
supersaturated   298
superwhite   44
surround   105
    dark, compensation in film   118
    effect   116
    very dim   428

SVGA   92
SVM (scan-velocity modulation)   383
sweep   98
swing   41
   full   41
   see also excursion
switch
   vertical interval   442
      in 480*i*   442, 448
      in 576*i*   460
switched-mode power supply (SMPS)   390
switcher   442
   production   387
SXGA   92
Symes, Peter   504, 535
symmetry
   definition   207
   of filter impulse response   207
sync   90
   block, in VTR   508
   combined   90
   composite   90
   datum
      line sync *see* 0_H
   picture:sync ratio   132, 381
   trilevel (in HD)   433, 468, 475
syntactic hierarchy (of MPEG-2)   533
syntax, MPEG-2 bitstream   533
system clock
   in MPEG-2   557
system clock reference (SCR)   557

T

T (talbot)   576
Table 3 (of ATSC A/53)   143 (table), 560
taboo channels   559
taking primaries   298, 348
talbot (T)   576
tau (τ), transmittance   574
Taubman, David S.   150
Td (troland)   252
tearing artifact   414
telecine   406
   inverse   408, 411
telephony   38
television lines (measure of horizontal
   resolution)   104
template
   filter
      BT.601   213
      for HD   488
      for oversampling   225

lowpass filter   212 (sketch)
temporal
   axis   237 (sketch)
   coherence   150, 513
   domain   237 (sketch)–238 (sketch)
Thornton, William A.   272
three-chip (3 CCD)   299
three-pass algorithm (in DV)   511
threshold discrimination   250
thumb, astronomers' rule of   99
Thunderbolt   167
time
   blanking   85
   coincidence, of *R'G'B'*
      in 720*p*   485
   retrace   85
timebase
   error   139
timecode   399–404
   in 2-3 pulldown   406
   burnt-in timecode (BITC)   399
   dropframe   392, 400
   in MPEG-2 GoP header   534
   longitudinal   399, 402
   vertical interval (VITC)   402
   VITC (vertical interval timecode)   400,
      402
      in 480*i*   447
      in 576*i*   459
timing reference signals (TRS)   433
TINT control, see HUE control
TOD file   557
.tod (file extension)   557
tone
   reproduction curve (TRC)   *see* transfer
      function
   scale   315
      see also gamma; transfer function
top field (in MPEG-2)   132
top/bottom field   88
   in MPEG-2   132, 517
Topiwala, Pankaj N.   548
train, impulse   199, 218
transcode   95, 130
transfer function   27–35, 315–334
   cinema   119
   EOTF,   *see* EOCF
   in JPEG/JFIF   503
   modulation (MTF)   241
   OETF   *see* OECF
   SMPTE 240M   322
   in sRGB   323

transform
    between *RGB* and CIE *RGB*   307
    Bradford   309
    chromatic adaptation (CAT)   309
    DCT (discrete cosine transform)   240, 495
        in MPEG-2   525
        linear and nonlinear data   36, 494
    Fourier   196, 200
        discrete (DFT)   240
        self inverse property   198
    Laplace   196
    lapped   482
    matrix
        among *RGB* systems   309
        to compute colour difference   359, 370
    projective   276
transformer, flyback   390
transition
    band   211
    bandwidth (of a filter)   212
    blanking   451
    mix/wipe   387
    ratio (of a filter)   212
    samples   87, 378–379, 388
transmission
    primaries   *see* interchange primaries
transmittance (τ)   574
transport stream (TS)   167, 556
transverse domain   238
trap (filter)   203–204
TRC (tone reproduction curve)   *see* transfer function
trellis coding   561
triad   289
triangle, of *RGB* primaries   290
triangular window   214
trichromacy   247, 266
trilevel sync   433, 468, 475
Trinitron   289, 298, 309
    SPD   303 (graph)
tristimulus   28
    calculation by matrix multiplication   273
    CIE *XYZ*   272
    and SPD   267
troland (Td)   252
Troxel, Donald E.   243
TRS (timing reference signals)   433
truecolour   68
    and compression   149
    and number of colours   284

    and quantization   33
    raster image   68
truncation
    of filter coefficients   208
    of filter impulse response   208
.ts (file extension)   557
TS (transport stream)   167, 556
Tschichold, Jan   xxxvii
TSP (transport stream packet)   557
Tufte, Edward R.   xxxvii
tungsten illumination   280
TV lines (TVL/PH)   104
twitter   89
    filter   89
two-level   *see* bilevel
two's complement   46, 377, 495

U

μ-law   38
u*v*   *see L*u*v**
u'v'   282
Ultra-HD   397
unassociated foreground   388
underflow, buffer, in MPEG-2   532
undershoot   365
    see also footroom; headroom
uniform colour space   280
    lightness component of, CIE *L**   262
uniformity, perceptual   8, 27–36
    in DCT/JPEG   494, 502
    in MPEG-2   525
unit, IRE   381
Unser, Michael   228
unshaped foreground video   388
upconvert   96
upsampling   221, 223 (sketch)
    in keying   388
    negative weights in   245
    with 1:2 ratio   226
    see also resampling
UV components
    confusion with CIE *u*v**, *u'v'*, and *uv*   357
uv, CIE 1960 (obsolete)   281
UXGA   92

V

V(λ), *see* luminous efficiency function
V flag bit (in TRS)   434
vacuum tube   48
valid   339

value
    of a colour   28
    in *HSV*   28
    Munsell   260
van Dam, Andries   569–570
van Nes, Floris L.   251
VANC   431 (sketch), 437
    colour   313
vanRyper, William   66
variable bit-rate (VBR)   531
variable-length encoding (VLE)   499
    in DV   510
    in MPEG-2   524, 527
VBI (vertical blanking interval)   85
VBR (variable bit-rate)   531
VBV (video buffering verifier)   532
    delay   532
VC-1   160
VC-2,   *see* Dirac PRO
VD (vertical drive)   90
vector image   3
vertical
    axis   237 (sketch)
    blanking interval (VBI)   85
    centre of picture
        in 480i 446
        in 576i 458
        in 720p 468
        in 1080i, 1080p 478
    DCT transform   495
    domain   237 (sketch)–238 (sketch)
    drive pulse (VD)   90
    filtering   241
    interval
        switching point
            in 480i 442, 448
            in 576i 460
        test signal (VITS)   86, 380
        timecode (VITC)   400, 402
            in 480i 447
            in 576i 459
    resampling   134
    resolution   104
    retrace   85
    size
        in MPEG-2   517
        see also L_A (active lines), N_R (image
            rows)
    sync
        datum (0_V)   448
        in 480i 447
        in 576i 459

V flag bit (in TRS)   434
VESA   380
vestigial sideband (VSB)   561
VGA   92
$V(\lambda)$ 257 (graph)
$V'(\lambda)$ 257 (graph)
video buffering verifier (VBV)   532
video usability information (VUI)   176
viewing
    angle   80, 84, 100–101, 104–106
    and chroma subsampling   347
    distance   101 (sketch)
        and angle   80, 100–101, 104–106
        in computing   104
        Lechner distance   105
        and oversampling   244
    environment   115, 117, 248
        and sRGB   323
        and white   280, 311
    and flicker   83
violet   275
visibility
    of AC line frequency   389
    of luminance detail   99
    of luminance differences   30, 249
    of modulated chroma   391
vision
    acuity   247
        colour   121, 335
        and pixel structure   77
    central   84
    and DCT/JPEG   497
    foveal   84
    fundamentals of   266
    night   247, 257
    principle of superposition in   288
VITC
    DVITC   404
VITC (vertical interval timecode)   86, 380,
        400, 402
    and film   410
    in 480i 447
    in 576i 459
VITS (vertical interval test signal)   86, 380
VLE (variable-length encoding)
    in DV   510
    in MPEG-2   524, 527
.vob (file extension)   556
VOLUME control   8
von Hann window   214
VP8   162
VSB (vestigial sideband)   561

VTR (videotape recorder)   481–483
    D-5 HD   481–482
        compression   482
    D-6   481–482
    D-7   150
    D-9   150
    D-11   481–482
    D-12   481–482
        compression   482
    D-12 HD
        compression   482
    D-15   481–482
    D-16   481, 483
    Digital-S   150
    DVCPRO HD   481–483, 512
    HDCAM   481–482
    HDCAM SR   481
VUI (video usability information)   176

W

Wandell, Brian A.   78, 247
Watkinson, John   96, 535
wave number   266
wavelength (λ)   256, 266, 574
weave (technique for deinterlacing)   414–
    415 (sketch)
Weber
    contrast   48
    Weber's Law   48
WebM   162
Weiss, S. Merrill   564
Weston, Martin   416
Whitaker, Jerry C.   558, 564
white
    balance   278
    CIE Ill. D_{65}
        in EBU Tech. 3213   279
    CIE Ill. C, in NTSC (obsolete)   279, 293
    CIE Ill. D_{65} 267 (graph), 273 (table), 277
        in EBU Tech. 3213   279, 293
        in BT.709   292
        in SMPTE RP 145   293
    CIE Ill. E   278
    and colour temperature   277
    diffuse   115, 117, 249
    peak   42
    point   see white reference
    reference   42, 277 (graph)–279 (graph),
        310
        in JPEG   503
        and luma coefficients   346
    SPD   277 (graph)–279 (graph)

Whittaker, E.T.   193
wideband
    filter, optical   269
    I chroma modulation, in NTSC   352
    monochrome component, in composite
        video   337
    $P_B P_R$ components   453
widescreen   5
    HD   14
    SD   133
width
    blanking   380
    cycles per picture   see C/PW
    of image   4, 72
    samples per picture   see S_{PW}
    spectral   200
    of spot   81
Wiegand, Thomas   548
Wilkins, Paul   552
window   383
    function
        in deinterlacing   418
        of filter   214
    "Hanning"   214
    method, of filter design   214
    rectangular, triangular, von Hann
        ("Hanning"), Kaiser   214
    windowed sinc   216
wipe   387
WM9   160
WM10   160
Wolberg, George   214
Woodward, Phillip M.   197
wrap
    of frequency, upon sampling   198
    of sample values, at edge of picture   378
wraparound   46, 377
WTW (whiter-than-white)   44
Wuenschmann, Juergen   552
WUXGA   92
WXGA   92
Wyszecki, Günter   286

X

[x, y] chromaticity   275–276
$\bar{x}(\lambda)$ 257, 270–271 (graph), 273 (table), 296
X (tristimulus component)   272
x.v.Color, x.v.Colour   see xvYCC
XDCAM   159
XGA   92
XLR connector   402
Xu, Yaowu   552

Xvid   159
xvYCC   292, 354, 373
XYZ tristimulus components   272

Y

$\bar{y}(\lambda)$ 257 (graph), 270, 273 (table), 296
Y (relative luminance)
    defined   258
    tristimulus component   272
Y'   *see* luma
$Y'C_BC_R$ 94, 123
    notation   344
    in HD   145, 371
    in SD   361
    see also C_BC_R components; chroma
        subsampling
Y'IQ   123
    confusion with Y'UV   367, 571
    see also IQ components
$Y'P_BP_R$ 94, 123
    notation   344
    colour cube   339 (sketch)
    for HD   370
    for SD   359
    see also P_BP_R components; chroma
        subsampling
Y'UV   123
    confusion with Y'IQ   367, 571
    see also UV components

yellow
    always appears light   258
    appearance of tungsten illumination
        280
    and colour temperature   277
    negative excursion of B'-Y'
        in HD   370
        in SD   359
YouTube   xxxv, 165
.yuv (file extension)   173, 571

Z

$\bar{z}(\lambda)$ 270–271 (graph), 273 (table), 296
Z (tristimulus component)   272
zero
    of filter   204
    setup   382
    zero-order hold   243
zero-H (0_H, line sync datum)   437
    in 1080*i*, 1080*p*   475
    in 480*i*   447
    in 576*i*   459
    in 720*p*   468
zero-order hold (ZOH)   219
zero-V (0_V, vertical sync datum)   90 (sketch),
    448
zigzag scanning
    in DV   508, 510
    in JPEG   498
    in MPEG-2   527
ZOH (zero-order hold)   219

About the author

sketch by Kevin Melia

Charles Poynton is an independent contractor specializing in the physics, mathematics, and engineering of digital colour imaging systems, including digital video, HD, and digital cinema. Apart from his professional work, he is a PhD candidate at Simon Fraser University.

In the early 1980s, Charles designed and built the digital video equipment used by NASA to convert video from the Space Shuttle into NTSC. In 1990, he initiated Sun Microsystems' HD research project, and introduced color management technology to Sun. He was Sun's founding member in what a few years later became the International Color Consortium (ICC).

Charles was a key contributor to current digital video and HD studio standards; he originated the number 1080 (as in 1080*p*60) in HD standards. A Fellow of the Society of Motion Picture and Television Engineers (SMPTE), he was awarded the Society's prestigious David Sarnoff Gold Medal for his work to integrate video technology with computing and communications.

Charles has taught many popular courses on video technology, HD, colour image coding, and colour science, including many SIGGRAPH courses.

Charles lives in Toronto with his wife Barbara – a psychotherapist. Their twenty-something daughter Quinn is back in Toronto after stints in Paris and New York. Their teenager Georgia is an undergrad at Dalhousie University in Halifax. It is owing to pressure from all three family members that he has reverted to spelling *colour* with a *u*. The sketch in the margin was made many years ago, just prior to Charles granting Georgia's ninth-birthday wish to shave off his beard.

This book is set in the Syntax typeface. Syntax was designed by Hans Eduard Meier, and first issued by Stempel in 1969. This book uses Linotype's revision issued in 2000 that includes bold italics, small caps, and old-style figures. The body type is 10.2 points, leaded to 12.8 points, set ragged-right.

The mathematical work underlying this book was accomplished using *Mathematica,* from Wolfram Research. The illustrations were executed in Adobe *Illustrator;* for raster (bitmap) images, Adobe *Photoshop* was used. The equations were set using Design Science *MathType.* Text editing, layout, and typesetting were accomplished using Adobe *FrameMaker.* Adobe *Acrobat* was employed for electronic distribution.

The work was accomplished using various Apple Macintosh computers.